REVISE PEARSON EDEXCEL AS/A LEVEL
Politics
REVISION
GUIDE AND WORKBOOK

Series Consultant: Harry Smith

Authors: Sarra Jenkins; Andrew Mitchell; Kathy Schindler; Adam Tomes

Also available to support your revision:

Revise A Level Revision Planner   9781292191546

The **Revise A Level Revision Planner** helps you to plan and organise your time, step-by-step, throughout your A level revision. Use this book and wall chart to mastermind your revision.

A small bit of small print

Pearson Edexcel publishes Sample Assessment Material and the Specification on its website. This is the official content and this book should be used in conjunction with it. The questions have been written to help you practise every topic in the book.

For the full range of Pearson revision titles across KS2, KS3, GCSE, Functional Skills, AS/A Level and BTEC visit:
www.pearsonschools.co.uk/revise

Contents

UK POLITICS

1 Representative democracy
2 Direct democracy
3 How healthy is UK democracy?
4 Participation crisis
5 Reforming UK democracy
6 Group politics
7 Methods used by pressure groups
8 Factors influencing the success of groups
9 Groups and democracy
10 Rights in the UK
11 Are our rights protected?
12 Political parties
13 Enhancing democracy and funding
14 The history of the Labour Party
15 The Labour Party today
16 The history of the Conservative Party
17 The Conservative Party today
18 The Liberal Democrats
19 Emerging and minor parties
20 Other emerging and minor parties
21 Parties and party systems
22 Factors affecting party success
23 The role of elections in democracy
24 First-past-the-post
25 Supplementary Vote
26 Additional Member System
27 Single Transferable Vote
28 Use of referenda
29 Impact of different electoral systems
30 Trends in voting behaviour
31 Short-term factors affecting voting behaviour
32 Case study: the 1997 general election
33 Case study: the 2017 general election
34 The influence of the media
35 Media and electoral outcomes

CONSERVATISM

36 Pragmatism and tradition
37 Human imperfection and the organic state
38 Paternalism and libertarianism
39 Traditional conservatism
40 One Nation conservatism
41 New Right
42 Neo-liberalism and neo-conservatism
43 Key thinkers: 1
44 Key thinkers: 2
45 Exam skills

LIBERALISM

46 Individualism and freedom
47 The state and rationalism
48 Equality/social justice and liberal democracy
49 Liberalism and freedom
50 Liberalism and the state
51 Liberalism and the economy
52 Contradiction of continuation?
53 Key thinkers: 1
54 Key thinkers: 2
55 Key thinkers: 3
56 Exam skills

SOCIALISM

57 Collectivism and common humanity
58 Equality
59 Social class and workers' control
60 Revolutionary socialism
61 Social democracy
62 The Third Way
63 Key thinkers: 1
64 Key thinkers: 2
65 Key thinkers: 3
66 Exam skills: the conclusion
67 Exam-style practice

UK GOVERNMENT

68 Types of constitutions
69 Sources of the UK constitution
70 Constitutional reforms since 1997
71 UK devolved bodies
72 Devolution and its impact
73 Are further reforms desirable?
74 Other possible reforms
75 Parliament
76 The structure of the Houses
77 Functions: legislating and debating
78 Representative function
79 Composition and powers of the Houses
80 Relative power of the Houses
81 The legislative process
82 Parliamentary scrutiny
83 Backbenchers
84 Structure and role of the executive
85 The Cabinet
86 Collective ministerial responsibility
87 Individual ministerial responsibility
88 The power of the prime minister
89 The Cabinet and the prime minister
90 The executive and coalition government
91 The Supreme Court

92 Judicial neutrality and independence
93 The influence of the Supreme Court
94 Important Supreme Court cases
95 Aims and influence of the EU
96 Impact of the EU on UK government
97 Sovereignty in the UK
98–103 UK AS Exam skills
104–109 UK A Level Exam skills
110–113 UK AS Exam-style practice
114–115 UK A Level Exam-style practice

ANARCHISM

116 Rejection of the state
117 Liberty and order
118 Economic freedom and utopianism
119 Collectivist anarchism: anarcho-communism
120 Mutualism and anarcho-syndicalism
121 Individualist anarchism
122 Anarchist key thinkers
123. Exam skills

ECOLOGISM

124 Ecology and holism
125 Environmental ethics and consciousness
126 Materialism, consumerism, sustainability
127 Deep green ecology
128 Shallow green ecology
129 Social ecology
130 Agreement and tension within ecologism
131 Ecologist key thinkers
132 Exam skills

FEMINISM

133 Sex and gender
134 Patriarchy and 'the personal is political'
135 Equality and difference feminism; intersectionality
136 Liberal and socialist feminism
137 Radical feminism
138 Post-modern feminism
139 Differences within feminism
140 Feminist key thinkers
141 Exam skills

MULTICULTURALISM

142 Politics of recognition
143 Culture and identity
144 Minority rights
145 Diversity
146 Liberal multiculturalism

147 Pluralist multiculturalism
148 Cosmopolitan multiculturalism
149 The conservative criticism
150 Multiculturalist key thinkers
151 Exam skills

NATIONALISM

152 Nations
153 Self-determination and nation-states
154 Culturalism and racialism
155 Internationalism
156 Different types of nationalism
157 Liberal and conservative nationalism
158 Expansionist and anti/post-colonial nationalism
159 Differences within nationalism
160 Nationalist key thinkers
161 Exam skills
162 Exam-style practice

POLITICS OF THE USA

163 Comparative theories
164 The US Constitution
165 The constitutional framework
166 The amendment process
167 Principles of the US Constitution
168 Federalism
169 Evaluation of the US Constitution
170 The US Constitution and democracy
171 Federalism today
172 Constitutions compared
173 The structure of Congress
174 Powers within Congress
175 Representative function
176 Legislative function
177 Oversight function
178 Effectiveness of representation
179 Changing role and powers of Congress
180 The effectiveness of Congress
181 Legislatures compared
182 The US president
183 Informal sources of power
184 Executive Office of the President
185 Relationship with other institutions
186 Limits on the president's power
187 Achieving their aims
188 The imperial presidency
189 The president and foreign policy
190 Executives compared
191 Nature of the Supreme Court
192 The appointment process
193 Public policy

194 Political role of the Court
195 Rights today
196 Race and rights
197 Affirmative action
198 Judicial vs. political
199 Effectiveness of rights protection
200 Immigration reform
201 Judiciaries compared
202 Rights compared
203 The electoral process
204 The Electoral College
205 Significance of the electoral process
206 Incumbency
207 Campaign finance and reform
208 Electoral reform
209 Elections compared
210 Party principles
211 Party factions
212 Party power
213 Voters
214 Two-party system
215 Democracy compared
216 Significance of interest groups
217 Resources and tactics of interest groups
218 Interest group typology
219 Interest groups and democracy
220 Interest groups and influence
221 Interest groups compared
222–230 Exam skills
231 Exam-style practice

GLOBAL POLITICS

232 The state: nation-state
233 The state: national sovereignty
234 The state and globalisation
235 Economic and cultural globalisation
236 Political globalisation
237 Globalisation and international law
238 Humanitarian and forcible intervention
239 Globalisation and the nation-state
240 The impact of globalisation
241 Globalisation and contemporary issues
242 The United Nations (UN)
243 The UN Security Council (UNSC)
244 UN General Assembly, ECOSOC and ICJ
245 North Atlantic Treaty Organization (NATO)
246 The IMF and the World Bank
247 IMF and World Bank: significance and reform
248 The World Trade Organization (WTO)

249 The G7(8) and G20
250 Global governance and poverty
251 Poverty and development
252 Global governance and contemporary issues
253 International law and human rights
254 International Court of Justice
255 UN tribunals and the ICC
256 Human rights and international justice
257 Humanitarian intervention
258 Humanitarian intervention: controversy
259 The UNFCCC and Kyoto Protocol
260 Other international agreements
261 The IPCC
262 International cooperation
263 Competing views
264 Power and hard power
265 Soft and smart power
266 Classification of state power
267 Polarity
268 Changing nature of world order
269 A multipolar world
270 Different systems of government
271 Failed and rogue states
272 Global developments
273 Contemporary political issues
274 Different forms of regionalism
275 Regionalism and globalisation
276 Regionalism and sovereignty
277 NAFTA and the AU
278 The Arab League and ASEAN
279 European integration
280 The development of the EU
281 Key treaties of the EU
282 Key debates about the EU
283 The EU as a global actor
284 Regionalism and global issues
285 Realism in global politics
286 Realism in international anarchy
287 Conflict and the balance of power
288 Liberalism in global politics
289 Complex interdependence and global governance
290 Realism vs liberalism
291 The anarchical society
292 Globalisation and global governance
293 Global governance and regionalism
294 Power and developments
295–302 Exam skills
303 Exam-style practice

304 Answers

320 Glossary

Published by Pearson Education Limited, 80 Strand, London, WC2R 0RL.

www.pearsonschoolsandfecolleges.co.uk

Copies of official specifications for all Pearson qualifications may be found on the website: qualifications.pearson.com

Text and illustrations © Pearson Education Limited 2018
Typeset and illustrations by Tech-Set Ltd, Gateshead
Produced by Hart McLeod
Cover illustration by Eoin Coveney

The rights of Sarra Jenkins; Andrew Mitchell; Kathy Schindler and Adam Tomes to be identified as authors of this work have been asserted by them in accordance with the Copyright, Designs and Patents Act 1988.

First published 2018

25 24 23 22 21
10 9 8 7 6 5 4 3

British Library Cataloguing in Publication Data
A catalogue record for this book is available from the British Library

ISBN 978 1 292 22156 4

Printed by Neografia in Slovakia

Acknowledgements
The authors and publisher would like to thank the following individuals and organisations for permission to reproduce copyright material:

Text Credit(s):
p13: The Electoral Commission 'Political parties' 2016 financial accounts published (2017). Contains public sector information licensed under the Open Government Licence v3.0;**p32:** British Election Study(BES), © 1997, British Election Panel Survey [CREST]; **p74:** Make-up of House of Lords to be based on election results, © 2017, The Times; **p94:** Lord Neuberger on the Supreme Court Five Key Cases from its First Five Years by Chris Green © Independent 12 October 2014; **p94:** https://europa.eu/european-union/about-eu/eu-in-brief_en: The EU in brief: Goals and values of the EU, © 1995- 2018, European Union; **p100:** https://www.gov.uk/government/news/e-petitions: Adapted from E-Petitions Department for Digital, Culture, Media and Sport, © 2011, Contains public sector information licensed under the Open Government Licence v3.0; **p104:** Referendums are great . . . if you're a dictator, David Aaronovitch; *The Times*, Oct 19 2017, © 2017, Times Newspapers Limited; **p112:** https://www.parliament.uk/about/how/committees/select/: Select Committees; www.parliament.uk, (c) Parliamentary Copyright , Contains public sector information licensed under the Open Parliament Licence v3.0; **p114:** Election 2015: turnout crucial for Tories as Labour supporters stayed at home, © 2017, The Guardian; **p115:** https://www.parliament.uk/business/news/2010/12/elect-select-or-reject-the-future-of-the-house-of-lords-reform-options-pros-and-cons/: Lords reform options: pros and cons, www.parliament.uk (c) Parliamentary Copyright , Contains public sector information licensed under the Open Parliament Licence v3.0; **p128,264:** Report of the World Commission on Environment and Development: Our Common Future, © 1987, United Nations; **p149:** PM's speech at Munich Security Conference, © 2011, Crown Copyright, Contains public sector information licensed under the Open Government Licence v3.0; **p175:** https://www.opensecrets.org/overview/reelect.php: Re-Election Rates over the Years, © 2016, Center for Responsive Politics; **p179:** http://media.cq.com/votestudies/: 'Unity Vote Frequency Up in Senate and Down in House', © 2013, CQ Roll Call Inc; **p200:** http://www.pewhispanic.org/2017/09/18/facts-on-u-s-latinos/#hispanic-pop: Facts on U.S. Latinos, © 2015, Pew Research Center; **p209:**'Political Party Spending at Previous Elections', © 2017, Electoral Commission. Contains public sector information licensed under the Open Government Licence v3.0; **p233:** From Article 2 (4) - Prohibition of threat or use of force in international relations, by Repertoire of the practice of the security council, ©2017 United Nations. Reprinted with the permission of the United Nations; **p233:** From Article 2 (7) - Non-intervention in domestic affairs by the United Nations, by Repertoire of the practice of the security council, ©2017, United Nations. Reprinted with the permission of the United Nations ; **p251:** http://www.worldbank.org/en/topic/poverty/overview: The World Bank: Available under Creative Commons CC-BY 4.0; p321- 325 Pearson Edexcel Level 3 Advanced GCE in Politics – Specification – Issue 1 – March 2017 © 2017 Pearson Education Limited.

Pearson acknowledges use of the following extracts:
p33: From How Britain voted at the 2017 General Election, © 2017, YouGov; **p36:** Oakeshott, Michael, Rationalism in politics, and other essays, Methuen, © 1962, Methuen Publishing; **p47:** Russell, Bertrand, Why I Am not a Christian: And Other Essays on Religion and Related Subjects, © 1967, Taylor & Francis; **p125:** Leopold Aldo, The land Ethic, © 1949, Estate of Aldo Leopold; **p133:** https://www.businessinsider.com/sandberg-controversial-quotes-2013-3?IR=T: The 10 Most Controversial Things Sheryl Sandberg Just Said, Sandberg Sheryl, 2013 (c) Sheryl Sandberg; **p137:** Dworkin Andrea, Strong feminist voice was hardly a man hater, Houston Chronicle © 2005, Estate of Andrea Dworkin; **p138:** Richards Amy and Baumgardner Jennifer, Manifesta [10th Anniversary Edition]: Young Women, Feminism, and the Future, © 2010, Farrar Strauss and Giroux; **p138:** Femen, www.femen.org, © 2018, Femen; **p140:** De Beauvoir Simone, The Second Sex, © 1949, 2015, Vintage Classics; **p140:** Rowbotham Sheila, Resistance and Revolution: A History of Women and Revolution in the Modern World (Radical Thinkers), © 2014, Penguin Random House; **p142:** Parekh Bhikhu, Parekh Report, © 2000, Runnymede Trust; **p143:** https://blacklivesmatter.com/about/what-we-believe: What we believe, © 2018, Black Lives Matter; **p165:** Neustadt Richard, Presidential Power and the Modern Presidents: The Politics of Leadership from Roosevelt to Reagan, © 1964, 1990, Free Press; **p264:** Nye Joseph, Soft Power: The Means to Success in World Politics, © 2004, Public Affairs; **p274:** https://au.int/en/about/vision : Vision of the African Union, © 2004, African Union; **p279:** Monnet Jean, Estate of Monnet Jean, © 1970; **p285:** Morgenthau Joachim Hans, Politics Among Nations: The Struggle for Power and Peace, © 1960, Knopf; **p285:** Robert J Art, ''War with Iraq is not in America's National Interest'', © 2003, Robert J Art and Others

Credit(s)
Photographs
(Key: T-top; B-bottom; C-centre; L-left; R-right)
123RF: Georgios Kollidas 51l, Scanrail 52l, Karel Miragaya 52r, Andreanita 95b, Sanchai Loongroong 125c, platongkoh 125, **Shutterstock:** 8tr, 8br, 87b,182, Ben Cawthra 8tl,138br, Photofusion 8bl, Equinox Features 15b, James Gourley 17t, **David Fowler** 22bl, **Wavebreakmedia** 46b, **Everett Historical** 51r, 60br, justasc 68tr, 164, RMV 72, Andy Rain / EPA 90tl, Leonello calvetti 127,128, M-SUR 134, Ms Jane Campbell 138tr, Alva Viarruel 146, Paul Brown 152tl, Everett Historical 184, Peter Foley/Epa-Efe 186, AP 191, railway fx 245, photocosmos1 246bl, Krysja 246br, Nerthuz 266, AlexLMX 277tl, Claire Doherty/Sipa USA 91br, **Alamy Stock Photo:** Homer Sykes Archive 22tl, Lee snider 57b, World History Archive 60tr, Ian Dagnall Computing 69t, carol moir 143, Chronicle 155, Kelly Neilson 157cl, Mark Thomas 157cr, Pictorial Press Ltd 158 tr, Stacy Walsh Rosenstock 169, dpa picture alliance 177, John Frost Newspapers 188, Thabo Jaiyesimi 196, Alex Arnold 218br, Heritage Image Partnership Ltd 232, Olekcii Mach 233, Max McClure 242, PeerPoint 273, Nick Fox 277tr,**Getty Images:** Peter Macdiarmid 9l, AFP Contributor 76br, Handout 85c, WPA Pool / Pool 90cl, AFP / Stringer 91bl, Handout 85, Miguel Villagran 149, PAU BARRENA/AFP Contributor 152br, Scott Olson 218cl, Laurent Van Der Stockt/ Gamma-Rapho 238, Jerry Cooke/Pix Inc./The LIFE Images Collection 279tr, **Newscom:** Robert Eames B433 9r, Pa/ZUMA Press/Newscom 76tc, **Bridgeman Images:** Granger 158bl, **Pearson Education Ltd:** Jules Selmes 274, **Barry Deutsch cartoonist:** 197

Notes from the publisher
1. While the publishers have made every attempt to ensure that advice on the qualification and its assessment is accurate, the official specification and associated assessment guidance materials are the only authoritative source of information and should always be referred to for definitive guidance.
   Pearson examiners have not contributed to any sections in this resource relevant to examination papers for which they have responsibility.
2. Pearson has robust editorial processes, including answer and fact checks, to ensure the accuracy of the content in this publication, and every effort is made to ensure this publication is free of errors. We are, however, only human, and occasionally errors do occur. Pearson is not liable for any misunderstandings that arise as a result of errors in this publication, but it is our priority to ensure that the content is accurate. If you spot an error, please do contact us at resourcescorrections@pearson.com so we can make sure it is corrected.

Representative democracy

'Democracy' is a catch-all term which has no precise meaning other than that the people (*demos*) are involved in their own rule (*kratia*).

Definition of democracy

Abraham Lincoln famously described democracy as 'government of the people, by the people, for the people'. With this statement, he clarified the principles of democracy:

1 *of the people* – this suggests that the people governing must be 'ordinary people'

2 *by the people* – this suggests that the people must have a say in choosing who rules over them

3 *for the people* – this suggests that those in charge must govern in the interests of the people.

The two most common forms are **representative democracy** and **direct democracy** (see page 2 for more on direct democracy).

Representative democracy

DECISION

the people

Parliament

the politician

In representative (indirect) democracy, the people elect representatives who take decisions on their behalf.

Advantages and disadvantages

Advantages	Disadvantages
Professional politicians make complex decisions	Citizens are disengaged from politics
Minority views are considered and upheld	Tightly controlled parties result in politicians lacking independence
Elected politicians are held to account by the people	Politicians are skilled at swerving accountability and passing the buck
The most practical form of democracy	Politicians are open to corruption and self-interest

Features of representative democracy

Features	Is the UK a representative democracy?
The election of representatives should be regular, competitive and secret, and carried out without force and with universal adult suffrage.	In the UK, elections must be held every five years, using **first-past-the-post (FPTP)**. They are held in secret and the results are legally binding.
Civil liberties must be protected. For example, freedom of assembly, press, etc.	There are established rights and freedoms, now enshrined in UK law by the Human Rights Act 1998 (see page 10 to read more about civil rights in the UK).
Elections must be contested by numerous political parties.	There are numerous political parties that contest elections. For example, Labour, Conservative, Liberal Democrats (Lib Dems).
Constitutional checks exist to prevent a concentration of government power.	The UK **constitution**, although **uncodified**, sets the boundaries of the democratic system (see pages 68–74 for more on the constitution).
An assembly exists which reflects the make-up of society and passes laws.	Political decisions are made by Members of Parliament (MPs); they sit in a parliament and are expected to represent the views of the electorate.
Pressure groups should have the opportunity and freedom to put forward their views.	Pressure groups are seen as an integral part of the UK democratic, representative system.
An independent judiciary should exist.	In the UK, the judiciary is separated from the **executive** and legislature (see page 92 for more on the judiciary's independence).

Now try this

Identify two ways the UK is a representative democracy.

Direct democracy

Direct democracy does not currently exist in any country. However, it is important to understand it as an alternative model of democracy. In calling **Parliament**, Edward I proclaimed: 'What touches all, should be approved of all.'

→ DECISION

In direct democracy, the people make decisions for themselves. In its purest form, there is **no** government.

Advantages and disadvantages

Advantages	Disadvantages
Everyone in society participates	Impractical to achieve securely as it requires all citizens to be involved in decision-making daily
People directly make decisions in their interests	Citizens become apathetic if they are asked to participate too often
All citizens' voices are equal	People will vote in their own interest, not society's
It is the purest form of democracy	No minority voices can be heard, resulting in the tyranny of the majority

Athenian democracy

The population of Ancient Athens (508–322 BC) was around 250,000 people. Of these, only male citizens, 18 years or over, could speak and vote in the Assembly.

The Assembly

The Assembly, formed of around 30,000 people, was regularly attended by perhaps 3,000 citizens. At times, attendance at the Assembly was paid in order to encourage citizens who lived far away or couldn't afford the time off to attend. Thucydides, an Athenian historian and general, stated: 'We alone consider a citizen who does not partake in politics... useless.'

Checks and balances

- These processes were to ensure **checks and balances** to potential abuses of power.
- By using sortition to select positions, and sticking to strict term limits, it was difficult for any individual or small group to dominate.
- Corruption was reduced as no one ever knew who would be selected to serve next.

How it worked

- The assembly met two to three times a month and could accommodate around 6,000 citizens.
- The *boulé*, formed of 500 citizens, decided the topics to be discussed in the Assembly. They were chosen by lot (known as sortition) and each served for a year.
- Any citizen could speak to the Assembly and vote on decisions.
- The majority won and the decision was final.
- Presidents, elected by lot, organised the proceedings and assessed the voting.
- The Assembly could also vote to ostracise (banish) any citizen who had become too powerful and dangerous.

Evaluation

👍 Democracy in Ancient Athens was a revolutionary system.

👍 It gave all citizens equal political rights, regardless of wealth, social standing, education, ancestry, etc.

👎 Only adult, male citizens could apply for the privileges and duties of government; women were totally excluded.

👎 Of the 250,000 people in Athens, approximately 3,000 actively participated in politics.

👎 Of this number, as few as 100 citizens – the wealthiest, most influential and the best speakers – dominated the political arena.

👎 The people were too often swayed by a good orator or got carried away with their emotions.

👎 They often lacked the necessary knowledge to make informed decisions.

👎 The citizen body was still a closed political elite.

 Now try this

Identify two differences between direct and representative democracy.

How healthy is UK democracy?

While no one disputes that the UK is a democracy, it is useful to assess how well the system functions.

Elections

👍 Free and fair, based on universal franchise/suffrage, choice and party competition.

👍 FPTP (see page 24) has strengths such as simplicity, speed, constituency–MP link.

👍 The use of proportional representation (PR) for devolved elections is an improvement.

👎 FPTP is disproportionate and leaves minor parties under-represented. It also leads to wasted votes.

In 2015, for example, 50 per cent of votes cast were cast for a losing candidate.

👍 Turnout is not high but is in line with many other Western democracies.

For example, 69 per cent in 2017.

👎 The health of representative democracy has been called into question by **general public apathy towards politics** (see page 4).

Representation

👍 The UK Parliament represents constituents **and** holds the government to account on behalf of the electorate (see page 87).

👎 Parliament can be ineffective in holding the government to account as it is dominated by a government with an overall majority (see page 75 for more on the role of Parliament).

👎 The unelected House of Lords has the ability to delay laws (see page 80 for more on its power and limitations).

👍 All citizens are **represented by an MP** and can expect their concerns to be taken up.

👎 Many MPs can ignore their constituents' concerns because they hold 'safe seats' and want to remain loyal to their party.

👎 Women, ethnic minorities and the working class are **under-represented** in Parliament.

Citizens' rights

👍 There are extensive freedoms and rights incorporated in the **Human Rights Act 1998** (see page 10).

👎 The Human Rights Act is not fully entrenched; governments can ignore judges' rulings.

👍 The **Freedom of Information Act 2000** requires the government to reveal information on how and why decisions were taken on behalf of the people (see page 10).

👎 The Freedom of Information Act has too many exemptions which governments use to further their own interests.

Pressure groups

👍 Pressure groups supplement democracy by giving a voice to minorities, allowing citizens to exert influence between elections (see page 6 for more on pressure groups).

👎 Wealthy and powerful pressure groups may pursue their own interests, which may not benefit the majority of the population.

👍 Pressure groups enhance democracy by ensuring political diversity.

👎 The leaders of pressure groups are not elected, accountable, or under public scrutiny.

Limited government

👍 The UK constitution is effective at limiting government and adapting to changing circumstances (see page 68).

👎 There is no codified constitution, so power distribution is undefined.

👎 The fusion of executive and legislature creates an over-powerful executive (see page 84).

Independent judiciary

👍 The rule of law is protected by judicial independence to protect citizens and limit government (see page 92).

👍 All governments are subject to law, upheld by judges via judicial review and the Human Rights Act (see page 93 for more on the Supreme Court).

👎 Government has a role in appointing judges.

Now try this

What is meant by (i) limited government and (ii) judicial independence?

3

Participation crisis

One of the key concerns over the last few decades with the UK's democracy is the extent to which citizens have been getting involved in decision-making. This has led many to ponder whether the UK is facing a **participation crisis**.

Falling participation

There is evidence of falling participation levels in elections over the last 50 years:

👎 Turnout in general elections has been falling since 1979.

   It was 76 per cent in 1979 (84 per cent in 1950); in 2001, it was 59 per cent.

👎 European, local and other elections have seen even lower turnouts – 35.2 per cent in 2014 European elections; 36% in 2018 local elections; 15.1 per cent for police commissioner elections in 2012.

👎 In 2011, on average only 42 per cent bothered to vote in some referenda.

Further evidence

There is evidence of falling participation in other areas:

👎 Party membership has fallen since the 1980s. There are fewer party activists, leading to difficulties in recruiting candidates locally.

👎 The public is disillusioned with the lack of core differences between the parties, leading to **partisan dealignment** (see page 30 for more on voting trends).

👎 Voter registration among young people is lower than among older people.

👎 Public trust in politicians has been undermined by, for example, sexual harassment allegations.

Positive participation

Turnout levels may not be so bad:

👍 Turnout levels have risen in general elections, from 59 per cent in 2001 to 69 per cent in 2017.

👍 If we combine voting for all new elections, political participation has risen (though it is still not as high as in the 1970s).

👍 The Scottish Independence referendum (2014) saw an engaged population and turnout at 85 per cent; 75 per cent of 16- and 17-year-olds voted. The **European Union (EU)** referendum in 2016 had a very high turnout of 72.2 per cent

👍 Some argue that the election of Jeremy Corbyn as leader of the Labour Party has reinvigorated young people. The 2017 general election saw large numbers of young people registering to vote and then voting.

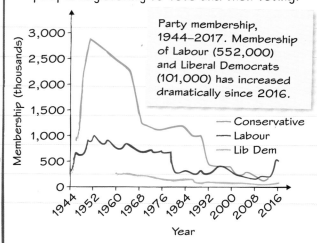

Party membership, 1944–2017. Membership of Labour (552,000) and Liberal Democrats (101,000) has increased dramatically since 2016.

Increasing participation

Other signs that participation is growing are:

👍 The number and membership of pressure groups has increased, suggesting participation has changed.

👍 There have been over 26,000 e-petitions on the government's website, showing high levels of engagement.

👍 Protesting and campaigning via Facebook has also become a popular way of participating.

👍 Using Twitter to engage with MPs, commentators and journalists.

Anti-politics

Anti-politics is often used to describe: **distrust** of politicians; **dislike** of party politics; **disaffection** with democracy. It is caused by:

👍 complacency in rich Western nations

👍 a lack of interest in political institutions (especially in the young)

👍 people feeling they are being taken for granted and turning away from political elites who seek power and break promises with impunity

👍 voters not being committed to any party.

Now try this

How has 'anti-politics' resentment shown itself across the Western world?

Reforming UK democracy

The UK has been accused of having a **democratic deficit**. A number of reforms have been suggested to remove the deficit (see pages 73–74 for more on democratic reforms).

Steps to improve democracy

Between 1884 and 1928 the UK moved from a system of voting for privileged landowners to universal adult suffrage. However, democracy and participation could be further improved by making voting compulsory for all adults, lowering the voting age to 16 and making use of the internet.

Compulsory voting

MPs would be more representative and legitimate. However, to force someone to vote may be unfair as there may be no real choice for them.

👍 Governments could claim greater **legitimacy**.

👍 Political participation is a civic duty; compulsory voting would have wider educational implications as all of society would be aware of this fact.

👍 The greater the level of political participation, the greater the likelihood that citizens will think and act as full citizens.

👎 Compulsory voting would simply mask deeper engagement issues.

👎 It could encourage non-serious voting.

👎 It could be considered a violation of individual freedom (which includes the right **not** to vote).

Lowering the voting age

Matching the voting age to other 'maturation' levels is fair and will develop political engagement. However, are 16 year olds experienced enough to make that choice?

👍 Voting at 16 would match other aspects of citizenship available at this age.

👍 The needs, views, concerns and interests of 16–17 year olds are marginalised.

👍 It may help re-engage young voters by strengthening their interest.

👎 Age 16 is too young. Most are in full-time education and living with their parents.

👎 Young voters are less likely to vote than other age groups and this will result in a decline in turnout percentage.

eDemocracy

eDemocracy is the use of the internet to increase and enhance citizens' engagement in democratic processes.

Examples include e-petitions, blogs and Twitter, as well as e-campaigns.

👍 Citizens can express their views without having to leave home.

👍 New technology enlarges citizens' access to information, making possible a truly free exchange of ideas and views.

👍 eDemocracy creates a genuinely democratic process in which citizens become active, not passive, participants in politics.

👎 The risk of hacking could undermine the legitimacy of elections.

For example, hacking allegedly took place in the 2016 US presidential election.

👎 It threatens to turn democracy into a series of push-button referendums, like a reality TV show, eroding its importance.

Other possible reforms

Greater use of referenda to give legitimacy to decisions. However, referenda can be very divisive.

Change to the voting system would make citizens' votes more valuable. However, where PR has been introduced it has not delivered increased turnout.

Constitutional reform of the organisation and structure of government may improve both participation and democracy (see page 77 for more on recent constitutional reforms).

Now try this

Give three examples of eDemocracy.

Group politics

Group politics refers to the many different types of groups seeking to exert pressure on the government.

Types of pressure groups

Sectional/interest groups
Membership is often restricted to particular sections of society, e.g. teachers, lawyers. They aim to look after the interests of that particular group.

Outsider groups
Outsider groups are not closely associated with government and are largely excluded from political consultation and contact. They usually concentrate on mobilising public opinion to put pressure on government.

Promotional/cause groups
Membership tends to be open – seeking to gain a mass of support. Cause groups tend to have altruistic policies, i.e. they benefit wider society.

Insider groups
Insider groups have a special relationship with government. Their aims are usually compatible with government.

Other collective organisations

Corporations

Large companies seek to lobby the government to encourage them to legislate (or not legislate) in certain areas.

For example, after the recent decision to revoke its licence in London, Uber took to heavy lobbying to convince the public and authorities that Transport for London had made the wrong decision.

Think tanks

Think tanks refer to privately funded, non-profit organisations that conduct research with a view to changing political policies. Arguably, good think tanks are as rigorous as academic research and as accessible as journalism. Well-known think tanks in the UK include:

- The Centre for Policy Studies
- The Adam Smith Institute
- The Centre for Social Justice

Lobbyists

Lobbyists are companies who get paid to gain access to government for their clients. Lobbying companies often employ ex-politicians who know how to access decision-makers. The ethics of this style of lobbying is often questioned, as companies can afford to pay lobbying companies' fees in order to influence government.

Parliament and big business

Well known in the USA, the issue of a 'revolving door' between Parliament and big business has recently come under criticism. The number of former ministers taking up jobs outside Parliament rose by nearly 60 per cent in 2017.

In 2017, for example, former Chancellor George Osborne was criticised for becoming editor of the *Evening Standard* and other roles such as a £650,000-a-year advisory post at BlackRock.

Access points

Access points refer to the places pressure groups try to exert influence.

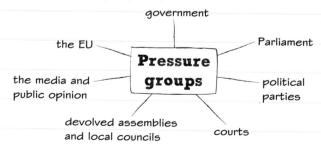

Now try this

Explain how Uber can be considered a pressure group.

Methods used by pressure groups

The methods used by pressure groups vary depending on their relationship to the government.

Insider methods

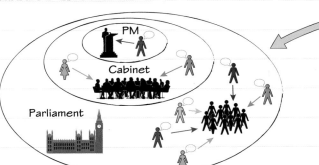

Outsider methods

The public   Pressure group

Insider methods seek to influence the government **directly** by having contact with politicians and decision makers. Methods are 'quiet' as they already have access to government (advising, sharing research).

Outsider groups influence government **indirectly** by informing and persuading the public to support them, hoping this will influence the government. They use 'loud' methods.

Pressure groups may:

- try to access key decision-makers – the prime minister (PM), **Cabinet** and civil servants – to argue the case directly
- provide specialist information and advice when the government is considering new legislation; this provides pressure groups with access to influence governments
- try to target and influence specific members of the House of Commons, Lords, EU and so on.

  For example, many UK policies regarding farming are made at an EU level. The National Farmers Union therefore lobbies Brussels, not Westminster.

Methods include:

- mass public campaigns such as marches and demonstrations to put pressure on government, for example, the Stop the War and anti-austerity demonstrations in London
- **publicity stunts** of various kinds
- **social media**, **e-petitions** and the **internet** to voice their concerns and raise public support
- the **use of celebrities** to contribute to news and current affairs television programmes
- **civil disobedience** and **illegal activities** (see below).

Direct action

Direct action is where the public actively becomes involved in politics as opposed to dealing through a representative or simply voting in elections. Direct action takes many forms:

- **marches and demonstrations** to show objection or support, for example, anti-Brexit marches or 'Day of rage' Grenfell Tower protests
- trade unions may go on **strike**, for example, junior doctors striking to protest against the imposition of new contracts

- **sit-ins**, for example, Occupy London
- **illegal acts**, for example, against animal testing, such as grave violation or harassing animal laboratories. They are used when other non-direct methods have failed and to attract the media spotlight.

Civil disobedience

Civil disobedience is a form of direct action and is the refusal to obey certain laws. It is one of the many ways people have rebelled against what they deem to be unfair laws.

It has been used in many **non-violent resistance** movements in India and the American Civil Rights Movement. Fathers4Justice, who climbed famous buildings wearing costumes, is a modern example.

Now try this

Why do different pressure groups use different methods?

Factors influencing the success of groups

Here we look at why some pressure groups are more successful than others.

Insider

Insider groups are consulted by governments. Their aims tend to be compatible with government and if they are important to the economy, they will get a sympathetic hearing from government.

The Confederation of British Industry (CBI) works very closely with government to help achieve economic growth and prosperity.

Social status

An important social position in society can be key to success, including doctors, nurses and the police. These are groups who may not have economic power but have instead high social status (social power).

Nurses demonstrating against cuts in the NHS receive support from the population, which recognises the key role they play in society.

Wealth

Wealth can be decisive. Large industries, trade unions and charities command large funds for campaign purposes. They can afford to hire expensive lobbyists who advise on how best to conduct their campaign.

Unison is a wealthy trade union with over 1.2 million members.

Celebrity

Having a celebrity endorsement can be a real help in publicising a campaign.

For example, Jamie Oliver's campaign for good food in schools revolutionised our attitude to school meals, with governments getting on board to support his campaign.

Another example of this is Joanna Lumley and her successful fight for Gurkhas' rights.

Public support

Some groups are successful because they enjoy public support and sympathy. Even if the government is not concerned about the issue, it would feel under pressure from the public to act.

For example, the NSPCC campaigns against cruelty to children and has widespread public support, so the government is sympathetic to the issues it supports.

Size

The size of a pressure group is a key factor. Groups with mass memberships or which clearly represent a large proportion of the electorate are more likely to enjoy success.

For example, Age UK represents 12 million pensioners. As older people have the highest percentage turnout in elections, pensioners are usually well looked after by successive governments.

Now try this

Put your top three factors in order of importance and explain your order in one sentence.

Groups and democracy

It is important to be able to assess and evaluate the significance of pressure groups for democracy.

Strengths of pressure groups

Groups enhance democracy in several ways.

👍 They enable individuals to **participate in the political process** between elections.

The Plane Stupid campaign to prevent a third runway at Heathrow involved 13 campaigners shackling themselves together on a runway in 2015.

👍 Pressure groups reflect the system of pluralist democracy, which **gives citizens another voice** in the decision-making process beyond parties.

👍 Pressure groups counter-balance the **tyranny of the majority** by lobbying on behalf of minorities. They ensure that minorities, such as gay people, the elderly and students, can have their voice heard.

For example, Stonewall has been campaigning for decades to get equality for gay people. In 2014, David Cameron legalised gay marriage, which Stonewall had been campaigning on.

👍 They can bring **expert knowledge** to the government's attention on an important issue. Ministers and MPs are rarely experts on every issue.

👍 Pressure groups keep government on its toes, and encourage government to be responsible, democratic and answerable. They act as a **limit to government** power.

👍 Pressure groups promote debate and **educate and inform the electorate**. They ensure healthy debate occurs.

Weaknesses of pressure groups

Groups also undermine democracy in several ways.

👎 They can be divisive and **selfish**. One powerful group can dominate an issue.

For example, when trade unions strike, as the BMA did in 2012, the Fire Brigade's Union did in 2013 and NHS workers did in 2014.

👎 Pressure groups are very good at **stopping things which others feel are needed**.

Opposition to High Speed Two (HS2) raised concerns that it could affect house prices and noise levels, and spoil the countryside. Supporters argue that this is outweighed by the economic benefits the line would bring to the country.

👎 Pressure groups are **not accountable to the public** as a whole despite the fact that their influence on policy can be large. They often work with governments behind closed doors.

For example, the British Bankers Association has very close links with the government. It is suggested that the heavy lobbying done by the group in the aftermath of the banking collapse stopped severe punishments to the banking sector and individual bankers.

👎 Pressure groups have **reduced the power of Parliament** and undermined its sovereignty by working closely with ministers and civil servants (see page 97 for more on how sovereignty is exercised). By the time Parliament sees legislation, it is all but decided.

👎 They make the country **difficult to manage** and govern. 'Hyper-pluralism' depicts the difficulty a government may encounter when it is perplexed by a multitude of pressure groups blocking their actions.

Now try this

Identify one strength and one weakness of pressure groups to democracy.

Rights in the UK

Part of a healthy democracy is protection of rights. The UK is unusual in that it does not have a codified, entrenched bill of rights. So, what are our rights, and where can we find them?

What are civil liberties?

Civil liberties are the rights that citizens have in a democracy.

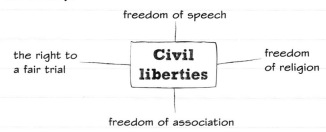

freedom of speech

the right to a fair trial — **Civil liberties** — freedom of religion

freedom of association

In many democracies, these freedoms are enshrined in a Bill of Rights. In Britain, civil liberties are simply part of the law of the land and can be changed by governments.

Human Rights Act (1998)

The Human Rights Act (HRA) is one of the most important ways that rights are protected.

- It incorporated the European Convention on Human Rights (ECHR) 1950 into UK law.
- Citizens can now challenge laws in UK courts rather than having to go to the European Court of Human Rights (ECHR).
- UK courts can issue a 'declaration of incompatibility', which can put pressure on the government to back down (see pages 3 and 77 for more on constitutional reform).
- The ECHR is nothing to do with the European Union, and Brexit will have no effect on the Human Rights Act (HRA) and the ECHR.

Freedom of Information Act (2000)

- It was introduced to create a more open system of government.
- It gives citizens the 'right to know' information regarding how and who made decisions.
- It allows the public to access files from any government body. Any person can request information and has a right to have that information given to them.
- However, it has some major exceptions to it, particularly if it affects national security.

The Equality Act (2010)

This combined earlier legislation making it illegal to discriminate in nine areas.

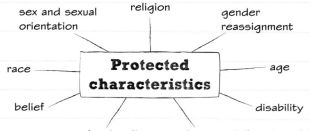

sex and sexual orientation   religion   gender reassignment

race — **Protected characteristics** — age

belief   disability

pregnancy and maternity   marriage or civil partnership

How are rights protected in the UK?

Judicial review

- Judicial review is a review of ministers and officials' decisions to ensure they are lawful.
- Ministerial decisions and actions can be declared unlawful when they are *ultra vires*. That is, when the minister is acting beyond their powers.
- Anyone can apply for a judicial review for one of three reasons: authority has been exceeded, procedural impropriety or acting in an 'irrational' or 'unreasonable' way.

Conflict between individual and collective rights

What makes rights protection complicated is the conflict between individual and collective rights. Whose rights should prevail?

Common law

- Common law refers to rules that have been established through customs.
- Judges have decided that some rules are so firmly rooted in 'commonly held' traditions that they have the force of law. It is therefore left for judges to interpret what they are.
- Statute law takes precedence over common law.

Common-law marriage, the right to hunt with foxes and the right to roam began as common law but were subsequently superseded by statute law.

Individual rights	Collective rights
Right to privacy	Freedom of the press
Freedom of expression	Upholding religious/racial tolerance
Right to protest	Right to peaceful existence
Freedom of movement/ assembly	Security of the nation

Now try this

How did the Human Rights Act give us positive rights?

Are our rights protected?

While our rights have increased, critics have recently argued that some rights are under threat.

How well are rights protected in the UK?

👍 The HRA and other laws mean that rights are set out clearly and in detail.

👍 A rights-based culture has been established.

👍 This allows the judiciary to be active in defending rights.

👍 Pressure groups, such as Liberty, work to stop governments undermining rights.

👎 Citizens' rights have been restricted as governments seek to protect citizens from terrorism.

👎 The right to protest near Parliament has been restricted.

👎 The government has also introduced 'control orders' to restrict freedom of movement.

👎 The media undermines rights protection by portraying Acts like the HRA as restricting rights.

Possible threats to civil liberties in the UK

Threat	Use
Surveillance	The UK has more surveillance cameras than any other country in Europe. In 2010, it was estimated that there is one CCTV camera for every 14 people.
Stop and search	Police now have the power to stop and search any suspected person without having to record why they have done this.
Freedom of expression	Laws against incitement to racial or religious hatred are often seen as threats to free speech.
Political demonstrations	Police are increasingly using powerful public order laws to prevent legitimate protests.
Anti-terrorism	It is claimed that anti-terrorism has led the police to make excessive use of powers of search and interrogation on the grounds of national security.

Rights protection cases

The Abu Qatada case (2012)

A 2012 ECHR judgement prevented the deportation of the radical Islamist cleric to Jordan where he risked being tortured and tried. He was finally removed in 2013, and was tried and acquitted. Theresa May, then Home Secretary, said he would have been removed earlier had the ECHR not 'moved the goalposts' by establishing new, unprecedented legal grounds for blocking his deportation.

The Belmarsh ruling (2004)

Law Lords ruled 8–1 against the government's indefinite detention of terrorist suspects in Belmarsh prison. Lord Hoffmann ruled that there was no 'state of public emergency threatening the life of the nation' – the only basis for Britain opting-out of Article 5 of the European Convention, the right to liberty.

The Poundland case (2013)

Cait Reilly won her claim that it was unlawful to force her to work for free at Poundland as a condition of her claiming jobseeker's allowance. The court ruled that the government had acted unlawfully by not giving unemployed people enough information about the penalties they faced if they refused to work unpaid.

Segregation in schools ruling (2017)

The court ruled that a co-educational faith school in Birmingham had caused unlawful discrimination by separating boys and girls. Ofsted argued that the school had breached the Equality Act 2010 by segregating pupils, teaching them in different classrooms and making them use separate play areas.

Now try this

Pick one of the cases above and name the right (or rights) being threatened.

Political parties

A political party is a group of people who want to win elections to become the government. You need to know how political parties are defined.

Functions

Political parties perform several functions:

- **Representation**: they represent the views and beliefs of large sections of society and act in their interests.

- **Participation**: parties enable individuals to participate effectively in the political process, and to influence the decisions that affect their lives.

- **Elections**: they offer the electorate choice in elections.

- **Government**: they hold government office and run the country.

- **Organisation**: they organise and bring together a variety of demands into a coherent political programme.

- **Education**: parties educate and inform the general public.

Features

There are four features that usually distinguish political parties from other social groups:

1. Parties aim to become a government by putting candidates up for election and mobilising support.

2. Parties are organised bodies with a formal membership.

3. Parties typically adopt a broad-issue focus, addressing major issues of government policy.

4. To varying degrees, parties are united by shared political preferences and a shared ideological identity.

Left wing

Left-wing political ideas are those associated with a desire to introduce change into the political system. Left-wing ideas look to make society more equal and favour the group solution above the individual, and thus support state intervention and collectivism. They are usually associated with welfare, economic intervention and wealth redistribution.

Right wing

Right-wing political ideas emphasise a widespread acceptance of the status quo and the need for stability in society. Right-wing ideas seek to give individuals more freedom and favour the individual in preference to the group, and thus favour the market and individualism. They would therefore support low taxes, limited welfare and free market economics.

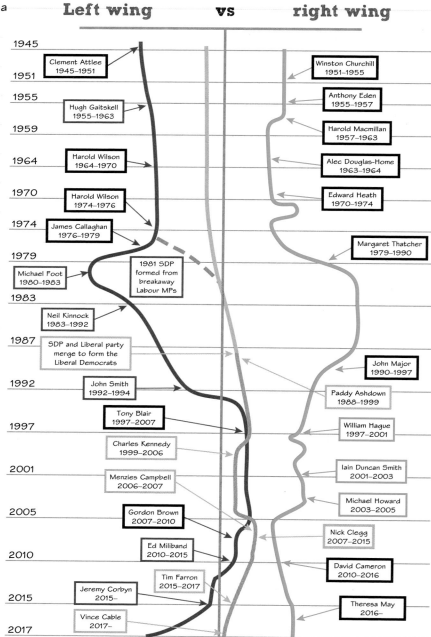

Left wing   vs   right wing

Year	
1945	Clement Attlee 1945–1951
1951	Winston Churchill 1951–1955
1955	Anthony Eden 1955–1957
	Hugh Gaitskell 1955–1963
1959	Harold Macmillan 1957–1963
1964	Harold Wilson 1964–1970 / Alec Douglas-Home 1963–1964
1970	Harold Wilson 1974–1976 / Edward Heath 1970–1974
1974	James Callaghan 1976–1979
1979	1981 SDP formed from breakaway Labour MPs / Margaret Thatcher 1979–1990
	Michael Foot 1980–1983
1983	Neil Kinnock 1983–1992
1987	SDP and Liberal party merge to form the Liberal Democrats
	John Major 1990–1997
1992	John Smith 1992–1994 / Paddy Ashdown 1988–1999
1997	Tony Blair 1997–2007 / William Hague 1997–2001
	Charles Kennedy 1999–2006
2001	Menzies Campbell 2006–2007 / Iain Duncan Smith 2001–2003
2005	Michael Howard 2003–2005 / Gordon Brown 2007–2010
	Nick Clegg 2007–2015
2010	Ed Miliband 2010–2015 / David Cameron 2010–2016
2015	Tim Farron 2015–2017 / Jeremy Corbyn 2015– / Theresa May 2016–
2017	Vince Cable 2017–

Now try this

Identify one feature of left-wing ideas and one of right-wing ideas.

Enhancing democracy and funding

Political parties are a vital part of the UK's representative democracy. One democratic feature of the UK political system is the funding of political parties.

Do political parties enhance or threaten democracy?

Enhance democracy	Threaten democracy
Political parties **encourage people to participate in politics** via party activity, election campaigning, voting and standing for office.	Political parties engage in adversarial politics, which threatens to reduce Parliament and politics to silly rituals and point-scoring.
They **provide voters with choices**, and help to make electoral choice clearer and more coherent.	Turnout at elections is not particularly high, which may indicate that the public's faith in political parties is low.
They help to **educate and inform** the electorate about key political issues through political debate and by presenting a range of arguments.	Parties may sometimes **oversimplify issues** or present information in a misleading way, especially in election campaigns.
They **uphold the authority of Parliament** and reinforce respect for political institutions.	The need for increasing amounts of finance for election campaigns creates a situation in which **rich interest groups** ('big business', media organisations or trade unions) **become excessively influential**.
They **facilitate representation** by serving as a channel of communication between government and people.	They fail to reflect the society they 'represent'. Women and ethnic minorities are under-represented, particularly in senior party roles.
They **administer** elections, encouraging people to vote and presenting election issues clearly to the electorate.	
Legitimate political parties ensure that there is a **peaceful transition of power** after elections.	

Funding of parties

While MPs are paid by the state, political parties must fund their own activities, which usually consists of membership fees and donations.

Political party income in 2016

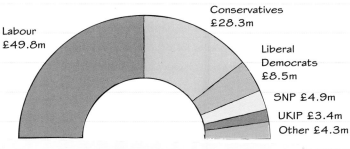

Labour £49.8m
Conservatives £28.3m
Liberal Democrats £8.5m
SNP £4.9m
UKIP £3.4m
Other £4.3m

The Electoral Commission keeps a record of every donation to political parties above £7,500.

Donations

Political parties can accept donations if they come from 'permissible sources'. That is:

- someone on the UK electoral register
- a UK registered company
- a registered political party
- a registered trade union or building/friendly society.

There are no rules limiting the amount of money that individuals may give, as long as the donation is declared and the donor is permissible. It is the amount that parties may spend that is limited.

Should parties receive state funding?

👍 It stops wealthy groups influencing parties.

👍 Parties can focus on representing the electorate, not fundraising.

👍 Smaller parties will get fair financial support.

👍 Less wealthy pressure groups will get a more equal hearing by parties.

👎 Politicians may be less interested in what pressure groups have to say.

👎 Taxpayers should not be funding political parties.

👎 There would be disagreement over how funding would be allocated.

Now try this

Give two ways in which political parties enhance democracy.

The history of the Labour Party

The Labour Party was founded in 1900 and declared itself to be a socialist party committed to a peaceful, parliamentary route to socialism. It has historically shown a commitment to a milder version of socialism, known as social democracy (to learn about the principles of social democracy see page 61). This type of socialism seeks to reform capitalism, not overthrow it.

Old Labour (social democracy), 1945–1994

Ideas and principles	Examples of ideas and principles reflected in policies
Equality – people are of equal worth and there should be no unjustified privilege or inequality in society	• Tax and welfare should be used to reduce differences in income • Wealth should not give anyone unjustified access to power
Collectivism – humans are social animals who prefer to work collectively	• The welfare state to be funded by taxes and all should be equally entitled to it • Strong trade unions are needed to defend workers' interests
Capitalism – capitalism must be controlled	• Key industries should be nationalised • Control capitalism to limit its exploitation of the working class
Social justice – all should have access to a decent standard of living	• Free education and welfare are at the heart of social justice • Strong laws to guarantee equal rights and outlaw discrimination
Class and society – recognise class divisions as problematic in society	• Highly progressive taxes and welfare to make society more economically equal • Firm economic management to control unemployment

New Labour (Third Way), 1994–2010

Ideas and principles	Examples of ideas and principles reflected in policies
Individualism – greater emphasis on the ability of the individual to realise their own potential	• Low income tax to be retained to encourage work • Home ownership to be encouraged • Small business to be encouraged and supported
Free market – accepted as the best form of wealth creation	• No more nationalisation and some further privatisation • Reduce corporate taxes to encourage enterprise • Trade unions should be weak to ensure free labour markets
Welfare state – support welfare state and increased spending	• Increased spending on health and education • Education to maximise ability of individuals • Welfare to be targeted to most needy and as an incentive to work
Social justice – all should have access to a decent standard of living	• Welfare state to guarantee living standards • Strong laws to guarantee equal rights and outlaw discrimination • Minimum wage
Communitarianism – all have responsibility to care for the community collectively	• Caring attitude towards the environment • Emphasis on schools and strong social services • State support for local voluntary associations

Now try this

Identify one way that Old and New Labour disagree.

The Labour Party today

Since Tony Blair stepped down in 2007, the Labour Party has moved leftwards ideologically, first very subtly with Brown, then Miliband and more recently a quite radical shift under Corbyn.

Gordon Brown (2007–2010)

When Brown took over from Blair, he attempted to recreate the party in his own image. He was committed to social justice. Despite this, he was involved in a dispute with his party over abolishing the 10p tax rate, which would have affected the poorest in society. His short premiership will be known for two things:

- presiding over and handling the banking collapse of 2008
- his unpopularity with the public and constant threats of coups and leadership challenges from within his party.

He failed to form a **coalition government** with the Lib Dems after the 2010 election and resigned as PM. This led to the first peacetime coalition between the Conservatives and Lib Dems in UK history.

Jeremy Corbyn (2015–)

The Labour Party under Jeremy Corbyn has taken a sharp turn to the left. In 2017, it supported left-wing policies, including:

- the re-nationalisation of water, railways and Royal Mail and regulation of the energy market
- the reintroduction of the 50p tax rate
- an increase in corporation tax
- the establishment of a National Investment Bank with £250bn for infrastructure
- the re-introduction of maintenance grants for university students and the abolition of tuition fees.

However, the **manifesto** also included:

- support for Trident's renewal
- a commitment to spend 2 per cent of GDP on defence in line with NATO.

As the party moved more towards the left, moderate and Blairite MPs found themselves out of place in their former home. Many quit (Tristram Hunt, Jamie Reed), some went to chair select committees (Hilary Benn, Angela Eagle) and a few retired (Gisela Stuart) or resigned themselves to the role of ex-MPs (Douglas Alexander).

Ed Miliband (2010–2015)

In 2010, Ed Miliband won the Labour leadership at the age of 40, infamously beating his older brother David to the leadership. Miliband was left an uncomfortable legacy of a party with a reputation for being involved in an unnecessary war and economic incompetence after the recession in 2008. He never succeeded in personally endearing himself to the electorate. It was seen as crucial to appeal to both middle and working classes to win a majority, as Blair had demonstrated. Miliband struggled to balance his more left-wing views with a desire to appeal to the centre ground.

Momentum

- Momentum is an organisation credited with mobilising supporters online and on the doorstep during the 2017 election campaign.
- It was founded by John Lansman and Adam Klug. They built Momentum into a movement to support the pro-Corbyn wing of Labour local branches and made links with the unions to provide funding and infrastructure.
- Momentum is peopled by young activists, who focus on inventive social media messages. Youthful protest and the organisational power of the unions appears to be a winning combination.
- Critics of the group claim its activists have taken over constituency Labour parties and stirred up trouble against sitting MPs who are critical of Corbyn.
- As of January 2018, momentum had 35,000 activitsts and 15 members of staff.

Momentum is the name of a group founded following Mr Corbyn's victory in the Labour leadership race in October 2015.

Now try this

Suggest how the Labour Party has shifted to the left since 2007.

The history of the Conservative Party

Conservatism is an idea which developed in the 18th and 19th centuries. It prioritises order and security and doesn't like extreme ideas. It seeks traditional, evolutionary and pragmatic solutions to political problems.

One Nation conservatism

One Nation conservatism influenced the Conservative Party in the 19th (Disraeli) and 20th centuries (Harold Macmillan and others; see page 40 for more on this philosophy). It is based on ideas of paternalism, pragmatism and consensus. It sought to introduce social reforms to reduce social inequalities, with the rich fulfilling an obligation (noblesse oblige) to the needs of the poor.

Thatcherism and the New Right

Thatcherism and the New Right combined ideas of neo-liberalism and neo-conservatism (to find out more about these ideas see pages 41–42). It favoured the individual as opposed to the state, as shown through free-market economics, reduced welfare and lower taxes. It also had a strong nationalistic character and was intolerant of 'alternative' lifestyles, believing instead in traditional values.

Cameron's Conservative Party (2005–2016)

When elected party leader in 2005, Cameron urged his party to 'stop banging on about Europe' and tried to present a new image, one that cared about the environment and socially disadvantaged young people. In 2010, he become the UK's first peacetime coalition PM. This, alongside the need to reduce the UK's budget deficit, restricted his ability to create 'Cameron's Britain'. Nonetheless, he adapted well to coalition, with some suggesting he used the Lib Dems as his excuse for not carrying out some of the more right-wing manifesto promises. Despite making progress on reducing the UK's budget deficit, winning the Scottish Independence referendum and detoxifying the Conservative brand, Cameron will be remembered for his decision to hold (and then lose) the EU referendum in June 2016.

How Conservative ideas shaped policy

	Traditional and One Nation conservatism	Thatcherism	Cameron
Ideology	Pragmatic – opposed to fixed political principles	Prefers a highly ideological, dogmatic approach	A preference for pragmatism over dogmatism
Welfare	Support welfare as part of a 'one nation' outlook	Sees excessive welfare as a threat to enterprise and work	Defence of welfare mainly as incentive to work
Tax	Preference for low tax	Against high taxes	Preference for low tax
State	State should be used to improve the lot of the very poor	Reduce state control and local government	State needed to help the most deprived, but as minimally as possible
Society	Believe in organic society and the need to preserve 'one nation'	See society as a collection of unconnected individuals	'Big Society': communities to take on roles carried out by the state.
Economy	More likely to 'manage' the economy	Support laissez-faire policies with a reluctance to interfere	A belief in the power and desirability of free markets
Law and order	Take a strong position on law and order	Take a strong position on law and order	Strong position on crime but consider the causes as well
Values	Believe in traditional values, especially relating to morality and the family	Believe in traditional values, especially relating to morality and the family	Believe in importance of family, but that can include gay couples
Property	Support property rights	Support property rights	Support property rights

Now try this

Would you argue that David Cameron was a One Nation Conservative or a Thatcherite?

The Conservative Party today

Since David Cameron's shock resignation in 2016, the Conservative Party has been in turmoil. Where does it go from here?

May's Conservative Party (2016–)

The Conservative Party in 2017 was in turmoil. Theresa May's decision to call an early general election to gain her own **mandate** could be understood in April 2017, when she was 20 points ahead in the opinion polls and facing one of the weakest opposition Labour leaders since 1983. However, Cameron's 2016 slim majority became a minority, needing the support of the Democratic Unionist Party (DUP) to prop up the government.

With regards to policy, May often spoke about a group known as JAMs – those **J**ust **A**bout **M**anaging – and seemed to prefer a more interventionist approach than Cameron, wanting to create an industrial strategy and setting a price cap for energy prices. At the same time, however, she wanted to reintroduce grammar schools and repeal the fox-hunting legislation, giving a mixed message. Nonetheless, the May period in office is unlikely to be remembered for much else other than Brexit.

The party was also split over a hard or soft Brexit and a transition or no transition period. Add a poor response to the Grenfell Tower fire (14 June 2017), a disastrous conference speech and a failed coup-attempt, and May's position appeared untenable.

'Big beasts' in the Conservative Party

Boris Johnson

Johnson has been a thorn in both Cameron's and now May's side. Johnson was resurrected by May when she made him Foreign Secretary in June 2016. By appointing him, she gave one of her most serious rivals experience of government. He was not able to stick to collective responsibility and undermined her on Brexit on a number of occasions, eventually leading to his resignation in June 2018.

Amber Rudd

Rudd (Home Secretary 2016–2018) was one of May's staunchest allies in the Cabinet. She did not hesitate to speak up in favour of the PM. Unfortunately for May, Rudd had to resign in light of the Windrush scandal in the Spring of 2018, leaving May with even fewer allies in the cabinet. While Rudd may have longer-term leadership ambitions, her small constituency majority makes her an unlikely contender.

Michael Gove

The environment secretary is suggested as a possible post-brexit PM. Michael Gove is a political enigma. He's famous for saying on the record, on many occasions, that he didn't want to be PM, but then standing to run against Johnson in 2016. Hated by many (for example, for changes he made to education), respected by some (for example, both lawyers and environmentalists have been on record as saying they thought he did a great job when he held their respective Cabinet positions), he has some support within the Conservative Party with many saying he saved them from the prospect of a Johnson premiership.

George Osbourne

Despite no longer being an MP, Osborne has continued to challenge the PM from his new position as editor of the *Evening Standard*. Sacked by May in June 2016, his critical headlines and columns have helped to make her position extremely weak.

Philip Hammond

Hammond and May are not best friends. A staunch remainer and soft Brexiteer, he and the PM have disagreed over the direction of economic policy. He was widely rumoured for the sack if she won a huge majority in June 2017, however the result made his position safer than hers.

Sajid Javid

After Amber Rudd resigned as Home Secretary she was replaced by Sajid Javid. He is, famously, the son of an immigrant, who on arrival in Britain, worked as a bus driver. Javid is a classic self-made, rags to riches story. He is not an ally of Mrs May. In his short time as Home Secretary he has made it clear that he disagreed with the government's handling of the Windrush affair specifically, and immigration in general. He also opposed her wishes on a customs union. Some suggest that he would make a creditable leader.

Now try this

What are 'big beasts' and why are they significant?

Had a look ☐   Nearly there ☐   Nailed it! ☐

The Liberal Democrats

The Liberal Democrat Party (Lib Dems) was reinvented in 1988 through a merger of the Liberal Party and the Social Democratic Party (SDP). The Liberal Party, in existence for 129 years, had been in power under many famous leaders, including Gladstone, Lloyd George and Asquith. A breakaway group of centre-left MPs from the Labour Party formed the SDP in 1981.

Liberal Democrat values

The Lib Dems are a socially liberal party that supports constitutional reform, membership of the EU and human rights. The principles of liberalism on which it is based are:

- **Tolerance**: a belief that a wide variety of beliefs, lifestyles and religions should be tolerated.
- **Liberty and rights**: individual freedom and rights should be strongly safeguarded.
- **Equality of opportunity**: unfair advantages in society should be removed and all should enjoy equal life chances.
- **Social justice**: though there should be capitalism, there should be social justice established through the redistribution of wealth, but not at the expense of individual liberty.
- **Constitutionalism**: a strong constitution should guarantee the separation of political power. Government power should be limited by laws and decentralised.

Social liberals

- They are traditionally seen as being the centre-left wing of the party, associated with the ideas of modern liberals (see pages 49–52 for more on the principles of modern liberalism).
- They are more associated with the desire to increase social justice through the state.
- They would rather see higher spending on the disadvantaged to reduce inequality.
- They include Tim Farron, Simon Hughes and Charles Kennedy.

Orange Book liberals

- They lean more towards the centre, supporting greater choice and competition. To a small extent they are linked to the individualism espoused by classical liberals (the tenants of classical liberalism can be studied on pages 49–52).
- They aim to increase social mobility through increasing economic freedom for those from disadvantaged backgrounds.
- They tend to favour cutting taxes for the poorest in order to increase opportunity.
- They include Nick Clegg, Ed Davey, David Laws and Danny Alexander.

Clegg's Liberal Democratic Party (2010–2016)

In 2010, Nick Clegg became deputy PM alongside David Cameron in the first peacetime coalition. Clegg saw the role of the Lib Dems as being the moderators of Conservative policy, pulling them towards the centre. They felt they had a role to play in putting the country back on its feet economically after the deep recession of 2008. They were also able to direct the Conservatives towards tax cuts for the poorest in society, raising the threshold of income tax from £6,475 in 2009 to £11,000 in 2015.

However, the Lib Dem Party paid a heavy price for its U-turn on university tuition fees while in coalition, and for failing to win the referendum on electoral reform or making headway on House of Lords reform. In 2015, they were reduced from 57 MPs (in 2010) to just eight. History may remember Clegg as the man who made a brave decision in the country's interest but paid a heavy political price for it.

Now try this

For what reason did the Liberal Democrats U-turn over tuition fees?

Emerging and minor parties

There has been a rise in the importance and impact of minor parties on the UK political system, including the SNP and UKIP (below), the DUP, Green Party and Plaid Cymru (see page 20 to find out more about these parties).

SNP

Independence referendum

The fortunes of the Scottish National Party (SNP) changed dramatically in 2011 when the results of the Scottish Parliament election gave them an overall majority. It quickly became very clear that they would use this result to demand a referendum on independence from the UK. This referendum took place in September 2014. After a hard-fought campaign, the result for independence was:

✗ No: 55 per cent

✓ Yes: 45 per cent

Support following the general elections

Despite a vote to keep the status quo, the Scottish referendum resulted in seismic change in Scottish politics, including the obliteration of Labour's support in Scotland. In the 2015 general election, the SNP swept up 56 out of 59 Scottish seats in Westminster. However, the ensuing Brexit debate complicated support for the SNP, despite a 62 to 38 per cent Remain vote in Scotland.

The Scottish Parliament and general elections in 2016 and 2017 showed a drop in support for the SNP. They became a minority government in Scotland, with many suggesting they will lose their position as governing party in 2021. This led Nicola Sturgeon, the leader of the SNP and First Minister of Scotland since 2014, to drop her demands for another independence referendum for the foreseeable future.

	SNP	Lab	Cons	Libs
2003	27	50	18	17
2007	47	46	17	16
2011	69	37	15	5
2016	63	24	31	5

Seats won by the SNP in the Scottish Parliament.

	SNP: seats	SNP: votes
2010	6	0.49m
2015	56	1.5m
2017	35	0.98m

Seats won in the UK general elections (out of a total of 59 seats).

UKIP

For a party that has never held more than two seats in Westminster, the impact of the UK Independence Party (UKIP) on the UK political system has been dramatic. UKIP managed to defy those who wrote the party off as 'fruitcakes and loonies' (Cameron).

	UKIP	Lab	Cons
2004	12	19	27
2009	13	13	26
2014	24	20	19

Seats won in European elections.

Since the 1999 European elections, UKIP has made a steady rise into the nation's consciousness to win the 2014 European election outright, with 27.5 per cent of the vote. UKIP became the third most popular party at the 2015 general election, and managed to persuade 17m to vote to leave the EU in 2016.

Nigel Farage has been a thorn in the side of the Conservative Party, David Cameron, the European Parliament and mainstream politics in general since becoming UKIP's leader in 2006. Farage made UKIP's focus the impact of Britain's 'open door' immigration policy causing a shortage of housing, healthcare, school places and jobs for young people. He wanted UKIP to be a home for the disenfranchised, who were alienated by the rapid social change caused by mass immigration, as well as working-class voters left behind in the hunt for jobs, those who felt silenced and ignored by the liberal political elite.

	UKIP: seats	UKIP: votes
2010	0	0.9m
2015	1	3.8m
2017	1	0.5m

Seats won by UKIP in UK general elections.

David Cameron's decision to hold an in/out referendum was seen as an attempt to halt the rise of UKIP, which he feared could stop the Conservatives winning an overall majority in 2015, as well as defections from his party. Farage's focus on immigration during the referendum campaign was not to everyone's liking, but it became a defining issue and led to the historic 52–48 per cent win for the Leave campaign.

Now try this

Suggest why there is a disparity between the number of people who voted for UKIP in 2015 and the number of seats won.

Other emerging and minor parties

This page examines the share of the vote achieved and impact of the Democratic Unionist Party (DUP), the Green Party and Plaid Cymru over recent decades on UK politics.

DUP

The DUP is a Northern Ireland party which is unionist – it supports remaining a part of the UK.

- It is the largest party in the Northern Irish Assembly.
- It has consistently blocked attempts to introduce gay marriage or more liberal abortion laws to the province.
- The DUP was the only party in the Stormont power executive to campaign for Brexit.
- However, the party want to avoid a hard border with Ireland and has spoken against a 'hard Brexit'.

	DUP	SF	SDLP	UU
2011	38	29	14	16
2016	38	28	12	16
2017	28	27	12	10

Seats won in the Northern Ireland Assembly elections (out of a total of 108 seats, 90 in 2017).

	DUP: seats	DUP: votes
2010	8	0.17m
2015	8	0.18m
2017	10	0.29m

Seats won by the DUP in UK general elections.

Green Party

According to their 2017 manifesto, the Green Party identified the following key principles:

- A green economy that works for everyone.
- To protect our environment.
- Membership of the EU.
- NHS and public services – it is time they belonged to all of us.
- Education for all – education is a right, and should therefore be available to all.
- A safe, affordable, secure and warm place to call home.

	Green: seats	Green: votes
2010	1	0.28m
2015	1	1.16m
2017	1	0.52m

Seats won by the Green Party in UK general elections.

Plaid Cymru

Plaid Cymru's 2017 manifesto sought to get the best deal for Wales. It argued that Wales's economy, identity and its devolved legislature need protecting.
Its key aims were as follows:

- To ensure that Wales can continue to buy and sell to Europe without any costly barriers.
- To introduce a £7.5b investment programme to fund vital infrastructure projects throughout Wales.
- A social care rescue plan to help people live independently and increase the role of community hospitals.

	PC	Lab	Cons	LD
2007	15	26	12	6
2011	11	30	14	5
2016	12	29	11	1

Seats won in the Welsh Assembly elections (out of a total of 60 seats).

	PC: seats	PC: votes
2010	3	0.17m
2015	3	0.18m
2017	4	0.16m

Seats won by Plaid Cymru in UK general elections.

Impact of minor parties on politics in the UK

- **Policy**: UKIP was a major influence on why the EU referendum was called, which led to the triggering of Article 50.
- **Parties**: the fall of Cameron and the current splits in the Conservative and Labour parties can all be linked to UKIP's influence on the Brexit referendum.
- **Governing**: the DUP are currently holding up the Conservative minority government.
- **Devolved assemblies**: there have been many minor parties in government, either on their own or, more usually, with a main party.
- **The UK**: the SNP pursued a policy of independence, which nearly led to the break-up of the UK.

Now try this

Identify one way a minor party has influenced UK politics.

Parties and party systems

Party systems attempt to define how many parties play a role in governing the country and how large a role they play.

Features of party systems

Two-party system	Multi-party system
Two major parties dominate the political system; each has a chance of gaining power.	More than two parties competing for power with a realistic chance of gaining power.
Usually, one of these two parties can secure a majority to govern alone.	The outcome of an election is most likely to be a coalition.
Usually, one party is victorious with the other forming the official opposition.	Parties' electoral strength tends to fluctuate and new parties can gain power more easily.
Government power regularly alternates between the two parties, but not necessarily at each election.	The distinction between major and minor parties is harder to identify.
Other parties may exist but they have low representation in Parliament.	Office-holding can and does change at election time but can also fold in between elections, and new coalitions are set up.
The Westminster system in the UK, for example, has been characterised for much of the 20th century as having a two-party system.	Many countries in Europe have multi-party systems – Italy, for example. In the UK, we would look to the devolved assemblies to see evidence of multi-party systems at work.

One-party dominant system

A one-party dominant system is where the party in power has been there for a long time, winning successive elections, and where it is unlikely that they will be defeated in the near future.

It could be argued that the UK has had spells of one-party dominance, such as in the 1950s, 1980–1990s and the 1990–2000s. Eventually, however, the pendulum swings back to the other party.

The two-and-a-half party system

Two major parties take turns to form government plus a 'third party', which is electorally much smaller, but bigger than other minor parties. The UK could be described as having this system, with the Lib Dems playing the role of the third party since the 1970s. After losses in 2015 and 2017, however, third-party status was conferred on the SNP.

Westminster governments and devolved assemblies

Aside from the 2010–2015 coalition, there is a two-party dominance in Westminster, where a FPTP system applies. In Wales and Northern Ireland, however, a PR system applies, which provides wider representation to parties. This, in turn, affects the types of governments formed. Coalitions are routine in the devolved assemblies, whereas the 2010–2015 coalition government was the only one in peacetime history since the Second World War.

Welsh Assembly since 1999

Term	Governing party
1999–2003	Labour and Lib Dems
2003–2007	Labour
2007–2011	Labour and Plaid Cymru
2011–2016	Labour
2016–	Labour

Northern Ireland Assembly, 2017

Party representation	Seats
DUP	28
Sinn Féin	27
SDLP	12
Ulster Unionist Party	10
Alliance Party	8
Green Party	2
Traditional Unionist	1
Independents	1
People Before Profit	1

Now try this

Which system best describes UK general elections?

Factors affecting party success

You need to know about the reasons parties are electorally successful. The section on voting behaviour and the media on pages 30–35 is also very useful when looking at this area.

Policies

A party's policies should be the most important factor when deciding how to vote.

WE'LL ALL WIN WITH THE CONSERVATIVES.

Thatcher's radical agenda in 1979 (pictured) enthused the country, as did Blair's in 1997. In a different way, May's policies in 2017 played a significant role in the election.

Campaign

In general, campaigns rarely make a significant difference to the outcome of elections. There may be a slight widening or tightening in opinion polls but, generally, a party with a clear lead in the polls at the beginning of a campaign tends to win, even if there are occasional mishaps (such as John Prescott's punch in 2001). When polls are tight, however, the campaign can make a difference. On these occasions, one party wins by just a small margin.

However, 2017 broke all political assumptions, showing just how significant a campaign can be. May was 20 points ahead in the polls when she called the election in April 2017. By 8 June, she had lost her parliamentary majority and was seen as an ineffective leader and PM.

Jeremy Corbyn smashed another widely accepted fact that once the electorate have made their mind up about you, it is impossible to change. He ended the campaign being hailed as the new socialist messiah.

Leaders

Leadership can make a key difference to the success of a party. Charismatic leaders are often trusted more by voters (read about valence on page 31), which may result in voters ignoring other factors.

Leaders who look 'strong' and 'fresh', such as Blair in 1997, tend to be successful, whereas leaders who appear weak, such as Ed Miliband, often struggle to get the voters' attention.

Media

The influence of the media cannot be underestimated in modern politics. It had been said that if you have the support of *The Sun*, you have a good chance of winning an election (see page 34 for more on the influence of the media). More recently, social media platforms have taken on the older media and are seen as a force to be reckoned with. This was certainly true in 2017.

Wider political context

The context of a campaign can be crucial in determining an election. If a party has been in power for a long time, brand fatigue may set in and governing parties are likely to make mistakes and lose credibility with voters.

For example, in the run-up to the 1979 and 2010 elections, the governing party had gained a poor reputation for economic competence, and voters reacted badly to this.

The electorate also doesn't like politicians to engage in sleazy activities, whether they are scandals relating to sex, financial misconduct or expenses.

In the 1992, 1997 and 2010 elections, this had an impact on the result.

Party unity

Disunity in political parties is damaging. Voters like to feel that the party they vote for has a clear vision for governing.

The Conservatives under Major, the Blairite/Brownite split in New Labour (pictured) and the Conservatives under May are all examples of the damage that governing parties at war within themselves can do.

Opposition

The quality of the opposition has an effect on how successful a party may be. On the one hand, the opposition has less experience than the government, which holds the experience and status of office. Equally, however, the government has a track record, which a skilful opposition can exploit to their own advantage.

The success of Labour in 1997 was partly down to their ability to exploit the Major government's weaknesses, and they ran a slick campaign to become elected.

Now try this

Which factors were the most important in the 2017 general election?

The role of elections in democracy

You need to know the key features of a representative democracy, and consider whether elections promote democracy.

Elections

Elections have various roles and functions:

- They are a device for ensuring that the will of the majority is made clear.
- They **confer legitimacy** on government and politicians.
- They help to **form governments**. If a party wins a general election, it secures the right to govern. The party that loses recognises the loss and leaves.

- They provide **a choice** of political programme in their **manifesto**.
- They are a means by which **citizens can actively participate** and feel involved in political life.
- They **provide representation** by ensuring that MPs are accountable to their constituents at regular intervals.
- They are a means of holding an incumbent **government to account**.

Mandates and manifestos

Electoral mandates

An electoral mandate refers to the authority extended to the winning party or candidate following success in an election. A mandate grants permission to act or produce legislation in accordance with the promise or manifesto offered for consideration and choice at the election. As such, winning parties in an election claim they have a mandate or authority to introduce legislation as it has popular support from the electorate.

Do elections promote democracy?

👍 Elections **educate the public** as political parties try to explain current issues and how they would deal with them if voted into office.

👍 Popular participation is a core feature of democracy and elections **encourage participation** at various levels.

👍 Elections also offer the electorate **choice**. Instead of having elections where only a single party can stand, as in China, in the UK the electorate can choose between many different parties.

👍 Through elections, MPs are individually and government is collectively responsible to the people. This ensures they are all acting in the interests of the electorate rather than just to further their own aims.

👍 Political changeover via elections ensures that there is a **peaceful change**. Democracy requires that those who have lost an election accept the authority of those who have won.

👍 Elections are the **ultimate expression of the popular will**. In a representative system they are the occasion when the people are able to show a preference between different candidates, parties and political programmes or ideologies.

👎 Elections can **fail to educate** the wider electorate; it rather misinforms them with biased facts and propaganda.

👎 Elections are also a form of indirect democracy, and **take decision-making away from the people**. There is no guarantee that politicians will abide by their mandate.

In the run-up to the 2010 general election, for example, the Lib Dems pledged not to raise tuition fees. However, after joining the Conservative Party in coalition government, 27 Lib Dem MPs voted to increase fees.

👎 At general elections, it is accepted that the winning party has a mandate to carry out its manifesto. However, elections do not indicate which aspects of a manifesto the voters approve of.

👎 It could be said that the choices presented at elections are largely an illusion because there are **so few differences between the main parties**. Democracy in Britain today is much more a case of pluralist group politics than party politics.

Now try this

What is an electoral mandate and why is it important?

First-past-the-post

First-past-the-post (FPTP) is used to elect the Westminster Parliament. It is also used for local government in England and Wales.

Plurality electoral systems

In a plurality electoral system, each voter can vote for only one candidate. The candidate who achieves the most votes (a plurality) is elected. It is also known as winner-takes-all as no matter how close the vote, they win. A candidate can get much less than 50 per cent of the vote in a constituency but still become the MP.

Safe seats

A **safe seat** or safe constituency is one which is regarded as secure by a party. In such seats, there is very little chance of the seat changing hands from one party to another.

In 2017, for example, Labour retained Liverpool Walton with 85.7 per cent of the vote.

Marginal seats

A **marginal seat** or constituency is one held with a very small lead. These seats only require a small amount of votes to change hands for the seat to be lost/won. Money and campaigning almost always focuses on marginal seats.

In 2017, for example, the SNP won North East Fife by only 2 votes.

How FPTP works

The UK is divided up into 650 constituencies.

⬇

To stand in elections under FPTP, the candidate has to pay a deposit. This is returned if 5 per cent of the vote is obtained.

⬇

Electors cast their vote for one candidate in **single-member constituencies**.

⬇

Each voter has one vote and indicates their choice by an '**X**' next to a candidate's name.

⬇

The winner need only achieve a **plurality** of votes (one more than their nearest rival). The winner is the one with the **most** votes in their constituency; this may **not** be above 50 per cent of votes cast.

⬇

For a party to win the overall general election, they aim to have a majority over all other parties in the Commons. Thus, they need to get at least 326 MPs elected (out of 650) to be in that position.

Advantages and disadvantages

👍 It creates stability and strong governments, able to make coherent decisions, yet retaining the flexibility necessary to adapt to changing circumstances.

👍 MPs have a close relationship with constituents; they meet them regularly at 'surgeries', represent their concerns in Parliament and deal with their grievances.

👍 The candidate who most people prefer wins the seat.

👍 It is simple and easy to operate. All that is required is an 'X' in the desired voter choice.

👍 It is quick to produce a result.

For example, Newcastle Central was the first constituency to declare a result in 2017 at 11 pm, only 60 minutes after the polls closed.

👍 FPTP has the effect of keeping out small, extremist parties by discriminating against them.

👎 FPTP discriminates in favour of the two main parties, particularly those with concentrated support, so government is unrepresentative.

👎 Votes are wasted on losing candidates or on huge majorities in safe seats, so not everybody's vote is 'worth' the same.

👎 Other systems also offer constituents good local members to represent them. For example, **Single Transferable Votes (STV)** (find out more about how STV works on page 27) and **Additional Member System (AMS)** (see page 26 for more on the workings of AMS).

👎 Most MPs do not achieve 50 per cent of the votes in their constituency, so they are not representative of their constituency.

👎 Electronic voting today means the ease and speed of operation of FPTP is overrated.

👎 It discriminates against moderate small parties with legitimate causes and ideologies.
UKIP, the Green Party and the Lib Dems have all suffered at the hands of FPTP.

Now try this

1 What is a safe seat and why do some consider them a problem?

2 Why does first-past-the-post 'waste votes'?

Supplementary Vote

The London mayor and other elected mayors, as well as police and crime commissioners, are elected using Supplementary Vote (SV). It is a **majoritarian system** (see below).

Majoritarian electoral systems

In a majoritarian electoral system, candidates **must** gain a majority of the votes to be elected.

- Parties can get a majority of the seats without necessarily obtaining a majority of the votes cast, which means that governments are often formed without the support of 50 per cent of those who voted.

- This type of representation often ensures that one party obtains a majority of the seats in a legislature.

- It is associated with strong, single party government as it tends to give a 'winner's bonus' to the party with the most seats.

How SV works

> Voters have two preferential votes. They place '1' in the first column for their first choice and '2' in the next column for their second choice.

> If a candidate wins more than 50 per cent of the first-choice votes, they are elected.

> If no candidate wins 50 per cent of the votes, all but the top two candidates are eliminated.

> Second preference votes for the two remaining candidates (on ballot papers of the eliminated candidates) are then counted.

> The candidate with the most first and second choice votes is elected.

London mayoral election results, 2016

Candidates	Sadiq Khan	Zac Goldsmith	Siân Berry
Party	Labour	Conservative	Green
1st round vote	1,148,716	909,755	150,673
1st round percentage	44.2%	35.0%	5.8%
2nd round vote	1,310,143	994,614	Eliminated
2nd round percentage	56.8%	43.2%	Eliminated

Advantages and disadvantages of SV

👍 It encourages moderate campaigning, as gaining second-choice votes is important.

👍 It is a relatively simple system to understand and use.

👍 It is the system that could most easily replace FPTP. All that would change would be the way the ballot cards were marked.

👍 All MPs would have the support of a majority of their voters.

👍 It reduces tactical voting as you can vote for your first-choice candidate without fear of wasting your vote.

👍 As it uses single-member constituencies it ensures good MP–constituency links.

👎 It promotes voting for candidates from the main three parties because only two candidates can make the cut; therefore smaller parties will not secure enough first preferences.

👎 If there are more than two strong candidates, voters must guess which two will make the final round. If they guess incorrectly, their second-choice vote will be wasted.

👎 Voters may need to vote tactically if they want their vote to count.

👎 It may mean that not all MPs secure the support of a majority of voters, because some of the second choices will be for previously eliminated candidates.

Now try this

Why is the Supplementary Vote a majoritarian system?

Had a look ☐ Nearly there ☐ Nailed it! ☐

Additional Member System

Additional Member System (AMS) is a proportional electoral system used in the devolved regions of Scotland and Wales and for the London Assembly. This system is a **hybrid system**, which combines the FPTP system (see page 24 for an overview of FPTP) and the list system.

Proportional electoral systems

- Parties should be represented in proportion to their overall electoral strength. The percentage of seats they win should be similar to the percentage of votes they gain.
- No wasted votes – all votes are used and the voter feels more valued.
- Coalition governments are the normal outcome of this system.

List system

Parties list their candidates in order of importance. Depending on the percentage of votes each party receives, they will be allocated seats (if a party wins 50 per cent of the vote and there are 100 seats, the party will be allocated 50 seats; candidates 1–50 on the list will fill these).

In a **closed list**, electors have no say in the order of the candidates on the list; in an **open list**, voters have some say over the order.

How AMS works (using the Scottish Parliament as an example)

With AMS, the voters have **two separate votes**. (There are 129 seats in the Scottish Parliament.)

The first is used to choose a member for their **local constituency** (using FPTP). The person with the most votes wins. (73 MSPs are chosen this way.)

The second vote is used to select a political party (using the party list). They are known as 'top-up' members. (56 MSPs are chosen using a closed party list, elected from eight **regions**.)

This produces two types of representative, one local and one regional. The party-list element is used to 'top up' the constituency vote, making the overall result more proportionate.

Government in the Scottish Assembly

Term	Governing party
1999–2003	Labour and Lib Dems
2003–2007	Labour and Lib Dems
2007–2011	SNP
2011–2016	SNP
2016–	SNP

Scottish Parliament election results, 2016

Turnout: 56 per cent	Constituency		Combined	
	% of vote	Seats (%)	% of vote	Seats (%)
SNP	47	59 (81%)	45	63 (49%)
Conservatives	22	7 (10%)	23	31 (24%)
Labour	23	3 (4%)	21	24 (19%)
Greens	1	0 (0%)	4	6 (5%)
Lib Dems	8	4 (5%)	7	5 (4%)
Total seats		73		129

Advantages and disadvantages of AMS

- 👍 It is proportional.
- 👍 Each voter has a directly accountable single constituency representative.
- 👍 It gives voters a wider choice.
  For example, they may choose a candidate from one party for their first vote, and choose a different party for their second vote.
- 👍 A coalition government is more likely (this can also be a disadvantage).

- 👎 List members are chosen by the party and are answerable to it rather than voters, giving more control to the party.
- 👎 Having two different types of representative may create animosity between them. Those elected via the party lists may be seen as having 'got in via the backdoor'.
- 👎 It can be complicated; people may be confused over what to do with their two votes.
- 👎 Smaller parties are less well represented than under a fully proportional system.

Now try this

Explain how, in the 2016 Scottish results, 'top-up' MSPs affected the overall result.

Single Transferable Vote

The **Single Transferable Vote** (STV) is used in the Northern Ireland Assembly and for Scottish Local Council elections. It is a highly proportionate electoral system.

How STV works

STV uses multi-member constituencies (MMCs) and voters number their choices preferentially: 1, 2, 3.

⬇

In order to be elected, a candidate needs to get more votes than a quota, which is derived by using the Droop formula:

the number of votes cast
the number of seats + 1

⬇

Surplus votes (i.e. those above the quota) are proportionally redistributed to second preferences.

⬇

If no one reaches the quota, the least popular candidate is eliminated and the second preferences of those who voted for them are redistributed.

⬇

This process is continued until all the seats are filled.

STV in Northern Ireland

The province is divided into 18 multi-member constituencies.

⬇

Each constituency elects five members, to make 90 in total.

⬇

Voters cast their votes preferentially, up to a maximum of five.

⬇

A quota is then calculated in each of the 18 regions.

Northern Ireland Assembly results, 2017

Party	Seats	Vote share
DUP	28	28.1%
Sinn Féin	27	27.9%
SDLP	12	11.9%
Ulster Unionist Party	10	12.9%
Alliance Party	8	9.1%
Green Party	2	2.3%
Traditional Unionist	1	2.6%
Independents	1	1.8%
People Before Profit	1	1.8%
Progressive Unionist	0	0.7%
Conservatives	0	0.3%
Others	0	0.8%

Advantages and disadvantages of STV

👍 Fewer votes are 'wasted', so most voters will have helped to elect one representative.

👍 Greater choice – voters can choose between parties or between candidates in the same party.

👍 It offers voters more than one representative to approach with their concerns post-election.

👍 There are no safe seats under STV, meaning candidates cannot be complacent and parties must campaign everywhere, not just in marginal seats.

👍 There is no need for tactical voting.

👍 A coalition government is more likely (also a disadvantage), so parties have to work together (for example, power-sharing is a feature of NI assemblies).

👎 Counting the results takes longer, so results take a while to be announced.

👎 It can lead to 'donkey voting', where voters vote for candidates in the order they appear on the ballot.

👎 In MMCs, ballot papers can get big and confusing. Many ballot papers were spoiled in Scotland when it was introduced for local government.

👎 MMCs mean lines of accountability for representatives are less clear.

Now try this

Identify complications caused by multi-member constituencies.

Use of referenda

A referendum is a vote on a particular issue. Referenda are tools of direct democracy, but used in a representative democracy.

Arguments for and against the wider use of referenda

👍 They enable the electorate to **decide on big constitutional issues** and act as a form of entrenchment.

👎 They **undermine the authority of Parliament**, as Parliament is sovereign and it may be side-lined by the overuse of referenda – the Brexit court case was on this precise issue (read more about this case on page 93).

👎 They may impose a decision on a reluctant government/Parliament (which may also be an advantage).
For example, the EU referendum returned a Leave result despite the Conservative government officially backing Remain.

👍 They can **settle long-standing disputes** and disagreements.
For example, the referendum on alternative vote (AV) in 2011 has stopped electoral reform for now.

👎 Referenda **can be asked more than once** until the 'right' answer is received.
For example, the possibility of another Scottish independence referendum, a second Brexit referendum.

👎 Referenda can be very divisive in society, as was shown by the EU and Scottish referenda.

👍 They help to create a more engaged and **better educated and informed** electorate.

👎 However, **campaigns can be misleading** or may oversimplify complicated issues.
For example, both the Remain and Leave campaigns in the 2016 EU referendum made claims that fact-checkers found to be extremely misleading.

👍 They strengthen democracy by allowing the **public to speak for themselves**.

👎 They place political decisions in the hands of those who **lack specialised knowledge**.

👎 They **simplify and distort** issues, reducing them to questions that have a simple yes/no answer.

👍 Referenda **promote participation** and give everyone an equal voice.
The 2014 referendum on Scottish independence had 84.5 per cent turnout.

👎 Too regular use of referenda might result in voter **disillusion and apathy** or fatigue.
Turnout in the 2016 EU referendum was slightly lower in Scotland. Some suggested it was due to voter fatigue.

Brexit referendum – the case for no more referenda?

The EU referendum of June 2016 possibly changed the outlook for wider use of referenda for a generation. In May 2016, PM Cameron called a referendum on the divisive issue of UK membership of the EU after pressure from within his party. This issue was of huge significance and Cameron did not take into account the risks of his gamble going wrong. It was also an issue of enormous complexity to which there are no clear answers (see page 33 for an in-depth look at this referendum).

Post-referendum consequences

- It undermined the authority of Parliament and brought judges into the political arena (for example, the Article 50 court case; see page 100 to read more on this).

- It caused a huge chasm in the heart of Labour Party supporters.

- It risks the break-up of the UK. Scotland voted overwhelmingly to remain in the EU, leading the SNP to discuss a second vote for independence.

- The 52 per cent to 48 per cent result showed the country was hugely divided.

- It created an enormous issue over the Irish border as when the UK leaves the EU, the only hard border between the UK and the EU will exist between Northern Ireland (part of the UK and hence no longer a member of the EU) and the Republic of Ireland, which will still be a member of the EU.

- It caused the resignation of David Cameron.

Now try this

Why did David Cameron call the EU referendum?

Impact of different electoral systems

Since the arrival of electoral reform in the UK, many changes have occurred to party representation and types of government.

Third parties

Proportional and hybrid/mixed electoral systems are much fairer for third parties. The use of AMS in the Scottish Parliament, Welsh Assembly and London Assembly elections has helped third parties to turn their considerable but thinly spread support into seats.

For example, UKIP failed to win any constituency seats in the 2016 Scottish Parliament, Welsh Assembly and London Assembly. However, it had enough support across Wales and London to win seven 'top-up' seats in Wales and two 'top-up' London Assembly seats.

Seats reflect votes

AMS has ensured that the number of seats won more closely reflects votes. In the 2016 Scottish Parliament elections, the SNP won 59 of the 73 constituencies with just 47 per cent of the vote. But the party only received four list seats, despite winning 42 per cent of the regional vote. Most of the list seats went to Labour and the Conservatives, who won a combined 45 per cent of the constituency vote, but only 10 out of 73 constituency seats. The end result was much more proportionate and reflective of the vote: Scottish Conservatives had 31 seats (24 per cent) and Scottish Labour 24 seats (19 per cent) (see page 26 for more on how AMS works in practice).

Coalitions

The use of more proportional electoral systems has made majority government less likely as PR systems tend to produce multi-party systems, meaning that parties work together in **coalition governments** or alone in **minority governments**. Some argue that past Scottish and Welsh governments have proven that minority and coalition government can be effective.

- The 2011 Scottish Parliament election resulted in an SNP **majority government**, the 1999 and 2003 elections produced a Labour/Lib Dem **coalition**, and the 2007 and 2016 elections resulted in an SNP **minority government**.
- The 1999 Welsh Assembly election resulted in a Labour/Lib Dem **coalition**, while the 2003 and 2016 elections resulted in a Labour **minority government**.

Multi-party system

STV in **Northern Ireland** results in a multi-party system. In the Northern Ireland Assembly, there is a complex process of power-sharing intended to include both Unionist and Nationalist parties.

- In 2011, there were five parties represented in the NI Executive (like a Cabinet) and a First and Deputy Minister of different parties. This was also true in 2007.
- Five of the larger parties all achieved significant representation in the Assembly and were awarded places in a power-sharing government.
- STV elected representatives from eight different parties as well as independents in NI Assembly elections.

Majoritarian systems

👍 Majoritarian systems give stronger individual mandates (see page 25 for more information on how this works). Majoritarian systems, like the Supplementary Vote, place much greater emphasis on winning a majority of the vote.

Electoral reform

👎 Electoral reform does not necessarily increase turnout. Despite the greater choice given by the AMS and SV electoral systems, none of the 2016 elections had turnouts close to the 69 per cent who participated in the 2017 general election.

Gender balance

👍 Electoral reform encourages greater descriptive representation. The Scottish Parliament and Welsh Assembly both have a much better gender balance than Westminster, where only 32 per cent of MPs are female.

Spoiled ballots

👎 Electoral reform can see an increase in spoiled ballots. Many regions reported alarmingly high numbers of spoiled ballot papers in the PCC elections in 2016. In many contests, the numbers range from 2 per cent to 4 per cent. In Gwent, however, 12.5 per cent of ballot papers were rejected as spoiled.

Now try this

Give an example of how different electoral systems affect party representation.

Trends in voting behaviour

There are many **long-term trends** and **social factors** that influence the way people vote.

Class voting

Certain classes have a connection with specific political parties, and will principally vote for them. Traditionally, working-class voters (also known as C2, D, E) have voted with the Labour Party, whereas middle-class voters (also known as A, B, C1) have voted Conservative.

The 1950s were a high point for partisan alignment. Since then, there has been a blurring of class identification with a rising aspirational middle class, which was evident in the 1979 election and increased in the 1980s–1990s. Nonetheless, even as recently as 1992, middle-class voters were still significantly more likely to vote Conservative than Labour. The real change occurred in 1997 when there was a huge switch across classes to Labour under Blair.

Class and partisan dealignment

- Class alignment (or **class dealignment**) refers to individuals identifying (or not) with a certain class.
- Partisan alignment (or **partisan dealignment**) refers to the attachment (or not) that exists between an individual and a certain political party.

Class alignment normally coexists alongside partisan alignment. So, when people strongly identify with a social class, they also strongly associate with a certain political party (for example, the working class and the Labour Party in the 1950s). Equally, as people stop identifying so strongly with a social class, they stop identifying strongly with a political party (for example, the many working-class voters who voted Conservative in 1979).

Regions

Regional voting is closely associated with class, with parties having electoral heartlands and electoral deserts.

2015

The north of England and large urban towns and cities tend to vote Labour; the south and rural areas tend to vote Conservative. Traditionally, Scotland has been a Labour electoral heartland, but that changed after the independence referendum and the SNP won 56 out of 59 Scottish Westminster seats in the 2015 general election.

Age

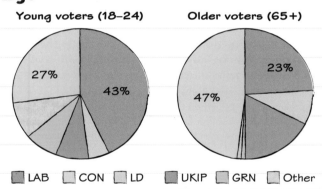

Young voters (18–24)   Older voters (65+)

☐ LAB ☐ CON ☐ LD ☐ UKIP ☐ GRN ☐ Other

Trends show that young people tend to vote Labour and older people vote Conservative. This could be because older people may have a greater interest in maintaining the status quo.

Age also influences election turnout. The older you are, the more likely you are to vote. This was even true in the 2017 general election.

Gender

Female voters tend marginally to favour the Conservatives. The difference, however, is small. Over the past five elections, the disparity between the percentage of men and women voting either Labour or Conservative hasn't gone over 4 per cent.

Ethnic groups

Evidence suggests that ethnic groups are more likely to vote Labour (for example, approximately 60–70 per cent of black and minority ethnic (BME) voters voted Labour in the last four elections). There is an overlap here with class, as poorer ethnic minority groups vote Labour and the more prosperous groups favour the Conservatives.

Now try this

Why is there a link between class and regional voting?

Short-term factors affecting voting behaviour

Several short-term factors have an effect on people's voting behaviour.

Rational choice theory

Voters act like individual consumers, choosing the most suitable 'product' on offer. Voters consider how they would be affected by having different parties in government, and make their decision based on who will benefit them and their families. Therefore successful parties are able to adapt their policies to ones that are popular with most of the electorate.

For example, Thatcher changed the Conservative Party's policies for the 1979 election, as did Blair for New Labour in 1997.

Rational choice theory combines **issue voting** and **valence** (trust), which may be seen as a more accurate way of analysing voting behaviour.

Issue voting

Voters make decisions on a range of issues by going through several stages:

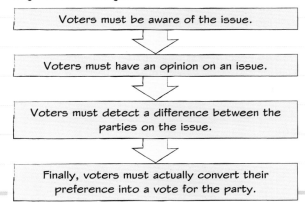

Voters must be aware of the issue.

↓

Voters must have an opinion on an issue.

↓

Voters must detect a difference between the parties on the issue.

↓

Finally, voters must actually convert their preference into a vote for the party.

Issue voting is problematic as it relies on a high level of political engagement from voters. It is also not particularly good in explaining voting patterns (for example, in 1987 and 1992, voters preferred Labour's policies but the Conservatives won the elections).

Valence

Valence is the idea that people support the party best able to deliver on issues they care about. So, valence suggests that voters aren't solely concerned with policies, but also on how much they **trust a party to deliver** those policies. This might be summed up with three questions:

1 Which party leader do I trust?

2 Which party do I trust to manage the economy?

3 Which party has been/will be most competent in government?

In 2017, many voters questioned whether the Labour Party could deliver economic prosperity, even though they liked their policies of abolishing tuition fees, renationalising industries and giving the NHS more funding.

Party leader

The charisma and personality of party leaders is now crucial to a party's success – they are the 'brand' of their party and are often put in good positions for 'photo opportunities'.

For example, in 1997 the young, energetic, family man Blair was seen in stark contrast to Major.

The 2010 televised debates reinforced this view when leaders tried to avoid saying anything controversial, and began to look less 'human'. Voters started to trust them less, being unable to identify with them. Voters seemed willing to vote for an 'authentic' character who would tell the truth in a language they understood, almost irrespective of the policies they supported.

Economic management

It is widely accepted that voters are more likely to support a party if it has managed the economy successfully while in government or it is thought likely to be able to deliver economic prosperity. Equally, voters are less likely to support a governing party which they feel has been responsible for mismanaging the economy.

For example, the 1978 'winter of discontent' played a key role in Thatcher's victory in 1979. In 2010, the Conservatives were able to blame Labour under Brown for the 2008 financial crisis.

Governing competency

Governing competency is an assessment of how effective a party has been in government.

- **Control of events**: Major's government lost power in 1997 when voters felt they were stumbling from one crisis to another and seemed unable to control events.

- **Policy**: the Thatcher government (1979–1990) stuck firmly to its promises to change the economic model and was rewarded with electoral success.

- **Party unity, strong leadership**: the Labour Party under Blair (1994–2007) is an example of how voters rewarded the party who had a clear vision and a united party.

Now try this

Explain how valence was a factor in the 1997 election.

Case study: the 1997 general election

You need to look at three case studies of general elections from three different periods, two of which your teacher will choose. The 1997 general election is **compulsory study**. You need to know about the factors that explain the outcome. For other factors affecting party success, see page 22.

Key points

The 1997 general election was a landslide victory for New Labour over Major's Conservatives, for several reasons:

- The Conservatives suffered internal divisions, poor leadership and failed to seem relevant to contemporary society. Voters felt that they had not dealt well with the 1990s financial crisis.
- Blair modernised the Labour Party, appealed to more middle-class voters, moved away from traditional policies such as nationalisation and emphasised constitutional reform – in common with the Liberal Democrats, thus enabling some tactical voting.

The Liberal Democrats emerged as a significant third party.

Party	Number of seats	Increase/loss of seats	% of popular vote
Labour	418	+ 145	43.2
Conservative	165	− 178	30.7
Liberal Democrats	46	+ 28	16.8

1997 general election results.

Age

Labour achieved more votes across all age groups than the Conservative Party, with the highest percentage coming from the 18–34 age group. This was particularly seen in the 18–24 female age group, with 53 per cent voting Labour as opposed to 24 per cent voting Conservative. The Conservatives' largest reduction in votes was in the 35–54 age group (down by 16 points).

Media

The press largely turned against the Conservative Party, with most media backing Blair. The Conservatives also faced a number of well-publicised financial and sexual scandals. In contrast, Labour had a highly polished campaign, focused on Blair. Public-relations experts dealt with the media, focus groups were used to understand public opinion and marginal seats were targeted. For more on the influence of the media, see pages 34–35.

Gender

In 1997, the gap between male and female voting habits closed, with the male/female vote for Labour being 45/44 per cent. Reasons may include:

- More women were working by the 1990s, particularly in the public sector.
- New Labour's more family-friendly policies, such as free nursery places.

Class

Historically, voters in Britain had been strongly influenced by their social class background. This all changed in 1997, as can be seen in the chart below.

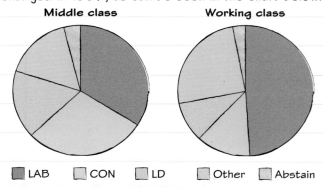

Middle class   **Working class**

■ LAB   ☐ CON   ☐ LD   ☐ Other   ☐ Abstain

Labour's win in 1997 was aided by Blair's ability to appeal to middle-class voters as well as the working-class base.

Employment status

Around 45 per cent of those in all types of employment voted for Labour, as did 64 per cent of the unemployed. The percentage was slightly lower for the self-employed and those working in the private sector. The Conservative vote was nearer 30 per cent from the employed and 15 per cent from the unemployed.

Ethnicity

70 per cent of all non-white voters voted for Labour in 1997, as opposed to just 18 per cent for the Conservatives. Labour gained 66 per cent of Asian votes and 82 per cent of black votes.

Now try this

What were the key factors in the 1997 election?

Case study: the 2017 general election

This case study looks at the factors that explain the outcome of the 2017 general election. For other factors affecting party success, see page 22, and for more on the influence of the media on the general election, see pages 34–35. You need to revise the case study elections that you have covered in class.

Age

Age was a key factor. In the ten constituencies with the highest proportion of 18–24-year-olds, there were increases of 14 per cent in the Labour vote. Despite an increase in youth turnout, young people were still less likely to vote than older people.

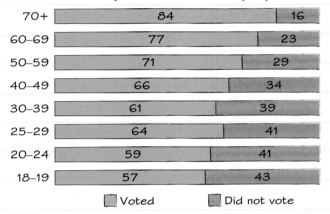

Age	Voted	Did not vote
70+	84	16
60–69	77	23
50–59	71	29
40–49	66	34
30–39	61	39
25–29	64	41
20–24	59	41
18–19	57	43

☐ Voted   ☐ Did not vote

While 57 per cent of 18- and 19-year-olds voted in 2017, for those aged 70+ the turnout was 84 per cent.

Class

Class is no longer a good indicator of voting intention. In 2017, Labour was only 4 per cent behind the Conservatives in the top three socio-economic grouping (ABC1) and 2 per cent behind among the bottom three (C2DE). That said, Labour did best among semi- and unskilled-manual workers, unemployed people and those in the lowest-grade jobs (DE).

Gender

There was only a small gender gap between men and women. Women were equally split between Labour and the Conservatives (43 per cent to 43 per cent) and men slightly more in favour of the Conservatives (45 per cent to 39 per cent).

Employment status

In 2017, the Conservative Party was 39 points ahead among retirees and Labour was 45 points ahead among full-time students.

Labour was also ahead among those who work: 4 points ahead with part-time workers and 6 points ahead with full-time workers. Conservatives are still having to rely on the 'grey' vote.

Education

Education was a key factor in 2017. While the Conservatives' support decreased the more educated a voter was, the opposite was true for Labour and the Liberal Democrats. Among those with low qualifications (GCSE or below), the Conservatives beat Labour by 22 per cent, and among those with high qualifications (degree or above), Labour led by 17 points.

Brexit

May called the 2017 election the 'Brexit election' and in many ways it was, as one of the biggest factors in helping voters decide how to cast their ballot was withdrawal from the EU.

Percentage of voters who named Brexit as the top election issue.

Con	UKIP	Lib Dem	18–24s	SNP	Labour
48%	33%	31%	15%	13%	8%

- Brexit cut across party loyalties and contributed to the revival of the Conservative and Labour parties at the expense of UKIP, the SNP, Plaid Cymru and the Greens compared to 2015.

- The Conservatives' position on Brexit, combined with the loss of Farage as leader, saw the UKIP vote collapse and most of its support go to the Conservatives, with over half of UKIP's 2015 voters switching to them, 18 per cent to Labour and 18 per cent remaining with UKIP.

- Despite a clear pro-EU position, the Lib Dems failed to pick up the Remain votes that they were hoping for.

- Labour was seen as the soft-Brexit party, winning many Remainers from the Conservatives, Greens and Lib Dems.

Remember, you need to revise the three election case studies you have studied.

Now try this

What were the key factors affecting the 2017 general election?

The influence of the media

The media is of vital importance in a democracy as it brings issues to the public's attention. You need to know what it is and how it has changed in recent years.

What is the media?

The media is not a cohesive whole; it is made up of a variety of types:

Newspapers are the most traditional form of media. Until recently, they were the most important and powerful form of political media.

Television has come to dominate political debate with huge coverage during election campaigns, as well as daily and weekly current affairs shows. In 2010, the election leaders debate was watched by just under 10 million viewers.

Social media is the newest and arguably most powerful media platform. It has begun to play a huge role in politics both here in the UK and in the USA.

Media bias

There are strict laws governing political broadcasting on TV and radio to ensure fair representation of all parties. The Office of Communications (Ofcom) states that:

- coverage of parties during the election period must be fair and appropriate
- all discussion and analysis of election and referendum issues must finish when the poll opens
- broadcasters must wait until polls close on polling day before they publish the results of opinion polls
- a list of all candidates must be included in any constituency discussions.

However, newspapers are under no such obligation. Most national newspapers, except *The Guardian*, *iNews* and the *Mirror*, support the Conservatives, and these newspapers have the largest readership.

Social media and fake news

One of the largest platforms for media bias has become social media. Fake news has become a big issue; it was particularly influential in the US 2016 presidential election, but also affects the UK media. In 2016, Facebook was the top social network site for news across 26 countries. In the UK, 28 per cent of young people cited social media as their main news source, compared with 24 per cent for TV. Facebook has been criticised for not taking its role as a media platform seriously enough, with Amber Rudd, the then Home Secretary, suggesting they should be treated the same as publishing companies.

Opinion polls

Opinion polls assess the popularity of political parties by asking a sample of people how they intend to vote. Public opinion polls are now a key part of our electoral experience, but the main political parties also conduct their own private polls. Opinion polls have come in for criticism for getting their predictions spectacularly wrong. A hung parliament was widely predicted in 2015, and in 2017 May was expected to get a majority of around 50+. Still, opinion polls are widely read and valued.

Exit polls seem to be the most accurate opinion polls. John Curtice's exit polls are legendary in their ability to successfully predict the outcome of elections, usually within a handful of seats.

Now try this

What does the 2017 general election tell us about the influence of print media?

Media and electoral outcomes

It is important to consider whether the media creates and shapes political opinion or whether it simply reflects the prevailing political views.

Winning elections: the media vs parties

👍 The public gain most of their information from the media; very few read **manifestos**.

👍 The public are more swayed by persuasive headlines in the media than party policies.

👍 Politicians are conscious of their media image, and seek to control the news agenda.

👍 The winning party at the 2015 and 2017 elections was supported by the majority of the press.

👍 The power of the media, whether papers, TV or social media, continues to grow.

👎 The public make up their mind from many media sources.

👎 The issues that dominate election campaigns come from the parties, not the media.

👎 Parties now use the different media platforms to 'broadcast' directly to voters, uniting party and media in one.

👎 The public tend to choose media sources which reflect their views, not vice versa.

👎 Many argue that the media follows and reflects the public's views rather than creates them.

The 2017 general election

The 2017 general election heralded the arrival of **social media** as a political force to be reckoned with. It even appeared to outflank the power of the populist *Daily Mail* and *Sun* newspapers to create a balance for the Corbyn campaign. Social media came of age in 2017.

Due to the number of newspapers, the Labour Party received the majority of negative **traditional media** coverage in the weeks leading up to the election, with a particular focus on Corbyn. In another era, such an assault would have been fatal. But social media gave Corbyn's supporters a powerful weapon.

Labour spent more on their social media campaign than the Conservatives, with a strategy that harnessed social media to bolster support. The scale of their supporters' **Facebook** operations stood out: Corbyn's official page has more than double the 'likes' of May's. When combined, there are hundreds of thousands of 'likes' for pages like these.

Whereas Labour's was a very polished social media presence, the Conservatives' came across as unprepared and unresponsive. While Labour used social media to build and motivate its voter base, the Conservatives focused on anti-Corbyn attack ads.

Labour didn't merely use social media, they dominated it. Pro-Labour **memes**, **slogans**, **videos** and **articles** saturated social media. They used humour – such as the viral video of Corbyn eating a Pringle! – as well as slogans and serious messages. Together, they made millions of people feel connected to a common project. They made Corbynism feel like a community.

Labour had a positive, hopeful message, and they used social media to build a movement. Social media can provide the glue for people to be bound together. It energised people and got the supporters out. The Conservative strategy of poking holes in the other side didn't evoke the same emotion of togetherness.

On polling day, Labour spent considerable money promoting #*forthemany* on **Twitter** to rally the younger vote, which played a huge part in Labour's performance.

Crucially, however, this community didn't just exist online. Young people – the heaviest users of social media – turned out in greater numbers than usual, and they voted overwhelmingly for Labour.

The Canary

The Canary is an online blog which publishes pieces that spread more widely than mainstream media and pay their writers partly based on their click numbers. In the early weeks of the election campaign, *The Canary* was one of the most popular news sources on Facebook, at times drawing in numbers comparable to the BBC and national newspapers to some of its stories. Kerry-Anne Mendoza, editor of *The Canary*, is a big supporter of Corbyn.

Now try this

Why did Labour focus on social media in 2017?

Pragmatism and tradition

Conservatism aims to conserve society as it is and is suspicious of change. Pragmatism and tradition are two core values of conservatism; they are strongly linked to traditional and One Nation Conservatism and associated with writers Edmund Burke and Michael Oakeshott.

Pragmatism

Pragmatism rejects ideology and theory in favour of decisions made on the basis of **practical experience** and 'what works'. It implies a **flexible** political approach that considers what is acceptable to, and in the best interests of, the people, and what ensures social stability and cohesion. According to Edmund Burke (see page 43 to find out more about Burke's influence on conservatism): 'Example is the school of mankind, and they will learn at no other.' Likewise, Michael Oakeshott (for more on Oakeshott, see page 44) said: 'To be a Conservative is to prefer the tried to the untried.'

Tradition

Tradition refers to the institutions, customs and beliefs of a society that has **developed over time**. The term also implies that such practices will be **passed on from generation to generation**. According to G.K. Chesterton (1874–1936): 'Tradition means giving votes to the most obscure of all classes, our ancestors. It is the democracy of the dead. Tradition refuses to submit to the small and arrogant oligarchy of those who merely happen to be walking about.'

Arguments in favour of pragmatism

Human nature: humans lack the intellectual ability to fully understand the complex realities of the world. Theories, abstract ideas or ideologies that claim to 'explain' or 'improve' the condition of human life are rejected as potentially destabilising.

Society: abstract ideas and principles such as 'equality' and 'rights' are dangerous because they can lead to radical change (often through revolution) that produces worse rather than better conditions.

The state: a pragmatic approach that emphasises caution, moderation, gradualism and continuity will introduce necessary change or reform without endangering social cohesion or stability.

The economy: the One Nation conservative approach to the economy is described below.

Arguments in favour of tradition

Human nature: tradition provides humans, who are weak and security-seeking, with the social framework to make sense of society and their place within it.

Society: long-established institutions, customs and practices give communities and nations a strong sense of **identity** that encourages social cohesion and security. Any attempt to remove the 'traditional' base of society will lead to insecurity and instability.

The state: tradition represents the **accumulated wisdom** of the past. State institutions and practices that have proved 'fit for purpose' over time (for example, the monarchy, constitution and House of Lords) should be preserved for the benefit of future generations.

The economy: the capitalist market system has endured as an efficient, dynamic and productive form of economic organisation. It should be maintained as long as it doesn't undermine conservative values.

Pragmatism: traditional and One Nation conservative approaches

There are two strands of conservative thinking on pragmatism:

1 **Traditional conservatives** such as Burke argue that cautious pragmatism enables a society to adapt to changing circumstances by introducing moderate changes/reforms rather than reject change completely and risk revolution. A key aim of this **change to conserve** policy is to safeguard the essential features of society such as property, order, tradition and established institutions, such as the monarchy.

2 **One Nation conservatives** (see page 40 to find out more about this philosophy) adopt a pragmatic 'middle way' economic policy that combines market competition with government regulation. They argue that this promotes growth and social stability by creating wealth through the private sector and generating the funding for state welfare provision.

Now try this

Why do conservatives favour pragmatism?

Human imperfection and the organic state

Conservatives, such as Oakeshott (see page 44), view humans as flawed, unchanging and incapable of achieving perfection. **Human imperfection** has to be reined in because of people's capacity for evil. Furthermore, since humans are dependent and insecure, they can only exist in an **organic state or society**.

Three aspects of human imperfection

1 Psychological

As limited and dependent beings, humans desire familiarity, safety and the security of knowing their place in society. Consequently, people need **social order** rather than liberty. An **ordered society** provides security, predictability and stability. Liberty brings choice, change and uncertainty.

2 Moral

As naturally selfish beings, humans are morally imperfect. Thus, **human nature** accounts for anti-social or criminal behaviour, not social or economic deprivation. A tough law-and-order system that punishes such conduct is the only deterrent capable of tackling human moral imperfection.

3 Intellectual

Humans lack the intellect and powers of reasoning to understand a complex world. Conservatives therefore reject theories or ideologies that claim to explain or predict the development of human society. Instead, humans should be **pragmatic** and rely on history, tradition and practical experience to understand their place in the world.

Links to human nature

Due to the weakness of human nature, conservatives argue that:

- **the state** has to impose tough law-and-order policies to deter criminal behaviour and pursue foreign policies based on national security, not 'liberal' notions of international cooperation and harmony

- **society** has to be based on authority, hierarchy and paternalism in order to provide people with stability, predictability and security

- an **economy** based on capitalism is a more powerful motivator than altruism since humans are self-interested.

The organic state or society

Conservative support for an organic society or state is based on the view that humans are dependent and security-seeking.

Authority: top-down **authority** shapes relations between the different social groups and permeates all social institutions, such as schools and families. Authority provides humans with **direction** and **security**, promotes **social cohesion** by showing people where they 'fit in' and offers **leadership roles** to be admired and respected.

Living organism: society functions like a living organism with all its carefully balanced parts working together in harmony to ensure that the 'body' remains healthy, social cohesion is preserved and **atomism** avoided.

Traditional institutions: long-standing institutions play a key role in preserving the 'health' of **society** and the **state** and meet the **human need for security**. They should not be radically changed or abolished.

Features of an organic society

Paternalism: the most advantaged (in terms of financial rewards or status) have the greatest social responsibilities. For example, managers are paid more than their workers because their role is more demanding but they are obliged to protect the jobs and economic well-being of their workforces. In this way, **economic inequality** is justified.

Hierarchy: a **hierarchy** based on fixed ranks and inequalities, partly because humans vary in terms of their **intellect, skills,** etc., and partly because different groups or classes have to perform different roles in society such as political leadership, business management or manual work.

Now try this

How does the organic society complement the conservative view of human nature?

Paternalism and libertarianism

Paternalism and libertarianism are opposing conservative core ideas. **Paternalistic** conservatism was perhaps best exemplified by Harold Macmillan's Conservative government (1957–1963). **Libertarianism** informed the policies pursued by UK Prime Minister Margaret Thatcher (1979–1990) and US President Ronald Reagan (1981–1989).

Paternalism

Paternalism is the traditional conservative belief that government should be conducted by those best equipped to lead and make decisions through birth, inheritance and upbringing. Paternalism is strongly linked to conservative views on hierarchy, order and the organic society. In short, it represents a form of benign power exerted from above by the state that governs in the interest of the population as a whole. One Nation conservatism softened this notion (see page 40).

Libertarianism

Libertarianism is a strand of conservative thinking influenced by Adam Smith's arguments for **economic liberalism**. It advocates:

• individual liberty

• maximum economic freedom

• minimal government or state regulation.

Now more commonly known as the liberal new right or **neo-liberalism** (see page 42), it rejects paternalism. Key libertarian thinkers include Friedrich von Hayek, Ayn Rand and Robert Nozick (see page 44).

Arguments in favour of paternalism

Human nature: in the past, **traditional conservatives** (such as Burke) argued that the innate or hereditary abilities of the social elite gave them the authority to make decisions on society's behalf and impose on them an obligation to care for the less fortunate (see page 39). Modern **One Nation conservatives** similarly maintain that, since human ability is not evenly distributed, the successful are entitled to their rewards but they also have a social responsibility to look after those who are unable to look after themselves (see page 40).

The economy: One Nation paternalistic conservatism, originally introduced by Disraeli (see page 40) and recently exhibited by the Cameron and May governments, has argued that government regulation of the economy and social welfare measures are necessary to improve conditions for the poorest.

Society: conservative paternalism blends principle with pragmatism (see page 36) – the privileged in society have a social responsibility to look after the less fortunate and, in so doing, they aim to preserve their position, strengthen the hierarchical nature of society and remove threats to the social order.

The state: since 1945, One Nation conservatives have argued that the modern state is the most appropriate agency through which to deliver social welfare and economic regulation in the interests of all (see page 40). Paternalism (notably in its state-directed form) can be **soft** when recipients give their consent or **hard** when it is imposed regardless of consent or opposition.

Arguments in favour of libertarianism

The economy: the free market is the only mechanism that can:

• efficiently supply goods and services on the basis of consumer demand

• determine the 'natural' level of unemployment.

Inflation poses the biggest threat to the market economy because it inhibits economic and business activity. To curb inflation, government spending has to be cut to control the money supply.

The state: state involvement in the mixed economy, welfare programmes and public ownership are rejected as too expensive and inefficient. Instead, 'supply side' economic policies (see page 42) should be pursued to boost production. Obstacles such as government regulation, high taxation and trade-union influence over the labour market should be removed to release the wealth-creating potential of the free market. Taxation represents a form of legalised 'state robbery' by transferring property (income) from one individual to another without consent, thereby undermining property rights.

Human nature: humans are naturally competitive, autonomous, individualistic, self-interested and rational. For this reason, social welfare provision is rejected on moral grounds since such programmes create a 'dependency culture', undermining personal responsibility, freedom and initiative.

Now try this

How would a paternalistic conservative criticise libertarianism?

Traditional conservatism

Traditional conservatism emerged in the late 18th century as a critical response to the **French Revolution** and the **Enlightenment**. Edmund Burke's famous book *Reflections on the Revolution in France* (1790) is the classic work in favour of traditional conservatism.

What is traditional conservatism?

Living organism: society is an **organic** or 'living' body with complex interconnections and relationships between its component parts.

Tradition institutions: tried and tested traditional institutions (e.g. the Church, the monarchy and the family) represent the accumulated experience and wisdom of the past. These bind society together through ties of duty, loyalty and affection.

Traditional conservatism

Hierarchy: an organic society has to be organised as a **hierarchy** because people are not equal (e.g. in terms of their ability and work rate). Different jobs are rewarded differently depending on the contribution they make (see page 36).

Pragmatism: any attempt to create a perfect society using abstract theories and principles will fail since such an approach is not based on previous human experience and **pragmatism** (see page 37).

Gradual reform: change or reform has to be introduced gradually over time and be based on past experience in order to preserve the balance or 'fabric' of the organic society; sudden or radical change is likely to be harmful.

Rule by the 'natural aristocracy'

Burke maintained that the 'true natural aristocracy' should govern. These are the people with the ability, experience and inclination to lead the nation wisely in the interest of the whole society. Burke thought this small governing elite would be largely (but not exclusively) drawn from the hereditary aristocracy.

Traditional conservative defence of aristocratic rule

Rule by the aristocracy was natural since, for generations, the upper class had been raised and educated to govern at all levels in society. As large property holders, they also had a significant stake in society.

The longstanding practice of aristocratic rule was based on paternalism (see page 38) and the concept of noblesse oblige. This meant that those in authority were best placed, and had a duty, to make decisions on behalf of society as a whole.

During the late 18th and early 19th centuries, traditional conservatives argued that the 'natural' leaders of society were the aristocracy.

French Revolution

A major upheaval in France between 1789 and 1799 that violently removed the monarchy and the privileged position of the aristocracy and the Church. Traditional conservatism was a reaction to the French Revolution by the British ruling elite to justify their own privileged position and thereby avoid the same fate as their French counterparts.

The Enlightenment

The Enlightenment was an 18th-century European intellectual movement that stressed the importance of human reason and the need to examine critically existing ideas, institutions and traditions. Traditional conservatives rejected much Enlightenment thinking on the grounds that it would encourage rapid, indiscriminate and destabilising change.

Reflections on the Revolution in France

Edmund Burke's 1790 classic study of the French Revolution attacked the assumption that a system of government could be created on the basis of abstract principles and theories (such as liberty and equality). In his view, the French Revolution illustrated the dangers of sudden and far-reaching change. The removal of the monarchy and aristocratic privilege by popular revolution undermined the stability of French society by challenging established notions of authority, tradition, hierarchy and property. Furthermore, he feared that France's new leaders would lack the experience, restraint and understanding to perform their role. As a result, the country would be plunged into chaos.

Now try this

On what grounds did traditional conservatives defend aristocratic rule?

One Nation conservatism

One Nation conservatism emerged in the 19th century in response to the impact of **laissez-faire capitalism** and **industrialisation**. It is an updated version of traditional conservatism. Benjamin Disraeli, Conservative prime minister in 1868 and from 1874–1880, is generally regarded as the founder of One Nation conservatism.

Emergence

There were two key reasons for the emergence of One Nation conservatism:

1 The rise of laissez-faire capitalism in the 19th century led to fears that a self-interested individualism was undermining the basis of the organic society and the idea of social responsibility.

2 Growing industrialisation during the same period led to concern that Britain was becoming '**two nations**' (the rich and the poor) and that this division would destabilise society, sharpen class conflict and possibly lead to revolution. One Nation conservatism softened the ideas of paternalism, seeing it as the responsibility of the well-off to look after those who are less fortunate.

Disraeli's analysis

Disraeli wanted to reconcile the 'two nations'. He argued that conservatism would have to respond to these social and economic changes by renewing its commitment to reform and social obligation. His motives were both pragmatic and principled:

- Reforms to improve conditions for the poorest would reduce social discontent, preserve the position of the upper classes, and probably increase working-class support for the Conservative Party.

- The most privileged social groups had a moral and paternalistic duty to help the poor. This included social welfare measures to preserve 'one nation'. This is often understood as the idea of noblesse oblige.

Three key ideas

Disraeli's One Nation conservatism

Maintenance of traditional institutions	**Support for imperialism**	**Social and other reforms for the working class**
Disraeli was determined to protect traditional British institutions (e.g. the monarchy, Church of England) because they had proved themselves over time, provided stability and created a sense of national loyalty and identity across the classes.	Disraeli argued that the British Empire strengthened national pride and Britain's influence in the world. Imperialism appealed to all classes and linked conservatism with the emerging 'mass' politics of the late 19th century.	Reforms were introduced (e.g. housing, food safety, voting rights) to create an alliance between the traditional ruling class and the workers, offset the negative effects of laissez-faire capitalism and reduce social discontent.

Conservative government, 1951–1964

This was the high point of One Nation conservatism:

- The government used **Keynesian economics** (see page 51 for more on this approach to the economy) to maintain high employment, accepting the mixed economy and supporting the welfare state.

- Harold Macmillan referred to this One Nation approach as a 'middle way' between unrestrained liberalism (individualism and the free market) and socialist collectivism (extensive state control and planning).

- R.A. Butler, a 1950s–1960s One Nation conservative minister, stated that government policy at the time was designed to bring Disraeli's two nations 'into a single social entity'.

Harold Macmillan (1894–1986)

- Conservative prime minister (1957–1963).

- His classic study, *The Middle Way* (1938), proposed a 'halfway house' between unrestricted capitalism and state socialism, to include public ownership of key industries, government direction of investment and state-funded welfare to establish a minimum standard of living.

- He argued that a managed economy and 'orderly capitalism' would preserve the cohesion of the 'one nation' and prevent social unrest.

- One Nation conservatism remained the dominant strand in conservative thinking from the 1950s to the 1970s.

Now try this

Why have modern One Nation conservatives endorsed the mixed economy?

New Right

New Right conservatism emerged in the 1970s as the main rival to One Nation conservatism (see page 40 for a discussion of this approach). The New Right brought together two distinct strands – **neo-liberalism** (or liberal New Right) and **neo-conservatism** (or conservative New Right).

Rise of the New Right

- New Right thinking gained momentum in the 1970s as the interventionist policies of Western governments (based on welfare provision and Keynesian techniques; see page 51) failed to combat **stagflation** (an economy experiencing rising inflation, little or no growth and rising unemployment).

- New Right conservatism was prominent in the 1980s in the UK and the USA and became popularly linked with UK PM Margaret Thatcher (1979–1990) and US President Ronald Reagan (1981–1989).

- This New Right perspective was frequently referred to as 'Reaganism' or 'Thatcherism'.

Neo-liberalism and neo-conservatism

```
        ┌─────────────┐
        │  New Right  │
        └─────────────┘
         ┌──────┴──────┐
```

Neo-liberalism	Neo-conservatism
An updated form of classical liberalism (see page 49) that calls for a free market economy, a minimal state and individual freedom and responsibility.	A modernised version of traditional conservative social thinking that emphasises social order, traditional values and public morality.

For more on neo-liberalism and neo-conservatism, see page 42.

Features of the New Right

The New Right contains radical, traditional and reactionary elements. For this reason, some have argued that the New Right is not a coherent doctrine as it contains apparently incompatible features.

② Traditional
Neo-conservatives endorse traditional views such as family values, respect for authority, and the benefits of hard work.

③ Reactionary
The New Right often appear to regard the 19th century as a 'golden age' of economic freedom and individual moral responsibility. A reactionary person or attitude favours a return to an earlier situation or period on the grounds that it possessed positive features that are currently lacking. The term is usually associated with right-wing politics.

① Radical
The New Right opposes economic and social intervention by the government and adopts **anti-permissiveness** regarding social attitudes and moral choices.

Losing Ground: American Social Policy 1950–1980

Charles Murray's (1984) influential study of post-war US social policy argued that state welfare provision had created a dependency culture, which sapped the notion of individual responsibility and enabled the feckless to evade their obligations (as fathers or partners, for example). Murray, an American political scientist, also maintained that the legal neutrality and liberal nature of the welfare state encouraged a moral relativism and **permissive** outlook that undermined the traditional nuclear family and made alternative lifestyles financially viable.

Now try this

Why have some maintained that the New Right is not a coherent doctrine?

Neo-liberalism and neo-conservatism

Neo-liberalism gained ground during the 1970s, promoted by economists such as Milton Friedman and Friedrich von Hayek. Neo-conservatism emerged at the same time as a reaction against the 'liberal' 1960s in the West.

Neo-liberalism: key principles

Free market

The **free-market economy** is the only mechanism that can meet consumer demand effectively, make maximum use of resources and produce the greatest overall prosperity. Government intervention cannot do this and creates or exacerbates economic problems.

The free market has to be protected against:

- **inflation**, which discourages economic activity and investment
- industrial or business **monopolies**, which reduce economic competition and consumer choice
- **government intervention**, which creates inflation by introducing too much money or credit into the economy.

Inflation

The government's vital economic role is to tackle inflation. Thatcher and Reagan adopted Friedman's **monetarist** policy in the 1980s to reduce inflation by controlling the money supply through cuts in public spending. This neo-liberal approach is generally known as '**supply side**' economics (see page 38 to read more about libertarianism).

Rejection of government intervention

State planning, nationalisation and high taxation lead to economic inefficiency and lack of incentive. State welfare provision expands, irrespective of demand, due to the vested interests of the professionals concerned (for example, doctors) and political parties (promising increased welfare spending in elections). The result is rising taxation and inflation, and increasingly inefficient state welfare services.

Atomistic individualism

Individuals are rational, self-interested and self-sufficient. Individual freedom can only be safeguarded by opposing collectivism and 'rolling back' the state, to release human potential and create natural harmony through free relations.

For example, extensive welfare provision creates a dependency culture that undermines atomistic individualism.

Neo-conservatism: key principles

Social order

The 'liberal' 1960s, with its progressive reforms, ideas and attitudes, undermined the social order by threatening society with fragmentation (for example, the decline of authority and respect, rising crime rates and increased anti-social behaviour). Social order can only be safeguarded by:

- strong political leadership and a renewed emphasis on government authority
- re-introducing discipline, hierarchy and respect throughout society to re-establish the authority of the family and other traditional social institutions.

Traditional values

Traditional values, such as respect for authority and the law, and the benefits of hard work, have to be upheld to strengthen society and restore social discipline. To achieve this, the 'strong state' has to be promoted, with greater police powers and tougher penalties to combat crime and public disorder. During the 1980s, Thatcher and Reagan took a tough stance on law and order, believing that such an approach would deter those who were tempted to commit illegal acts and thus challenge the traditional values of society.

Public morality

The permissive 'anything goes' culture that developed in some Western countries in the 1960s undermined public morality by allowing people to make their own moral choices and suggesting there is no objective right and wrong.

If an individual is allowed to make their own moral or lifestyle choices, two problems arise:

- The person may adopt an 'immoral' code or lifestyle.
- If people are free to choose different moral positions, this undermines the development of common moral standards and threatens social cohesion.

Thatcher ('Victorian values') and the Moral Majority in the USA (traditional values) illustrate the neo-conservative concern with public morality.

The Road to Serfdom

Friedrich von Hayek's (1944) pioneering study was addressed to 'the socialists of all parties'. It argued that state interventionism and collectivism, even if pursued moderately, would erode individual liberty and create a new form of serfdom or slavery. Free individuals would become dominated by, and dependent on, the state (via welfare provision). Hayek's study became a key text for supporters of the free market and opponents of Keynesian-style interventionism and state welfare provision, including British conservatives Keith Joseph and Margaret Thatcher.

Now try this

Why do neo-liberals oppose state intervention?

Key thinkers: 1

Hobbes and Burke are regarded as two of the key conservative thinkers.

Key thinkers and ideas

Thomas Hobbes (1588–1679)

Key ideas

In his book **Leviathan** (1651), Hobbes developed two important conservative ideas:

 Order: an ordered society should balance the human need to lead a free life.

 Human nature: humans are needy, vulnerable and easily led astray in their attempts to understand the world around them.

Uses

The ordered society

- In a 'state of nature', humans are free from authority. A 'restless desire for power' would lead to war.

- Rational people would therefore sacrifice their freedom and natural rights for security through the establishment of political authority.

- Government is therefore established by the joint consent of the people, and authorises those in power to preserve order and peace.

Human nature

Humans demonstrate needy and vulnerable characteristics by:

- competing violently to obtain the basic necessities of life and other material gains

- fighting out of fear to ensure their personal safety

- seeking reputation, both for its own sake and to avoid being challenged by others.

Human capacity to reason is fragile. People's attempts to interpret the world are distorted by self-interest and the concerns of the moment.

Hobbes asked: *'How could a state be governed, or protected in its foreign relations if every individual remained free to obey or not to obey the law according to his private opinion?'*

Key thinkers and ideas

Edmund Burke (1729–1797)

Key ideas

In **Reflections on the Revolution in France** (1790), Burke developed two key conservative ideas:

 Change to conserve has to be undertaken with caution and mindful of the delicate balance inherent in an organic society.

 Respect tradition and empiricism because they represent practices passed down from one generation to the next.

Uses

Cautious change

- The state resembles a living organism like a plant that may be changed through gentle 'pruning' or 'grafting' in order to preserve the stability and harmony of the social and political order.

- Reform should be limited and cautious, and be based on **empiricism** and tradition, rather than new abstract principles.

- Revolutionary change threatens to cut off the 'roots' of the organic society (such as the institutions and customs that gave it stability), leading to social and political breakdown. For more on Burke's views on the French Revolution, see page 39.

Tradition and empiricism

- They represent the accumulated and 'tested' wisdom of the past residing in society's longstanding institutions, customs and practices.

- Continuing respect for tradition and empiricism promotes social continuity and stability and provides the essential reference points for 'necessary' change.

- They encourage social cohesion and security because they offer people a sense of being 'rooted' in, and tied to, their particular society.

According to Burke: *'It is with infinite caution that any man ought to venture upon pulling down an edifice which has answered in any tolerable degree for ages the common purposes of society, or on building it up again without having the model and patterns of approved utility before his eyes.'*

Now try this

In what ways are the views of Hobbes and Burke similar?

Key thinkers: 2

Oakeshott, Rand and Nozick are also key conservative thinkers.

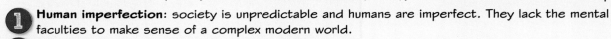

Key thinkers and ideas

Michael Oakeshott (1901–1990)

Key ideas

In *Rationalism in Politics* (1962) and *On Human Conduct* (1975), Oakeshott stressed two concepts:

1 **Human imperfection**: society is unpredictable and humans are imperfect. They lack the mental faculties to make sense of a complex modern world.

2 **Pragmatism**: conservatism is about being pragmatic.

Uses

Society

A 'rationalist' political leader is inclined to make decisions based on the 'authority' of his own reason (rather than practical experience). This encourages the dangerous idea that the leader fully understands society and how it should be changed, as was the case, for example, in fascism and communism.

The state

Political thinking and action should be guided by pragmatism and practical experience to ensure public acceptance, maintain social stability and cohesion and respond flexibly to shifting circumstances; the British parliamentary system is a good example of what can result from this thinking.

Key thinkers and ideas

Ayn Rand (1905–1982)

Key ideas

Rand's novels *The Fountainhead* (1943) and *Atlas Shrugged* (1957) advocated:

1 **Objectivism**: rational self-interest is a virtue. The pursuit of rational self-interest is morally right, based on 'the virtue of selfishness'.

2 **Freedom**: support for a completely unregulated, laissez-faire economy, compatible with the free expression of human rationality.

Uses

You can use Rand when discussing human nature and the economy (as above).

Key thinkers and ideas

Robert Nozick (1938–2002)

In *Anarchy, State and Utopia* (1974), Nozick promoted:

1 **Libertarianism**: individuals have rights to their lives, liberty and the rewards of their labour (based partly on the ideas of Immanuel Kant, 1724–1804). They cannot be treated as things or used against their will.

2 **Self-ownership**: individuals own their own bodies, talents, abilities and labour. This is threatened by enforced taxation to fund welfare (it gives others part of the individual's rewards) and by state regulation over the individual (for example, anti-smoking measures).

Uses

You can use Nozick when discussing human nature, the state and the economy.

The state

Taxes levied for state welfare are immoral because they treat individuals as a means/resource (rather than an end in themselves). Only a minimal state can be justified.

This is threatened by enforced taxation to fund welfare (it gives others part of the individual's rewards), and by state regulation over the individual (for example, anti-smoking measures).

Now try this

What are the key differences between Oakeshott's conservatism and that of Rand and Nozick?

Exam skills: the introduction

This question will help you to revise for **Section B** of your A Level **Paper 1** exam. This section consists of two 24-mark essay questions – you will need to choose **one** of them to answer.

Section B

- You should aim to spend around 30 minutes on this essay.
- Your essay needs to be fully structured, including an introduction and a conclusion.
- Aim to show clear links between your points and use examples to support them.
- You will be assessed on AO1, AO2 and AO3 skills.
- You **must** use at least **two** relevant key thinkers as outlined in the relevant section of the specification.

Introduction

Your **introduction** should show that you understand what you have been asked to do. It should therefore define key terms (if necessary), outline what you are going to discuss and identify what you intend to argue.

Questions

Questions will explore the extent of agreement within the ideology **or** tensions within the different strands over one of the four key areas (the state, society, the economy and human nature). You need to cover all three AOs, which are equally weighted:

- set out the nature of the debate on both sides – show you understand how the content relates to the question (AO1)
- examine the ideology/strands in relation to the question, this also means showing similarities and differences within the strands (AO2)
- make judgements: explore (evaluate) the extent of the similarities and differences and come to a judgement (AO3). This should be clear throughout your essay, not just in the conclusion.

Worked example

To what extent do One Nation and New Right conservatives agree over the role of the state?

You must use appropriate thinkers you have studied to support your answer and consider both sides in a balanced way.   **(24 marks)**

Conservative attitudes to the state vary and some sharp differences exist, particularly between One Nation and neo-liberal conservatives, but also between neo-liberals and neo-conservatives within the New Right. Disagreement over the role of the state highlights fundamental differences between these two strands of conservatism, and in particular their contrasting views of human nature. Thus, One Nation conservatives and neo-conservatives agree (for different reasons) on the importance of the state. Having said this, the New Right and One Nation strands cannot be reconciled on the appropriate level of state involvement in the economy...

Steps to planning

1 **Introduction**: define key terms and introduce the argument.

2 **Body**: which concepts or strands are you going to discuss and which key thinkers are you going to use to support your argument? Identify the key similarities and differences between the strands that you plan to discuss.

3 **Conclusion**: make a final summary judgement, drawing on the concepts and strands from your essay.

This introduction includes the two relevant strands of conservatism identified in the question.

The areas of agreement and disagreement regarding One Nation conservative and New Right attitudes to the role of the state are identified. This suggests excellent understanding of the issue targeted by the question.

The final sentence gives a hint as to how the student will argue. An introduction like this identifies that a student understands all three of the assessment objectives and sets the essay up excellently.

Command words: To what extent

Questions will explore the tensions within conservatism or differing views within conservatism. You need to show that you know and can set out the nature of the debate (AO1), can analyse (AO2) and evaluate (AO3) the similarities and differences between the different strands or tensions within the idea.

Individualism and freedom

Liberalism is seen as a product of the Enlightenment, recognising humans as rational creatures capable of understanding the world and making decisions. The key core values are a belief in individualism and freedom or liberty.

Individualism

Liberals stress the importance of **the individual** over the claims of any social group or collective body. Individuals possess self-awareness, capabilities, personality and free will to decide their own destiny.

Freedom or liberty

Freedom (or liberty) for liberals implies the ability and right of an individual to make decisions in his or her interests. Such freedom, however, is not absolute and has to be exercised under the law.

Arguments in favour of freedom or liberty

Human nature: early liberals argued that the **human need** for individual freedom overrode the claims of authoritarian governments to make decisions for the people and regulate their lives.

The state: however, liberals past and present maintain that freedom is not absolute and must be exercised under the laws of the state.

Society:

* Utilitarian thinker Jeremy Bentham (1748–1832) argued that individuals are able to make decisions based on **rational self-interest** and that human actions are driven primarily by a desire to **pursue pleasure** and **avoid pain**. Government or the state should only intervene if people's decisions/actions undermine others' ability to make choices. Applied to **society** at large, this principle established 'the greatest happiness for the greatest number' (but could mean that minority interests are disregarded in favour of the majority).

* Classical liberal thinker John Stuart Mill (for more on Mill, see page 54) advocated **negative freedom** – individuals should only be subject to external restraints (for example, the **state**) when their actions may adversely affect others.

* Later liberals rejected Mill's view of liberty as too limited because it reduced society to a collection of independent individuals. T.H. Green (1836–1882) argued that society was organic and people pursue both the common good and their own individual interests. This led to the concept of **positive freedom** – individuals should control their own destiny, develop personal talents and reach self-fulfilment. **Limited state intervention** was required to facilitate this.

Arguments in favour of individualism

Human nature:

* All individuals are **unique** and have equal worth. They should not be treated as instruments to achieve a particular goal, but should be regarded as having their own intrinsic value.

* Classical liberals emphasise *egoistical individualism* – the idea that people are basically self-seeking and self-reliant.

Society: a more modern liberal justification downplays the pursuit of self-interest by stressing **developmental individualism**, a concept that links individual freedom with the creation of a society where every human can experience personal growth and achieve their potential.

The state: developmental individualism has been used to justify limited state intervention in society to help the disadvantaged.

Individualism and tolerance

For liberals, individualism is linked to **tolerance** – where a person is prepared to accept values, customs and beliefs with which one disagrees. Liberals believe this is a natural right all humans should have.

Liberals have argued for toleration within society of a growing range of views and practices, including different religious beliefs, ethnic cultures and 'alternative' lifestyles such as gay relationships.

Now try this

Why do liberals stress the importance of the individual?

The state and rationalism

Liberals view the state as essential but problematic and regard rationalism as central to their outlook.

The state

Liberalism has a complex relationship with the state (defined as a sovereign body that exerts authority over all individuals and groups living within its defined geographical limits). Liberals tend to see the state as a 'necessary evil', but also seek to limit its power and scope.

Rationalism

Rationalism maintains that humans are (or should be) guided by **reason** rather than emotion, instinct or prejudice. Rationalism was central to Enlightenment thinking, which rejected unquestioning acceptance of traditional authority and religion (see page 39 for more on rationalism and the Enlightenment).

Liberal attitudes to the state

- The state is necessary because it prevents **social disorder** and the **exploitation** of the disadvantaged and vulnerable.

- However, state power is suspect because, as **human nature** is fundamentally self-seeking, people may use any position of power to benefit themselves at the expense of others.

- The concentration of state power has to be opposed since it encourages people to pursue their own self-interest and to use other people for their own ends.

- As such, **limited government** has to be established, based on constitutionalism, the separation of powers, checks and balances, and a bill of rights.

- **Devolution** (see page 68) and **federalism** (see page 164) can be used to prevent the concentration of state power.

Liberal attitudes to rationalism

- **Humans need to be free** to make decisions about their own interests without being directed by external agencies (for example, the **state** or Church).

- Individuals benefit from **taking responsibility for themselves** rather than relying on external guidance.

- Rationalism fosters a **progressive society** because the personal development of the individual promotes wider social advancement.

- Reasoned discussion and debate should be used to resolve disputes and conflicts. For example, arbitration in employer-trade union **economic** disputes.

The liberal view of the economy

Arguments for the limited role for the state also heavily influence liberal views on the economy:

- 18th- and 19th-century liberals embraced **laissez-faire capitalism**. Economic competition, based on individuals striving to generate their own profits, benefits everyone. Government should keep intervention in the economy to a minimum.

- In *The Wealth of Nations* (1776), the economist Adam Smith argued that human self-interest was a key driving force behind economic growth.

Liberals on the state and rationalism

John Stuart Mill (see page 54 for an overview on Mill's influence on liberalism): 'The most cogent reason for restricting the interference of government is the great evil of adding unnecessarily to its power.'

Liberal philosopher Bertrand Russell (1872–1970): 'Religion is something left over from the infancy of our intelligence, it will fade away as we adopt reason and science as our guidelines.

Now try this

Explain why rationalism is central to the liberal outlook.

Equality/social justice and liberal democracy

Liberalism maintains that individuals are of equal value and should be treated impartially and fairly by society. Although they have some reservations, liberals generally support democracy.

Equality and social justice

Liberals argue that humans share the same essential nature and are therefore equal. Having said this, liberals are divided over what equality actually means in practice. Modern liberals emphasise **justice** – a morally justifiable distribution of wealth that implies a desire to limit inequality in society to some extent.

Liberal democracy

Most liberals back the concept of liberal democracy based on:

- free elections
- a neutral state with limited powers
- recognition of civil liberties and toleration of different viewpoints.

Liberal attitudes to equality and social justice

Equality of opportunity: everybody should have the same chance to rise or fall in society. Differing outcomes are acceptable. Humans have different abilities and potential, which they should be free to fulfil.

State intervention: modern liberals believe some state intervention is acceptable to enable individuals to fulfill their potential role and be treated fairly by society. Complete equality of outcome is neither achievable nor desirable.

Equality and social justice

Foundational equality: all people are born equal. They possess inalienable human rights which are universal and cannot be removed by the state or social groups.

Social inequality: liberals believe some social inequality is acceptable as people with different talents require different rewards. Society benefits because individuals have an incentive to strive and fulfil their potential, creating a **meritocracy** where social position is achieved by effort and ability.

Formal equality: in society, people should have the same legal and political rights, based on equality before the law and equal voting rights.

Arguments for and against liberal democracy

👍 Government lacks legitimacy without the consent of the people.

👍 A **social contract** should operate between the people and their rulers whereby the people freely give, and renew, their consent to be governed (for more on Locke and the social contract, see page 53).

👍 Citizens can hold the government to account.

👍 Democracy enhances popular participation and promotes the **personal growth and development of individuals**.

👍 Democracy encourages political stability and consensus in **society** by giving a political voice to different groups and interests.

👎 In the 19th century, liberals such as Robert Lowe (1811–1892) argued that the poorly educated were incapable of voting in an informed way.

👎 Since democracy was collectivist, it would lead to an **expanded role for the government and state**, requiring higher taxation and **stifling individual initiative**.

👎 Democracy may result in the 'tyranny of the majority', **undermining minority rights or individual freedoms** and imposing a grey conformist culture.

👎 Most modern liberals endorse democracy but insist it is subject to constitutional constraints and protects individual and group rights.

Now try this

Why are some liberals uneasy about liberal democracy?

Liberalism and freedom

Classical and **modern liberalism** are the two key strands of liberal ideology. You need to know how their views of freedom differ.

Classical liberals and freedom

Classical liberals advocate **negative freedom**. This belief is linked to several features of the classical liberal approach:

- Endorsement of **egoistical individualism** (see page 46).
- Belief that freedom can be maximised by limiting state power; that way, individuals take greater responsibility for their own lives instead of depending on the state.
- Reliance on the state takes away a person's self-respect and undermines the human entrepreneurial drive essential for economic growth.

Modern liberals and freedom

Modern liberals reject negative freedom on its own because individuals who are disadvantaged through no fault of their own require help to overcome these obstacles. Modern liberals endorse the concept of **positive freedom**, which:

- regards freedom as self-realisation
- supports limited state intervention in society and the economy (for example, through education and welfare provision) to release individuals from social deprivation and give them greater opportunities to realise their potential
- reinforces **developmental individualism** (see page 46).

Classical liberalism

Classical liberalism dates back to the 18th century and is linked to the emergence of **industrial capitalism**.

Classical liberals maintain that:

- there should be negative freedom (see page 46 for more on liberal views of freedom) and a **minimal state** or 'night watchman' state
- the state has an essential obligation to protect property because property ownership is a fundamental freedom
- individual behaviour should be as unrestricted as possible, so long as social stability is maintained
- economic activity should be based on free-market and laissez-faire principles
- large-scale welfare should be rejected because it leads to immoral or self-indulgent behaviour and encourages dependency on the state.

Key classical liberal thinkers include Mary Wollstonecraft (1759–1797) and John Stuart Mill (1806–1873). For more on Wollstonecraft and Mill, see page 54.

Modern liberalism

Modern liberalism emerged in the early 20th century as a reaction against **free-market capitalism**. Modern liberals believe that the free market has not produced freedom for everybody because freedom cannot be defined as just being left alone by the state. They argue that the market has to be regulated to combat inequality and poverty.

Modern liberals maintain that:

- formal equality does not lead to equality of opportunity because it permits significant inequalities (wealth and living standards) that prevent real equality of opportunity
- developmental individualism should be promoted by society through an interventionist state and a managed economy (go to page 46 to find out more on liberals' views on individualism)
- individualism (a person's potential) can be assisted through collective action such as state intervention to alleviate the effects of poverty and social deprivation
- positive freedom (see page 46) is required to establish real equality of opportunity
- economic management of capitalism (based on government spending and fiscal policies to regulate demand) rather than the free-market approach is needed to ensure the smooth running of the economy (read more about liberals' approach to the economy on page 51).

Key modern liberal thinkers include John Rawls (1921–2002). For more on Rawls, see page 55.

Now try this

Why do classical liberals support negative freedom?

Liberalism and the state

Although classical and modern liberals share some common views on the nature of the state, they differ in certain respects about the role the state should play.

Liberal views on the nature of the state

Classical and modern liberals believe that the state should:

- function according to pre-set regulations and practices
- be decentralised so that power is fragmented and dispersed (for example, through devolution)
- guarantee citizens' rights and protect civil liberties
- exercise its authority subject to the consent of the governed.

They also believe that the state is based on mechanistic theory – the idea that the state was created by people to serve them and act in their interests.

The role of the state

Classical liberalism (as advocated by Mill; see page 54)	Modern liberalism (as advocated by Rawls; see page 55)
Take a minimalist view of the role of the state.	Call for an enabling state.
The state should simply establish a stable framework for human activity and leave everything else to individuals and businesses.	The state should play a larger role in order to help individuals to be free and achieve their potential.
This minimal or 'night watchman' state should focus on maintaining social order, ensuring contract compliance and providing protection against external attack.	The state has a social responsibility to reduce or remove social and economic disadvantages if individuals are held back by their social circumstances.
State intervention in social and economic life should be kept to a minimum in order to protect individual liberty.	An enlarged state, using taxation to provide welfare, health and education enhances equality of opportunity in society.
The state's role is to maintain an orderly environment for private trade, sustain the value/stability of the currency and establish conditions under which the free market can flourish.	The enabling state should improve the lot of the poorest in society without introducing equality of outcome so that considerable scope is left for individual liberty and self-fulfilment.

The 'survival of the fittest'

By the late 19th century, some classical liberals were linking their arguments in favour of negative freedom and the minimal state with Social Darwinism (Charles Darwin's principles of natural selection applied to human society), which emphasised the 'survival of the fittest'. In *The Man versus the State* (1884), Herbert Spencer maintained that individual success or failure rested on a person's ability to adapt to the prevailing economic conditions. Through this process, society would eventually be based on rational self-reliance and individual freedom. An important implication of Spencer's work was that people should not be supported by state welfare.

Examples of modern liberal state intervention

1 The UK Liberal governments of 1906–1914 introduced welfare reforms, including a state pension and health and unemployment insurance.

2 Economist John Maynard Keynes's call for state-directed capitalism influenced the UK government economic strategy from 1945–1979 (see page 51 for more on the liberal approach to the economy).

3 William Beveridge's *Beveridge Report* (1942) proposed state provision to tackle the 'five giant' evils threatening personal freedom and the realisation of individual potential (poverty, unemployment, poor education, inadequate housing and poor healthcare). The UK Labour government (1945–1951) created the welfare state based in part on this report.

Now try this

Why do liberals oppose and embrace the state?

Liberalism and the economy

Classical and modern liberals agree on the fundamental need for a capitalist economy, but there are also important economic differences between the two forms of liberalism.

Shared views on the economy

Classical and modern liberals believe in a market-based capitalist economy because it:

- reflects the liberal conviction that private property is a natural right
- complements liberal individualism through economic self-striving
- is seen to benefit everyone, in keeping with liberal optimism and belief in progress.

Classical liberalism on the economy

Classical liberals' support for negative liberty and a minimal state, as well as their optimistic view of human nature, led them to endorse **laissez-faire capitalism** (see page 47 for more on liberal rationalism). The classical liberal perspective became the economic orthodoxy of the 19th century.

Adam Smith's *The Wealth of Nations* (1776) is the most famous classical liberal statement on the economy.

1 Laissez-faire capitalism, operating through the 'invisible hand' of market forces, would make individuals and society more prosperous.

2 As long as the state adopts a 'hands off' approach to the economy, the wealth of successful individuals would 'trickle down' to the rest of society, improving the lives of the rest of the population.

3 For this reason, all forms of domestic economic protection, such as duties and tariffs, had to be scrapped to promote free-trade globally and bring about the 'wealth of nations'. Under such conditions, countries and their business communities could engage in unrestricted trade to their mutual benefit.

4 This laissez-faire economic approach rested on egoistical individualism and human rationalism/virtue; the latter prevented destructive selfishness and competition.

Modern liberalism on the economy

Modern liberals advocate government or state intervention in the economy, drawing on **Keynesianism**.

John Maynard Keynes's ideas, developed in works such as *The General Theory of Employment, Interest and Money* (1936), influenced President Franklin Roosevelt's 'New Deal' in the USA in the 1930s and UK government economic policy from 1945–1979.

1 The capitalist economy has to be preserved but the free market is not self-regulating since it is prone to cyclical slumps, which bring mass unemployment and a consequent loss of individual freedom.

2 State- or government-directed capitalism (also known as *dirigisme*) is required to guide the economy and regulate demand to deliver sustainable economic growth and maintain full employment.

3 To prevent a slump, governments should manage the level of demand in the economy to preserve full employment. When facing a slump, governments should introduce public spending programmes to create jobs and stimulate the economy.

4 This Keynesian economic approach was partly designed to prevent economic depression leading to the creation of illiberal regimes (such as communist and fascist dictatorships).

Now try this

Identify two ways liberals agree and two ways they disagree on the economy.

Contradiction or continuation?

It is often claimed that modern liberalism has departed from the principles of classical liberalism. To some extent this is true, but the two forms of liberal thought also agree on several key issues.

Similarities and differences between classical and modern liberalism

👍 Both classical and modern liberals have an optimistic view of human nature based on the idea that each individual is unique, has their own intrinsic value and the ability to reason. Humans are self-aware, and capable, possess personality, and have the free will to shape their own destiny.

👍 Both classical and modern liberalism regard individualism as the essential feature of politics and society (although they disagree on how to promote it) and regard the claims of social groups and collective bodies as less important.

👍 Both classical and modern liberals advocate tolerance – being prepared to accept values, customs and beliefs with which one usually disagrees. Liberals regard this as a natural right to which all humans are entitled.

👍 Both classical and modern liberalism maintain that capitalism is the best economic system because it:
- strengthens the natural right to private property
- reinforces liberal individualism
- benefits everybody in society.

👍 Both also oppose state ownership of the economy.

👍 Both classical and modern liberals believe in a constitutional state to limit government power and protect natural rights. They also call for government by consent.

👎 Classical liberals define liberty in terms of negative freedom, with individuals free from external interference (for example, by the state). Modern liberals, in contrast, see liberty in terms of positive freedom, which means that people are free only if they are actively enabled through outside intervention, usually by the government or the state.

👎 Modern liberals often view increased taxation as an important means of achieving positive freedom through intervention. Classical liberals frequently view taxation as a form of 'state robbery' and attempt to restrict it.

👎 Modern liberals endorse a Keynesian-style approach to capitalism where the state attempts to manage market forces and level of demand in the economy. Classical liberalism embraces laissez-faire capitalism and advocates minimal state involvement in economic affairs.

👎 Modern liberals support liberal and representative forms of democracy. Classical liberals are more ambivalent about democracy, fearing the 'tyranny of the majority' and a culture of grey conformism.

👎 Modern liberals reject classical liberalism's emphasis on a minimal state restricted to areas such as national defence and the protection of private property. They call instead for an enabling state with a larger social and economic role.

Now try this

Assess the view that classical liberalism has little in common with modern liberalism.

Key thinkers: 1

John Locke is commonly regarded as one of the founders of liberal thought and a key figure in **classical liberalism**.

Key thinkers and ideas

Key ideas

Locke's most important work was *Two Treatises of Government* (1690), in which he developed two key liberal ideas:

 Social contract theory: society, state and government are based on a voluntary agreement or contract. Citizens obey the state's laws on the understanding that the state will guarantee them certain rights. If these rights are not upheld by the state, the governed are no longer obliged to obey the state's laws.

 Limited government: government should be limited by a constitution's rules and procedures, and be based on consent from below. The concept of limited government rejected the arbitrary rule of medieval monarchs and the idea of 'divine right' to rule.

Uses

The state

- Locke did not accept the traditional view that the state was God-given or that monarchs had a 'divine right' to govern.
- He also rejected the idea that ordinary people were 'subjects' of the state who were expected to submit to the monarch's wishes.
- He argued that the 'true' state would be established by humans to serve their interests, and this state would rest on the voluntary consent of those governed by it.
- Locke maintained that people would accept the authority of this 'true' state as long as the latter fulfilled its side of the 'contract' by upholding natural rights such as the right to property and liberty.
- He concluded that if the state broke its contract with the people (by disregarding their natural rights), they would be entitled to oppose or even remove it.
- Locke's 'social contract' was based on reason: rational people would not willingly submit to arbitrary rule (power without legal restraints) because it was not in their interests to do so. The state should serve the individual, not the other way round.

The state and limited government

- Locke argued that the contractual nature of the state embodied the concept of limited government, whereby the governed are guaranteed certain rights.
- Under this social contract, the government is limited to representing the interests of the people and gaining their ongoing consent.
- The limited nature of the state would be achieved by dispersing its powers between the Executive, legislature and judiciary. In this way, the state would not become overbearing.

Although Locke argued forcefully in favour of a social contract and limited government, his political ideas only went so far.

- He was not a democrat in the full modern sense since he accepted that the right to property led to inequality in terms of possessions and power. However, he did believe in the people's right to remove an unjust government, and this is often cited as an influence on the US Declaration of Rights.
- Although he argued that government should exercise tolerance in religious matters and the area of private conscience, Locke was against extending toleration to atheists.

Now try this

What are the key features of Locke's social contract?

Key thinkers: 2

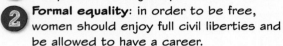

Mary Wollstonecraft (1759–1797)

Mary Wollstonecraft is rightly regarded as an important feminist writer but her work was firmly grounded in liberal philosophy.

Key ideas

1. **Reason**: women are rational and independent beings capable of reason.

2. **Formal equality**: in order to be free, women should enjoy full civil liberties and be allowed to have a career.

Uses

In her best-known book, *A Vindication of the Rights of Woman* (1792), Wollstonecraft drew on Enlightenment philosophy to argue that women were guided by reason.

Human nature

Human nature should be viewed in optimistic terms and, since both men and women are able to act in a rational way, women should be entitled to the same rights as men.

The state

- 18th-century state measures and social attitudes assumed women were not rational and so they could not enjoy individual freedom.
- Few women owned property or had rewarding jobs, and, within marriage, they were not legally independent.
- Women were not permitted to vote, which contradicted the concept of 'government by consent'.

Society

- To be equal and free, women should enjoy full civil liberties and be able to pursue a career, rather than be economically dependent on men.
- Formal education was vital in this process since it would give women (and men) self-respect and help them to realise their potential.
- Marriage had to be a truly equal partnership so that women could choose freely between having a family or a career.

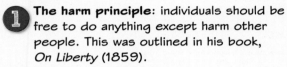

John Stuart Mill (1806–1873)

John Stuart Mill was arguably the greatest 19th century British liberal thinker, whose work signalled the transition from classical to modern liberalism.

Key ideas

1. **The harm principle**: individuals should be free to do anything except harm other people. This was outlined in his book, *On Liberty* (1859).

2. **Tolerance**: being prepared to accept values, customs and beliefs with which one usually disagrees with.

Uses

Mill's **harm principle** was closely linked to the classical concepts of negative freedom, limited government and tolerance.

Human nature

- Human actions are either 'self-regarding' (affecting only the person undertaking the action) or 'other-regarding' (affecting other people).

  Examples of self-regarding actions include religious observance or the airing of personal views. Other-regarding actions include violence or disruptive behaviour.

Society

Mill endorsed tolerance and the right to hold a minority view – a widely-held opinion did not always make it correct.

The state

- The state or other individuals should not interfere with self-regarding actions (even if they cause harm to the individual) because they do not harm other people
- However, the state and other individuals should curb other-regarding actions if they harm the freedom of others.
- Self-regarding actions and 'unharmful' other-regarding actions should be tolerated by the state.
- Tolerance of diverse views would promote new ideas and expose flawed ones.

Now try this

Explain how Wollstonecraft's feminist ideas are linked to liberalism.

Key thinkers: 3

John Rawls (1921–2002)

John Rawls, author of *A Theory of Justice* (1971), was a **modern** liberal who attempted to construct a society where individual freedom coexisted with limited inequality.

Key ideas

1 **Theory of justice**: society must be just and guarantee each citizen a life worth living.

2 **The veil of ignorance**: individuals agree on the type of society they want from a position where they lack knowledge of their own position in society.

Uses

Use Rawls when discussing society and the state.

Society

To create a just society, individuals need formal equality and greater economic and social equality.

The state

- This requires an **enabling state** to redistribute wealth, increase public spending and adopt progressive taxation.
- The state should improve the condition of the poor but inequalities of outcome would remain to reflect individual differences. This is tolerable as long as deprivation does not worsen.

Society/state

- Humans, being rational and empathetic, would devise a new society where the poor received better treatment
- People would **choose** a fairer, more equal society (partly because the 'veil' would prevent them knowing their position in society). The enabling state required would be based on government by consent.

Human nature/society

Most people would still *expect* scope for individual freedom. So, although the state would improve the condition of the poor, the gap between the top and bottom of society would not automatically be reduced.

Betty Friedan (1921–2006)

Friedan's major work is *The Feminine Mystique* (1963).

Key ideas

1 **Legal equality**: women and men are of equal worth and are equally capable, and oppressive laws and social views must be rejected.

2 **Equal opportunity**: women are restricted in their choices and opportunities by social conditioning through the family and agencies such as the education system and the mass media.

Uses

Use Friedan when discussing society and the state.

The state

- Legislation and official regulations should criminalise discrimination. This will prevent women from having their freedoms 'harmed' by others.
- Legal change is the only realistic way to make progress; confrontation is counter-productive.
- Legal equality represents a modern form of the longstanding liberal belief in tolerance, as advocated by social liberalism.

Society

Conditioning emphasises unfulfilling domestic roles rather than careers. More extensive opportunities and a shift in social attitudes is needed.

The state

Legal measures will secure greater equality of opportunity for females and enable women to compete with men on equal terms.

Now try this

In what ways is Friedan's feminism liberal?

Exam skills: the main body

This question will help you to revise for **Section B** of your A Level **Paper 1** exam. This section consists of two 24-mark essay questions – you will need to choose **one** of them. See also page 45. This page provides an example of two paragraphs from the main body of an answer to a question about liberalism.

Worked example

To what extent do classical and modern liberals agree on human nature?

You must use appropriate thinkers you have studied to support your answer and consider both sides in a balanced way. **(24 marks)**

... Classical and modern liberals share an optimistic view of human nature, arguing that people have the capacity to bring about progress and continually enhance human happiness. They base this assessment on the assumption that individuals are principally driven by rationalism or reason. John Locke, for example, believed that humans were innately blessed with the faculty of reason, and although they were self-interested, this rational element of human nature prevented people from disregarding the interests of others. Betty Friedan argued that women were just as rational and capable as men, and that cultural conditioning based on irrational assumptions had disadvantaged females. Such conclusions lead both classical and modern liberals to maintain that humans can solve all sorts of problems through discussion, debate and critical scrutiny.

Furthermore, for all liberals, human rationalism ensures that people can plan to shape their own destinies in a preconceived way rather than passively accept what happens to them as 'God's will' or 'fate'. Finally, since all liberals regard rationalism as an essential feature of human nature, they tend to believe that reasoned discussion leads to general agreement or consensus. As such, liberals believe that human rationalism promotes peace, harmony and mutual understanding. As shown, classical and modern liberals agree that rationalism is central to human nature...

 Excellent use of political vocabulary and related concepts.

 The only thinkers that can be formally recognised are those listed on the relevant section of the specification. The ideas of two key liberal thinkers are used here in their correct context.

Good identification of key areas of agreement between classical and modern liberalism on 'rational' human nature.

Clear evaluation at the end of this paragraph about the level of agreement between the two liberal strands on the 'rational' element of human nature.

You now need to discuss where classical and modern liberals **differ** on human nature. For example, classical liberals believe humans are innately blessed with rational characteristics whereas modern liberals (such as Rawls) view rationalism as a potential feature of human nature to be developed or enabled by enlightened intervention.

Coming to a judgement (AO3) – what does it mean?

- It is not enough to show both sides of an argument and to conclude in a neutral way that both sides have various merits and demerits. Instead, you have to pick a side and argue, throughout the essay, why, in your opinion, that side is more convincing. **But**... you have to do it in a balanced way.

- This means that you cannot ignore the views expressed on the opposing side of the argument. You need to address them, but explain why 'your side' is better.

Your answer should make judgements based on evidence about the significance of the differences and similarities, leading to a clear and justifiable conclusion.

Collectivism and common humanity

Socialism is generally opposed to capitalism. Socialism seeks to create a society founded on key ideas, including collectivism and common humanity, which inform other socialist values and principles such as equality, welfare and common ownership.

Collectivism

Collectivism maintains that humans can achieve their political, social and economic objectives more effectively through **collective action**. It also suggests that society can only be transformed by collective endeavour.

Arguments in favour of collectivism

Human nature: humans are social creatures with a natural tendency to work together to achieve their goals, tied together by the bonds of **fraternity**.

Society

- The interests of the group (for example, society or community) should take priority over individual self-interest.
- People are defined by the social groups they belong to, so membership of a community/society offers fulfilment.

The economy

Collective endeavour utilises the economic potential of society more efficiently than wasteful competitive individual effort.

The state

Collective action via the state ensures a fairer distribution of goods and services (via **state intervention** and **state planning**) than free-market forces.

Collectivism in practice

Different strands of socialism vary in their commitment to collectivism.

Marxists

Marxists advocated collective action based on the principle of 'from each according to ability, to each according to need' (for example, the communist regimes of the USSR and North Korea).

Revisionist socialists

Revisionist socialists accept some degree of free-market capitalism and pursue collectivism in a more limited way (for example, the 1945–1951 UK Labour government nationalised key industries but left much of the economy in private hands).

 Collectivism suppresses human individuality and diversity.

 It leads to the growth of arbitrary state power and erodes individual freedoms.

Common humanity

Socialists see humans as social creatures with a tendency for cooperation, sociability and rationality. The individual cannot be understood without reference to society, because human behaviour is determined by people's place in society.

Arguments in favour of common humanity

Cooperative effort

Humans are naturally inclined to work together for the common good because cooperative effort:

- produces the best results for **society**
- enables people to form connections based on respect, understanding and mutual support
- is superior to **capitalist** competition which sets one person against another and undermines our common humanity.

Moral motivation

Humans can be driven by a desire to contribute to the betterment of society.
For example, cooperative effort to boost economic growth increases living standards for the working population **and** provides the funds (through taxation) to finance welfare measures.

Example of collectivism

The cooperative movement began in Britain with the Rochdale Society of Equitable Pioneers (1844). Cooperatives are voluntary associations designed to provide economic assistance for their members. They are owned and run by workers or consumers (rather than investors), who benefit in the form of shared earnings or cheap goods secured through the cooperative.

Cooperatives include farming and wholesale cooperatives (as above), mutual insurance companies, credit and banking cooperatives and housing associations.

Now try this

On what grounds do socialists support collectivism?

Equality

The pursuit of **social equality** or **equality of outcome** is, arguably, the fundamental value of socialism. Equality underpins most areas of socialist thought.

Equality

The key socialist idea of equality is based on two key principles:

 1 **Social equality/equality of outcome:** the equal distribution of economic rewards such as income and wealth.

 2 **Egalitarianism:** a theory or practice (best viewed in a relative sense) designed to remove or reduce inequalities and ensure everyone has a fair chance in life.

Debates about equality

Revolutionary socialists

The state: revolutionary socialists demand **absolute equality** (in terms of material rewards and life opportunities), the abolition of private property and replacement with **common ownership** of all means of production.

Social democrats

Economy: social democrats call for the **relative equalising** of society within a reformed capitalist economy via welfare measures, government spending and progressive taxation to remove absolute poverty.

Human nature: material incentives continue to play an important role in human motivation, and greater emphasis is placed on **equality of opportunity**.

Arguments in favour of equality

- **Ensures fairness:** economic inequality is due to the structural inequalities in capitalist society, rather than innate differences of ability among people.

- **Reinforces collectivism, cooperation and solidarity:** human beings are more likely to co-exist harmoniously and work together for the common economic good if they share the same social and economic conditions.

- **Satisfies basic human needs:** the more equal distribution of wealth and resources, via the redistributive state, will promote human fulfilment and realise human potential.

Common ownership

Socialists argue that common ownership of the means of production ensures that all can participate and benefit. They argue that wealth is created by communal effort so it should be owned collectively. Conversely, private property encourages materialism and the false belief that personal wealth will bring fulfilment. It also generates social conflict between 'have' and 'have not' groups.

The nature of equality

Socialists disagree about the nature of equality.

	Equality of outcome	Absolute equality	Equality of opportunity	Universal welfare
Nature	People's experiences of society should be more or less the same. Associated with social equality and economic equality.	Everyone who contributes to society will receive the same rewards. Over time, each person's contribution will be roughly equal.	Everyone has an equal chance to make the best of their abilities, with no artificial barriers to progress for those who work hard and have ability and talent.	Inevitably, human society is unequal. However, all individuals have an equal minimum standard of living guaranteed by state welfare provision.
Supported by...	fundamentalist socialists, who reject capitalism.	Marxists, who support **communism**.	The Third Way (see page 62) on meritocratic grounds.	social democrats as it protects the most vulnerable.
Rejected by...	social democrats and the Third Way as artificial social and economic levelling.	social democrats and the Third Way as impractical and potentially destabilising.	Marxists because it does not remove capitalism. Social democrats who support greater social equality/justice.	Marxists because it does not remove capitalism. The Third Way as they support targeted welfare.

Now try this

Why do different socialists disagree about the nature of equality?

Social class and workers' control

For socialists, **social class** explains the most important divisions in society, and the idea of **workers' control** has influenced various strands of socialist thought, including **Marxism** and **syndicalism**.

Social class

Socialists believe that members of a social class share similar outlooks and aims. Social classes are therefore the **principal agents** of change.

Socialism is ideologically committed to represent the interests of, and improve conditions for, the working class.

Workers' control

Socialists use the term 'workers' control' in two ways:

- The complete or partial ownership of an enterprise (such as a factory, company or workshop) by employees, including real decision-making powers.
- Control of the state by the workers – a wider and more political concept.

Differing socialist views on class

Marxists

A person's class position is **economically determined** by their relationship to the means of production. Conflict is inevitable between the owners of productive wealth (the capitalists/bourgeoisie) and those who sell their labour to survive (the working class/proletariat). The ruling bourgeoisie use the **state apparatus** (the political and legal system) to maintain their dominance. Eventually, class conflict leads to a proletarian revolution, which overthrows capitalism, resulting in a **classless, equal society** and the **state withers away**.

Social democrats

They define social class more flexibly, emphasising **income and status differences** between non-manual and manual occupational groups. Socialist objectives can be achieved through targeted government intervention to narrow (but not remove) class distinctions. The **state** provides welfare and redistribution schemes to reduce class inequalities. Unlike Marxists, social democrats advocate **class consensus in society and peaceful social improvement**.

Socialist justifications for workers' control

Human nature: workers' control is based on socialist views about **human nature** as it promotes collective effort and the pursuit of group interests. It also tackles workplace alienation (for more on working-class struggles, go to page 63) and challenges the capitalist view that the workforce is simply a commodity in the production process.

Economy: workers are the most important element in economic production, so they should have the right to control the means of production and thus either dilute or replace capitalist control of the **economy**. By the early 1900s, for example, French syndicalists were calling for full workers' control over the economy based on the trade unions and proletarian political institutions.

Society: it is an important step towards a **socialist society**. 'Moderate' workers' control (such as increased trade-union influence over managers' decisions) enables the introduction of limited social and economic reforms. Industrial self-management by workers living under state socialism reinforces the idea that a socialist society should raise the condition and status of the working class.

Decline of the socialism–working-class link

In recent decades, the connection between socialist ideology and working-class politics has weakened considerably because of:

- **deindustrialisation**, which has reduced the size of the working class and weakened the trade-union movement
- the rise of the **post-industrial service and information economy**, together with an expanding middle class.

Consequently, moderate socialist political parties have adapted their programmes to appeal to non-manual workers.

Criticism of workers' control

- 👎 Businesses don't just rely on workers; they also depend on people who are prepared to take commercial risks and invest money.
- 👎 Workers may not have the entrepreneurial qualities required to make their workplace a thriving concern.
- 👎 By assuming responsibility for functions, such as appointments, promotions and dismissals, manual employees may lack the appropriate managerial expertise, thereby undermining the economic prospects of their workplace.

Now try this

Explain the difference between Marxist and social democratic views on the importance of social class.

Revolutionary socialism

You need to know about the differing views and tensions within socialism. **Revolutionary socialism**, such as Marxism (see pages 58–59 for more on the tenets of revolutionary socialism) or Blanquism, rejects the use of democratic methods to achieve a socialist society in favour of overthrowing existing political structures.

Background to revolution

The revolutionary road to socialism was popular in the 19th century for two reasons.

1 Early industrialisation and capitalism brought poverty, exploitation and unemployment. This was expected to radicalise the working classes.

2 Workers were largely excluded from political participation and so had little ability to influence policies in governments that were usually dominated by the aristocracy or bourgeoisie.

After 1945, national liberation movements in Africa, Asia and South America tried to adopt revolutionary socialism to:

- remove colonial powers and dismantle outdated social and economic systems
- bring about rapid modernisation to enable these societies to catch up with more prosperous and technologically advanced industrial countries.

For example, Mao's Chinese communists, the Viet Cong and Castro's Cuban insurgents (pictured).

Justifications for revolution

1 The bourgeois state is an instrument of class oppression, which upholds capitalist interests and is reinforced by the state apparatus (see page 59 for more on how the state exploits workers).

2 Gradual change will not lead to a socialist society because the ruling class and bourgeois values are too entrenched in the capitalist state and society.

3 A total transformation of society is required as the ruling class won't give up its power without a fight. Revolutionary socialists often resort to violence to establish their regimes.

For example, the civil wars in Russia (1918–1921), China (1946–1949) and Mexico (1910–1920).

4 Attempts to reform a capitalist society would undermine the principles and objectives of socialism, since capitalism is based on inequality and exploitation.

The results

Revolutionary socialism has usually resulted in **fundamentalist** regimes that have claimed to be based on socialist principles. However, the key issue is that these states replaced private property with state ownership not **common ownership**. Without genuine common ownership, no further stages of Marxism were able to occur and these regimes used the term 'communist' to justify brutal suppression of opposition in their country.

The end?

Marxist theory has undergone a rebirth since the economic crash of 2007–2008, with a huge increase in sales of their books. The collapse of the USSR in the late 1980s allowed Marxist theory to be severed from the totalitarian Soviet Union once and for all.

Case study: Blanquism

Inspired by Louis-Auguste Blanqui (1805–1881), a French radical socialist, **Blanquism** called for:

- a rapid seizure of power by a small, secret, elite group of armed socialist conspirators rather than a mass organisation
- a temporary dictatorship, formed by this group, to dispossess the bourgeoisie and place industry and business under state control
- a socialist programme imposed on the population, by force if necessary
- state-assured equal conditions for workers who would be organised in industrial and agricultural producer associations.

Lenin's revolutionary socialism was influenced by Blanquism.

Now try this

Why has revolutionary socialism tended to produce fundamentalist socialist regimes?

Social democracy

After 1945, social democracy emerged as Western socialist parties moved towards electoral politics and adopted the more limited aim of reforming and humanising, rather than abolishing, capitalism.

What is social democracy?

Social democracy is a revisionist form of democracy and attempts to reconcile free-market capitalism with state intervention, based on four assumptions:

1 Capitalism is a dependable creator of wealth, but distributes that wealth unfairly.

2 State intervention in economic and social affairs protects the public and remedies capitalism's weaknesses.

3 Peaceful constitutional methods should be used to bring about social change.

4 Socialism is morally superior to capitalism and should focus on **social justice**.

The evolution of socialism

In the late 19th century, some socialists concluded that Marxism was flawed. Eduard Bernstein's **revisionist** study, *Evolutionary Socialism* (1899), argued that capitalism was not developing along Marxist lines. The capitalist system was resilient and not succumbing to economic crises or promoting ever-deepening class conflict.

→

Bernstein concluded that capitalism was not brutally exploitative. It could be reformed peacefully through electoral politics. He called for state ownership of key industries, legal safeguards and welfare measures to protect workers.

→

In the 20th century, Western socialist parties recognised the dynamism and productivity of the market economy and pursued a revisionist policy of reforming capitalism.
For example, the West German Social Democratic Party (1950s).

Social democracy in practice

Championed by modern socialist thinkers such as **Anthony Crosland** (see page 65 for more on Crosland's ideas), social democracy adopted a programme with three key elements:

1 A **mixed economy**, with only key strategic industries nationalised.
For example, as under the Attlee Labour government of 1945–1951.

2 Keynesian economics (more on liberal economic theory can be found on page 51) as a means of regulating the capitalist economy and maintaining full employment.

3 **Reform** (not removal) of capitalism, using the welfare state, to redistribute wealth and tackle social inequality and poverty.

The decline of social democracy

After 1945, social democracy was a balancing act, trying to deliver both economic efficiency and egalitarianism. This tension was concealed during the early post-war boom-decades when economic growth, high employment and low inflation delivered both rising living standards and the tax revenues to expand welfare programmes.

→

Economic downturn in the 1970s–1980s exposed this central tension. Unemployment rose and demand for welfare increased as tax-based funding for social support declined (due to fewer people in work and falling company profits). Social democrats faced a critical dilemma: reduce inflation and taxes to stimulate the economy or prioritise the funding of welfare.

→

The shift to a service-based economy in the 1980s–1990s, and the contraction of the working class due to deindustrialisation, reduced social democracy's electoral base. The collapse of the Soviet communist bloc (1989–1991) and rejection of its system discredited forms of socialism that looked to the state to deliver economic and social reform.

Now try this

Why did social democracy find it difficult to sustain both dynamic economic growth and fairness in society?

The Third Way

Following the crisis of social democracy, from the 1980s reformist socialist parties in Europe and elsewhere moved away from traditional social democratic principles and policies to embrace **the Third Way**.

What is the Third Way?

The Third Way or 'neo-revisionism':

- represents an ideological 'middle ground' alternative to traditional social democracy and free-market neo-liberalism in the context of a modern globalised economy
- advocates the primacy of the market, community, consensus and the competition state
- was first introduced in the UK by the Labour Party or 'New Labour' under Tony Blair in the 1990s. Peter Mandelson (New Labour politician) said: *'We are intensely relaxed about people getting filthy rich... as long as they pay their taxes.'*

Its chief intellectual proponent is the academic Anthony Giddens (see page 65 for more detail on Giddens's work).

Five key features of the Third Way

Stresses the primacy of the market over the state and rejects 'top down' state intervention	1 Endorses a dynamic market economy and an enterprise culture to maximise wealth creation, thus showing some ideological overlap with neo-liberalism.
	2 Downplays the socialist policy of redistributing wealth through progressive taxation.
Values community and moral responsibility	1 Distances itself from the moral and social 'downside' of neo-liberal economics – a market-driven free-for-all.
	2 Emphasises communitarian liberalism whereby personal autonomy operates within a communal context based on mutual dependence and benefit so that rights have to be balanced by responsibilities.
Supports a social model based on consensus and harmony	1 This clearly differs from the traditional socialist focus on class differences and inequality.
	2 Endorses what might otherwise be seen as opposed values or concepts. For example, champions self-reliance and mutual dependence, and the market economy and fairness.
Promotes social inclusion rather than the socialist commitment to equality	1 Emphasises equality of opportunity and a meritocratic social system.
	2 Does not oppose great individual wealth if it helps to improve society's overall prosperity.
	3 Welfare should target socially marginalised groups and provide the assistance people need to enable them to improve their own situation.
Advocates a competition (or market) state	1 Aims to develop the national workforce's skills and knowledge base.
	2 Focusing on social investment, the competition state emphasises the importance of education because it improves a person's job prospects and boosts economic growth.

Evaluation of the Third Way

Although New Labour was electorally successful in 1997, 2001 and 2005, many socialists criticise Third Way thinking because, in their view:

👎 it lacks real socialist content (for example, its watered-down commitments to equality and redistribution of wealth)

👎 neo-revisionism was essentially a Labour rebranding exercise to attract middle-class voters and business interests following four consecutive UK general election defeats

👍 Third Way ideas have influenced various left of centre parties, including the German SDP and the South African ANC

👍 under New Labour, neo-revisionism introduced important measures that promoted social justice and improved the position of the most disadvantaged in society (for example, the minimum wage and family tax credits).

Now try this

How socialist is the Third Way?

Key thinkers: 1

Karl Marx and Friedrich Engels are the most famous revolutionary socialists. Their influential works include *The Communist Manifesto* (1848) and *Capital* (1867, 1885, 1894).

Key thinkers and ideas

Karl Marx (1818–1883) and Friedrich Engels (1820–1895)

Key ideas

In their writings, Marx and Engels developed several influential ideas, including:

 Social class is central to socialism.

 Human nature is socially determined and can only be expressed under communism.

Uses

Social class

Social class underpins three key elements of Marxism:

- **Historical materialism**: historical and social development can be explained in terms of economic and class factors. The economic system (such as capitalism) influences or 'conditions' all other aspects of society.

- **Dialectic change**: each stage of human history has its own economic system and class structure. Within each stage, dialectical change is propelled by the struggle between the exploiters and the exploited. This only ends with the establishment of a communist society.

- **Revolutionary class consciousness**: the exploited class must acquire a revolutionary class consciousness in order to overthrow their oppressors. The proletariat must become a 'class for itself', aware of its own interests and determined to pursue them.

According to Marx and Engels:

'Let the ruling classes tremble at a communist revolution. The proletarians have nothing to lose but their chains. They have a world to win. Working Men of All Countries, Unite!'

'The history of all hitherto existing society is the history of class struggles.'

Human nature

- Humans are essentially social beings, whose behaviour and potential are influenced more by nurture than by nature. Humans are sociable, rational and cooperative, with the capacity for significant personal and social development.

- Humans are productive and capable of leading satisfying lives based on fulfilling work, where the conditions for free creative production exist. These do not exist under capitalism, which leads to human alienation by separating people from their true selves.

- Under capitalism, workers are alienated from:
  - the product of their labour because they do not own what is produced
  - their work colleagues due to capitalism's competitive ethos and division of labour
  - the production process because it doesn't represent the human power of creative transformation
  - their human capabilities and potential since they cannot freely create and enjoy beautiful things.

- Under communism, workers are freed to realise their true human potential by engaging in many activities, benefiting from increased leisure time, pursuing creative work in cooperation with others and providing socially necessary and meaningful work that meets others' needs. Alienation disappears and the 'cooperative man' is established.

Now try this

Why is social class central to Marxism?

Key thinkers: 2

Beatrice Webb (1858–1943)

Beatrice Webb, a Fabian socialist, rejected the Marxist theory of class struggle in favour of the 'inevitability of gradualness'.

Key ideas

1 The 'inevitability of gradualness': establishing socialism peacefully by passing democratic reforms gradually through existing parliamentary institutions.

2 The 'economic side of democracy': the expansion of the state, rather than its overthrow, will deliver socialism.

Uses

Human nature

- Webb believed that workers were limited, selfish and uninformed, so democracy should be representative.

- Representative democracy was preferable (to direct democracy and 'self-interested' workers' control) because it would lead to a skilled 'socialist' governing class subject to democratic constraints.

The state

The gradual growth of state power was evidence that collectivism would bring in a new socialist age. The expanding state had *'silently changed its character... from police power to housekeeping on a national scale'*.

Society

The state's ability to deliver socialism would depend heavily on highly trained specialists and administrators to organise society and the economy.

Rosa Luxemburg (1871–1919)

Rosa Luxemburg, a Marxist revolutionary, opposed *evolutionary socialism* and disagreed with Lenin over key features of Marxism.

Key ideas

1 Social reform: evolutionary socialism and revisionism are not possible as capitalism is based on economic exploitation.

2 Class consciousness: struggle by the proletariat creates the class consciousness needed to overthrow the capitalist society and state.

Uses

The economy

Luxemburg believed that any evolutionary or revisionist socialist strategy would leave the capitalist system of economic exploitation intact. Revolution was therefore necessary to effect true change.

According to Luxemburg: *'The masses are the decisive element. They are the rock on which the final victory of the revolution will be built.'*

Human nature

- In *The Mass Strike, the Political Party and the Trade Unions* (1906), Luxemburg argued that class consciousness would develop naturally from within the workers themselves. Proletarian discontent against state control would erupt in numerous unsuccessful and successful strikes, culminating in a spontaneous mass strike that would radicalise the workers and bring about a socialist revolution.

- Unlike Lenin, she did not believe that a small, disciplined party was needed to lead workers in revolution.

Now try this

How did Beatrice Webb and Rosa Luxemburg differ over the 'correct' path to socialism?

Key thinkers: 3

Key thinkers and ideas

Anthony Crosland (1918–1977)

Anthony Crosland was the leading post-war revisionist theorist of British socialism with works such as *The Future of Socialism* (1956).

Key ideas

1 **Modern capitalism lacks inherent contradictions**: these are required to drive social change or bring about revolution; managed capitalism can deliver greater social equality.

2 **State-managed capitalism**: the state must manage capitalism to deliver greater social equality, provide a more egalitarian distribution of rewards, status and privileges and remove class barriers.

Uses

The economy

Governments pursuing Keynesian economics could maintain high employment, ensure low inflation and promote continuous growth. Rather than collapsing, as Marx predicted, capitalism had produced rising living standards.

The state

High levels of government spending is required on welfare services and the redistribution of income and wealth.

The economy

Economic expansion is required to fund welfare and social spending to improve living standards for those at the bottom of society, while preserving those of the more affluent.

Key thinkers and ideas

Anthony Giddens (1938–)

Anthony Giddens, through books such as *The Third Way: The Renewal of Social Democracy* (1998), was an important intellectual figure in the development of the Third Way.

Key ideas

1 **The rejection of state intervention**: social democracy must be modernised due to the impact of globalisation, the new knowledge economy and more individualistic aspirations.

2 **The 'social investment' state**: Giddens rejected the economic and social engineering that underpinned the state welfare and redistribution programmes of previous social-democratic governments.

Uses

The economy

The free market is the most efficient system of production (and economic growth would benefit everyone) and it encourages desirable personal qualities, such as responsibility.

The state

Equality of opportunity over equality. For this market-driven system to be fair, everyone needs an equal opportunity to better themselves through their ability and effort. Government action would be required to control the inevitable widening inequalities of outcome.

The state

State welfare and redistribution foster a culture of dependency. Instead, a 'social investment' state is needed – a 'contract' between the state and the citizen. The state benefits from growth so must invest in infrastructure and education. The people must take advantage of this and help themselves.

Human nature

Community and responsibility, rather than class conflict, are important to offset the negative effects of the free market and promote social cohesion, shared values and individual and social responsibility.

Now try this

What, according to Giddens, is the role of the modern state?

Exam skills: the conclusion

This question will help you to revise for **Section B** of your A Level Paper 1 exam. This section consists of two 24-mark essay questions – you will need to choose **one** of them to answer. Look back at pages 45 and 56 before continuing here.

Conclusion

The conclusion must continue to give a clear answer to the question and show how you reached it – it must be more than simply 'yes' or 'no'. This exam skills page provides an example of a concluding paragraph from an answer to a question on socialism.

The essay so far

In the main body of the essay, the student has argued that other socialists have disagreed with Marxists on the economy.

Moderate socialists (in the post-war years):

- temper interventionism with qualified acceptance of the productive potential of capitalist economics
- accept a degree of free-market capitalism to stimulate the economic growth needed for welfare provision and favour a mixed economy of nationalised key industries and privately owned enterprises
- support Keynesian interventionist techniques to enable governments to regulate capitalism and maintain employment, and also welfare policies to redistribute wealth.

The Third Way: with the crisis of social democracy in the 1970s and the end of the Cold War, the Third Way has endorsed the free-market economy as the most efficient system of production, rejecting state intervention because it discourages investment and stifles entrepreneurial initiative.

Worked example

To what extent are different socialists in agreement on the economy?

You must use appropriate thinkers you have studied to support your answer and consider both sides in a balanced way.   **(24 marks)**

... In evaluating whether different socialists are in agreement on the economy, it should be noted that most socialists endorse some type of intervention in the capitalist economy on the grounds that the profit-driven free market cannot allocate wealth and resources fairly. Marxists however call for capitalism to be abolished and replaced with an economy based on common ownership of the means of production. Hence it can be seen that there are fundamental differences between Marxists and the other socialists, as Marxists reject that socialism can be reconciled with capitalism in order to make society fairer and more equal.

The opening line of the conclusion shows the student understands the broad context of the question – they are not simply repeating what they have already written.

Both sides of the argument are referenced but a clear case is made for supporting one of those sides. This shows the student is making a justified argument.

The final sentence directly addresses the question and places the whole question in its current context.

Remember: conclusions should not be unexpected, because a third of your marks come from AO3; you should be evaluating and making judgements throughout your essay.

Conclusion checklist

Have I...

- ✓ answered the question directly?
- ✓ explained how and why I reached this conclusion?
- ✓ written a conclusion that matches the tone of my essay?

Have I avoided...

- ✗ simply repeating paragraphs or examples?
- ✗ writing only one sentence?
- ✗ introducing new information?

Exam-style practice

Practise for **Section B** of **Paper 1** of your A Level exam with these exam-style questions. There are answers on page 307. Section B consists of a choice of two questions and you will have to answer **one** question. Aim to spend around 30 minutes answering the question.

1 To what extent do conservatives agree on human nature?
You must use appropriate thinkers you have studied to support your answer and consider both sides in a balanced way.

 Allow time to do a quick bullet-point plan of your answer, to ensure you are looking at both sides of the debate.

 Your essay needs to be fully structured, including an introduction and a conclusion.

 Aim to show clear links between your points and use examples (evidence) to support them.

(24 marks)

2 To what extent do classical and modern liberals agree on the economy?
You must use appropriate thinkers you have studied to support your answer and consider both sides in a balanced way.

 Make sure you use at least **two** relevant key thinkers as outlined in the relevant section of the specification.

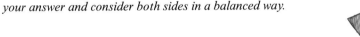 You need to show that you know and can set out the nature of the debate. You also need to analyse and evaluate the similarities and differences between the different strands or tensions within the idea.

(24 marks)

3 To what extent do socialists agree on the nature of society?
You must use appropriate thinkers you have studied to support your answer and consider both sides in a balanced way.

 Pick a side and argue, throughout the essay, why that side is more convincing. Make sure you do this in a balanced way.

 You need to make judgements based on evidence about the significance of the differences and similarities, and use these to come to a clear and justifiable conclusion.

(24 marks)

Types of constitutions

Simply put, a **constitution** is the rules by which the 'game' of governing is played. Governments and all other parts of the state must play by the rules of the constitution.

The nature of uncodified and codified constitutions

Uncodified constitutions	Codified constitutions
An **uncodified** constitution refers to a constitution where parts are written down, but there is no one single document outlining the constitution of the state. The UK Constitution is uncodified – it draws on a variety of sources. 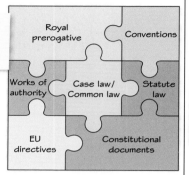	A **codified** constitution is a constitution in which the key constitutional structure and arrangement in a state are collected together within a single legal document (see page 164 to read about the US Constitution).  The US Constitution is codified and was written in 1787.
Flexible: the UK Constitution is **flexible** as any of its sources can be changed without any lengthy or difficult process. However, this is in the context of **the rule of law**, one of the 'pillars' of the UK constitution, which is the idea that the government is limited by law (see page 92 to find out more on judicial independence).	**Rigid**: a **rigid** constitution is one that requires a lengthy and difficult process to alter it. For example, in the USA an amendment requires a two-thirds majority vote in Congress plus three-quarters of state legislatures.
Unentrenched: the UK Constitution is **unentrenched**, meaning that constitutional laws are no different from **statute laws**. **Parliament** is sovereign so can change the constitution by passing statute law (see page 69). Constitutional provisions do not have a higher legal status than ordinary laws, so laws which modify the constitution are passed by a simple majority in Parliament.	**Entrenched**: the provisions of a codified constitution are **entrenched**, in that it is difficult to amend or remove them. Codified constitutions are considered 'higher' law, usually the highest law of the land. This leads to a two-tier legal system in which the constitution stands above law made by the legislature.
Non-judiciable: the UK Constitution is **non-judiciable** – judges cannot challenge Parliament's ability to make or amend statute laws.	**Judiciable**: codified constitutions are **judiciable**, in that a constitutional court decides if government action or laws passed by the legislature are 'constitutional'.
Unitary: a **unitary** system is based on the principle of **parliamentary sovereignty** – one of the 'twin pillars' of the UK constitution. This means that supreme power remains in the hands of a single source. Lower government bodies are subordinate to the sovereign body and powers can be taken back from them. In the UK, the power of the Scottish and Welsh parliaments could be taken away from them by Parliament in Westminster. For more on sovereignty, see page 97.	**Federal**: in a **federal** state, authority is constitutionally divided between various regions. Central government may have the more important responsibilities but the regional governments are sovereign within their constitutionally defined areas of responsibility. Clashes between central and regional governments are resolved by the constitutional court.
Evolutionary: an **evolutionary** system is one which has evolved over centuries, constantly changing and adapting to the circumstances. Evolutionary systems do not normally have clear rules and principles governing the country, but as they evolve they tend to fulfil the democratic requirements of the time.	**Revolutionary**: a 'revolutionary' constitution is one which has been created following a dramatic overthrow of power. Revolutionary systems are usually carefully and clearly designed to ensure all aspects of a democracy are included within it from the beginning.

Now try this

Why would a codified constitution undermine parliamentary sovereignty?

Sources of the UK Constitution

This page looks at the five main sources that make up the UK Constitution and the relationship between them.

Key historical documents

Constitutional documents are very old (sometimes ancient) laws which signify an important stage in the UK's democratic history and still bear some relevance today. They include:

- Magna Carta (1215)
- Bill of Rights (1689)
- Act of Settlement (1701)
- Acts of Union (1707)
- Parliament Acts (1911 and 1949)
- The European Communities Act (1972).

Magna Carta introduced the concept of *habeas corpus* – the right to be brought before a court to hear the charges against you, and especially to secure release unless lawful grounds are shown for the detention.

 Statute law

Arguably, the most significant source of the UK's constitution are **statute laws**. These are laws passed by Parliament; as Parliament is sovereign, this means statute laws are sovereign.

For example, the Freedom of Information Act is an example of statute law.

2 **Works of authority**

Authoritative works refer to books written to help explain the workings of the UK's uncodified and somewhat complicated constitutional arrangements. These books have become so vital to our understanding that they are now considered part of the UK constitution.

For example, authoritative works include Erskine May's *Parliamentary Practice* (1844).

 Common law and case law

Common law exists where judges make decisions based on long-established practices or form an opinion of a fair and just outcome. The UK judicial system works on the principle of precedence, which means that once the senior judiciary have decided on a case, similar cases will be considered in the same light.

 Conventions

Conventions are traditions and customs that have developed over centuries throughout the UK's evolutionary system. They are not laws. For example, while all rules relating to elections are laws, the idea that a prime minister should resign after they have lost an election is in fact a convention, not a law. Does that mean it would be OK if the PM didn't resign? Clearly not! Just because something isn't a law in the UK's constitutional structure does not make them any less significant than laws.

 EU treaties/law

European Union (EU) **treaties** are an additional source of the UK Constitution.

The Treaty of Rome 1957, the Maastricht Treaty 1992 and the Lisbon Treaty 2009 are all examples.

Relationship between the sources

- EU laws currently take precedence over all other sources, although they will be replaced by statute laws after Brexit.
- Statute law supersedes all other sources (except EU law until Brexit).
- Common law cannot contradict statute law, but has equal authority to it.
- Authoritative works and conventions are not binding but are considered extremely strong guidance, which are usually adhered to.

Now try this

Why are some sources seen as being more rigid than others?

Constitutional reforms since 1997

Constitutional reforms refer to any reforms of the system of government, but specifically to changes made since 1997 by the Blair and subsequent governments. You need to know the significance of these reforms.

How the constitution has changed since 1997

Reforms that enhance democracy	Reforms that decentralise power
• **House of Lords (HoL) reform 1999**: took away power from the most undemocratic element of the HoL, the hereditary peers. • **Electoral reform**: introduced proportional representation (PR) in all devolved assemblies, leading to much fairer representation of the people's views. • **Recall**: the 2015 Act introduced a process by which an MP can be recalled by their constituency to face a by-election. • **Reforms in the House of Commons**: the **Wright Reforms** redistributed power to **backbenchers** (see page 83 for more on the role of backbenchers) and from the government. • **English votes for English laws (EVEL)**: that laws concerning England only have a greater input from MPs representing English constituencies.	• **Devolution**: devolved powers to Scotland, Wales and Northern Ireland put local representatives in charge of local issues. • **Exiting the EU**: returned all decision-making powers back to Parliament, which is directly accountable to the British people. • **Elected mayors**: gave powers over large areas to locally elected mayors. For example, London, West Midlands, Liverpool, Manchester. • **Police and crime commissioners (PCC)**: elected representatives who are responsible for the efficient and effective policing of an area.
Reforms that enhance rights	**Reforms that modernise the system**
• **Human Rights Act 1998**: made the European Convention on Human Rights (ECHR) law accessible in UK courts, making it easier for UK citizens to access the rights. • **Freedom of Information Act 2000**: provided public access to documents held by public authorities.	• **Fixed-term Parliaments Act 2011**: fixed the dates of UK general elections to once every five years to reduce the PM's prerogative power (see page 88 for more on the PM's power). • **Constitutional Reform Act 2005**: established the **Supreme Court** in place of the Law Lords and separated the role of Lord Chancellor into three separate roles and people.

🔍 Case study Focus on Wright Reforms

The **Wright Committee** was established in 2009 to improve the procedures and relevance of Parliament. It made a number of recommendations, which included:

• Chairs of departmental and other **select committees** (read about how Parliament scrutinises the government on page 82) should be directly elected by secret ballot of the **House of Commons**.

• Members of select committees should be elected from within party groups.

• Backbench business should be scheduled by the House rather than by **ministers**.

• The House should decide its sitting pattern for itself.

• An effective e-petitions system should be introduced, including the possibility that members of the public might be able to compel an issue to be debated in the House.

• One backbench motion per month should be routinely scheduled for debate.

The aim was that the House of Commons should have more scope to choose and schedule its activities. The Wright Committee was introduced in full in 2010 by the coalition government.

Now try this

What effect did electing chairs and members of select committees have?

UK devolved bodies

Since 1998 there have been devolved assemblies in three of the four component nations of the UK. However, their role and powers differ radically.

Scottish Parliament and government

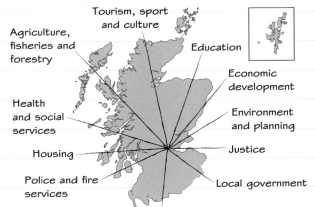

Tourism, sport and culture
Agriculture, fisheries and forestry
Education
Economic development
Health and social services
Environment and planning
Housing
Justice
Police and fire services
Local government
Some aspects of transport policy

- The Scotland Act 1998 gave primary powers and income tax-varying power, ± 3p per pound.
- The Scotland Act 2012 gave a small extension of powers, increase of tax-varying power to ± 10p and **devolution** of some additional taxes.
- The Scotland Act 2016 extended powers in relation to transport, energy and social security benefits, and to set income tax rates and thresholds, as well as to receive the proceeds of national VAT.

Welsh Assembly and government

Culture, including the Welsh language, and sport
Planning (except major energy infrastructure)
Education and training
Agriculture, fisheries and forestry
Economic development
Local government
The environment
Health
Housing
Fire and rescue services
Transport

- The Wales Act 1998 gave secondary legislative powers to the Assembly.
- The Wales Act 2006 provided for an additional referendum on primary legislative powers.
- The Welsh devolution referendum in 2011 voted 'yes' to give the Welsh Assembly direct law-making power in 20 devolved areas, such as health and education.
- The Wales Act 2014 gave minor tax powers and a referendum on income tax-varying power.
- The Wales Act 2017 provided for a reserved powers model and a transfer of further powers in transport and energy, and gave income tax-varying power to ± 10p without a referendum.

Northern Ireland Assembly and Executive

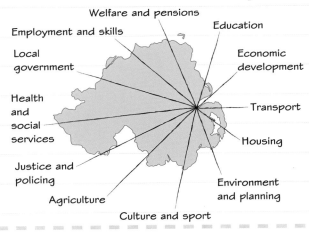

Welfare and pensions
Employment and skills
Education
Local government
Economic development
Health and social services
Transport
Housing
Justice and policing
Agriculture
Environment and planning
Culture and sport

- The Northern Ireland Act 1998, based on the Belfast Agreement, created the Assembly and related institutions and gave the Assembly power to legislate in transferred matters.
- The St Andrews Agreement (2006) renewed devolution in 2007.
- Devolution of policing and criminal justice in 2010.
- The Corporation Tax (Northern Ireland) Act 2015 devolved power to set corporation tax.

Primary and secondary legislation

Power to make **secondary legislation** is set out in primary legislation. Primary legislation provides the framework while secondary legislation adds the detailed rules and procedures. The devolved Parliament and Assemblies have different areas over which they can make primary legislation.

Now try this

Why does the Scottish Parliament have more powers than the Welsh Assembly?

71

Devolution and its impact

Since the Blair government introduced devolved assemblies at the end of the 1990s, there has been sufficient time to assess whether devolution has been a success or not.

Devolution in England: elected mayors

In 2000, the Blair government established an elected mayor in London, supported by the Greater London Assembly. The government tried to extend this by creating elected regional assemblies, but the idea failed to win support. Only one referendum took place, in the north-east, where the idea was heavily defeated by a 78 per cent 'no' vote in 2004.

The coalition government (2010–2015) tried to reintroduce the idea with directly elected 'metro mayors' to develop what the then chancellor George Osborne called the 'northern powerhouse'. Twelve cities held referenda: Leicester and Liverpool established mayors, Bristol elected its first mayor in 2012 and the remaining nine cities rejected mayors.

In 2017, metro mayors were elected in Greater Manchester (Lab), Liverpool City Region (Lab), the West Midlands (Tory), Tees Valley (Tory), West of England (Tory), and Cambridgeshire and Peterborough (Tory); Sheffield City Region elected Labour MP Dan Jarvis as its mayor in 2018.

The powers of the new metro mayors vary but they include developing an economic growth strategy and making policy on housing, skills and transport.

Andy Burnham, mayor of Greater Manchester, speaking at a concert for victims of the Manchester Arena bombing in 2017.

Mayors have responsibilities and powers across the city regions, unlike existing city mayors or local council leaders, who only make decisions for their local authority. This does not include the mayor of London and the Greater London Authority, who have quite different powers.

Has devolution been a success?

Has not led to the break-up of the UK.

Different policies were necessary to support the different devolved regions in distinct ways.

Devolved assemblies are very popular in the regions and there are no main parties suggesting it should be overturned.

England has been short-changed in the devolution settlement.

Has devolution been a success?

Welsh interest in devolution has increased, as has their demand for greater powers for their Assembly.

It has left the West Lothian question unresolved (see page 73).

Has secured a peaceful environment in NI for 20 years – a huge achievement.

Interest in devolved assemblies is low, as shown by turnout.

Scottish desire for independence has increased dramatically since the arrival of the Scottish Parliament.

Elected mayors have led to greater regional identity in England.

Now try this

Why may metro mayors help economic regeneration in an area?

Are further reforms desirable?

You need to consider whether reforms introduced since 1997 have been extensive enough or whether there is scope for more reform.

Arguments for and against introducing a codified constitution in the UK

👍 The major principles of the constitution would be **entrenched**, safeguarding them from interference by the government of the day.

👍 With an entrenched constitution, **individual liberty would be more securely protected**. Despite the Human Rights Act (for more on this important legislation see page 10), rights are still not adequately protected since they lack entrenchment.

👍 The power of the **executive would be constrained** by a rigid, codified document. Codification would provide a counter-balance to the power of the executive.

👍 In a codified system, independent **judges** are able to protect the constitution to ensure that its provisions are upheld.

👎 A codified constitution would be **less responsive** and adaptable than an uncodified one. Since 1997, many constitutional reforms have been enacted to update the UK Constitution.

👎 The US Constitution has had an entrenched Bill of Rights for centuries but it didn't stop African-Americans being lynched without any kind of trial – entrenched constitutions do not guarantee people's rights in practice.

👎 Government power may **be more effectively constrained by regular elections** than by a constitutional document.

👎 **Judges** are not the best people to regulate the constitution because they are unelected and socially unrepresentative. An uncodified constitution protects against the tyranny of the unelected judiciary.

Arguments for and against greater devolution to or in England

👍 It would provide a solution to the West Lothian question. This asks whether Scottish, Welsh or Northern Irish MPs have the same right to vote at Westminster as English MPs on matters concerning England, while English MPs cannot vote on matters affecting only the devolved assemblies.

👍 It would facilitate a more federal model of government. (This can also be seen as a disadvantage.)

👍 It would provide stronger regional identity in parts of the UK.

👍 England is the largest and most prosperous part of the UK, but it is the only nation without a devolved body.

👍 Under the current system, England receives less money per person than the other parts of the UK.

👍 EVEL (see page 70) does not resolve the West Lothian question and makes Scottish MPs second-class representatives at Westminster, weakening the unity of the UK.

👍 Some parts of the UK have a very strong identity and would want the ability to make more decisions for their regions locally.
For example, Devon and Cornwall.

👎 It could complicate the relationship between the regions and Parliament.

👎 It would result in even more asymmetric devolution. This refers to devolution arrangements that are unbalanced. In the UK, devolved powers differ sharply between territories – Scotland has the most devolved powers and England has the least.

👎 There is little public support for an English Parliament and the idea is not supported by any major political party.

👎 England would dominate a federal assembly and its relationship with Westminster would be complicated.

👎 EVEL has resolved the West Lothian question and been used in Westminster to pass English-only legislation.

👎 As the largest component in the UK, most English people don't make a clear distinction between England and the UK.

👎 Many areas of England don't have a strong local identity, seeing themselves as English or even British.

Now try this

Why would an English Parliament resolve the West Lothian question and improve the symmetry of devolution in the UK?

Other possible reforms

An additional area in which to consider further reforms of the UK Constitution is within the two chambers in Parliament.

Reform of the House of Commons

Weakness	Proposed reform	Possible consequences
The prime minister is not sufficiently accountable	Reform PM's Questions and increase regularity of the Liaison Committee	Create more meaningful, rational debate of issues
Departmental select committees are still often ignored and not valued	Give them enforcement powers	More accountable government
MPs have little control over legislation	More power to legislative committees and remove membership from whips	Legislative committees become more independent, better scrutiny of legislation
Government majorities render the House of Commons useless	A change in the electoral system might improve the House of Commons's operation	Coalitions and minority government might empower MPs
MPs lack research facilities	Increase research support	Commons would be more effective in making ministers accountable

Should the House of Lords be reformed?

👍 Full or partial election would raise the **legitimacy** of the second chamber.

👍 The current process for the selection of Lords is controlled by the prime minister and benefits the governing party.

👍 An elected chamber would be a **more effective check on the executive**, since the Salisbury Convention (see page 80 for more on the relative power of the Houses) would not exist.

👍 An elected second chamber might **create a balance** against the power of the Commons, which is largely controlled by the executive.

👍 Elections might inject a **more 'professional'** element into the second chamber.

👍 Reducing the size of the Lords would make it a more effective chamber.

👎 If elected it might **Challenge the authority of the Commons**.

👎 Election would **eliminate the many experts who sit in it**, including the experience of the ex-ministers and PM in the Lords.

👎 The **current Lords more closely mirrors the popular vote** at the last general election than the Commons.

👎 The **current chamber works well**. It is the most active chamber in the world. It sits for longer and meets more frequently than any other.

👎 Since 1999, the Lords has proved to be a **useful check on the executive-dominated Commons**. If elected, it would be dominated by parties and less likely to hold the Commons to account.

An alternative 'reform' of the Lords?

The cost of running the House of Lords has been criticised – members can claim £300 a day with little scrutiny of the work they actually do. The size of the Lords soared after Cameron created many new peers (295 between 2010 and 2017).

Devised by a committee led by Lord Burns in 2017, the reform suggests:

- reducing the size of the Lords to 600 within ten years and maintaining this until at least 2047
- new peerages will be restricted to a 15-year term
- political peers should be appointed in relation to a party's election performance, taking into account the number of seats it wins as well as the vote share it achieved.

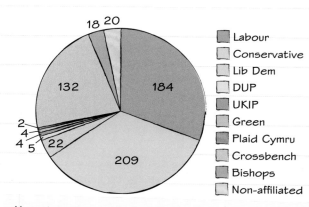

How the House of Lords would look were it reduced and based on parties' 2017 election performance.

Legend: Labour, Conservative, Lib Dem, DUP, UKIP, Green, Plaid Cymru, Crossbench, Bishops, Non-affiliated

Values shown: 18, 20, 132, 184, 2, 4, 4, 5, 22, 209

Now try this

Why would reform of the Lords enhance the legitimacy of Parliament?

Parliament

All representative democracies have three aspects to their state: a legislature, an executive and a judiciary.

Legislature, executive and judiciary

The UK is unusual as the legislature and executive are fused (joined together), as shown below. This means that its executive (government) sits in the legislature (Parliament). This is known as a 'parliamentary system' and has many consequences, as you will find out.

Legislature — The body that has the power to make, revoke and change laws. It also has the role of scrutinising the executive and holding them to account. In the UK, this is Parliament.

Executive — The body that runs the country and proposes laws to the legislature. In the UK, this is called the government and consists of the PM, Cabinet, junior ministers, their advisers and civil servants.

Judiciary — The body that interprets and applies the law. It does this to uphold the rule of law in society.

Parliamentary government

The UK Parliament is made up of three parts: the House of Commons (for more on this chamber see page 76), the House of Lords (see page 76) and the monarchy. The terms 'parliament' and 'government' are often misunderstood and sometimes used interchangeably. It is essential to clearly understand the difference between these two terms.

- Parliament is sovereign (for a discussion of sovereignty in the UK, go to page 97). This means that there is no higher authority in the UK. All laws must be passed by Parliament; no other authority can make, amend or unmake their laws.

- Parliamentary systems are based on a fusion of powers between the legislature and the executive. This means that government governs in and through Parliament.

- The prime minister is not directly elected, but is selected by being the leader of the largest party in the Commons.

- The prime minister is head of government, but not head of state.

- The prime minister heads a Cabinet, the vast majority of whom are elected and are individually accountable for their actions. The prime minister controls their appointment and dismissal (see page 88 for more on the power of the PM).

- All members of the Cabinet and the government are from the Commons or Lords and are accountable to that House.

- The government can be removed by Parliament – despite fixed terms, if a government loses a vote of no confidence an election is called.

Confidence and supply – in the event of a minority government, the government can rely on a limited agreement with another party (or parties) to keep itself in office. The supporting party will provide backing on a vote of no confidence, and will vote through the government's budget ('supply').

Now try this

Outline a difference in the role of the executive and the legislature.

The structure of the Houses

The two Houses of Parliament are very different in their composition despite both playing a key role in passing legislation and holding the government to account.

The House of Commons

Office holders and other roles in Parliament

1 Speaker: chair of the Commons or Lords, who runs its proceedings. An MP or Lord who is elected Speaker by fellow MPs/Lords, but is expected to act with impartiality.

2 Prime minister: the leader of the largest party in the Commons, usually commanding a majority.

3 Cabinet: the 20 or so most senior ministers in the government, most of whom will run their own department of state.

4 Government ministers: junior ministers who work under a Cabinet minister in a specific department. In the Lords they are known as government spokespeople.

5 Whips: both main parties have whips who are responsible for ensuring that **backbenchers** vote with their party.

6 Backbenchers: they are not part of the government, but are MPs or Lords in the governing party. Their role is to hold the government to account, but are usually torn between this and a desire to support their party.

7 Opposition benches: this consists of all the other MPs or Lords who are not members of the governing party. In the UK, it normally includes Her Majesty's Official Opposition and four or five smaller parties. Included within these benches is:

8 Leader of the Opposition and Shadow Cabinet: they are included in the **opposition** benches and consist of 20 or so senior members of the official opposition who 'shadow' government ministers.

9 Crossbenchers: these are unique to the Lords and are peers who are not part of any party.

The House of Lords

Now try this

What is the role of the whips?

Functions: legislating and debating

You need to understand the **functions** of Parliament and how they are carried out. You also need to **evaluate** how effectively each function is carried out, using up-to-date examples. This page looks at legislating and debating.

Functions of Parliament

Legislating

- Both Houses of Parliament review the laws government wishes to pass and, after debating and scrutinising them, Parliament is generally expected to pass them.
- The Commons can amend legislation and ultimately veto it.
- The Lords can suggest amendments, but does not have the power to veto laws, only to delay them for a year.

Debating

- Debates are a way for Parliament to hold the executive to account. Each bill is debated in its second reading.
- As well as legislation, backbenchers and the opposition also debate the significant issues of the day.
- Adjournment debates are held at the end of every day, when an MP can raise a matter that affects their constituency with a minister.
- Emergency debates can be held, such as after the phone-hacking scandal.

Evaluation

Legislating

👍 The May government was defeated in the Lords over 14 times between April and June 2018 on the EU Withdrawal Bill. This resulted in it returning to the Commons where rebels managed to get concessions from the government over a final parliamentary vote on the Brexit deal.

👍 The May government's 'working majority' is just 13, so the PM needs to work hard to ensure her MPs back her. If opposition parties work together, they need only seven unhappy Conservatives and/or DUPs to join their side and the government risks defeat.

👍 The government doesn't always get its way. For example, in 2015, Cameron's government suffered its first defeat in the Commons on the rules surrounding the EU referendum.

Under the coalition, the 2010–2015 Parliament was the most rebellious in the post-war era – coalition MPs rebelled in 35 per cent of votes.

In 2005, backbench MPs defeated Blair's plans to extend the detention of terrorist suspects to 90 days – it was his first ever Commons defeat.

👎 Usually, governments enjoy majority control of the Commons and are rarely defeated. This undermines the effectiveness of Parliament.

For example, Blair did not lose a vote in the Commons from 1997 to 2005.

👎 The coalition was only defeated twice on legislation in the Commons.

👎 Backbenchers vote with their party because their career prospects are in the hands of the PM.

Debating

👍 Due to implementation of the Wright Committee recommendations (see page 70 for more on this constitutional reform), MPs now have more control over the parliamentary agenda via the Backbench Business Committee. Parliament now engages more in debates on the great issues of the day. For example, wars in Syria and Iraq, and the London riots of 2011.

👍 PMs have become reluctant to initiate military action without Parliament. In recent years, Parliament has been given a chance to debate the matter.

For example, in 2013, Cameron wanted to order military action in Syria. Instead of giving the order, Parliament was given a chance to debate it – the motion was defeated 285 to 272.

In 2014, Cameron recalled Parliament from its summer recess to debate a motion on using air strikes against ISIS in Iraq. This motion was successful.

In 2015, Parliament was again given the opportunity to debate the issue of air strikes in Syria. MPs voted to approve air strikes after a ten-hour debate in the House of Commons.

👎 However, there is limited time for genuine debate and the whips control and curtail the independence of MPs.

Now try this

How much overlap is there between these two functions?

Representative function

Representation of the people is one of the core **functions** of Parliament and a fundamental **role** of MPs.

Is Parliament democratically representative?

👍 Each MP in the Commons represents an area in the UK.

👎 First-past-the-post (FPTP) distorts the representation of parties, so MPs are often elected by less than half their constituents.

👎 The Lords is unelected and is unrepresentative.

Does Parliament 'look like' the UK?

👎 White, middle-class men dominate Parliament, with 442 out of 650 MPs being men. Ethnic minorities fair even worse, with only 52 MPs being from an ethnic minority in 2017.

👍 However, things are improving with all parties encouraging a more diverse group of people to stand as candidates.

Who do MPs represent?

There are three ways an MP can be a representative:

1 **The Burkean idea of representation**: MPs deciding what they think is best for constituents and constituents trusting them to do so.

2 **The delegate model**: MPs are essentially the 'mouthpiece' of their constituents.

3 **The doctrine of the mandate**: MPs represent their party, which was elected with a mandate to carry out their manifesto.

How effective is MP representation?

👎 UK elections are focused on parties, not candidates. Voters rarely notice the name of the candidates, voting for the party they prefer.

👍 Social media increases pressure on MPs to respond to constituents, making the relationship more direct. They can contact MPs on Twitter, encouraging them to act as delegates.

For example, this occurred with gay marriage legislation in 2013 and air strikes on Syria in 2016.

👎 Under the coalition, Conservative and Liberal Democrat MPs supported policies that their constituents may have voted against. Many Liberal Democrat voters ended their membership of the party after it supported rises in tuition fees.

👍 Free votes on issues allow MPs to have more ability to listen to the views of constituents or their conscience.

For example, in 2013 the Marriage (Same Sex Couples) Act was passed, despite 136 Conservative MPs voting against and 40 abstaining, perhaps due to personal views or constituency pressure.

Legitimation

All legislation must be approved by Parliament. This is essentially giving the consent of the people to laws they are expected to obey. Without this consent, laws would lack authority. Parliament is legally sovereign, so all laws that have been passed by Parliament have full legal authority.

Scrutiny and accountability

This involves Parliament and its committees checking how government is operating. Scrutiny also means investigating that the government is acting in the public interest. The government must present all decisions and policies to Parliament (see page 83 for a detailed look at Parliamentary scrutiny).

Now try this

Outline two ways Parliament carries out its representative function.

Composition and powers of the Houses

There is a significant difference between the people who sit in the House of Commons and those in the House of Lords, and the subsequent powers they have.

Composition of the Commons and Lords (2018)

	House of Commons	House of Lords
Total	650 MPs	791 Lords
Representatives	MPs only	• Life peers – appointed for their lifetime only (676) • Hereditary peers – title passed down for generations (89) • Lords spiritual – bishops and archbishops of the Church of England (26)
Social representation	442 men 208 women 52 ethnic minorities	585 men 206 women 48 ethnic minorities
Party representation	318 Conservative 262 Labour 35 SNP 12 Liberal Democrats 10 DUP 13 others	250 Conservative 188 Labour 98 Liberal Democrats 182 Crossbenchers 46 others

Powers of the Commons and Lords

The 'exclusive' powers of the House of Commons are shown in **bold**.

House of Commons	House of Lords
The Commons can **veto legislation**.	The Lords can only delay legislation for a year (Parliament Act 1949).
The Commons can amend legislation.	The Lords can amend legislation, but needs Commons approval (this can lead to 'ping-pong', see page 81).
The Commons can reject any legislation, even manifesto pledges.	Salisbury Convention – The Lords won't vote against manifesto pledges. However, under the coalition, the Coalition Agreement (2010) was not a manifesto, so the Lords was more obstructive.
The Commons **approves government's budget**.	The Lords has no jurisdiction over financial matters.
The Commons can **dismiss a government under extreme circumstances** with a vote of no confidence.	The Lords has no power to dismiss a government.
The Commons is run on party lines, so its ability to legitimise government is limited.	The Lords is more independent with less loyalty to parties; 179 crossbenchers have no party loyalty. Also, whipping is less effective.
The Commons **represents constituency interests**. On the whole, MPs represent their parties' policies.	The Lords does not represent constituencies, but other interests.
The Commons has the key role of **legitimation of the government and its laws**. This means the Commons is the Senior House, being elected and thus accountable.	The Lords cannot legitimise as it lacks democratic authority. However, since the **1999 reforms** it has more democratic legitimacy. As it gains legitimacy, it uses its powers more.
The vast majority of ministers are selected from the Commons.	The Lords can, on rare occasions, provide the government with ministers (e.g. Lord Mandelson) – it is a good way of bringing talent into the government, However, it is seen as undemocratic.

Now try this

What are crossbenchers and why are they significant in the Lords?

Relative power of the Houses

While we may look at how effective Parliament is in general, in reality sometimes the Commons is more effective than the Lords, or vice versa.

The Lords is more effective than the Commons

The Lords was reformed in 1999 when most hereditary peers were removed. Since then, it has been more willing to challenge the government as it believes it is more legitimate. The House of Lords has also been noticeably more active since the 2015 election. The Cameron government had a majority of 12 in the Commons, and May leads a minority government.

Party discipline is weaker in the Lords so it is more independent. The Lords has a large number of crossbenchers, so more freedom for peers to debate and express their own views.

For example, the Lords defeated the government:
- 14 times in 2018 over the EU Withdrawal Bill
- twice in 2017 over the European Union Bill (Article 50)
- in 2016 over the Dubs Amendment on child refugees
- in 2012, by voting against a £26,000 benefit cap.

Between 2010 and 2012, the Lords defeated the coalition 48 times, while the Commons did not defeat the executive on any proposed legislation.

Scrutiny: Lords spend most of the time scrutinising legislation, unlike MPs in the Commons. Between 2010 and 2015, for example, the Lords voted against reforms to constituency boundaries, the NHS, the House of Lords, the Alternative Vote referendum and caps on welfare payments.

Legislation: the government has lost some legislation in the Lords. Several controversial pieces of legislation have been effectively dealt with in the Lords.
For example:
- tax credits
- NHS reform
- welfare reform.

The Lords also defeated the government:
- in 2012 over its Welfare Reform Act
- in 2013 over its plans to cut legal aid.

The Lords can also force the government to amend bills. The Lords has been most active in challenging the government over Brexit legislation, defeating the government 14 times – a modern-day record for one piece of legislation.

Expertise: the Lords is more effective in its scrutinising role for checking the government than the Commons. Many Lords are appointed (as Lords) due to their expertise.

For example, Lord Walton, the former president of the BMA; Lord Hogan-Howe, the ex-police chief.

The Commons is more effective than the Lords

Parliament Acts 1911 and 1949: these made the Lords less powerful than the Commons, preventing the Lords from rejecting legislation and only allowing them to delay for a year. For example, the Lords forced a delay in the (fox) Hunting Act 2004.

Any Lords amendments that are rejected three times by the Commons become ineffective. For example, in 2012 the Lords returned the Welfare Reform Act to the Commons with seven amendments; all the amendments were defeated.

Salisbury Convention: the Salisbury Convention emerged during the 1945–1951 government. The Convention means that the Lords does not try to vote down a government bill mentioned in an election manifesto.

Legitimacy and representation of constituents: the Lords is **unelected**, so they lack a mandate.

Liaison Committee: this is part of the Commons and checks the power of the prime minister, which the Lords cannot do.

Committees: the Commons select committees have grown in influence and authority. Since 2010, they have become much more effective in scrutinising government departments. For example, the Health Committee brought about changes to the coalition's Health and Social Care Bill; Margaret Hodge, while chairing the Public Accounts Committee, called Starbucks (as well as other big businesses) to account over the amount of tax they pay. There are no departmental select committees in the Lords.

Scrutiny: the Lords is less effective in scrutinising the government. PM's Questions and ministerial question time only happen in the Commons, while there are only government spokespeople in the Lords. This allows the Commons to directly scrutinise the government (see page 82 for more on parliamentary scrutiny).

Media: the media still concentrates more on the Commons and its role in making government accountable.

Now try this

Explain reasons for the growing significance of the Lords.

The legislative process

In order to become an Act of Parliament, a **legislative bill** must go through a number of stages.

Stages of a bill

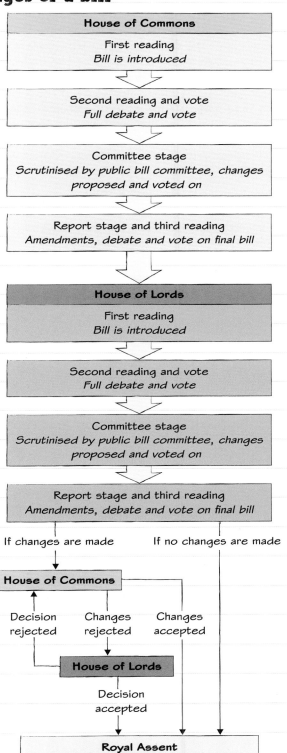

House of Commons

First reading
Bill is introduced

Second reading and vote
Full debate and vote

Committee stage
Scrutinised by public bill committee, changes proposed and voted on

Report stage and third reading
Amendments, debate and vote on final bill

House of Lords

First reading
Bill is introduced

Second reading and vote
Full debate and vote

Committee stage
Scrutinised by public bill committee, changes proposed and voted on

Report stage and third reading
Amendments, debate and vote on final bill

If changes are made   If no changes are made

House of Commons

Decision rejected   Changes rejected   Changes accepted

House of Lords

Decision accepted

Royal Assent
Bill signed by monarch and becomes law

Interaction between the Commons and the Lords

A bill can go back and forth between the two Houses for up to a year before it becomes law.

This is known as '**ping-pong**':

- the Lords can propose amendments to the Commons
- the Commons can accept them or send them back to the Lords
- the Lords can then accept the Commons' will, or send the bill back.

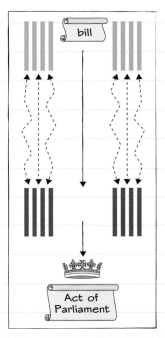

bill

Act of Parliament

Parliamentary 'ping-pong' between the Commons and the Lords.

Invoking the Parliament Act

The Parliament Acts of 1911 and 1949 removed the power to veto a bill from the Lords. Instead, the Lords could delay a bill by up to two years (1911), which was further reduced to one year in 1949. The Act also stated that the Lords cannot amend or delay 'money bills'. In line with the Act, the elected Commons can reintroduce the bill the following year and pass them without the consent of the Lords.

Now try this

What do you think is the most important stage of a bill and why?

Parliamentary scrutiny

One of the key functions of Parliament is to scrutinise the executive. There are a number of ways they do this.

Questioning

👍 Parliament requires that ministers, including the prime minister, answer questions by backbenchers in the Commons.

👍 PM's Questions (PMQs) forces the PM to be well informed about policy and the wider news agenda. It gives the leader of the opposition the chance to ask several questions.

👍 The opportunity to regularly question the PM is significant, and quite unique. While not always entirely civilised, PMQs is still an important opportunity for the Commons to challenge the PM. For example, in 2017 Jeremy Corbyn (opposition leader) used PMQs to effectively overturn the premium-rate number used to call Universal Credit.

👍 The Speaker can raise 'urgent questions', which allow the Commons to demand the attendance of the relevant minister so they can answer questions and face criticism.

👎 PMQs is political theatre rather than proper scrutiny. The Speaker often has to intervene to address the behaviour of MPs.

👎 Too many questions are from 'friendly' government backbenchers.

👎 PMQs has become an exercise in point-scoring. It is 'Punch and Judy' politics, with MPs jeering and shouting in a highly childish manner.

Legislative committees

After its second reading in the Commons, a bill reaches a committee stage. **Public bill committees** are formed to scrutinise a bill and consider any amendments.

👍 Public bill committees were strengthened in 2007, improving the scrutiny of legislation.

👎 They are far less independent than select committees as their membership is still dominated by party whips.

👎 Amendments that are contrary to a majority government's wishes are rarely accepted.

Other forms of scrutiny

• In extreme circumstances, the Commons can **pass a vote of no confidence** in the government and dismiss it.

• Individual MPs draw attention to **grievances of constituents**.

• Debating (see page 77).

Select committees

Select committees allow for the scrutiny of government departments. Committees reflect the composition of the Commons, so a government with a majority will also have a majority on the committee. They have the power to send for 'persons, papers and records'. Due to implementation of the Wright Report (see page 70 for more on this and other constitutional reforms), the executive no longer controls membership of select committees. They can act independently and scrutinise departments effectively.

👍 They have an interrogative style of questioning and witnesses have no notice of questions.

👍 Committee members tend to be independently minded, so feel freer to be critical.

👍 Chairs of committees get paid well and so the position attracts career- and independently-minded politicians.

👍 Select committee reports receive a lot of publicity, especially when they are critical.

👍 Successes include Margaret Hodge and the Public Accounts Committee (PAC) who, in 2013, held Amazon, Starbucks and Google to account for the limited tax they pay in the UK.

👎 They often review problems after they have occurred and criticise the government for this.

👎 The government is not obliged to act upon the recommendations of select committees.

👎 Ministers have a huge amount of support, whereas MPs have very little research support.

Activities of the opposition

The ability of the opposition to scrutinise the executive is often affected by factors beyond its control, such as the size and unity of the governing party and the length of time the government has been in office. However, oppositions can still influence the popularity and power of a government in certain circumstances.

• For example, the Blair opposition (1994–1997) was very effective in highlighting weakness in the Major government as well as presenting itself as a good alternative government.

• The Cameron opposition (2005–2010) managed to underline divisions in the final years of the Blair premiership, as well as throughout the Brown one.

Now try this

Outline two criticisms of parliamentary questioning as a form of scrutiny.

Backbenchers

Traditionally, backbench MPs (**backbenchers**) have been seen as 'lobby fodder' – there to vote and do as their party says. In recent years, however, backbenchers have evolved their role.

Parliamentary privilege

Parliamentary privilege refers to the fact that, within the walls of Parliament, MPs are free to speak without fear of prosecution for slander. Allegedly, it is the origins of the phrase: '*would you like to step outside and say that?*'

Backbench Business Committee, 2010

The role of backbenchers has increased as they are now able to choose topics for debate 35 days a year. Topics can be chosen by individual backbenchers or via e-petitions signed by the public, giving backbenchers more say and power over debates in Parliament.

Independence

 1 Since 2007, backbenchers seem to have become more independent when voting in Parliament than in previous decades. This is not always reflected in government defeats as backbenchers often negotiate with governments to get amendments to legislation before they agree to vote for them.

2 Select committees show backbenchers' independence. Since the Wright Reforms of 2010 removed the whips' power over the selection of members, select committees have used their limited powers to maximum effect, often causing embarrassment to the government or other bodies (see page 82 for more on the role of select committees).

3 Speaker John Bercow has been a champion of backbenchers' rights since assuming the chair in 2009.

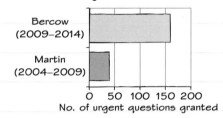

No. of urgent questions granted

One way he has done this is by reinstating **urgent questions** into the Commons (read more about urgent questions on page 82).

Limits to backbenchers' powers

Whips: their role is to encourage backbenchers to vote with their party. Whips have lots of 'carrots' to entice backbenchers, such as sending them on fact-finding trips to exotic locations and giving positive reports to PMs for the next reshuffle of their government. They are also well known for the 'sticks' they use, such as refusing to 'pair' MPs, revealing information they hold on MPs to newspapers and scuppering their chances of any promotions.

Resources: compared to the government, backbenchers have relatively few resources to rely on. They have limited research and admin staff, and a meagre budget to explore personal interests.

Majority: a government with a large Commons majority means a lot of MPs are needed to make governments pay attention to them. Usually, backbenchers accept the government's legislative programme and vote with them, even if they disagree at times. This is especially true if the government has just been elected and/or is popular with the electorate.

Factors that affect whether backbenchers will vote with their government

The difference between the power of May and Blair in the Commons can be shown by backbenchers' attitudes towards these.

	May	Blair
Ambition: if they think the PM is there for the long term, as the PM appoints the Cabinet and government, ambitious MPs will vote with the PM to please them.	✗	✓
Keeping their seat: an MP with a more marginal seat will be more likely to support a popular PM, who will enhance their chance of re-election.	✗	✓
Likes the PM's agenda: supporters of the PM on the backbenches will vote with them simply because they like them and agree with their policies.	✗	✓
Dislikes the PM's agenda: equally, backbench MPs who don't like the PM or where they are taking the party are less likely to vote with them.	✗	✓

Now try this

Why is the size of the government majority so significant to backbenchers' power?

Structure and role of the executive

You need to understand the difference between **the government** and **Parliament**. In the UK system, the government sits *in* Parliament (see page 75 for more on the workings of Parliament). This does **not** mean they are the same thing. We describe the UK system as having a **fusion of powers**.

Who are the executive?

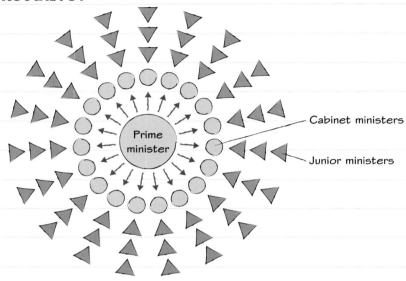

Prime minister

Cabinet ministers

Junior ministers

In the UK, the **executive** (also known as the government) consists of approximately 100 ministers (who must be MPs or Lords), as well as the civil servants who support them.

- **Prime minister**: appoints all **ministers**, chairs the **Cabinet**, organises the structure of government departments.

- **Cabinet ministers**: approximately 25 ministers. Each heads a **government department**. Support is provided by...

- **Junior ministers**: approximately 75–100 ministers who work under Cabinet ministers in specific government departments. Each department is responsible for an area of policy.

For information about the structure of the Commons and where ministers sit on the benches, see page 76.

Role of the executive as a whole

The role of the executive (government) is quite distinct from the role of the legislature (known as Parliament in the UK). There are three main functions:

1. **Proposing legislation**: bills are proposed to Parliament, which they usually, but not always, agree to pass.

2. **Proposing a budget**: this is presented to the House of Commons by the Chancellor of the Exchequer to pass (the Lords has no power to delay 'money bills').

3. **Running the country**: this refers to the day-to-day decisions made by members of the executive.

Role of a minister

A minister is a person appointed to perform a government function.

- Senior ministers usually have a role in the Cabinet. This may involve them in reaching or endorsing final decisions on major issues, helping to resolve disputes between government departments or participating in Cabinet committees.

- Their role is to formulate policy and coordinate the work of their department.

- Junior ministers support the senior minister in their department. They may stand in for the senior minister in Parliament (such as when the senior minister is unable to attend PM's Questions).

- Junior ministers are usually in charge of specific areas within the department whereas the Cabinet minister is responsible for the work of the whole department.

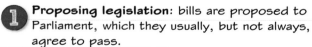

Now try this

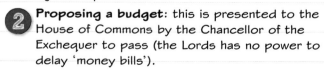

Why is it easy to confuse the terms 'Parliament' and 'government' in the UK?

The Cabinet

The **Cabinet** is the highest tier of the executive (government) and includes the prime minister, who chairs the Cabinet.

Role of the Cabinet

The Cabinet has several functions:

1 **Making formal decisions**: policy becomes 'official' once it is approved by the Cabinet.

2 **Coordinating government policy**: ensuring that there is an overview of developments.

3 **Providing a forum**: in particular, for disagreements between ministers.

4 **Managing parliamentary business**: which is facilitated by the Chief Whip and Leader of the Commons and Lords in Cabinet. This means planning when different bills will be put to Parliament to cover the various stages needed

5 **Managing emergencies**: for example, the 2017 Westminster attacks.

The Cabinet, 2016

Cabinet committees

Cabinet committees are groups of Cabinet ministers designed to allow discussions and decisions to take place with fewer ministers than in the full Cabinet. The prime minister has the power to set up Cabinet committees and is responsible for appointing their members. There are approximately 25 main Cabinet committees, which are chaired by the PM, Deputy PM, Chancellor or Home Secretary. Committees report back to the Cabinet with their decisions, which the Cabinet usually feels obliged to accept.

Examples of Cabinet committees include the:

- National Security Council
- Home Affairs Committee
- Economic Affairs Committees
- Scotland Committee
- Social Justice Committee.

Is the Cabinet still important?

👍 Cabinet discusses the government's general strategy and goals.

👍 In some circumstances, the Cabinet makes key decisions (perhaps rarely) (for example, whether to hold an election in 2017).

👍 Some Cabinet ministers in charge of large departments are powerful in their own right (such as the Chancellor of the Exchequer).

👍 No PM can survive without Cabinet support, and in some circumstances Cabinets are able to exert a lot of influence (for example, May's Cabinet deciding on the type of Brexit to have).

👍 The Cabinet can overrule the PM or even remove them (for example, Thatcher's Cabinet famously aided her departure).

👍 The Cabinet is the only effective place where disputes between ministers can be dealt with out of the public eye.

👍 Under coalition, the Cabinet reconciles the differences between coalition partners (see page 90 for more on coalition government in the UK).

👍 Under coalition, the Cabinet is much more significant.

👍 It is the Cabinet which deals with emergencies or crises (known as Cobra – **C**abinet **O**ffice **B**riefing **R**oom **A**), not the PM alone.

👎 The PM has significant powers of patronage over the Cabinet.

👎 PMs rely less on their Cabinet for policy advice, preferring to use special advisers.

👎 Collective responsibility gives PMs power to silence dissenters in the Cabinet.

👎 The Cabinet meets for less time now and tends to rubber stamp decisions made elsewhere.

👎 PMs control the workings of the Cabinet by shaping the Cabinet's agenda as well as chairing meetings.

👎 PMs decide the number and nature of Cabinet committees.

👎 The growth of Cabinet committees is seen as a way for the PM to bypass the Cabinet as a form of 'inner cabinet'.

👎 A Cabinet united behind its PM gives a PM enormous power.

Now try this

Why do Cabinet committees reduce the importance of the Cabinet?

Collective ministerial responsibility

Collective responsibility or collective ministerial responsibility (CMR) extends to all members of the government. The convention requires that they all stick to an agreed policy and do not question it in public.

Collective responsibility

Collective responsibility is necessary because:

- it ensures ministers present a united front against opposition
- it means that discussions inside the Cabinet remain private and disagreement remains confidential
- it binds the government together as ministers collectively shoulder responsibility for their actions and policies
- it can enhance prime ministerial power by silencing critics within the government.

Any member of the Cabinet who will not accept these restraints is expected to resign. For example, in March 2016 Iain Duncan Smith resigned as Secretary of State for Work and Pensions; in August 2014, Baroness Warsi resigned from Cameron's government over policy on the escalation of violence in Israel.

Collective responsibility under strain

CMR has come under strain with ministers disagreeing with government policy but not resigning. The past decades have seen several internal Cabinet battles and some of these have led to the ultimate downfall of a PM. The lesson from history is clear — a PM must maintain at least the semblance of Cabinet unity if they wish to maintain their position as leader of the country.

 Case study **The Blair years (1997–2007)**

The biggest split in Blair's Cabinet was between Blair and Gordon Brown, which reflected deep personality rivalries. Their arguments were often very public and their supporters were always keen to leak details of the disagreements, but there was never any suggestion of resignations or sackings. The Blair–Brown years reinforced the need for CMR. In the 1990s, the split in Cabinet between Euro-sceptics Michael Portillo, Peter Lilley, John Redwood and Jonathan Aitken and Euro-enthusiasts Kenneth Clarke, Douglas Hurd and Michael Heseltine was well publicised in the media. No one resigned.

 Case study **May's Cabinet**

Throughout 2017 and 2018, May's Cabinet appeared to be on the brink of open civil war as some of the government's most important ministers – Chancellor Philip Hammond, Brexit Secretary David Davis and Foreign Secretary Boris Johnson – publicly aired their differences over Brexit.

- Hammond and Davis suggested different timetables for how long a transitional phase ought to last: Hammond suggested four years once the UK ceased to be an EU member, while Davis argued for two years.
- There was also a rift over the issue of free movement of people after Brexit. Hammond claimed there was 'broad acceptance' in the Cabinet that free movement would end in name only three years after Brexit. However, International Trade Secretary Liam Fox dismissed the idea that a consensus had been reached on the issue. This led Vince Cable (Lib Dem) to say that the Cabinet was 'in a state of civil war'.

May's failure to retain a parliamentary majority diminished her authority, allowing moderates like Hammond to push for a soft Brexit and derailing the harder Brexit desired by Davis, Johnson and Fox. By June 2018, both Davis and Johnson had resigned.

There are other examples of CMR being under strain in May's Cabinet:

- **Saudi Arabia** (December 2016): Johnson claimed Saudi Arabia was waging a proxy war in the Middle East. He did not resign.
- **Brexit** (December 2016): while appearing on *The Andrew Marr Show*, Johnson repeatedly refused to support suggestions made by Davis that Britain may pay contributions to the EU after Brexit for access to the single market.
- **Heathrow** (October 2016): May announced that Cabinet ministers who disagree with the Heathrow decision will be given a 'derogation' (exemption) from collective responsibility.
- **Brexit** (June 2016): Cabinet ministers were given permission to disagree in the 2016 referendum on the UK's membership of the EU.
- **'Trojan Horse' plot** (June 2014): Gove and May had a public disagreement over allegations of a hard-line Muslim plot, with each one suggesting it was the other's responsibility.

Now try this

Why was collective responsibility weakened in June 2017?

Individual ministerial responsibility

In **individual responsibility**, or individual ministerial responsibility (IMR), ministers have a responsibility for their own conduct in office as well as to Parliament. There are two distinct strands to IMR: legal and political.

 Legal responsibility

- Ministers are responsible for all that goes on within their own department, whether or not they are directly concerned.

  For example, David Cameron resigned as PM after the UK had voted to leave the EU in June 2016 and he had campaigned to stay. However, Theresa May did not resign as Home Secretary in 2011 over lapses in border controls as she argued that a civil servant, Brodie Clark, acted beyond the guidelines she gave him.

- They must give accurate information to Parliament; if they knowingly mislead Parliament, they are expected to resign. For example, Amber Rudd resigned as home secretary in 2018 because she inadvertently misled Parliament over the question of whether she knew about targets to remove illegal immigrants. Liam Fox had to resign in October 2011 as information regarding the influence of his close friend Adam Werrity (and his backers) in Ministry of Defence business came into the public domain. However, Jeremy Hunt remained Culture Secretary in 2012 when it was suggested that his closeness to James Murdoch made him biased.

- Ultimately, the PM decides how long a minister remains in office.

  For example, in 2002 Estelle Morris resigned as Education Secretary after failing to meet government targets on literacy and numeracy tests. However, May remained Home Secretary in 2012 despite confusion over deadlines for appeals against Abu Qatada's deportation to Jordan.

 Political responsibility

Ministers are responsible for their own personal conduct. In this situation, ministers may be forced to resign because of some personal failing, which is not necessarily related to their performance as a minister. Their fate depends on:

- how serious an issue is perceived to be (for example, Maria Miller resigned as Culture Secretary in 2014 after a row over her expenses; in 2014, Immigration Minister Mark Harper resigned after it emerged his cleaner did not have permission to work in the UK; Chris Huhne resigned in 2012 as he was told he would face a criminal charge for avoiding a speeding offence)

- how critical Parliament is about the matter and any media response (for example, in 2014 for example, the Conservative MP Brooks Newmark stepped down as a minister over a newspaper report that he sent an explicit image of himself to an undercover reporter)

- how the PM responds to the issue (for example, Peter Mandelson was forced to resign over the allegation that he abused his position to give the Hinduja brothers passports. The PM told him he had to resign without waiting to see how accurate such allegations were).

IMR and CMR under the coalition

Under the coalition, IMR was 'reinterpreted' for Vince Cable. Instead of being sacked, the Business Secretary was stripped of all responsibilities for competition and policy issues related to media, broadcasting, digital and telecoms after he boasted to undercover reporters that he had 'declared war' on Rupert Murdoch. Cable managed to retain his Cabinet seat despite being called by the PM to Downing Street to be told that he would have no further role in the decision on BSkyB.

The coalition government also had important implications for CMR as it was suspended on some issues where the coalition parties disagreed fundamentally:

- the Alternative Vote referendum – each party was free to campaign as they wished

- nuclear power stations, tax allowances for married couples, tuition fees – Liberal Democrat MPs were permitted to abstain

- renewal of Trident – Liberal Democrat MPs could campaign against this policy.

Vince Cable also had an impact on CMR. He was able to speak out in a way that would not normally be tolerated in a Cabinet minister. In July 2017, he was elected leader of the Liberal Democrats.

Now try this

Is individual ministerial responsibility still a significant convention?

The power of the prime minister

The prime minister is head of the executive (government) in the UK. Most of the PM's powers come through Parliament, although they are able to exercise a few independently.

Role of the prime minister

- The PM is head of government – they appoint all ministers and are responsible for promotions, demotions and sackings.
- They direct government policy and provide national leadership, particularly in times of crisis.
- They are chair of the Cabinet (*primus inter pares*).
- They are responsible for setting up, reorganising and abolishing government departments.

- The PM is the main figure in the Commons. They make statements and answer questions from Parliament.
- They exercise **royal prerogative** powers.
- They have an international role in negotiating with foreign states.

Royal prerogative powers

Royal prerogative powers are exercised on behalf of the monarch by the PM and the executive.

- They do not require the permission of Parliament.
- Such prerogative powers have existed over a long period of time and are therefore traditional in nature.
- Most prerogative powers are now exercised by the PM.
- In 2011, the PM's royal prerogative power to call elections was removed by the Fixed-term Parliaments Act.

Patronage

Make treaties with other countries

Royal prerogative powers

Deploy the military

Head of the civil service

Call an election

Selecting ministers

- They may be **close allies** of the PM and will have supported the PM's rise to high office.
  For example, Gordon Brown possibly appointed Ed Balls (his former personal adviser) for this reason.
- They may be a key figure in the parliamentary party, with a substantial following – a '**big beast**'.
  For example, Boris Johnson was in David Cameron's 'political' Cabinet and Vince Cable was in the coalition Cabinet.
- The **ability** of the minister.
  For example, as suggested by the appointment of Lord Mandelson by Gordon Brown in 2008. He made him a lord just so he could have him in his Cabinet.
- A PM might want an ideologically balanced Cabinet, in which case they would appoint members from different sections of the party, **with different political views**.
  For example, Theresa May has had to manage the Brexit/ remainer balance in her Cabinet very carefully so as not to upset either side.

- Occasionally PMs promote **political adversaries** in order to 'silence' them by making them subject to CMR.
  For example, Theresa May appointed Boris Johnson to silence him. Gordon Brown's appointment of David Miliband to Foreign Secretary showed why it was a good idea to bring a rival into the Cabinet – CMR prevents them from being obstructive.
- A PM might wish to have a **socially balanced** Cabinet.
  For example, David Cameron promoted two women to his Cabinet in October 2011 as he was trying to increase his popularity among women voters. Theresa May made sure to have women in top jobs, appointing Amber Rudd as Home Secretary in 2016.
- Ministers have to be **good parliamentarians**, able to face close scrutiny within Parliament. So, they need to show good experience in the House, their past experience being useful.
  For example, William Hague was well known as an outstanding debater in Parliament.

Now try this

What are the key factors a prime minister considers when choosing a Cabinet?

The Cabinet and the prime minister

Almost all the PM's powers are balanced by limits. However, these limits don't apply consistently across different PMs. The ability of a PM to stretch their powers (and thus ignore the limits) tends to be dependent on a number of factors.

Patronage and other prerogative powers

The PM appoints, shuffles and dismisses Cabinet ministers as well as all ministers in government.

Limits

- 'Big beasts' have to be included.
- Both 'wings' of the party should be represented.
- Rivals may have to be included.
- Botched reshuffles can cause problems.

Powers over the Party

Party, Cabinet and Parliament are loyal to the PM as leader of the party, which usually commands a majority in the Commons.

Limits

- Loyalty is dependent on the possibility of electoral success.
- Backbench rebellions in the Commons are possible.
- There is a risk of a leadership challenge.

Factors affecting the prime minister's powers

Personality: is the PM charismatic or not? This affects their ability to persuade colleagues and the electorate.

Events: even the most powerful PM can be derailed by an unexpected event, which can turn everything on its head.

Media: a PM that is able to be an effective media performer can be seen as more powerful than one who is not.

Variable factors

Cabinet and Party: if they are prepared to give the PM a lot of leeway, this will enhance a PM's power.

Majority: a large majority in the Commons gives PMs huge power, while the opposite is also certainly true; coalitions can work both ways.

Opposition: a weak opposition allows the PM to be more dominant.

Popular: popular PMs are given more freedom by their party than unpopular ones.

Institutional support for the PM

There has been a large increase in personnel to support the PM. This is known as the growth of a 'PM's Office' and now includes the No. 10 Policy Unit, Press Office and Cabinet Office. The use of special advisers to provide the PM with additional support has also increased.

Limits

- There is still no formally structured PM Department.
- Power of other large, rival departments by far overshadows the size of the PM's office (for example, the Foreign Office and the Treasury).
- The PM's Office is miniscule compared to the huge personnel available to support the US president.

Powers over the Cabinet (and government)

PMs call, chair and set the agenda for Cabinet meetings. They also establish Cabinet committees, hold bi-laterals (meetings between the PM and another minister) and sofa governments (Blair's unique informal bi-laterals) and use these to bypass Cabinet. Collective responsibility is also used by PMs to silence difficult cabinet members. Some feel that the executive is dominated by the PM, giving rise to a **presidential government**.

Limits

- Requires Cabinet support on major or controversial issues.
- 'Big beasts' have their own authority.
- Any threat of resignation can damage a PM.
- Ultimately, a PM's position is dependent on Cabinet support.

Elective dictatorship

Lord Hailsham used the term **elective dictatorship** in a Dimbleby Lecture in 1976 to describe the way that Parliament is dominated by the government of the day if it has a substantial overall majority. It refers to the fact that government bills virtually always pass the Commons because of this majority, which FPTP allocates via the so-called 'winner's bonus'. When this is combined with strict party discipline, the result is a form of 'elective dictatorship'. In other words, if the government has a large majority, it has the powers of a dictator.

Now try this

Take one prime minister that you have studied and see how they fared on the variable factors.

The executive and coalition government

You need to study in detail the influence of one PM before 1997 and one PM after 1997. In 2010, the UK saw its first ever peacetime coalition government. The effect on the power of the PM and the Cabinet were great. (You will need to revise the studies you have learned in class.)

Patronage

For the first time ever, the PM's patronage powers were constrained by a written document:

- The PM could not appoint Cabinet members himself.
- Cameron had to consult Clegg on reshuffles.
- Cabinet committee membership was determined by Cameron in consultation with Clegg.

The 2010 Cabinet was agreed between Cameron (PM) and Clegg (deputy PM).

The Quad

The Quad was the top four Conservative and Lib Dem ministers in the coalition government: Cameron (PM), George Osborne (chancellor), Clegg (deputy PM) and Danny Alexander (chief secretary to the Treasury).

The role of the Quad was to 'iron out' contentious matters prior to Cabinet meetings. They met to discuss issues, with each considering the consequences for their party. According to James Forsyth (political editor of *The Spectator*):

- decisions taken by the Quad were handed down to other ministers to implement
- the Quad decided all major matters of policy (for example, the 2013 Budget)
- the Quad was more like Blair's sofa government than Cabinet government – intimate, relational and highly political (for example, the strength of Osborne and Alexander's relationship apparently led Clegg to complain that Alexander's brain had been taken over by Treasury officials).

The Coalition Agreement

The **Coalition Agreement (2010)** was a policy document drawn up following the 2010 general election. It formed a programme for governing under coalition for the 2010–2015 period. The programme had been negotiated by the two parties in the days following the election. It meant that the Conservatives dropped some policies that the Lib Dems didn't like (such as abolishing the Human Rights Act) and agreed to support some policies that the Lib Dems wanted (such as holding a referendum on electoral reform), and vice versa.

Cabinet

Coalition saw a significant change in the workings of the Cabinet. For the first time in many years, the Cabinet became a forum for proper and full discussion again:

1. The PM had to consult coalition partners on policy and Cabinet business.

2. The Cabinet had an additional function of settling differences between coalition partners.

3. The PM had to consider both coalition parties' views when formulating policy.

Parliament

Coalition government made getting legislation through Parliament quite a challenge.

👎 The PM was more vulnerable to rebellions, both from within his own party and from his coalition partner.

👎 This was compounded by increased activity and activism by the Lords as they considered the coalition government's mandate to be weak.

👎 The PM was aware of the precarious nature of his position and the possibility of a coalition breakdown.

👎 The PM had to consider backbench opinion as coalition makes government control of Parliament more fragile.

👍 The coalition gave the PM a solid majority in the Commons. They lost only six votes in the Commons during government.

👍 Policies, arguably, had additional authority as they were supported by two parties who together were elected by a majority of the electorate.

Now try this

Why were the Quad significant in the coalition?

The Supreme Court

The UK has traditionally had a fusion of powers (see page 75 to learn about how the functions of the different branches of government overlap). In 2009, however, the **Supreme Court** was established to create a greater separation of powers.

Role of the Supreme Court

The highest court in the UK was previously in the House of Lords. Under the **Constitutional Reform Act 2005**, the Supreme Court took on the roles previously performed by the Law Lords:

1 To act as the final court of appeal in England, Wales and Northern Ireland.

2 To hear appeals on issues of public importance surrounding arguable points of law.

3 To hear appeals from civil cases in England, Wales, Northern Ireland and Scotland.

4 To hear appeals from criminal cases in England, Wales and Northern Ireland.

Constitutional Reform Act 2005

The Act brought about several changes:

- It changed the role of the Lord Chancellor, removing him from his position as head of the judiciary (who appointed other judges) and the House of Lords speakership. The aim of this change was to ensure more independent appointments.

- It created an independent Supreme Court – the Act separated the Court from the legislature to create more independence.

- It established the independent Judicial Appointments Commission (JAC). This vets proposals for appointments to senior judicial posts and ensures the political independence of nominees. The JAC removes much of the political influence of the PM and Lord Chancellor, who used to have the final say over senior appointments.

The reforms became more necessary after the passage of the Human Rights Act (see page 93 to learn about how this helped changed the role of the Supreme Court) and the extension of judicial review which followed.

The Supreme Court in action.

Appointment of justices

- The Supreme Court consists of 12 members, but cases are heard by an odd number of justices in order to reach a majority verdict.

- The most senior judge is designated as the President. For example, Lady Hale became President in 2017.

- When a vacancy occurs, nominations are made to the JAC. The Lord Chancellor either confirms or rejects the person put forward. The appointment is also confirmed by the PM and the monarch. Supreme Court justices (like all judges) retire at 70 if they were appointed as a judge after 1995, or at 75 otherwise.

- Members of the Supreme Court do not sit in the House of Lords until their term has come to an end.

Lady Hale became president of the Supreme Court in October 2017, taking over from Lord Neuberger. The other 11 justices were made up of ten men and one woman. All the justices were white.

Now try this

How did the Constitutional Reform Act enhance independence of the judiciary?

Judicial neutrality and independence

Judicial neutrality and judicial independence are key operating principles of the Supreme Court.

Judicial neutrality

This refers to the principle that judges should not be politically active or motivated, and should show no personal bias. Judges should reach decisions on the basis of law alone and should show no favour or prejudice against any group.

How is judicial neutrality upheld?

👍 The Judicial Appointments Commission (JAC) identifies and eliminates from promotion any judges who demonstrate a lack of neutrality.

👍 The process of legal training and their lengthy experience is intended to ensure that judges operate according to a set of professional ethics that enable them to keep personal prejudices and biases to one side.

👍 Attempts in recent years have been made to broaden the judiciary in terms of their backgrounds and life experiences.

👍 The use of legal precedent and the possibility that cases may go to appeal help restrict the influence of personal views.

👎 Judges are demographically unrepresentative – 'male, pale and stale'. In 2017, a quarter of judges in the Court of Appeal and a fifth of those in the High Court were female; the proportion of black, Asian and minority ethnic judges was still well below one in ten. There was also a drop in the percentage of non-white barristers, the largest source of future judges.

👎 Judges are seen as 'Establishment', inclined to uphold the status quo. This is the main thrust of arguments put forward by J.A.G. Griffiths in his book *The Politics of the Judiciary* (first published in 1977 but updated regularly).

👎 Growing judicial activism can be seen as lacking neutrality.

Judicial independence

This is the principle that the actions and decisions of judges should not be influenced by pressure from the executive and Parliament. It implies a strict separation between the judiciary and other branches of government.

How is judicial independence upheld?

👍 **Lord Chancellor**: bound by oath to preserve the principle of judicial independence.

👍 **Security of tenure**: judges are appointed until retirement and can only be removed by a joint address in both Houses of Parliament if they break the law.

👍 **Appointment**: judges are appointed by the JAC using a procedure which is free from political involvement.

👍 **Decisions**: the remarks and sentences of judges in court cases should not be subject to criticism in Parliament and are immune from any legal action.

👍 **Fixed salary**: this is not subject to party political debate in Parliament so that politicians cannot threaten to reduce judges' salaries.

👍 **Human Rights Act**: provides a guide to rights cases which is externally determined and can be used in an independent way.

👍 **Supreme Court**: a separate body from Parliament.

👎 Government retains some role in the final decision of appointing judges, which could be abused.

👎 There has also been a growing trend of ministers being prepared to criticise judges' rulings.

For example, in 2017, politicians (and newspapers) criticised the Supreme Court's ruling on the Article 50 case (see page 93 for more on the operations of the Supreme Court).

The rule of law

The rule of law is one of the two pillars of the UK's uncodified constitution (see page 68). It is the principle that the law should 'rule'. It is a core principle of liberal democracy, upholding limited government and preventing arbitrary government. It should apply equally to **all** members of society, regardless of whether they are private citizens or public officials. Its core features include:

- everyone is entitled to a fair trial and no one should be imprisoned without due legal process
- all citizens must obey the law and are equal under it
- public officials are not above the law and they can be held to account by the courts
- the judiciary must be independent of political interference.

Now try this

Why is judicial independence so important?

The influence of the Supreme Court

The role of judges within an uncodified constitutional system is limited as they cannot rule the actions of Parliament as unconstitutional. Judges in the UK therefore have a narrower capacity to constrain Parliament and the executive than judges in the USA (learn about the political role played by the US Supreme Court on page 194), but they still have some influence over them.

Judicial review

Judicial review is a review of the actions of ministers and other government officials to ensure that they conform to law. Ministerial decisions and actions can be declared unlawful when they are *ultra vires*, that is, when the minister is acting beyond their powers.

The Human Rights Act 1998

The Human Rights Act (HRA) made it possible for the Supreme Court to issue a 'declaration of incompatibility' if it believed that an Act of Parliament conflicted with it. Parliament can still ignore the Supreme Court, but these declarations bring significant political pressure to bear on Parliament to review the issue.

 Case study

Miller v Secretary of State for Exiting the European Union [2017]

In 2016, Theresa May told Parliament of her intention to trigger **Article 50** (the mechanism to start the formal process of Brexit). Like many, May assumed this was part of her royal prerogative powers (read more about the PM's powers on page 88). However, she faced a legal challenge by those who argued that only Parliament could take the UK out of the **European Union (EU)**, as membership of it had introduced constitutional rights for UK citizens, which only Parliament could remove. The case went to the High Court, which upheld Miller's claim, and was passed to the Supreme Court when the government appealed.

The case was heard by all 11 Supreme Court Justices – the first time ever – and they upheld the earlier ruling in Miller's favour. Despite suggestions of pro-EU bias on the benches and that they were acting against the will of the people, the Supreme Court was simply reasserting the constitutional principles governing how Brexit should be carried out.

Is the Supreme Court influential?

👍 The Supreme Court can stop executive action according to the principles set out for judicial review.

👍 Their position as the 'final court of appeal' dealing with the most significant matters affords them significant power. For example, the Article 50 ruling in 2017 (see below).

👍 Since the Human Rights Act, the Supreme Court has increased its ability to protect citizens' rights, usually from government actions. As a result, the Court has become more involved in human rights debates, being generally more aware of issues of civil liberties.

👍 Senior judges have become influential by making public comments about major issues. For example, about sentencing policy and human rights.

👍 The Supreme Court has acquired a reputation for standing up for rights, which has led critics to suggest that they are 'reading rights into' laws that were not intended by governments. This has led to charges of judicial activism.

👍 In freedom of information cases, the Supreme Court has upheld decisions to publish information against the wishes of ministers. For example, Prince Charles's 'black spider' memos.

👎 There are no 'higher' constitutional laws, so the Supreme Court cannot strike down statute law.

👎 If the Supreme Court sets aside decisions by ministers or public bodies, Parliament may pass legislation which allows such decisions. For example, Belmarsh and Poundland (see page 11 for more on these cases).

👎 The Supreme Court cannot be pro-active – it must wait for cases to be brought before them.

👎 The Supreme Court cannot make judgements beyond the law, even in the interests of natural justice. For example, right to die cases.

👎 Supreme Court Judges are unelected and understand their constitutional role in relation to elected politicians.

👎 Parliament is sovereign, which means that it decides if it wishes to amend laws in line with the Supreme Court's 'suggestions'.

👎 The Supreme Court cannot overturn statutes even if they go against the ECHR.

Now try this

Explain why the Article 50 case is an example of the Supreme Court being influential.

Important Supreme Court cases

In 2014, Lord Neuberger, then president of the Supreme Court, was asked to select the most significant cases the Supreme Court had heard since it was set up in 2009. Had he been writing today, Miller v Secretary of State for Exiting the European Union [2017] would, without doubt, have been on his list.

R v Horncastle [2009]

The focus: the use of 'hearsay' – statements from absent witnesses, who are not under oath at the time and are not able to be cross-examined – has long been permitted in British courts.

The case: this case centred on a clash between the UK courts' and the European Court of Human Rights' (ECtHR) view of 'hearsay'. The ECtHR (Strasbourg) ruled if a person was convicted on the strength of hearsay evidence, then their human right to fair trial would be infringed.

The decision: the UK government felt this stance posed a real risk to **justice** – and the Supreme Court justices agreed. 'Although normally we follow the Strasbourg cases, in the Horncastle case we didn't,' said Lord Neuberger. 'We explained in some detail why we thought our system was fair and that Strasbourg had in fact gone wrong.' As a result of the ruling, the ECtHR altered its original decision. Lord Neuberger showed 'there can be genuine, civilised and constructive dialogue between the UK courts and the ECtHR'.

Nicklinson v Ministry of Justice [2014]

The focus: Tony Nicklinson (and two others) had locked-in syndrome, having been paralysed in a road accident, and wished to go to a Swiss suicide clinic. 'They all felt condemned to a life that was worthless, demeaning and sometimes even rather painful,' said Lord Neuberger.

The case: the Supreme Court had to decide whether the **Suicide Act 1961**, which made it illegal to encourage or aid another person to commit suicide, should be ruled unlawful. The men claimed the Act infringed their right to decide when to die.

The decision: nine justices took part, showing the importance of the case. Although there were differences of opinion, the court decided against the men by seven to two, agreeing the issue centred on a **moral judgement** which should be addressed by Parliament.

Al Rawi v Security Service [2011]

The focus: this case raised the conflict between human rights and national security.

The case: some inmates of US-run prisons tried to bring claims against the UK security services for contributing to mistreatment while in detention. The security services wanted to give evidence in secret in the interests of national security. However, this would result in the prosecution never seeing the evidence against them.

The decision: the Supreme Court decided this 'simply wasn't possible', adding: 'However sympathetic one might be to the security services wanting to produce evidence to exonerate themselves, we felt we simply couldn't approve a trial process which undermined one of the most fundamental principles of a fair trial: that each side hears and sees all the evidence and arguments put before the judge by the other side.'

HS2 Action Alliance Ltd v Secretary of State for Transport [2014]

The case: campaigners opposing High Speed Two (HS2) sought a judicial review of the government's plans to see if they complied with **EU environment directives**.

The decision: the Court unanimously dismissed the case, saying that until Parliament reached a final decision on the HS2 scheme, its merits remained open to debate. Lord Neuberger said, 'We criticised the EU court for saying the directives meant something different from that which they naturally meant. We said that was wrong in principle. That's not what a court should do. The law should be made by the European Commission and the ministers, not the judges rewriting directives.' The Supreme Court also criticised observations made in Strasbourg that courts should monitor parliamentary debate. Lord Neuberger described this as 'completely contrary' to the long-established British view that judges shouldn't 'poke their noses into what's going on in Parliament', adding: 'We thought this was risking blurring that important separation.'

Now try this

Why would judges monitoring parliamentary debates blur the separation of powers?

Aims and influence of the EU

Here, we look at the aims of the EU and the ways the EU has influenced many areas of UK government, in particular, policy. For more on the impact of the EU, see page 96.

Aims of the EU

The EU is a political and economic union of 28 (soon to be 27) countries in Europe. The EU aims to:

- promote peace, its values and the well-being of its citizens
- offer freedom, security and justice without internal borders
- offer sustainable development based on balanced economic growth and price stability
- offer a highly competitive market economy with full employment and social progress, and environmental protection
- combat social exclusion and discrimination
- promote scientific and technological progress
- enhance economic, social and territorial cohesion and solidarity among member countries
- respect its rich cultural and linguistic diversity
- establish an economic and monetary union, the currency of which is the euro.

The four freedoms

The **four freedoms of the EU** lie at the heart of the EU and underpin the single market. They include:

1 **Free movement of workers**: this is the most controversial freedom and has been at the centre of the EU referendum debate. It gives EU nationals the right to live and work in any EU member state.

2 **Free movement of goods**: this exists through the removal of customs duties and other trade tariffs. Its aim is to create an area without internal borders so goods can move freely as if it were a single country.

3 **Free movement of capital**: this allows capital and payments to move freely between member states.

4 **Free movement of services**: this allows EU companies to set up in other EU countries and provide services in those countries.

These freedoms are the key to understanding the Brexit debate and negotiations regarding the UK's departure from the EU.

Overview

The EU has had an impact on many areas of the UK.

Governing
Citizens' rights
Parties
Public opinion — **Impact of the EU** — Policy
Economy
Sovereignty
Devolution

Policy

- International trade has been the most affected area of EU membership – around 40 per cent of the UK's trade is with the EU.
- Membership of the single market (but not the single currency, the euro) has affected the UK's ability to control free movement of goods, services and capital.
- Immigration policy has been affected by the single market's requirement of free movement of people but, by opting out of the Schengen Agreement, the UK has been able to have more control of its borders.
- Agriculture and fisheries policies have been dramatically affected by EU membership because of the Common Agricultural Policy (CAP) and Common Fisheries Policy (CFP).

- Welfare, health and education policy have not really been affected.

The environment is an area where we see an impact from EU membership, with cleaner beaches and pollution controls.

Now try this

Outline two policy areas that have been affected by EU membership.

Impact of the EU on UK government

As Brexit goes ahead, its impact will become evident in the UK in many areas in years to come.

Rights

The **Social Chapter** was the most significant EU measure to protect workers' rights. When Blair came to power in 1997, one of Labour's first actions was to sign up to the Social Chapter.

Increased workers' rights

Entitlement to paid annual holidays

Social Chapter

Limited working hours

Parental leave

Led to the minimum wage

Equal rights for part-time and full-time workers

Devolution

As the UK devolved powers to the nations of the UK, so the relationship with the EU became complicated. Many devolved areas are areas that the EU has a large say in over the UK government, including agriculture, fisheries and the environment. Thus, Westminster had to consult Edinburgh, Cardiff and Belfast when it negotiated Brexit. In addition, Scotland and NI both voted to remain in the EU, while Wales voted to leave. This has led to a complicated relationship between the component nations and Westminster in trying to negotiate a smooth exit from the EU.

Parties

Few political parties have remained unscathed by the EU and subsequent Brexit debate.

- **Conservative Party**: has been internally split over the EU for many decades. Cameron was not its first leader to lose his job to party infighting. Thatcher, Major and now May have found it difficult to manage the Europhiles and Europhobes.
- **UKIP**: the EU issue gave rise to a new political party, UKIP, which, in 2014, gained 24 seats in the European elections.
- **Labour**: divisions within the party in the 1970s led Wilson to renegotiate European Commission (EC) membership in 1974 and to call the 1975 referendum. The Brexit referendum caused huge issues for the party, whose support is divided between two very distinct groups – one very 'remain', the other staunchly 'leave'.
- **Liberal Democrats**: have always been the UK's most pro-European party. Tim Farron believed he could harness the 'remain' vote as the only party with a clear pro-EU position going into the 2017 election, but they picked up only four seats and he resigned after the election.

Sovereignty

There is little debate that sovereignty (see page 97 for more) was affected by membership of the EU and this may have been the key factor in the referendum outcome. While the UK was a member, EU law took precedence over UK law, as was shown by the Factortame ruling (see below). The greater use of qualified majority voting (QMV) instead of a national veto furthered the loss of sovereignty.

Public opinion

The UK has always been the 'awkward' member of the EU and this has been mirrored by large public scepticism towards Brussels. Historical as well as geographical factors may explain why its citizens don't usually describe themselves as European, and feel strongly that there is a distinction between the UK and the rest of Europe. The UK press may also have influenced the public's euro-scepticism with *The Daily Mail*, *The Sun*, *The Telegraph* and *The Times* being broadly Eurosceptic in their outlook.

🔍 Case study Factortame case

Factortame was a court case regarding the compatibility of UK law (in this case, the Merchant Shipping Act 1988) and EU law.

The case: a group of Spanish fishermen claimed that the UK had breached EU law by requiring ships to have a majority of British owners if they were to be registered in the UK. The European Court of Justice (EJC) argued that UK courts must set aside the Merchant Shipping Act because it was in conflict with EU law. UK courts had to decide between upholding parliamentary sovereignty or accepting EU legislative supremacy.

Decision: the Law Lords nullified the Merchant Shipping Act of 1988, arguing it was enforcing the will of the 1972 Parliament to voluntarily limit its sovereignty by joining the EU, thus upholding the principle of Parliamentary sovereignty and adhering to the principle of EU supremacy.

Now try this

Why was Factortame such a significant case?

Sovereignty in the UK

Legal sovereignty

Legal sovereignty is defined as that person or body who makes laws and whose laws are final, recognised by courts and enforced by the executive.

Political sovereignty

Political sovereignty refers to the person or body who makes decisions in reality. It ignores where legal sovereignty may lie and concentrates on who realistically can exercise power within the state.

Parliamentary sovereignty

1 Parliamentary sovereignty is a form of legal sovereignty: it means that Parliament has the ability to make, unmake or remove any law it wishes.

2 No Parliament can bind its successor. Thus, the current government could, if it so wished, repeal the Human Rights Act, the Fixed-term Parliaments Act, etc.

3 No other institution has the authority to challenge an Act of Parliament.

4 Power which has been transferred either upwards or downwards can be reversed. *For example, devolution can be repealed by a simple Act of Parliament.*

5 The absence of a codified constitution ensures that there is no higher authority than Parliament.

Limits to Parliamentary sovereignty

The European Union

👎 Legal sovereignty has been affected as EU law takes primacy over all UK law covered by treaties. Therefore, the EU does not need the prior approval of Parliament.

👍 The UK will leave the EU (in 2019) and Parliament will be sovereign again.

👍 Some argue that membership of the EU enhanced political sovereignty, as the UK pooled its sovereignty with other nations and enjoyed benefits and rights that were not in the power of the UK Parliament.

Human Rights Act 1998

👎 Since its introduction, judges have had the power to review cases and declare Acts incompatible.

👎 It requires judges to interpret all UK laws, as far as possible, to be compatible with the ECHR.

👍 The UK Supreme Court cannot strike down laws.

👍 The Human Rights Act can be repealed.

👍 Despite repeated rulings in Hirst v UK, Parliament refused to amend the law.

👍 The UK could withdraw from the ECHR.

Devolution

👎 Devolution of legislative power to Scotland, Wales and NI greatly limits Parliament.

👎 Devolution was not a one-off event; subsequent Acts devolved more powers.

👎 Policy differences continue to multiply in Scotland, NI, Wales and England.

👍 Devolution has not altered the legal sovereignty of Parliament. The UK remains a unitary state.

👍 Devolution Acts state that Parliament retains the right to make laws on any matter.

👍 Devolved powers can be restored to London.

Referenda / 'the people'

👎 In a democracy, the people hold ultimate power; Parliament needs to be sensitive to the wishes of the electorate.

👎 The Brexit referendum and Parliament vote to trigger Article 50 saw popular sovereignty triumph.

👍 Popular sovereignty is not absolute; Parliament can ignore a referendum.

👍 Many MPs and Lords voted against triggering Article 50 in defiance of the referendum.

Executive dominance

👎 Our fused executive and legislative branches mean that, in practice, the executive is sovereign.

👎 A PM with a large majority in the Commons can enjoy considerable power. *For example, Blair didn't lose a vote from 1997 to 2005 and the sovereignty of Parliament was limited.*

👍 This is never a constant situation – sometimes the executive dominates, sometimes the Commons.

👍 The triggering of the Article 50 court case showed the limits of executive power. As it is sovereign, only Parliament could amend or repeal an existing Act of Parliament.

Now try this

Explain two ways Parliament's sovereignty is undermined.

Had a look ☐   Nearly there ☐   Nailed it! ☐

AS Paper 1, Section A

This question will help you to revise for **Section A** of your AS Level **Paper 1** exam. The first question you will encounter in Paper 1 will ask you to **describe** an aspect of UK politics.

Section A

- Section A of your Paper 1 exam consists of two 10-mark questions and you will need to choose **one** of them to answer.
- You will be assessed on AO1 skills only.
- You should aim to spend around 15 minutes on your answer.

Assessment objective

- **AO1 knowledge and understanding.** You need to express what you know and show you understand how it relates to the question you are answering.
- Marks can be achieved by producing either depth of detail and/or breadth, and questions can be asked on any section of the full specification.

Command word: Describe

Provide clear and factually correct information about the features and functions of institutions or processes, or the characteristics of a political idea. Knowledge must be precise and show understanding of the topic.

Planning

It is not really necessary to plan a 10-mark question. However, picking the right question is crucial. You could make a brief plan of three bullet points that identify the factor you will discuss in each paragraph.

Worked example

1 Describe the main methods used by pressure groups in the UK.   **(10 marks)**

One of the main methods used by insider pressure groups is lobbying ministers. This means arranging meetings with them and outlining their support or objections to proposed legislation. This is a very effective method as it puts pressure groups in direct contact with decision-makers. An example of this is the British Bankers' Association, which is an insider group that effectively lobbied the government after the financial crash in 2008 to limit the harshness of regulations against bankers as a punishment for the crash. However, this method is only available to pressure groups that have insider status or are able to pay for the professional support of lobbying companies.

A key method used by outsider pressure groups is protest marches. Many pressure groups march through the streets of main cities, especially London, in order to show their support or dissatisfaction with an area of government policy. Recently, we have seen marches against tuition fees, austerity and Brexit, as well as the earlier protest against the war in Iraq. The aim of these marches is to show the government that there is a lot of support for the view in order to persuade them to reconsider...

 An important word here is 'main', so make sure you only focus on the **main** methods.

 These questions do not need an introduction, but notice how the student has used an introductory phrase as part of their first paragraph.

 At the beginning of each paragraph, clearly identify the factor that you are going to discuss – in this case, 'lobbying ministers'.

The student has identified what lobbying is **and** explained what that means.

 The student not only describes the main methods, but also associates them with insider and outsider pressure groups, showing both knowledge and understanding.

 Using examples is important, but they must have some sort of explanation to make the most use of them. Here, the student has explained the aim behind the recent examples given.

 You should be aiming for **three** paragraphs to answer this question.

 To complete this answer, you could go on to discuss celebrity endorsement of pressure groups and how this is a method used mainly by outsider groups to gain publicity.

AS Paper 2, Section A

This question will help you to revise for **Section A** of your AS Level **Paper 2** exam. The first question you will encounter in Paper 2 will ask you to **describe** an aspect of UK government.

Section A

- Section A of your Paper 2 exam consists of two 10-mark questions and you will need to choose **one** of them to answer.
- You will be assessed on AO1 skills only.
- You should aim to spend around 15 minutes on your answer.

Assessment objective

- **AO1 knowledge and understanding.** You need to express what you know and show you understand how it relates to the question you are answering.
- Marks can be achieved by producing either depth of detail and/or breadth, and questions can be asked on any section of the full specification.

Command word: Describe

Provide clear and factually correct information about the features and functions of institutions or processes, or the characteristics of a political idea. Knowledge must be precise and show understanding of the topic.

Worked example

1   Describe the main features of the UK Constitution.   **(10 marks)**

Plan:
- uncodified
- flexible
- unentrenched

One of the main features of the UK's constitution is that it is uncodified. This means that it is not written down in a single document. As a result, it is made up of a number of different sources. One of the main sources is statute law, which is passed by Parliament. This is one of the written aspects of the UK Constitution, for example the Human Rights Act. Conventions are also part of the uncodified constitution, which are unwritten, e.g. collective ministerial responsibility. These work as customs and traditions that are widely kept, despite having no force in law.

The UK Constitution is also considered to be flexible, which means that it is easy to adapt to changing circumstances as it has no complicated procedure to go through to be amended. Flexibility is a crucial element of the UK's constitution, as it is an evolutionary system...

You could make a very brief plan of three bullet points that identify the factor you will discuss in each paragraph.

An important word here is 'main', so make sure you only focus on the **main** features.

 You do not need to include an introduction for this type of question – get straight on with your first feature.

 At the beginning of each paragraph, clearly identify the factor that you are going to discuss – in this case, 'uncodified'.

 The student has explained what 'uncodified' means, showing knowledge, and then explained a consequence of this feature, showing understanding.

 Using examples is important, but they must have some sort of explanation to make the most use of them.

 The student has introduced the second point without making the answer sound like a list.

 To complete this answer, you need to finish this paragraph by giving an example of the flexibility of the UK Constitution. Then add a third paragraph which could cover the importance/effect of the UK Constitution being unentrenched with a single-tier legal system.

AS Level Section B, question 2

Section B of your AS Level **Paper 1** and **Paper 2** exams consists of **two compulsory questions**. Question 2 is a 10-mark **source** question. This will ask you to explain an aspect of UK politics (Paper 1) or government (Paper 2). The question on this page is related to Paper 1, UK Politics. However, question 2 of Paper 2 will follow the same style and will require the same skills.

Section B

- Section B consists of two 10-mark source questions. You must answer **both** questions.
- You will be assessed on AO1 and AO2 skills, each worth 5 marks (see below).
- You should aim to spend around 20 minutes on your answer to question 2.

Command word: Explain

You need to look in detail at the issue in the question (in this case, e-petitions) and make its meaning clear in order to identify how this concept is (in this instance) improving democracy.

Assessment objectives

AO1 knowledge and understanding. You need to:

- identify and show understanding of the points **made in the source**
- show depth and breadth of knowledge
- enhance and extend points, as long as they have their origin in the source.

AO2 analysis. You need to:

- show how the points relate to the question
- develop a robust examination: expose the facts behind the point, show criticism/analysis of the point, differences and similarities, and question its merit/validity.

Worked example

2   *Source 1 is adapted from a news story from the Department for Digital, Culture, Media and Sport website. It explains how e-petitions can be used.*

> **Source 1**
>
> If you have a strong opinion about an issue relating to policies which you'd like to raise you can register it as an e-petition. E-petitions are an easy way for you to influence government policy in the UK. You can create an e-petition about anything that the government is responsible for and if it gets at least 100,000 signatures, it will be eligible for debate in the House of Commons. All e-petitions will be accepted and published on the e-petition website, providing they meet the criteria.

Using the source, explain the way e-petitions improve democracy.

*In your response you must use knowledge and understanding to analyse points that are only in the source. You will **not** be rewarded for introducing any additional points that are not in the source.* **(10 marks)**

E-petitions were introduced to improve democracy in the UK. According to the source, e-petitions enable members of the public to raise issues they feel strongly about. One of the most signed e-petitions was over a second EU referendum in June 2016, which was signed by 4,150,260. The topic was debated in September 2016 but the government announced that it would not be pursuing a second referendum. Despite the fact that the e-petition was not successful, millions of people were able to make their feelings heard by the government, which improved democracy in the UK...

This source raises the following issues:

- It's a way for members of the public to raise issues they have strong opinions about.
- They are an easy way to influence government policy.
- You can create an e-petition about anything the government is responsible for.
- If it's accepted, it may be debated in the House of Commons.

All the points you develop **must** originate from the source. Highlight the key points to help guide you.

This question does **not** need an introduction.

Aim to identify three points from the source to make up your answer.

The student has used an example very effectively to illustrate their point.

The key aspect of this question is **how e-petitions improve democracy**, not just what e-petitions are.

You now need to discuss another two points, such as how e-petitions influence government policy and the wide remit of e-petitions, to complete your answer.

AS Level Section B, question 3

This question will help you to revise for **Section B** of your AS Level **Paper 1** and **Paper 2** exams. This section in **both** papers consists of **two compulsory questions**. Question 3 is a 10-mark **source** question. This will ask you to **assess** an aspect of UK politics (Paper 1) or government (Paper 2). This question is for UK Politics but the style of question and skills required are exactly the same for UK Government, question 3, Paper 2.

Section B

- Section B consists of two 10-mark source questions. You must answer **both** questions.
- You will be assessed on AO2 and AO3 skills, each worth 5 marks (see below).
- You should aim to spend around 20 minutes on your answer to question 3.

Worked example

3 *Sources 2 and 3 are adapted from the Conservative and Labour Parties' manifestoes in 2017. Each source outlines their policies, which they wanted voters to consider when casting their vote in the 2017 general election.*

Source 2

Conservative Party manifesto policies, 2017

Economy and taxation
- Eliminate the deficit by 2025.
- Increase the income tax personal allowance.
- Cut corporation tax.

Work and education
- Increase schools budget by £4bn by 2022.
- Lift ban on selective schools.
- Provide free breakfast to all schoolchildren.
- Increase national living wage to 60 per cent of median earnings by 2020.

Brexit
- The UK will leave the single market and the customs union.
- 'Vast annual contributions' would end.
- 'Secure the entitlements' of EU citizens living in the UK and Britons living in the EU.

Source 3

Labour Party manifesto policies, 2017

Economy and taxation
- Eliminate the deficit within five years.
- Increase corporation tax.
- Raise taxes for top earners.

Work and education
- Ban unpaid internships and zero-hour contracts.
- Increase the minimum wage.
- Abolish university tuition fees.
- Provide free meals to schoolchildren.

Brexit
- 'Strong emphasis on retaining the benefits of the single market and the customs union'.
- Guarantees rights for EU nationals and secure reciprocal rights for UK citizens.

Command word: Assess

This means you need to discuss both the similarities **and** the differences and come to a judgement (in this case, as to how similar or different the policies are).

Assessment objectives

AO2 analysis. You need to:

- look at the two sides given in the source
- make effective analytical comparisons (a key aspect)
- show a full appreciation of both sides in the debate.

AO3 evaluation. This aspect is about reaching a conclusion. You need to:

- say which side of the debate you support and why
- explain why you reject or doubt the alternative position
- try, where possible, to link the judgement to the analysis you have made.

This worked example continues on the next page.

AS Level Section B, question 3
continued...

This is a continuation of the question given on page 101. Read the question and sources on that page before continuing below.

Worked example

Using the sources, assess the similarities in policy between the Labour and Conservative parties.

In your response you must compare and contrast similarities and differences and consider competing points by analysing and evaluating them; only knowledge which supports this analysis and evaluation will gain credit. **(10 marks)**

Paragraph 2

... According to the sources, there are a number of similarities, for example both parties seek to eliminate the deficit within a decade. This can be seen to confirm that both parties are working towards balancing the UK's budget. However, the sources also show that they have different ways of seeking to do so which shows a profoundly different attitude to the economy. The Labour Party seeks to balance the UK's budget by increasing corporation tax and raising taxes for top earners, whereas the Conservative Party seeks to cut corporation tax and balance the budget by further austerity. These two approaches, while similar in outcome, show fundamentally different approaches to the economy and reflect clear ideological differences between the parties...

All the points **you analyse and evaluate must** originate from the sources. Here, we can see these similarities:
- eliminate the deficit
- increase the minimum wage
- provide free meals in schools
- secure the rights of EU and UK citizens.

We can also see differences:
- corporation tax
- abolition of tuition fees
- selective schools
- single market and customs unions.

The student has analysed the sources (AO2) by showing areas where the parties are similar as well as where they are different. Remember, you must support your point with evidence from the sources, and any contrasts or comparisons you make must be based on evidence from the sources.

In addition, the student has evaluated (AO3) the similarities and differences and **come to a judgement**, suggesting that the differences are much more fundamental than the similarities.

To complete the answer, you would need to discuss another two similarities or differences between the two parties. For example, their approach to Brexit and their plans for student tuition fees.

AS Level Section C, question 4

Section C of the AS **Paper 1** and **Paper 2** exams consists of two 30-mark questions. You will need to choose **one** to answer. The question on this page is related to Paper 2, UK Government.

Section C

- Aim to spend around 50 minutes on this essay.
- Your essay needs to be fully structured, including an introduction and a conclusion.
- You will be assessed on AO1, AO2 and AO3.
- Your essay should flow well and be persuasive in its argument and structure.

Note that in Paper 1 (UK Politics) you will **not** be instructed to link to UK government. For tips on how to plan your answer, see page 105.

Assessment objectives

- **AO1 knowledge and understanding**. You need to express what you know and show you understand how it relates to the question you are answering.
- **AO2 analysis**. You need to show how the factor you are examining can be broken down and how it relates to the question. You should also show comparisons, similarities, differences and parallels.
- **AO3 evaluation**. This is your ability to debate the different sides and come to a judgement. This should be clear **throughout your essay**, not just in the concluding paragraph.

Worked example

4 'The UK would be better served with a codified constitution.'

How far do you agree with this view of the UK government?

In your answer you must:
- *refer to **both** codified **and** uncodified constitutions*
- *consider this view and the alternative to this view in a balanced way*
- *draw on relevant knowledge and understanding of the study from Component 1: UK politics.* **(30 marks)**

The UK is unusual in having an uncodified constitution, which means that it's not all written in a single document. Instead, the UK's constitutional arrangements are made up of many sources, some of which are written (e.g. statute law) and some are unwritten (e.g. conventions). There have been worries over the UK's constitution, but this essay will argue that the UK is best served by its uncodified constitution.

One highly important reason why the UK is best served by an uncodified constitution is that it works very well. In the UK, Parliament is sovereign as only it has the ability to make and unmake laws. A codified constitution requires a Supreme Court to decide if the normal laws are in line with the constitution. This would lead to unelected judges overruling elected politicians. In the UK, if MPs act in a way that goes against the wishes of the people, they can remove them from office at the next election. For example, when the Article 50 legislation went through Parliament, MPs voted to pass it even though most MPs preferred to remain in the EU. This shows that the UK would not be better served by a codified constitution, as politicians are kept in line by elections...

This essay could include the following points:
Better served by being codified:

👍 Makes the system more rigid

👍 Restricts government activity

👍 Independent judges uphold the constitution

👍 Protects rights more effectively

Better served by <u>not</u> being codified:

👎 Retains flexibility

👎 Upholds parliamentary sovereignty

👎 The people check government via elections, not judges

👎 Rights are effectively checked in the UK's system.

Remember that you must also draw on relevant knowledge from UK Politics.

Finally, you need to come to a conclusion and make a judgement as to how far you agree with the statement, based on the argument you've made.

This definition is very thorough and shows the student knows the difference between a codified and an uncodified constitution.

Saying that this is a 'highly important reason' shows evaluation.

This is excellent interpretation and analysis of the case, highlighting the impact of the example and its relevance to the question.

The final sentence shows what the student thinks and the direction from which they will argue.

A Level Section A, question 1

The first question on A Level **Paper 1** (UK Politics) **and** A Level **Paper 2** (UK Government) consists of a 30-mark source question. You will be given two questions and will need to choose **one** of them.
The question on this page is for UK Politics but the style of question and skills you will need are exactly the same for UK Government, question 1, Paper 2.

Worked example

1   *This source is adapted from an article published in* The Times *on 19 October 2017.*

> Direct democracy is growing in popularity but there is no substitute for well-informed decisions made by parliaments.
>
> Representative democracy seems, to a lot of people, a flawed model. It brings you the professional politicians vying for your vote. It offers tedious slanging matches between largely interchangeable professionals. It's dreary, is what it is. Direct democracy feels like the coming thing. If for no other reason than that we're developing the technology that allows us, with minimum effort, to cast a vote for or against any proposition. Away with the elite! Long live the masses!
>
> A decade or so ago I would have counted myself among the direct democracy advocates. Turnout at elections was falling, there was a long-term secular decline in party membership, experts were talking about the need for a re-connection. In response, the representative democrats implemented some direct democratic reforms to draw people back into politics.
>
> But this system has a problem… It means that people can decide issues having been involved in absolutely no discussion at all. In practice, it has always meant the same thing: that those with the best organisation, the loudest voices and nothing else to do on the night, get to win. And who else has the time? Direct democracy… doesn't of itself require debate.
>
> In 1965, the Commons voted against the popular will and abolished the death penalty. If we'd had a referendum we'd almost certainly have kept it. The reason for the difference wasn't that MPs were an out-of-touch elite, but that they had debated it, heard the evidence at length and, critically, that they would have had to take responsibility for it. They, unlike the electorate at large, would be proxy executioners if they voted to retain capital punishment.
>
> Here in the UK we are in the greatest mess of the post-war years because a referendum was passed which, as most elected representatives know, cannot be enacted without incredible disruption and substantial loss. It's not exactly an advertisement for them.

Using the source, evaluate the view that referenda are not effective in a representative democracy.

In your response you must:
- *compare and contrast the different opinions in the source*
- *examine and debate these views in a balanced way*
- *analyse and evaluate only the information presented in the source.*   **(30 marks)**

Section A
- Aim to spend around 45 minutes on this essay.
- Your essay needs to be fully structured, including an introduction and a conclusion.
- You will be assessed on AO1, AO2 and AO3 skills.
- Your essay should also flow well and be persuasive in its argument and structure.

Assessment objectives
- **AO1 knowledge and understanding**. You need to express what you know and show you understand how it relates to the question you are answering.
- **AO2 analysis**. You need to show how the factor you are examining can be broken down and how it relates to the question. You should also show comparisons, similarities, differences and parallels.
- **AO3 evaluation**. This is your ability to debate the different sides and come to a judgement. This should be clear **throughout your essay**, not just in the concluding paragraph.

Timing
Allow yourself some time to get to grips with the source as your whole answer will be based on it. Spend a few minutes planning your answer and also proofreading it at the end. This will ultimately help you produce a better and more effective answer.

Read the source **thoroughly**. In the source you will find two points of view relating to the question. Use two different coloured highlighters to highlight the different views in the source.

This worked example continues on the next page.

A Level Section A, question 1
continued...

This is a continuation of the question given on page 104. Read the question and source on that page before continuing below. The question is for UK Politics but the style of question and skills required are exactly the same for UK Government, question 1, Paper 2.

Choosing the question

The 30-mark source question tests a number of skills. The first one is choosing which question to answer. It is not advisable to read both sources before choosing as you do not have time. Instead, read both questions and then decide based on which topic you know best. Look back at page 104 to remind yourself of the question.

Steps to planning

1 **Introduction:** define key terms and introduce the argument.

2 **Body:** what factors are you going to discuss and what examples are you going to use to support your work?

2 **Conclusion:** make a final summary judgement, drawing on the overarching themes you can draw from your essay.

Plan

The two views in the source on page 104 give reasons why referenda are a good idea and reasons why they are not. Use the two views as your plan. In this case it will look something like this.

	For	Against
Representative democracy	✓ (If we'd had a referendum on the death penalty we'd almost certainly have kept it) ✓ MPs were not an out-of-touch elite ✓ They had debated it, heard the evidence at length ✓ They would have had to take responsibility for it ✓ Here in the UK we are in the greatest mess of the post-war years because a referendum was passed	✗ Professional politicians vying for your vote ✗ Tedious slanging matches ✗ Interchangeable politicians ✗ It's dreary ✗ Turnout at elections was falling ✗ Decline in party membership ✗ Need for a re-connection
Direct democracy	✓ Developing the technology ✓ Away with the elite! Long live the masses!	✗ People can decide issues not having been involved in any discussion at all ✗ Those with the best organisation, the loudest voices and nothing else to do on the night, win ✗ Direct democracy doesn't of itself require debate.

Your job now is to formulate these points into a coherent, structured argument, but you must also come to a judgement (AO3).

This worked example continues on the next page.

Command word: Evaluate

AO3 requires you to evaluate both sides of the argument and **come to a judgement**.

- It is not enough to show both sides of an argument and to conclude in a neutral way that both sides have various merits and demerits.
- Instead, you have to pick a side and argue, **throughout the essay**, why, in your opinion, that side is more convincing.
- BUT... you have to do it in a balanced way. This means that you cannot ignore the views expressed on the opposing side of the argument. You must address them but explain why 'your side' is better.

A Level Section A, question 1

Look back at page 104 to remind yourself of the question. Read the question and the sample student plan on page 105 before continuing below. Remember that question 1 is the same style in both Papers 1 and 2. This question relates to UK Politics.

Worked example

Until 2016, it was widely considered that referenda were a device that enhanced democracy in the UK. However, the EU referendum in June 2016 changed that perception. As the source outlines in detail, referenda can have a severely detrimental effect on a society. As such, this essay will argue that referenda are not effective in a representative democracy...

Your introduction is crucial to your answer as it sets the tone for the whole essay. You need to set out the case that will continue **throughout your essay**. Here, the student has referenced the source and has made a judgement showing how they are going to argue.

... According to the source, referenda enhance democracy as they reduce the power of elites in society and give more power to the masses. Referenda create a more pluralist society, as every citizen's vote is of equal value. With representative democracy, wealthy corporations or special interest groups have the 'ear' of the government and are able to influence policy more than a regular voter, whereas with referenda all citizens are of equal value. This argument was seen during the Brexit referendum, when Michael Gove argued that the people were 'sick of experts'. He was identifying a phenomenon where so-called 'experts' would bombard the ordinary citizens with frightening statistics about the consequences of them voting the 'wrong' way. This was known as 'Project Fear'...

The student uses the point from the source and then elaborates using their own knowledge.

How to structure your paragraphs most effectively is a personal choice. This example is an effective way of outlining your paragraph in order to get maximum usage across all three AOs.

This is a good example and explanation of its relevance to the point being made.

... However, the source counteracts this by arguing that MPs are professional politicians who spend a great deal of time researching, debating and discussing key issues before coming to a judgement. MPs may appear to be above ordinary citizens (an elite), but they are charged with making complicated decisions on our behalf, so they can, in some ways, be considered to be more knowledgeable than ordinary citizens. They are elected to make decisions on our behalf, yet referenda take the decisions out of their hands. In reality, British politicians have spent many years debating our relationship with the EU, so they probably do know better than most of us. Also, they don't necessarily have a personal agenda – they are arguing from a perspective of what they think is best for the whole of the UK. Hence it can be seen that referenda are not an effective way of making decisions in a representative democracy. A representative democracy places that responsibility in the hands of elected representatives and they should be the ones making the decisions...

Most of your paragraphs will follow the same basic structure. Try to discuss three or four points in this way. Your third and fourth points may be debated in less detail than here.

The student counters the point made in the first paragraph and elaborates on the point from the source with their own knowledge.

This shows an 'interim judgement', summing up the points above and coming down very clearly on one side of the argument.

... So, to conclude, it can be seen that referenda are not an effective way of enhancing a representative democracy for the many reasons outlined above. Referenda are a tool of direct democracy and, when used in a representative democracy, they can cause conflicts of mandates and deep divisions in society. Ultimately, as the source suggests, an ill-advised referendum has left the UK in the 'greatest mess of the post-war years'.

If you have argued effectively, using good evaluation throughout your essay, your conclusion will merely be a formality of summing up what you have previously answered.

Here, the student is again countering the point made in the first paragraph and exemplifying the point with an example.

A Level Section A, question 2

The second question of your A Level **Paper 1** (UK Politics) and A Level **Paper 2** (UK Government) gives you a choice of two 30-mark essay questions – you will need to choose **one** of them. The question style and the skills you will need are the same for both Paper 1 and Paper 2. The question on this page is for UK Government.

Section A

- Aim to spend around 45 minutes on this essay, including time planning and proofreading your answer.
- Each essay needs to be fully structured, including an introduction and a conclusion.
- You will be assessed on AO1, AO2 and AO3 skills.

Steps to planning

1. **Introduction**: define key terms and introduce the argument.
2. **Body**: what factors are you going to discuss and what examples are you going to use to support your work?
2. **Conclusion**: make a final summary judgement, drawing on the overarching themes you can draw from your essay.

Worked example

2 Evaluate the extent to which the UK would be better served with a codified constitution.

In your answer you should draw on relevant knowledge and understanding of the study of Component 1: UK Politics and Core Political Ideas and consider this view and the alternative to this view in a balanced way.
(30 marks)

The UK is unusual in having an uncodified constitution, which means that it is not all written in a single, authoritative document. Instead, the UK's constitutional arrangements are made up of a number of different sources, some of which are written (e.g. statute law) and some are not (e.g. conventions). There have been a number of concerns that the uncodified nature of the UK's constitution has led to it being too flexible, allowing governments to exercise too much power and at times resemble an 'elective dictatorship'. This essay is going to argue, however, that the UK is better served by its uncodified constitution rather than by a codified one...

The final sentence of this introduction shows what the student thinks and the direction from which they will argue.

Assessment objectives

- **AO1 knowledge and understanding**. You need to express what you know and show you understand how it relates to the question you are answering.
- **AO2 analysis**. You need to show how the factor you are examining can be broken down and how it relates to the question. You should also show comparisons, similarities, differences and parallels.
- **AO3 evaluation**. This is your ability to debate the different sides and come to a judgement. This should be clear **throughout your essay**, not just in the concluding paragraph. Your essay should also flow well and be persuasive in its argument and structure.

Command word: Evaluate

This command word will be followed by a statement that suggests one side of an argument. You need to show that you **know and understand** (AO1), can **analyse** (AO2) and **evaluate** (AO3) this and the other side of this argument. You need to review the factors that affect your argument and judge their importance or effectiveness.

Introduction

Your introduction should show that you understand what you have been asked to do. It should therefore define the key terms of the question, outline what you are going to discuss and identify what you intend to argue.

Note that in Paper 1 (UK Politics) you will **not** be instructed to link to UK Government.

This definition is very thorough and shows the student knows the difference between a codified and uncodified constitution.

The exemplification of the UK's uncodified nature by using two examples of sources enhances the student's introduction.

This worked example continues on the next page.

Section A, question 2
continued...

Read the question and sample student answer on page 107 before continuing below.

Worked example

... In the UK, our constitution works very well so there is no need for it to be replaced by a codified constitution. Our constitution makes sure that Parliament is sovereign and that elected politicians are always in charge, e.g. the Gina Miller case. Parliament has been elected by the people and it is only right that Parliament, and not unelected judges, should be in charge.

On the other hand, a codified constitution would allow judges to decide what was right and wrong as sometimes politicians aren't brave enough to make difficult decisions, e.g. gay marriage in America. Politicians can be too scared of the electorate, whereas judges don't have to listen to the people and can just do what is right.

Thus there are valid arguments on both sides...

Never underestimate the importance of language when writing your answer. This section is entirely correct, but the lack of a more sophisticated language style lets it down.

While the student has identified the points correctly, the essay lacks the depth of explanation that's needed.

While examples have been included, they are poorly used. Elaborating on the example will add depth to your explanation.

This final sentence does little more than repeat the question.

Improved sample answer

... It can be argued that the UK is best served by its uncodified constitution, which works extremely effectively. In the UK's unitary constitutional set up, Parliament is sovereign as only it has the ability to make and unmake laws. A codified constitution requires a special constitutional court to arbitrate between the regular laws passed by the legislature and higher laws as set out in the constitution. This would lead to unelected judges overruling elected politicians. In the UK, if MPs act in a way that goes against the wishes of the people, they can remove them from office at the next election. We can see evidence for this when the Article 50 legislation went through Parliament. Most MPs preferred to remain in the EU, but mindful of the wishes of the people, they voted overwhelmingly to trigger Article 50. This shows that the UK would not be better served by a codified constitution, as regular elections are sufficient to keep politicians in check.

However, the UK could be said to be better served by a codified constitution as in certain circumstances there is a limit to what politicians are prepared to do, precisely because they must be mindful of the wishes of the electorate. Politicians have to be careful not to offend their constituents specifically and the electorate in general. For example, in the USA, it was down to judges to legalise same-sex marriage as the elected branches were apprehensive about the backlash if they were too fervent in their support for it.

Despite this, it can be seen that judges in America are too powerful and political, as it is impossible to stay above the fray. Moreover, controversial rulings by judges can often be rejected by that part of the population who disagree. In the UK, same-sex marriage was legalised by elected politicians and as a consequence, has not been surrounded by the controversy it has in America...

A clear opening that uses the wording of the question.

Excellent use of political vocabulary and related concepts.

This is excellent interpretation and analysis of the case, highlighting the impact of the example and its relevance to the question.

Clear evaluation of the point and excellent use of political vocabulary.

Here, the student relates directly back to the point made in the first paragraph but shows the negative aspect of it.

Good use of the example, which elaborates on the point being made.

While they have given a balanced argument, the student ends by maintaining their original argument and evaluating which side of the argument is stronger.

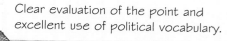

This worked example continues on the next page.

Section A, question 2
continued...

Here, we conclude looking at **question 2** of your A Level **Paper 1** (UK Politics) and **Paper 2** (UK Government) exams, and the UK Government question you were asked on page 107.

Completing the essay

To finish off the essay, you would need to make another two or three points, evaluating both sides of the argument, before coming to a final judgement. These points might include:

Better served by being codified:	Better served by not being codified
👍 Restricts government activity	👎 Retains flexibility
👍 Protects rights more effectively	👎 Maintains parliamentary sovereignty
👍 Educates the public	👎 Judges not involved in politics
👍 Makes the system more rigid	👎 Adapts according to changing times
👍 Independent judges uphold the constitution	👎 Keeps the people powerful via elections

Conclusion

The conclusion should show a definitive answer to the question and show how you reached that conclusion. With the command word 'evaluate', the conclusion must be more than simply 'yes' or 'no'. Look back at page 107 to remind yourself of the question. Read the question and sample student answer on pages 107–108 before continuing below.

Improved sample answer

... While there is no doubt that the UK presents as an anomaly with its uncodified constitution, that in itself is not a justification for change. The UK is an interesting mix of conservative and liberal approaches. It values its traditions and organic approach to change, as well as the simple fact that its current constitutional arrangement works remarkably well, and certainly no worse than alternative codified systems. Moreover, it has adopted greater liberal principles – separation of powers, rights protection and devolution – through constitutional reforms in recent years, which have enhanced its system of government. Thus, it can be concluded that the UK would not be better served with a codified constitution.

The opening line of the conclusion shows the student understands the broad context of the question.

Here, the student uses synoptic analysis of the core ideas of conservatism and liberalism from Component 1: UK Politics.

The conclusion directly addresses the question but places the whole question in context.

Just like the introduction, you will not be awarded marks for your conclusion alone. The conclusion should, however, be predictable. From how you have written your essay, it should be reasonably clear what you are going to conclude.

Conclusion checklist

Have I...

✓ answered the question directly?

✓ explained how and why I reached this conclusion?

✓ written a conclusion that matches the tone of my essay?

Have I avoided...

 simply repeating paragraphs or examples?

 writing only one sentence?

✗ introducing new information?

In A Level Papers 1 and 2 you will also have to answer a 24-mark question in Section B on political ideas. Turn to pages 123, 132, 141, 151 and 161 for more on this.

AS exam-style practice 1, Paper 1

Practise for **Paper 1**, **Section A** (question 1) and **Section B** (question 2) of your AS Level exam with these exam-style questions. There are answers on page 308–309. Paper 1 covers Component 1: UK Politics. It is made up of three sections, and in total you will have to answer **four** questions: **one** from Section A, **two** from Section B and **one** from Section C.

Section A

1 Describe the main features of political parties in the UK today.

 Aim to spend around 15 minutes answering question 1.

(10 marks)

Section B

2 *Source 1 is adapted from an article on the Politico website titled 'The Trouble with Referendums', by Kristi Lowe and Kelsey Suter in August 2016.*

 This question should take you about 20 minutes.

Source 1

One of the main issues with referendums is that confusion can hijack the issue. Although the question is a simple yes or no answer, the actual policy question at stake is often highly complex. The result can appear clear cut in terms of votes but it can be hard to interpret what the vote over a particular issue really means in practice. Turnout in referendums is often lower than in elections and this means the side with the most energised voters wins rather than reflecting the real balance of public opinion. In such cases, referendums are decided by the minority not the majority. The campaigns around referendums see the public bombarded from all sides with information by groups and individuals that they have little knowledge of. These campaigns often aim to simplify complex issues into hot button issues in order to capture the public agenda. This can steer the campaigns and the attention of the public away from the real and complex issues at stake. The result of this is that many voters can feel a sense of voter regret at the way they cast their vote or the way that the government implements their decision. In the end referendums are direct democracy but their results do always give a clear direction.

 Your answer should use information provided in the source, include examples and be made up of three or four paragraphs.

 All the points you develop **must** originate from the source. Highlight the key points to help guide you.

Using the source, explain the problems with using referenda in the UK.

 You will be assessed on AO1 and AO2 skills, each worth 5 marks.

*In your response you must use knowledge and understanding to analyse points that are only in the source. You will **not** be rewarded for introducing any additional points that are not in the source.*

(10 marks)

AS exam-style practice 2, Paper 1

Practise for **Paper 1, Section B** (question 3) and **Section C** (question 4) of your AS Level exam with these exam-style questions. There are answers on page 309.

Section B

Aim to spend around 20 minutes answering question 3.

3 *Source 2 is adapted from the Electoral Reform Society.*

> ### Source 2
>
> In the Scottish Independence Referendum, 16- and 17-year olds were given the right to vote and they used it. Seventy five per cent of those asked were said to have voted, with 97 per cent saying they would vote in future elections. This was a higher turnout rate than for 18- to 24-year olds, which was estimated at 54 per cent. There is also evidence that they engaged with a wider variety of news sources and information than any other voting age group. The very nature of their engagement appears to have changed wider public opinion from 30 per cent supporting the lowering of the voting age in Scotland pre-referendum to 60 per cent post referendum. There may be no one solution to improving participation in politics, but involving people directly in politics during their formative years is crucial for our democracy.

All the points you analyse and evaluate must originate from these sources. Highlight the key points to help guide you.

Source 3 is adapted from Michael White, 'Should 16-year-olds be allowed to vote?' on The Guardian *Politics Blog in 2015.*

> ### Source 3
>
> It is conventional wisdom to say the young are disengaged and disillusioned with politics and letting them vote will help. Voter turnout among the 18–24 age group has dropped from 60 per cent in 1970 to 43 per cent in 2015. Yet there is not enough clear evidence that lowering the voting age will make things better. Only one-third of the UK public back the change and Dr Philip Cowley, political scientist, sees no evidence the change would make a difference or that the young are more politically mature than in the past. Secondly, across the UK, the devolved assemblies and Westminster have introduced many new laws and regulations to protect under 18s, as they are still seen as children not adults. To change the voting laws at this stage would be inconsistent.

Once you have highlighted the key points, sort them into two lists: similarities and differences.

Using the sources, assess whether the voting age should be lowered in the UK for general elections.

You will be assessed on AO2 and AO3 skills, each worth 5 marks.

In your response you must compare and contrast similarities and differences and consider competing points by analysing and evaluating them; only knowledge which supports this analysis and evaluation will gain credit.

You need to reach a well-argued judgement and come to a conclusion.

(10 marks)

Section C

Allow about 50 minutes for this question.

4 'The United Kingdom still has a two-party system.'

How far do you agree with this view of the UK party system?

Your answer should be properly structured, with an introduction and a conclusion, and include examples.

*In your answer you must refer to **at least** two elections and consider this view and the alternative to this view in a balanced way.*

(30 marks)

AS exam-style practice 3, Paper 2

Practise for **Paper 2, Section A** (question 1) and **Section B** (question 2) of your AS exam with these exam-style questions. There are answers on page 309. Paper 2 covers Component 2: UK Government. It is made up of three sections, and in total you will have to answer **four** questions: **one** from Section A, **two** from Section B and **one** from Section C.

Section A

1   Describe the main roles of backbenchers in the House of Commons.

Aim to spend around 15 minutes answering question 1.

Your answer should be made up of three or four paragraphs and include examples.

(10 marks)

Section B

2   *Source 1 is adapted from the Parliament website on Select Committees.*

This question should take you about 20 minutes.

You need to look for differences, similarities, causes or consequences in the source.

Source 1

There is a Commons Select Committee for each government department, examining three aspects: spending, policies and administration. There are also some select committees that cross departmental boundaries such as the Public Accounts Committee. These committees have a minimum of 11 members, who decide upon the line of inquiry and then gather written and oral evidence by calling witnesses, including Ministers, Civil Servants and outside witnesses. These sessions enable the Committee to question witnesses in depth over an extended time period. Findings are reported to the Commons and the government usually has 60 days to reply to the recommendations made in the Committee's report. These reports often get a high level of attention from the media such as the 2013 PAC's report into tax payments made by Amazon, Starbucks and Google. The Committees act largely free of party politics and aim to produce reports that are agreed upon unanimously by all members, Since the Wright reforms, Chairs are elected by their fellow MPs and receive an additional salary for their work, which provides an attractive career opportunity. Membership of the Committees is in line with party strength in the overall House with the members elected by MPs from their own political party, removing the power of the Whips to decide the membership.

Your answer should use information provided in the source, include examples and be made up of three or four paragraphs.

Using the source, explain the main strengths of Select Committees in the House of Commons.

*In your response you must use knowledge and understanding to analyse points that are only in the source. You will **not** be rewarded for introducing any additional points that are not in the source.*

You will be assessed on AO1 and AO2 skills, each worth 5 marks.

(10 marks)

AS exam-style practice 4, Paper 2

Practise for **Paper 2, Section B** (question 3) and **Section C** (question 4) of your AS exam with these exam-style questions. There are answers on page 309.

Section B

3 *Source 2 is adapted from* The Daily Telegraph *article: 'The House of Lords is working fine – don't fix it'.*

Aim to spend around 20 minutes answering question 3.

Remember, both questions in Section B are compulsory.

All the points you analyse and evaluate must originate from these sources.

> ### Source 2
> If we were designing a system to deliver effective government today, we would not come up with the House of Lords. Yet, the House does an excellent job amending legislation created by the government that started in the Commons for the greater good. This is possible due to the wealth of experience and expertise available in the House that is not matched in the House of Commons. Importantly, the electorate seems remarkably unconcerned that the House of Lords is not elected. A wholly elected chamber would certainly be less effective in the role as it would lose the expertise and become either an echo chamber for the Commons and the government, just meekly accepting its legislative programme or would become a direct challenge to it, leading to potential gridlock. In the end, the bottom line remains for the House of Lords, if ain't broke, don't fix it.

Source 3 is adapted from 'Lording it up', by Meg Russell.

> ### Source 3
> The Lords has displayed increased confidence since the 1999 Labour reforms. It defeated the government of Blair and Brown over 450 times, at an average of 40 defeats per year. It is estimated by the University College London, that about 50 per cent of these defeats stick and the legislation is amended. Yet the Lords, as it is unelected, remains very sensitive to public opinion and the opinions of the backbench MPs from the governing party. Its opposition will melt away when the opposition from backbenchers from the governing party disappears. As such an elected second chamber would become more conventionally political and lose some of its expertise but it would less likely to back down in its conflicts with government and the Commons.

Highlight the key points in both sources and then sort them into two lists: similarities and differences.

Using the sources, assess whether the House of Lords would be more effective if it was elected.

In your response you must compare and contrast similarities and differences and consider competing points by analysing and evaluating them; only knowledge which supports this analysis and evaluation will gain credit.

You will be assessed on AO2 and AO3 skills, each worth 5 marks.

You need to reach a well-argued judgement and come to a conclusion.

(10 marks)

Section C

4 'Constitutional reforms since 1997 have proved inadequate.' How far do you agree with this view of constitutional reform?

You need to include analysis and evaluation and reach a well-argued judgement.

In your answer you must:

- *refer to **at least two** constitutional reforms*
- *consider this view and the alternative to this view in a balanced way*
- *draw on relevant knowledge and understanding of the study from Component 1: UK Politics.*

Assessment objectives: AO1 (10 marks), AO2 (10 marks), AO3 (10 marks).

Remember that for Paper 2, you must link back to Component 1: UK Politics.

A Level exam-style practice 1, Paper 1

Practise for **Paper 1, Section A** (UK Politics) of your A Level exam with these exam-style questions. There are answers on pages 309. You must answer **two** questions from Section A and one from Section B (see pages 123, 132, 141, 151, 161 and 162 for more on Section B).

Section A

1 *This source is taken from* The Guardian *newspaper, 22 May 2015. It offers an analysis of the results of the 2015 general election.*

> The Conservatives were not only best at holding on to their 2010 voters, they were also the most successful party among those groups with high turnout.
>
> With voters aged 65 or above, the highest turnout group (78%), they gained a 5.5 point swing from Labour since 2010. And among ABs – the social class with the highest turnout (75%), defined as "households with higher and intermediate managerial, administrative, professional occupations" – the Conservatives registered a three-point swing from Labour. Within the 65-and-over age group, the Conservatives won 47% of the vote compared with Labour's 23%. With ABs the Tories captured 45% of the vote, and Labour 26%. In both cases a far greater margin than the overall election result (38% to 31%).
>
> Meanwhile, Labour were only able to achieve a substantial swing in their favour among young people – registering a 7.5 point swing from the Tories among 18- to 24-year-olds, and a four point swing among 25- to 34-year-olds – and renters.
>
> Labour only had a clear lead over the Conservatives among 18- to 34-year-olds, voters in social class DE (the 'semi-skilled and unskilled manual occupations, unemployed and lowest grade occupations'), among private and social renters, and black, Asian and minority ethnic (BAME) voters.
>
> But among all these groups, turnout was lower than the overall level of voter turnout (66%).

Using the source, evaluate the view that age was the most important factor in determining the outcome of the 2015 general election.

In your response you must:
- *compare and contrast the different opinions in the source*
- *examine and debate these views in a balanced way*
- *analyse and evaluate only the information presented in the source.*

(30 marks)

2 Evaluate the extent to which a pressure group's access to resources is the most important factor in determining its level of influence.

You must consider this view and the alternative to this view in a balanced way.

(30 marks)

Allow about 45 minutes for planning and writing your answer to this question.

Do not start writing straight away. Take 5–10 minutes to read through the source carefully, annotating it with comments, which may form part of your answer. If it is a piece of data, for example, jot down any trends that you notice.

You will be assessed on AO1 (10 marks), AO2 (10 marks) and AO3 (10 marks) skills.

All the points you develop **must** originate from the source.

Your answer must include analysis, evaluation and reach a well-argued judgement.

You will be assessed on AO1 (10 marks), AO2 (10 marks) and AO3 (10 marks) skills.

You need to make connections between relevant areas of politics drawn from across the specification.

A Level exam-style practice 2, Paper 2

Practise for **Paper 2, Section A** (UK Government) of your A Level exam with these exam-style questions. There are answers on pages 309–310. You must answer **two** questions from Section A and one from Section B (see pages 123, 132, 141, 151, 161 and 162 for more on Section B).

Section A

1 *This source is taken from the Parliament.uk website, December 2010.*
It offers a variety of views on House of Lords reform.

> **Lords reform options: pros and cons**
> Some of the potential positions on the options for reform are:
>
> **Fully appointed**
> A fully appointed House would remove the remainder of the hereditary peers leaving just the appointed Lords
>
> **Supporters say**
> It will help maintain the current broad range of membership of the Lords. Would Lord Sugar or Baroness Grey-Thompson stand for election?
> It doesn't threaten the democratic supremacy of the Commons.
> Appointment is more cost effective than election.
>
> **Opponents say**
> It's undemocratic to have unelected Members of the Lords involved in passing legislation.
> The UK is the only country, other than Canada, that has an unelected second chamber.
> A more democratic system is worth investing in.
>
> **Fully elected**
> Members would have to win their place through an election.
>
> **Supporters say**
> It addresses the democratic deficit, giving the Lords a full mandate to initiate and amend legislation.
> More people will be given the opportunity to stand for Parliament, giving a greater range of representation.
> More young people will sit in the Lords.
>
> **Opponents say**
> It causes more problems than it solves: with two elected chambers, the Commons would no longer be supreme.
> The chamber would be full of professional politicians rather than attracting individuals with knowledge and experience in a vast range of fields.
> It isn't clear how often elections should be and any additional costs.
>
> **Hybrid**
> A mixture of elected and appointed Members of the Lords
>
> **Supporters say**
> It combines the best of both systems: addressing the democratic deficit while retaining individuals with expertise and experience in valuable fields.
> The Commons would retain its democratic supremacy.
> It would be a more straightforward system to introduce.
>
> **Opponents say**
> It is undemocratic to retain any unelected Members of the Lords.
> It will create a two-tier Lords with elected and non-elected Members causing friction.
> The system would cause additional confusion as to where power does and should lie.

Using the source, evaluate the view that the Lords should remain an unelected house.

In your response you must:
* *compare and contrast the different opinions in the source*
* *examine and debate these views in a balanced way*
* *analyse and evaluate **only** the information presented in the source.*

(30 marks)

2 Evaluate how far the concept of ministerial responsibility remains an important feature in UK government.
In your answer you should draw on relevant knowledge and understanding of the study of Component 1: UK Politics and Core Political Ideas and consider this view and the alternative to this view in a balanced way.

(30 marks)

Read the source carefully. All the points you develop **must** originate from the source.

You need to show in-depth knowledge and understanding, as well as perceptive comparative analysis, with a fully substantiated argument leading to a focused and justified conclusion.

Your answer should be properly structured with an introduction and a conclusion.

You will be assessed on AO1 (10 marks), AO2 (10 marks) and AO3 (10 marks) skills.

Make sure you include examples in your answer.

You must draw on your knowledge from Component 1: UK Politics **and** Core Political Ideas (see pages 1–65) in your answer.

Rejection of the state

A core principle of anarchism is the rejection of the **state**. Anarchists maintain that the state has to be abolished because it is unnecessary and/or evil and corrupting. All forms of authority based on hierarchy, such as the Church and capitalism, have to be removed.

Aspects of the state

Government
A system of rule, from monarchism to dictatorship to liberal democracy, based on deceit and violence.

The state

Authority
The right of one person or institution to influence the behaviour of others.

Power
The instruments (the law, the police, the use of ideology) by which the state and other social institutions secure their authority.

Anarchist views of the state

The state is immoral: it restricts liberty and is oppressive. It therefore denies that people are rational sovereign individuals.

Power of the state must be resisted: power cannot be exercised by one person over another because individuals only exercise power over themselves.

Political participation: democratic government is based on deceit, supported by the threat of violence. Democratic voting is a fraud designed to deceive people into thinking they are decision-makers, while encouraging conformism and obedience to the ruling elite.

How the state can be overthrown

Anarchists do not all agree on the means of overthrowing the state. Examples include:

- **Direct action**: non-payment of taxes, non-compliance with conscription orders and the mass strike, to bring about a revolution (endorsed by Mikhail Bakunin; see page 122 for a more detailed look at anarchist key thinkers).

- **Establishing a moral society**: education would create 'perfect' humans who could be relied on to exercise their private judgement well. This would make the state irrelevant and it would wither away (endorsed by 18th-century anarchist philosopher William Godwin).

- **Peaceful and gradual abolition of the state**: achieved through a democratic political process as anarchist ideas gained in popularity. People would vote to dismantle the state (endorsed by Pierre-Joseph Proudhon; see page 122).

- **Withdrawing from society to become an autonomous individual**: the state would have no relevance for, or hold over, a person (endorsed by 19th-century anarchist thinker Henry Thoreau).

Application

Human nature

The state must be rejected due to its impact on human nature. It is:

- **Commanding**: the state can coerce a person to act against their will, forcing the individual to suspend their reason and removing their **autonomy**.

- **Controlling**: authority control suppresses initiative and creativity and stifles individual self-realisation.

- **Corrupting**: those with authority lose contact with their 'true' human nature (collaborative and altruistic) because of their wealth, power and status.

- **Corrupting**: the state abuses those under its authority because of its defence of inequality and reliance on force to impose its will.

The economy

Anarchists argue that the state is unjust and exploitative in its defence of economic inequality.

Anarcho-individualists (see page 121 for more on this strain of anarchism): taxation is no more than state 'robbery' imposed by the veiled threat of force.

Anarcho-collectivists (see page 119 to read about collectivist anarchism): globally, the state protects the elites of industrially developed countries through institutions such as the G20 and World Bank.

Anarcho-collectivists: the state protects private property and the privileged position of the wealthy.

Now try this

On what grounds do anarchists reject the state?

Liberty and order

Liberty and order are regarded as important features of a stateless society and both are linked to a positive view of human nature.

Liberty

For anarchists, liberty is incompatible with any form of political authority in the state, society or economy. Liberty is critical to human nature. It is freedom for individuals to pursue their own best interests and freedom from state control.

Order

Most anarchists want to establish an ordered society, or look forward to its natural development, because order promotes freedom and security. The capitalist state encourages disorder because those oppressed by the ruling class will try to topple it.

Liberty and human nature

The anarchist perspective on liberty draws on liberal and socialist concepts of freedom and human nature.

Individualist anarchists argue that humans are rational, autonomous, competitive and self-interested individuals.

As all forms of authority are:
- commanding, a person cannot engage in autonomous and rational decision-making
- controlling, a person is deprived of the freedom to explore their individuality.

People therefore have to be freed from the control exerted by hierarchical authority.

Collectivist anarchists maintain the state prevents humans from being unselfish and collaborative. A person can only be really free when everyone is free to fulfil their potential. So, liberty only exists if equality is present. People then treat each other equally, enjoy economic equality and contribute equally to workplace or community decision-making. Thus freedom is attained by toppling the class-based, hierarchical society with its socio-economic inequalities.

Society and social order

Social order occurs naturally and spontaneously, based on rational, social and cooperative human nature. An anarchist society would:
- not contain a centralised controlling body, any official hierarchical authority or coercive agencies to enforce laws
- be based on some type of decentralised association of independent self-governing districts, where free and equal individuals would cooperate voluntarily and participate directly in decision-making.

Differing views on liberty and order

Anarchist views on liberty and order differ according to their position on the individualist–collectivist spectrum.

Liberty	Order
Anarcho-individualists such as Stirner (see page 122 to read about anarchist key thinkers) advocate unrestrained, individual liberty free from all constraints, with some voluntary associations but only for their own personal interest.	**Anarcho-individualism**: individuals should act freely without legal, political, social, moral or religious constraints. A stateless society will promote rationalism, autonomy and self-interest to guarantee social order.
Anarcho-communists such as Kropotkin (see page 122) argue that liberty is absolute, but that freedom is achieved through mutually supportive communities. Members attain individual liberty by sharing concepts of natural law, making imposed laws redundant.	**Anarcho-communism**: the divisive nature of capitalism undermines human **altruism**. Common ownership and mutualism encourage cooperative **altruistic** behaviour, which maintains natural order.
Mutualist Proudhon (see page 122) sought to balance individualism and collectivism to create a condition of complete liberty.	**Anarcho-capitalism**: the free market will enable competitive, rational, self-interested individuals to make decisions in their own best interests, establishing natural order.

Now try this

How does anarchism's view of human nature underpin the anarchist perspective on liberty?

Economic freedom and utopianism

Economic freedom and utopianism are linked to anarchism's positive view of human nature and its hostility to the state.

Economic freedom

Anarchists advocate economic freedom so that people can conduct their economic affairs **autonomously** without state ownership, regulation or intervention. This position, based on the anarchist rejection of the state, means opposing all existing forms of capitalism and state socialism. For example, the USA, UK, China or North Korea.

Utopianism

This is a set of political beliefs that creates a model of an ideal or perfect future society. Anarchists use utopianism to develop a critical analysis of existing society. For anarchists, the utopian society rests on a **positive view** of human nature and its potential for development. The key features of this perfect society will be peace, harmony, order and complete freedom.

Anarchist objections and solutions to capitalist and state socialist economies

	Capitalist economy	State socialist economy
Collectivist anarchist (Proudhon, Kropotkin and Bakunin)	**Objection**: capitalism is based on inequality, exploitation and private property. It uses the state to protect the privileged and oppress the masses so real freedom cannot exist. **Solution**: replace capitalism, especially private ownership with collective ownership or **mutualism** (see page 120 for an in-depth look at mutualism) to encourage human altruism, and develop liberty and natural order.	**Objection**: under state socialism, the state has become the exploiting power over the masses, simply replacing the capitalist ruling elite, so no real freedom exists. **Solution**: replace state socialism with genuine collective ownership or mutualism to encourage human altruism and develop liberty and natural order.
Anarcho-capitalist (Murray Rothbard, David Friedman)	**Objection**: state intervention in the economy restricts competition, choice and liberty by skewing the market and creating public and private monopolies. **Solution**: remove the state to allow an entirely free competitive market (including private property). Rational, autonomous and self-interested individuals can then make judgements in their own best interests, creating natural order.	**Objection**: the reliance on state planning and state ownership of production rejects property rights and liberty. **Solution**: replace state socialism with a wholly free competitive market (including private property) since individuals can experience economic freedom only through free competition with no outside interference.

Anarchist utopianism

Collectivist anarchists propose removing capitalism. Common ownership, economic equality and **mutual aid** will foster altruism.

Individualist anarchists call for the removal of the state, with no social or economic organisations, to allow autonomy to flourish.

Anarcho-capitalists propose a stateless society based on 'natural' and unregulated economic competition, including the pursuit of property.

Criticisms

👎 The perfect anarchist **stateless society** is **unachievable** – no anarchist social order has been created to date. Anarchists point to anarchist initiatives. For example the Zapatista uprising (Mexico, 1994) and during the Spanish Civil War.

👎 Anarchist utopianism is **unrealistic**. It relies on an over-optimistic view of **human nature**. People are selfish and competitive, so an anarchist **society** and **economy** would be dominated by the wealthy, powerful and ruthless. Anarchists assert that, without state involvement, humans have the potential to act collectively and altruistically. For example, the Occupy movement – an international socio-political movement.

Now try this

Why do anarchists oppose capitalism?

Collectivist anarchism: anarcho-communism

Anarchists agree on many things, such as the rejection of the state, but they also have some key differences. Collective anarchism is associated with Bakunin and anarcho-communism with Kropotkin (see page 122 for more on anarchist thinkers).

What is collectivist anarchism?

Collectivist anarchism asserts the superiority of the collective. It calls for the abolition of the state, where common ownership will promote the rational, altruistic and cooperative aspects of human nature. This is closely linked to socialism. Collectivist anarchism is divided into three sub-strands: **1** Anarcho-communism, **2** Mutualism and **3** Anarcho-syndicalism (see page 115 for more on these latter two strands).

What is anarcho-communism?

Anarcho-communism advocates full communism in the pursuit of liberty, economic freedom and natural order. An anarcho-communist society would be based on human cooperation and solidarity, freely formed small-scale autonomous communities, direct democracy, common ownership of the wealth produced and economic equality.

Application

	Collectivist anarchism	Anarcho-communism
Human nature	'True' human nature is sociable, cooperative and altruistic. Relationships are naturally based on mutual assistance, social unity and harmony.	Anarcho-communists, such as Kropotkin, reject the view that people are self-seeking and competitive. Instead, they argue that humans are naturally empathetic, sociable and cooperative.
The state	The state has to be abolished/overthrown as it rules through coercion and deception, defends capitalist economic inequalities and has a negative impact on human nature. Most collectivist anarchists call for revolutionary action.	Humans are capable of peaceful and harmonious self-government and therefore do not need to be subjected to state control. People would practise mutual aid (cooperation not competition).
Society	Society would be organised into voluntary communities of producers and consumers. These would be responsible for the production and distribution of goods.	Anarcho-communist communities would make decisions collectively using a localised form of direct democracy to reflect the wishes of a specific community.
Economy	Capitalism has to be destroyed and replaced with more collective and equal economic arrangements. Private property would be abolished and land and the means of production collectively owned. The individual would own the products of their labour. The sub-strands of collectivist anarchism differ in their approach to the economy, but all stress the importance of self-sufficiency and cooperation.	Capitalism and private property are rejected because of the oppression and inequality they create. Instead, all land, means of production and wealth would be held under common ownership by communities. This leads to the principle of 'from each according to their ability, to each according to their need', reinforcing the human capacity for cooperation and altruism.

Key disagreements

1 **Marxists** argue that, post-revolution, a temporary socialist state should protect the gains of the revolution and prepare the way for stateless communism. **Collectivist anarchists** maintain that all forms of the state are immoral, unjust, coercive, controlling and corrupting.

2 **Collectivist anarchists** disagree with **individualist anarchists** on two key points:
- They reject the view that social and economic problems can be remedied by the individual or the free market.
- They also regard revolution as the only way to overthrow authority – the state and private property.

 Now try this

In what ways is collectivist anarchism similar to, and different from, socialism? (Look back at pages 57–65 to remind yourself about socialism.)

Mutualism and anarcho-syndicalism

Mutualism and anarcho-syndicalism are also types of collectivist anarchism. Anarcho-syndicalism has been able, in certain circumstances, to attract temporary mass support.

What is mutualism?

Mutualism (sometimes known as 'contractualism') is a more moderate sub-strand of collectivist anarchism, based on the ideas of Proudhon (read about him and other anarchist thinkers on page 122). It provides a link between collectivist and individualist anarchism. Under mutualism, self-governing producers (either individuals or groups) reject profiteering and exploitation, and exchange goods and services equitably and fairly. Mutualism opposes large-scale property ownership (because it leads to exploitation and inequality) but allows small-scale private property based on use or possession.

What is anarcho-syndicalism?

Anarcho-syndicalism is based on the work of Georges Sorel (1847–1922), an important French syndicalist theorist. Anarcho-syndicalists argue that **trade unions** are the vehicle for revolutionary change. As democratic, voluntary organisations, trade unions would form the basis of a stateless, free, stable and classless anarchist society. Anarcho-syndicalism attracted notable support during the Spanish Civil War (1936–1939).

Application

	Mutualism	Anarcho-syndicalism
Human nature	Offers a positive view of human nature. Humans are characterised by their productive abilities and creativity as producers. They are seen as cooperative with a firm belief in social solidarity.	Has a positive view of human nature, but places greater emphasis on people's capacity for social solidarity, and regards work and creativity as essential to human existence. People with similar occupations naturally join together in associations.
Society	People would be bound together in small communities or associations by mutually beneficial economic and social relations. These would be based on possession, ensuring producers are entitled to the products of their labour and have the necessary means (land or tools) for work.	This would resemble trade union organisations since groups of workers with similar jobs would form self-governing federations. This occupational solidarity would guarantee a stateless ordered society.
The state	The state is oppressive and must be peacefully abolished through a democratic process as mutualist ideas become more popular. Mutualist communities would form a federation and operate a bottom-up political system, based on voluntary agreements and free from central authority.	They argue that both the state and capitalism are oppressive. By using the weapon of the general strike, together with mass demonstrations and acts of violence, the workers would destroy the state.
Economy	An economic system with individuals and small worker associations engaging in mutually beneficial exchange based on contracts freely entered into. Workers would receive the 'true value' of what they produced based on labour input. A non-profit People's Bank would make credit available to the associations.	The self-governing workers' federations would become the owners of their own means of production and engage in the mutually beneficial exchange of goods and services, based on the real value of the labour it took to make them.

Now try this

What are the main differences between mutualism and anarcho-syndicalism?

Individualist anarchism

Individualist anarchism first emerged in America and Europe almost 200 years ago.

What is individualist anarchism?

It is on the libertarian right of the political spectrum, taking classical liberalism to an extreme end point. Individualist anarchists view society as a loose grouping of separate autonomous individuals. To protect this personal autonomy, the state has to be abolished. Freed from restrictions such as taxes, individuals will behave rationally, working together voluntarily to settle disagreements via reason rather than conflict. This approach would establish natural order and a stable, harmonious society. Two important sub-strands of individualist anarchism are **egoism** and **anarcho-capitalism**.

Differences with collectivist anarchism

Collectivism	Individualist anarchism
Suppresses individuality and personal autonomy by forcing people to belong to a community and relinquish private property.	Endorses **private property** and the pursuit of free economic **competition** to safeguard **individual autonomy**.
Revolutionary violence flouts personal autonomy and individuality due to the forcible seizure of property.	Calls for the **gradual** replacement of the state through education, non-violent protest and grassroots 'takeover' organisations.

Application

	Egoism	Anarcho-capitalism
	Associated with Max Stirner (see page 122 for more on anarchist thinkers), it is the most radical form of individualist anarchism.	Appeared in the 1970s–1980s, championed by economists Murray Rothbard and David Friedman.
Human nature	Humans are self-interested, lack morality and want total personal autonomy. They are driven by egoism and should act in any way they see fit without restriction. Nihilism (the most extreme form of egoism) sees humans as naturally individualistic, not sociable.	Humans are rational, competitive, autonomous and economic. An innate sense of entitlement motivates them to work to acquire private property. People naturally act in a self-interested way and engage in free, self-serving economic relationships.
The state	The revolutionary overthrow of the state is necessary because state control and coercion limit individualism and personal autonomy. Individuals should reject social conventions, laws and religious principles.	The state has to be removed and its functions taken over by the free market. State intervention threatens economic freedom and competition. State taxation violates the right to private property and represents a form of institutionalised theft.
Society	Organised society is incompatible with individualism and personal autonomy. Nevertheless, egoism argues that rational, self-interested individuals would form voluntary 'unions of egoists' when they needed to make agreements or cooperate, in order to benefit themselves. These would not constitute a real society.	Anarcho-capitalists envisage a competitive society where the wealthy benefit most. But free competition would establish social balance and stability because people have an obvious interest in avoiding disorder. Important services (such as education and health) would be provided by the free market.
Economy	Egoism rejects capitalism because employees are exploited and alienated. Free individuals would reap the full benefits of work and trade with each other based on the pursuit of rational self-interest. The accumulation of property would be a key feature since humans naturally desire possessions.	An unregulated free-market capitalist economy is needed for economic growth and innovation. It is the most effective mechanism to supply and distribute goods, services and private property. It provides competition, keeps prices low and quality high, and responds to consumer demand.

Now try this

How do individualist and collectivist anarchists differ over human nature?

Anarchist key thinkers

This section looks at how anarchist key thinkers have shaped the idea of the different strands within anarchism.

Key thinkers and ideas

Max Stirner (1806–1856)

Stirner was the leading figure in the **egoist** sub-strand of individualist anarchism (see page 121 to find out more about this strand).

Key ideas

1. **The ego**: the rational and self-interested individual takes precedence over everything else.

2. **The Union of Egoists**: a new society will be created by **insurrection**, not the overthrow of the state.

Uses

Stirner can be used when discussing liberty, egoism, human nature, the state and society.

Key thinkers and ideas

Pierre-Joseph Proudhon (1809–1865)

The work of Proudhon provided an important link between individualist and collectivist anarchism.

Key ideas

1. **Opposition to private property and collectivism**: these should be replaced by mutualism.

2. **Rejection and overthrow of the state**: the immoral state should be **rejected** and removed but by peaceful means.

Uses

Proudhon can be used when discussing mutualism, the economy, society and the state.

Key thinkers and ideas

Mikhail Bakunin (1814–1876)

Bakunin was an important founding figure in collectivist anarchism, an uncompromising opponent of capitalism, private property, religion and the state.

Key ideas

1. **Humans are naturally sociable**: private property should be abolished and replaced with collectivisation.

 2. **Propaganda by the deed**: this is needed to trigger a revolution and abolish the oppressive state.

Uses

Bakunin can be used when discussing collective anarchism, human nature, the economy, society and the state.

Key thinkers and ideas

Peter Kropotkin (1842–1921)

A key theorist in the anarcho-communist movement, Kropotkin used a scientific approach to support his arguments in *Mutual Aid: A Factor of Evolution* (1902).

Key ideas

1. **Mutual aid** is based on a scientific approach and allows human nature to flourish.

2. **Revolution** is needed to replace the state and private property with a utopian future society.

Uses

Kropotkin can be used when discussing anarcho-communism, human nature, the economy, society and the state.

Key thinkers and ideas

Emma Goldman (1869–1940)

Goldman advocated communal individuality which attempted to fuse elements of individualist and collectivist anarchism.

Key ideas

1. **The state is a cold monster**: it is immoral and should therefore be rejected.

2. **Revolution is essential**: political participation in the state and society by men and women is both futile and corrupting.

Uses

Goldman can be used when discussing the state and society.

Now try this

How far do Goldman's and Proudhon's views on the state overlap?

Exam skills

This question will help you to revise for **Section B** of your A Level **Paper 2** exam. You will be given two 24-mark essay questions for each political idea – you will need to choose **one** from your chosen idea.

Section B

- You should aim to spend around 30 minutes on this essay.
- Your essay needs to be fully structured, including an introduction and a conclusion.
- You **must** use at least **two** relevant key thinkers as outlined in the relevant section of the specification.

Questions

Questions will explore the extent of agreement within anarchism **or** tensions within the different strands over one of the four key areas (the state, society, the economy and human nature). The command words for the questions are always '**To what extent**'. You need to cover all three AOs, which are equally weighted:

- set out the nature of the debate on both sides – show you understand how the content relates to the question (AO1)
- examine the ideology/strands in relation to the question – this also means showing similarities and differences within the strands (AO2)
- make judgements – explore (evaluate) the extent of the similarities and differences and come to a judgement (AO3). This should be clear throughout your essay, not just in the conclusion.

Worked example

3 To what extent do collectivist anarchists and individualist anarchists agree about the nature of future society?

You must use appropriate thinkers you have studied to support your answer and consider both sides in a balanced way.   **(24 marks)**

Collectivist and individualist anarchists agree about the nature of future society in two ways. First, both call for future society to be stateless as they believe the state is oppressive and undermines individual sovereignty. Second, nearly all anarchists seek to establish an ordered society or wait for it to emerge spontaneously. However, there are also divisions regarding the nature of future society. Collectivist anarchists wish to create a natural stateless society. In contrast, individualist anarchists maintain that social organisation threatens the individual. These disagreements outweigh any consensus on future society...

... Unlike collectivist anarchists, who stress the communal, sociable and altruistic nature of future society, egoists (uncompromising individualist anarchists) maintain that any organised society is incompatible with individualism and personal autonomy. According to Stirner in *The Ego and His Own* (1845), since the essence of human nature is the self-interested ego, each individual should be free from all constraints and able to use other people for their own purposes. Nevertheless, Stirner also argues that humans, being rational and self-interested, will form voluntary 'unions of egoists' to make agreements or cooperate to benefit themselves. Such unions, however, will not threaten individual liberty or constitute a real society. By rejecting collectivism and human sociability, egoists are significantly at odds with collectivist anarchists regarding the nature of future society...

...Collectivist and individualist anarchists agree future society should be stateless and naturally ordered to promote freedom and security, but fundamental disagreements exist. Collective anarchists see future society as a decentralised entity of voluntary communities organising production and distribution in the common interest. In contrast, individualist anarchists distance themselves from collectivism, sociability and altruism. Egoists maintain the individual has to be free from all restrictions and constraints and nihilists believe humans are not sociable creatures. Lastly, anarcho-capitalists envisage a competitive capitalist society of self-interested rational individuals. As such, the disagreements between the two anarchist strands over the nature of future society clearly outweigh any consensus.

The introduction identifies the areas of agreement and disagreement.

The final sentence hints at how the student will argue and sets up the essay.

Correct use of political vocabulary.

Correct use of one key thinker to explain the egoist position. Use Kropotkin or Bakunin to consider collectivist anarchism.

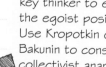

Next explain further the areas of agreement, identify disagreements between collectivist anarchists and egoists, and differences between anarcho-capitalists and collectivist anarchists, before coming to a final judgement.

Ecology and holism

Ecology and **holism** are two core ideas and principles that challenge the human-centred thinking of traditional ideas like conservatism, socialism and liberalism (see pages 36–65 for more on these key ideologies).

Ecology

- In political terms, the message from ecology is that all living and non-living parts of nature are interdependent, interrelated and need to co-exist in harmony to maintain the natural balance of the Earth.
- This is a direct challenge to the anthropocentrism of the traditional political ideologies, although the lessons of ecology are applied differently by **deep** and **shallow greens** (see pages 127–128).

Anthropocentrism	Enlightened anthropocentrism	Ecocentrism
Traditional ideas have viewed humankind as the master of nature. Nature only has value as a resource to be exploited by current society; it is this view that is fuelling ecological disaster.	**Shallow greens** argue that nature has more value than just as a resource. Nature should be protected to support present and future generations, making humanity the steward of nature.	**Deep greens** see humanity as neither master nor steward of nature, but just one species among many. It is a nature-centred approach, aiming to maintain ecological balance, not human goals.

Holism

- Holism is closely linked to ecology, as it challenges the **mechanistic world view** of post-Enlightenment science that nature can be viewed as a machine, whose parts can be studied, fixed or replaced in isolation (read about Merchant on page 131).
- Holism sees nature as deeply complex, interdependent and each part can only be understood through its relationship to the whole (see Carson on page 131).

Deep and shallow greens have different views on holism:

Limited holism

Shallow greens:
- argue that humanity should only intervene in nature with caution as all life is connected
- focus on environmental issues, such as resource depletion, individually
- look for ways to reduce humanity's impact on nature for current and future generations.

Deep greens:
- argue for a more radical view that sees all ecological issues as related
- so tackling each issue separately will lead to failure
- instead, a radical change is needed in humanity's understanding of its relationship to nature.

Radical holism

Application

Human nature

Ecologists argue that human nature has become separated from wider nature, through the **anthropocentric** belief that humanity is above and separate from nature. There needs to be a change to recognise that human nature is interdependent and interrelated with wider nature.

- For **shallow greens**, humanity's survival is dependent on respecting and protecting nature – enlightened anthropocentrism.
- For **deep greens**, this means a radical inner revolution within human nature (study Leopold on page 131) to challenge the mechanistic world view and to recognise the individual's deep connection to nature, leading to an **ecocentric** world view.

Society

Social ecology opposes both anthropocentrism and ecocentrism. It argues that only a radical change in society to end oppression, such as sexism, racism and capitalist exploitation, can allow for a new society to emerge that would have a harmonious relationship with nature.

Bookchin (see page 131) attacked the idea that he must choose between anthropocentrism and ecocentrism. He sees anthropocentrism as the domination of nature and ecocentrism as saying humans and non-humans both deserve equal consideration, and so both ideas are flawed.

Now try this

How does enlightened anthropocentrism differ from ecocentrism?

Environmental ethics and consciousness

The core principles of environmental ethics and **environmental consciousness** challenge the traditional moral framework of society and human nature's relationship to wider nature.

Environmental ethics

Within traditional political ideas, **ethics** (the moral principles that govern behaviour) are anthropocentric (see page 124 to read about anthropocentric beliefs). Green thinking has been developing new moral standards and values for human relations in three ways:

1 **Intergenerational equity:** shallow green ecologism gives rights to future generations, meaning that currrent economic development must not stop future generations meeting their own needs. This still views nature in terms of its value to humanity.

2 **Animal rights:** extends rights to animals. Moral philosopher Peter Singer argues that rights should be extended as animals are able to feel pain. Tom Regan (moral philosopher) believes animals have rights as they are 'subjects of a life', where what happens to them matters to them.

3 **Holistic ethics:** far more radical and associated with deep green ecologism. This extends right to life much further to include all living organisms as well as non-living nature such as the land, water and ecosystems. This is **biocentric equality** (see Leopold, page 131).

Environmental consciousness

Within deep ecology, it has been argued by some that extending the moral community is the wrong approach. The key is a paradigm shift (fundamental change) in how individuals see the self and the world, brought about by a radical transformation in human nature to create an environmental consciousness. This consciousness will come from a deep identification of the self with nature and lead to individuals living in harmony with nature as it will allow them to reach spiritual fulfilment.

This idea has drawn heavily on eastern mysticism, and in particular Zen Buddhism and the interconnectedness and unity of all things. This consciousness will act as the basis for a new form of society, state and economy.

Application

Society

- Shallow greens argue for the principle of intergenerational equity as they see that the emission of greenhouse gases today will have a far bigger impact in the future. Some greens have extended the moral community to include animals.

- Holistic ethics would extend intrinsic value to all living and non-living nature.

Human nature

Some deep greens, arguing for environmental consciousness, are really arguing that only a change in human nature, not the extending of ethics, can change the state, society and economy to tackle the ecological problems.

Leopold (see page 131) extended the moral community to include 'soils, waters, plants, and animals, or collectively: the Land'. This idea of **biocentric equality** means all living and non-living nature has intrinsic value – value in its own right, irrespective of its value to humanity. Any action is only right where it preserves the integrity, stability and beauty of the biotic community.

The economy

Bookchin (see page 131) dismisses this debate as irrelevant and sees environmental consciousness as 'eco-la-la'. He focuses on replacing the capitalist economy and the state with a society in which people live in harmony with each other and with nature.

Now try this

How has ecologism moved beyond traditional ethical thinking?

Materialism, consumerism, sustainability

The core principles of post-materialism, anti-consumerism and sustainability offer challenges to traditional approaches to economic thinking and society. Sustainability in particular raises the issue of the role of the state in tackling the ecological crisis.

Post-materialism and anti-consumerism

Materialism	Consumerism	Environmental degradation

... links happiness to the consumption of material goods

... increasing consumption is good for the economy and the individual, so consumerism keeps creating new needs

... increasing consumption drives the production of goods, resource depletion and pollution

Green thinking opposes materialism and consumerism, wishing to break the link between consumption and human happiness.

- For **shallow greens**, this involves a commitment to developing a more environmentally sound and technologically smart capitalism so society can still do more but with less (see page 128).
- For **deep greens**, there must a radical transformation in human nature to value quality of life over quantity of goods so society does less with less (see Schumacher and other key thinkers on page 131).

Sustainability

Sustainability is the capacity of the Earth to maintain its health over time. Ecologists argue that:

- mass production, faith in technology and limitless growth of industrialism, supported by traditional political ideas is unsustainable
- there are limits to growth as the Earth's resources are finite.

Green thinking is very divided on what sustainability means:

Weak sustainability

Shallow greens:
- Growth should meet the needs of the present and future generations.
- Natural capital (Earth's resources) can be used up to create manufactured capital (infrastructure).
- Strong belief in technological solutions to environmental problems.

Deep greens:
- Opposes economic growth, materialism and consumerism.
- Natural capital should be preserved.
- Living economies that work well within the limits of the Earth.
- Technology cannot solve all environmental problems – radical change is needed.

Strong sustainability

Application

The economy and state

Shallow greens believe this can be achieved by the **state** intervening in the economy through managerialism or withdrawing from the economy, allowing for market-based solutions – green **capitalism**. In either solution, there is strong belief in technology as a basis for sustainability.

Schumacher (page 131) argues for a total break from materialism and consumption. He advocates a new form of Buddhist economics based on right livelihood – creating well-being from creative work and minimum of consumption. Leopold (page 131) argues economics has no satisfactory way of handling concepts like wilderness, beauty or land health.

The state, economy, human nature

For deep greens and social ecology, the **state** and existing **economies** are part of the problem not the solution. This involves a paradigm shift away from the false **human nature** created by consumerism and materialism to ecocentrism, radical holism and a zero growth an economy.

Society

In social ecology, the solution lies in radical change to **society** and its social structures – overthrowing capitalism for ecosocialists, overthrowing the state and hierarchy for ecoanarchists and overthrowing patriarchy for ecofeminists (see page 129).

Now try this

Why do greens regard consumerism and materialism as key causes of environmental damage?

Deep green ecologism

Deep green thinking argues that ecological problems can only be tackled by a fundamental change in our relationship to nature, and in our social, political and economic life.

Deep green thinking

There are four key ideas that are central to deep green thinking:

Environmental consciousness: the move to ecocentrism is reliant on a paradigm shift in humanity's understanding of its relationship to nature.

Ecocentrism: the lessons from ecology are incompatible with any form of anthropocentrism. There needs to be a move to ecocentrism, where nature has intrinsic value, independent of any value placed on it by humankind.

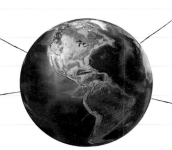

Strong sustainability: opposition to industrialism, consumerism and materials, and emphasis on zero-growth economies.

Ecology and holism: all things are interdependent and interrelated. Humanity is not distinct from or superior to any other part of nature, and a new world view is needed based on radical holism, not the mechanistic world view of post-Enlightenment science.

Application

Human nature

Consumerism, materialism and the mechanistic world view has changed human nature. It has created a view that humanity is both separate from and superior to nature, which only has value as a resource to be exploited for human gain. Deep greens argue for a paradigm shift in our understanding to an **ecocentric** world view to create 'a new kind of people' (Leopold), through:

- extending rights to the land, as Leopold argued, so there is **biocentric equality**, where all 'life', including rivers, landscapes and ecosystems, has intrinsic value, or

- a radical transformation to an **environmental consciousness**, where there is a deep identification of all individuals with 'life' – this view is closely associated with ethicist and philosopher Warwick Fox.

The state

Deep greens advocate decentralised societies (see Bookchin's thoughts on this on page 131). These are living democracies, which are local communities organised around bioregions (areas naturally defined around ecosystems), not states. Decisions will be taken locally so they are environmentally sound and socially responsible. The existing state structure is part of the problem, not the solution.

Society

Present human interference in nature is excessive and the situation is rapidly getting worse. Deep greens oppose the consumerism and materialism of society and wish to replace this with a society that focuses on life quality rather than an increased standard of living – so these will be zero-economic-growth societies. This future society will be based around **ecocentrism**.

The economy

Deep greens oppose industrialism and its belief in large-scale production, limitless growth and technological solutions, and support living economies. These economies will be based on **strong sustainability**, local production to meet vital needs using only a minimum of local resources. Work should be fair, creative and bring people close to the land so it increases life quality. This approach draws inspiration from the ideas of **Schumacher** (study Schumacher and other key thinkers on page 127).

Now try this

1 What is meant by the term 'ecocentrism'?
2 Define 'intrinsic value'.

Shallow green ecologism

Shallow green thinking argues that environmental problems can be solved by applying the lessons of ecology and holism but without any fundamental changes in the key values, modes of production or level of consumption of modern capitalist society.

Shallow green thinking

There are four key ideas that are central to shallow green thinking:

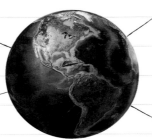

Weak sustainability: this involves economic growth but at a slower pace and using technology to limit the impact of growth on sustainability.

Stewards of nature: a commitment to intergenerational equity to meet 'the needs of the present without compromising the ability of future generations to meet their own needs' (Brundtland Report, 1987). This places humans as the steward of nature, not its master.

Enlightened anthropocentrism: accept the lessons of ecology and holism and adopt enlightened anthropocentrism and limited holism.

Limits to growth: there are limits to growth as the Earth is finite, so resource depletion and pollution threatens the possibility of continued economic growth and increasing standards of living.

Application

Human nature

Shallow greens accept the lessons of ecology and holism (see Carson's ideas on this on page 131) to argue that humanity needs to adopt a principle of **enlightened anthropocentrism**. The individual has an obligation to protect nature in order to promote the well-being of both the current generation and future generations. For some shallow greens, this can involve an obligation to take into account the well-being of animals, as argued by Regan and Singer (see page 125 to read about environmental ethics).

The state

Many shallow greens see a growing and vital role for the state in adopting a managerialist approach. Managerialism uses green taxes to encourage businesses to operate in a more environmentally friendly way, as well as environmental regulations and targets to limit environmental impact such as the UN Framework Convention on Climate Change and the Climate Change Act of 2008 in the UK. Others argue for a limited role for the state and stress market-based solutions.

Society

Present human interference in nature is damaging and the situation is getting worse. Shallow greens want a society based on **limited holism** and **enlightened anthropocentrism** (see page 124) that looks to limit the impact of humanity on nature. Society should place less emphasis on materialism and consumerism and focus more on quality of life, aiming for slower and environmentally smart economic growth driven by technological innovation.

The economy

Shallow greens argue for **weak sustainability**, where the economy will grow more slowly and in a more environmentally friendly way. This could be achieved in two ways:

1 Green taxes and regulations can be used to place a financial cost on companies for using finite resources or polluting – hopefully driving business to use new technologies to become more sustainable.

2 The market can deliver sustainability as ethical consumer spending and the rising cost of increasingly scarce resources, like oil, drive companies to adopt a more environmentally friendly approach, using more sustainable technologies, in order to make a profit.

Now try this

How do shallow greens disagree among themselves over the role of the state in the economy?

Social ecology

The current ecological crisis driven by the domination of nature by humanity can be linked to the oppression of human by human and sustainability can only be resolved through a process of radical social change.

Social ecology

All strands of social ecology argue that ecological disaster is caused by existing hierarchical structures in society based on the domination of human by human. The only way to achieve a society that is in harmony with nature is for radical social change to take place. This should aim to change how humans treat each other and build new societies based around the principles of ecology. There are three main strands to social ecology: eco-anarchism, ecosocialism and ecofeminism.

Eco-anarchism

> Lessons of ecology show that harmony and balance develop naturally.

- Criticises all forms of hierarchy and domination such as the state, sexism, racism and capitalism.
- Sees the key issue as the domination of human by human, leading to a domination over nature.
- Aims to overthrow the state, hierarchy and capitalism.
- Harmony and balance in society will develop from self-managing communes built around the principles of **decentralisation**, direct democracy and anarcho-communism (see page 114).
- Eco-anarchism is argued by **Bookchin** in his concept of ecotopia (see page 131 for more on Bookchin).

Ecosocialism

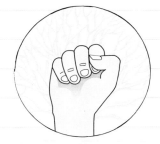

> Green capitalism is a myth.

- Capitalism requires exponential growth, which is unsustainable, and technology cannot save the Earth, as innovation is driven by profit not the needs of the environment.
- The concept of private property makes humanity see nature as property to be owned and used.
- It leads to commodification, where nature only has value as an economic resource to be bought and sold.
- Capitalism should be overthrown to be replaced by socialism built around collective ownership.
- Sociologist **John Bellamy Foster** argues an environmental proletariat suffering ecological and economic oppression will overthrow capitalism.

Ecofeminism

> Sees the domination of women through patriarchy as causing the domination of nature by humanity.

- Prior to the Enlightenment, nature was female, living and nurturing.
- In the Scientific Revolution, nature remained female but was seen as inert and a resource to be exploited.
- So the mechanistic world view must be overthrown.
- The new society needs to be post-patriarchal and nature should no longer be seen in gender terms.
- This new holistic society will be a partnership of nature and humanity, as **Merchant** argues (see page 131 for an overview of ecologist key thinkers).
- Ecofeminism in India: 111 trees are planted for every baby girl born in the village of Piplantri.

Now try this

1 What unites eco-anarchism, ecosocialism and ecofeminism?
2 In what ways does the future society of eco-anarchism look like the future society of deep greens?

Agreement and tensions within ecologism

This section looks at the extent to which ecologism has more that unites it than divides it.

Key areas of agreement

Ecology and holism

The lessons of ecology and holism must be applied to tackle the ecological crisis.

Traditional ethics

Humans and society must change their ethical framework to live in harmony with nature so it maintains its natural balance, which is the basis for all life. This challenges the **anthropocentric** idea, which underpins the traditional ethics of society that humanity is the master of nature and nature is just an economic resource to be exploited.

Sustainability

Future society needs to be sustainable in order to be in harmony with nature so it can maintain its natural balance and health.

Industrialism

There are limits to growth and **industrialism** is a key cause of ecological destruction because it is built on the following principles:

- An anthropocentric view of the world.
- The commitment to the idea that unlimited growth is possible and desirable.
- Materialism and consumerism drive the idea that consumption is linked to happiness.
- A mechanistic world view based on the belief in science and technology to study, fix and repair elements of nature in isolation as if it was a machine.

Key areas of disagreement

	Shallow greens	Deep greens	Social ecology
Anthropo-centrism	Look to balance the lessons of ecology with anthropocentrism to reach a view of enlightened anthropocentrism and limited holism.	Reject the idea that the principles of ecology are compatible with anthropocentrism, adopting an ecocentric view and radical holism.	Rejects both anthropocentrism and ecocentrism.
Sustainability	See the future society as being based on weak sustainability.	Wish to build a future society based around strong sustainability.	Also emphasises strong sustainability.
Traditional ethics	Support intergenerational equity to extend rights to future generations while some extend rights to animals.	Argue for holistic ethics, where all living and non-living nature has intrinsic value, while some dark greens argue for a radical revolution in human nature to achieve an environmental consciousness.	Sees overthrowing the societal structures of oppression as the key to returning society and humans to way of life that is in harmony with nature.
Materialism	Emphasise quality of life, but do not completely break from materialism. Future society will aim to get richer but more slowly and in a more environmental way, by emphasising the role of technology and either the market or managerialism to deliver green growth.	Are totally opposed to materialism and consumerism, believing that the idea of green growth of shallow greens is part of the problem, not the solution. Deep greens emphasise life quality over increasing consumption.	Is in agreement with deep green thinking on materialism and consumerism.

Now try this

1. Define 'industrialism'.
2. Why might critics of deep greens regard their belief in holistic ethics and environmental consciousness as unrealistic?

Ecologist key thinkers

Key thinkers and ideas

Aldo Leopold (1887–1948)

Leopold's ideas are crucial to the development of deep green ecologism and can be used to discuss ecology, environmental consciousness and environmental ethics.

Key ideas

1 *The Land Ethic* **(1949)**: extends the right to life to the environment as a whole. This biocentric equality is the ethical basis for a new form of society and economy.

2 **Conservation fails**: traditional economic models are unable to protect and value beauty, biodiversity or the wilderness. A land ethic attitude to nature is needed to radically alter the state and society and move to a new human–land relationship.

Key thinkers and ideas

Rachel Carson (1907–1964)

In *Silent Spring* (1962), Carson used ideas of ecology and criticism of anthropocentrism to show how the use of chemical pesticides was damaging wildlife and humans. Use her views when discussing holism, ecology, environmental ethics and sustainability.

Key ideas

1 **Balance of nature**: profit and production create a poisoned planet and a sick society. Humanity needs to ensure the balance of nature to protect humanity – a form of enlightened anthropocentrism.

2 **Nature should be seen holistically**: the mechanistic world view of controlling nature is human arrogance. Humans need to accept the lessons of ecology and take a more holistic view to create a sustainable society.

Key thinkers and ideas

E.F. Schumacher (1911–1977)

Schumacher has played a key role in developing criticisms of industrialism, capitalism and consumerism. Use him when discussing sustainability, post materialism and consumerism.

Key ideas

1 Buddhist economics: society should adopt a new form of economics around the idea of 'right livelihood' – economics as if people mattered, where maximum life quality is achieved with minimal consumption.

2 **Traditional economics**: traditional economics favours economic growth, based around consumerism and materialism. New economics should underpin a society built around quality not quantity and creative, fulfilling work, not drudgery.

Key thinkers and ideas

Murray Bookchin (1921–2006)

Bookchin has influenced both the anarchist and ecologist movement through the development of social ecology. Use Bookchin when discussing ecology, environmental consciousness, sustainability, post materialism and anti-consumerism.

Key ideas

1 **Domination**: the existing oppressive social structures, built on the domination of human by human, leads people to be self-interested, competitive and arrogant to nature. Radical social change is needed.

2 **Ecotopia**: a new society of decentralised, self-governing communes. Ecotopia would allow human nature to develop to be more in tune and harmonious with nature.

Key thinkers and ideas

Carolyn Merchant (1936–)

Merchant's ideas are influential in the criticism of the mechanistic world view of post-Enlightenment science and her extension of the analysis of feminism to environmental issues. Use Merchant when discussing ecology, holism and sustainability.

Key ideas

1 **Mechanistic world view of science**: this treats nature as a dead, inert resource to be exploited and dominated.

2 **Patriarchy** (see page 134): the domination of women and nature must be overthrown and replaced by a society where there is a sustainable partnership between all humanity and nature.

Now try this

Label each thinker as either a deep green, shallow green or social ecologist based on which strand in ecologism has been most shaped by their ideas.

Exam skills

This question will help you to revise for **Section B** of your A Level **Paper 2** exam. You will be given two 24-mark essay questions for each political idea – you will need to choose **one** from your chosen idea.

Section B

- You should aim to spend around 30 minutes on this essay.
- Your essay needs to be fully structured, including an introduction and a conclusion.
- You **must** use at least **two** relevant key thinkers as outlined in the relevant section of the specification.

Questions

Questions will explore the extent of agreement within ecologism **or** tensions within the different strands over one of the four key areas (the state, society, the economy and human nature). The command words for the questions are always '**To what extent**'. You need to cover all three AOs, which are equally weighted:

- set out the nature of the debate on both sides – show you understand how the content relates to the question (AO1)
- examine the ideology/strands in relation to the question – this also means showing similarities and differences within the strands (AO2)
- make judgements – explore (evaluate) the extent of the similarities and differences and come to a judgement (AO3). This should be clear throughout your essay, not just in the conclusion.

Worked example

4 To what extent do ecologists disagree about the economic approach that is needed to protect the environment?

You must use appropriate thinkers you have studied to support your answer and consider both sides in a balanced way. **(24 marks)**

Within ecologism, there is agreement that the current economic approach, based on materialism, consumerism and unlimited growth, is not sustainable. Shallow greens wish to reform the current economy, based on the principle of weak sustainability, while both social ecology and deep green thinking argue for a radical transformation of the economy, based on the principle of strong sustainability. The disagreements are so fundamental over the economy that deep greens view the shallow green approach as part of the problem, not part of the solution...

... There is clear agreement within ecologism with the idea suggested by Carson that the existing economic model, based on profit and production, is poisoning the planet and society. Consumerism and materialism, which underpin the economy and link human happiness to the consumption of goods, are driving ever increasing production, which depletes resources and increases pollution in a world that is finite. The solution, which emerges from the thinking of Schumacher, is to break with materialism and consumerism, to offer an economy that is built around quality and not quantity and takes into account the lessons of ecology and holism...

... In the end, ecologists agree that the existing economic model is unsustainable and needs reform but the agreement ends here. Shallow greens believe capitalism can be greened, while social ecologists and deep greens argue that capitalism can never be greened. This faith in greener growth and technology can only lead to continued environmental destruction. Only a radical transformation to living economies that are zero growth and built around the principle of strong sustainability can protect the environment.

Take a few minutes to plan your answer.

The introduction identifies the areas of agreement and disagreement between all the strands of ecologists regarding the economic approach to protecting the environment.

The final sentence hints at how the student will argue. This shows they understand the assessment objectives and sets the essay up excellently.

The ideas of two key thinkers are used here in their correct context.

Correct use of political vocabulary in the right context here, which reveals clear understanding.

Having identified agreement over what is wrong with the existing economy, the student can move on to identify the differences between shallow greens, deep greens and social ecologists over how the economy should be transformed in order to reach a conclusion.

Throughout your essay, it should be clear which side you think is most convincing. Your conclusion should sum this up and be justified by your argument.

Sex and gender

Feminism generally is an ideology that aims for gender equality. There are numerous strands of feminism. This page looks at one of the core ideas and principles of feminism: sex and gender. These core ideas largely stem from **radical feminism**, which you can read more about on page 137.

The history of feminism

The history of feminism is described as occurring in four waves.

1 **First wave (1850s–1940s):** focused on the legal and political rights of women, most famously in the UK through the suffragette movement, which culminated in equal suffrage with men in 1928 (see page 5 for more on efforts to reform democracy in the UK).

2 **Second wave (1960s–1980s):** focused on the different roles that society expected of men and women. Many books on feminism were written, including *The Second Sex* (1949) by **Simone de Beauvoir**, *The Feminine Mystique* (1963) by **Betty Friedan** and *Sexual Politics* (1970) by **Kate Millett**.

3 **Third wave (1990s):** was concerned that feminism had failed to identify and recognise the concerns of women of other cultures. Authors such as **bell hooks** in *Ain't I a Woman* (1981) wrote about the experiences of women of colour and wanted feminism to widen its embrace to understand how cultural variations affect women's oppression.

4 **Fourth wave (2008 onwards):** is feminism entering a fourth wave, reacting against online misogyny? For example, Laura Bates's website The Everyday Sexism Project seeks to document everyday examples of sexism; Project Unbreakable seeks to give a voice to victims of sexual violence by posting photographs on Instagram of quotes from their attackers.

Sex and gender

Feminists argue that there is no justification for gender stereotypes to be ascribed to people, despite clear biological differences. In a patriarchal society (see page 134), the gender roles given to women are to keep them in an inferior, less powerful position to men.

Sex...	Gender...
refers to biological differences between men and women: body shape, size, sexual and reproductive organs	refers to the social and cultural differences between men and women
is categorised by the words 'male' and 'female'	is categorised by the words 'masculine' and 'feminine'
remains the same regardless of time and culture	expectations differ across time and culture

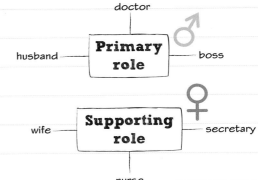

Women are traditionally seen as caregivers and supporters of men's roles. Feminists identify gender roles in the home to have done the most harm. In 2013, the CEO of Facebook, Sheryl Sandberg, said: 'I want every little girl who's been told she is bossy to be told she has leadership skills.'

Application

Human nature

There may be a dispute between those who believe that both sex and gender are natural biological issues and those who reject the idea.

The state

It could be argued that the state has slowly played a role in passing laws outlawing gender discrimination and promoting more positive roles for women.

Society

The issue of sex and gender refers to the way feminists see patriarchal society as it exists currently and how they would like to change it.

The economy

As gender roles have become less clearly demarcated than in the past, so women's role in the economy has expanded.

Now try this

Make a list of words traditionally used to describe men and women, which reinforce the blurring of sex and gender.

Patriarchy and 'the personal is political'

The ideas of patriarchy and 'the personal is political' are also key ideas of feminist ideology. There is significant overlap between the two ideas.

Patriarchy

Feminists identify patriarchy as a system run by and for men. Sylvia Walby in *Theorizing Patriarchy* (1990) identified six areas through which patriarchal ideas dominate society:

1 **The state**: women have been denied representation and are underrepresented in the formal positions of power.

2 **Household**: women have been discouraged from occupations outside the home.

3 **Culture**: society has always reinforced messages to women through culture. Adverts emphasised a woman's domestic role. There are now unrealistic expectations of women's appearance.

4 **Sexuality**: women were made to feel abnormal for having sexual feelings while encouraging men to fully explore their sexuality.

5 **Paid work**: when women were allowed to take up paid jobs, they were pushed towards low-paid or part-time jobs, or jobs that put them in an assistant position to men.

6 **Violence**: domestic abuse has only recently been taken seriously in society; previously, it was considered a private matter.

The personal is political

Feminists challenge the idea that what goes on between men and women in the **private sphere** ('personal' relationships) has nothing to do with the rest of society. These 'private' issues include:

- household division of labour
- attitude towards women who want to work
- 'morality' associated with women's sexuality
- objectification of women.

Feminists argue that in fact these 'private' issues were all ways of keeping women in their subordinate place in society. This distinction between the **public sphere** (society) and private sphere (home) were therefore about power, and were thus 'political'.

'The personal is political' is a slogan that arose with second-wave feminism, which sought to challenge all of society's views about women, specifically the public and private sphere.

Application

		Patriarchy	Personal is political
	Human nature	Difference feminists (read about equality and difference feminism on page 135) argue that men are, by their very nature, predisposed to oppress women. As such, they argue for a complete separation from men.	Feminists reject the view that women's nature makes them more suited to domestic roles and are naturally less capable than men.
	The state	The state perpetuates patriarchy by reinforcing patriarchal values. State institutions are dominated by men who, argue feminists, legislate in their own interests.	Feminists argue that the state perpetuates the artificial distinction between private and public oppression.
	Society	Any issues to do with feminism and society would usually relate to a discussion of patriarchy. Radical feminists (see page 137 to read more about radical feminism) in particular want patriarchal society overthrown and believe that women will not be treated equally under any other conditions.	Feminists seeks to change society by removing the distinction in patriarchal society to enable oppression in the private sphere to be removed.
	Economy	Feminists argue that patriarchy is the reason that: • women have historically been restricted to the home • women's jobs have traditionally been considered less important and thus less well paid than men's.	Feminists believe that women are restricted from entering the economy as equals to men because of misconceptions that their key role should be at home.

Now try this

How does the media perpetuate patriarchy?

Equality and difference feminism; intersectionality

Equality and difference feminism as well as intersectionality are also key ideas of feminism.

Equality vs difference feminism

Equality feminism

Most feminists studied come under the heading of 'equality' feminists (see page 137 for an overview of different types of feminists), meaning that they believe that the differences between men and women are irrelevant and both can be considered equally capable of fulfilling all roles in society (bar child-bearing).

Difference feminism

This is also known as essentialism. Difference feminists argue that the differences between men and women are innate (natural). They argue that equality feminism has encouraged women to reject 'womanhood' and instead to try to be like a man, replicating male behaviour (see page 137).

Equality feminism	Difference feminism
Men and women are basically the same.	Men and women are fundamentally different.
There is no such thing as male characteristics and female characteristics.	Women approach things in a different way to men.
Any character differences between men and women are a result of nurture, **not** nature.	Women's role as creators of life gives them a unique perspective on the world.
Women should seek to throw off the yoke of gender roles and take their equal place alongside men in society.	Women should be encouraged to explore their own unique powerful characteristics rather than suppress them and attempt to act like men.

Application

Human nature

Primarily, difference feminism relates to the issue of human nature, as there is a dispute between difference feminists who believe there are innate differences between men and women and equality feminists who reject this idea.

Society

Difference feminists seek to create a world where men and women's different characters are seen as being of equal importance in all areas of society, rather than an 'equal' society based on women being like men. A tiny minority of extreme difference feminists argue for men and women to live separately as their aims can never be reconciled when living together.

Intersectionality

Intersectionality in feminism emerged in the 1980s and criticised feminism for considering only the concerns of white (largely middle-class) women and ignoring all other classes and cultures. Intersectionality suggested that feminism needed to embrace women of different ethnicities, religions and classes. This movement, identified by bell hooks among others, argued that the feminist movement had left 'women of colour' and other differences (class, ethnicity, religion, etc.) feeling estranged as their experience of oppression was different to that discussed by feminists so far.

Application

Society

Intersectionality refers to the way feminism has evolved in society. Traditional feminism has ignored the role of all but white, middle-class women in society and framed feminism in a way that is only familiar to these women.

The economy

Feminism must embrace the position of women in developing-world economies, which is much worse than women in the West enjoy.

bell hooks chose not to capitalise her name in order to place focus on her work and her ideas, not her personality.

Now try this

Identify and explain two groups in society whose experience of oppression could be different from white, middle-class women.

Liberal and socialist feminism

There are many different types of feminism. This page will look at **liberal** and **socialist** feminism.

Liberal feminism

Liberal feminism was an early form of feminism (see page 133 to revise first-wave feminism) primarily associated with the demand for women's right to vote. Its core ideas and principles include:

- **Individualism**: women (like all humans) should have the freedom they need to become autonomous individuals in society.

- **Equality of opportunity**: ensuring that women and men have equal chances in life.

- **Foundational equality**: all humans are of equal moral worth and value. In the eyes of the law, all humans, whatever their sex, are entitled to the same rights as each other, for example to vote, protest, and so on. This is known as **legal equality** and **political equality**.

- **Reformist**: society does not require fundamental or even radical change. As society progresses, inequalities will be rectified. This will happen by changes in the law, leading to changes in attitudes and the process of 'role-modelling' (that is, seeing women in non-traditional roles which challenge the inherent bias of society).

- **Discrimination**: women are discriminated against, not oppressed.

Socialist feminism

Socialist feminism believes that gender inequality in society stems from economics and capitalism. Its core ideas and principles include:

- **Eradication of capitalism**: capitalism creates patriarchy and subordinates women in order to fulfil the role of a **reserve army of labour**, do domestic work for free, reproduce children and socialise them into capitalist values, and look after their husband at home and replenish his energy for a full day's work.

- **Economic and social equality**: women should be liberated through a socialist revolution. When capitalism is removed, women will be treated equally.

- **Radical/revolutionary**: socialist feminism is a revolutionary or a radical movement as they wish to overthrow capitalism and replace it with a socialist society. Only then will women be equal to men.

- **Marriage and family**: a key area of women's oppression. Removing women from the workforce makes them financially dependent on their husbands. Monogamy guaranteed the paternity of any children who would inherit property.

Liberal feminist Betty Friedan (1921–2006)

In *The Feminine Mystique* (1963), Friedan discussed the idea of 'the problem with no name', which resulted in many (white, middle-class) women questioning their role in society and demanding change. Friedan believed in **foundational equality** (women are as capable as men). She fought for legal and political equality as well as equality of opportunity in education and the workplace. She wanted women to fulfil their potential and have the freedom and chances in society to do so. See page 55 for more on Friedan's views.

Betty Friedan is a **key thinker in Liberalism** and must be used as such. However, she can be studied in addition as a major influence to Liberal feminism.

Socialist feminist Juliet Mitchell (1940–)

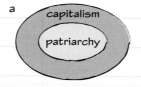 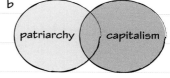

Socialist feminism sees patriarchy as being created by capitalism (a); modern socialist feminists such as Mitchell argue that capitalism and patriarchy work side by side as dual systems of female oppression (b).

Mitchell argues that women are oppressed in four ways: reproduction, sexuality, socialisation of children and production. She argues that women should fight both capitalism and patriarchy to create a classless society. Only when all four areas are transformed will women be truly free.

Now try this

What did Betty Freidan mean by 'the problem with no name'?

Radical feminism

Radical feminists are the only feminists who define society solely as patriarchal. They believe that the biggest problem facing society is gender inequality.

Gender inequality and patriarchy

Radical feminists are united by their insistence that society has a single source of female oppression – patriarchy. They reject the liberal and socialist view that feminism can be understood in association with any other ideology. Patriarchy is an independent system of oppression. They believe that only through a radical sexual revolution can patriarchy be removed and women be free.

Beyond this core belief, it is important to see radical feminism as a collection of unique contributions and extensions to this core, unifying belief.

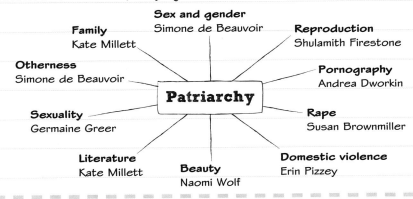

Family
Kate Millett

Sex and gender
Simone de Beauvoir

Reproduction
Shulamith Firestone

Otherness
Simone de Beauvoir

Pornography
Andrea Dworkin

Patriarchy

Sexuality
Germaine Greer

Rape
Susan Brownmiller

Literature
Kate Millett

Beauty
Naomi Wolf

Domestic violence
Erin Pizzey

Some influential radical feminists and their area of interest. They all argue in different ways that the personal is political (see page 134). This highlights the idea that patriarchy pervades every aspect of society.

Types of radical feminism

While difference and separatist feminism receive widespread coverage, they account for a tiny proportion of feminist thought.

Equality radical feminism

The vast majority of radical feminists are 'equality' radical feminists who are often outraged by the views expressed by difference feminists. Some feel that it gives men an opportunity to 'put women back in the kitchen', while others feel that the 'man hating' of some separatist feminists turns many women away from feminism.

Difference feminism (or cultural feminism)

Difference feminists (also known as cultural feminists or essentialists) make up a very small strand of radical feminists. They suggest that women should stop denying their own, distinct female nature by trying to imitate men (see page 135 for an overview of difference feminism). Instead, they should embrace their female values, which patriarchal society has taught them to hate.

Separatist feminism

A much more extreme version of these ideas are separatist feminists, whereby women seek to separate themselves from men, believing that men are naturally pre-disposed to dominate women.

Andrea Dworkin (1946–2005)

Dworkin is known for her views and writings on pornography, particularly *Pornography: Men Possessing Women* (1981). Dworkin analysed years of pornography and argued that it was complicit in violence against women in patriarchal society, by encouraging men to fantasise over the domination, humiliation and abuse of women – pornography was essentially about male supremacy. She passionately denied that she thought all men were rapists, arguing that 'I don't believe rape is inevitable or natural. If I did, I would have no reason to be here... I'm here because we believe in your humanity.'

Erin Pizzey (1939–)

Pizzey, a key figure of the women's movement in the 1970s, did groundbreaking work on domestic violence. She founded the first women's refuge in Chiswick and her book, *Scream Quietly or the Neighbours Will Hear* (1974), was a terrifyingly blunt account of domestic violence and the way it is ignored by patriarchal society. A documentary was made to accompany the book in 1974.

Now try this

Why do equality radical feminists reject difference feminists' views?

Post-modern feminism

Post-modern feminism is about being different, but not in the same way as difference feminism. It argues that patriarchy appears in many different ways depending on a woman's race, class or identity, and therefore supports a wider understanding of the experiences of women. This was the key issue of third-wave feminism (see page 133 for an overview of the different stages of feminism).

Different experiences

By applying post-modern ideas to feminism, post-modern feminism recognised that it is impossible to generalise about a single 'women's experience' because there is too vast an array of different experiences. Post-modern feminism is therefore linked to the concept of **intersectionality** (read more about intersectionality on page 135), which seeks to highlight that women of different colours, religions and classes all have uniquely different experiences of partiarchal oppression. Gender is not the only issue to affect women and must be seen alongside these experiences.

bell hooks criticised the second-wave 'sisterhood', which gave white, middle-class women a voice and bond, but discouraged women of colour from speaking about their different experiences (see page 133 for more on third-wave feminism).

Individual definitions

Post-modern feminism is also about women being able to define feminism for themselves. Richards and Baumgardner, in *Manifesta* (2000), argued that in each generation, young women would rediscover and re-establish what feminism meant for them.

'We're not doing feminism the same way that the seventies feminists did it; being liberated doesn't mean copying what came before, but finding one's own way – a way that is genuine to one's own generation' (Richards and Baumgardner, 2000).

Post-modern feminism and conflict

The idea of post-modern feminism has led to many different interpretations of what being a 'feminist' is. In turn, this has led to a certain degree of conflicting views.

Nudity

One of the biggest areas of conflict is views towards nudity. While some feminists think public nudity is degrading and oppressive to women, others see it as empowering – that women are owning their bodies and their sexuality.

For example, Femen is a radical feminist group known for its topless protests. Its website states that 'the right to her body by the woman is the first and the most important step to her liberation. Female nudity, free of patriarchal system, is a grave-digger of the system.'

Other feminists believe that public displays of female nudity are playing into the hands of patriarchy. They argue that all it does is titillate men, who don't register the protest.

For example, in March 2017 Emma Watson found herself at the centre of a row over her semi-topless cover for *Vanity Fair* magazine. Watson has a high profile as a feminist campaigner and was caught in the crossfire of the nudity and feminism debate.

Appearance

SlutWalk originated in Canada after a police officer suggested that 'women should avoid dressing like sluts' as a precaution against sexual assault. They were protesting against excusing rape by referring to a woman's appearance.

Another area of conflict is the wearing of a burqa, hijab or other forms of dress worn by Muslim women. Many feminists see this as a sign of patriarchal oppression being forced on women. Some Muslim women reject this, arguing that they feel freed from the oppressive focus on appearance of Western society.

SlutWalk is a protest group who march dressed as 'sluts'.

Now try this

How do the types of feminism discussed on this page relate to post-modern feminism?

Differences within feminism

It is useful to see the different views towards the core principles of the different strands of feminism.

Patriarchy, sex and gender, the 'personal is political'

	Liberal feminists	Socialist feminists	Radical feminists	Post-modern feminists
Patriarchy	Don't really recognise the term as systematic oppression. They see it as discrimination, which will be eradicated by society making small, gradual adjustments.	Recognise patriarchy as systematic oppression, but they argue it is primarily caused by capitalism, not men.	Patriarchy is the deepest, most politically important division. It is a systematic, institutionalised and pervasive form of male power.	Patriarchy is pervasive in society and it mutates according to class, ethnicity and religion. Society needs to recognise the different forms that patriarchy takes.
Sex and gender	All humans are rational creatures, and so the distinction of sex and gender is artificial. Women are as capable as men and should have equal chances in society.	Reject and seek to eradicate gender stereotypes, which are required by capitalism as it needs women to do free domestic work and fulfil other functions.	Gender roles are created by patriarchy to subjugate women. Women are duped into believing that childcare and household work are their natural roles.	Gender roles are forced upon women by society. Those imposed on black and working-class women are different to those imposed on white, middle-class women.
Personal is political	Reject 'the personal is political'. Their focus is discrimination in the public sphere. They want to see **all** barriers to entry in the public sphere removed.	The personal **is** political. Women are forced into domesticity to help reproduce the labour force and other functions for capitalism.	'Politics' is found wherever there is an imbalance of power and women are suppressed in both public and private spheres through male domination.	Support the radical feminist view of society as political, but see 'politics' in a wider way than other radical feminists.
Difference vs equality	Equality feminists; all humans are of equal moral worth and entitled to the same rights.	Equality feminists; they believe in sexual and class equality. Sexual equality is meaningless without class equality and equality must be seen in economic terms.	Most are **equality feminists**: gender inequality is created by patriarchy. **Difference feminists**: women should not seek to replicate male behaviour and should be free to be 'women'.	Equality feminists; the different experiences of women are crucial in understanding the different ways women are oppressed.
Intersection-ality	**All** women, no matter what their class, religion or ethnicity, should be treated equally.	Capitalism oppresses all women and working-class men. They must unite to remove capitalism and patriarchy from society.	**All** women are equally oppressed by patriarchy, albeit in different ways.	Different groups of women experience different types of oppression.
Reform or revolution	Reformist; society will change gradually as women gain greater rights and take on more roles usually associated with men.	Only an economic and social revolution will rid society of capitalism and hence patriarchy.	A social revolution is needed to eradicate society of the entrenched patriarchal values that are pervasive.	Agree with radical feminists, and the oppression of different classes and ethnicities needs to be eradicated too.

Now try this

What do all feminists agree on?

Feminist key thinkers

Key thinkers and ideas

Charlotte Perkins Gilman (1860–1935)

Gilman was an American socialist feminist. She can be used when discussing socialist feminism, patriarchy, sex and gender roles, personal is political, the economy and society.

Key ideas

1. **Societal pressure**: gender stereotyping from childhood is wrong and little boys and girls should not wear different clothes, play with different toys, do different activities or be pushed into different roles.

2. **Economic independence**: women's dependency on their husbands for money is at the heart of their oppression.

Key thinkers and ideas

Simone de Beauvoir (1908–1986)

De Beauvoir was a writer and political activist. She can be used when discussing sex and gender roles, human nature, patriarchy and society.

Key ideas

1. **Socialisation**: society moulds (or socialises) women into their behaviour. According to de Beauvoir, 'one is not born, but rather becomes, a woman'.

2. **Otherness**: men are the norm and women are 'other'. Women have accepted this and therefore their subordinate position in society.

Key thinkers and ideas

Kate Millett (1934–2017)

Sexual Politics (1970) is often credited with launching radical feminism. She was one of the first feminists to analyse the role of the traditional family in patriarchy. Use her to discuss patriarchy, radical feminism, society and the personal is political.

Key ideas

1. **The family**: the family and other influences work together to reinforce patriarchal values teaching girls their 'role'.

2. **Portrayal of women in art and literature**: patriarchal culture has produced writers and literature that degrade women. The language used to describe sex demonstrates the subjugation of women, and women are commodities silenced by the freedom of men to sexually possess them.

Key thinkers and ideas

Sheila Rowbotham (1943–)

Rowbotham is a socialist feminist, arguing that capitalism is part of the system of female oppression. Use Rowbotham to discuss economy, society, patriarchy and socialist-feminism.

Key ideas

1. **Sexism and capitalism**: the oppression of women predates capitalism so it cannot have 'created' patriarchy. But sexism and capitalism are closely linked and a 'revolution within the revolution' is needed to eradicate both.

2. **The family**: is a place where men take refuge from alienation in a capitalist economy. Women are oppressed economically and culturally.

Key thinkers and ideas

bell hooks (1952–)

American author and social activist hooks, campaigned for the cultural concerns of women of colour to be heard in mainstream feminism. Uses: intersectionality, society, patriarchy, sex and gender roles and human nature.

Key ideas

1. **Gender boxes/socialisation**: children are forced into unnatural gender boxes.

2. **Intersectionality**: mainstream radical feminism ignores women's different cultural and class experiences.

Now try this

Label each thinker as either liberal, socialist, radical or post-modern feminist based on which strand has been most shaped by their ideas.

Exam skills

This question will help you to revise for **Section B** of your A Level **Paper 2** exam. You will be given two 24-mark essay questions for each political idea – you will need to choose **one** from your chosen idea.

Section B

- You should aim to spend around 30 minutes on this essay.
- Your essay needs to be fully structured, including an introduction and a conclusion.
- You **must** use at least **two** relevant key thinkers as outlined in the relevant section of the specification.

Questions

Questions will explore the extent of agreement within feminism **or** tensions within the different strands over one of the four key areas (the state, society, the economy and human nature). The command words for the questions are always '**To what extent**'. You need to cover all three AOs, which are equally weighted:

- set out the nature of the debate on both sides – show you understand how the content relates to the question (AO1)
- examine the ideology/strands in relation to the question – this also means showing similarities and differences within the strands (AO2)
- make judgements – explore (evaluate) the extent of the similarities and differences and come to a judgement (AO3). This should be clear throughout your essay, not just in the conclusion.

Worked example

5 To what extent is feminism more united than divided?

You must use appropriate thinkers you have studied to support your answer and consider both sides in a balanced way. **(24 marks)**

Feminism is a cross-cutting ideology. There are some areas of agreement but many areas of disagreement between liberal, socialist, radical and post-modern feminists, as well as disagreement within radical feminism. This essay will therefore argue that feminism is more divided than united.

Feminists are united in the belief that women and men are not treated equally in society. Even in societies where there are equal laws and rights for men and women, women are still not treated equally. Liberal feminist Friedan argued that society must work hard to give equal opportunity to women, as well as legal and political equality. However, radical feminists such as Millett have rejected liberal feminists' analysis of society. Instead, they argue that society needs to look beyond the public sphere towards the private sphere, especially the family, to see key areas of women's oppression. Radical feminists have long argued that 'the personal is political' and encouraged liberal feminists to recognise that the oppression of women in all aspects of society will not be removed by legal and political means alone. Hence, despite general agreement that women are not treated equally in society, it is clear that radical feminists fundamentally reject the premise on which liberal feminists believe this. This uncovers significant areas of division between radical and liberal feminists...

... In evaluating whether the divisions between feminists are greater than the similarities, it can be seen that despite superficial similarities between feminists, the deeper one digs into the different strands of feminism, the more the illusion of unity is shattered.

Take a few minutes to plan your answer.

The introduction introduces all the strands within feminism. The final sentence shows what the student thinks and the direction from which they will argue.

An area of unity between feminists is effectively outlined.

This paragraph suggests excellent understanding of feminist differences. The student critically compares the liberal view to the radical feminist view, identifying key areas of division.

It is essential to understand that the only thinker that can be formally recognised in this section is Kate Millett because she is a key thinker in the feminism section. **Betty Friedan cannot count towards your allocation of two key thinkers,** as she is a key thinker in the liberalism section.

The student sums up this section by identifying that the divisions are greater than the similarities, as suggested by the introduction.

You could go on to discuss the differences (and any similarities) in feminist views on the significance of patriarchy.

Throughout your essay, it should be clear which side of the argument you think is most convincing. Your conclusion should sum this up and be justified by your argument.

Politics of recognition

The politics of recognition is based on the idea that the recognition of an individual's identity and culture is a human need, crucial to our sense of self. Recognition allows the individual to feel that society is committed to them, so they can commit to society.

Multiculturalism

A **multicultural society** is a society where there is cultural, religious and ethnic diversity. This is **not** the same as multiculturalism, which refers to a political idea that attempts to explain and respond to the challenges related to cultural, ethnic and religious diversity. Multiculturalism attempts to provide a solution to the legitimate competing demands of **diversity** and unity in order to achieve a society which has political unity without cultural uniformity. The idea prescribes a state-led policy programme that provides fairer terms for integration into society for immigrants to create a 'community of citizens and a community of communities' (*The Future of Multi-Ethnic Britain: The Parekh Report*, 2000).

Human nature

Humans can only understand themselves through the **culture** they grew up and function in, and their self-worth and identity is shaped dialogically. This means the sense of self emerges out of dialogue with or struggle against how others see us. Social recognition of culture is crucial to human development. Misrecognition in the form of racism, stereotyping and stigmatisation can inflict serious damage on the individual's sense of self-worth. It can damage the commitment to the political community and the quality of citizenship as individuals withdraw from the wider community out of a fear of rejection or ridicule, or a sense of alienation.

Equal dignity and recognition

The starting point of the politics of recognition is the idea that minority groups can suffer legal and political oppression (see Taylor on page 150) but also a deeper cultural marginalisation. The 'politics of recognition' has two separate elements that work together to tackle this oppression and ensure that minority groups can achieve citizenship in terms of rights and a sense of belonging to the wider community:

Equal dignity: the equal dignity of all citizens involves the granting of **formal equality** in line with liberal thinking, where there are equal legal and political rights for all to ensure there are no second-class citizens. This is based on the idea that all humans are alike and should be treated alike; it is 'difference-blind'. For example, the Civil Rights Act 1964 and Voting Rights Act 1965 in the USA enforce these principles.

Equal recognition: everyone should be equally recognised for their own unique identity and this moves beyond liberal thinking as it focuses on the politics of difference. As our identity can only be understood in the context of our **culture**, this means giving status and recognition to a diversity of cultures that are fundamentally different. For example, specific rights and protections are allocated by the state to particular groups, such as the laws in Canada to ensure the collective survival of the French Quebecois.

Application

The state

The state passes laws to ensure that legally and politically all are treated equally and cultures are recognised and allowed to survive and flourish, by granting specific rights or protections to particular groups. Charles Taylor advocates a liberal view that the dominant culture can be appealed to through moral and intellectual argument to adopt the 'politics of recognition' (see page 150).

Society

Bhikhu Parekh dismisses this, arguing that recognition requires an extensive critique of the majority culture hand in hand with a radical political and economic restructuring by the state to create a fair and equal distribution of political and economic power for minorities (see page 150 for an overview of multiculturalist key thinkers).

Now try this

What is meant by the term 'misrecognition'?

Culture and identity

The 'politics of recognition' is part of a much wider discussion in political thinking about the politics of culture and identity.

Culture and identity debate

This debate centres on the idea that individuals with pride and confidence in their own culture, which is publicly valued by the wider community, will have a sense of belonging. Where the state and society do not value and cherish the diversity of cultures, individuals do not feel committed to the wider political community because it is not committed to them. This debate is shaped by two main ideas: **communitarianism** and identity politics.

Communitarianism

Communitarianism is a challenge to the liberal view that human nature has innate qualities and humans can be understood outside of society. Multiculturalists such as Taylor argue that humans are culturally embedded as they are shaped by the communities they grow up and live in. Culture deeply shapes the individual and their view of themselves and the world. Culture is so significant that the state must recognise different communities or risk alienating both individuals and cultures from wider society.

Black Lives Matter

The Black Lives Matter movement that emerged in 2013 reflects the politics of culture and identity.

Identity politics

Identity is taken to mean an individual's sense of who they are and what is important about them as a human being. It is argued that the culture of Western, liberal societies is based around the identities of the dominant culture: white, male, heterosexual, able-bodied and bourgeois. Individuals in immigrant populations and other minority groups are marginalised by the dominant culture and oppressed through one-size-fits-all stereotyping that creates a sense of 'us' vs 'them'. While culture is a tool of oppression, it can also be a positive force. Minority groups can reshape their identity by taking control of it, building positive images and a sense of pride. This form of identity politics can confront and defeat oppression, giving minorities a real sense of their own authentic identity and allow them to feel part of the wider society.

'We are unapologetically Black in our positioning. In affirming that Black Lives Matter, we need not qualify our position. To love and desire freedom and justice for ourselves is a prerequisite for wanting the same for others.'

Conservative criticisms

👎 The **politics of identity** and culture creates cultural balkanisation – a process of creating strong and competing cultures within the state that create problems for the unity of society.

👎 In reshaping their identities, minority cultures express difference not similarity and become inward- not outward-looking, and this stops different cultures exploring what they have in common.

👎 Minority groups develop a distrust of each other and the majority group, while the majority culture sees minority cultures as a potential threat to its way of life.

Application

Human nature

As human nature is culturally embedded, culture becomes so significant that the state must recognise cultures or risk alienation of minority groups from society. Culture can be a positive force, allowing minority groups to create an authentic identity and feel part of wider society, creating political unity.

Now try this

What is meant by the term 'communitarianism'?

Minority rights

Minority rights break from liberalism by granting collective rights to groups rather than individuals. These collective rights, referred to as **group differentiated rights**, are specific to a particular group and so may be meaningless to other groups.

Group differentiated rights and the state

The state should put in place policies and laws that promote group differentiated rights to promote cultures as a source of integration, not division:

Self-government rights	**Polyethnic rights**	**Representation rights**
Granted to national minorities or indigenous populations who want political autonomy or territorial control. Groups will be geographically concentrated, have suffered historical oppression and desire self-government. *For example, Native Americans in the USA.*	These meet the demands of immigrant groups who want to maintain their cultural identity. These rights provide the basis for individuals from minority groups to integrate into society. *For example, they are protected by anti-discrimination law like the Equality Act 2010.*	These are used to tackle the exclusion of minorities from public life to counterbalance historical exclusion. **Positive discrimination** allows minorities to fully engage in society and enables public life to reflect the diversity of cultures within the state. *For example, affirmative action in the USA.*

How are minority rights justified?

In *Multicultural Citizenship: A Liberal Theory of Minority Rights* (1995), Will Kymlicka defends minority rights from within the tradition of liberalism (see page 150 to read about multiculturalist key thinkers).

- Minority rights ensure **justice** through equality between groups as the state is naturally aligned with the majority culture, even where it claims to be neutral. The cultural background of the majority culture is reflected in the state's decisions, leaving minority cultures at a disadvantage.
  For example, the official language for schooling and legal documents, and the limits placed on some groups through law, like the banning of the niqab and burqa.

- Group differentiated rights are a guarantee of individual freedom and autonomy. Cultures must be maintained as they provide the context within which the individual makes meaningful choices about the life they want to lead. This autonomy to choose and revise beliefs, interest and desires is a key value as it is central to human development.

While Kymlicka argues that culture is key to human development and minorities have a right to their culture, others, like Parekh, have argued that a diversity of cultures is a good in itself. Minority rights counter oppression, especially where there is a power imbalance between minority and majority cultures, and protect and promote minority cultures.

Conservative criticisms

Minority rights have been seen as a source of division, not integration:

👎 Representation rights are a form of reverse discrimination that undermines minority achievement and creates resentment among the majority culture.

👎 Minority rights create **segregation**, not integration, as they make minority cultures inward- not outward-looking. Is the burqa a symbol of cultural identity or difference?

👎 Minority rights can contradict individual rights where an illiberal minority culture restricts the freedoms of its individual members. Should the state intervene in this case to protect individual rights?

Application

The state

The state should promote minority rights to enable different cultures to live together harmoniously in society. By granting group differentiated rights to minority cultures, the state secures their commitment and consent.

Now try this

1 How can the state be seen as aligned with the dominant culture?
2 Explain three ways in which minority rights can be seen as a source of division.

Diversity

There is a growing diversity within society due to globalisation and international migration. Multiculturalism argues that diversity and unity can and should be balanced, although there is disagreement about the exact nature of that balance.

The different justifications for diversity

1 It should be promoted and celebrated as culture is essential to human development. Individuals must have access to their culture to make decisions about the customs, practices and beliefs they want to adopt in leading their life.

2 Culture provides a sense of identity and belonging to individuals and so contributes to human well-being. This underpins the building of stable societies.

3 It benefits society as it generates vibrancy, creativity and energy in society based on the variety of different cultures. Cross-cultural exchange promotes understanding, **tolerance** and a respect for difference, weakening divisions and distrust within societies.

How far should diversity extend?

Multiculturalists are divided on how far diversity should be extended:

 Shallow diversity

Liberal multiculturalists promote diversity, but it must exist within a framework of liberal values. Diversity does not extend to promoting cultures which are illiberal and restrict individual freedom and autonomy.

Pluralist multiculturalists see diversity as a value in its own right. Liberal ideas are just one set of ideas and are not morally superior to other cultures. So a society that is united and inclusive must start from the point that all cultures have some moral worth and value.

Deep diversity

The criticisms of cultural diversity

Diversity is the promotion of difference, which some have argued can lead to **segregation** and discrimination within society. These dangers must be challenged as diversity undermines unity, so the state must adopt one of two approaches to ensure unity:

1 Assimilation: the state must encourage minorities to conform to the majority culture to create a strong, homogenous national identity that is necessary for unity.

2 Individualist integration: the state tolerates minorities, nurturing their identities in the private sphere. In public life, however, the state encourages them to see themselves as individuals, not a minority group. The state will grant equal individual rights, pass anti-discrimination laws but not pass laws that recognise difference or provide funding to support minority cultures.

The multiculturalist response

Assimilation has a history of failure in practice as it ignores the importance of culture and identity to the individual. Assimilation is likely to generate alienation, inequality and the perception of injustice among minority cultures, which will undermine the unity of society and the state. **Individualist integration** is one approach, but it does not go far enough as it is difference-blind. There must be support for state approaches that recognise difference in order to balance diversity and unity.

Application: the state and diversity

Kymlicka and Taylor would argue that the state needs to move beyond **individualist integration** to **multicultural integration** based on group differentiated rights and the politics of recognition to balance diversity and unity. Parekh and Modood (see page 150 for an overview of multiculturalist key thinkers) would go further, arguing that the state should not just tolerate diversity but actively promote it by subsidising public services that promote diversity, such as faith schools. In *The Future of Multi-Ethnic Britain: The Parekh Report*, Parekh argues that the principle of equal moral worth in diversity can only develop if economic and social inequality is challenged head on by the state.

Now try this

What is the difference between shallow and deep diversity?

145

Liberal multiculturalism

You need to know about the different types of multiculturalism. Liberal multiculturalism is a broad ideology that endorses diversity, but within the framework of liberal values and liberal democracy.

The liberal framework

Three key liberal ideas provide the basis of support for cultural diversity within society:

1 The neutrality of the state

The state is difference-blind. In the private sphere, individuals can celebrate their cultural identities and diversity is supported. In public life, the state promotes equal rights and anti-discrimination law and individuals sign up to the values of the society (for example, the Oath of Allegiance in the USA).

2 Tolerance

Cultural practices, beliefs and values are examples of self-regarding actions in the views of J.S. Mill (read about key liberal thinkers on pages 54–55). As such, these actions should be tolerated – this is the basis for supporting diversity and opposing assimilation.

3 Liberal democracy

Liberal democracy is the only type of state that can support diversity as it is based on formal equality, tolerance, autonomy, liberty and the consent of the governed.

Liberal multiculturalism has developed a further two arguments to support state intervention to protect and promote different cultures within society: **autonomy** and **justice**.

Autonomy

Kymlicka's approach to multiculturalism is based on the liberal principle of individualism (see page 46 for more on this strand of liberalism). The individual's key interest is leading a good life and this involves autonomy:

- The individual should be able to lead their life in line with their beliefs and values.
- The individual has the ability to question, revise or change their beliefs.

As humans are cultural beings, culture provides the context in which humans make decisions about their values and beliefs so they can choose their version of the good life. This provides the basis for the state to move beyond granting formal equality and anti-discrimination laws to accommodating group identities and cultures through group differentiated rights.

Justice

There is recognition that even if the state is neutral, its decisions will reflect the culture of the majority group through its choice of official language, education curriculum and which religious and cultural days are public holidays. This means minorities are subject to the tyranny of the majority and minorities may feel like second-class citizens. The allocation of group differentiated rights and the politics of recognition ensure that minority cultures are treated equally with the majority culture in line with the principle of justice. This enables minorities to feel a sense of belonging and commitment to the state and society.

The problem of tolerance

The liberal state is tolerant of different customs, practices and beliefs. However, this acceptance of diversity can only go so far (shallow diversity). **Tolerance** does not extend to cultural practices that are regarded as illiberal: practices that are themselves intolerant or oppressive. For example, tolerance does not extend to groups that wish to replace the liberal democratic state with a state based on religious law or to practices such as forced marriages or female dress codes if they are seen to contradict individual rights, in particular autonomy and freedom.

In 2009, President Sarkozy of France banned the niqab and burqa, on the grounds of protecting women's individual rights.

Now try this

1 What is the principle of autonomy?
2 How far does tolerance extend for liberal multiculturalists?

Pluralist multiculturalism

Pluralist multiculturalism values diversity in its own right, based on the principle that all cultures should be viewed as having some value and so are due respect. Unity is only possible if different cultures are encouraged.

Deep diversity

Pluralist multiculturalists favour deep diversity. Their starting point is that all cultures have some worth and are due respect, not just those which practise liberal values. There are two justifications for this: value pluralism and the attack on universalism.

Value pluralism

Based on the work of Isaiah Berlin (read about Berlin and other multiculturalist thinkers on page 150), some pluralists support the idea of value pluralism. There are many absolute values, such as liberty, equality and courage. Conflict between them is inevitable and there is no singular approach to resolve that conflict. So, when an individual makes a choice about their values, beliefs or interests, there is no right or wrong answer. In order to reflect this, the state must recognise a variety of different cultures in order to reduce this conflict within society.

Attack on liberal universalism

Liberal universalism sees liberal values, such as autonomy, as absolutes that are applicable to all individuals and societies, regardless of culture or any other difference. Parekh attacks this idea, using a three-step process:

 1 Human beings are culturally embedded, as they grow up and function in a culturally structured world, which deeply shapes their values and identity.

 2 Every culture has a particular view of what the good life should be, but is inherently limited as it cannot grasp a true understanding of the complexity and richness of humanity. This true understanding of humanity emerges from dialogue within and between cultures to allow each to develop a deeper understanding of itself. The state must promote cultures and dialogue between cultures.

 3 Liberalism is embedded in culture, so only offers one limited version of the good life. It cannot provide the basis for the true understanding of humanity, so deep diversity must be supported.

Ultimately, the liberal multiculturalist approach is not a sound basis for cultural diversity. This absolutises autonomy (makes it an absolute value that all cultures must subscribe to) and assumes that individuals can choose between different cultures to achieve the good life. However, our culturally embedded nature means that most other cultures are not options that are open or available to us. Diversity is a value of itself as it enables the conversation between cultures to enrich, develop and deepen each individual culture and this enriches society for all. This is the basis for developing a shared sense of unity.

The national story

Parekh and Modood argue that state support of cultural diversity is the best approach to balancing unity and diversity. Modood sees the dialogue between cultures as crucial to rethinking the national story of individual states that in the past have often been linked to nationalism and excluded minority groups. Continuous dialogue between cultures, promoted by the state, can create a new national story that is inclusive and respectful of all cultures to create a sense of unity within society.

Now try this

What is 'universalism'?

Cosmopolitan multiculturalism

Cosmopolitan multiculturalism argues that diversity allows cultural mixing, which leads to the emergence of multicultural individuals who increasingly come to see themselves as global citizens.

Difference

Cosmopolitan multiculturalists, such as Jeremy Waldron, value difference. Individuals are not constrained by membership of one culture. Any inherited identity which labels people into identities that they have not chosen should be refused. This refusal is justified as inherited identities restrict individual choices and splits society up into antagonistic blocks. Individuals can 'pick and mix' from different cultures to create new identities. This mixing allows individuals to develop multiple, fluid identities that truly are a multiculture: made from different elements from different cultures. This can be seen to be dissolving old identities, such as nation or race, and providing maximum freedom for the individual.

Diversity

Cosmopolitan multiculturalists support a diverse society. They see a key role for the state in promoting and protecting cultures through positive discrimination and minority rights. This maintains the diversity of cultures, which individuals 'pick and mix' from in order to create their new identities. These new identities mean that individuals from both majority and minority cultures no longer see themselves as having one single identity from one culture.

For example, individuals may enjoy Spanish food, meditate, listen to reggae music and seek spiritual fulfilment through Buddhism.

Cosmopolitan integration and citizenship

Cosmopolitan integration allows individuals the widest possible freedom to mix with, borrow and learn from different cultures. The result will be a citizen who no longer has one strong attachment to a culture or race, but rather feels a greater sense of unity and loyalty to fellow global citizens. This is the basis for unity. In essence, the 'pick and mix' element creates unity between individuals across the globe while dissolving cultural groups and undermining the very diversity that it is built on.

Tensions

Cosmopolitan multiculturalists fit with the other strands of multiculturalism in their support of difference, diversity and the politics of identity. However, there are some clear tensions:

👎 **Culture is embedded**: culture is seen as a matter of choice for individuals, who can create and develop fluid identities, and this clashes with the idea that the individual is culturally embedded. As Parekh argues, culture deeply shapes the individual, who can revise or change some of its influences but will necessarily view the world from within it. Individuals rarely adopt other cultures as they are not viable options for them.

👎 **Detachment**: the 'pick and mix' nature of cosmopolitanism creates hybridity (a mix of cultures) that detaches people from their own culture and group. It can create identities that are not authentic, weakening the sense of belonging, which is central to the well-being of the individual and stability of society.

👎 **Dissolving groups**: cosmopolitanism celebrates difference but both criticises and wishes to disband groups.

Now try this

How might cosmopolitan multiculturalism be seen to undermine diversity?

The conservative criticism

Conservatism, of all the core ideas, is most at odds with multiculturalism, which it sees as breeding fear and **segregation** that threatens to fracture society and undermine national values.

Conservatism and human nature

Conservatives view humans as limited in their understanding of the world, fallible in their decision-making and security-seeking. As a result, humans should rely on history, tradition and practical experience to guide their behaviour and desire familiarity, safety and order within society. Consequently, conservatives fear diversity and difference, arguing that stable societies emerge from shared values and a common culture.

The state and the economy

Multiculturalism advocates state intervention to protect cultures and promote diversity. Parekh's idea of state intervention (for example, subsidising minority cultures) conflicts with One Nation, pragmatic conservative ideas. It is an example of state intervention, based on abstract principles and ideas, which generally makes things worse rather than better and endangers social cohesion and stability.

Diversity and society

Diversity in society has undermined the concept of the organic society (see page 37 for more on the organic state) as it creates cultural balkanisation (read about culture and identity on page 143). Strong cultures emerge within society with competing values, beliefs and practices that undermine unity. These groups tend to be inward- not outward-looking, and this provokes fear and distrust between groups, while the majority culture sees minority cultures as a threat to its way of life. In particular, multicultural integration, with its constant revision of the national story (see page 147 on pluralist multiculturalism), can be seen as undermining the nation's past, associating it with **imperialism/colonialsm**, racism and exploitation. Some conservatives have attacked the idea of tolerance, seeing it more as permissiveness that fails to recognise that there is right and wrong. Conservatives believe that any practices, values or beliefs that run counter to a nation's values should not be tolerated.

Conservative strategies

Conservative strategies for dealing with the issue of diversity and unity involve establishing a strict immigration policy and assimilation. **Assimilation** encourages individuals from minority cultures to conform to the majority culture. This flattens cultural difference and creates a strong, homogenised national identity that is the basis for a stable society. This process means that there is very little or no change at all for the majority culture in society and the laws and institutions of the state.

Multiculturalism in the UK

In 2011, the Conservative prime minister David Cameron delivered this attack on multiculturalism:

'Under the doctrine of state multiculturalism, we have encouraged different cultures to live separate lives, apart from each other and apart from the mainstream. We've failed to provide a vision of society to which they feel they want to belong. We've even tolerated these segregated communities behaving in ways that run completely counter to our values.'

Cameron at the Munich Security Conference in 2011

Now try this

What is meant by the term 'assimilation'?

Multiculturalist key thinkers

Isaiah Berlin (1909–1997)

Berlin's key contribution is his support for value pluralism. Uses: pluralist multiculturalism, diversity, culture and identity and minority rights.

Key ideas

1 **Value pluralism:** some values of different communities conflict. These values are of equal worth and conflict cannot be resolved. The state should allow communities to hold different values.

2 **Liberty:** only liberal democratic states can ensure the liberty to choose between different values and beliefs.

Charles Taylor (1931–)

Taylor uses communitarianism to criticise liberalism. Our sense of identity is formed by our community. Use Taylor when discussing culture and identity, politics of recognition and diversity.

Key ideas

1 **Equal dignity:** all humans should be treated alike via equality and anti-discrimination laws.

2 **Politics of recognition:** all humans should be recognised equally for their unique identity. Specific rights should be allocated to particular groups, but not others, and diversity should be promoted.

Bhikhu Parekh (1935–)

Parekh challenged liberal multiculturalism and developed pluralist multiculturalism. Uses: pluralist multiculturalism, culture and identity, the politics of recognition, diversity and minority rights.

Key ideas

1 **The rejection of universalist liberalism:** humans are culturally embedded and each culture is valuable but limited. Liberalism has only a narrow view of the good life, so there is the need for deep diversity. Attempts to get cultures to sign up to one value system will fail and create disunity.

2 **Cross-cultural dialogue:** allows cultures to learn from others to deepen, enrich and develop their own. Dialogue can help create a shared commitment to the political community and a vibrant society.

Tariq Modood (1952–)

Multiculturalism is essential to a successful society and the state has a crucial role in achieving this. Uses: culture and identity, unity through diversity, minority rights and pluralist multiculturalism.

Key ideas

1 **Integration:** individual cultures are internally diverse and society is multicultural, so no one method of integration works for all. Assimilation, individualist, cosmopolitan and multiculturalist integration, are all valid if they are the choice of the individual or the group.

2 **National identity:** strong identities are positive, but an inclusive national story is needed that weaves together these cultures. The state must support cultures, (for example through faith schools and in promoting cultural dialogue).

Will Kymlicka (1962–)

Will Kymlicka is the most influential writer in shaping liberal multiculturalism. Use him to discuss liberal multiculturalism, minority rights, diversity.

Key ideas

1 **Group differentiated rights:** the state should provide self-government, polyethnic and representation rights to ensure full and equal participation of all groups in society, resulting in real integration for all.

2 **The justification for these rights:** is through the liberal principles of justice and autonomy – multiculturalism works with a liberal framework. Minority rights ensure, individuals will consent and commit to the state and society.

Now try this

Explain the four possible methods of integration.

Exam skills

This question will help you to revise for **Section B** of your A Level **Paper 2** exam. You will be given two 24-mark essay questions for each political idea – you will need to choose **one** from your chosen idea.

Section B

- You should aim to spend around 30 minutes on this essay.
- Your essay needs to be fully structured, including an introduction and a conclusion.
- You **must** use at least **two** relevant key thinkers as outlined in the relevant section of the specification.

Questions

Questions will explore the extent of agreement within multiculturalism **or** tensions within the different strands over one of the four key areas (the state, society, the economy and human nature). The command words for the questions are always '**To what extent**'. You need to cover all three AOs, which are equally weighted:

- set out the nature of the debate on both sides – show you understand how the content relates to the question (AO1)
- examine the ideology/strands in relation to the question this also means showing similarities and differences within the strands (AO2)
- make judgements – explore (evaluate) the extent of the similarities and differences and come to a judgement (AO3). This should be clear throughout your essay, not just in the conclusion.

Worked example

6   To what extent does multiculturalism build social harmony within a diverse society?

You must use appropriate thinkers you have studied to support your answer and consider both sides in a balanced way.   **(24 marks)**

Take a few minutes to plan your answer and ensure you have chosen the right question.

The conservative criticism identifies multiculturalism as undermining shared values and common culture, which are necessary for a stable and peaceful society. In contrast, multiculturalists reject the idea that multiculturalism creates conflict, arguing that it is the only viable approach to creating social harmony in increasingly diverse societies. In fact, it is the denying of minority rights and the refusal to grant minority rights and recognise minority identities by the state and society which increases tension and conflict within society...

The introduction identifies the areas of agreement and disagreement between the conservative criticism and multiculturalism and introduces the debate.

The final sentence hints at how the student will argue. This shows they understand the assessment objectives and sets the essay up excellently.

... Multiculturalists argue strongly that multiculturalism is the only way to build social harmony in society, by recognising diversity. Within liberal multiculturalism, Kymlicka argues that the giving of group differentiated rights will ensure that minority cultures are treated fairly and equally, in line with the majority culture. This provides the basis for minorities to feel a sense of belonging and commitment to the state and society, which is the basis for social harmony. However, this acceptance of diversity does not extend to cultural practices that are viewed as illiberal as this would undermine the freedom and autonomy, which are essential to a harmonious society. Pluralists, like Parekh, while agreeing that multiculturalism reduces tension, go beyond liberal multiculturalism by arguing that deep diversity is needed to develop the shared sense of unity needed for a harmonious society...

It is really important that you refer to the ideas of two key thinkers listed on the multiculturalism section of the specification. The ideas of two key thinkers (Kymlicka and Parekh) are used here in their correct context.

Correct use of political vocabulary in the right context here, which reveals clear understanding.

Having identified agreement between multiculturalists, this section starts to identify how multiculturalists disagree about how best to create a harmonious society.

The essay would then explore the pluralist approach in more detail before covering the conservative criticism in order to reach a conclusion.

Nations

Unlike the core ideologies you have studied, nationalism is not a cohesive ideology. All nationalists believe that the world is best understood as being divided into different nations. How to respond to that fact, however, differs greatly from nationalist to nationalist.

Nationalism

Nationalism is an idea that is highly relevant in society today. Wherever there is conflict between countries, and often within countries, nationalism is probably the motivation behind it.

For example, the passions aroused in Catalonia in 2017 were to do with how a nation is defined and the self-determination of a nation.

Another example is Brexit. The views on both sides of the Brexit debate are inspired by different notions of nationalism, internationalism and the nation-state.

Application

Human nature

The idea of the nation is linked to human nature as different nationalist views of the concept of the nation, namely civic or ethnic, are to do with their view of human nature, that is, rational or irrational.

Society

The way a nation is defined will relate to the type of society that exists. Rational, civic definitions of nationhood will lead to a highly inclusive society, whereas a nation defined by race or **ethnicity** will be the most exclusive type of society.

Nations

Any understanding of nationalism is only possible when the concept of 'a nation' is understood.

- The term refers to a community of people who consider themselves to be connected together.
- This connection is different for different nations. Some nations feel connected due to shared values for society or a shared history, others a shared culture or religion or language.
- However, there is no objective understanding of what constitutes a nation, and this is where problems start.

Confusions over nationhood

A nation is defined as a group of people who consider themselves to be a nation. A nation is, therefore, **self-defined**. However, when a group of people consider themselves to be a nation, but others do not, these differing opinions can often lead to conflict.

- The conflict in Northern Ireland (1968–1998) is an issue of defining nationhood.
- The desire for independence in Scotland is also to do with distinct understandings of nationhood.
- Recent conflicts in Catalonia, Spain, are about nationhood.
- The Russian invasion and annexation of Crimea (2014) is also about definitions of nationhood.
- Aspects of the Brexit referendum may be down to preservation of the British nation and rejection of European nationhood.

🔍 Case study Catalonia, 2017

In 2017, Catalans felt so strongly about their national identity as Catalonian and not Spanish that the regional government held an illegal independence referendum. The national government in Madrid rejected the Catalans defining themselves as a distinct nation and was outraged by the calling of the referendum.

So, is there a clear way to decide who has the right to call themselves a nation? Can Spain insist that Catalans are Spanish as well, and the two identities are not mutually exclusive?

The Spanish government sent extra police and military troops into Barcelona to stop people voting in the illegal poll.

Now try this

Outline two ways a group may consider themselves a nation.

Self-determination and nation-states

Two principles closely linked to the nation are the ideas of self-determination and the **nation-state**.

Self-determination

Self-determination is the desire to make decisions for oneself. In other words, **autonomy**.

- Self-determination is the primary aim of most nations.
- This is because most nations believe that only they know what they want and so only they can make decisions that will benefit them.
- Self-determination is associated with 18th-century philosopher Jean-Jacques Rousseau's idea of 'general will', where he argued that a community of people was a recognised political unit who had rights and should be heard (see page 160 for more on Rousseau and other nationalist key thinkers).

Nation-state

When a nation's desire for self-determination is realised, a nation-state is born.

- A nation-state is when a nation rules itself within a geographical area that it controls.
- Most countries in Europe are considered to be nation-states. For example, Italy, Austria and Denmark are all areas controlled respectively by Italians, Austrians and Danes.
- Today, we may see the nation-state as a relatively uncontroversial term. Yet many conflicts concern this innocuous sounding term.

 Case study **Former Yugoslavia**

Yugoslavia was created after the First World War, in 1918. Many people growing up in the post-War era may have mistakenly assumed that Yugoslavia consisted of a nation of Yugoslavs. In fact, it brought together Serbs, Croats, Bosnian Muslims, Albanians, Slovenes and others.

Former Yugoslavia, 1918.

In 1991, after the Cold War, Communist-controlled Yugoslavia became embroiled in a bloody and violent war between the different nations, all seeking to assert the right to self-determination and create independent nation-states. Around 100,000 lives were lost between 1991 and 1999, with millions FORCED from their homes in a drive for 'ethnic cleansing'.

Yugoslavia has now disappeared from the map of Europe, to be replaced by six nations and the disputed territory of Kosovo.

Application of self-determination

Human nature

Self-determination is considered to be a rational idea and hence can be seen to be connected to human nature.

Society

Self-determination can be linked to society as it is suggesting that the nation is a genuine political community capable of self-government.

Application of nation-state

The state

The concept of the nation-state supports the idea that nations should rule themselves in their own state.

Economy

A nation-state also has control over its own economy and can seek either a mutually interdependent model with other nations or autarky (economic self-sufficiency).

Now try this

Name two countries in Europe that are considered nation-states and explain why.

Culturalism and racialism

The ideas of culturalism and racialism both look at different ways of identifying a nation. These are more irrational than the liberal idea of civic nationalism.

Culturalism

Culturalism is the way some nations identify themselves. It is the idea that each nation has a unique and powerful mix of shared values and history, which, when seen as a whole, are their culture.

- 18th-century philosopher Johann Gottfried von Herder argued that a nation's culture is crucial in understanding its volksgeist (see page 160 to revise nationalist key thinkers).

- Some nations do not seek self-determination, preferring instead to be a component part of a larger nation as long as they are given the freedom to practise and protect their unique cultural heritage; for example, the Welsh.

- Culturalism thus emphasises the emotional links people have with their nation and are grounded in more mystical, emotional ties.

Racialism

A few nations, historically, have identified themselves as such on the basis of race.

- Racialism is the belief that there is not a single human race. Instead, there are a number of distinct races.

- Such beliefs argue that race is biological and, as such, **unchangeable**. One is born into a specific race. (Only a very small group of nationalists believe this.)

- Forms of nationalism which use race as their determining factor are highly **exclusive** as no one can be a part of the nation unless they are born into it. Nazi Germany is an example of racialism.

- It is useful to note than the notion of racialism can be seen as a perversion of the idea of culturalism, turning culturalism into something far darker than is accurate.

 Case study **The Risorgimento and culturalism**

The Risorgimento (1815–1871) was the movement that brought about Italian unification, consolidating the different states into a single, unified nation. It was a cultural movement that aimed to awaken the national consciousness of the Italian people via cultural association. 'Young Italy', a key group in the movement, was founded by propagandist and revolutionary Giuseppe Mazzini in 1831. The group hoped to educate Italian people to a sense of their nationhood and encourage the masses to rise against the existing regime.

Italy had not been unified since the 5th century and foreign influence was pervasive.

The Risorgimento sought to evoke the romantic, nationalist and patriotic ideals of an Italian Renaissance via Italian culture and create a unified political identity.

The final unification of Italy took place in 1870, but author and statesman Massimo d'Azeglio (1798–1866) argued that centuries of foreign domination had created large differences in Italian society and the role of the new government was to create a unified Italian society. He famously said, 'Italy has been made. Now it remains to make Italians.'

Application of culturalism

Human nature

Culturalism connects to human nature as it relates to how humans understand themselves and the belief that being part of a nation is an emotional link.

Society

Culturalism supports the view that society should encourage and promote the unique culture of the nation.

Application of racialism

Human nature

Racialism is based on the idea that one's human nature is entirely connected to one's race, and that different races have different innate qualities.

Society

Racialist approaches to nationhood envisage a segregated society in which different races live separately, fulfilling their separate roles in society.

Now try this

Why are culturalism and racialism considered exclusive forms of nationalism?

Internationalism

The concept of internationalism looks beyond the nation and nationalism to the wider world. Two types of internationalism – **liberal internationalism** and **socialist internationalism** – have starkly different conclusions as to the role of nationalism in the world.

Liberal internationalism

For liberal nationalists, internationalism has a crucial role to play in maintaining peace and stability in the world.

- While liberals believe that all nations should have self-determination if they want it (read more about liberal nationalists on page 157), this sits alongside a belief that nations must be encouraged to be interdependent.
- This combination of independence and interdependence may appear odd, but it reflects liberal thinking towards the individual. Society must allow individuals autonomy but, at the same time, individuals cannot act as they wish.
- Liberal internationalism is the 'harm principle' (see page 54 to see how liberal key thinkers argued this view) for nations. That is, nations should be as free as possible provided they do not cause harm to other nations.

Liberal internationalism in practice

So, how have liberal nationalists attempted to bring about this combination of independence and interdependence?

- Liberals recognise that nations, like individuals, should rule over themselves.
- The League of Nations (1920–1946) was based on the liberal internationalist view of creating 'supranational' institutions to police the world.
- The United Nations, its successor, has the same role now.
- Perhaps the most successful 'supranational' institution has been the EU. Created in the 1950s to avoid Europe ever going to war with itself again, the EU realised that economic interdependency among nation-states creates positive relationships between these countries, which is the most likely way to avoid war.

Application

Human nature

Internationalism is based on the view that there is one world and one human race, with a single human nature. Some see nationalism as divisive, seeking to divide humans into separate groups.

The economy

Liberal internationalism is based on economic interdependency as a way to maintain peace and order.

Socialist internationalism

Socialists, generally, are opposed to nationalism. Instead, they support internationalism.

- Socialists believe nationalism divides the working class across the world and creates artificial divisions between them, encouraging them to see fellow workers not as comrades, but as enemies.
- Internationalism, therefore, should be encouraged. As Marx famously said, 'Workers of the world unite. You have nothing to lose but your chains!'
- Socialist internationalism argues that we should look beyond the geographical boundaries of nations and see instead multi-national working classes being exploited across the globe.
- When workers understand their strength as a worldwide class, they will feel empowered to challenge it.

⊜ Case study · Lenin, *Imperialism, the Highest Stage of Capitalism* (1917)

Lenin wrote about imperialism, claiming that it was the highest stage of capitalism. He argued that capitalism had temporarily avoided collapse by exploiting the proletariat in colonies and 'buying off' the indigenous population. This enabled the bourgeoisie to improve working conditions and provide welfare at home while ruthlessly exploiting the raw materials and people in the colonies. Hence, for socialists, there can only be internationalism as nationalism is a way of oppressing the proletariat.

The Berlin Conference: the German Chancellor Otto von Bismarck is about to divide up the 'cake' of Africa between the different powers of Europe.

The state

Liberal internationalism sees the world as made up of independent nation states, freely cooperating with each other.

Now try this

Why is liberal internationalism considered consistent with liberal nationalism?

Different types of nationalism

Some say that nationalism is a chameleon, cross-cutting ideology. Over the next few pages, we will look at how the core ideas and principles on pages 152–55 relate to the four different types of nationalism: liberal, conservative, anti/post-colonialism and expansionist nationalism.

The four types of nationalism

The diagram below shows how varied the views are between the different nationalists. They are frequently diametrically opposed to each other.

Rational ← Liberal nationalism / Anti/Post-colonialism ... Conservative nationalism ... Expansionist nationalism → Irrational

Inclusive ← Liberal nationalism / Anti/Post-colonialism ... Conservative nationalism ... Expansionist nationalism → Exclusive

Civic ← Liberal nationalism / Anti/Post-colonialism — Cultural — Ethnic — Expansionist nationalism / Racialist nationalism -Nazism → Racial

Self-determination ← Liberal nationalism / Anti/Post-colonialism ... Expansionist nationalism → Expansionist

Multicultural ← Liberal nationalism / Anti/Post-colonialism ... Conservative nationalism ... Expansionist nationalism → Monocultural

Progressive ← Liberal nationalism / Anti/Post-colonialism ... Conservative nationalism ... Expansionist nationalism → Regressive/reactionary

Rational or irrational

These terms relate to whether an idea is based on logical reasoning (rational) or on emotional responses (irrational). Whether a form of nationalism is rational or irrational largely controls the remainder of its attributes (as seen above).

Progressive or regressive/reactionary

Progressive refers to whether an idea is forward looking. Regressive refers to an idea which hangs on to or seeks to return to past ways or ideas. This is usually in a regressive way.

Inclusive or exclusive

Inclusive nationalism is open to all; anyone can join. Exclusive nationalism seeks a shared culture, history or even language in order for someone to be considered part of a nation. The most exclusive forms of nationalism are those based on race because if you are not considered part of a race, you cannot become part of the nation.

Self-determination or expansion

Liberal and anti/post-colonial nationalism believe in self-determination for all nations. In contrast, chauvinistic nationalism tends not to, believing instead in colonising weaker nations and ruling over them (see page 158 for a discussion on expansionist and anti/post-colonial nationalism). Conservative nationalism is unconcerned with other nations as its primary concern is to preserve a cohesive sense of nationhood in its own nation.

Multicultural or monocultural

These terms relate to whether a form of nationalism allows different cultures to flourish in society or seeks to have one culture (mono) dominating society.

Civic, cultural, ethnic or racial

These different types of nationalism relate to how one can be part of a nation. Civic nationalism requires 'members' to support the values of society. Cultural nationalism requires shared values, such as language, culture, tradition. Ethnic nationalism requires more than cultural assimilation, it requires a shared heritage and ancestry. Racial nationalism requires racial 'purity' within the nation, as it rejects the view that there is only one human race.

Now try this

What makes a type of nationalism inclusive or exclusive?

Liberal and conservative nationalism

Liberal nationalism is associated with the creation of independent nation states. Conservative nationalism usually occurs in nation-states that have been in existence for a very long time.

Liberal nationalism

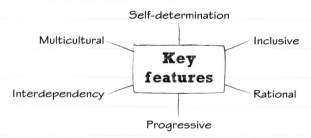

Self-determination

Multicultural — **Key features** — Inclusive

Interdependency — **Key features** — Rational

Progressive

Conservative nationalism

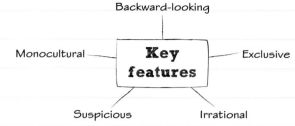

Backward-looking

Monocultural — **Key features** — Exclusive

Suspicious   Irrational

Features explained

Self-determination: liberal nationalism is primarily concerned with ensuring that all nations can rule themselves in their own state, if they wish to.

Support for Scottish independence.

Inclusive: liberal nationalism has an inclusive, civic understanding of nationhood. That means anyone who shares the values of a nation should be able to become part of it relatively quickly.

Rational: like liberalism itself, the ideas of liberal nationalism are based on rational principles like self-determination.

Progressive: liberal nationalism is forward-looking in that it sees society advancing and improving in the future, promoting and protecting the rights of people. It is a force for peace in the world.

Interdependency: liberal nationalism is unique in seeking independence alongside interdependence (see page 155 for more on internationalism), believing both are necessary for a peaceful world order.

Multicultural: liberal nationalism supports the practising of different cultures in society, supported by their strong belief in diversity, pluralism and tolerance. Their only requirement is that the cultures are supportive of the wider values of the nation.

Features explained

Backward looking: conservatism sees nationalism as a way to bind society together as one nation. It is essentially backward-looking and seeks to maintain traditions of the past.

Exclusive: the nation has a shared history and culture. This makes it somewhat exclusive as it takes time to become part of the nation. You need to have shared some history and immersed yourself in the culture until you are able to feel part of that nation.

Irrational: conservative nationalism is most certainly irrational as it is based on an emotional connection with one's nation. Human identity is understood as part of the community that is the nation.

Commemorating the Queen's Diamond Jubilee in 2012.

Suspicious: the cohesiveness of the nation is of crucial importance. Hence, conservative nationalists are extremely suspicious and hostile towards any attempt to change the uniqueness of the nation. This links closely with their support for monoculturalism.

Monocultural: in order to maintain cohesiveness, new cultures or traditions should not be introduced into society. This explains conservative nationalists' anxiety towards immigration. When immigrants are allowed to settle, they must adopt society's dominant culture and reject the culture of their home nation.

Now try this

Why does liberal nationalism support multiculturalism and conservative nationalism support a monoculture?

Expansionist and anti/post-colonial nationalism

Expansionist nationalism tends to exist in nations which consider themselves superior to other nations (this is chauvinism). Anti/post-colonial nationalism is a form of nationalism unique to those countries that have experienced colonial rule.

Expansionist nationalism

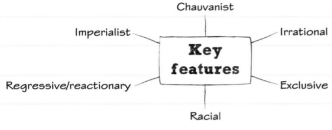

Chauvanist
Imperialist
Irrational
Key features
Regressive/reactionary
Exclusive
Racial

Features explained

Chauvinist: expansionist nationalism is highly chauvinistic. This means it considers itself superior to all other nations.

Irrational: expansionist nationalism is highly irrational, believing myths of national greatness to inspire the nation.

Exclusive: expansionist nationalists believe their nation is unique and special and membership of the nation is usually restricted to inheritance.

Racial: in some cases, expansionist nationalism takes on a racial tone, suggesting only people who belong to the same 'race' can be members of the nation. This is not the same as being born in the particular country – sometimes, even this is not sufficient.

Regressive/reactionary: expansionist nationalism is highly regressive and reactionary as it is seeking to return aspects of society to a less advanced state, often restricting or removing rights of people. It also seeks to look back to a previous era, wishing to emulate it in many ways.

Imperialist: the chauvinistic character of expansionist nationalism leads it towards imperialism.

Imperialist countries seek to dominate and control weaker nation-states for their own benefit.

Anti/post-colonial nationalism

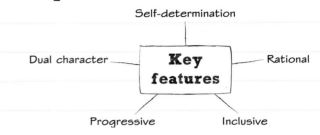

Self-determination
Dual character
Rational
Key features
Progressive
Inclusive

Features explained

Self-determination: like liberal nationalism, anti/post-colonial nationalism is concerned with ensuring that nations who wish to may rule themselves in their own state.

Mahatma Gandhi was the main leader of India's anti-colonial or independence movement.

Rational: the ideas of anti/post-colonial nationalism are based on rational principles like self-determination or civic nationalism.

Inclusive: anti/post-colonial nationalism has an inclusive, civic understanding of nationhood – anyone who shares the values of a nation should be able to become part of it.

Progressive: anti/post-colonial nationalism is forward-looking, in that it seeks to advance society and make it better for all in the future, promoting and protecting the rights of people.

Dual character: as the name suggests, anti/post-colonial nationalism has a dual character:

- Anti-colonialism is the ideas found in liberal nationalism as applied to the phenomena of colonialism. These colonies sought to be free from their colonial oppressor.

- Post-colonialism refers to the period after independence has been achieved. Here, the former colonies seek to reject the traditions of their oppressors and create a new nation-state based on the culture, traditions and customs of their own nation.

Now try this

Why is it accurate to say that anti-colonial nationalism is the rejection of expansionist nationalism?

Differences within nationalism

It is helpful to be able to categorise the different strands of nationalism according to the following terms.

Differences between different strands of nationalism

	Liberal and anti/post-colonial nationalism	Conservative nationalism	Expansionist nationalism
Rational or irrational?	Can be seen to be the most rational.	Has a more emotive understanding of nationhood and nationalism.	The most irrational – adopts an integral form of nationalism to heighten emotional understanding of it.
	It is suggested that **all forms of nationalism** are irrational as the very essence of nationhood is the belief in feeling a connection with one group of people over another – an emotional, irrational notion.		
Progressive or recessive?	Progressive forms of nationalism that are seen to be forward-looking, seeking to improve, free and advancing society.	Seems to be nostalgic, looking to the past in deciding how to act in the future. It isn't necessarily regressive or reactionary, but it certainly seeks to hang on to past experiences and tradition.	Seeks to return society to a less advanced state, often restricting or removing rights of people or nations. Many **expansionist forms of nationalism** were also driven by a plan for the future, often world domination, and so cannot solely be seen as backward-looking.
Inclusive or exclusive?	They have an inclusive understanding of nationhood, although anti/post-colonial nationalism is perhaps slightly less so.	More exclusive as 'membership' of the nation cannot be immediate; it takes time to fully integrate into a nation's customs.	They believe their nation is superior to others and therefore membership is highly exclusive. Only **racial** understandings of nationhood are more exclusive.
Self-determination or expansion?	They strongly believe in the concept of self-determination for all nations; it is a fundamental value for them.	Unconcerned with the status of other nations, being solely interested in the cohesiveness of their own nation.	Does not support the right of self-determination for other nations, believing instead that they are superior and should conquer and control other nations.
Multicultural or monocultural?	Support a diverse society where citizens are free to have different cultures and values. However, these diverse views cannot challenge the overall values of society.	Doesn't support multiculturalism, believing instead that all members of the nation must fit in with the dominant culture in society by assimilating and dropping their past customs and traditions.	They revere their superior culture, believing all other cultures are degenerate.
Civic, cultural, ethnic or racial?	They have a civic understanding of nationhood. The only requirement for 'membership' is to want to be part of the nation, accepting their values.	Has a cultural approach, believing a single culture is essential to promote cohesiveness. Some may also support an ethnic approach, believing that ancestry is also important.	Sees ancestry as significant in defining nationhood. The most extreme forms of expansionist nationalism take a racial (biological) understanding of race.

Peace or war?

Overall, you need to consider these ideas in trying to determine whether a form of nationalism would lead to a more peaceful world or one consumed by war. It would be straightforward to assume that **liberal and anti/post-colonial nationalism** always lead to peace and that **expansionist nationalism** always leads to war. While the latter is most certainly true, it is also the case that many wars and conflicts have been fought on the basis of **liberal nationalism** and **anti-colonialism**.

Now try this

Is it accurate to call nationalism a coherent ideology?

Nationalist key thinkers

Key thinkers and ideas

Jean-Jacques Rousseau (1712–1778)

Rousseau was a French Enlightenment philosopher whose writings had an enormous impact on early nationalism. Use him when discussing liberal nationalism, civic nationalism and self-determination, nation-states and nations and the state and society.

Key ideas

1. **General will**: the people (the nation) are sovereign and their 'will' is what is best for the state as a whole. Government must enforce, not direct, the collective will of the people.

2. **Civic nationalism**: Rousseau believed that the validity of a (nation) state was based on the participation of its citizens.

Key thinkers and ideas

Johann Gottfried von Herder (1744–1803)

Von Herder was a German philosopher who was passionate about the role of culture in nationhood. Use him to discuss culturalism, irrationality, conservative nationalism, human nature and society.

Key ideas

1. **Culturalism**: a nation's culture is a unique and precious commodity. Each nation should value and respect its own culture as well as others.

2. **Volksgeist**: Herder used the word to mean the unique cultural essence and spirit of a nation. 'Volk' refers to the people. The people are the root of national culture.

Key thinkers and ideas

Giuseppe Mazzini (1805–1872)

Mazzini was an Italian nationalist who was committed to the cause of Italian unification. Use him to discuss liberal nationalism, nations, self-determination and nation-states as well as the state, human nature and society.

Key ideas

1. **Self-determination**: the nation can only be free when it has the ability to express itself through its own state.

2. **Patriotism**: patriotism must be the primary focus of all citizens, with every other matter being secondary.

Key thinkers and ideas

Charles Maurras (1868–1952)

Maurras was a French ultra-nationalist whose views are considered far-right wing. Use him when discussing irrational, exclusive, expansionist and chauvinistic nationalism, as well as the economy, human nature, the state and society.

Key ideas

1. **Integral nationalism**: this is the idea that citizens must immerse themselves completely within the nation, putting the needs of the nation above their own.

2. **Expansionism**: or a strong military ethos; Maurras's form of nationalism was chauvinistic and expansionist, believing that national pride was tied in to conquest.

Key thinkers and ideas

Marcus Garvey (1887–1940)

Garvey was an African nationalist who was committed to the cause of black nationalism. Use him when discussing anti/post-colonial nationalism, self-determination and culturalism, as well as the economy, human nature and the state.

Key ideas

1. **Pan-Africanism**: all Africans must unite together to end imperial rule and create strong economies and societies in Africa for black people

2. **Black pride**: black people should feel proud of their black heritage and not succumb to dominant white cultural attitudes of their assumed inferiority.

Now try this

Label each thinker as either liberal, conservative, expansionist or anti/post-colonial nationalism based on which strand *has been most shaped by their ideas.*

Exam skills

This question will help you to revise for **Section B** of your A Level **Paper 2** exam. You will be given two 24-mark essay questions for each political idea – you will need to choose **one** of them from your chosen idea.

Section B

- Aim to spend around 30 minutes on this essay. Plan your answer (page 104).
- Your essay needs to be fully structured, including an introduction and a conclusion.
- You **must** use at least **two** relevant key thinkers as outlined in the relevant section of the specification.

Questions

Questions will explore the extent of agreement within nationalism **or** tensions within the different strands over one of the four key areas (the state, society, the economy and human nature). The command words for the questions are always '**To what extent**'. You need to cover all three AOs, which are equally weighted:
- set out the nature of the debate on both sides – show you understand how the content relates to the question (AO1)
- examine the ideology/strands in relation to the question – this also means showing similarities and differences within the strands (AO2)
- make judgements – explore (evaluate) the extent of the similarities and differences and come to a judgement (AO3). This should be clear throughout your essay, not just in the conclusion.

Worked example

7   To what extent does nationalism encourage peace?

You must use appropriate thinkers you have studied to support your answer and consider both sides in a balanced way. **(24 marks)**

The idea of nationalism is represented by many different strands. While it may be reasonable to suggest that only some strands encourage peace in society, namely liberal and anti/post-colonial nationalism, with conservative nationalism seeking stability above all, expansionist nationalism is primarily responsible for many wars and conflicts. This essay will argue that all forms of nationalism undermine the peace and stability of the world in some way or another.

The best case in favour of the view that nationalism encourages peace can be found in liberal nationalism. Liberal nationalists are totally committed to worldwide peace as they believe that all nations should rule themselves in their own state – national self-determination. They echo Rousseau's notion of the nation being a genuine political community able to express its own will. The ability of nations to rule themselves is supported by anti-colonial nationalists who argue that indigenous populations have been oppressed for too long by their colonial rulers, which causes conflict in society; peace will only prevail when independent nation-states are created across the world. Mazzini argued that nations are only truly free when they have their own state.

However, other forms of nationalism are much more closely associated with war, showing that nationalism does not encourage peace. As its name suggests, expansionist nationalism rejects the liberal nationalist idea that all nations are entitled to self-determination and instead seeks to expand beyond the borders of its own nation-state by invading other (usually) sovereign nation-states. They believe that their nation is superior to other nations, who are undeserving of the right to rule themselves, contrasting sharply with the views of anti-colonialist nationalists...

... In evaluating whether nationalism encourages peace, it can be seen that although it appears that liberal and anti-colonial nationalism stand for noble values which certainly appear to support peace, stability and international order, the reality of attempting to achieve these aims is almost always a violent, bloody war where many innocent people lose their lives in the name of peace. Thus, the beliefs of some forms of nationalism may support peace more than the reality.

An introduction like this shows that the student understands the assessment objectives and sets the essay up excellently. The final sentence hints at how the student will argue.

Suggesting that this is 'the best case' for the view shows evaluation.

A key thinker is correctly referenced and used successfully to expand on the point. Make sure you refer to **two** key thinkers.

A contrast is shown to the views in the first paragraph. Expand this by using examples and referencing Maurras.

Next, discuss how liberal and anti-colonial nationalism do not always promote peace and stability.

Throughout your essay it should be clear which side you think is most convincing, so your conclusion should sum this up and be justified by your argument.

Exam-style practice

Practice for **Section B** of **Paper 2** of your A Level exam with these exam-style questions. There are answers on page 312. Section B consists of two questions for each non-core political idea and you will have to answer **one** question on the political idea that you have studied.

Anarchism

3 To what extent do collectivist anarchists and individualist anarchists agree about the state?

   You must use appropriate thinkers you have studied to support your answer and consider both sides in a balanced way. **(24 marks)**

Remember, you need to allow around 30 minutes to answer this question.

Your essay needs to be fully structured, including an introduction and a conclusion.

Ecologism

4 To what extent do ecologists agree that human nature needs to change to protect the environment?

   You must use appropriate thinkers you have studied to support your answer and consider both sides in a balanced way. **(24 marks)**

Don't forget to quickly plan your answer. Aim to draw up a four-point essay plan to ensure that your answer is balanced.

Feminism

5 To what extent do all feminists agree over patriarchy in society?

   You must use appropriate thinkers you have studied to support your answer and consider both sides in a balanced way. **(24 marks)**

Make sure you include key terms and the main ideas of at least two key thinkers.

You should also aim to include evidence about the significance of the differences and similarities **between the different views**.

Multiculturalism

6 To what extent do multiculturalists agree over the role of the state in balancing diversity and unity?

   You must use appropriate thinkers you have studied to support your answer and consider both sides in a balanced way. **(24 marks)**

Read over your answer at the end to make sure your points are logically linked and your essay flows.

Remember to explore **both** the agreements and the tensions (both sides of the argument). Don't ignore the views expressed on the opposing side of the argument, but address them to explain why 'your side' is better.

Nationalism

7 To what extent is nationalism more united than divided?

   You must use appropriate thinkers you have studied to support your answer and consider both sides in a balanced way. **(24 marks)**

Your conclusion should be focused and justified by your argument. Make clear which side you think is most convincing, though this should already be clear throughout your essay.

Comparative theories

When comparing the political situations in two or more countries, you need to identify the similarities and differences and show **why** they occur. In every case, you are looking to explain an **outcome**. Three theoretical approaches – **rational**, **cultural** and **structural** – can help you to explain the similarities and differences between the government and politics of different countries.

Rational theory

The key to understanding rational theory is to focus on **individuals**.

- Individuals will act selfishly to protect their best interests.
- They will evaluate options and pick the one that has the best outcome for them.

Identifying rational theory

The key word here is **selfish**. If you can explain the actions of individuals in a political system because they have been selfish, this is **rational**.

For example, citizens might argue for better protection of rights as their rights have been infringed, rather than for the common good.

Cultural theory

The key to understanding cultural theory is to focus on **group and shared ideologies**. This could have two interpretations:

- Groups act to protect and advance a common ideology. Therefore, outcomes can be explained by groups acting together.
- Cultural norms or expectations might guide the outcomes of a political system and the individuals within it.

Identifying cultural theory

The key word here is **shared**. If you can explain a political outcome (similarities and differences) because it was expected, or because a group acted with a shared ideology, this is **cultural**.

A good example of this is the difference in constitutions between the USA and UK. While the UK is governed culturally by conventions, the US culture is that the entrenched and sovereign Constitution is superior to political wrangling.

Structural theory

The key to understanding structural theory is to focus on the **institutions and processes**.

- Outcomes can be explained by looking at the processes that had to be followed within institutions of power.
- These institutions and processes are the best explanation of political action and outcome.

Identifying structural theory

The key word here is **institutions**. If you can explain political outcomes because of the processes in place, this is **structural**.

An example of this might be the loyalty of MPs to their party but Congressmen to their state – the party discipline structure is strong in the UK but weak in the USA.

Applying the theories

It is important to remember that you have to **use** these theories to explain differences and similarities **between** governments and political systems – they do not explain outcomes in one country alone. It is also important to remember that more than one theory might be used to explain the same outcome. In this case, you have to judge which is **more** suitable. For more on the application of these theories, see pages 172, 181, 190, 201–202, 209, 215 and 221.

Now try this

1 Using the 'key word' for each definition, explain why each theory is best understood using these words.
2 Explain how you would include any of these theories in an exam answer.

The US Constitution

The US **Constitution** was written in 1787 and ratified in 1789. Since then, the government of the United States of America has been regulated by the rules and principles laid out in the Constitution.

Key features of the US Constitution

- At 7,000 words, the US Constitution governs a country nearly 10 million square kilometres in size with a population of over 300 million people.

- To avoid becoming outdated, the language in the Constitution is vague, allowing it to be interpreted and adapted over time.

- Unlike the UK constitution, the US Constitution is **codified**. In the USA, therefore, **sovereignty** resides in the Constitution as the source of political authority and power.

- The US Constitution is **entrenched**, meaning it is protected by law. This makes the Constitution **judiciable** (see page 68 for a more general look at constitutions). Article V outlines the amendment process to the Constitution.

The US Constitution has been formally amended 27 times.

Case study **The 2nd amendment**

The right to bear arms, the 2nd amendment, can often be a cause of controversy.

The Founding Fathers may have considered a militia 'necessary' as the newly freed states had a very small regular army, having overthrown the British.

Having fought and won the War of Independence, the USA was now 'free'. However, it still faced military threat from the British, Spanish and French, who held adjoining territories.

Amendment II: *A well regulated Militia, being necessary to the security of a free State, the right of the people to keep and bear Arms, shall not be infringed.*

The Founding Fathers were referring to the guns and rifles available at that time, primarily muskets.

Having spent decades under the tyranny of the British, some of the Founding Fathers wanted to ensure the rights of citizens could not be removed by any future government.

The 2nd amendment today

The situation today is very different. The USA has the largest army and nuclear arsenal in the world, they no longer face such continental threats from other armies and the variety and lethality of guns available has vastly increased. Changing the Constitution is incredibly difficult so, despite instances of terrible gun crime in the USA, the 2nd amendment remains in place.

Now try this

1 Using the key features, explain the benefit of each feature of the US Constitution.
2 Name two ways in which the US Constitution could be considered to be outdated.

The constitutional framework

The Constitution gives each of the three branches of government – executive, legislature and judiciary – a set of **enumerated powers**.

Enumerated powers

Executive branch: President
Recognises other countries
Negotiates treaties
Grants reprieves and pardons
Vetoes legislation
Nominates federal justices
Commander-in-chief

Can reject and approve appointments

Can amend, delay or reject legislation

Can impeach the president

Can use the veto override

Can rule actions of the executive branch unconstitutional

Nominates judges

Can veto bills

Send nominations and treaties to Congress

Can issue pardons

Legislative branch: Congress
Collects taxes
Borrows money
Declares war
Regulates trade
Ratifies treaties and appointments

Can rule legislation unconstitutional

Approves judicial appointments

Can create lower courts

Can suggest constitutional amendments

Judicial branch: Supreme Court
Inference of judicial review

The power of judicial review was not formalised until Marbury v Madison (1803) and Fletcher v Peck (1810).

All other powers not outlined in the Constitution were given to the states to exercise (10th amendment).

 **Synoptic link**   The separation of powers in the USA can be contrasted with the UK's fused executive and legislative branches (see page 75 for more on the UK Parliament). However, at times, both create an overly powerful executive.

Separated powers or sharing powers?

Political theorist Richard Neustadt claimed in 1960 that the **separation of powers** in the Constitution was misleading: 'The Constitutional Convention of 1787 is supposed to have created a government of separated powers. It did nothing of the sort. Rather it created a government of separated institutions sharing powers.'

This does not mean that 'separation of powers' and **checks and balances** are the same thing (read more

about the principles of the US Constitution on page 167). Rather, the powers themselves have been broken up and shared, as shown above. For example, the president can suggest and veto legislation, Congress can make and veto override legislation, while the Supreme Court can declare it unconstitutional. All branches of government therefore have a 'part' of this legislative power.

Now try this

1 Explain, with examples, the powers of each branch of government according to the Constitution.
2 In what ways can Congress's power be evaluated as a 'reactive' to the president?

The amendment process

The US Constitution can only be amended formally through the process laid out in Article V **entrenchment**.

The process

The amendment process has two stages:

1 A proposal stage at national level.

2 A ratification stage at state level.

Congress can place a time limit on the ratification, typically seven years. This should avoid events like the 27th amendment, which took more than 202 years to ratify.

Two-thirds of both houses of Congress must agree to a proposed amendment. For example, 33 amendments have passed this stage.

Two-thirds of states must call a National Constitutional Convention and adopt the proposed amendment. This stage has never been used.

Three-quarters of state legislatures need to ratify the amendment. This stage has been used for all but one amendment.

Three-quarters of state constitutional conventions need to ratify the amendment. This stage has only been used once – for the 21st amendment, which repealed prohibition.

Evaluation of the process

Of the amendment process, constitutional Founding Father James Madison claimed: 'It guards equally against that extreme facility, which would render the Constitution too mutable; and that extreme difficulty, which might perpetuate its discovered faults.'

 Madison meant that the process would prevent the Constitution being too flexible or too rigid.

But was he correct? The process has a range of advantages and disadvantages.

👍 The process works, with 27 amendments having been added.

👍 The Constitution and its principles have endured the test of time, with the amendment process protecting these principles.

👍 The process requires **bipartisanship** (see page 167 on principles of the US constitution), which prevents the tyranny of one party or opinion.

👍 The process protects federalism by preventing federal government gaining too much power.

👎 The requirement for super-majorities has made the process too difficult.

👎 The unelected Supreme Court gains too much power through interpretative amendments.

👎 The process can allow for a tyranny of the minority, with just a few members of Congress or states able to hold up amendments.

👎 The process means it is difficult to incorporate new and evolving ideas into the US Constitution, making it increasingly out of date.

👎 The process has allowed for poor amendments, such as the 18th which was repealed just fourteen years later by the 21st.

 **Synoptic link**   The **codification** of the US Constitution means a formal amendment process is necessary. The uncodified nature of the UK constitution makes it far more flexible.

Now try this

1 Explain why the US Constitution has so few amendments.

2 Analyse the arguments for changing the amendment process, given how much the USA has changed since 1787.

Principles of the US Constitution

The Constitution has a number of underlying 'principles', which are effectively the things the Founding Fathers aimed to achieve through their words. Most of the 'principles' are not named in the Constitution, but are implicit in the wording.

Five key principles of the Constitution

Meaning	In the Constitution	Effectiveness today
① Separation of powers		
Governmental powers are divided between three branches of government, all of which can act independently and interdependently.	The powers that are outlined in Articles I, II and III. The three branches are physically separate.	👍 The branches remain completely separate from one another and can act independently. 👎 The president has usurped some of Congress's power (for example, dominating military actions).
② Checks and balances		
Each of the three branches of government can exercise control over the other branches.	The checks laid out in Articles I, II and III.	👍 Use of checks such as the veto and override demonstrate their continued importance. 👎 Checks and balances can lead to gridlock and, ultimately, government shutdowns.
③ Bipartisanship		
The requirement of political parties to act together (as some Founding Fathers disliked parties altogether!)	The two-thirds requirement for amendments and the veto override.	👍 Use of the veto override demonstrates bipartisanship can be achieved. 👎 The USA seems more partisan than ever, with three government shutdowns in the last six years.
④ Limited government		
The requirement that government should be as big as necessary but no bigger.	Enumeration of powers limits governmental power; the Bill of Rights protects citizens' rights from the government.	👍 Supreme Court decisions have protected citizens' rights rather than congressional legislation. 👎 Guantanamo Bay remains open, infringing citizens' rights.
⑤ Federalism		
The shared sovereignty outlined in the Constitution between federal and state government.	States have the right to run their own elections (Article I); powers not enumerated go to the states (10th amendment).	👍 States have successfully used the Supreme Court to maintain their own power (for example, Texas v US [2016]). 👎 Federal government has increasingly grown in size (for example, 'Obamacare').

Guantanamo Bay

The Founding Fathers, fearful of the tyranny from which they had just freed themselves and determined to protect their states, wrote the Constitution to create a 'limited government'. The case of Guantanamo Bay therefore raises some questions.

👍 Guantanamo Bay allows the USA to try and deal with the emerging threat of terrorism and protect its citizens.

👍 Individual states would not be well placed, in terms of money and resources, to deal with such a threat.

👍 As Guantanamo Bay is not on US soil, the Bill of Rights does not apply.

👎 Guantanamo Bay breaches the US principled belief in protection of rights, especially against cruel and unusual punishment.

👎 It creates an overly powerful federal government, which shows no sign of shrinking.

👎 Guantanamo Bay is only the third time in US history that *habeas corpus* (the right to free and fair trial by a jury) has effectively been suspended nationally.

Now try this

1 Explain the difference between 'separation of powers' and 'checks and balances'.

2 Analyse which of these five principles is most under threat today and explain why.

Federalism

Federalism is the sharing of sovereignty between federal government and individual state governments. The Constitution enumerates powers allocated to these governments. By doing so, it also tries to achieve a limited government.

Powers of the states

> **Amendment X:** The powers not delegated to the United States by the Constitution, nor prohibited by it to the States, are reserved to the States respectively, or to the people.

The 10th amendment was designed to protect states against an overly powerful federal government and allow them to retain their own state cultures and practices. Power was therefore 'reserved' – it belonged to the states.

State powers

In practice today, this means that states can control:

- their election practices
- local law enforcement and criminal codes
- regulate the lives of their citizens.
  For example, the age of consent.

Concurrent powers

There are also a number of powers that the states hold concurrently with the federal government, and which they must exercise together.
For example, the right to levy taxes and to borrow money, and making and enforcing laws.

The federal–state relationship

The 'necessary and proper' clause has allowed federal government considerable growth. For example, the government today has 15 departments, up from three when the Constitution was written, the latest being Homeland Security added in 2002.

With growing globalisation, the federal government alone has the funds to deal with issues such as terrorism and natural disasters. For example, just the physical damage of 9/11 has been estimated at $55bn. The annual budget for the whole of New York was around $80bn in 2001; they needed federal money to help clean up after the attack.

Factors affecting federal–state relationship

The 'commerce' clause allows the federal government to regulate interstate trade. Wide interpretation of this has granted more power to federal government. For example, Obamacare was possible because of this clause.

If state and federal law conflict, federal law usually triumphs, but the Supreme Court is the final referee. For example, the Supreme Court ruling of Texas v US [2016] ruled Obama's immigration executive order (DAPA) unconstitutional.

 Case study **The death penalty**

While the death penalty remains controversial, states have managed to uphold their own legislation on this punishment, supported by federal government:

- It is legal in 31 states and illegal in 19 states.
- All states use legal injection, but the back-up method varies from state to state.
  For example, firing squad (Utah), hanging (Washington), electric chair (seven states) or gas inhalation (California and Arizona).

- States have had to trial various combinations of drugs for lethal injection as some drug companies are trying to prevent their drugs being used for the death penalty. This led to controversies such as the death of Clayton Lockett in 2014 (see page 171 to read how this case highlights the controversial nature of the death penalty).
- The Supreme Court has upheld the use of lethal injection, most recently in Glossip v Gross in 2015.
- Three states had initiatives on their 2016 ballot, with Californians and Nebraskans voting to keep the death penalty, and Oklahomans voting to include the punishment in the state constitution.

Now try this

1 Explain how the Constitution protects the powers of both state and federal government.
2 Analyse whether state government or federal government is ultimately more powerful today.

Evaluation of the US Constitution

Interpretations of the US Constitution have led to considerable controversy over time. When considering these debates, it is important to put any discussion into context. You need to explain, for example, why rigidity is a problem today, rather than just generally.

Strengths and weaknesses of the US Constitution

There are many strengths and weaknesses which could be discussed but this is a good start:

👍 Interpretive amendments allow the Constitution to remain flexible in response to 21st-century challenges.
For example, in Obergefell v Hodges, same-sex marriage was ruled constitutional for the whole of the USA.

👍 The interpretation of the Constitution by the Supreme Court allows for non-partisan interpretation.
For example, Obamacare was upheld only because the Supreme Court ruled it was a valid tax under the Constitution.

👍 The amendment process has allowed for significant change while protecting the Constitution against frequent, and unwarranted, change.
For example, allowing for an elected Senate (17th amendment in 1913).

👍 States have remained largely independent, with a wide range of laws, cultures and practices in existence across the USA.
For example, the variety of state legislation regarding the death penalty and marijuana.

👍 The federal government has been prevented, largely, from amassing vast, unquestioned power.
For example, the Supreme Court ruling against the federal government in Texas v US [2016].

👍 Citizens' rights remain mostly protected, even when they are controversial.
For example, the 'right to bear arms' has been upheld despite recent mass shootings such as the Orlando nightclub (2016) and Sandy Hook (2012).

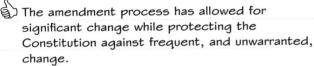

Each of these 'strengths' is simply a matter of interpretation. The same points could also be interpreted as weaknesses. This is the key A Level skill of 'analysis' (AO2).

The ruling in Obergefell v Hodges made same-sex marriage legal in the 13 states that had made it illegal.

👎 Interpretative amendments have trampled on the rights of the individual states.

👎 The role of the Supreme Court grants almost entirely accountable power to nine unelected Justices.
For example, in striking down Obama's executive order DAPA (Texas v US [2016]) they ignored Obama's electoral mandate.

👎 The amendment process has prohibited necessary change.
For example, given the increasing number of mass shootings in the USA, the 2nd amendment is arguably out of date today and in need of review.

👎 States have increasingly found their powers diminishing.
For example, laws such as Obamacare took supremacy over state healthcare systems

👎 In practice, the federal government has demonstrated wide, unchecked power.
For example, Obama negotiated the Iran deal with almost no Congressional input.

👎 The rights of citizens often conflict.
For example, the controversy over the 'right to bear arms' protects weapons, but not the many who lose their lives each year to gun violence.

It is important to try to link different interpretations in the same paragraph – it shows better analysis and evaluation (AO2 and AO3).

Now try this

1 Explain why the Constitution could be considered to be 'out of date'.
2 Evaluate which strength and which weakness of the Constitution is the most convincing.

The US Constitution and democracy

When discussing the extent of democracy in the US Constitution, it is important to remember there are differing kinds of democracy.

Types of democracy

Some aspects of the US Constitution can be compared to different types of democracy.

	Representative (people elect representatives to act on their behalf)	Liberal (focuses on protection of rights, tolerance and limited government)	Pluralist (policies based on a compromise of different views and interests)
Checks & balances	👎 Super-majorities can encourage tyranny of the minority	👍 Checks and balances should create a limited government	👍 Super-majorities encourage bipartisanship and therefore tolerance
Federalism	👍 Federalism allows government to be kept close to the people	👎 Federalism has not prevented the growth of federal government	👍 Federalism allows local beliefs to be enshrined in local law
Bill of Rights	👎 This can protect the minority over the majority	👍 This can protect the minority over the majority	👍 This can protect the minority over the majority
Supreme Court	👎 The Supreme Court is unelected and therefore unrepresentative	👍 The Supreme Court is able to protect the rights of individuals against all levels of government	👎 Appeal to the Supreme Court is not a right
Elections	👎 The Electoral College (see page 204 on the role of this institution) can prevent the people's vote being enacted	👎 The separate election and therefore mandate of Congress and president limits their respective powers	👎 The use of FPTP (read about this electoral process on page 24) and the Electoral College encourages a two-party system

Impact of the Constitution today

The Constitution is well over 200 years old. It is important to be able to evaluate its impact on government and politics in the USA today. The impact can be assessed against these key areas:

Power and role of each branch of government

👍 Each branch of government retains and uses the enumerated powers in the Constitution.

👎 During some circumstances it has seemed that one of the branches has been more dominant.

Effective protection of rights

👍 The Bill of Rights gives clarity and also a basis from which citizens can appeal to the Supreme Court.

👎 Protection of rights is often sacrificed for the sake of 'national security'.

Federalism and state powers

👍 The Constitution continues to allow diversity in state laws and practices.

👎 Federal government has increasingly encroached upon state laws, including Supreme Court rulings.

Now try this

1 Explain which type of democracy the US Constitution is most effective at upholding today.

2 Explain how the US Constitution undermines the principles of a representative democracy.

Federalism today

While the US Constitution protects states' rights, it is up for debate how effectively it achieves this today.

Is the US federal today?

👍 Each state is able to decide upon and enforce a wide variety of laws. For example, the recreational use of marijuana is legal in nine states.

👍 The Supreme Court has ruled in favour of states against federal government. For example, Texas v US [2016] overturning DAPA.

👍 Electoral practices vary and are developing. For example, the testing of online voting in West Virginia.

👍 Political parties remain 'broad churches' (see page 210 for more on the principles behind parties) as both Democrats and Republicans have dramatically different ideologies across the country. For example, the 'Freedom Caucus' within the Republican Party is considerably further right than members such as Susan Collins.

👍 Appealing to the Supreme Court is not a right, so state courts remain important. In 2017, for example, the Supreme Court refused to hear a case on whether sexual discrimination in the workplace extends to discrimination on the basis of sexual orientation.

👎 The growth of federal government seems to increasingly encroach upon state 'reserved powers'. In Kentucky, for example, a clerk was imprisoned for refusing to issue same-sex marriage licenses after it was legalised (revise the strengths and weaknesses of the Constitution on page 169).

👎 The Electoral College and House of Representatives place great importance on a few states. For example, California is worth 55 Electoral College Votes, Texas 38 and Florida 29, so these states are heavily targeted by candidates, often at the expense of the seven states worth just three votes each.

👎 Only the federal government has the resources to deal with terrorist attacks, market crashes and natural disasters. For example, it is projected that Hurricanes Harvey and Irma may have caused upwards of $200bn of damage.

👎 The Supreme Court has also ruled for federal government, further centralising political power. In upholding Obamacare in the NFIB v Sebelius case, for example, the federal government seems now to have vast power over healthcare.

In many ways the USA does remain federal today. However, the nature of federal–state relationships and changes over time suggests that the answer is not simply 'yes' or 'no'. Rather, it depends on the issue, the governments and the national circumstances.

Case study: The death penalty and midazolam

The controversy over the use of the death penalty has meant that it has become increasingly difficult for states to get hold of the three drugs required for an execution (see page 168 for more on this process). In 2014, this difficulty made national headlines after an execution in Oklahoma went wrong.

Background: Clayton Lockett was convicted of murder and his execution took place in April 2014. The drug cocktail used was untested, including the use of **midazolam** which is supposed to make the inmate unconscious. Lockett took 43 minutes to die, with a combination of the drugs used and difficulty in finding a vein both cited as reasons for this occurrence.

The case: further executions in Oklahoma were put on hold and ultimately **Richard Glossip**, who was due to be executed in Oklahoma in 2015, brought a Supreme Court case (**Glossip v Gross**) to challenge the use of midazolam as 'cruel and unusual' under the 8th amendment.

Decision: the case held 5–4 that the use of midazolam was not 'cruel and unusual', upholding Oklahoma's use of the drug and placing Glossip back on death row.

This case highlights the controversy of the death penalty and the different ways in which states are seeking to overcome drug shortages, as well as support from federal government for these continued differences.

Now try this

1 Using the two case studies on the death penalty (above and on page 168), explain how they show the extent of federalism in the USA today.

2 Analyse whether the Supreme Court or the Electoral College poses a greater threat to federalism.

Constitutions compared

As the guiding principles by which a country is governed, constitutions form the basis for political processes and engagement. Yet, the US and UK constitutions appear vastly different.

 **Synoptic link** The UK constitution is covered in component 2: UK Government (pages 68–74). You can link to this to compare the US and UK constitutions, principles, federalism and devolution.

Nature of the constitutions

Similarities	Differences
Both constitutions can be amended, either informally or formally.	The US Constitution is codified, while the UK's constitution is uncodified.
Both constitutions are to an extent judiciable: the USA's through the Supreme Court; the UK's through acceptance of the Human Rights Act.	The US Constitution is entrenched through Article V, while the UK's constitution is not.
Both constitutions consist of written documents in some guise. While the US formal document is written, the addition of Supreme Court rulings could be compared to the vast array of written sources in the UK.	In the UK, sovereignty rests with Parliament in a unitary system. Comparatively, the USA sees sovereignty rest ultimately in the Constitution, but split between states and federal government.
Both constitutions allow for the explicit protection of citizens' rights, and both countries have also infringed upon rights in the name of national security.	Rights protection in the USA is far more extensive, with an entrenched Bill of Rights and an effectively sovereign Supreme Court. In the UK, rights are effectively given and taken by the government, despite acceptance of the Human Rights Act.

Principles

Similarities	Differences
Both have separation of powers to some extent, especially after the UK's Constitutional Reform Act of 2005.	Checks and balances are limited in the UK due to fused powers of executive and legislature, but are strong in the USA.
The growth in power of the House of Lords could be compared to divided government in the USA, both suggesting an effectiveness of checks and balances.	Bipartisanship is enforced through supermajorities in the US Constitution, but is usually unnecessary in the UK due to large electoral majorities of the winning party.
Checks and balances do exist in both countries, with the Supreme Court of both the UK and US successfully challenging elected branches.	The US government is limited through separation of powers and checks and balances, which can lead to government shutdowns. The power of the UK executive in the legislature can lead to an 'elective dictatorship' (Hailsham, 1976).

Federalism and devolution

Similarities	Differences
US states are reliant on grants from the government to supplement their budgets in the same way that the four UK nations are reliant on money from central government.	Each state in the USA can have a vast array of varying legislation and criminal punishments; most of the UK criminal law is centralised or strikingly similar across all four nations.
The national government maintains a degree of supremacy over the smaller, regional governments.	The states of the USA have their sovereignty protected whereas devolved bodies are dependent on Parliament for their existence.
Both states and devolved regions have notable differences in legislation to other parts of their respective countries.	UK devolved bodies have limited recourse to appeal to the Supreme Court, while US states frequently successfully challenge the US federal government in the Supreme Court.

Now try this

1 Explain why the constitutional amendment process is different in the USA and the UK.
2 Can you explain these differences using the comparative theories on page 163? Are the differences between federalism and devolution best explained using cultural or structural theory?

The structure of Congress

Congress is a bicameral legislative branch of government, meaning that it is made up of two Houses: the House of Representatives ('the House') and the Senate.

The membership of Congress

Congress	111th		112th		113th		114th		115th	
	2009–2011		2011–2013		2013–2015		2015–2017		2017–2019	
	Reps	Sen	Reps	Sen	Reps	Sen	Reps	Sen	Reps	Sen
Total number	435	100	435	100	435	100	435	100	435	100
Number of women	76	17	77	17	83	20	88	20	89	23
Total percentage	17.4%		17.5%		19.3%		20.2%		20.9%	
Number of African-Americans	41	1	43	0	43	2	46	2	48	3
Total percentage	7.9%		8%		8.4%		9%		9.5%	
Number of Hispanics	28	1	29	2	33	4	34	4	41	5
Total percentage	5.4%		5.8%		6.9%		7.1%		8.6%	
Average age	57.2	63.1	56.7	62.2	57	62	57	61	57.8	61.8

Population of USA from 2010 census
- Women: 50.9 per cent
- African-Americans: 14 per cent
- Hispanics: 16.3 per cent

The Federation of American Scientists (fas.org) publishes a 'membership of Congress' document every two years. Use this to research the latest statistics.

The election cycle

The House of Representatives

... shall be composed of Members chosen every second Year by the People of the several States.

Each state must have at least one Representative, but the number that each state receives depends on their population.

House members are elected in small districts, with a population ranging from 500,000 to a little over 1 million people. Their role is to represent their district in Congress.
- 435 voting members
- two-year term
- constitutional requirements – 25 years old, citizen of the USA for 7 years.

The Senate

... they shall be divided as equally as may be into three Classes... so that one third may be chosen every second Year.

Every state in the USA elects two Senators. The 'senior' Senator – the one who has served the longest time – goes on to represent the state.
In each state, Senators are up for re-election at different times. Senators are graded as Class I, II or III based on when their election is.
- 100 members – two Senators per state
- six-year term (one-third of Senators elected every two years)
- constitutional requirements – 30 years old, citizen for 9 years.

Safeguards

The Senate was originally unelected. The Founding Fathers harboured a concern about populism (too much power to ordinary people). Therefore they included safeguards in the Constitution like the Electoral College (see page 204). The Senate was not made an elected chamber until 1913, by the 17th amendment.

Now try this

1. Explain the trends in representation in Congress since 2009.
2. Compare the the membership of Congress table with the population data from the 2010 US census – how effective is Congress at representation?

Powers within Congress

The Constitution awards a number of powers to Congress. These powers are either **concurrent** or **exclusive**.

Concurrent powers

Concurrent powers are powers that are exercised by both the House of Representatives and the Senate together.

Constitutional amendments: two-thirds of **both** Houses must agree to a constitutional amendment before it can be put to the states for ratification. Of around 11,000 proposed, only 33 have passed this hurdle.

Confirming a new vice-president: if the office of the vice-president becomes vacant (through becoming the president or resignation), a majority vote in the House and the Senate is needed to approve a new vice-president.

Concurrent powers

Passing legislation: all legislation, including the budget and the veto override, must pass through **both** Houses, which have equal power in terms of passing legislation. When using the veto override, two-thirds of both Houses (290 in the House of Representatives and 67 in the Senate) must vote to override the president's veto.

Declaring war: both Houses must be in agreement for the USA to declare war. This power has been used 11 times since 1789, lastly in 1941 for the Second World War.

Don't forget that 'legislating' is arguably Congress's most important power, and this is jointly exercised.

Exclusive powers

Exclusive powers are powers exercised by only one of the legislative bodies.

Initiate money bills: bills must be approved by both Houses, but only the House of Representatives can initiate it as representatives of the taxpayers.

Elect president if the Electoral College is deadlocked: in two elections, 1800 and 1824, the House of Representatives chose the president.

The House of Representatives

Sole power to bring cases of impeachment: the House brought charges of 'perjury' and 'obstruction of justice' against Bill Clinton in 1998. They have only brought proceedings against three presidents.

Confirm presidential appointments: this includes the confirmation of judicial nominees, cabinet appointments and ambassadors.

Elect vice-president if the Electoral College is deadlocked: in two elections, 1800 and 1824, the Senate chose the vice-president.

The Senate

Ratify treaties: treaties must be ratified by a two-thirds (67) vote in the Senate.

Try cases of impeachment: the Senate requires a two-thirds (67) vote to convict and remove a president. They acquitted Bill Clinton of both charges in 1998.

Avoid the trap of believing the Senate is simply more important than the House. The most important Congressional powers (legislation, war and even impeachment) are all shared **equally**.

Synoptic link While the two Houses of US Congress are largely equal, with a few exclusive powers, the UK Houses of Parliament are quite different, with the House of Commons being superior through the Salisbury Convention (revise the powers of the UK Houses of Parliament on pages 76–80).

Now try this

1 Explain the ways in which the Senate limits the power of the president.
2 Explain the ways in which the House of Representatives could be considered superior to the Senate.

Representative function

Congress is responsible for representing the people, creating law (legislation) and maintaining **oversight** of the government. With 535 elected representatives, Congress has the key role of representing the districts and states across the USA and the 320 million US citizens.

Congressional elections

With elections every two years, Congress must pay attention to its constituents or face the possibility of being unelected at an impending election. However, evidence suggests that constituents are more loyal to their Congressional politicians than this process is supposed to allow for. **Incumbency** rates suggests that once a Congressional politician is elected, they are likely to retain their seat in future elections. For more on the advantages of incumbency, see page 206.

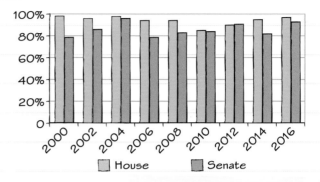

☐ House   ☐ Senate

Incumbency rates in Congress.

Significance of incumbency

In congressional elections, the incumbent frequently wins their seat again at the next election. There are several reasons for high incumbency re-election rates:

- name recognition – among the incumbent's constituents but also bringing in interest-group campaign money
- legislative record allowing the incumbent to demonstrate the gains achieved for the constituency
- congressional franking privileges
- gerrymandering – whether the boundaries of a congressional constituency have been manipulated to help one particular party
- House- or Senate-dedicated website.

Features of congressional elections

- Every two years; in the year when no presidential election is taking place, congressional elections are called **mid-term elections**. They are often seen as a referendum on how well the president is doing and have a much lower turnout than elections in a presidential year.

- To become a Congressional politician, a candidate must first win a primary to become the Democratic or Republican candidate for a seat, and then win the seat on election day under FPTP.

- While third parties do exist, they seldom do well in US elections.

Factors that affect voting in Congress

Several factors affect how Congressional politicians vote on the powers Congress can exercise.

Constituency
- Public opinion due to re-election cycles
- State/district ideology

Pressure groups and lobbyists
- Shared ideology
- Campaign finance
- Mobilising the public

Factors affecting voting in Congress

Party and partisanship
- Shared ideology
- Party leadership
- Party discipline

Congressional caucuses
- Party factions
- State or issue factions

Now try this

1 Explain what the incumbency rates in the graph above suggest about congressional elections, and why.
2 Analyse which factor is likely to be most significant for a Congressional politician when considering how to vote.

Legislative function

The key power and function of Congress is to create, scrutinise, amend and delay legislation.

The legislative process

House of Representatives	Senate
Introduction A bill can go through the Houses consecutively (one House and then the other) or concurrently (both Houses at the same time).	**Introduction** A bill can go through the Houses consecutively (one House and then the other) or concurrently (both Houses at the same time).
Committee Including sub-committee hearings and mark-up. Committee chairs can 'kill' a bill by pigeonholing it (i.e. leaving it untouched). The House Speaker's power in choosing a committee can determine a bill's fate.	**Committee** Including sub-committee hearings and mark-up. Committee chairs can 'kill' a bill by pigeonholing it (i.e. leaving it untouched).
Timetabling By the House Rules Committee, which is dominated 2-to-1 by the majority party. This stage is dominated by the majority party.	**Timetabling** By the Majority leader. The 'timetabling' stage is therefore dominated by the majority party.
Second reading and vote A simple majority is all that is required.	**Second reading and vote** A simple majority is all that is required. However, a **filibuster** can prevent this in the Senate.
Third reading and vote A simple majority is all that is required.	**Third reading and vote** A simple majority is all that is required. However, a filibuster can prevent this.

Conference committee
The conference committee is made up of an equal number of House and Senate members who reconcile the bills, which then need agreement from both Houses.

House approval	Senate approval

Sent for presidential action
The president can sign, veto or leave the bill on his desk for ten days. A two-thirds majority in both Houses can override any presidential veto.

Strengths and weaknesses

👍 High level of scrutiny

👍 Protects states' rights

👍 Prevents a tyranny of the majority

👍 With **unanimous consent** in the Senate, bipartisanship is required

👎 Incredibly slow

👎 Lack of bipartisanship leading to **gridlock**

👎 Congressional politicians often choose to focus on re-election over legislation

Now try this

Explain the differences between the House and the Senate passages of legislation.

Oversight function

As part of the checks and balances system, Congress also provides **oversight** of the executive branch. This means monitoring what they are doing, investigating their actions and using checks and balances to prevent abuse or overuse of executive powers.

Oversight powers

Impeachment and removal of members of executive branch (e.g. the attempted impeachment of Bill Clinton in 1998)

Investigation of actions of the executive branch (e.g. the 'Russia' investigation; see below)

Determining the funding available and agreeing on the budget for the president (e.g. the 2018 shutdowns)

Oversight powers

Ratification of treaties (Senate only) (e.g. the START Treaty 2010)

Ratification of federal justices and other appointments (Senate only) (e.g. Neil Gorsuch in 2017)

Declaring war (e.g. in the Second World War). Mostly this power is now exercised by granting approval for military action rather than issuing a formal declaration of war.

While amending/delaying or veto overriding legislation is technically a form of oversight, leave this for your paragraph or essay on legislation. Use other checks to illustrate oversight.

 Case study   **The 'Russia' investigation**

Following President Trump's election in 2016, allegations surfaced about Russian interference in the US election. Russian confirmation of meeting with members of the Trump campaign, and Trump's unexpected firing of FBI director James Comey, led to a number of investigations being launched into potential Russian interference in US elections by the:

- House Intelligence Committee
- Senate Intelligence Committee
- House Oversight Committee
- Senate Judiciary Committee.

Most investigations are ongoing and have called in high-ranking officials such as Comey to give evidence.

Of the claims, Comey said: 'There should be no fuzz on this whatsoever: the Russians interfered in our election.'

Congress and the presidency

Effective Congressional oversight over the executive branch depends on:

- whether the House of Representatives, Senate and presidency are presided over by the same party or not
- when the next election is, as Congress may be more focused on pleasing constituents than oversight
- which branch has the most recent mandate
- the poll ratings and popularity of the president, which can make Congress more or less likely to scrutinise him
- national circumstances, as in times of national crisis, Congress often defers to the president.

Oversight of the Supreme Court

Congress has some methods to oversee the action of the Supreme Court:

- the ratification of judicial nominees, following hearings by the Senate Judiciary Committee
- the creation of lower courts
- justices can be impeached if they do not act in line with the constitutional requirement of 'good behaviour'
- Congress determines the number of justices on the Supreme Court
- Congress can initiate a constitutional amendment to overturn a Supreme Court ruling.

Now try this

1 Analyse the effectiveness of Congressional oversight over the Supreme Court.
2 Explain the biggest challenge to effective Congressional oversight.

Had a look ☐   Nearly there ☐   Nailed it! ☐

Effectiveness of representation

Congress does not 'look like' US society. While this has improved over recent decades, this calls into question the **adequacy** of their representational ability.

Representative role

In terms of descriptive representation, US Congress does not 'look like' US society (as shown in the table).

Given this, it is possible to raise questions about the effectiveness of Congressional representation – how can Congressional politicians adequately represent people with whom they do not share a life experience?

115th Congress			
	No.	%	USA %
Women	112	20.9	50.8
African-Americans	52	9.5	12.1
Hispanic/Latino	46	8.6	16.7
Bachelor's degree	519	97	32.0
Christian	524	90.7	70.0

A brief demographic analysis of the 115th (2017–2019) Congress and the USA.

Who does Congress represent?

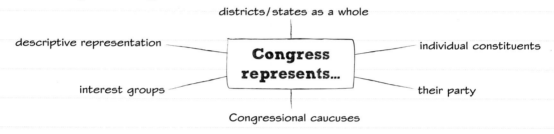

descriptive representation   districts/states as a whole   individual constituents

Congress represents...

interest groups   Congressional caucuses   their party

Effectiveness of the two Houses

While Congress should act as the one branch, it is possible to debate the effectiveness of each House individually.

House of Representatives

👍 Shorter election cycle makes House members more responsive to constituents.

👍 Congressional politicians represent smaller numbers of people (usually).

👍 Party discipline is stronger in the House than in the Senate.

👍 As representatives are based on population, more populous states can be better represented.

The Senate

👍 Senators represent the view of the whole state, not minor districts.

👍 Unanimous consent allows individual senators to be powerful in representing their state.

👍 Unanimous consent also makes party discipline weaker so Senators can represent their state better.

👍 Six-year terms means they can 'get on with the business of government'.

Remember that when it comes to legislation, the Houses are equal.

 **Synoptic link**   The comparison of the two US Houses can be extended to a comparison of the UK's House of Commons and House of Lords (see pages 76–80), and looking for similarities and differences.

Now try this

1 In what ways does the US Constitution try to ensure adequate representation of the US population?
2 Analyse which House is more effective at **representation**.

Changing role and powers of Congress

In the years since the Constitution was written, the role of Congress has evolved. The powers given to Congress have developed and the 'broad church' nature of parties in the USA means that they have varying significance.

Changing role

Constitutional power	Changing circumstance	Power today
Declaration of war	Developments in weapons and technology mean wars are no longer fought or launched in the same way	Authorisations for the use of military force are more common than a formal 'declaration of war'
Passing the budget	Increased bipartisanship in Congress	Arguments over the budget are so frequent now that continuing resolutions have become more common place
Passing legislation	A lack of bipartisanship has led to record low production of legislation, a power being usurped by some presidents through executive orders	A decrease in legislative output and a focus on the president as the head of government rather than a separation of powers

It is important to remember that Congressional power is often reactive – this means the president acts first (proactive) then Congress reacts. This still affords Congress lots of power. For example, stripping abortion out of Obamacare or refusing to ratify the appointment of Merrick Garland to the Supreme Court.

The public view of Congress and the president is very important to their power. While congressional approval ratings languish around the 10 per cent mark, if a president has low opinion poll ratings, Congress becomes more willing to challenge the president. Congress's role is thus dependent on how popular they, and the president, are.

The changing significance of parties

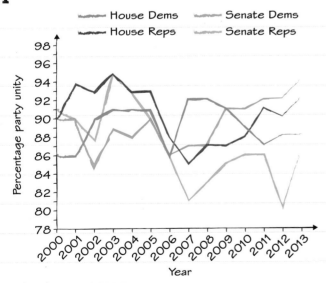

Party unity scores, 2000–2013. This graph shows how often a member of the House of Representatives or the Senate voted with the majority of their party. It shows that the role of parties is becoming increasingly important as it may determine how someone will vote.

The relative importance of parties

Parties are important because:

👍 increased **partisanship** is clear, and has led to a fall in legislative output, and even government shutdowns

👍 differing parties control the presidency and Congress

👍 they control significant appointments and roles, especially in the House.

Parties are not important because:

👎 parties are 'broad churches' – liberals and conservatives exist within both parties (see page 210 for more on party principles)

👎 party discipline is weak due to state loyalties

👎 unanimous consent gives individual senators greater individual power.

Now try this

1 Explain why circumstances affect the power of Congress.

2 Does the US two-party system make parties more or less important? Explain your answer.

The effectiveness of Congress

In judging 'effectiveness', it is important to focus on what Congress is **supposed** to do.

Oversight function

The power of investigation (joint power)	
👍 Congress can investigate any aspect of the executive branch and highlight problems that need correcting.	👎 Investigations end in recommendations and Congress cannot bring criminal proceedings, meaning it can only apply pressure.

Ratifying justices (Senate only)	
👍 As the Senate must approve nominees, they are usually thoroughly vetted, meaning the Senate should not have to reject nominees often, although they still can and do.	👎 The Senate is reactive in this power and can only act once the president has nominated someone; they cannot continually reject nominees otherwise they look partisan.

Electing the president if the Electoral College is deadlocked (House only)	
👍 The House has successfully exercised this power in 1800 and 1824.	👎 This is largely a defunct power, but one that remains 'just in case'.

Ratifying treaties (Senate only)	
👍 The Senate has ratified (e.g. START Treaty, 2010) **and** rejected treaties (e.g. Convention on the Rights of Persons with Disabilities, 2012).	👎 The president can manoeuvre around this power by not using the phrase 'treaty', as Obama did with the Iran deal.

Impeachment	
👍 While impeachment is rarely used, it is an effective threat and Congress has shown it is willing to use this power.	👎 In all three full cases, the president was found 'not guilty'. Failure to successfully impeach makes it a weaker power.

Declaring war	
👍 Congress has used this power 11 times (though not since the Second World War) and authorises presidential military action.	👎 Congress arguably has little choice in authorising action, especially if their constituents favour action, such as after 9/11.

Analysing **both** positively and negatively is a key skill and a great way to revise.

Legislative function

👍 Legislation is well scrutinised through a lengthy process.

👍 With the increased likelihood of **divided government**, it reduces the tyranny of one branch.

👎 There is a lack of legislative output by Congress.

👎 It is difficult to overturn a president's veto.

👎 The likelihood of presidential bills passing is largely unhindered.

Context is key

Congress is not simply 'effective' or 'ineffective'. Its effectiveness changes over time – show this in your writing. Circumstances such as the timing of the next election, poll ratings and national events all affect effectiveness.

Now try this

At which function is Congress **most** effective? Explain your answer.

Had a look ☐   Nearly there ☐   Nailed it! ☐

Legislatures compared

The UK and US legislatures share the same basic functions – legislation, scrutiny and representation.

 **Synoptic link** Information about the UK Parliament is covered in component 2: UK Government (pages 82–90). You can link to this to compare the legislative branches of the USA and the UK.

Powers of the legislative branches

UK Parliament	US Congress
Can declare war	Can declare war
Passes legislation based on the leading party's manifesto	Passes legislation based on the president's, and its own, electoral platform
Scrutinises the government, which (usually) holds a majority in the House of Commons	Scrutinises the executive branch, which is completely separate from Congress
A vote of no confidence can be held to remove the government and force an election	A president can be impeached but fixed terms mean his vice-president will take over

Strengths and weaknesses of each House

		Strengths	Weaknesses
UK Parliament	House of Commons	👍 More powerful chamber 👍 Strong backbench power 👍 Strong constituency links	👎 Strong party whip 👎 Executive dominance 👎 Government majority in committees
UK Parliament	House of Lords	👍 More time to debate 👍 Reduced party discipline 👍 Increasingly willing to challenge the House of Commons, especially post-reforms.	👎 Unelected and includes hereditary peers 👎 Salisbury convention (see page 80) 👎 The size of the House of Lords membership
US Congress	House of Representatives	👍 Strong constituency links 👍 Representation by population 👍 Effective control by the majority party	👎 Short election cycle 👎 Power of the Speaker means the minority party can be ignored 👎 Shared legislative power
US Congress	Senate	👍 Unanimous consent 👍 Power of the filibuster 👍 Six-year terms enable continuity 👍 Representation of state interests, not just the electorate	👎 Shared legislative power 👎 Unanimous consent can cause gridlock 👎 Overrepresentation of smaller states and underrepresentation of big ones

Some similarities and differences

Similarities	Differences
Bicameral nature of the two legislatures	Level of party discipline
Limited powers to scrutinise, with outcome, the executive branch	Equality of power between the chambers
Strong constituency links in the lower chambers	Legislative output

Now try this

1 Explain whether the House of Commons or the House of Representatives is more powerful.
2 Analyse which legislature exercises better control over the executive branch, Congress or Parliament.

The US president

Article II of the Constitution lays out the role and power of the president. Importantly, the Founding Fathers put the president second to Congress, to demonstrate the primary importance of Congress.

Presidential powers

> The executive Power shall be vested in a President of the United States of America.

Opening line of Article II.

Importantly, this Article vested powers in 'a President' – a singular individual in which all power rests. While the **executive branch** is made up of many parts – the president, vice-president, Cabinet, Executive Office of the President (EXOP) and Federal Bureaucracy – the only person with constitutional power is the president.

The Constitution makes the president commander-in-chief of the 'Army and Navy'. Interpreting this today to include the Air Force shows the flexibility of the Constitution.

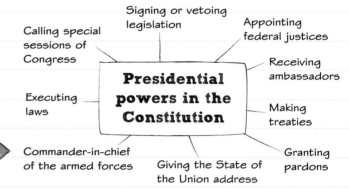

Presidential powers in the Constitution

- Signing or vetoing legislation
- Appointing federal justices
- Receiving ambassadors
- Making treaties
- Granting pardons
- Giving the State of the Union address
- Commander-in-chief of the armed forces
- Executing laws
- Calling special sessions of Congress

Head of state vs head of government

Head of state

As head of state, the president is the representative of the USA to the world. This involves roles such as:

- granting pardons
- attending global summits (e.g. the G7)
- being 'consoler-in-chief' during times of national crises
- receiving and nominating ambassadors.

In this role, the president is best understood as a **public figure**. For example, at the World Economic Forum in Davos, Trump met with other world leaders and spoke on behalf of the USA as the head of state.

Head of government

As head of government, the president commands the executive branch and **domestic politics**. This involves roles such as:

- signing, vetoing and executing legislation
- appointing his Cabinet
- delivering the State of the Union address to Congress.

In this role, the president is best understood as a **political figure**. For example, at the annual State of the Union address, the president outlines his legislative agenda for the coming year, acting as the head of government.

Commander-in-chief

The role of commander-in-chief could be seen as both head of state and head of government. As commander-in-chief of the US military, the president is a key global public figure and can act to 'defend' the USA. Equally, however, he is dependent on money and approval from Congress, making it more about 'governing'. This helps to illustrate the 'grey areas' between the roles of head of state and head of government.

In addressing the US military, Trump is acting as the head of state with control over foreign policy, but he is also talking to his own citizens and so is also acting as a head of government.

Now try this

1 Explain the ways in which the Founding Fathers made the president reliant on Congress.
2 Analyse which role is more important for a president – head of state or head of government.

Informal sources of power

In addition to Constitutionally granted powers, the president is able to garner considerable **informal powers** from other sources.

Electoral mandate – a president who wins the election convincingly can often exercise more power than someone who scrapes a win. For example, Obama won the 2008 election with 52.9 per cent of the vote, while Trump 'won' the 2016 election with 46 per cent of the vote – 3 million fewer votes than his opponent, Clinton. Trump has struggled to achieve legislative victories with this weaker electoral mandate.

Informal sources of power

Executive orders – these are directives to a department on how to carry out a law. While not new legislation, many appear very similar. For example, Trump used executive orders to restrict abortion, attack Obamacare and institute a travel ban, signing 49 executive orders in 266 days.

National events – in times of national crisis, the president often gets a popularity bump. This could be due to a national tragedy, natural disaster or global event. For example, George W. Bush gained a huge popularity bump the day after 9/11 terrorist attack, which allowed him considerable personal control over the national response to this crisis.

The vice-president and Cabinet – despite lacking constitutional power, the individuals in the Cabinet can lend the president power if they have popularity. For example, vice-president Biden's popularity and connections were of huge importance to Obama's foreign policy; while Hillary Clinton, as secretary of state, played a big role in negotiating the START Treaty of 2010.

Powers of persuasion

'He'll sit there all day saying "do this, do that", and nothing will happen. Poor Ike, it won't be a bit like the military. He'll find it very frustrating.'

President Truman's comments about the newly elected President Eisenhower, 1953.

Despite the powers given to the president in the Constitution, separation of powers and checks and balances mean that often they cannot act simply as they please. Instead, they rely on their **powers of persuasion** to get things done. This means the president must bargain with those around him to get his way – he is the 'bargainer-in-chief'. The president has more persuasive power when he is popular, as other branches gain some reflected glory by doing what the president wants. Conversely, he is often less persuasive when he is unpopular. This explains why the informal sources of power are so crucial for a president.

 Case study ### Successful powers of persuasion

Obama campaigned on healthcare reform throughout the 2008 electoral campaign. With a clear electoral mandate gained in November 2008, he was able to get the Patient Protection and Affordable Care Act (PPACA, or 'Obamacare'), passed in 2010 – quite a feat given how slow Congress can be (see page 187 for more details on the creation of Obamacare). Some of this success was due to his bipartisan appeals to Republicans, healthcare summits at the White House and because Democrats controlled both the House of Representatives and the Senate and wanted some of the popularity that Obama had gained for themselves.

 Case study ### Unsuccessful powers of persuasion

Trump campaigned on repealing Obamacare. Like Obama, his party won control of both Houses of Congress, yet 'repeal and replace', which would get rid of Obamacare, failed to pass into law. This was partly due to a lower electoral mandate, meaning that Trump's party had less reason to work with him so his powers of persuasion were lower. In addition, Trump consistently achieved the lowest approval ratings and had the lowest in history after one year, meaning his party was less united behind him and his persuasion became, therefore, less convincing.

Now try this

1   Explain how each of the 'informal powers' could both improve and reduce the president's popularity.

2   Analyse why Obama was able to successfully get his healthcare bill through Congress, while Trump could not.

Executive Office of the President

The Executive Office of the President (EXOP) consists of those staff and bodies that immediately surround the president and which help him carry out his duties.

EXOP

The EXOP was created following the Brownlow Committee's recommendation in 1937 that 'the President needs help.' The components of EXOP are most commonly found in the 'West Wing' of the White House, or in the Eisenhower Executive Office Building next door, and include the National Security Council (NSC), the Office of Management and Budget (OMB) and the White House Office (WHO).

The White House West Wing, which has 400–500 people working in it.

National Security Council

NSC

- Established in 1947.
- To coordinate military, foreign policy and security information and policy for the president.
- Headed by the national security adviser (NSA).
- Briefs the president daily.
- Its importance varies depending on the president and whether they want to rely on the NSC, Defense or State Departments.
- For example, Susan Rice was interviewed as Obama's NSA in the aftermath of the Benghazi attack.

Office of Management and Budget

OMB

- Established in 1970.
- Advises the president on the budget and oversees federal department spending.
- Headed by the Senate-confirmable OMB director.
- Ensures that all presidential legislative initiatives are budgeted and fit into the presidential policy goals.
- For example, Trump's OMB Director Mick Mulvaney commented that a 'good shutdown' might be needed in 2017.

White House Office

WHO

- Most trusted presidential advisers who work in direct proximity to him in the White House.
- Headed by the White House Chief of Staff, and includes the press secretary
- Act as a link between president and Cabinet members and their departments.
- Control access to the president.
- Act on behalf of the president, giving interviews on his behalf, briefing the press and organising access to him.
- For example, Stephen Miller defended Trump's actions in a 'State of the Union' interview with Jake Tapper.

Steve Bannon and the NSC

Trump controversially appointed Steve Bannon to the NSC in January 2017. This was deemed unusual as Bannon was a chief strategist for Trump, ideologically very right wing and with almost no national security experience. This led some to accuse Trump of politicising the NSC when traditionally EXOP is seen as 'honest brokers'. By April 2017, Bannon had been removed and traditional roles were restored, seen by some as the influence of Trump's second NSA, Lieutenant General McMaster.

Now try this

1. Using the case study, explain the importance and impotence (lack of power) of the role of the EXOP!
2. Analyse how the importance of the key parts of the EXOP may vary due to changing national circumstances.

Relationship with other institutions

To achieve any of his policy agenda, the president must work with **Congress** and, occasionally, the **Supreme Court**. His relationship with these institutions changes depending on a range of factors.

Factors affecting presidential relationships

Elections: not only does Congress have its own mandate from the people, it also has more frequent elections and must therefore look to its constituents as well as to the president. For example, the veto override of 97–1 (in the Senate) of the 9/11 Victim's Bill 2016.

Persuasion: if the president is popular, he might find it easier to persuade Congress to act with deference; but the opposite can be true, too. For example, Obama failed to persuade Congress to act on gun control, despite mass shootings.

Divided government: the majority party in Congress might be different to the president's, straining the relationship. For example, Obama's failure to get immigration reform through a divided Congress. Sometimes, even in **unified government**, the president and his party do not always agree and have a differing legislative agenda.

Separation of powers: the president is utterly dependent on Congressional agreement for money, war, legislation and much more. For example, Trump's failure to pass 'repeal and replace' of Obamacare.

Congress

Supreme Court

Presidential action: executive orders and recess appointments can often cause tension as the president is seen to usurp Congressional roles. For example, Obama used executive orders to get limited immigration reform.

Appointments: a fortunate president may get a chance to shape the Court with an appointment that reflects his own ideology. For example, George W. Bush was able to replace Sandra Day O'Connor (a centrist justice) with Samuel Alito (who was more conservative).

Judicial review: as the final interpreter of the Constitution, the Supreme Court can thwart the president by ruling against him. For example, the Supreme Court struck down Obama's DAPA executive order in Texas v US [2016].

In the media: some justices have had an increasing tendency to speak out about political events, often causing political tension. For example, Justice Alito spoke out against the ruling in Snyder v Phelps [2011].

The lame-duck president

Officially, a president is a 'lame duck' once his successor has been elected (in November), but he remains in power until January. During this time, the president effectively has no mandate. Congressional sessions during this time are also lame ducks.

The informal lame-duck president

A president is often referred to as a lame duck when they are unable to get anything done. Most commonly, presidents may become lame ducks after the six-year mid-terms, when the US public starts to look towards the next presidential race. This is by no means certain, however. For example, Obama failed to get immigration reform passed, but did use his veto during his last two years.

Now try this

1 During a formal lame-duck session, which branch holds the most power?
2 Which factor is most important to determining presidential power?

Limits on the president's power

The Constitution gives the president a set of enumerated, formal powers. His ability to execute these is not unlimited, however. While the powers themselves never change, the circumstances in which a president finds himself can have a huge effect on his power in reality.

Factors affecting presidential power

1 **Presidential popularity:** a president who experiences high popularity is more likely to be successful in his policy proposals than an unpopular president. If a congressional politician's constituents support the president, then by supporting the president the politician is likely to also be more popular – this is known as the **coat-tails effect**. The opposite is also true. In his 2014 campaign, Democrat Senator Mark Pryor highlighted his differences with Obama on gun control in order to appeal to his constituents.

Despite the scale of the Sandy Hook tragedy, Obama didn't manage any meaningful change to gun control and other tragedies such as the shooting at Stoneman Douglas High School in Florida in 2018 continued to occur.

2 **The election cycle:** with fixed-term elections, a president has to always have one eye on the electoral calendar. Mid-terms might deliver him a **divided government**, which will make passing his legislative agenda more difficult. His own re-election campaign for a second term is an important consideration for his actions throughout his first term. All of these elections can act as 'referendums' on his performance up to that election. Finally, once the invisible primary begins at the end of his second term, his power inevitably wanes as the public look to the next president.

3 **National events:** the crises a president faces and his reactions to them can have a hugely limiting effect on the president. The response to a terrorist attack, mass shooting (for example, at Sandy Hook Elementary School) or natural disaster (for example, Hurricane Maria) can not only knock the president's popularity, it can also derail his legislative agenda by making the response more important than any other goals or considerations.

These limitations, and the factors that affect presidential relationships, must all be considered together to understand their impact.

 Case study ## Obama and Sandy Hook

In 2012, a gunman entered Sandy Hook Elementary School and killed 20 schoolchildren and six staff. In the midst of the public outcry, Obama acted as 'mourner-in-chief' for the nation, before suggesting changes that were needed to gun laws in the USA. Despite the scale of the tragedy, Obama never managed any meaningful change to gun control, and other tragedies such as the Orlando night club shooting in 2016 and the 2017 Las Vegas shooting continued to occur. He was unable to battle the Constitution, the cultural attachment to guns, the NRA and the Republican Party, despite these tragic circumstances.

 Case study ## Trump and Hurricane Maria

In 2017, Hurricane Maria hit and devastated Puerto Rico. In the aftermath, Trump sent a Tweet criticising the leadership of the Puerto Rican mayor, saying that the Puerto Ricans wanted 'everything done for them'. When he followed this up with a visit, he was further criticised for the video of him throwing out kitchen roll to a population that had not yet restored running, clean water. This led to a 20-point drop in his ratings concerning handling national disasters, a key role of the president. However, the effect on his popularity rating more generally was negligible.

Now try this

Using the case studies, explain the reasons why each president managed to achieve relatively little.

Achieving their aims

Given all the factors that can limit a president, being able to analyse whether they have ever managed to achieve their aims is crucial. You only need to look at the presidents since 1992: Clinton, Bush, Obama and Trump.

What did they achieve?

To say that each president 'achieved' or 'did not achieve' their aims is rather too simple. For each of their aims, most presidents got some way towards their goal, or in many cases actually got the legislation they wanted. The effectiveness of this, however, questions their success.

President Bill Clinton (1993–2001)

👍 Raising tax on the wealthiest
👎 Affordable healthcare
👎 Expansion of civil rights
👍 Smaller federal government
👍 Economic growth
👍 Bringing down the deficit
👍 Responsibility for the environment

President George W. Bush (2001–2009)

👍 Increasing defence spending
👍 Tax cuts
👍 Healthcare reform
👍 Education reform
👎 Social security reform
👍 War on terror (post 9/11)

President Barack Obama (2009–2017)

👍 Healthcare reform
👍 Stimulating the economy
👎 Minimum wage
👎 Gun control
👎 Immigration reform
👍 Ending the war in Iraq
👍 Reforming nuclear weapons

President Donald Trump (2017–)

? 'Build a wall'
? Immigration reform
? Travel ban
? Renegotiating NAFTA
? Renegotiating Iran deal
? Applying tariffs
👍 Tax reform
👎 Repeal and replace Obamacare

🔍 Case study Obama and healthcare reform

In 2008, Obama proposed universal coverage healthcare in which employers would contribute to the cost. Those who could not get employer coverage would be able to purchase healthcare at affordable prices, which were not based on their medical history. This became the PPACA (see page 183), or 'Obamacare'. However, the law itself was full of compromises. There was no 'public option', which effectively meant universal coverage was not a reality and abortion was not federally funded as Obama had wanted. Once Republicans took Congress entirely in 2014, there were frequent attempts to repeal Obamacare. Trump has encouraged 'repeal and replace' and has used executive orders to partly dismantle Obamacare.

Now try this

1 Which president was most successful in achieving their aims? Explain why.
2 What factors would prevent a president achieving his aims?

The imperial presidency

Arthur M. Schlesinger Jr's book *The Imperial Presidency* (1973) includes coverage of events under the presidency of Nixon and has brought into question whether the limits placed on a president are actually effective.

Traditional imperial powers

The president has a number of powers which have only limited, if any, checks upon them, including:

- executive orders and agreements
- signing statements
- pardons.

These powers could be seen as those of an **imperial presidency**.

Changing circumstances

As the USA has evolved and developed since 1787, so the Constitution has been interpreted and reinterpreted. This has enabled the president to gain additional 'imperial powers'. In doing so, the effectiveness of Congress to limit the president is seemingly weak.

 Case study **The commander-in-chief (part 1)**

The role of commander-in-chief is supposed to be checked by Congress's power to declare war. Congress has not, however, formally declared war since 1941, but the USA has been involved in numerous conflicts since then. The development of weaponry and the changing nature of diplomacy made 'traditional' wars less common, meaning Congress's power was less effective, allowing the president to dominate in international relations. Obama's negotiation of the Iran deal with little reference to Congress is a good example of this.

Congress declared war against Japan after Japanese Navy planes attacked Pearl Harbor in December 1941.

The imperilled presidency

A president is unlikely to be 'imperial' for the duration of his presidency. With circumstances being crucial to dictating the power of a president, he can find himself imperial at one point, only to become 'imperilled' (weak) due to changing circumstances.

 Case study **The commander-in-chief (part 2)**

Much of the president's ability to act in foreign policy matters depends on national circumstances. While Congress might not have declared war, it still controls the purse strings. For example, Congress effectively brought an end to the Vietnam War by withdrawing funding and tried the same with Iraq in 2007 when the war had become unpopular with the public. Congress has, however, authorised most military action taken by a president, including an 'Authorisation for the Use of Military Force' for Iraq (2003). In this way, the president is not imperial, but rather the Constitution has been reinterpreted for the 21st century.

So, which one?

Ultimately, most presidents will have elements of imperial and imperilled power over the course of their four- or eight-year term, depending on their popularity, control of Congress and national circumstances.

No recent president has been entirely imperial or imperilled; being able to show the change over time, or context, is crucial to a top-level answer.

Now try this

1 What is meant by the term 'imperial presidency'?
2 Analyse the constitutional structures which make an 'imperial presidency' difficult to maintain.

The president and foreign policy

Control over foreign policy must be headed by the president, but the extent of his power in this area is debatable.

Presidential controls

his choice of Cabinet secretaries (e.g. the secretaries of state and defense)

the US armed forces, as commander-in-chief

the NSC

The president controls...

the ability to negotiate treaties

executive agreements, which do not need Senate approval

the ability to receive ambassadors and therefore recognise countries

Congressional controls

the power of the purse, crucial for any military action

the right of the Senate to approve treaties

Congress controls...

the power to declare war

the right of the Senate to approve Cabinet members (e.g. the secretaries of state and defense)

The balance of power

'Our forefathers knew you couldn't have 535 Commanders-in-Chief and Secretaries of State. It just wouldn't work and it won't work.' (President Gerald Ford, 1974–1977)

Ford's quote is insightful when considering foreign policy. Many situations, such as the threat of war or invasion, require swift action, but Congress has rarely been accused of being decisive. Instead, the workings of Congress are slow and deliberate.

For this reason, negotiations with foreign nations are best left to one representative of the USA. As head of state, it is more commonly accepted that this is the president, or his representative, usually a Cabinet secretary.

This seems to place the balance of power with the president. However, in the aftermath of any foreign policy intervention by the president, he is likely to face high levels of scrutiny at home, which may negatively affect his popularity and therefore power.

Case study — Obama and Syria

Obama came in for considerable criticism after ordering air strikes in Libya in 2011. Having become less popular, when he wanted to follow the same action in Syria in 2013, he took the unusual step of asking Congress for its approval. One reason for this may have been the international precedent set when David Cameron asked the UK Parliament the same question – one which they rejected, highlighting the importance of circumstance.

While Obama asked Congress, he also said, '... I believe I have the authority to carry out this military action without specific congressional authorisation'. This served both to reinforce his constitutional power and remind Congress that he was not setting a precedent in doing this. Congress never actually voted on the issue, but was clearly reticent to give permission.

Case study — The War Powers Resolution

In 1973, recognising that they were losing some of their power and control over foreign policy, Congress passed the War Powers Resolution to try to reassert their power. This required the president to notify Congress within 48 hours if he had agreed to commit the US military to any action. Following this, Congress would either authorise the action, declare war or demand withdrawal, giving the president just 60 days to begin withdrawing the committed troops.

Congress has hoped this would re-establish their power over foreign policy, having lost control to the president over the Vietnam War. However, there remain questions over whether the Resolution is even constitutional, given that it encroaches upon the president's constitutional power of commander-in-chief. While the resolution remains, it is commonly cited that it has never been used successfully and that the balance of power remains firmly with the president, especially in the short term.

Now try this

1 Explain the meaning of Gerald Ford's quote and show how this is seen in the Constitution.
2 Who holds the balance of power when it comes to foreign policy?

Executives compared

The executives of the USA and UK are notably different in political theory. The US president has separate powers and a separate mandate, while the UK prime minister has power only because their party is the leading party in the House of Commons.

> **Synoptic link** The roles and powers of the UK prime minister and executive are covered in component 2: UK Government (pages 84–90). You can link to this to compare the executive branches of the USA and UK.

Roles and powers

UK Prime Minister	US president
Head of government	Head of state and head of government
Party mandate from being leader of the largest party in Commons, but can serve any number of terms	Personal mandate from a direct election, but can only serve two terms
In reality, the Prime Minister acts as sovereign as a leader with a majority (in theory, this is the Queen)	Both in reality and in theory, the president is sovereign with Constitutional powers
Collective executive as *primus inter pares* ('first among equals') within the Cabinet	Singular executive, but appoints a Cabinet and EXOP to support him
Commander-in-chief through royal prerogative	Commander-in-chief of the US Armed Forces according to the Constitution
Draws up the legislative agenda and writes the Queen's Speech each year	Delivers the State of the Union address which serves as the legislative agenda, but has no power to force it through Congress
Has no need to veto legislation due to (usually) having a majority; however, has an effective veto through this majority	Has the veto, according to the Constitution

Impact on politics and government

The 'roles and powers' of both the US president and the UK prime minister have an impact on their respective governments. In both countries, the executive serves as the political figurehead for the country, driving the political agenda. Their ability to push through their desired changes is, however, very different. With the USA having separation of powers, the president has limited legislative ability. The UK's fused power (read about the role of Parliament on page 75) gives the PM sometimes seemingly limitless legislative ability. Nonetheless, as public figures, both can use 'persuasion', popularity and the media to pressure the legislature into agreeing to their legislative agenda.

Accountability to the legislature

Similarities	Differences
Executive power depends on their control of, and majority size in, the legislature.	Constitutionally separated powers give Congress a final say on many issues such as approval of cabinet ministers. While Parliament is in theory sovereign, the executive dominance means Parliament is often subservient to the government.
The role of the legislature in both countries is to scrutinise policy proposals, and in both countries the legislature has made notable changes to government proposals.	Government in the UK can be removed with a vote of no confidence (in the House of Commons rather than the whole of the legislature), and has been so twice in the 20th century. Impeachment proceedings have only been brought three times against a president, and none successfully.
While both legislatures can remove the government, both legislature have not effectively exercised this power for centuries.	While the State of the Union is a suggestion of what the president would like achieved, the separated powers means he has little muscle to force Congress to act upon it, unlike the UK government, which writes the Queen's Speech as the legislative agenda for the coming year.

Now try this

1 Explain which executive is more dependent on 'persuasion' to achieve their goals.
2 Analyse the effectiveness of each legislature to limit the executive.

Nature of the Supreme Court

The role of the Supreme Court is to uphold the US Constitution. Article III of the Constitution states that the 'supreme court' has power over: 'all Cases, in Law and Equity, arising under this Constitution, the Laws of the United States, and Treaties made, or which shall be made…'.

Judicial review

Judicial review is often considered to be a principle of the Constitution. In reality, however, Article III is incredibly vague. Formally, the Supreme Court took the power of judicial review over national law in Marbury v Madison (1803) and over state law in Fletcher v Peck (1810). Since then, the Supreme Court has been able to use judicial review to rule on whether state law, federal law or the actions of any branch of government have been unconstitutional. As the Constitution is sovereign, by ruling anything unconstitutional, it becomes 'null and void', meaning it is no longer enforceable.

Independence

The Constitution identifies a number of ways in which the independence of the Supreme Court is protected:

- **Separation of powers:** the Supreme Court has its own power in Article III of the Constitution.
- **Life tenure:** justices leave the Supreme Court only through death, retirement or impeachment.
- **Protected salary:** the Constitution says that justices 'shall, at stated Times, receive for their Services, a Compensation, which shall not be diminished during their Continuance in Office'. In 2018, this is $255,300.
- **Appointment process:** this ensures that the justices are qualified enough to be on the Supreme Court (see page 192 for a more detailed discussion on the appointment process).

The judicial review process

Judicial review gives the Supreme Court the power to rule on any law or action of the executive. The Court is only allowed to rule whether these laws are constitutional or unconstitutional. In ruling anything unconstitutional, this law immediately becomes ineffective – it does not need to be repealed, it simply ceases to be functional. The Supreme Court receives around 8,000 cases a year, but it only hears between 60 and 100 of them; increasingly towards the lower end of this figure since Chief Justice John Roberts took office in 2005 (a conservative and therefore more restrained). In the rest of the cases, the decision of the lower court stands and that is the end of the appeal – in the USA, there is no right to appeal to the Supreme Court.

- The 'rule of four' is applied to decide whether to hear a case or not – just four of the nine justices have to agree.
- If the case has been heard in a lower court, all the documents are sent to the Supreme Court.

- Plaintiff, defence and *amicus curiae* briefs (filed by someone who is not directly involved but is interested in the case) briefs are collected.
- On a set date, the plaintiff and defence are given 30 minutes of oral arguments to put forward their case.
- The Supreme Court will reach a majority verdict (five or more, unless someone is recused because they have heard the case before they joined the Supreme Court), and write both a majority and dissenting opinion. The majority opinion outlines the ruling to be upheld and why the verdict was reached; the dissenting opinion outlines the reasons that some justices voted the other way. All the reasoning must be drawn from the Constitution.

Chief Justice John Roberts.

Now try this

1 Explain what is meant by the power of judicial review.
2 Analyse the extent of independence of the Supreme Court.

The appointment process

There have been nine justices on the Supreme Court since the Judiciary Act of 1869. When a vacancy occurs, the chance to appoint a new justice affords the president considerable opportunity and power.

The appointment process

A vacancy occurs: as justices are appointed for life, vacancies only occur through death, retirement or impeachment. For example, the last death was Antonin Scalia in 2016. The last resignation was Anthony Kennedy in 2018. There have been no successful impeachments; the only justice to have proceedings brought against them was Samuel Chase in 1805.

Presidential nomination: the president, taking advice from the White House, Cabinet, Senators (known as 'senatorial courtesy') and looking at a variety of recruitment pools, announces his nominee. For example, Obama nominated Merrick Garland for Scalia's seat; this was not confirmed, so President Trump nominated, and got confirmed, Neil Gorsuch in 2017.

ABA rating: while not a constitutional step, the American Bar Association (ABA) will rate the nominee as 'not qualified', 'qualified' or 'well qualified'. For example, Clarence Thomas is the only sitting justice with a 'qualified' rather than 'well qualified' rating. This may have had an impact on his Senate Judiciary Committee (SJC) and Senate votes (see SJC below).

Senate Judiciary Committee (SJC): again, not constitutional, but the SJC will hold hearings, including a number of days interviewing the candidate. They will then vote on the nominee, which serves as a recommendation to the whole Senate. For example, over four days of hearings, Sonia Sotomayor spoke for just 34 per cent of the time in her SJC interviews. Clarence Thomas received a split vote of 7 for and 7 against his 'approval' from the Committee.

Full Senate vote: this is the final constitutional element, the Senate providing 'advice and consent'. A simple majority is needed for the approval of the candidate. For example, Neil Gorsuch passed the Senate by 54–45, a not dissimilar pattern to the previous four nominees. Older nominees were able to garner almost unanimous consent from the Senate.

Strengths and weaknesses

👍 Ensures independence

👍 Ensures individuals are qualified

👍 Role of elected branches gives some accountability

👎 Politicised by the president

👎 Politicised by the Senate

👎 Role of the media, which can hinder the chances of a nominee through their coverage of them

Judicial ideologies

When appointing a justice, the president may consider their ideology:

- A **liberal justice** is one who interprets the Constitution to favour liberal values such as protecting rights or advancing socially progressive policy.

- A **conservative justice** interprets the Constitution to favour conservative values such as government authority and national security or the right to bear arms.

- A **swing justice** falls, ideologically, in the middle of the nine justices. The 'swing justice' may change with any new appointment to the court.

The justices are unlikely to refer to themselves by these terms and they frequently vote in ways that may seem to go against these ideologies.

Now try this

1 Explain why having a chance to nominate a justice is so important for a president.
2 Analyse the factors a president might consider when nominating a justice.

Public policy

Public policy is simply the policy and legislation that affects the lives of US citizens. When the Supreme Court rules to uphold or strike down a law, it invariably alters these policies and this has an impact on the people. Typically these are public policy issues such as the death penalty, abortion, **affirmative action** (see page 197) and same-sex marriage.

What can the Supreme Court do?

The Supreme Court effectively has three potential impacts on public policy:

1 By upholding the constitutionality of a case, it protects existing policy.

2 By striking down the constitutionality of a case, it removes existing policy.

3 Occasionally, by doing either of these, it sets entirely new policy for the whole nation.

Cases post-2005

  Case study — **Obergefell v Hodges [2015]**

The case: this case effectively made same-sex marriage a legal right in every state. This had a reasonable impact as 13 states did not already have such a law. However, its impact should not be overstated as almost three-quarters of states already had this law.

Impact: set a new policy.

 Case study — **Texas v US [2016]**

The case: the Supreme Court sided with the state of Texas against President Obama, striking down the constitutionality of his executive orders regarding Deferred Action for Parents of Americans (DAPA).

Impact: struck down presidential action.

 Case study — **NFIB v Sebelius [2012]**

The case: the Supreme Court upheld 'Obamacare', ruling that the provisions mandating that individuals take out healthcare were not prohibited by Constitutional requirements regarding tax.

Impact: upheld an existing policy.

 Case study — **Whole Woman's Health v Hellerstedt [2016]**

The case: the Supreme Court struck down the full implementation of a Texas law that may have reduced the number of abortion clinics in the entire state to just seven.

Impact: struck down an existing policy.

Controversies

A ruling of the Supreme Court can be hugely controversial as it is unelected and therefore unaccountable.

- When the Supreme Court strikes down a state or congressional law, it is effectively overruling the will of the elected branches, and doing so in a way that is almost irreversible.
- The only way to overturn a Supreme Court ruling is to amend the Constitution; this has only happened once, with the 16th amendment. For example, the Supreme Court had struck down the Congressional Income Tax Act of 1894 in the case of Pollock v Farmers' Loan & Trust Co. To enable Congress to raise income tax, they added the 16th amendment to the Constitution.

- The effect of the power of judicial review is to make the Supreme Court effectively 'sovereign', known as **quasi-sovereign**. This means that, in reality, as they interpret the sovereign document of the Constitution, the rulings of the Supreme Court are themselves sovereign.
- It is therefore arguable that the Supreme Court is 'imperial' – just like with a president (see page 188 on the imperial presidency). This means that the checks and balances to which the Court is subjected are weak and ineffective, allowing them far more power than was intended. On the other hand, the power of judicial review does allow the Supreme Court to protect the rights of everyone in the USA, regardless of the view of the majority.

Now try this

1 Explain why the Supreme Court is considered to be quasi-sovereign.
2 How does the case of NFIB v Sebelius demonstrate the power of the Supreme Court?

Political role of the Court

While the Supreme Court is supposed to be independent, it is clear that its rulings have a political impact. The justices themselves are often described by their political leanings and in many cases the outcome can be explained by these ideologies.

Judicial activism and judicial restraint

Judicial activism and **judicial restraint** are theories that are applied to the actions of Supreme Court justices. They are one way of trying to understand how a justice votes and what they believe their role should be. For example, using their position as a justice to achieve what they deem to be the right aspirations for society (activism) or believing a ruling should have a limited impact (restraint).

Remember that these are just theories. Most justices would not describe themselves in these terms; this is our interpretation of their actions.

Activism or restraint?

There are a number of reasons a justice might believe that activism or restraint is the correct approach.

Activism

- 👍 Elected branches often shy away from controversial issues as it may cost them votes.
- 👍 Current problems need solutions now, and Congress is often slow to act.
- 👍 Without interpretation, the Constitution will become irrelevant.
- 👍 The Founding Fathers could not imagine the challenges of the 21st century.
- 👍 Ignoring issues could lead to breaches of the Constitution and constitutional rights.

Restraint

- 👍 The Supreme Court is unelected and unaccountable, and therefore should refrain from big decisions.
- 👍 No one can adequately know what the Founding Fathers intended.
- 👍 Previous Court decisions have already interpreted the Constitution – reinterpretation suggests the justices are using personal views which is not what a court is supposed to do.
- 👍 Limited ways to check the Court means they should act in a limited fashion.
- 👍 Activism undermines their independence and neutrality.

Remember that the 'good things' about judicial activism are the 'bad things' about judicial restraint, and vice versa. For example, the Supreme Court **should** act in a restrained manner as they are unelected; but this is also the reason that they **should not** be activist.

Living Constitution vs originalism

In a similar vein, the two prominent views on how the Constitution should be interpreted are **living Constitution** and **originalism**.

Living Constitution

- Argues that the Constitution is essentially an evolutionary document to be interpreted by its principles. Using the 14th amendment, for example, the Supreme Court upheld abortion under the 'due process' clause and same-sex marriage under the 'equal protection' clause, yet no mention of abortion or same-sex marriage is in the Constitution.
- Living Constitution is closely related to the **loose constructionist** philosophy.

Originalism

- Argues it should be interpreted more literally, by the words written or the original intent of those words.
  For example, the gun rights in the 2nd amendment continue to be upheld because it states the 'right to bear arms' in the amendment.
- Originalism is closely related to the **strict constructionist** philosophy.

Now try this

1 Explain whether conservative justices are more likely to be activist or restrained.
2 Analyse whether this explanation changes with different issues, for example gun control or abortion.

Rights today

The US Constitution enshrined the Bill of Rights in 1791, and over the coming centuries another 17 amendments were added. These, and their interpretation, outline the **constitutional rights** that US citizens share today.

The Bill of Rights

Amendments ratified in 1791.

1st amendment	Freedom of speech, association, press, religion and redress of grievances (the five freedoms)
2nd amendment	'As a well regulated Militia, being necessary to the security of a free State, the right of the people to keep and bear Arms, shall not be infringed'
3rd amendment	No quartering of soldiers
4th amendment	Freedom from unreasonable searches
5th amendment	The right to not self-incriminate
6th amendment	The right to speedy trial
7th amendment	The right to trial by jury
8th amendment	The right to no cruel and unusual punishment
9th amendment	The Bill of Rights does not represent all rights
10th amendment	Reserved rights of the states

The Bill of Rights today

Some of these rights are more important today than others and some may need to be interpreted to be relevant. For example:

- **Upheld:** 1st amendment and the right to free speech – even in controversial cases such as Snyder v Phelps [2011], this right was upheld.
- **Controversial:** 8th amendment – the death penalty and Guantanamo Bay raise questions as to whether 'cruel and unusual punishment' is truly outlawed in the USA.
- **In need of interpretation:** 3rd amendment – there is no real danger of the government quartering soldiers in citizens' houses today, but could this be interpreted as a 'right to privacy', which does not exist in the Constitution?

Later amendments

13th amendment (1865) 14th amendment (1865)	Making slavery unconstitutional and guaranteeing equal protection of everyone before the law
15th amendment (1870)	The right to vote regardless of race
19th amendment (1920)	The right to vote regardless of sex
24th amendment (1964)	The right to vote regardless of paying tax
26th amendment (1971)	The right to vote at 18

Additional rights

While many of the additional amendments deal with the right to vote, other 'rights' today are protected by Supreme Court rulings.

For example:

- Abortion: Roe v Wade [1973] and subsequent rulings
- Euthanasia: Gonzales v Oregon [2006]
- Same-sex marriage: Obergefell v Hodges [2015] (see page 193 for more on this case).

The Supreme Court has, however, upheld gun ownership and the death penalty, albeit with some limitations.

Effectiveness

Ultimately, the protection of rights, usually by the Supreme Court, is limited by the few cases the Court hears each year, a lack of initiation of cases and often the public opinion on a matter, which can affect the justices' willingness to rule.

Now try this

1 Outline two amendments which cause controversy in their use in the USA today.
2 Analyse whether the Supreme Court is an effective protector of rights in the USA.

Race and rights

Following the Civil War and the 14th and 15th amendments, African-Americans gained the right to vote and to be considered as equals before the law. However, this has not always been the case in practice. Today, **race rights** extend beyond African-Americans. The two largest groups hoping for **racial equality** in the USA are African-Americans and Hispanics.

Timeline

1861–1865 American Civil War

1865 13th amendment

1868 14th amendment

1870 15th amendment

1896 Plessy v Ferguson, which allowed for 'separate but equal', meaning facilities could be segregated but had to be of equal quality

1948 Executive Order 9981 desegregating the US military

1954 Brown v Board of Education of Topeka, disallowing 'separate but equal', as many states had 'separate' facilities, but they certainly were not 'equal'

1955 Rosa Parks's actions led to the Montgomery bus boycott

1963 Martin Luther King Jr.'s 'March on Washington for Jobs and Freedom' on Washington DC

1964 Civil Rights Act

1967 Loving v Virginia struck down laws prohibiting interracial marriage

1965 Voting Rights Act

1971 Swann v Charlotte-Mecklenburg Board of Education upheld busing

1978 Regents of the University of California v Bakke, upheld **affirmative action** in college admissions

2003 Grutter v Bollinger upheld race as a factor in college admissions

2012 Obama signs Deferred Action for Childhood Arrivals (DACA) executive order (see page 200)

2013 Fisher v University of Texas upheld race as a factor in college admissions

2014 Obama extended DACA and introduced Deferred Action for Parents of Americans (DAPA) (see page 200)

2016 Fisher v University of Texas (II) again upheld race as a factor in college admissions

2016 Texas v US strikes down Obama's executive order DAPA

2017 Trump rescinds DACA executive order

Methods and effectiveness

People have used a range of **methods** to fight for race rights, including:

- using the courts, notably the Supreme Court
- civil disobedience and mass demonstrations, such as the Black Lives Matter campaign
- action through the ballot box – by having the vote, this made elected representatives more likely to listen to their demands and act through elected branches.

The Black Lives Matter campaign, formed shortly after the murder of Trayvon Martin in 2012, aims to highlight systematic racism that still exists.

However, the **effectiveness** of this today is questionable:

- There are currently 23 majority-minority African-American districts, with all but one represented by an African-American.
- There are currently 30 majority-minority Hispanic districts with all but six represented by a Hispanic American.

These outcomes suggest that in order to gain representation, race groups still rely on support from their own groups, rather than across the board. Even following the election of Obama, the issue of racial equality remained a key controversy:

- In 2009, 4.7 per cent of African-American males were in prison; more than double any other race.
- In the 115th Congress, 8.3 per cent of Congress was Hispanic, compared to 16.7 per cent of the US population.

Now try this

1 To what extent has the issue of racial equality for African-Americans been overcome?

2 Outline an argument showing why the Supreme Court should be 'activist' when advancing racial rights.

Affirmative action

In 1961, President Kennedy signed Executive Order 10925, which stated that: 'The contractor will take **affirmative action** to ensure that applicants are employed and that employees are treated during employment, without regard to their race, creed, color, or national origin.'

What is it?

There is no single policy that encompasses **affirmative action** (AA). Kennedy introduced AA to try to redress the historic injustices faced by race groups in America and to ensure they had equality of opportunity in the USA. In 1965, President Johnson took this further, signing Executive Order 11246, which required government departments to hire more women and racial minorities.

How does it work?

AA works to favour those who come from a historically disadvantaged group. Commonly, this has been achieved through quotas.

For example, in the Regents of the University of California v Bakke case [1978], the medical school put 16 of their 100 spaces aside for racial minority applicants. Allan Bakke argued he had scored more highly than some of the minority applicants and yet had been denied a place. The Supreme Court sided with the university.

Public opinion on affirmative action

 A 2014 survey showed 63 per cent of Americans support AA in colleges.

 Numerous Supreme Court cases have upheld AA in higher education, most recently Fisher v Texas II [2016].

 A 2009 survey showed that a majority of Americans favoured AA (although not preferential treatment!).

👎 The same 2014 survey showed a majority of Democrats in favour of AA, while a majority of Republicans opposed AA.

👎 The case of Grutter v Bollinger [2003] suggested that in 25 years or fewer, AA would not be necessary.

👎 Schuette v Coalition to Defend Affirmative Action [2014] upheld Michigan's right to outlaw AA.

Public reaction to affirmative action

AA has arguably worked in creating a more equal America. However, it is not universally well received. In the case of Fisher v Texas, for example, Clarence Thomas (the only African-American justice) argued AA was discriminatory: 'The alleged educational benefits of diversity cannot justify racial discrimination today.' However, some note that Clarence had himself benefited from Affirmative Action when he was accepted to Yale Law School, partly due to AA (though Thomas wrote in his memoir that he felt stigmatized by the preferential treatment).

Now try this

1 Explain the meaning of the cartoon above; is it accurate today?

2 Analyse whether affirmative action has any place in America today.

Judicial vs political

As the judicial branch, the Supreme Court evidently has a judicial role in the USA. However, it also has wide ranging impacts in the political sphere.

The Supreme Court is judicial

- Justices can only rule based on the Constitution, and can only rule that something is constitutional or unconstitutional (see page 191).
- The Supreme Court cannot enforce its rulings; it relies on elected branches for that.
- The Supreme Court has no initiation power – it can only rule on cases brought to them, not start them itself.
- Justices are appointed based on their judicial experience, and rated as such by the ABA (see page 192 to read about such ratings).
- The Constitution guarantees the justices' independence through life tenure and protected salaries (see page 191).
- Justices do not reliably vote on party or ideological lines (see pages 192 and 194).
- The Supreme Court places emphasis on *stare decisis* – previous court decisions.

The Supreme Court is political

The Supreme Court has been accused of acting more like a political than a judicial body. The Court is often said to be 'legislating from the bench' or composed of 'politicians in robes'. Importantly, these quotes are about the **role and impact** of the Court, **not** about how much power they have.

- The Court is usually ruling on a law or action of an elected branch.
- Justices can be divided into liberal and conservative ideologies (read about how political beliefs affect the Court on page 192).
- The impact of justices extends far beyond the plaintiff and defendant in a case (see page 191).
- Justices are chosen and approved by political branches, and chosen for their predicted ideology (read more about this on page 192).
- The president, Congress and interest groups all try to influence the Court through the media and *amicus curiae* briefs (see page 191 for an overview of influences on the Court).

Is the Supreme Court an 'imperial judiciary'?

The imperial judiciary debate is all about **power**. This looks at the power the Supreme Court justices have and discusses the checks and balances to establish whether they have **too much** power or not.

- 👍 The power of judicial review allows the Court to overrule elected branches (see page 191).
- 👍 Judicial review is almost impossible to overturn, having only occurred once by constitutional amendment.
- 👍 Justices are appointed for life and are almost impossible to remove (see page 191 for more on the working conditions enjoyed by justices).
- 👍 Justices can act with judicial activism (see page 194).
- 👍 The Supreme Court often chooses to decide on the cases that have the biggest public impact.

- 👎 With no enforcement power, the Court 'may truly be said to have neither FORCE nor WILL' (Federalist No. 78).
- 👎 The Court can only rule on the Constitution and nothing more (read about the remit of the Court on page 191).
- 👎 The Court can only hear about 80 cases a year (see page 191).
- 👎 The Court has been reluctant to rule on some particularly controversial issues. For example, there have only been three notable cases on gun control since 1990.
- 👎 The Court is subject to checks and balances (see page 193).
- 👎 Many cases are dull and not landmark.

Note that there are similarities in the two debates, but you must understand the differences.

Now try this

1 Explain the meaning of 'legislating from the bench'.
2 Analyse whether the case of Obergefell *v* Hodges (see page 193) shows the Supreme Court to be more political or judicial in nature.

Effectiveness of rights protection

When considering the effectiveness of the Supreme Court in rights protection, it is important to remember that they can only protect Constitutional rights and these are rights for everyone, not just racial minorities.

Rights protection

	Protected	Not protected
Free speech	Snyder v Phelps [2011]: free speech is protected, even when the speech is controversial. Citizens United v FEC [2010]: electoral donations are a form of free speech.	Citizens United directly contravenes McConnell v FEC [2003], which said campaign donations were not free speech, which itself contravened Buckley v Valeo [1976].
Gun control	DC v Heller [2008]: the 2nd amendment protects an individual's right to gun ownership irrespective of militia membership. Chicago v McDonald [2010]: right to gun ownership is protected.	The Supreme Court has not ruled recently on a case that limited the rights of gun owners. In the 2010 ruling, however, Alito said that it was not a right to 'any gun, anywhere, anytime'.
Cruel and unusual punishment	Hamdi v Rumsfeld [2004], Hamdan v Rumsfeld [2006] and Boumediene v Bush [2008] all struck down aspects of Guantanamo Bay, namely the right to access civilian courts in the USA.	That the Court had to rule three times, and that Guantanamo is still open, speaks to the Court's lack of effective power.
Abortion	Roe v Wade [1973]: the right to have an abortion. Whole Woman's Health v Hellerstedt [2016]: struck down a Texas law which would have placed 'undue burden' on women seeking an abortion.	Numerous court cases have chipped away at this right. Gonzales v Carhart [2007]: upholding a ban on partial birth abortion. Burwell v Hobby Lobby [2014]: allowing employers to opt out of providing contraception in healthcare coverage on the grounds of religion.
Affirmative action	Fisher v Texas [2016] and Grutter v Bollinger [2003] – see page 196 for more on the significance of these cases.	Schuette v Coalition to Defend Affirmative Action [2014] – read more about how this affected affirmative action on page 195.
Protection of states' rights	Texas v US [2016]: upheld a Texas challenge to Obama's DAPA executive order.	NFIB v Sebelius [2012]: upheld the constitutionality of Obamacare as a form of tax.

 Case study **Gun control views**

It is important to remember that whether a right is 'protected' or not depends on political perspective. There may be disagreement between conservatives and liberals, activists and restrained, and living constitutionalists and originalists. Take the case of the 2nd amendment of the Constitution: 'A well regulated Militia, being necessary to the security of a free State, the right of the people to keep and bear Arms, shall not be infringed.'

Originalists: gun rights have been upheld in accordance with the 'right to bear arms'.

Living constitutionalists: the lack of interpretation of this right today is concerning.

Judicial restraint: Congress and the president can rule on this as elected branches; it should not be down to the Court.

Conservatives: the right to bear arms is crucial to the protection of the state and individual rights.

Liberals: the Founding Fathers did not mean any gun, for anyone.

Judicial activists: Congress and the president have failed to act while mass shootings have become commonplace, so someone should act.

Now try this

Explain why it is difficult to establish whether constitutional rights have been protected.

Always check the question. If it is asking about the Bill of Rights, your answer should only cover the first ten amendments. If it is about 'constitutional rights', it is any right from the whole document and all 27 amendments.

Immigration reform

Around 11 million unauthorised immigrants live in the USA today. Reforming immigration was a key policy for Obama.

Obama's reforms

Much of the history of 'immigration reform' in the USA has been about making it harder, not more inclusive. Hispanics were a key part of Obama's 2008 victory – following campaign promises of immigration reform, 67 per cent of the Hispanic vote went to him.

However, the record of immigration reform since Obama's election has been little better than those who came before him (see the timeline). The steps that he did take through executive order have either been struck down by the Supreme Court or reversed through subsequent executive orders.

DACA and DAPA

Deferred Action for Childhood Arrivals (DACA) and Deferred Action for Parents of Americans (DAPA) were policies which would have protected around 5 million (of the 11 million) undocumented immigrants in America from deportation. They were not, as some thought, programmes designed to give immigrants citizenship in the USA.

DACA was for immigrants who:

• were brought to the USA before they were 16 years old

• lived in the USA continuously since 2007

• were born after 16 June 1981 (i.e. aged under 31).

In 2014, **DAPA** extended the programme, removing the 31-year age limit. It was for immigrants who:

• had a child that was a lawful resident

• had lived in the USA since 2010.

Timeline

2008 Obama: 'I can guarantee that we will have, in the first year, an immigration bill that I strongly support'

2009 DREAM Act reintroduced into Congress (Development, Relief, and Education for Alien Minors Act)

2010 Obama's State of the Union address looks to 'fix our nation's broken immigration system'

2010 DREAM Act defeated (effectively three times) in Congress

2010 Arizona passes SB1070 ('it is a misdemeanour if you are not carrying your immigration paperwork with you')

2011 DREAM Act reintroduced, again, into Congress

2012 Supreme Court strikes down parts of SB1070, but allow Arizona's 'show me your papers' part. They uphold the federal government supremacy on immigration

2013 'Gang of 8' (Senators) author a bipartisan immigration reform bill. It passed the Senate but House Speaker John Boehner refused to hear it on the floor of the House

2013 Obama delivers an immigration reform speech in Las Vegas

2014 Obama extends DACA and introduces DAPA using executive order

2015 US District Court places an injunction on DAPA

2016 Texas v US strikes down DAPA

2016 Trump elected, having campaigned heavily on anti-immigration policies, including 'build a wall'

2017 Trump effectively undoes DACA by executive order

Hispanic population in the USA

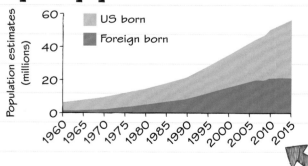

US born
Foreign born

Population estimates (millions)

60 / 40 / 20 / 0

1960 1965 1970 1975 1980 1985 1990 1995 2000 2005 2010 2015

This graph demonstrates the growing Hispanic population in the USA, which is estimated to reach 106 million by 2050. It is for this reason that immigration reform and Hispanic racial equality has become an issue, gaining prominence over affirmative action.

Now try this

1 Explain the methods by which immigration reform have been attempted.

2 Outline the factors that make immigration reform so important today.

Judiciaries compared

The unitary nature of the UK's constitution means the UK Supreme Court is notably less powerful than its US counterpart.

 **Synoptic link**   The UK Supreme Court is covered in component 2: UK Government (pages 91–97). You can link to this to compare the Supreme Courts of the USA and UK.

Power of the UK and US Supreme Courts

UK Supreme Court	US Supreme Court
Established in Constitutional Reform Act 2005; opened in 2009	Established in Article III of the US Constitution
The 2005 Act meant a greater separation of powers in the UK government	Completely separate branch of government
Power of judicial review does not give it the power to overrule the UK Parliament	Power of judicial review gives it quasi-sovereign power to strike down elected branches
Judicial review allows the Supreme Court to interpret the actions and laws of government to ascertain whether they have acted *ultra vires* (beyond their power)	Judicial review allows the Supreme Court to interpret the Constitution and compare laws and actions to the limits therein
UK citizens could appeal onwards to the ECJ or ECHR	Final court of appeal in the USA, with no right to appeal to this Court guaranteed
Despite the Court's lack of sovereignty, it is unlikely the government would ignore a Supreme Court ruling	Despite a lack of enforcement power, it is unlikely the government would ignore a Supreme Court ruling

Relative independence

Similarities	Differences
Both have independence of buildings and personnel	US justices' salaries are protected by the Constitution. The UK Supreme Court budget is set by the Ministry of Justice
Both have a rigorous appointment process	
Both countries give their justices security of tenure – the USA by death, retirement or impeachment; the UK largely by an upper age limit	The USA selects justices through elected, political branches, while the UK uses the independent Judicial Appointments Commission. This can have a knock-on effect on cases ruled upon. For example, Bush v Gore [2000]
Both countries face pressure from elected branch and interest groups in their rulings	
Both are willing to rule against the government and these rulings have stood (see examples below)	The USA can overrule elected branches, questioning their independence, which the UK cannot

 Case study   ## Supreme Court cases

Revise these cases on pages 93 and 193.

Miller *v* Secretary of State for Exiting the European Union [2017]
Decision: Parliament had to be consulted on the final Brexit deal.

Texas *v* US [2016]
Decision: Obama had acted unconstitutionally by passing the DAPA executive order.

Similarities	Differences
Both cases highlight the power of the judiciary over the elected governments.	While DAPA immediately became 'null and void', the UK government continues to try and manoeuvre around Parliament.
Both cases allowed for direct challenge of the government.	
Both governments abided by the ruling of the Supreme Court.	The US Court was split 5–4 on ideological lines, whereas the UK Court was 8–3.

Now try this

1 Explain how independence is ensured for both Supreme Courts.
2 Analyse whether the UK and US Supreme Courts have more in common than differences.

Rights compared

The judiciary is a key player in the protection of rights in both the USA and the UK. In both countries, they have challenged the government in order to protect rights and can protect the racial minority against the 'tyranny of the majority'.

> **Synoptic link** The topic of UK civil rights is covered in component 2: UK Government (pages 91–97). You can link to this to compare civil rights in the USA and UK.

Effectiveness of rights protection

UK

👍 The Human Rights Act has given justices a codified document on which to make their rulings.

👍 UK citizens can appeal beyond the UK Supreme Court to the ECHR.

👍 In reality, Parliament is unlikely to ignore justices – they have 'moral authority'.

👎 Parliament remains sovereign.

👎 The ECHR rulings have been ignored in the UK. For example, Hirst v UK on prisoners' rights.

👎 The role of justices and the Supreme Court is far less widely understood.

USA

👍 The US Supreme Court has a constitutional foundation, giving it quasi-sovereign power.

👍 The Constitution is the basis for Supreme Court rulings, which are difficult to change.

👍 Rulings are unlikely to be ignored or not enacted.

👎 Rulings have been ignored, such as those on Guantanamo Bay.

👎 The Court can hear relatively few cases a year.

👎 Citizens have no right to have their case heard by the Supreme Court.

👎 Judges seem more ideologically motivated than their UK counterparts.

Examples of rights protection

	UK	USA
Abortion	Application by the Northern Ireland Human Rights Commission for Judicial Review, 2017 – dismissed	Whole Woman's Health v Hellerstedt [2016] – right to abortion upheld
Gay rights	Lee v Ashers Baking Company Ltd [2018] – to be decided	Masterpiece Cakeshop v Colorado Civil Rights Commission [2018] – found for religious rights over gay rights
Euthanasia	R (Nicklinson) v Ministry of Justice [2014] – euthanasia is not allowed	Gonzales v Oregon [2006] – allowed for euthanasia in Oregon
Terrorism	HM Treasury v Ahmed [2010] – freezing of terror suspects' assets is not allowed	Boumediene v Bush [2008] – terrorist suspects held in Guantanamo Bay have a right to challenge their detention in a US civilian court

Effectiveness of interest groups in the protection of civil rights

UK	USA
Interest groups are increasingly relevant in court cases; for example, the right to die cases	Groups more frequently bring cases to the Supreme Court; groups can give *amicus curiae* briefs to the Supreme Court
UK respect for civil rights, while not entrenched in one document, predates the US Bill of Rights, meaning action from interest groups has been heeded more frequently	A codified Bill of Rights has made rights clearer and more culturally engrained
Increasing devolution gives interest groups more access points	Greater number of access points

Now try this

1 Explain the access points available to US and UK pressure groups trying to protect rights.

2 Has quasi-sovereignty allowed the US Supreme Court to better protect rights?

The electoral process

For US federal elections, the **first-past-the-post (FPTP)** electoral system is used. However, the process of becoming the president is far more complex than a vote on one day. You need to be able to analyse each part of the process.

The electoral process

Announcement/invisible primary: usually 12–18 months before election day. This is an intra-party campaign – candidates from the **same party** campaign to establish themselves as viable candidates for their party's presidential nominee.

Primaries and caucuses: these take place at state level between February and June. Candidates from the same party compete against each other in a public vote to decide who will be the party's presidential candidate.

National party conventions: usually take place in July. They confirm each party's nominee for the president and vice-president and agree a **party platform** (the policies on which a party is campaigning). In reality, the presidential candidate is almost decided by the time of the convention due to **front-loading** of primaries (primaries are occurring earlier and earlier in the calendar, so the winner of the primaries is apparent long before the conference). Party conventions are also a chance to rally support and enthuse those loyal to the party.

The campaign: between July and November the announced candidate from each party campaigns for the presidency.

Election day: on the Tuesday following the first Monday in November. Voters are **not** directly electing the president. They are nominating the electors from their state to the **Electoral College** (see page 204), to whom their state's Electoral College votes will go.

Electoral College: on the Monday following the second Wednesday in December.

Inauguration: on 20 January of the following year, when the president is sworn in and officially takes on the role.

The president and the Constitution

The Constitution states that the president must be:

- at least 35 years old
- a natural-born US citizen
- a resident of the USA for 14 years.

The 22nd amendment of the Constitution limits the president to two terms.

Primaries vs caucuses

The presidential election is best understood as 50 state-based elections. Early in the process, each party must nominate one candidate. Some states do this through **primaries** – an intra-party election. Some states use **caucuses** – local party meetings in which open voting takes places. States also differ between 'open' methods (any resident can take part in any party's primary or caucus) and 'closed' methods (you must be a registered member of that party to take part).

Now try this

1 What is meant by front-loading?
2 Analyse why the electoral process is so long.

The Electoral College

The election for the US president is not a direct election, meaning the people are not voting for the president himself. Instead, they are voting for 'electors' from their state who will elect the president on their behalf.

How the Electoral College works

- Each state is allocated a number of Electoral College Votes (ECVs). There are a total of 538 ECVs in the Electoral College.

- The number each state gets is dependent on their population and it is the same as the number of Senators plus the number of Representatives that state has.

- On election day, the electorate in each state are voting to decide which party their state's ECVs will go to.

- In 48 states, the party with the most votes gets all of that state's ECVs. In Maine and Nebraska, ECVs are allocated by district.

- To win, a presidential candidate must achieve 270 ECVs. The popular vote in the country does not matter.

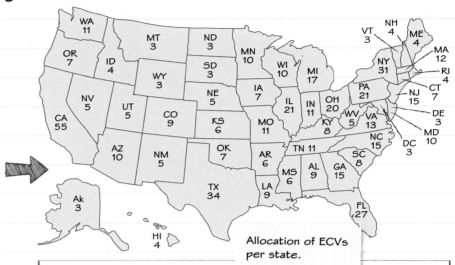

Allocation of ECVs per state.

Rogue voters

A 'rogue voter' (also known as a 'faithless elector') is an elector who does not cast their ECV for the candidate that their state voted for. This action is illegal in 30 of the 50 states. There were seven rogue voters in 2016.

🔍 Case study The 2016 US election

In 2016, presidential candidates Trump and Clinton were competing for the presidency. On election day in November 2016, Trump gained nearly 63 million votes (46 per cent) and Clinton gained nearly 66 million votes (48 per cent). However, Trump won 30 states, worth a total of 306 ECVs, whereas Clinton won just 20 states, worth a total of 232 ECVs. Despite getting fewer votes nationally, therefore, Trump was announced as the winner and inaugurated in January 2017.

This has happened only once before in the previous five US presidential elections. In 2000, Al Gore won more votes than George W. Bush, but lost in the Electoral College.

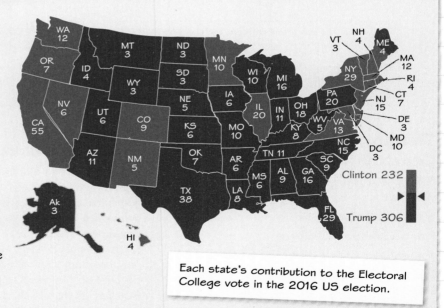

Clinton 232

Trump 306

Each state's contribution to the Electoral College vote in the 2016 US election.

Now try this

1 Explain why the presidential election is not a 'direct' election.
2 How did Trump win in 2016 with fewer votes than Clinton?

Significance of the electoral process

Debates about possible reform of the electoral system have been increasingly discussed following the 2000 and 2016 elections, in which the candidates who won in the Electoral College did not win the popular vote.

Advantages and disadvantages of the electoral process

	Advantages	Disadvantages
Invisible primaries	👍 Identifies candidates able to gain enough support/money 👍 Allows for a range of candidates 👍 Candidates well scrutinised	👎 Those able to raise the most money are not necessarily the best candidate 👎 The length of the process can cause apathy
Primaries and caucuses	👍 Maintains federalism 👍 Allows intra-party choice 👍 Caucuses allow for genuine party involvement 👍 More participation in 'open' primaries and caucuses	👎 Open primaries and caucuses can be 'sabotaged' 👎 Low turnout in both, but especially caucuses 👎 Calendar affects the importance of a primary, which has led to front-loading
National party conventions	👍 Formally announce the party candidate 👍 Engage the party faithful 👍 A poll 'bounce' (gain in the poll ratings) 👍 TV coverage allows for national involvement	👎 Increasingly presidential and vice-presidential candidates are already known, as is the party platform 👎 TV coverage increasingly reduced to acceptance speeches and little more
Electoral College	👍 States with a small population are still important 👍 Decisive outcome 👍 Usually this results in the winner gaining a majority of the popular vote 👍 Promotes a two-party system (see page 204 for more on the workings of the Electoral College) 👍 It works, largely, as the Founding Fathers intended	👎 Complex; and recent problems have caused more apathy 👎 The winner may not have a majority of the votes 👎 The winner-takes-all nature of state electors mean the population is not adequately represented 👎 Swing states (where either of the two major political parties are likely to win) overly powerful 👎 Disadvantages third parties

You must have examples for each of these points and be able to explain **why** they could be considered a 'pro' or 'con' – this is analysis.

When it comes to the **Electoral College**, avoid the simplistic argument that 'it doesn't work'. Instead, try to explain for whom it does or does not work. Also, think about why the Founding Fathers created the Electoral College and what it was designed to do.

Now try this

1 Explain, using examples (see page 204), the arguments for and against the Electoral College.

2 Analyse which part of the electoral process is most in need of reform.

Incumbency

A candidate, for either the presidency or Congress, is far more likely to be successful if they are the **incumbent** – this is the person already holding that office (see page 175 for more on the representative function). For presidents, this means seeking their second election due to term limits. In the last 11 elections that had incumbents running, eight of them won.

Incumbent advantages

Name recognition: incumbent candidates are already largely well known to voters. While this can be a danger if they have not proved popular in their first term, usually this enables them to gain media attention with greater ease than their opponents.

Fundraising: the fact that an incumbent president faces so few challengers means they do not have to worry as much about fundraising. That said, the ability of a president to fundraise, as the single candidate of a party, is far greater than his opponents'.

Single candidate: the incumbent is usually unchallenged from their own party, or such challenges are minor. In comparison, the opposing party has to go through the gruelling, and public, primary season in which they expose each other's weaknesses in an attempt to win nomination. This can destroy unity within the opposing party.

Government control: as the head of government and head of state, the incumbent president is able to undertake vote-winning behaviour in the run up to the election. For example, Obama introduced DACA in August 2012, just months before the election.

Incumbent advantages

Risk aversion: American voters can sometimes be seen as unwilling to change. This, coupled with increasing party polarisation, means that the likelihood of an incumbent being defeated is minimal except in the case of something tangible that affects voters' lives, such as a failing economy.

Campaign experience: the incumbent candidate has already been through, and won, a campaign. They should be more polished and better rehearsed than a competitor.

Presumed success: given the history of incumbent success, there is a good degree of belief that the incumbent will be successful regardless of other circumstances. This links closely with risk aversion.

Obviously, for the president, these incumbent advantages can only occur once as they have a two-term limit.

Case study: Obama in 2012

Despite the inherent advantages an incumbent has, their campaign can be precarious. While Obama won a second term in 2012, he faced a number of issues that were quite unusual by incumbents' standards:

- The polling was particularly close, with rarely more than a five-point difference and often less. Romney took the lead after his convention and arguably had a lead in some swing states.
- Romney spent more than Obama; initially, Romney was raising more money.
- Obama was said to have performed poorly in at least the first televised debate.

Nonetheless, Obama went on to win the campaign, perhaps underlining the significance of incumbency even in challenging circumstances (see page 175 for more on the significance of incumbency).

Now try this

1 Explain what is meant by 'government control' and why it might cause difficulty in a presidential campaign.
2 Explain why the advantage of 'presumed success' might actually be a disadvantage.

Campaign finance and reform

You need to know about the role of and current legislation on **campaign finance**.

Campaign donations

Money has always been a prominent feature in US politics. The first billion-dollar presidential election campaign took place in 2008, with the total spend being around $8 per vote cast. The year 2012 saw each candidate raise more than a billion dollars, with each vote costing around $20. There was a slight decline in election costs in 2016, but increasingly these vast electoral sums have come under scrutiny.

The main fundraising groups

- 527 groups (named after the tax code which exempts them from tax) raise **unlimited** money for political activities, but **not** specifically for or against a candidate.

- **Political Action Committees (PACs)** raise **hard money** to elect or defeat a specific candidate but are **limited** in their contributions to $5,000 per candidate per election.

- **Super PACs** raise **unlimited** money for political activities; they **can** support or oppose a candidate but **cannot** organise this with that person's campaign organisation.

Legislation

1974 Federal Election Campaign Act: placed legal limits on campaign contributions.

2002 Bipartisan Campaign Reform Act (McCain–Feingold reform): banned **soft money**.

2010 Citizens United v FEC: Supreme Court ruling which resulted in the development of Super PACS.

> ### 🔍 Case study   The 2016 election
>
> The candidate with the biggest 'war chest' usually wins a campaign, but the 2016 election seemed to buck that trend – Clinton raised $1.4 billion to Trump's $957.6 million. However, the *New York Times* calculated that Trump had gained nearly $2 billion of free media over his campaign to Clinton's $746 million. Factoring this in, it could still be claimed that the candidate able to mobilise more money did win in 2016.

Why is campaign finance reform so hard?

- **Supreme Court:** by interpreting the Constitution in Citizens United v FEC [2010], the Court has made it very difficult to constitutionally limit campaign spending.

- **Politicians:** those in a position to make the change are often the ones who have benefited from the current system in winning their seat.

- **Loopholes are constantly found:** in addition to Supreme Court rulings, the varying groups and 'types' of spending are simply tactics to get around spending limits.

- **Federal Election Commission:** the Commission is continually gridlocked and fails to work in a bipartisan manner, meaning it struggles to enforce the spending rules.

Potential campaign finance reforms

- As trialled in Seattle, a 'Democracy Voucher Program' with each voter having four $25 tax-payer funded vouchers to give to candidates.

- Small-donor matching funds, making smaller donations more lucrative.

- Make donor declarations more timely, rather than every quarter, which means that some figures are not released until after the election.

- Remove campaign finance limits – while this might allow further influence of the wealthy, it also would allow a greater range of voices.

Now try this

1. Explain the main differences between the three main types of campaign finance groups.
2. Analyse why campaign finance reform has rarely proved effective.

Electoral reform

Electoral reform in the USA is usually used with reference to the Electoral College – the reform of the system itself would have little impact without reforming the Electoral College.

Why reform?

Small states are over-represented

Swing states are given too much importance

Third parties are ignored

The Electoral College is outdated

Reasons to reform

The person who 'wins' might not have a majority of the vote, undermining their mandate. This has happened five times in US history, but twice in the last five elections.

Rogue voters (see their role within the Electoral College on page 204)

Winner-takes-all states distort the will of the voters

National Popular Vote Interstate Compact (NPVIC)

In 2014, New York became the 10th state to sign the NPVIC. This Compact is an agreement between these states and the District of Columbia, stating that they will give their 165 Electoral College Votes to whichever presidential candidate wins the popular vote nationally, rather than in their state. The hope is that this will ensure that the winner of the popular vote will triumph in the Electoral College. However, there has been little advancement since 2014 and the states that have signed up are almost solidly Democrat.

Types of reform

- Abolish the Electoral College and replace it with a direct, national vote. This would require a constitutional amendment, which can be difficult to achieve.

- Expand the NPVIC, but this would be non-enforceable due to the Constitutional outline of the Electoral College still being in place.

- Apportion electors by district (as Maine and Nebraska do) rather than by state. This would mean 'safe states' would be removed and the focus will be on districts instead.

But is reform necessary?

For states

👎 The Electoral College retains state power.

👎 It protects the voice of the small states.

👎 It ensures that all areas of a state – rural and urban – have a role.

👍 But larger states are under-represented.

For the people

👎 The Electoral College arguably is in line with the Constitutional principle of avoiding 'tyranny of the majority'.

👎 The two-party system encouraged by the Electoral College usually gives the people a real choice (see page 214 for more on the two-party system).

👍 But in two of the last five elections, the popular vote has not been respected.

For the president

👎 A decisive and accepted outcome is usually the result. Even in 2000, the transition was relatively smooth in the circumstances.

👍 But it encourages him to pay more attention to only swing states.

For the Constitution

👎 The Electoral College does work as the Founding Fathers intended, keeping the presidency away from a popular vote.

👍 But it makes the Constitution look outdated in 21st-century America.

Now try this

1 Explain how the NPVIC circumvents the Electoral College.
2 Analyse whether the Electoral College fulfils the role laid out in the Constitution.

Elections compared

While the USA and UK both use FPTP for their general elections, the outcome of these electoral systems is quite different.

 **Synoptic link**   The UK electoral system is covered in component 1: UK Politics (pages 23–34). You can link to this to compare elections in the USA and the UK.

Nature of UK and US electoral systems

Similarities	Differences
Both countries operate nationally on a two-party system.	The UK has a direct election for their MPs only; the leader of the party with a majority of seats becomes the prime minister. In the USA, the voters vote for both Congress and the president.
FPTP means that the winner may not have an outright majority of the popular vote.	
Both executives are effectively in place through indirect elections.	The elections at local and devolved levels in the UK involve more than two parties. In 2017, for example, the SNP did well in Holyrood, and also gained 35 seats at Westminster. The success of third parties in the USA is limited at all levels.
The chances of re-election of the incumbent are high in both countries.	The role of campaign finance is far greater in the USA than in the UK.
The two-party system is sustained by policy co-optation in both countries, where popular third-party policies are 'stolen' by the two main parties.	There are a far greater number of electoral systems in use in the UK.

Campaign finance

Elections in the UK are conducted on a far smaller financial scale than their US counterparts. A direct comparison can be difficult as UK figures focus on the cost to the public, whereas US figures focus on candidate spending. However, we can compare party spending.

UK			USA		
Election year	Labour spending	Conservative spending	Election year	Democrat spending	Republican spending
2010	£8.0m	£16.6m	2008	$760m	$358m
2015	£12.1m	£15.6m	2012	$721m	$450m
2017	£11.0m	£18.6m	2016	$969m	$564m

Both countries have suffered from scandals regarding electoral funding. In the most recent elections, for example, the UK Conservatives faced a police investigation for their 2015 election spending and the USA for their ever-growing cost of elections.

The state-funding debate

One way to remove electoral funding scandals would be to further the state funding of elections and parties and restrict outside cash influence. Both countries have tried this.

Arguments for

👍 Would encourage pluralism over elitism.

👍 Would be fairer to third parties.

👍 Could reduce public apathy.

Arguments against

👎 Would make parties less reliant on, and therefore less responsive to, voters.

👎 Could challenge party independence.

Now try this

1 Explain why providing state funding for parties would help third parties in the USA and the UK.
2 Analyse why the increasing cost of elections is controversial in the USA and the UK.

Had a look ☐ Nearly there ☐ Nailed it! ☐

Party principles

The **Democratic** and **Republican** parties of the USA are far broader in their ideological outlook than the UK political parties and each party encompasses a range of views. Nonetheless, each party does have some consistent ideological beliefs.

Key ideas and principles

	Issues	Democrats	Republicans
Social and moral issues	Abortion Same-sex rights Environment Crime	• More 'progressive' attitude • More supportive of abortion access and same-sex marriage	• More 'conservative' attitude • A good proportion of the party believe in the sanctity of life. They called the Obergefell ruling a 'judicial putsch' (a judicial rebellion against the government) (see page 194 on the political role of the Supreme Court).
Economy	Tax Economy Bank regulation Minimum wage	• In favour of tax cuts, but with a focus on the lower and middle classes • Accept government regulation as needed • Call for a federal minimum wage	• In favour of tax cuts across the board • Favour minimal government intervention and regulation with the exception of protecting US jobs and trade
Welfare	Health Education Pensions	• Support healthcare as a right and sought to expand Obamacare	• An overturned Obamacare to be replaced with a free-market equivalent • A strong preference for personal responsibility

The 'broad church' party

Parties in the USA have a broad ideological commitment. Some pressure groups give Senators score cards for their support of their issue. The four Senators in the table below are at the ideological extremes of their parties. Despite being either 'Democrat' or 'Republican', their support of a variety of issues is far from unified.

	Senators			
	Elizabeth Warren (Dem)	**Susan Collins (Rep)**	**Joe Manchin (Dem)**	**Ted Cruz (Rep)**
Human Rights Campaign – a group advocating for LGBTQ equality	100%	85%	85%	0%
American Civil Liberties Union (ACLU) – a group advocating for the protection of civil liberties	94%	58%	41%	5%
National Iranian American Council (NIAC) – a group advocating the voice of Iranian Americans	Grade A	Grade F	Grade F	Grade F
Americans for Prosperity – a group advocating for lower taxes and fewer government regulations	3%	49%	39%	98%

Now try this

Using the table above, explain why the parties in the USA can be described as 'broad church'.

Party factions

As the Democratic and Republican parties have such broad ideologies, each party can be seen as a collection of **factions**.

Factions

Importantly, the factions within parties develop and change over time and so will be different today compared to 30 years ago. In addition, most factions are constructs – we observe that factions exist, but most party members would not say they were part of a faction.

Democratic factions

Liberals:
* are more left-leaning members of the party
* aim for government intervention to achieve social justice
* favour provision of welfare
* support policies such as the more socialist policies advanced by Bernie Sanders in 2016.

Conservatives:
* are socially conservative but more fiscally liberal members of the party
* are known sometimes as Blue Dogs but there are a decreasing number of these.

Moderates:
* are willing to compromise on welfare and fiscal policy up to a point
* are often supported by minority groups or blue-collar workers
* accept capitalism and current market order.

Democratic factions

Republican factions

Social conservatives:
* favour traditional views on social and moral issues
* generally are anti-abortion, opposed to gay rights and anti-immigration
* emphasise law and order
* often includes members of the **religious right**.

Republican factions

Fiscal conservatives:
* favour only very limited government intervention in the economy
* argue for low tax and free trade
* as seen in the Freedom Caucus of the party.

Moderates:
* are fiscally conservative but socially more liberal members of the party, willing to accept advancements in gay rights and abortion
* are known sometimes as Republicans in Name Only (RINOs).

Case study — The Freedom Caucus

Formed in 2015, the House Freedom Caucus is a right-wing element of the Republican Party. Despite holding only about 30 seats in the House, they wield considerable power. In September 2015, they were unhappy with the leadership of Speaker Boehner (see page 217 on the resources and tactics of interest groups); they wanted him to go further on defunding planned parenthood. In the middle of a budget crisis, however, this would risk a shutdown of Congress. Ultimately, John Boehner (see page 217) resigned, demonstrating the power that factions of a party can have on its leadership.

Now try this

In what ways do the factions of the Republican and Democrat Parties overlap?

Party power

The organisation of the Democratic and Republican parties is very complex and reflects the federal nature of the USA.

Party organisation in Congress

Congressional leaders: the leadership positions in Congress are all held by partisan congressmen – the Speaker and Minority Leader in the House, the Majority and Minority Leaders in the Senate.

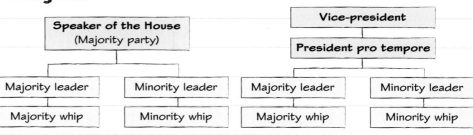

Speaker of the House (Majority party)		Vice-president	
		President pro tempore	
Majority leader	Minority leader	Majority leader	Minority leader
Majority whip	Minority whip	Majority whip	Minority whip

Organisation in Congress

The whips: to try to control the discipline within their party, both parties employ whips. These are more powerful in the House than the Senate due to the individual importance of Senators.

Caucuses: these are groups within Congress containing members that have shared interests. While some caucuses cut across party lines, some are intra-party such as the Freedom Caucus and these can affect party policy.

Congressional committees: each party has committees which oversee the policies it advances within Congress. These are known as policy and steering committees.

National organisation

The National Committees for the Democratic and Republican parties are in charge of organising the national party conventions. Outside of this election-year event, however, they have limited, if any, influence over party policy and direction.

State organisation

The most important element of party organisation occurs at state level. This is because the Constitution gives states the right to run their own elections. However, every state-based party will be run in a different manner.

Party decline and renewal

David S. Broder's 1972 book *The Party's Over: The Failure of Politics in America*, suggested that parties in America were in decline.

Arguments for parties being in decline	Arguments for party renewal
Presidential and vice-presidential candidates are largely chosen without the national party, having been selected through the increasing front-loading of primaries.	Nationalised election campaigns means that the main parties are the only ones politically and financially capable of fighting an election.
Issue voting has grown in importance, as seen by the growth of interest groups and the tripling of votes for third parties in 2016 (see page 214 for an overview of recent US voting habits).	Increasing political polarisation of the USA, with liberals and conservatives becoming more entrenched in their ideologies, has made parties more important.
Factions within parties seem to wield considerable power, meaning that parties are not united behind one ideological view (read about party factions on page 211).	Increasing partisanship evident in congressional voting patterns suggests that the party remains prominent (see page 179 for more on voters' relationship with Congress).
Due to primaries and caucuses, a party has little control over its candidate. For example, Trump was not the preferred party candidate, yet won anyway.	National parties still hold a nomination role, especially with the Democrats' 'super-delegates' having such a big influence at the national party conventions.

Now try this

1 Explain the difference between 'party decline' and 'party renewal'.
2 In what ways are parties important to the organisation of Congress?

Voters

Traditional voter patterns may have evolved, but it is still possible to see that certain groups of people tend to vote for certain parties or candidates.

Voter affiliation (percentages)

	2004		2008		2012		2016	
	Kerry (D)	Bush (R)	Obama (D)	McCain (R)	Obama (D)	Romney (R)	Clinton (D)	Trump (R)
Gender								
Male	44	55	49	48	45	52	41	53
Female	51	48	56	43	55	45	54	42
Race								
White	41	58	43	55	39	59	37	58
Black	88	11	95	4	93	6	88	8
Hispanic	53	44	67	31	71	27	65	29
Age								
Age 18–29	54	45	66	32	60	37	55	37
Age 30–44	46	53	52	46	52	45	50	42
Age 45–64	48	51	50	49	47	51	44	53
Age 65+	46	54	45	53	44	56	45	53
Education								
High school or less	N/A	N/A	53	46	51	47	45	51
College degree	46	52	50	48	47	51	49	45
Postgraduate	55	44	58	40	55	42	58	37
Religion								
Protestant	40	59	45	54	42	57	39	58
Catholic	47	52	54	45	50	48	45	52
Jewish	74	25	73	22	74	23	71	24
No religion	67	31	75	23	70	26	68	26

Voter tendencies

Race: black voters have consistently and reliably voted Democrat in the 21st century. More notably, the Hispanic vote, which began as reasonably evenly split, has veered far more towards the Democrats due to Democratic support for affirmative action and immigration policies, such as Obama and DACA, healthcare and the economy.

Gender: while the split between the two genders is only marginal, men are more likely to support the Republicans. Women are more likely to support the Democrats, potentially due to their greater support for socially progressive policies and women's rights.

Age: the broad trend remains that the older a person is, the more likely they are to vote Republican. However, there is also a narrowing of the split, especially in the 45–64 age group. Younger voters are often more liberal in their outlook, and more socially progressive than older voters.

Education: the broad trend is that those with a lower level of education vote Republican. However, the split between the groups is fairly narrow, with the exception of postgraduates in 2016, who often hold a more liberal outlook.

Religion: the split between Protestant and Catholic voters is limited but there is a more overarching trend that those who affiliate with a Christian religion vote Republican and those who do not vote Democrat. The Democrats have been more supportive of women's rights to abortion whereas Republicans have a more religious base, the 'religious right', and have been more pro-life in their policy stance.

Now try this

1 Explain how voting patterns have changed in the 21st century.
2 Analyse why each voting group may affiliate more closely to one party than the other.

Two-party system

The USA operates on a two-party system, where most of the seats in government, and most elections, are won by just the Republicans or the Democrats.

Party control

A 'unified government' refers to one party holding the presidency, the House of Representatives and the Senate. When these are controlled by different parties, this is 'divided government'.

	President	House	Independents	Senate	Independents
1992	D	D	1	D	0
1994	D	R	1	R	0
1996	D	R	1	R	0
1998	D	R	2	R	0
2000	R	D	2	R	0
2002	R	R	1	R	1
2004	R	R	1	R	1
2006	R	D	0	D	2
2008	D	D	0	D	2
2010	D	D	0	R	2
2012	D	D	0	R	2
2014	D	R	0	R	2
2016	R	R	0	R	2

Why is the USA a two-party system?

- The use of FPTP encourages a two-party system.
- The winner-takes-all nature of most states' allocation of Electoral College Votes.
- The cooptation of third-party policies means, even when a third party has a promotable policy, it is soon adopted by at least one of the major parties.
- The 'broad church' ideology of US political parties (see page 210 for more on party factions).
- The Electoral College, which encourages a two-horse race (read more about the Electoral College on page 204).
- The federal nature of the USA – if there were in fact two main parties from every state, the result in Congress could be a lack of a majority and therefore further gridlock.

In what ways is the USA not a two-party system?

- With each party being organised on a state basis, the argument could be made that neither the Republicans nor the Democrats are truly 'one' party.
- The breadth of both parties could mean that talking of 'two' parties is inaccurate, with the similarities being greater than their differences.
- Third parties have had an increasing impact on US politics, with their vote share tripling in 2016. Also, both the Libertarian Johnson and Stein of the Green Party argued to be allowed to take part in televised debates in 2016. This increase may have been partly due to the main party choice – Clinton or Trump – and to the early press that candidates such as Bernie Sanders gained.
- Some states are solidly Democrat or Republican, making the situation within those states effectively one-party.

Now try this

1 Explain why the third-party vote may have tripled in 2016.
2 Evaluate the most important reason that secures a two-party system in the USA.

Democracy compared

The UK and USA arguably both have **two-party systems** at national level: Republicans and Democrats in the USA, and Conservatives and Labour in the UK. However, both countries have seen a recent growth in third-party success, both at national and local level, challenging this political norm.

> **Synoptic link** The UK political parties are covered in component 1: UK Politics (pages 12–22). You can link to this to compare democracy in the USA and UK.

The impact of first-past-the-post

Both the USA and the UK use first-past-the-post (FPTP). This is a plurality system, meaning candidates simply have to gain the most votes in a district to win, not a majority. However, to gain a plurality, a candidate must gain considerable support in a district. When more than two parties run, it splits the vote in a district between more parties, meaning the amount needed to win is actually lower. In both the USA and the UK, this results in two-party dominance and, while third parties exist, they seldom have the means or opportunities to succeed highly.

A multi-party system?

It could be argued that the UK is a multi-party system. This, however, needs considerable qualification. In line with the definition of a **party system**, it is difficult to argue that Westminster is multi-party – while other parties are represented, they do not have a 'realistic chance of forming government'. Instead, perhaps it is possible to look at their **impact**.

Impact

👍 The rise of UKIP had a huge effect on the Conservative manifesto of 2015.

👍 The role of opposition days and urgent questions in the House of Commons gives third parties a genuine say.

👎 The size and breadth of Republicans and Democrats means third parties have little impact or power in the USA.

Parties compared

While both countries have two major parties, you **must not** simply assume the Democrats are similar to Labour and the Republicans are similar to Conservatives. While there are similarities, the whole of US politics is more conservative than UK politics.

Labour and Democrats

Similarities	Differences
Both favour a minimum wage and workers' rights	Labour under Corbyn is far more left wing than the current Democratic party
Both favour higher government intervention in the economy and welfare	Labour is more willing to increase taxes; Democrats accept but rarely want to advance tax

Conservatives and Republicans

Similarities	Differences
Both dislike government intervention, especially in the economy but also in welfare	The Conservatives have a more liberal view of many social issues than the Republicans, including gay rights and the environment
Both favour high levels of defence spending	The Republican Party has greater affiliation to religion than the Conservative Party does

Factions

Labour	Conservatives	Democrats	Republicans
Momentum	Thatcherites	Progressives	RINOs
Progress	1922 Committee	Blue Dogs	Freedom Caucus

Now try this

1 Explain how first-past-the-post (FPTP) relates to a two-party system.

2 Analyse which party is most unified – Labour, Conservatives, Democrats or Republicans.

Significance of interest groups

Interest groups in the USA have far more access points available to them than those in the UK. This means they are able to exert influence in a much wider political arena.

The significance of interest groups

Frequent election cycles give groups influence, especially since Citizens United v FEC [2010], as groups are now able to use Super PACs and campaign donations to gain influence (see page 207 on reforms to campaign finance rules).

Parties are weak and fractious, which allows interest groups greater access by targeting factions within parties. Party weakness also means parties' policies can be more flexible and responsive to pressure group influence.

Increasing political apathy towards the main parties in the USA, and increasing votes for third parties, signify a shift to issue-based voting. Interest groups have seen increased membership and significance as a result

Why are groups significant?

A large number of access points (a point at which groups can apply pressure to achieve change) means greater choice and a chance for a group to gain influence.

The federal nature of the USA means that groups can target change on a local level instead of having to worry about national politics. Marijuana, for example, has been legalised at state level, not federal level.

The Constitution protects the rights of groups to exist, but also gives them judicial recourse if their rights are infringed by challenging infractions in the Supreme Court.

Factors affecting group significance

Group finances	Group membership	Expertise
Money is crucial to interest groups' success. This may be used to hire lobbyists, launch advertising or media campaigns, or contribute to campaigns of those Congressional politicians who have been sympathetic to their issue. For example, the National Rifle Association (NRA) made nearly $350m in revenue in 2013, which allows them to donate to electoral campaigns and run adverts both for and against candidates. It ran an attack ad against Joe Manchin following his amendment to a bill on gun control.	The number of members a group has is important for two reasons: **1** The more members you have, the more voters a Congressional politician stands to gain by listening to you. **2** More members means more chance to organise events, protests, campaigns and so on. Obviously, more members also means more revenue from membership fees. For example, the American Civil Liberties Union (ACLU) has more than 1.6 million members. This means it has a wide financial base, as joining costs money, but can also claim to represent a wide spectrum of voters.	A group with a solid experience in their field is more likely to be able to offer useful reports and lobbying to Congress. For example, the NRA has an arm of the organisation dedicated to just this – the NRA-ILA (Institute for Legislative Action), which aims to educate lawmakers about gun ownership to prevent gun control measures from being passed.

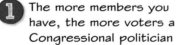

Now try this

1 Explain why the USA is such a hospitable environment for interest groups.
2 Analyse whether money is the single most important factor in interest group success.

Resources and tactics of interest groups

Given the vast array of access points, it is no wonder that lobbying is a key method for US interest groups. It is, however, far from their only tactic.

Lobbying

> Congress shall make no law... abridging the freedom... to petition the government for a redress of grievance.
>
> 1st amendment.

The seeking of 'redress of grievance' is really all lobbying is. In itself, this is not controversial; when money begins to get involved, however, it can get complicated.

Lobbying (using persuasion to influence an individual or organisation) in the USA has grown from seeking 'redress of grievance' into a vast corporate market. The individuals involved in this industry are commonly referred to as **lobbyists**.

- **Total lobbying spend:** averages about $3bn per year ($3.15bn in 2016)

- **Total number of registered lobbyists:** averages about 12,000 (11,167 in 2016).

 Case study John Boehner

John Boehner resigned from his role as the Speaker of the House of Representatives in 2015; in 2016, he joined lobbyists Squire Patton Boggs. This organisation was the sixth biggest lobbying firm, spending nearly $19m on lobbying in 2016 according to opensecrets.org. At the same time, This organisation was joined the board of directors of a huge tobacco company – Reynolds American. Having someone like Boehner associated with your lobbying company or business can help you gain access to the people still in Congress.

Who lobbies?

Lobbying can take place by firms like Squire Patton Boggs on behalf of interest groups or by interest groups themselves. In 2016, for example, the NRA lobbied Congress on 190 bills trying to prevent extensive gun control measures being introduced. Despite the tragic mass shootings of the 21st century, such as Sandy Hook in 2012 or the Orlando nightclub shooting in 2016, meaningful gun control reform has yet to be achieved.

Other methods to gain influence

Legal methods: either bringing a case to the courts or submitting *amicus curiae* briefs as part of a Supreme Court case (see page 191 for more on the workings of the Supreme Court). For example, the ACLU filed an *amicus curiae* brief in support of free speech in the Snyder v Phelps [2011] case.

Congressional report cards and funding: groups like the NRA rate Congressmen for their sympathy to their issue. A low rating may mean less funding or a loss of voters (see page 210 on voters' relationship with parties).

Other tactics

Protests and demonstrations: these could be an organised rally or may be mass online action through petitions or websites. For example, the Women's March on Washington organised a protest march against the NRA in 2017.

Publicity and media: advertising campaigns to try to influence voters, either into contacting their Congressional politician or into changing their voting behaviour. For example, the NRA ran an advert suggesting that if Obama's children deserved armed protection, so did many Americans.

Now try this

1 Explain what is meant by 'lobbying'.
2 Analyse why the existence of lobbying firms could be considered controversial.

Interest group typology

How interest groups are categorised is simply a construct of political philosophy. This means we need to look at the array of groups and identify those who have similarities to create the categories.

Policy groups

A **policy group** tries to exert influence over a whole policy area. For example, UnidosUS tries to exert influence over immigration policy, education, health and much more on behalf of Latinos. They labelled Obama as 'Deporter-in-Chief'.

> If you're struggling with what a 'policy area' is, think of it like a department. If a group is interested in lots of issues within one government department, it's a policy group. If it's interested in just one issue within a department, it's probably a single-issue group.

Professional groups

A **professional group** is one which represents the interests of its members, usually working in a specific area. These groups are similar to unions.
For example, the National Association of Broadcasters (NAB) was one of the biggest lobbying spenders in 2017, which is perhaps not surprising given Trump's comments on 'fake news'.

> As these 'typologies' are created by political scientists, it is possible to question the effectiveness of these categories. For example, the ACLU could perhaps be seen as a policy group given the breadth of its cases or a single-issue group given its single focus on 'civil liberties'.

Single-issue groups

A **single-issue group** tries to exert influence around one small, specific area. Given the size of the USA, these groups may be large themselves.

> You need to know at least one group from each of these categories. Make sure you can justify why the groups you have chosen fall into each category. It is also important to remember that what a group might claim to be a success can be difficult to prove. Take a look at the case study below.

The NRA could be deemed as a single-issue group. While it contacts Congress on many bills that may not appear to have a natural link to the 'right to bear arms', in almost all cases it is this and this alone that it is advocating. This NRA advert is campaigning against gun control and reflects the methods it uses to try to win support.

Case study: League of Conservation Voters

The League of Conservation Voters (LCV) is a group that aims to protect the environment. It lobbied the government on the Keystone Pipeline XL bill in 2015. When Obama rejected the pipeline, the LCV called the decision 'huge'. However, 124 unique organisations had registered to lobby on this bill, according to opensecrets.org, so attributing success to just one of them is challenging. In addition, with Trump in office and the pipeline back on, the success was short lived.

The LCV campaigning against Keystone.

Now try this

Explain the differences between the types of pressure groups.

Interest groups and democracy

With the clear impact that interest groups can have on the US political system, their impact calls into question whether their actions are good or bad for US democracy.

Types of democracy

Liberal	Representative	Pluralist	Constitutional
A democracy that places emphasis on the protection of rights, limited government and free and fair elections.	A democracy that places importance on the representation by elected officials.	A democracy that values the tolerance of views and wide dispersal of power.	A democracy in which all of the systems and processes are laid out in a written constitution.

Pressure group impact

It is possible to assess interest-group impact on democracy in a simple pros/cons list. However, a more nuanced way to do this is to look at types of democracy.

Scrutinising government	
👍 Interest groups scrutinise government decisions and protest them in their own interest. 👍 A successful outcome is an excellent result for the limited government of a **liberal democracy** and dispersal of power of a **pluralist democracy**.	👎 Changing the minds of those who have been elected on a platform could be seen as a negative argument for **representative democracy**. 👎 'Buying' access through lobbying could be seen to contravene the idea of 'free and fair' elections in the USA.

Increasing representation	
👍 The social make-up of Congress does not reflect society and therefore interest groups can represent under-represented groups.	👎 This directly undermines **representative democracy**, which places power in the hands of the elected; frequent elections in the USA give the electorate plenty of chance to change their representative. 👎 It can encourage a 'tyranny of the minority' which is contrary to pluralist democracy.

Encouraging participation	
👍 Interest groups allow the disaffected and apathetic to be involved in an area of politics which most interests them; this is especially important in the USA's two-party system as encouraged by the **constitutional democracy**.	👎 Illegal participation is inherently **illiberal** and undermines 'democracy' more generally.

Case study Citizens United v FEC [2010]

The interest group Citizens United argued against campaign finance limits for elections, saying they contravened freedom of speech. The Supreme Court ruled with them, protecting rights but potentially making elections less free and fair – **liberal** and **illiberal** at once.

Now try this

Outline one argument that interest groups are good and bad for each type of democracy listed here.

Interest groups and influence

With the volume of money spent by interest groups each year, it would be natural to assume that they do have considerable influence. However, are they **all** successful?

Influential or not?

Influential	Lacking in influence
👍 Groups can submit reports to Congress on proposed bills and may even be asked to give evidence in committee.	👎 It would be unusual for only one group to be involved in this manner, so allocating influence is difficult.
👍 Groups can bring cases to the Supreme Court.	👎 Ultimately, the Supreme Court decides which of the 8,000 cases it receives it will hear.
👍 Groups can donate money to campaigns and the additions of Super PACs allows for almost limitless involvement (read more about these funds on page 207).	👎 Direct campaign contributions are limited and the groups can only access a limited choice of candidates.
👍 Groups can arrange *amicus curiae* briefs for the Supreme Court (see page 217).	👎 The Supreme Court is ultimately only allowed to make its decisions on the basis of the US Constitution.
👍 Groups can rate Congressional politicians and launch campaigns for or against them in their districts.	👎 The power of incumbency suggests such campaigns are of limited value.
👍 There are a vast range of access points at local, state and national level for a group to utilise.	👎 At national level, while a group may find favour in one branch, checks and balances mean this needs to be reciprocated for them to be successful.
👍 Some interest groups have close relationships with current, or former, Congressional politicians or their staff, giving them insider access.	👎 The number of interest groups with such access is limited in number.
👍 Groups can provide Congress with expert information on their issue.	👎 This will be only one factor that Congress considers, especially in a system with a short election cycle.

Influence by branch

Congress	Presidency	Supreme Court
• Lobbying members of Congress • Giving evidence/information to committee • Proposing legislation with a member of Congress • Electioneering	• Lobbying (of the president, EXOP or executive branch) • Electioneering • Iron triangles, where a congressional committee, executive department and interest group all have similar aims and are therefore more able to achieve them given the power of this relationship	• *Amicus curiae* briefs • Protests outside of the Court • Taking a case to the Supreme Court • Lobbying on Supreme Court vacancies

Now try this

Explain the ways in which interest groups can be influential in US politics.

Interest groups compared

Interest groups (pressure groups in the UK) are prevalent in both the USA and the UK. However, their power, methods and influence can vary substantially.

 **Synoptic link**   The pressure groups are covered in component 1: UK Politics (pages 7–9). You can link to this to compare interest/pressure groups in the USA and the UK.

Power

Similarities	Differences
Groups in both countries are able to access members of the executive and legislature through lobbying.	Court cases are more commonly brought by interest groups in the USA and supported by them in the UK.
Free media in both countries means groups can buy advertising or use stunts to gain media attention.	The size of the USA makes mass protests more complex than in the UK.

Methods

Methods of groups in both countries are broadly similar.

Both court the support of current, or former, legislators as patrons for their group, or at the very least a sympathetic access point

Both can use lobbying to access the government

Similarities

Both organise protests and demonstrations as a show of public support

Both use media and advertising to create pressure and interest

Differences

US groups are more involved in elections than UK groups. It is far more common for groups in the USA to rate their Congressional politicians and advertise for or against their re-election than it is in the UK. It is also more common for groups to give money to election campaigns in the USA than in the UK.

Legal action carries more weight in the USA than it does in the UK. As the Supreme Court acts on a quasi-sovereign basis (see page 193 to read about how this works), it is far more powerful than its UK counterpart. This means that groups are far more likely to see the judiciary as a useful access point in the USA.

Influence

Similarities	Differences
Interest groups in both countries give evidence to committees in the legislative branch.	Groups in the USA have the Supreme Court as the final court of appeal. In the UK, groups can go to the ECJ or ECHR (until 2019) to achieve their ends.
Groups in both countries use the courts to exert influence on the government.	Judicial rulings in the UK can be ignored by the government.
Groups in both countries have more influence if they have more members and/or money.	A greater number of access points in the USA means a greater chance of achieving influence.

Now try this

1 Explain why US groups use electioneering and judicial methods more than UK groups.

2 Analyse in which country's groups are more powerful.

Exam skills 1: Section A

This question will help you to revise for **Section A** of your A Level **Paper 3** exam. The first question you will encounter in Paper 3 is the **comparative** question. This will ask you to compare factors, differences or similarities of an aspect of US and UK politics.

Section A

- Section A of your Paper 3 exam consists of two 12-mark questions and you will need to choose **one** of them to answer.
- You will be assessed on AO1 and AO2 skills, with each skill being worth 6 marks.
- You must make reference to **both** countries in your answer.
- You should aim to spend around 15 minutes on your answer.

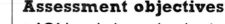

Assessment objectives

- **AO1 knowledge and understanding.** You need to express what you know and show you understand how it relates to the question you are answering.
- **AO2 analysis.** You need to show how the political aspect you are examining can be broken down and how it relates to the question. You should show comparisons, similarities, differences and/or parallels between the two countries.

Command word: Examine

You need to look in detail at the aspect of politics named in the question. You need to identify how this concept is different or similar in the UK and the USA, or what the causes or consequences of this aspect of politics are.

Planning

It is not really necessary to plan a 12-mark question. However, picking the right question is crucial. You could make a brief plan of three or four bullet points to identify the factor you will discuss in each paragraph to ensure you have enough factors to discuss before you begin.

Worked example

1 Examine the ways in which the US president and the UK prime minister can control foreign policy.

(12 marks)

Both the UK prime minister and the US president act as commander-in-chief. While the president holds this role constitutionally, the prime minister only has this role through royal prerogative and therefore is potentially weaker. The US president has used this role to control foreign policy alone, as shown when Obama authorised airstrikes on Libya in 2011 without any congressional approval. Conversely, the convention in the UK is that parliament should vote on such matters, meaning the prime minister should not be able to act alone. Nonetheless, the prime minister is usually able to use his/her position to gain enough support for any action, as Cameron did in 2011 winning a vote on Libya 557-13. In reality, the role of commander-in-chief for both executives affords considerable control...

This worked example continues on the next page.

These questions do not need an introduction.

The key word here is 'control' – not just what powers they have on paper, but whether they can **control** foreign policy.

At the beginning of each paragraph, clearly identify the factor that you are going to discuss – in this case, 'commander-in-chief'.

The student has identified a difference in where this power comes from and the consequences of this difference.

Using examples is important, but they must have a little explanation to make them relevant. Here, highlighting that Obama did not have congressional approval indicates his power.

Try to avoid summing up a paragraph by repeating the question. Here, the student has qualified their answer by saying 'in reality', indicating that despite theoretical differences, the power is similar.

Exam skills 2: Section A
continued...

This is a continuation of the sample answer given on page 222. Read the question and sample student answer on that page before continuing below.

Comparison

A 12-mark question should identify three or four points of **comparison**. It is important that each paragraph is actually a comparison. Make sure you include reference to **both** countries in every paragraph.

It is not enough for you to describe the two countries and leave your examiner to work out the comparison; **you** must explicitly show the comparison.

Timing

Make sure you know how much you can write in 15 minutes before you get into the exam. Practise at home in timed conditions as often as you can. There is not much point trying to write four long paragraphs if you know you are going to run out of time.

Worked example

... While power to declare war rests with the legislatures in the USA (constitutionally) and the UK (conventionally, since 2007), the executives can influence this decision. As the prime minister is the leader of the majority party, they should have a majority in the House of Commons. Using their party whips, they should be able to get approval for a declaration of war with relatively little difficulty. The US president, however, may find Congress is controlled by an opposing party and, given separation of powers in the USA, constitutionally only Congress can declare war. This would appear to limit the president's control over declaring war. Nonetheless, this congressional power has not been exercised since 1941, suggesting the president has grown in influence in this role given the number of conflicts that the USA has been involved in since this date...

Your answer to this question is likely to be about two sides in length in your exam booklet.

Most of your paragraphs will follow the same basic structure once you get into the flow of an essay. In this case, identify a method of control and show how it works in the UK and the USA using an example.

You must ensure your paragraphs are on different points. Here, the role of commander-in-chief and the power to declare war are closely related. This student has ensured that the first paragraph (see page 222) deals with the individual power of the president and the prime minister, while paragraph 2 deals with their relationship with their legislatures.

This worked example continues on the next page.

Exam skills 3: Section A
continued...

This is a continuation of the sample answer given on page 222. Read the question and sample student answer on that page before continuing below.

Answering the question

A key part of examining an idea or concept is making sure you are actually answering the question set. It is easy to become stuck in simply describing factors which, at best, is AO1 knowledge and understanding but, more commonly, it is often simply knowledge. Instead, you must show you can relate your factor to the words in the question. In this case, while 'foreign policy' is the factor, 'control' is the analytical term. Describing what powers the US president and the UK prime minister have is AO1; showing how this allows them to 'control' foreign policy is AO2.

Worked example

... Both executives act as their country's representative on a global stage. This allows them to influence foreign policy in a more peaceful sphere by, for example, being a representative of their country at international conferences. Obama and Cameron both attended the Paris Climate Change Summit in 2015, and both gave speeches and committed their countries to signing up to this agreement. Obama did so without consulting the Senate. Treaties in the USA are supposed to be put to the Senate for ratification; however, Obama used his executive powers to circumvent this. While Cameron was required to put the agreement before Parliament, he had already had an input at international level on the content of the agreement. It passed Parliament with no objections, suggesting that both executives have considerable influence over foreign policy in this manner despite this difference.

Remember, you are only being assessed on AO1 and AO2 in this question (see page 222 for details of the assessment objectives). You do not need to venture into assessing which executive has more power as this is evaluation, which is AO3.

The student has written three developed paragraphs. This is an acceptable approach and shows a good depth of knowledge. Alternatively, you might write four shorter paragraphs.

For each paragraph, ask yourself:
- ✓ Does this paragraph deal with a clear and unique factor?
- ✓ Have I shown an explicit comparison?
- ✓ Have I used a relevant example?
- ✓ Does my paragraph relate to the question?

This question does not need a conclusion.

Exam skills 4: Section B

This question will help you to revise for **Section B** of your A Level **Paper 3** exam. This section consists of **one compulsory question**. It is worth 12 marks and should be structured in roughly the same way as Section A (see pages 222–224). The key difference here is that you must deploy your **comparative theories** to help explain your answer.

Comparative theories

These are political theories that help to explain why similarities or differences exist between political systems. Each theory suggests that political outcomes can be explained by:

Rational theory: individual actions, presuming that individuals will act in a way that suits them best.
Remember: selfish actions!

Structural theory: the processes and institutions that govern political action.
Remember: institutions and processes!

Cultural theory: shared ideologies which explain how people choose to act.
Remember: shared beliefs!

Comparative theories

You can find more detail about each theory on page 163.

Which one should I use?

You only need to use **one** theory at some point during the essay. Which one you pick will depend on which one you think best explains why a similarity or difference exists. For some factors, only one or two theories are relevant at all. For others, you might be able to use all three theories – you just have to pick the best one.

The following examples show how these theories can be applied. In question 2B, you would need to decide which theory you think **best** explains the difference. Note: this is an example of how to address **one** paragraph of a full answer.

2A Analyse the differences in the US and UK constitutions.

In your answer you must consider the relevance of at least one comparative theory. **(12 marks)**

Could you use:

✗ ... rational theory? Not really. It is quite hard to argue that this difference exists because of selfish individuals.

✓ ... cultural theory? This is most relevant. An uncodified constitution is part of the UK political culture which has developed over hundreds of years. Comparatively, the USA experienced violent revolution which made a codified constitution more necessary.

✗ ... structural theory? Again, not really. As the constitutions themselves lay out political processes, it is difficult to argue this is what has caused the difference.

2B Analyse the similarities and differences between the US and UK legislative process.

In your answer you must consider the relevance of at least one comparative theory. **(12 marks)**

Could you use:

✓ ... rational theory? Yes, because MPs in the UK are more inclined to vote with their party to protect their jobs, whereas in the US constituent opinion may be more important.

✓ ... cultural theory? Yes, because UK parties are more ideologically coherent than the 'broad church' US parties.

✓ ... structural theory? Yes, because the whips in the UK and the threat of deselection means MPs can almost be forced into voting for their party, while primaries and caucuses in the USA make for weaker political parties.

Exam skills 5: Section B
continued...

Read the questions and accompanying information on page 225 before continuing below. While the essay structure, length and timing are the same as Section A, the inclusion of comparative theories in Section B makes your paragraphs look a little different.

The requirements

There are certain requirements you must ensure in order to maximise your marks.

- You must refer to both the USA **and** the UK.
- You must refer to **at least one** comparative theory.

Command word: Analyse

You need to look at the factor and break it down in order to show how its parts work together. In this kind of question, that means looking for similarities and differences and showing why or how they exist.

Worked example

2 Analyse the differences between federalism and devolution.

   In your answer you must consider the relevance of at least one comparative theory.   **(12 marks)**

One difference is the location of sovereignty. The US Constitution allows for the shared sovereignty between the states and federal government, meaning it is difficult for the federal government to infringe upon states' rights. Comparatively, the UK is a unitary system with sovereignty located in Parliament, so devolved bodies only exist because Parliament allows them to. This difference is best explained structurally, as the location of sovereignty in each country is determined by its constitution. The lack of a UK codified constitution results in the sovereignty of Parliament, while the US Constitution is itself sovereign – by enshrining states' powers, it enshrines them with a sovereignty of their own. The result of this structural difference is a lack of guaranteed power for devolved bodies, especially compared to US states...

These questions do not need an introduction.

The opening line clearly outlines the factor to be discussed. Note that it is brief and does not repeat the whole of the question – you have only limited time.

This sentence is a great example of the difference between knowledge and understanding. The first part shows knowledge, but everything after 'meaning' demonstrates understanding by the student as they have shown they can explain the point.

The student has explained which theory best explains this difference but also shows **why** they have picked this theory.

You do not need to include a theory in every paragraph, but you must include it in at least one paragraph.

To finish answering this question, you need to add two or three more differences. Examples include:

- the direction that power flows is different, explained using structural theory
- the power that devolved bodies have varies, but federal states have uniform power, explained using structural theory.

Exam skills 6: Section C

This question will help you to revise for **Section C** of your A Level **Paper 3** exam. This section consists of three 30-mark questions – you will need to choose **two** of them to complete. Importantly, these questions have a **synoptic** element, covering your whole course rather than just one topic. It is vitally important that you spend time planning your answer.

Section C

- You should aim to spend around 45 minutes on each essay.
- Each essay needs to be fully structured, including an introduction and a conclusion.
- You will be assessed on AO1, AO2 and AO3 skills.
- You only need to make reference to the USA in these questions – they are **not** comparative.

Assessment objectives

- **AO1 knowledge and understanding.** You need to express what you know and show you understand how it relates to the question you are answering.
- **AO2 analysis.** You need to show how the factor you are examining can be broken down and how it relates to the question. You should also show comparisons, similarities, differences and parallels.
- **AO3 evaluation.** This is your ability to argue how important the similarities or differences are. It should be clear **throughout your essay** how significant the divisions are, not just in the conclusion.

Planning

Planning is vital. It will ensure your essay makes sense, is focused and gains marks more quickly. More importantly, perhaps, you need to know if you can answer the question. Spend only a couple of minutes planning your essay. If it becomes clear that you do not have enough information to answer the question, quickly pick a different question to answer – this is not wasted time.

Steps to planning

1. **Introduction:** define key terms and introduce the argument.
2. **Body:** what factors are you going to discuss and what examples are you going to use to support your work?
3. **Conclusion:** make a final summary judgement, drawing on the overarching themes you can draw from your essay.

Worked example

3   Evaluate the extent to which constitutional rights have been effectively protected.

You must consider this view and the alternative to this view in a balanced way.   **(30 marks)**

Plan

Introduction: define 'constitutional rights' and outline both sides of the argument.

Body:

For	Against
• Free speech and Supreme Court, e.g. Snyder v Phelps [2011]	• Trump and free speech, e.g. NFL controversy
• 'Right to bear arms', e.g. Obama and Sandy Hook/DC v Heller [2008]	• Free and fair trial, e.g. Guantanamo Bay
• Same-sex marriage, e.g. 14th amendment/ Obergefell v Hodges [2015]	• Supreme Court and free speech, e.g. Citizens United v FEC [2010]

Conclusion: largely well protected but sometimes it takes time.

It is important to try to identify any links between opposing factors. Contrasting opposing factors can make for a very persuasive essay.

Note that the introduction identifies the key term to be defined.

The 'for' and 'against' columns have a number of references to 'free speech'. These should be put together in the essay so this order might need changing.

The conclusion has a clear answer; this should be reflected throughout the **whole** of your essay however, not just in the conclusion.

Exam skills 7: Section C
continued...

Read the question and plan on page 227 before continuing below.

Introduction

Your introduction should show that you understand what you have been asked to do. It should therefore define the key terms of the question, outline what you are going to discuss and perhaps even hint at what you may argue.

Command words: Evaluate the extent

This command word will be followed by a statement that suggests one side of an argument. You need to show that you **know and understand** (AO1), and can **analyse** (AO2) and **evaluate** (AO3) this **and the other side** of the argument. You need to review the factors that affect your argument and judge their importance or effectiveness.

Timing

Aim to spend 45 minutes on each 30-mark question. Use a few minutes to plan and proofread your work.

Worked example

Constitutional rights are any right that a US citizen has because it has been outlined in, or interpreted from, the US Constitution. Most commonly this is the Bill of Rights, but as the Supreme Court interprets the Constitution, they can interpret further rights. In an age dominated by the 'war on terror', there have been clear infringements of rights such as the continued use of Guantanamo Bay. Nonetheless, the Supreme Court has largely worked to ensure key rights, such as the 1st amendment, have been upheld. While the debate over whether rights have been protected may depend on the ideological view of differing sides, the continued existence of the Bill of Rights goes a long way to ensuring rights can be protected...

 This definition is very thorough and shows the student knows the difference between the 'Bill of Rights' and 'constitutional rights'.

 The reference to the 'war on terror' shows excellent contextual understanding of the USA and the political situation there.

 References to Guantanamo Bay and the 1st amendment give the examiner an idea of what the student is going to discuss.

 The final sentence gives a hint as to how the student will argue. This introduction shows a good understanding of the assessment objectives and sets up the essay.

... One constitutional right which has been well protected is the 'right to bear arms'. This is in the 2nd amendment of the Bill of Rights and allows Americans to keep weapons. Recent tragedies such as Sandy Hook in 2012 and Las Vegas in 2017 show that a right to bear arms has been upheld. Despite these tragedies, there have been very few successful attempts to gain greater gun control. Obama tried to increase gun control after Sandy Hook but Congress were unwilling to act. Additionally, in two landmark cases in 2008 and 2010, the Supreme Court sided with gun owners. Therefore, even in the face of gun violence, the 2nd amendment continues to be well protected, by at least two, and currently three, branches of US government...

 In this first paragraph, lots of examples are used but quite a lot of them are names rather than explained examples.

 Some attempt at evaluation is made, showing how and why the 2nd amendment has been well protected.

 By including the Supreme Court, they have shown a good deal of knowledge, but risk having only limited analysis.

 This final sentence repeats the question, but does try to offer an evaluative answer to it.

This worked example continues on the next page.

Exam skills 8: Section C
continued...

This is a continuation of the sample answer given on pages 227 and 228. Read the question and sample student answer on those pages before continuing below. Structuring the main part of your essay requires some individual style. The more you practise, the better at this you will become. Here the student improves on the paragraph on the previous page.

Improved sample answer

The freedom of speech is the very first freedom identified in the Bill of Rights. It is part of the five freedoms identified in the 1st amendment. The USA has a long tradition of protecting free speech, even when it has proved controversial. This has continued to be the case as recently as 2011, when the Supreme Court decided the case of Snyder v Phelps. In this case, the Supreme Court found in favour of the Phelps family, members of the Westboro' Baptist Church, even though many of the Church's protests have been highly controversial. The Supreme Court's power to interpret the sovereign Constitution, and this being their only role, has meant even when the public have perhaps found the defence of free speech unpalatable, the Supreme Court has been able to defend this right, as they did for the Phelps family. By interpreting the Constitution, the rulings of the Court take on a quasi-sovereign nature so their rulings are incredibly powerful and allow for a strong ability to protect rights.

 A clear opening that deals with the knowledge and understanding needed for this question.

 Clear evaluation of the point and excellent use of political vocabulary.

 While dealing with the same point, this student is showing an understanding of other viewpoints.

However, the same Court has ruled in other cases on free speech that seem to go some way to undermining the right to free speech. In Citizens United v FEC in 2010, the Court ruled that spending on political campaigns was covered by free speech. This allowed for the development of Super PACs which could spend unlimited amounts of money in supporting or opposing electoral candidates provided such spending was not done in cooperation with the campaign. While doing so may seem a defence of free speech, it also had the effect of equating money with speech. This could therefore be interpreted that this ruling effectively gave a greater right to 'free speech' to the wealthier Americans, and a diminished right to poorer Americans. Despite this, in practice this does still uphold free speech, and in electoral terms the USA still operates on 'one man, one vote', so while the wealthier might be able to aid candidates, they have no greater say than anyone else on election day. In these circumstances, the Supreme Court has largely protected free speech, even if it has done so controversially...

 This is excellent interpretation and analysis of the case, highlighting the **impact** of the case and its relevance to the question.

 While they have shown an alternative view, the student ends by maintaining their line of argument and evaluating which side of the argument is stronger.

This worked example continues on the next page.

Exam skills 9: Section C
continued...

This is a continuation of the sample answer given on pages 227–229. Read the question and sample student answer on those pages before continuing below.

Conclusion

Your conclusion should show a definitive answer to the question and how you reached that conclusion. With the command words 'evaluate the extent', the conclusion must be more than simply 'yes' or 'no'.

Worked example

... The ever-present concern over 'terrorism' in the USA has undoubtedly had a somewhat negative effect on the protection of rights, with both the president and Congress having played a role in infringing rights. Nonetheless, even in these cases, the Supreme Court has worked to try to ensure those in Guantanamo do have their rights respected. Across the vast majority of constitutional rights, not only has the Supreme Court played a similar role, the very existence of the Bill of Rights makes it pointless for any branch of government to try, or even to consider, infringing rights in the USA. Despite a few exceptional examples, rights have been reasonably well upheld, even in the face of an entirely new threat to national security.

The opening line of the conclusion shows the student understands the broad context of the question – they are not just repeating what they have already written.

Both sides of the argument are referenced but a clear case is made for supporting one of those sides. This shows the student is making a justified argument.

The final sentence directly addresses the question and places the whole question in context.

Just like the introduction, you will not be awarded marks for your conclusion alone. The conclusion should, however, be predictable. From how you have written you essay, it should be reasonably clear what you are going to conclude.

Conclusion checklist

Have I...

 answered the question directly?

 explained how and why I reached this conclusion?

 written a conclusion that matches the tone of my essay?

Have I avoided...

 simply repeating paragraphs or examples?

 writing only one sentence?

 introducing new information?

Had a look ☐ Nearly there ☐ Nailed it! ☐

A level
Politics of the USA
exam-style practice

Exam-style practice

Practise for **Paper 3** of your A Level exam with these exam-style questions. There are answers on page 316. Paper 3 is made up of three sections, and in total you will have to answer four questions: **one** from Section A, **one** from Section B and **two** from Section C.

Section A

1 Examine the differences in the power of the House of Lords and the US Senate. **(12 marks)**

Aim to spend around 15 minutes on the Section A question. It is worth 12 marks – 6 marks each for AO1 and AO2.

Write about three or four paragraphs and include examples.

Look for differences, similarities, causes or consequences (pay attention to what the question asks).

Section B

2 Analyse the differences in the principles of the US and UK Constitutions.

In your answer you must consider the relevance of at least one comparative theory. **(12 marks)**

Again, spend around 15 minutes on the Section B question. It is worth 12 marks – 6 marks each for AO1 and AO2.

You also need to write about three or four paragraphs and include examples. Look for differences, similarities, causes or consequences (pay attention to the question).

Make sure you include **at least one** explanation of which comparative theory (rational, cultural and/or structural) best explains your point.

Section C

3 (a) Evaluate the extent to which the Democratic Party is now more unified than the Republican Party.

You must consider this view and the alternative to this view in a balanced way. **(30 marks)**

(b) Evaluate the extent to which the US Constitution no longer lives up to its principles.

You must consider this view and the alternative to this view in a balanced way. **(30 marks)**

Aim to spend around 45 minutes on **each** of the Section C questions. They are worth 30 marks each – 10 marks each for AO1, AO2 and AO3.

Make sure your answers are properly structured, with an introduction and a conclusion, and that they include examples.

In both answers, include analysis and evaluation to help you reach a well-argued judgement.

Remember that each conclusion should have a clear answer; this should be reflected throughout the **whole** of your essay.

231

The state: nation-state

The **nation-state** brings together the political entity of the state and the cultural entity of a nation.

The state

The legal basis for the modern state was established by the Treaty of Westphalia in 1648. The state is a **territorially based political unit**, defined as having four key features.

The ability to enter into relations with other states, which requires recognition by other states

A legally defined territory

Key features

A stable population

An effective government

The nation

A nation is a community of people who are united together by shared values and traditions, such as language, history or customs, and generally occupy the same territory. Nationalism supports the idea that the proper basis for the state is the nation (see page 152 for a greater discussion of this idea). This is best expressed through the ideal of **national self-determination** – to each nation a state.

This process has happened in two stages:

1 **19th century**: the transformation of Europe into nation-states. For example, the Unification of Germany in 1871.

2 **20th century**: the collapse of Empire in Africa and Asia, and the collapse of the USSR in 1991, to be replaced by nation-states.

This has led to most modern states being seen as nation-states, which have authority and legitimacy as they embody and represent the nation.

 Case study **The Treaty of Westphalia (1648)**

The Treaty, which brought a conclusion to the brutal Thirty Years War in Europe, is seen as the starting point of both modern **international law** and international politics. The Treaty established three key principles:

1 The principle of **sovereignty** of states.

2 The principle of legal equality between states.

3 The principle of non-intervention by one state in the internal affairs of another state.

The '**Westphalian system**' is used to describe a state-centric view of the world, which sees states as central to international relations. This view is closely aligned with **realism** (read about realism in global politics on page 285).

The Treaty of Westphalia established the principle of the sovereignty of the state.

Evaluation of the nation-state

👍 States are seen as nation-states, with the right to rule themselves, and nations are the building blocks of global politics.

👍 Nations have the right to independence and democratic rule.

👎 The idea of a world of nation-states, where states represent a nation, is perhaps more fiction than fact.

👎 Many nations are struggling to gain recognition as a nation-state. For example, around 30 million Kurds, a mostly Sunni Muslim people who share a unique language, live in an area that spans Iraq, Turkey, Iran and Syria, making them the world's largest stateless nation.

👎 Most states are culturally and ethnically diverse, so do not represent a nation. For example, Iraq is so diverse that it can be seen as a state without a nation and the UK is a state that contains several nations.

Now try this

1 What is meant by the term 'nation-state'?

2 Why might this term be seen as problematic?

The state: national sovereignty

The fundamental characteristic of the nation-state is **sovereignty**.

National sovereignty

National sovereignty implies that the state has absolute and unlimited power both within its own territory (internal sovereignty) and in global affairs (external sovereignty).

Internal sovereignty	External sovereignty
• The power of a body within the state to make decisions that are binding on individuals and groups in the territory, and the ability to maintain order. • Philosopher Max Weber describes this as a monopoly over the use of legitimate violence within the state. Political economist Joseph Schumpeter adds to this – a monopoly over the ability to raise taxes within the state.	• There is no legal or political authority above the state. • The right of autonomy to make decisions within the territory of the state free from external interference. • No state or legal body has the right to intervene in the sovereign affairs of any nation-state.

Evaluation of national sovereignty

👍 Sovereignty has provided the basis for international law. For instance, in the **United Nations (UN)** General Assembly (see page 244), each nation-state has one vote and international law guarantees the territorial boundaries and autonomy of nation-states. For example, Article 2 (4) of the UN Charter says 'All Members shall refrain in their international relations from the threat or use of force against the territorial integrity or political independence of any state...' Article 2 (7) says the UN cannot intervene in 'the domestic jurisdiction of any state'.

👍 Sovereignty is also the basis for conflict. For example, the desire for the Palestinians to establish a nation-state in the same territorial space as Israel.

The traditional concept of state sovereignty and the billiard ball model have come under attack from:

👎 **globalisation** and growing levels of interdependence, which have led to state borders becoming increasingly porous and declining sovereignty (see page 234)

👎 the increasing role of **non-state actors** such as transnational corporations (TNCs) and **non-governmental organisations (NGOs)** (read more about contemporary views of global governance on page 252), which appear to work outside of the traditional limits of sovereignty

👎 the growing role of international institutions, especially the move from **intergovernmentalism** to **supranationalism** (for a discussion on this in the context of the EU see page 282) and **regionalism** (see page 274 for an overview of different forms of regionalism), which undermine sovereignty

👎 the growing tension between national sovereignty and **human rights** (read more about this clash on page 253), leading to the idea that states have the right to intervene in other states to protect those rights.

Billiard ball model

Realism (see page 285) sees states as billiard balls, with sovereignty being their key property and its key aim being maximum relative power. When the billiard balls collide, sovereignty allows the state to survive. Realism recognises that states have different levels of power, so the billiard balls can be different sizes, and this leads global politics to focus on the **great powers** (see page 266). The billiard ball model treats all states as the same and does not distinguish between 'good' and 'bad' states. For example, the motives of the USA and USSR during the Cold War are the same and are not driven by domestic political or economic factors.

The billiard ball model of global politics favoured by realists angers liberal theorists (see page 288).

Now try this

1 What is meant by the term 'national sovereignty'?

2 In what ways does national sovereignty form the basis of international law?

The state and globalisation

Globalisation is seen as the widening, deepening and accelerating of a complex web of **interconnectedness** (see page 236 for more on political globalisation) and is one of the most contentious issues in global politics.

The process of globalisation

Globalisation has created a 'shrinking world' that is increasingly interconnected and where geographical distance is increasingly irrelevant. So, decisions or events that take place at great distance from individuals and local communities increasingly shape their lives.
For example, conflict in Syria has increased the number of asylum seekers and migrants across Europe.

At the same time, globalisation has lessened the importance of the territorial borders of the nation-state as cultural, political and economic activities are organised across the global stage. The process has seen the rise of non-state actors, such as transnational corporations (TNCs) and non-governmental organisations (NGOs), as well as international institutions, such as the **World Bank** and **World Trade Organization (WTO)**, which challenge the state-centric approach.

The factors driving globalisation

Technology	Geographer David Harvey argued that technological innovations in travel and, in particular, communications infrastructure have created **space–time compression**. This has led to the creation of global financial markets and the global administration of TNCs. TNCs have created an increasingly uniform popular culture by using advertising to make their logos and trademarks into an international language understood by all.
Culture	Global cultures have been homogenised by global brands, global media, NGOs and migration to create a monoculture by crushing local production, companies, arts, music, literature and crafts. This **homogenisation and monoculture** is based around the ideals of liberal democracy, neoliberal economics and human rights (see page 235 for more on economic and cultural globalisation).
Economics	• According to Marxists, the expansionary logic of capitalism is driven by the constant thirst for profit or, according to liberals, the need to meet human nature's rational desire for improving living standards and economic security. • The development of global markets in goods and services, with TNCs like Apple having global supply chains. Apple products, for example, are designed in the US, their parts are sourced from across Asia and Europe, assembly takes place in China and they are sold globally. • The new global division of labour driven by TNCs has created patterns of economic specialism, with high technology manufactured increasingly in wealthier nations and agriculture, raw material production and low technology manufacturing in the poorer states.
Politics	The end of the Cold War has led to the spreading of neoliberal economic ideas, democratic ideals and the culture of individualism, consumerism and materialism.
People and countries	The growth of migration and the movement of peoples across the borders of countries. For example, the International Organization for Migration (IOM) calculates that there has been a 41 per cent increase in migration in the last 15 years and, in 2017, 3.3 per cent of the global population are migrants.
Institutions	The growing role of international organisations such as the WTO, which forces countries to operate within its free market rules, or the **European Union (EU)**, where decisions are made by European institutions rather than member states.

Now try this

Define the term 'globalisation'.

Economic and cultural globalisation

Globalisation includes three main processes that describe how change is taking place: economic globalisation, cultural globalisation and political globalisation (see page 236). These processes should not be seen as distinct but rather as overlapping.

Economic globalisation

Economic globalisation is the process whereby the economies of nation-states have been locked into a single 24-hour global market for production, consumption and distribution. There has always been the movement of goods, services and materials across borders, but economic globalisation is far greater than the interdependence of economies as it involves the emergence of a **single global economy**, which limits the economic sovereignty of the nation-state.

Causes	Evidence
• The underlying economic logic of capitalism. • The role of technological innovation, especially in ICT. • The political role of states and international institutions in promoting neoliberal policies of free trade, deregulation, privatisation, low tax and cuts to public spending. • The spread of pro-market values, consumerism and materialism.	• The growth in international trade, especially within TNCs across borders. • The growth of transnational production where design, manufacturing and assembly is globalised. For example, Apple. • The global division of labour by country, creating economic efficiency. • A globalised financial system where financial transactions are instant and oblivious to national borders.

Cultural globalisation

Cultural globalisation is the process whereby the cultural differences between nations are flattened out as the world becomes increasingly uniform. People across the globe are increasingly buying the same products, eating the same food, doing the same type of jobs, watching the same TV programmes and films and accessing the same news and information.

Causes	Evidence
• The role of technological innovation, especially in ICT. • The growth of TNCs, especially the growth of global media empires who may control the flow of news to propagandise. • TNCs have developed global goods and global brands: the Americanisation of the world. • The growth in migration and international travel and tourism. • The increasing roles of NGOs like Human Rights Watch. • States and institutions, especially the USA, promote lifestyles, ideas and needs that allow for the spread of global capitalism. • Increased wealth from economic globalisation increases the desire for political participation: democracy.	**Homogenisation and monoculture:** • Increasing uniformity of culture, described by political theorist Benjamin Barber in his concept of 'McWorld'. • An increasingly Westernised global culture based around individualism, materialism and consumerism. • The emergence of a human rights culture. The spread and protection of human rights is supported by the public and politicians. • Liberal democracy and neoliberal economic policies are the only options – political scientist Francis Fukuyama's idea in *The End of History and the Last Man* (1992). This is the idea that there is no alternative (TINA). • Global culture works across boundaries, weakening the state.

Now try this

1　In what way is economic globalisation different from trade between nation-states in the past?

2　How do cultural and economic globalisation overlap?

Political globalisation

Political globalisation is the growing importance of **international institutions** which operate in an international arena in a way that affects multiple states.

Political globalisation

These international institutions can be based on:

1 **Intergovernmentalism** (see page 282 for a discussion of this in an EU context): common institutions facilitate decisions by member states, but states remain in control of the process as decisions have to be unanimous.

2 **Supranationalism** (read more about this on page 282): common institutions are created that have independent decision-making ability and can impose both decisions and rules on member states.

Causes	Evidence
• The emergence of a human rights culture that places the rights of individuals above the power of states. • NGOs' growing role in watching and sharing information about human rights abuses by states (for example, Human Rights Watch). • The end of the Cold War. • The emergence of transnational political problems, for example, terrorism, ecological destruction and migration. • Economic globalisation has led to economic activity taking place in a 'borderless world' (Kenichi Ohmae, a Japanese theorist), reducing the power of the state to develop economic policy in isolation.	• The growth in regional trading blocs such as the EU, NAFTA (see page 276 to see how this affects sovereignty) and Mercosur. • The increasing emergence of **global governance** (the role of the UN here is discussed on page 242), which includes a wide range of cooperative problem-solving arrangements to tackle global issues. Examples include the UN, WTO, the **International Monetary Fund (IMF)** and the **International Criminal Court (ICC)**. • The massive growth in the number of institutions since the middle of the 20th century. There are estimated to be about 6,400 such organisations or networks. • The global spread of liberal democracy.

Evaluation of political globalisation

👎 Political globalisation is not as advanced as either economic or cultural globalisation as most international institutions are based on intergovernmentalism.

👎 While there might be emerging levels of global governance, there is little progress towards or desire for **world government**, due to the importance of state sovereignty.

Interconnectedness and interdependence

Major changes in the global system are noticeably different to earlier forms of globalisation in the widening and deepening of interconnectedness and interdependence, which have happened in three main ways:

1 Through technological change, the 24-hour global media and the emergence of a global financial market. For example, decisions taken in one organisation, such as the UK's decision to leave the EU, can have immediate worldwide effects on states and markets.

2 The growth in migration, international trade, NGOs, TNCs and intergovernmental institutions.

3 With political, economic and cultural activities crossing territorial borders and potentially the globe. For example, the impact of migration from the war in Syria. This widening and deepening leads to the idea that globalisation is moving towards a single worldwide system with the sovereignty of the state hollowed out.

Now try this

1 How can it be argued that political globalisation lags behind economic and cultural globalisation?

2 How does economic and cultural globalisation drive political globalisation?

Globalisation and international law

International laws are the formal rules of behaviour that govern states and other international bodies. These differ from laws inside a state as there is no world government to make laws or international police force to enforce them. Globalisation therefore presents a challenge to the sovereignty of states.

The development of international law

International law originated in the 17th century with the Treaty of Westphalia (1648), which developed the principle of national sovereignty (see page 232 for more on the origins of the nation-state). International law involves states being the main subjects and makers of the law. The law is based on the principles of:

1 the sovereignty of states

2 the legal equality of states

3 non-intervention in the internal affairs of other states.

The horrors of the Nazi and Stalinist states in the 20th century led to the development of international law based on moral principles, which national law should conform to. This has driven the rise in international humanitarian law, which has increased since the massacres and ethnic cleansing in Yugoslavia (1993) and the genocide in Rwanda (1994). The rise in international law can be seen as part of the process of globalisation as it is part of the complex web of interconnectedness between states.

Challenge to state control over citizens

The growth of international law in the late 20th and 21st centuries has challenged state sovereignty in three different ways:

1 Individuals are now the subject of international law, as well as states. For example, the development of international human rights law such as the Universal Declaration of Human Rights (UDHR).

2 International law looks not just to regulate relations between states but to manage how nation-states act within their own territorial borders. For example, the development of the principle of the Responsibility to Protect (R2P) (see page 238 to see how this works in practice).

3 International law is now about more than just international order; it has a moral component. For example, the 1951 Convention Relating to the Status of Refugees that is about global justice.

This raises the question whether the development of international law is compatible with state sovereignty and both Articles 2 and 7 of the UN (see page 233 for more on national sovereignty). This clash also arises with the creation of international institutions like the **International Court of Justice (ICJ)** (see page 254), the ICC (see page 255), special UN tribunals (see page 255) and the European Court of Human Rights (see page 256).

Evaluation

👎 From the realist perspective, any attempt to develop international law which is not based on the principle of national sovereignty will not be legitimate.

👎 International law will undermine the sovereignty of states and make the world a less safe place as it will break the principle that intervention in another state is only permitted in the case of self-defence.

👎 Conflict becomes more likely, not less.

👍 From the liberal perspective, the development of international law will increase the interconnectedness and interdependence of states by promoting the rules and norms of behaviour which all states will adopt, lessening the chance of conflict. This form of international law is also based on the liberal belief that all human beings have natural rights, as seen in the thinking of John Locke (see page 53 for an overview of his political theories).

Now try this

1 What has driven the rise of international human rights law?
2 How can international law be seen to challenge national sovereignty?

Humanitarian and forcible intervention

A key debate around globalisation and its impact on the state system concerns the principle of non-intervention in the affairs of other states and the moral case for intervention in the case of a humanitarian catastrophe.

Is humanitarian intervention justified?

The emergence of international human rights law raises the question of whether **humanitarian intervention** can be justified. Can intervention take place to prevent a mass atrocity crime or would standing aside and respecting state sovereignty be morally unacceptable? *For example, the decision to intervene in Libya in 2011 has been hugely controversial, as has the decision not to intervene in Syria in 2011.* There has been an attempt to move to a post-Westphalian consensus in order to deal with this problem through redefining sovereignty.

In the emerging norm of the Responsibility to Protect (R2P), formalised in 2005, states have a responsibility to protect their populations from mass atrocity crimes such as social cleansing or genocide.

Where a state fails, there is an obligation to intervene, provided there is a reasonable chance of success and intervention will do more good than harm.

The developing norms of international law, and the R2P in particular, suggest that state sovereignty has changed. It has become conditional on the state protecting its population and failure to do so invalidates that sovereignty, legalising external intervention.

 Case study Libya, 2011

In 2011, Human Rights Watch informed the world of crimes against the Libyan people by government forces under the control of Colonel Gaddafi. The UN Security Council authorised military intervention in Libya.

👍 Those supporting intervention argue that it saves lives by preventing mass atrocity crimes, such as a massacre.

👎 Critics argue legalised intervention is a cover for imperialism.

In the case of Libya, the intervention lasted far longer than the protection of Benghazi, finishing only when Gaddafi had been removed. So, did the intervention do more harm than good? Non-intervention would have led to catastrophe in Benghazi but intervention has left a **failed state** (see page 271 for more on failed and rogue states). In 2017, there were two rival parliaments, three governments, over 1,700 armed groups and

over 400,000 internally displaced people. Human intervention has also had global impacts, including:

👎 The large flow of refugees across the Mediterranean into Italy and other European countries.

👎 Tunisia and Southern Sudan have become destabilised; Algeria has suffered terror attacks.

👎 Weapons from Gaddafi's arsenal have made their way to Syria and into the hands of Boko Haram in Nigeria.

A coalition of US and European forces attacked pro-Gaddafi forces outside Benghazi (population 700,000).

Evaluation

👎 Humanitarian crises such as Libya (2011) have global implications in terms of the displacement of peoples and refugee crises, the destabilisation of local regions, the potential to bring global powers into conflict over what action to take and the creation of spaces where global terrorism may flourish.

👎 It brings into conflict the human rights of the individual with the principle of national sovereignty.

👎 Humanitarian intervention is often seen as an excuse to further the interests of powerful states. *For example, some believe that Libya was more about regime change and oil for the USA and the Western powers than it was about human rights.*

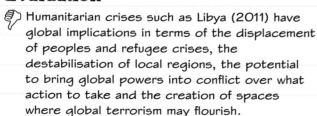 **Now try this**

How can state sovereignty and humanitarian intervention be seen as compatible?

Globalisation and the nation-state

The debate about the extent to which globalisation is happening and how it has affected the nation-state has been approached from three key perspectives: **hyperglobalisers**, **sceptics** and **transformationalists**.

Hyperglobalisers

Hyperglobalisers, whose ideas emerge from the liberal view, regard globalisation in a positive light and argue it will inevitably create a 'borderless world' (Ohmae) due to technological progress. Globalisation is therefore creating a new era in history where both the importance and authority of the nation-state is decreasing due the economic logic of a global market. The state's autonomy is in decline, as its ability to manage strategic economic activities decreases, due to the rise of global finance and TNCs as well as the rise of regionalisation and global governance.

Hyperglobalisers see three key benefits of globalisation:

1 The creation of a single, global market will bring wealth to all.

2 Growing economic interdependence makes the cost of war too great, creating peace.

3 The widening and deepening of interconnectedness will increase international understanding, spread the ideas of liberal democracy and a human rights culture which in the end may create a truly global civilisation.

Sceptics

Sceptics, who include realists, argue that the impact of globalisation has been over exaggerated. They point to 1870–1914 as the high point of globalisation. Sceptics have three main ideas about globalisation:

1 A large majority of economic activity takes place within the state so national economic policies are still highly relevant, with TNCs still primarily tied to their home nation-state. The majority of the globe's population, especially in the South, are becoming increasingly marginalised, not linked into the global economy. Although global trade has been increasing, Africa's share of world trade has been declining since the 1980s to less than 3 per cent.

2 The trend towards regionalisation and global governance remains weak as sovereignty still resides within states. Regional and international institutions are not a sign of state weakness, but are bodies through which states strive to grow their power and objectives.

3 The idea that globalisation is inevitable and there is no alternative is an ideology that has been constructed to allow the West, and the USA in particular, to achieve their goals.

Transformationalists

Transformationalists offer a middle way between hyperglobalisers and sceptics. They argue that globalisation is neither weakening the state nor strengthening it. Instead, the nature of the state has been changed and a new architecture of global politics is emerging. The state has been transformed in many different ways in different countries:

- Into a national security state to protect against global terrorism; a competition state that boosts education, skills and training to get ahead in a globalised economy; or a modernising state like China that mixes the free market and high levels of state control.

- In some instances, it has become a failed state, like Libya (see page 238), which cannot maintain internal sovereignty.

Globalisation has transformed the scale of human social organisation to extend cultural, political and economic activities across the world. Developments in one location can shape the life chances of communities in distant regions. It is uneven in its impact and it divides as much as it integrates. Globalisation may mean a shrinking world for some, but for others it creates a sense of distance as the power that shapes local communities becomes increasingly remote.

Now try this

1 How have transformationalists disagreed with hyperglobalisers and sceptics?
2 Outline three key disagreements between hyperglobalisers and sceptics.

The impact of globalisation

You need to know about the impact of globalisation and its implications for the nation-state and national sovereignty from the perspective of the key comparative theories of global politics.

Liberals

Liberals hold a positive view of globalisation. In economic terms, globalisation is the victory of the market over other forms of economic organisation.

> The emerging single global market will drive production and competition, producing increased wealth, which will benefit all.

> Increasing economic wealth and freedom will increase the desire for political freedom, leading to the spread of liberal democracy and human rights.

> The nation-state will decrease in importance as interdependence grows, leading to the emergence of international laws and international institutions, which will create a new global politics of peace and cooperation, sometimes described as the 'cobweb model'.

Realists

Realists remain sceptical about globalisation. They see growing interdependence, but argue that the state remains the key building block of global politics. For example, 9/11 may have increased the power of the state in relation to national security, while the global financial crash has illustrated the importance of the state in its provision of bailout packages. China also illustrates the continuing power of the state. It has undergone rapid growth both through opening up to the global market and maintaining strong political control.

In looking at the emergence of international institutions, realists argue that these were designed by states for states. In particular, these institutions were designed by powerful states, such as the USA, for themselves. Where globalisation is uneven, the domination of one state by another may increase, leading to conflict.

Has globalisation undermined state sovereignty?

Yes	No
State borders are increasingly porous to people, capital and culture so sovereignty has declined in significance.	The 'borderless world' is nonsense. Look at the huge number of migrants, asylum seekers and refugees who are stuck in holding camps and the creation of the Great Firewall of China to control the flow of information into the state.
There has been a rise in non-state actors, such as TNCs, NGOs and terror organisations, which operate outside the constraints of sovereignty and lessen states' power.	States remain the key actors on the world stage and nearly all states still have internal sovereignty, apart from failed states. The state has re-emerged in relation to 9/11 and the global financial crisis.
The trend towards regional and global governance to tackle global issues such as environmental degradation, poverty and humanitarian crises has undermined sovereignty.	Regional and global bodies are formed for states by states. By working together, states are not undermining sovereignty but pooling it with other states to increase their collective power. Trump and the idea of 'America First' in relation to **NATO**, NAFTA and the Paris Agreement threatens to weaken global governance.
The growing role of international law around human rights and a growing global-rights culture has seen the rise of bodies such as the ICC and of humanitarian intervention, which erodes state sovereignty.	While this move may be taking place in the West, China remains firmly wedded to its Five Principles of Peaceful Co-Existence, which includes mutual respect for territorial integrity and sovereignty. With China's rise in power, if it continues to assert sovereignty as a key principle, it will be a hammer blow to interventionists.

Now try this

1 Outline the realist view of globalisation.
2 Does globalisation increase the chance for peace and cooperation?

Globalisation and contemporary issues

Poverty, conflict, human rights and the environment are increasingly shared issues. You need to know the extent to which globalisation addresses and resolves these issues.

Economic globalisation and poverty, conflict, human rights and the environment

👍 The world economy is a globalising economy moving towards a single, global economy.

👍 Globally, economies are increasingly integrated into the market and poverty is falling.

👍 Globalisation has driven development and growth throughout most of the world, and drives cultural and political globalisation across the globe.

👍 States support the globally accepted rules of trade, and the bodies of global governance like the IMF, representing their commitment to economic globalisation.

👍 TNCs bring with them jobs, workforce training and upskilling and access to modern technologies and so are welcomed by states.

👎 Economic globalisation is uneven both between states and within states, creating inequality. Areas like sub-Saharan Africa are left behind, as are marginalised groups within states.

👎 Globalisation benefits developed states and TNCs but not the developing states, mostly located in the global South (see page 250 on global governance and poverty).

👎 Increasing and deepening global crises, with very negative impacts for the poor.

👎 The consequence of increasing inequalities is the higher chance of conflict both within and between nation-states.

Cultural globalisation and poverty, conflict, human rights and the environment

👍 Technology and TNCs, especially media corporations, have created a more uniform global culture, built around liberal values, global goods and global flow of news and information.

👍 There is a move towards a single global community where people feel a connection and obligation to each other, creating shared norms and views in areas like human rights, which are weakening state sovereignty and increasing cooperation and peace.

👎 A backlash to cultural globalisation has emerged in recent years, which has been seen as a form of cultural imperialism or Americanisation.

👎 There has been a rise in anti-globalisation, anti-capitalist and green movements, which see globalisation as responsible for poverty, inequality and environmental degradation.

👎 Ethnic nationalism (e.g. Chechyna) and cultural nationalism (e.g. Catalonia, Spain) has grown, and nationalism and the nation-state (e.g. Trump's 'America First' doctrine) has strengthened.

👎 There has been a rise in religious fundamentalism to combat cultural flattening by globalisation.

👎 This backlash is seen to threaten the existing global order, leading to an increased chance of conflict and weakens the ability of international institutions to tackle global issues such as poverty, human rights violations and environmental degradation.

Political globalisation and poverty, conflict, human rights and the environment

👍 Growing political globalisation has created a rule- and norm-based international system that limits sovereignty and restricts the behaviour of states, and is supported by most states.

👍 It comprises international institutions and international law, which breed cooperation, peace and harmony on the global stage.

👍 The spread of economic and political liberalism lessens the chance of conflict and human rights abuses.

👎 Without an authoritative, global decision-making body with enforcement powers, political globalisation struggles to deal with poverty and inequality, environmental degradation and human-rights abuses.

👎 Political globalisation is stalled by national sovereignty, which is the cornerstone of international order.

👎 9/11 and the global crises have decreased the importance of political globalisation and increased the importance of states.

Now try this

How can economic globalisation be seen as uneven?

The United Nations (UN)

Global governance is a system of global and regional institutions that have developed to tackle collective problems and to realise common aims. At the centre is the **United Nations (UN)**, along with other bodies such as the World Bank, IMF and WTO (see pages 246–248), and NGOs and TNCs (see page 233).

Global governance

Global governance is the collective effort by sovereign states, international organisations and non-state actors to tackle common challenges, such as poverty, and achieve common aims, such as peace. The question is whether real cooperation is possible under global governance in a global system that is anarchic (see page 285 for a discussion on realism in global politics) as it is composed of sovereign states.

The main aim of the UN is to maintain international peace and security.

Origins and development of the UN

The UN was established by 51 countries in October 1945 in the aftermath of the Second World War and now has expanded to 193 countries. Each member state that joins the UN signs up to its **1945 Charter**, which outlines its key purposes and principles:

Purposes (Article 1)	Principles (Article 2)
There are four purposes: to maintain international peace and security to develop friendly relations among nations to achieve international cooperation in solving international problems of an economic, social, cultural or humanitarian character, and encouraging respect for human rights and fundamental freedoms for all to be a centre for harmonising the actions of nations in the attainment of these common ends.	There are seven key principles, two of which are crucially important: The Organisation is based on the principle of the sovereign equality of all its Members. Nothing contained in the present Charter shall authorise the UN to intervene in matters which are essentially within the domestic jurisdiction of any state.

During the Cold War, the functioning of the UN was hampered by the ability of the USA or the USSR to use the veto on the **Security Council** (read about this body on page 243) whenever their interests were threatened. The UN's role was more restricted and focused on classical peacekeeping, involving placing a UN force between states after a ceasefire. Since the end of the Cold War, the role of the UN has changed in order to tackle new threats to global security, such as:

- civil war and the collapse of order within states; UN missions involve implementing complex peace agreements, stabilising security, reorganising the police and military and building democratic institutions within states, for example, Sierra Leone, 1999–2005

- political, economic and social conditions within states including poverty, inequality, humanitarian emergencies and violations of human rights, for example, Yemen, South Sudan, Somalia and northeast Nigeria

- non-state-based threats such as the rise of terrorism and the proliferation of arms and weapons of mass destruction, for example, the UN Office of Counter-Terrorism (OCT) works at preventing terrorists from acquiring weapons

- contemporary global issues such as environmental degradation and nuclear proliferation, for example, in Sudan and the Asia-Pacific region.

Now try this

How is state sovereignty protected in the UN Charter?

The UN Security Council (UNSC)

The UN **Security Council** (UNSC) is the UN's most powerful body, with primary responsibility for the maintenance of international peace and security.

UNSC membership and role

The Council is made up of 15 members:

When there is a threat to peace, the Council considers ways to settle the dispute peacefully. It can resort to economic sanctions and, if needed, authorise the use of force, under **Chapter VII** of the Charter. Each member has one vote. Resolutions must be passed by a majority of nine, and must include the P-5 members. Decisions passed by the Council are binding on all UN member states.

1 **The permanent members (P-5):** France, Russia, China, the USA and the UK. As all successful votes must include all P-5 countries, they effectively have a veto.

2 **Ten non-permanent members:** elected for a two-year term by the General Assembly.

Significance of the UNSC

Strengths	Weaknesses
In line with realist thinking, the P-5 recognises the importance of major powers to international politics. By granting the P-5 the veto, it ensures the participation of the major powers that are essential to make the UN work.	The principle of equality among states is violated by concentrating power in the UNSC, especially the P-5, which no longer represent the balance of power or a regional balance. Should the UK and France be replaced, perhaps with Brazil, an emerging economic power, to represent South America, or Nigeria to represent Africa?
Member states voluntarily provide funding and peacekeepers to enforce resolutions.	Where funding, troops and political will are lacking, this has been a key element of the failures of UN missions. For example, the failure to prevent the 1994 Rwanda genocide.
The absence of global war since 1945 can be seen as the UNSC's success in maintaining peace.	This may be more down to the balance of power established in the **bipolarity** (see page 267) of the Cold War world than the UN.
Establishes a system of collective security – the security of each state is the concern of all states, and all agree to join in a collective response to acts of aggression. For example, the UN action in the 1991 Gulf War.	Success has been very limited as the UNSC can do no more than its member states allow. The P-5 use the veto for their own ends rather than to build collective security. The UN Charter provides for the creation of a UN standing army; however, rivalries between the P-5 have made this impossible.
Peaceful resolution of international conflict through concerted UNSC action. For example, interventions in Sierra Leone (1999–2005) and in Burundi (1996 onwards).	The failures of the UN. For example, in Yugoslavia (particularly the massacre at Srebrenica where UN peacekeepers were based), Rwanda and Syria. The decision by the USA to invade Iraq, in the face of opposition from other leading members of the UNSC.

The veto

The veto powers of the P-5 have made it very hard for the UNSC to take action to deal with threats of aggression or threats to peace, as it becomes the mechanism through which the rivalries of the major powers are played out. During the Cold War (1947–1991), for example, the rivalry between the USA and the USSR saw 193 vetoes used, but only 12 were used between 1990 and 2003. In the Syrian conflict (2011–), the USA, the UK and France are generally aligned in support of the rebels, while Russia and China are aligned with Assad and the government. This has made UNSC action almost impossible in terms of condemning the violence against civilians in Syria, economic sanctions or military intervention. In future, a solution might be to ensure only a double veto (a veto by two of the P-5) can block a resolution. However, this would not have changed anything in the case of Syria, as Russia and China voted in concert.

Now try this

1 Outline three key weaknesses of the UN Security Council.

2 Why is the P-5 veto so problematic?

UN General Assembly, ECOSOC and ICJ

The **General Assembly** is where all 193 members of the UN are represented. The **Economic and Social Council (ECOSOC)** operates under the authority of the General Assembly, while the International Court of Justice (ICJ) is the principal judicial body of the UN.

The role of the UN General Assembly

In contrast to the concentration of power in the UNSC, the General Assembly is made up of all UN members and each country has a vote when they meet annually for the General Assembly session. In essence, the Assembly acts as a 'parliament of nations' and can make decisions, with a two-thirds majority, on the budget, admittance of new members and matters of peace and security. Decisions of the Assembly are recommendations only and are not binding.

The significance of the UN General Assembly

Strengths	Weaknesses
'One country, one vote' enshrines the principle of equality of all states and gives the Assembly legitimacy.	'One state, one vote' does not recognise the differing population size or powers and capabilities of states.
The Assembly is a genuinely global institution, which gives its recommendations moral authority and constrains the behaviour of states.	Its decisions are only recommendations and not binding, so the Assembly can be seen to lack power.
All member states can address concerns ranging from poverty and inequality to peace and security. This allows relations between states to grow, encourages international cooperation and develops a rule-governed international system.	The Assembly has been subject to bloc voting and criticisms of political posturing by those blocs. For example, the Assembly has been frequently criticised by the USA and Israel for disproportionally focusing on allegations of abuses by Israel.

The role of ECOSOC

ECOSOC's aim is to coordinate the economic, social and environmental work of the UN. It maintains a wide link to society with registered links to over 3,200 NGOs (in 2017). Bodies under ECOSOC include the World Bank, the IMF and the WTO, as well as specialised agencies, such as the World Health Organization (WHO), which coordinates work on public health across the globe, and programmes and funds, which respond directly to changing circumstances. This includes the UN Development Programme, which aims to promote global development, with a specific emphasis on the least developed countries.

The significance of ECOSOC

Strengths
It is an open forum for discussion at an international level where relations between states can develop and rules can be established.
It has confidence from global civil society (see page 252) and developing countries due to its development agenda.

Weaknesses
It lacks the ability to coordinate the various parts of a complex UN system.
It lacks the power to enforce decisions – that power really lies with the IMF and the World Bank in economic governance.

The role and significance of the ICJ

As the principal judicial body of the UN, the ICJ deals with legal disputes between states submitted to it by them and requests for advisory opinions on legal questions referred to it by UN bodies (see page 255 for a more in-depth look at the ICJ).

Now try this

How does the General Assembly differ from the UN Security Council?

North Atlantic Treaty Organization (NATO)

The North Atlantic Treaty Organization (NATO) is an alliance of countries from Europe and North America. Its main purpose is to guarantee the freedom and security of its members through political and military means.

The origin and role of NATO

NATO was formed in 1949, following the signing of the Washington Treaty by the 12 founding member states. The Treaty, derived from Article 51 of the UN Charter, gives states the right to individual or **collective defence**. Article 5 of the Treaty states: 'an armed attack against one or more of them in Europe or North America shall be considered an attack against them all'. This Article has only been triggered once, in response to the 9/11 attacks. Decisions are taken by consensus, meaning consultations take place until a decision that is acceptable to all is reached.

The Alliance now numbers 29 states, with Montenegro becoming a full member in 2017.

NATO's changing role

When NATO was established, its key role was to protect against aggression by the USSR and its military alliance, the Warsaw Pact. In practice, this meant that the USA took on the role as guarantor of the peace and security of Western Europe. After the end of the Cold War (1991), NATO had to reinvent itself, which it has done in three ways:

 1 Peacekeeping and humanitarian intervention. For example, NATO carried out 77 days of air strikes to remove Milosevic's Serbian troops from Kosovo in 1999.

 2 Expansion beyond Europe. For example, NATO commanded the UN mandated International Security Force in 2003–2014, and from 2015 has led the Resolute Support Mission to train, advise and assist Afghan security forces and structures.

 3 Eastward expansion. For example, ten countries which were part of the USSR or Warsaw Pact have joined NATO since 1999.

Significance

Strengths	Weaknesses
NATO is the world's most powerful military alliance, whose spending makes up over 70 per cent of global military spending. The USA remains the linchpin of NATO, with a huge defence spending budget of $569bn in 2015 compared to Russia's $53.2bn. In 2014, all non-US allies agreed to increase their defence spending to 2 per cent of GDP by 2024; in 2017, this figure stood at an average of 1.46 per cent.	NATO's increased size now makes decision-making very difficult (by consensus); it may have become a tool of some member states to pursue their own aims.
	Russia sees the eastward expansion as an attempt by the USA to encircle Russia. NATO strategy may have triggered Russia's annexation of Crimea in 2014 to prevent Ukraine joining NATO.
	NATO suffered from controversial and problematic missions in Afghanistan and Libya in 2011.
NATO achieved its goal of protecting Western states during the Cold War and can point to successes in Bosnia-Herzegovina from 1995–1996 and Kosovo in 1999 since the Cold War ended.	NATO is overly reliant on the USA (which provides 67 per cent of the defence spending of the Alliance). This has led to US criticism that NATO allies are not pulling their weight.
	In 2017, Trump suggested those who do not pay up cannot expect protection, undermining collective security.

Now try this

How has NATO reinvented itself since the end of the Cold War?

The IMF and the World Bank

The **International Monetary Fund (IMF)** and **World Bank** were conceived in 1944 with the aim of financing the rebuilding of Europe after the Second World War and saving the world from economic depressions, such as the Great Depression of the 1930s.

Roles and evolution

The **World Bank** (its proper name is the International Bank for Reconstruction and Development) was initially focused on post-war reconstruction but evolved in the 1960s–1970s to focus on development and tackling poverty.

The **IMF's** role was to maintain global economic stability, and was based on the economic experience of the 1930s that markets often do not work well. The IMF would provide loans to help states restart their economies and prevent mass unemployment.

In the 1980s, the work of the **World Bank** and the **IMF** became increasingly entangled, as both institutions were dominated by the **Washington Consensus** and focused on providing **Structural Adjustment Programs (SAPs)** – essentially loans that were made with conditions.

In the 1980s, the **IMF** evolved to focus on the transition of former Soviet bloc countries in Europe to market economies, as well as preventing global economic instability.

The Washington Consensus and SAPs

The Washington Consensus refers to the 'conditionality' policies of the IMF and the World Bank that are attached to SAPs. The policies involve austerity measures to reduce inflation, government spending and government involvement in the economy. They also include measures for privatisation, deregulation and the opening up of domestic markets, including financial markets, to foreign competition (trade liberalisation) as well as export-led growth. Transitioning and developing states were forced to accept austerity and trade liberalisation in return for loans. This reflects the fact that the World Bank and IMF had evolved from seeing markets as the problem to be tackled by state intervention, to government being the problem and free markets the solution. The Consensus is driven by bias in the decision-making process and structures of both bodies, which favour the interests of the USA, the West and TNCs.

Two key figures in the IMF. Both have been reappointed until 2021.

Managing director: Christine Lagarde

Lagarde, who is French, worked for the global law firm Baker McKenzie before joining the French government and becoming the first woman to hold the post of finance and economy minister in a G7 country. She became managing director in 2011.

First deputy: David Lipton

Lipton, an American, has worked for a global hedge fund Moore Capital Management and a global bank, Citi, before working in the Clinton Administration in the Treasury Department. He became first deputy in 2011.

Now try this

What are the main policy conditions attached to SAPs?

IMF and World Bank: significance and reform

The IMF and the World Bank have both strengths and weaknesses, but there is pressure for reform. See page 246 for more on the IMF and the World Bank.

Significance

Strengths	Weaknesses
The IMF and the World Bank were successful in maintaining the stability of the monetary system from 1945 to the 1970s, with economic growth rates and world trade both increasing, and post-war Western Europe reconstructed.	Both are dominated by the USA and Europe as vote share is calculated based on the size of a state's economy. For example, the USA has a 16.8 per cent vote share in the IMF, which is effectively a veto as decisions need 85 per cent support. Their headquarters are in Washington, USA. The IMF managing director is always a European, its deputy an American; the World Bank president is traditionally a US citizen.
They have 189 member states and have become the principal source of funds for developing countries. No country is forced to accept the loans – they are taken on the basis that the loans and conditions will promote growth.	The 'conditionality' of SAPs (see page 246) did more harm than good in most countries (for example, Tanzania). Loans did not improve financial crises but worsened them, (as in Indonesia and Thailand in 1997), and did not prevent financial contagion (as the Asian financial crisis spread to Russia in 1998).
From the 1980s, the IMF and the World Bank supplied loans with 'conditionality', to deliver long-term economic success and tackle poverty. Examples of success include Jordan, South Korea and Chile.	Conditionality was motivated by the powerful elites in Northern countries to further their own objectives of opening up markets. The implementation of SAPs in economies saw painfully high and persistent unemployment, growing levels of inequality and increased poverty.
The IMF is the 'lender of last resort', providing competitive loans to countries in trouble and preventing the spread of economic crises. For example, the Asian financial crisis of 1997.	Loans were knowingly made to dictatorships with poor human rights records and took little account of the environmental issues created by the Washington Consensus approach.
Since the global crash of 2007–2009, the IMF has taken on the role of global surveillance, identifying risks to stability and proposing solutions while the capital of the World Bank has been significantly expanded.	Global stability in the last 25 years has decreased with an increasing number of crises. SAPs damage state sovereignty – states have little choice but to accept these loans with the conditions limiting the nation-state's ability to make its own economic policy.

Pressure for reform and criticism

SAPs have a very weak record for tackling poverty and inequality. Countries that have prospered have refused loans (for example, Malaysia during the Asian crisis), or have used state intervention rather than neoliberalism (for example, China). The failures of the IMF and the World Bank were magnified by the global crash of 2007–2009. This has led to pressure for reform from the South and global civil society (see page 252).

The IMF and the World Bank have:

- replaced SAPs with **Poverty Reduction Strategy Papers (PRSPs)**, which are more flexible, seek to promote local ownership and control, are better adapted to particular needs and circumstances and focus more on poverty reduction
- made loans that are conditional on sustainable development (see page 263 for competing views on what this means), taking into account environmental concerns, as well as good governance and anti-corruption measures
- adapted their governance so that the voice of the developing world is better represented.

But are these reforms fundamental enough? Does global governance still reflect the power of the dominant interests – the USA, TNCs and global financial capital?

Now try this

How might the organisational structure of the World Bank and the IMF be said to favour the West and the USA in particular?

The World Trade Organization (WTO)

The World Trade Organization (WTO) was formed in 1995 to replace the General Agreement on Tariffs and Trade (GATT). The WTO aims to promote a multilateral trading system, built around the principle of free trade.

Role

All major decisions are taken by the membership (164 states in 2016) as a whole and generally made by consensus.

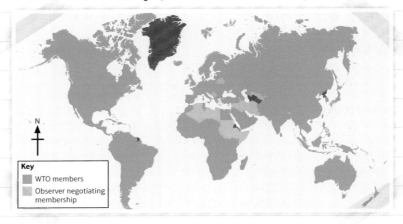

Key
- WTO members
- Observer negotiating membership

Significance

Strengths	Weaknesses
It has promoted an open trading system based on multilaterally agreed rules that has promoted world trade and economic growth. Protectionist tariffs have fallen steeply and now average less than 5 per cent in industrialised countries. Partly as a result of this, in the 25 years after the Second World War, world economic growth averaged 5 per cent per year and world trade grew by 8 per cent.	Its principle of free trade has been responsible for widening global inequality, as industrialised countries gain access to the markets of developing states without facing the prospect of growing foreign competition affecting them. Trade becomes about global needs and not meeting local needs, and places profit over the protection of the environment, local communities and workers' rights.
Unlike the IMF and the World Bank, the WTO is democratic with decisions made by consensus among all member states, its rules are negotiated by member states and enforcement is carried out in agreement by all members. This ensures the protection of developing countries, which make up around two-thirds of the membership.	The WTO lacks legitimacy as it favours the interests of the rich, industrially advanced states over developing states. Protectionist policies on agriculture in the North are often tolerated but are strongly opposed when adopted by developing countries. Both the USA's approach and the EU's Common Agricultural Policy (CAP) use quotas and tariffs to block imports of foreign foodstuffs while subsidising exports to undermine the livelihood of farmers in competitor countries.
Liberal trade policies sharpen competition, inspire innovation and breed success across the globe. English economist David Ricardo's principle of '**comparative advantage**' suggests that states prosper first by using their assets (human, industrial, financial and natural) to focus on what they can produce best, and then by trading these goods for goods that other countries produce best.	Negotiations are incredibly slow due to major disagreements between industrialised countries, such as the USA and the EU states, and emerging and developing states, such as China, India, Brazil and South Africa. In particular, there is conflict over agricultural protectionism. For example, this can be seen in the Doha round of negotiations, which started in 2001 but have stalled due to these issues and the need for consensus decision-making.

Now try this

1 How does comparative advantage work?
2 What are the strengths and weaknesses of consensus decision-making?

The G7(8) and G20

You need to know about the G7(8) and G20 and their ability to monitor and address developments in the world economy.

The origin and role of the G7/G8

The G7 was formed in the 1970s from the seven leading industrial states of the time (the USA, the UK, France, Germany, Italy, Canada and Japan). Russia was added in 1998 to create the G8, although it was later expelled in 2014 for its annexation of the Crimea. The main aim of the group is to consider economic policy issues and coordinate the system of global governance.

Significance of the G7(8)

Strengths	Weaknesses
It is a forum where the leaders and finance ministers of seven of the richest nations can discuss economic issues in an informal setting and devise new policy initiatives. For example, the G8 meeting at Gleneagles in 2005 saw a $50bn aid boost and debt cancellation deal agreed for the poorest countries.	Membership of the G8 is historically rooted so it does not reflect the changing nature of power in the global economy. There is no place at the table for China, India or Brazil so the G20 has come to be seen as a more effective tool for coordinating global governance.
	The group has been divided and unable to deal with emerging global issues such as climate change and growing inequality. The G8 has become the target for the anti-globalisation movement as seen in the protests in Genoa in 2001, which was marred by violence and led to the prosecution of 15 officials for mistreating protestors.

The origin and role of the G20

The G20, originally established in 1999, is a forum that brings together 19 of the world's leading industrialised and emerging economies and the EU. It was initially a meeting of finance ministers and central bank governors of member states. In 2008, the first meeting of heads of state or government took place in Washington to respond to the collapse of Lehman Brothers and the global financial crash. Its key role is to provide a forum for discussion around the global economy and economic governance, with much of the key business taking place in informal meetings.

Significance of the G20

Strengths	Weaknesses
It has great legitimacy as it reflects the nature of the current global economic order far better than the G7(8), the IMF and the World Bank.	While more representative, the G20 gives no voice to the poorer states and its ideology remains that of the liberal, orthodox theory of development which is seen by many to have failed. This has led to the G20 becoming a target for the anti-globalisation movement.
It includes nearly all the leading economies (accounting for 85 per cent of global GDP), has a good regional balance that represents the interests of industrialised and emerging economies and global population representation (two-thirds of world population).	
Its key success was its response to the global crash. Measures to inject £748bn into the global economy were agreed, as was a clean-up of financial markets and reforms of the World Bank and the IMF, including a stronger voice for the developing world, greater resources and a stronger role in supervising the global financial system.	Dealing with other global issues, such as debt, inequality and climate change, is likely to give rise to division, limiting its ability to act.

Now try this

How can the G20 be seen as more legitimate and effective than the G7(8)?

Global governance and poverty

You need to know about conflicting arguments in the poverty debate with a focus on the cause of poverty.

North–South divide

The North–South divide is a socio-economic and political divide between a relatively affluent North, where most of the world's economic activity takes place, and the increasingly marginalised South, where poverty and disadvantage exists.

The term is contested, as there is variation within both the North and the South. The South has seen poverty become more concentrated in sub-Saharan Africa, but also the emergence of China, Brazil, India and South Africa; all are now part of the G20. Globalisation has also created variations and inequalities within states, with women, ethnic minorities and the disabled being particularly disadvantaged, suggesting the term is increasingly meaningless.

It raises questions: has the marginalisation and poverty of the South been driven by globalisation or is it the result of too little globalisation? Dependency theory and world-systems theory both view underdevelopment in the South as a result of deliberate economic exploitation by the North.

Dependency theory

Dependency theory argues that the North and South are in a structural relationship with each other and it is a relationship of dependency that creates poverty.

> The North, during colonialism, created economies in the South based on the export of primary goods, like raw materials and food.

> Following decolonisation, market forces meant the South suffered from declining terms of trade, as the price of primary goods rises more slowly than the price of manufactured goods produced in the core.

> This leads to the South being economically drained by the North.

The process is neo-colonialism as it involves economic rather than political domination by the North, and is promoted by the SAPs of the IMF and the World Bank (read about these institutions on page 246). The solution was to use the state to nationalise or subsidise local industries and to implement protectionist trade policies to cut connections to the global market in order to drive development (import substitution industrialisation).

World-systems theory

World-systems theory, developed by the American sociologist Immanuel Wallerstein, rejects the idea of the North and South. Instead, it is a neo-Marxist analysis that sees the entire world as one single capitalist economy, based on the division of labour between the core, the semi-periphery and the periphery. Core regions benefit from capital and technology, exploiting the periphery for raw materials and cheap labour, while the semi-periphery acts as an intermediate as it is part core, part periphery. Poverty is an inevitable product of the world system and the system needs replacing by a more equitable one.

Core
Democratic government, welfare services, high wages, advanced technology, import primary products, export manufactured goods

Semi-periphery
Authoritarian government, limited welfare services, low wages, export and import primary products, export certain manufactured goods

Periphery
No democratic government, limited or no welfare services, below-subsistence wages, export primary products, import manufactured goods

cheap labour, raw materials

high profit goods

The three zones are in an exploitative relationship where wealth is drained from the periphery to the core.

Now try this

1 In what ways has the concept of the North–South divide been challenged?
2 What is import substitution industrialisation?

Poverty and development

You need to know about the extent of global poverty, the ways it can be measured and the different approaches to development.

Measuring poverty

Poverty remains a highly contested term. The orthodox view is that poverty should be measured in terms of absolute poverty, that is, not having the money to buy food and satisfy basic material needs. The best way to tackle poverty is development, which is measured by growth in GDP. This raises two issues:

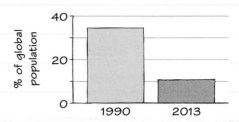

The World Bank measure of poverty is the number of people living on $1.90 or less per day.

- The GDP of a state can be increasing, but inequality within the state may also be increasing, creating relative poverty; people are considered poor if their income is substantially lower than a typical person in their country. This suggests that poverty and inequality are linked and both need to be tackled.

- This approach only measures income, not whether people's basic needs are being met. A wider measure is needed that takes into account human development: access to education and healthcare, gender equality, life expectancy, self-reliance (the ability to provide for oneself and one's family), as well as personal and food security. The UN Development Programme (UNDP) has created a new measure for poverty, the **Human Development Index (HDI)**, which is more focused on the capability to fulfil your own material and non-material needs rather than pure economic growth.

Orthodox development theory

Principles: the orthodox theory of development is rooted in liberalism. Unlimited growth is possible under the free market. Developing economies will reach a 'take off' and develop along the lines of Western countries, with wealth benefitting everyone by trickling down through society. Underdeveloped countries will become developed.

Measurement: economic growth, measured by GDP.

Process: top-down – reliance on expertise, technology and capital from outside the state – from Western states, the IMF, the World Bank and TNCs. This process has two different variants:

1 Classical theory, based on the ideas of Adam Smith and David Ricardo, believes free trade without government intervention and competitive markets will drive growth.

2 Neoclassical theory sees the failure of underdeveloped states to grow as a result of too much government intervention and regulation of the economy. Free markets, open economies and privatisation will open the state to international trade and trigger growth. This theory underpinned the conditionality of SAPs (read about how these are used on page 246).

Alternative development theories

Principles: development means becoming self-reliant, should be sustainable, locally controlled, engage with marginalised groups (such as indigenous groups) with local, democratic control. Its aim is human well-being. The increasing gap between rich and poor can be explained by structural imbalances in the world economy.

Measurement: the ability to fulfil both material and non-material needs through your own effort.

Process: bottom-up – local control, participatory, reliance on local knowledge and technology, inclusive and environmentally sound. It will often involve a far higher level of state intervention than is acceptable under the liberal model to end structural inequalities in the world economy. These ideas tend to reflect the views of the global South and have been used to criticise SAPs.

Now try this

How do the orthodox and alternative theories differ in their understanding of poverty?

Global governance and contemporary issues

You need to know about the effectiveness of global governance, as well as global civil society and non-state actors in tackling contemporary global issues.

Has global economic governance been effective?

👍 Economic governance focuses on the stability of the global economy. Global economic bodies have near universal membership and continue to thrive.

👍 Economic governance has implemented orthodox development theory, which underpinned the growth of Western economies and the Asian Tigers like South Korea. As a result, the number of people living in absolute poverty continues to fall, despite the global crash of 2007–2009.

👍 The IMF and the World Bank have been reformed to take emerging global issues more seriously with the change from SAPs to PRSPs and the emphasis on sustainable development.

👍 Economic governance has tackled global crises such as the 1970s recession and the 2007–2009 global economic crash. Global recovery after 2009 has been stronger than after the Wall Street Crash of 1929, with higher levels of international cooperation and opposition to moves to state protectionist policies (increasing taxes on imports).

👎 Economic governance protects the interests of the USA, the West and TNCs. It is based on the Washington Consensus, which benefits the North over the South by increasing structural dependency.

👎 Orthodox development theory has created wider issues such as climate change and has been ineffective at dealing with emerging global issues like poverty. For example, poverty rates have fallen in East Asia but remain high in sub-Saharan Africa.

👎 The effectiveness of global governance has been challenged by the increasing number and depth of economic crises and its responsibility for the banking and financial regulations at the heart of the 2007–2009 crash. For example, at the G20 meeting in 2010, the deal to cut interest rates and introduce a fiscal stimulus to pump money into the economy to drive growth collapsed with the threat of the debt crisis in Europe, causing some states to cut spending. The IMF struggled to offer ideas to promote growth and tackle the debt crisis in countries like Greece.

Global civil society and non-state actors

Global civil society has developed in parallel with international organisations such as the UN. It is seen as a bottom up, democratising force. Global civil society refers to the emergence of two main types of group and association that operate across the globe and are independent of states:

1 **Transnational movements**: these operate to challenge the institutions of global governance and globalisation. They cover issues such as human rights, women's rights, environmentalism, and the anti-globalisation and anti-capitalist movements.

2 **NGOs**: work within the institutions of global governance to influence the making and implementing of policy. There are over 3,380 NGOs, such as Médecins Sans Frontières (MSF, or Doctors Without Borders), registered to work with the UN through its various bodies.

Global civil society acts as a democratic counterbalance to the Washington Consensus by making sure the voices of the marginalised are heard. It has placed the alleviation of poverty on the agenda and forced the IMF and the World Bank to reform its approach. NGOs have also become the key channel for international aid to tackle humanitarian crises like famine and to help people lift themselves out of poverty, delivering healthcare and education programmes to the poorest on the planet. However, much of this funding comes from TNCs, states and international organisations, meaning NGOs are forced to work within the Washington Consensus, rather than challenge it. Aid has done little to boost economic growth or alleviate poverty as it does not tackle the structural imbalances in the global economy.

For example, sub-Saharan Africa receives $134bn every year in loans, foreign investment and aid, yet remains incredibly poor.

Now try this

What role does global civil society play in tackling contemporary global issues?

International law and human rights

International law is seen as binding on states and non-state actors in their interrelations. It establishes a framework for the practice of stable and organised international relations and is a key component in avoiding an anarchical system and protecting **human rights**.

Origins and development of international law

International law has its roots in the 1648 Treaty of Westphalia (read more about the implications of this Treaty on page 232), which defined statehood, sovereignty and the rules and limits for state action. Since the French Revolution (1789), international law has been informed by the values of political liberalism and is seen as the 'mutual will of nations'. It facilitates coordination and cooperation between states in order to escape the insecurity and constant threat of war that is a key part of **international anarchy**.

In the 20th and 21st centuries, international law has developed to include social justice, human rights and human development, with the **Universal Declaration of Human Rights (UDHR)** of 1948 as a key milestone. The idea of international law implies that states will face restrictions and this will impact on their sovereignty.

Sources of authority

International law has four key sources of authority, as established in Article 38 of the Statute of the International Court of Justice (ICJ). In order of importance, they are:

1 International conventions. For example, the 1968 Nuclear Non-Proliferation Treaty.

2 International custom – long-established practices of states. For example, the UDHR (see below).

3 The general principles of law – actions that are illegal within states are illegal in international law.

4 Judicial decisions and the teachings of the most highly qualified publicists of various nations.

Universal Declaration of Human Rights

The UDHR (1948) was the first time that the global community came together to define a comprehensive code of rights. The UDHR is not binding as it is not a Treaty, but is an example of customary international law. It means that states could no longer encroach upon human rights without the action being potentially taken up by the UN. The UDHR raises two issues:

1 Article 1 states all 'are born free and equal in dignity and rights'. This is seen as conflicting with state sovereignty as it violates the domestic jurisdiction of states.

2 The UDHR contains only civil and political rights as fundamental rights, as it is a liberal conception of rights. Economic and social rights, which are collective rights, are not included.

In 1966, civil and political rights became international law through the International Covenant on Civil and Political Rights, while economic and social rights were incorporated through the International Covenant on Economic, Social and Cultural Rights. The UDHR and both Covenants are collectively known as the International Bill of Human Rights. The inclusion of economic and social rights, such as the right to 'an adequate standard of living' and the right of peoples to 'self-determination', is a further challenge to state sovereignty.

Human rights

Human rights are commonly understood as fundamental rights to which a person is entitled simply because he/she is a human being, sometimes referred to as natural rights, as defined by John Locke (see page 53 for a discussion of Locke's ideas). This concept is controversial for a number of reasons:

- The infringement of human rights has resulted in **humanitarian intervention**, which is a violation of the principle of national sovereignty.

- There is disagreement about whether human rights are **universal human rights** and whether they should take into account cultural differences between societies and peoples. Should they take into account the differing values and legal systems of the Asian and Muslim world?

- Universal human rights can be seen as a form of neo-colonialism that seeks to replace the cultures of other societies with Western, liberal values.

Now try this

1 Describe the two most important sources of international law, giving examples.
2 Describe two ways in which human rights can be argued to be controversial.

International Court of Justice

You need to know about the role and significance of the International Court of Justice (ICJ) in supporting international law and focusing on the behaviour of states. For more on the development of international law, see page 237.

The role of the ICJ

The ICJ is the principal judicial body of the UN and was created in 1945. It deals with legal disputes between states (submitted by states) and requests advisory opinions on legal questions referred to it by UN bodies. It consists of 15 judges who must be elected by a majority of votes in both the General Assembly and the Security Council. Each judge serves a nine-year term. The make-up of the Court is representative of the regions of the globe, but the Court has always included a judge from each of the P-5 countries (see page 243 for more on the UN Security Council).

Significance of the ICJ

Strengths	Weaknesses
There is almost universal jurisdiction. It establishes the principles by which disputes may be judged, such as setting a just and equitable solution to maritime border issues. For example, Peru v Chile [2014].	The jurisdiction of the ICJ only applies to states, **not** non-state actors or individuals, which excludes a wide range of humanitarian issues.
It settles bitter international border disputes. States, even losing states, observe the decision of the ICJ, even though it has no enforcement power as decisions have moral power, with a high cost to the reputation and legitimacy of states who defy the Court. For example, Costa Rica v Nicaragua [2015], where the ICJ ruled that a patch of wetlands on the San Juan River, occupied by Nicaragua, was the property of Costa Rica.	The ICJ has no enforcement powers. States have to sign up to being bound by ICJ decisions and have the option to withdraw that commitment. In 1984, for example, Nicaragua brought a case arguing the USA had violated international law by supporting the Contras in their rebellion against the government. The ICJ found in Nicaragua's favour in 1986, but the USA said the Court had no jurisdiction.
Advisory opinions can shape international politics. In 2010, for example, the ICJ ruled that Kosovo's declaration of independence did not breach international law. This has led Kosovo to ratchet up its campaign for recognition as a state, and Catalonians have drawn parallels with their case for independence from Spain.	The ICJ appears to favour Western states and the P-5 in particular. Today, the distribution of 15 judges is: Africa three, Latin America and the Caribbean two, Asia three, Western Europe and other states five, Eastern Europe two.
The increasing number of cases brought to the ICJ, from an increasing range of states. By 1980, for example, the Court had commenced 65 cases; by May 2017, that had risen to 166 cases.	

🗨 Case study — Cameroon–Nigeria border dispute, 2002

In 2002, the ICJ ruled on a border dispute between Cameroon and Nigeria, which had sparked violent confrontation in the 1980s and 1990s. This area was heavily disputed due to the associated offshore fishing and oil rights. The ICJ ruled on the allocation of territory over the whole 2,100 km border, but most importantly awarded the Bakassi Peninsula to Cameroon. With the UN as a mediator, the dispute was resolved and Bakassi was handed over by Nigeria in 2008. This resolution is seen as a model for peaceful resolution of other border disputes, particularly in Africa, where only 30 per cent of borders are precisely drawn.

Now try this

What are the key weaknesses of the ICJ?

UN tribunals and the ICC

A series of international courts exist in support of international law. While the ICJ focuses on the actions of states (see page 254 for more on the ICJ), **international tribunals** and the **International Criminal Court (ICC)** focus on the actions of individuals.

Special UN tribunals

Key international criminal tribunals established after the Second World War include the Nuremberg and Tokyo trials (1945–1948). Following the end of the Cold War (1991), the UN Security Council (UNSC) established more tribunals to consider violations of international humanitarian law, where there was evidence of crimes of genocide, crimes against humanity and war crimes. For example, the International Criminal Tribunal for the former Yugoslavia (ICTY) was established in The Hague in 1993 and the International Criminal Tribunal for Rwanda (ICTR) in Tanzania in 1995.

62 sentenced

14 acquitted

10 referred to national jurisdiction for trial

3 fugitives referred to another tribunal

2 deceased prior to judgement

2 indictments withdrawn before trial

93 individuals have been indicted by the ICTR since 1995.

Evaluation of UN tribunals: ICTY and ICTR

👍 The trials focused attention on human rights violations. Attention was increased by global media coverage and the emergence of a 24-hour news cycle.

👍 Leaders cannot act above the law and can be held personally liable for crimes. For example, Jean Kambanda, the former PM of Rwanda, pleaded guilty to six charges of genocide and was given a life sentence.

👍 Crimes can be committed not just during war between states, but in civil war or even during periods of peace.

👍 Successful convictions act as an example to deter future crimes. For example, the conviction of Radislav Krstić for genocide at Srebrenica.

👎 Prosecutions are too slow – this is a major problem.

👎 The cost of special UN tribunals. For example, the ICTY costs rose from $267,000 in 1993 to $301m for the year 2010–2011.

👎 These court decisions, and the international humanitarian law they rest on, are culturally biased. They reflect Western, liberal values of human rights over other values.

👎 These courts and international humanitarian law are a threat to state sovereignty by intervening in their domestic jurisdiction.

👎 The courts are based on events in developing or transitioning countries, giving the impression that these countries are seen by the West as backward.

Origin and role of ICC

This evaluation led to global pressure to establish a permanent court with global jurisdiction to replace special UN tribunals. In 2002, the ICC was established by the Statute of Rome, devised by states, international institutions and NGOs. The ICC is located in The Hague, but it is not part of the UN family of institutions. It has the power to prosecute crimes against humanity, war crimes and genocide. It is a court of last resort, intervening only when national authorities cannot or will not prosecute.

Controversy and the ICC

Unlike special UN tribunals, the ICC is not reliant on the UNSC for its authority. The UNSC can only delay a prosecution for one year if the prosecution would obstruct the UNSC's efforts to secure peace. So no single P-5 state can block a prosecution – this has been controversial from the start. By 2016, 124 countries had ratified the Rome Statute but key states (the USA, China and Russia) had not as it conflicts with national sovereignty. Without these key powers, the ICC lacks the necessary legitimacy, power and jurisdiction to be fully effective.

Key ICC cases

- The ICC successfully prosecuted the Congolese warlord Thomas Lubanga for recruiting and using child soldiers from 2002 to 2003. He was sentenced for 14 years.

- The case against Kenya's President Kenyatta in 2014 was withdrawn.

- The case against the Ivory Coast's former President Laurent Gbagbo, on charges of murder, rape and other forms of sexual violence, persecution and inhumane acts is ongoing.

Now try this

How does the ICC differ from the ICTY and the ICTR?

Human rights and international justice

You need to consider the extent to which the **ICC** and the **European Court of Human Rights (ECHR)** can protect human rights and international justice.

The ICC and human rights

Does the ICC have the power and authority to uphold human rights?

Yes	No
Setting an example: it sends out the message that political and military leaders will be prosecuted for their actions and so should deter future crimes. This deterrence is difficult to measure.	**Cost and inefficiency**: the cost of the ICC is met by the individual contributions of states, based on their wealth. The burden on member states is great due to the absence of key powers like the USA. The first successful prosecution was ten years after the ICC was established.
Intervention: the ICC intervenes as a last resort, where states will not or cannot prosecute military and political leaders for committing crimes against their own citizens. This provides a defence of human rights across the globe.	**National sovereignty**: the Court will intervene in states, which is in conflict with the key international principle of national sovereignty (see page 233 for more on this principle). One issue is whether the jurisdiction of the Court extends to non-members if they break the law in a member state. For example, US soldiers in Bosnia.
The power of international law: international humanitarian law now has a court with global jurisdiction to enforce the law on crimes of genocide, crimes against humanity and war crimes.	**Western imperialism**: the ICC is based on Western values and principles, ignoring alternative world views. Its initial prosecutions appear to have an anti-African bias, according to the African Union, as it is only prosecuting black African leaders.
	Lack of jurisdiction: the lack of support from key powers reduces the legitimacy and jurisdiction of the ICC. The ICC also has no enforcement powers. For example, the African Union has instructed its members not to act on the arrest warrant for President Omar al-Bashir, President of Sudan.

The origin of the ECHR

The place where human rights are seen to be most effectively protected is Europe. The European Convention on Human Rights, which came into force in 1953, was developed from the UN Declaration and has 47 signatories. The Convention established the European Court of Human Rights (ECHR), based in Strasbourg. The ECHR has the jurisdiction to decide complaints submitted by individuals (most commonly) against states, concerning violations of the Convention.

Key ECHR key cases

- Othman (Abu Qatada) *v* the UK [2012], which ruled the radical cleric could not be deported to Jordan for fear he would be tried using evidence obtained by torture.

- S and Marper *v* UK [2008], which ruled that holding DNA samples of those arrested, but not prosecuted or later acquitted, is a violation of the right to privacy.

Significance of the ECHR

Strengths	Weaknesses
The high level of compliance with ECHR rulings by its signatory states.	The huge backlog of cases, due to the arrival of new states from central and Eastern Europe to its jurisdiction, where human rights protection is flawed. In 2013, 13,512 cases were referred from Ukraine alone and the backlog in the same year for the ECHR stood at 99,900 cases.
	The jurisdiction of the Court can be seen to clash with the sovereignty of the state – this is made worse where rulings against states are unpopular within that state.

Now try this

1 How does the absence of the USA undermine the ICC?

2 Why might the European Court of Human Rights be considered the most effective court at upholding rights?

Humanitarian intervention

Humanitarian intervention is a further example of a recent development, from the 1990s onwards, that has had significant impacts on state sovereignty but remains highly controversial.

Humanitarian intervention

Humanitarian intervention is military intervention within a state by another state or international organisations, like the UN. Its key purpose is to prevent crimes against humanity and is used where the intervention will result in an improvement for the people within the state.

Rise of humanitarian intervention

The end of the Cold War (1991) sparked the rise of humanitarian intervention, as the superpower rivalry between the USSR and USA on the UN Security Council came to an end. The world appeared to be moving towards a liberal, global order of peace where human rights were the responsibility of all.

However, the world quickly became unstable for two reasons:

1 The growing problems within states around inequality, rising ethnic nationalism, widespread corruption and the violent policies of dictatorships.

2 Growing global issues of debt, poverty, inequality and structural imbalances driven by economic globalisation and governance.

At the same time, states and international bodies became increasingly willing to intervene because:

- instability within states has global impacts and so it is in the best interests of states to take action to maintain regional stability, to stop refugee crises and to promote democracy

- the emergence of global media networks, the 24-hour news cycle and influential human rights NGOs (for example, Human Rights Watch) places pressure on states to take action

- the growing acceptance of the international community that international law is based on standards of conduct that states must comply with; the emergence of the Responsibility to Protect (R2P).

Development of the R2P

Human rights are seen as providing a moral framework for intervention, but it does not provide specific justifications or rules to apply to each case. In response to events in Rwanda in 1994, the **International Commission on Intervention and State Sovereignty** was established and it developed the ideas of the **R2P**, which were endorsed by world leaders at the 2005 UN World Summit. R2P can be seen as an emerging human rights norm which enables the protection of civilians from mass atrocity crimes. It has three key elements:

1 Basic principles	• State sovereignty implies the state has the primary responsibility to protect its peoples.	
	• When the state fails to stop serious harm coming to its peoples, the principle of non-intervention gives way to the international responsibility to intervene, which conflicts with the principle of state sovereignty.	
2 Just cause for military intervention	• Large-scale loss of life has happened or is likely to happen, with genocidal intent or not.	
	• Large-scale ethnic cleansing has happened or is likely to happen.	
3 Precautionary principles of intervention	• Intervention must be primarily for humanitarian ends, the last resort and proportional and must have a reasonable prospect of success.	
	• Intervention must be authorised by the UN Security Council.	

Now try this

1 How does the R2P attempt to balance sovereignty and humanitarian intervention?
2 Does this undermine the Treaty of Westphalia and the UN Charter?

Humanitarian intervention: controversy

You need to explore why humanitarian intervention is so controversial, and the role and significance of the global civil society and non-state actors in protecting human rights.

Controversy around humanitarian intervention

While there have been some instances of successful humanitarian intervention (such as in Kosovo or Sierra Leone) controversy remains for the following reasons.

Selective interventionism Intervention appears selective, taking place in some states but not in others. For example, intervention in Libya (2011) but not in Syria (2012) or Myanmar (2017). Libya had no regional or international allies so intervention was possible (see page 238 for more on the decision to intervene in Libya), while Syria was protected by its relations with Russia and China, who can veto any Resolutions on the UNSC.	**Western interests** Humanitarian intervention is a façade for neo-colonialism, so states will only execute humanitarian intervention when it is in their interests. For example, it is alleged that intervention in Iraq was really about the control of oil. Human rights, and therefore humanitarian intervention, are an example of Western 'cultural imperialism'.
Double standards On the one hand, there is intervention in Libya. On the other, there is failure to challenge human rights abuses by the Chinese in Tibet, as there is no prospect of success, or by Saudi Arabia in Yemen, as Saudi is an ally and weapons market for the USA and Western countries.	**Hypocrisy** The West's own record on human rights is controversial. For example, this can be seen in the USA's use of extraordinary rendition, torture and Guantanamo Bay.
State sovereignty Humanitarian intervention clashes with the principle of state sovereignty, which is the cornerstone of the established rules of world order. Realists would further argue that states should only focus on their own security, not pursue moral quests.	**R2P** Intervention involves the use of force and violence. Even if this is proportional, there will be civilian casualties. Even where there is a good chance of success (for example, Libya), the long-term outcome can still be failure. Libya has become a failed state (see pages 238 and 271).

Protecting rights: global civil society and non-state actors

Strengths	Weaknesses
NGOs such as Amnesty International and Human Rights Watch have campaigned to expose human rights abuses across the globe to exert international pressure on states to improve their human rights record.	NGOs cannot force governments to change, especially if those countries appear to be resistant to international pressure.
NGOs have used the growth of transnational media corporations and the 24-hour news cycle to focus global civil society's mind on human rights abuses.	NGOs have limited impact on the UNSC's decision-making, where the key decisions about intervention are made.
The influence of NGOs can also be felt in the establishment of the ICC, with NGOs witnessing the setting up of the Rome Statute, lobbying states to ratify the Statute and then supporting the role of the ICC by submitting legal opinions.	In 2017-2018, NGOs and global civil society failed to achieve coordinated UN action over the allegations of ethnic cleansing of the Rohingya Muslims in Rakhine State, Myanmar. The Rohingya Muslims are an ethnic minority in the largely Buddhist country, who have been in the region for generations but are denied citizenship. In August 2017, according to Médecins Sans Frontières, over 6,700 Rohingya were killed in violence led by troops and local mobs. This led to an estimated 671,000 Rohingyas fleeing between August 2017 and August 2018 to join the 307,500 already in refugee camps in Bangladesh. The UN described the offensive as a 'textbook example of ethnic cleansing', while the Myanmar government claimed to be fighting Rohingya militants not targeting civilians.
There has been increased support for human rights and humanitarian intervention in global civil society, and this has been reflected by UN support for intervention.	
There has been increased support for human rights and humanitarian intervention in global civil society, and this has been reflected by UN support for intervention.	

Now try this

1 Why is humanitarian intervention selective?
2 Name two human rights NGOs.

The UNFCCC and Kyoto Protocol

You need to know about the role and significance of the United Nations Framework Convention on Climate Change (UNFCCC) and the strengths and weaknesses of international agreements, including the Kyoto Protocol.

Climate change

Climate change is a high-profile, global environmental issue in the following senses:

- **Transnational**: greenhouse gas emissions by one state impact in other states.
- **Global effects**: the effects can only be tackled through international cooperation.
- **Global commons**: the exploitation of the global commons, such as the atmosphere, are shared by all countries.

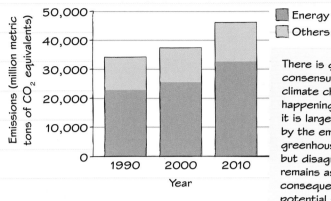

There is growing consensus that climate change is happening and that it is largely caused by the emissions of greenhouse gases, but disagreement remains as to its consequences and the potential solutions.

Role and significance of the UNFCCC

The Earth Summit took place in Rio de Janeiro in 1992. It was the largest environmental conference the world had seen, attended by 172 countries, with 108 heads of state and over 2,400 representatives of NGOs. It established a **Framework Convention**, which came into force in 1994 and has been ratified to date by 197 countries.

- **Recognition**: member states agreed to act in the interests of human safety, even though there was scientific uncertainty over climate change at the time.
- **Goal**: stabilise greenhouse gas concentrations at a level that would prevent human-induced interference with the climate system.

Strengths	Weaknesses
Industrialised states are responsible for most past and current emissions and so should cut emissions to pre-1990 levels by 2000.	It is a framework for further action and has no legally binding targets.
	Developing states were excluded and saw considerable rises in emissions, especially with the growth of China.

Significance of the Kyoto Protocol to the UNFCCC

In 1997, the Kyoto Protocol to the UNFCCC was negotiated and came into force in 2005.

- **Recognition**: increasing scientific consensus over climate change and the need to minimise its effects.
- **Goal**: binding targets for industrialised states to cut or limit their emissions by 2012.

Strengths	Weaknesses
Developed nations took more responsibility under the principle of 'common but differentiated responsibilities'. Developed states were set different targets, with an average reduction of 5 per cent below 1990 levels. An **emissions trading system** was set up: - Each state has a permitted number of carbon emission units. States under their targets can sell their remaining units to other states. - Developed states can reduce their emissions by investment in or technology transfer to emission-reducing projects in developing states.	The targets were arguably inadequate in preventing human-induced interference with the climate system.
	The failure of the USA, the largest greenhouse gas emitter at the time, to ratify it was a huge blow.
	There were no binding targets on developing states, like China, and their emissions continued to rise steeply in line with their economic growth.
	In 2008, China became the largest emitter and developing states accounted for more than 50 per cent of emissions by 2012.

Now try this

1 In what ways can climate change be seen as a global issue?
2 Why is the Kyoto Protocol considered as an important advance on the UNFCCC?

Other international agreements

Following the Kyoto Protocol, there have been more international conferences and agreements on environmental issues. You need to know about the strengths and weaknesses of these.

Copenhagen and Doha conferences, 2009 and 2012

The 2009 Copenhagen Climate Change Conference (COP15) was supposed to be the first step in creating a new protocol that went beyond Kyoto. However, no binding targets were set as countries failed to agree a common strategy due to great power politics and the economic pressures from the global financial crisis. At the 2012 Doha Conference, it was agreed to extend the Kyoto Protocol to limit or reduce targets that would apply from 2013 to 2020.

Paris Conference, 2015

At the 2015 Paris Conference, member states negotiated the Paris Agreement, which builds upon the UNFCCC. It came into force in November 2016; as of November 2017, it had been ratified by 168 member states. It brings **all** states into common cause to tackle climate change and to adapt to its effects.

- **Recognition**: climate represents an urgent and potentially irreversible threat to human societies and the planet.
- **Goal**: hold the increase in global temperatures to below 2 °C and aim to limit the temperature increase to 1.5 °C above preindustrial levels.

Strengths	Weaknesses
The negotiation process included China and the USA and the resulting agreement is binding on all signatory states, not just developing states so it has near-universal participation and acceptance of responsibility.	The bottom-up approach to setting NDCs enabled many more states to ratify the agreement. However, it is unclear whether the voluntary setting of targets by states will work.
The idea of Nationally Determined Contributions (NDCs) set by countries every five years. Developed states should aim to reduce emissions, while developing states limit them. Each successive NDC plan should progress beyond the previous one and reflect the highest possible ambition.	The timetable for reduction lies in the hands of the biggest polluters, like the USA, China and India, and there is no collective system to enforce targets. For example, this was highlighted in June 2017 when President Trump announced that the USA would withdraw from the deal as it was a threat to US economic interests and state sovereignty.
Finance and technology flows from the developed to support the developing world to build clean, climate resilient futures. $100bn was pledged to the Green Climate Fund.	Given the lack of specifics in the deal and the long history of broken promises in global governance on aid and funding, it is difficult to know how this aid will be raised and where, when and how it will be spent.

Protecting the environment: global civil society and non-state actors

NGOs have played a significant role in raising the awareness of the impact of human behaviour on the environment, thus increasing the relevance of environmental issues both nationally and internationally.

Strengths	Weaknesses
NGOs are important contributors to climate change conferences and Friends of the Earth played a key role in the adoption of the 1.5 °C aim in the Paris Agreement.	NGOs have been accused of over exaggerating the impact of climate change and its impact in order to further their own environmental agenda.

Now try this

1 Why was the 2009 Copenhagen Conference considered a failure? How is this failure explained?
2 What are the strengths and weaknesses of Nationally Determined Contributions (NDCs)?

The IPCC

The Intergovernmental Panel on Climate Change (IPPC) is the international body for assessing the science of climate change. You need to know about its significance in tackling climate change and why international cooperation is so difficult to achieve.

The role of the IPCC

The IPCC was set up in 1988 by the World Meteorological Organization (WMO) and the United Nations Environment Programme (UNEP) to provide regular assessment reports on:

- the science of climate change
- its impacts and future risks
- options for adaptation (policies to allow states to adapt to climate change) and mitigation (strategies to reduce greenhouse gas emissions).

The IPCC works and liaises with governments to provide scientific information to decision makers.

Significance of the IPCC

Strengths	Weaknesses
The Assessment Reports are comprehensive and objective and produced in an open and transparent way. The Fifth Report of 2014 upgraded its finding to say that it is extremely likely that human-centred emissions caused climate change (greater than 90 per cent probability).	The Reports use existing data and are slow to be produced (the next report is not due until 2022), meaning they quickly lose relevance and tend to underestimate climate change issues.
The Fifth Report states that if no action is taken, global temperatures will rise between 4 and 6 °C by 2100, with severe and widespread impacts such as substantial species extinction, large risks to global and food security, growing poverty and inequality.	The IPCC has been criticised by some for overestimating potential dangers in order to further a greenhouse emissions cuts agenda, and by others for getting the basis for its decisions wrong.
The growing consensus that climate change is a problem that cannot be avoided places pressure on countries like China and the USA to put aside differences and cooperate.	For example, many criticise its faith in revolutionary new technologies, like carbon dioxide capture, to deliver the level of mitigation needed to limit climate change.
Near-universal membership – 195 countries.	

Restrictions on international cooperation

Economic globalisation has spread capitalism across the globe. Inherent to capitalism is the belief in limitless growth, the constant desire for profit and the view that nature is just a pool of economic resources to be exploited by humanity. Any effective measure to tackle environmental issues will mean a move away from neo-liberalism and the free market to much tighter regulation at national and international level, which means that conventional economic wisdom will have to be overturned.

Cultural globalisation has spread the values of materialism and consumerism, which link happiness to increasing material consumption. These ideological positions underpin society, so it is not a matter of just asking people to consume less to protect nature; it is a matter of challenging the basic values of society.

Resistance to global governance

States pursue their own national interest, prioritising economic growth and national prosperity over wider global concerns, and this is a major cause of climate change and other environmental crises. States resist increased global governance on environmental regulation, or any moves towards world government as it threatens their sovereignty. For example, this can be seen in the resistance by states such as China and the USA to the setting of any binding targets or enforcement measures in the Paris Agreement. It is epitomised by Trump's withdrawal from the Paris Agreement in 2017, citing its impact on US sovereignty and economic competitiveness.

Now try this

How might economic and cultural globalisation be seen to make international cooperation on climate change difficult to achieve?

International cooperation

Disputes between developed and developing states, as well as the **tragedy of the commons**, make international cooperation on environmental issues difficult to achieve.

Disputes between developed and developing states

Views of developing states	Views of developed states
Environmental problems are historically caused by the industrialisation of developed states. As a result, developing states are both poorer and more likely to be impacted by climate change, as seen in the threat to Bangladesh of rising sea levels. Developed states are responsible for climate change and should shoulder the heaviest burden.	All states need to take responsibility and targets should be set based on the measurement of current emission levels only, especially as the South accounts for more than 50 per cent of emissions since 2012, and their emissions are growing as a percentage.
The measurement of environmental impact should be based on cumulative emissions, as this includes historical emissions. For example, the USA was responsible for 27 per cent and China 10 per cent of cumulative emissions by 2010.	They cannot be held responsible for emissions in the past, when there was no scientific evidence of the consequences.
The responsibility for tackling environmental problems should take account of population size. For example, in 2015 the USA was emitting twice as much carbon dioxide emissions per head as China and eight times more than India.	Measurement should be based on current emissions, with the USA responsible for 14 per cent and China 29 per cent in 2015; the biggest polluters have the greatest responsibility.
Developing states have the right to development and growth in order to tackle poverty and chronic hunger, as well as providing clean water and a decent energy source.	

🔍 Case study — The tragedy of the commons

In 1968, American ecologist and philosopher Garrett Hardin used the example of a common pasture ground to explain the inevitable ruin of the global commons (any shared resource such as the atmosphere, oceans or fish stocks). If each individual herdsman could increase their herd for a large individual gain (more profit) at a small cost (as the cost of overgrazing is shared between all herders), they would. As each herdsman acts in their best interest by adding more cattle, the commons will inevitably be ruined. Sovereign states, like herdsmen, act in their own best interests, rationally exploiting the global commons, as the environmental costs are shared by all states.

The tragedy of the commons and climate change

Climate change is a 'tragedy of the commons' problem. Protecting the global commons of the Earth's atmosphere is in the best interest of all states. Yet the costs of taking action, in terms of adaptation and mitigation strategies or lowering economic growth, are very high. States may thus act in their own self-interest, not the collective interest – they may not agree to binding targets or only to low targets, neither of which are enforceable. This will inevitably have catastrophic consequences for the global environment. Potential solutions include:

* Privatisation of the global commons, if it can be done. The owners would then have a clear interest in the conservation of resources.

* Establishment of global environmental governance to tackle environmental issues and manage the global commons. However, sovereign states are not legally obliged to obey an international law which they are not signatories to. A more radical solution would be to move to world government.

* Socialists and anarchists argue that private property, not the commons, is the issue, as indigenous peoples effectively manage the commons. Private property is the cause of selfishness, greed and seeing nature as only an economic resource. Common ownership would create greater human solidarity and a respect for nature.

Now try this

Why is climate change a tragedy of commons problem?

Competing views

Ecologism is a political ideology that shows all life needs to live in harmony and balance (see pages 124–131). Ecologism splits into two key approaches – **shallow** and **deep green ecology** – which offer competing views on how to tackle environmental issues and debates around sustainable development.

Shallow green ecology

Shallow green thinking (read about these ideas on page 128) takes the lessons of the science of ecology to mean that humans must live in harmony with nature. The environment is necessary for human prosperity and happiness, so must be protected. Nature's value is determined by its use to humanity, known as **enlightened anthropocentrism** (human-centred; see page 124). This makes humanity the steward, not the master of nature and focuses on slower, smarter growth that strikes a balance between the economy and the environment, that is **sustainable development**.

There are three main approaches:

1 **Green capitalism**: allows the market to resolve environmental problems. Ethical consumerism and the rising cost of scarce resources will drive TNCs to innovate and adopt corporate responsibility in order to keep making a profit.

2 **Managerialism**: use regulations and targets to limit environmental impacts and to manage the global commons by establishing global governance, such as the UNFCCC. At state level, this can involve setting targets or the use of green taxes.

3 **Strong faith in technology**: green technology can create an environmentally friendly form of capitalism and development.

Deep-green ecology

Deep green ecology (see page 127) rejects shallow green ecology as part of the problem, not part of the solution, because:

- nature cannot be balanced with the growth-orientated values that underpin global capitalism; industrialisation, consumerism, materialism and limitless growth are the problem
- the science of ecology teaches us that humanity is not the centre of life on Earth; humanity is not more important or superior to any other species or nature itself.

Deep green ecology can be realised in two ways:

1 A radical paradigm shift from the dominant world-view that gives priority to humans to an approach that gives priority to nature or the planet. This is known as **ecocentrism** (see page 124 for more on this view), where nature has value in its own right, independent of any value placed on it by humankind.

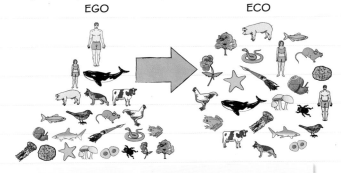

EGO   ECO

Anthropocentrism (EGO) to ecocentrism (ECO)

2 A rejection of modern global capitalism and its values. A move to strong **sustainability**, where happiness will be based on quality of life, not the consumption of material goods.

The sustainable development debate

Shallow green ecology: sustainable development was defined by the Brundtland Report (1987) as meeting 'the needs of the present without compromising the ability of future generations to meet their own needs'. This idea is now central to the World Bank and the IMF, which both support growth that is inclusive and environmentally sound so that it reduces poverty and meets the needs of today's population and future populations. This approach is referred to as **weak sustainability**.

Deep green ecology: favours **strong sustainability**, which preserves and sustains the Earth. This involves a negative growth economy for developed economies to significantly reduce their consumption and development for Southern states until basic needs are met. Then there will be a move to a zero-growth economy for all. This will be based around frugal but sufficient ways of living rather than material affluence with localised production to massively decrease the use of non-renewable resources (e.g. gas and coal) and pollution.

Now try this

1 What is the difference between the anthropocentric and the ecocentric view of nature?
2 What are the differing interpretations of sustainability?

Power and hard power

You will need to understand the debate about the nature of power as well as the use and effectiveness of different types of power, including **hard power**.

Power

American political scientist Joseph Nye describes power as 'the ability to influence the behaviour of others to get the outcomes one wants'. Power has usually been understood in three different ways:

1 **Power as capability**: the strength that a state possesses. Capability is typically measured in terms of population and territory, resource endowment, economic capability, military strength, political stability and competence.

2 **Power as a relationship**: the ability of one state to influence another to do something they have not chosen to do. This may be shaped by states' perceptions of each other's capabilities.

3 **Power as structural**: the power to shape how things are done. This involves setting the framework in which states and non-state actors operate, including influencing their beliefs and perceptions, controlling their access to credit or investment, shaping defence and economic development agendas.

The effectiveness of hard power

Hard power is **coercive** power, wielded through threats, such as **military intervention** or **economic sanctions** or inducements. For example, the promise of military protection or the reduction of trade barriers. Hard power is generally conceived in terms of capabilities.

The effectiveness of hard power

👎 The use of military power has damaged the credibility and international standing of the states that employ it.
For example, the collapse of the USA's international reputation after Afghanistan and Iraq, leading to a shift in policy under Obama.

Higher European approval ratings for the USA during the Obama administration.

👍 Realists see the world in terms of sovereign states aiming to guarantee their own survival, with military force as their ultimate instrument.
For example, Trump's policy of 'peace through strength', calling for an extra $54bn for tanks, ships and weapons systems in his first budget.

👎 Military conflict by stronger states against states with less capabilities have proved difficult to win due to the strategies of guerrilla warfare and terrorism.
For example, the issues faced by the USA in Iraq and Afghanistan.

👍 The response to acts of terrorism has been military force.
For example, air strikes on the Islamic State (Isis) in Iraq and Syria.

👎 Economic sanctions only work on smaller countries seeking access to the global economy.
For example, sanctions on North Korea have impacted their population, but not their foreign policy/pursuit of nuclear weapons.

👍 Economic globalisation makes state war too costly, so states compete through trade rather than war. Economic inducements are therefore cheaper and more effective.
For example, China has committed $74bn in aid since 2000 to strengthen its grip on Africa's natural resources.

Now try this

Why has there been a perceived move from the use of military power to economic power?

Soft and smart power

Soft power refers to the ability of a state to persuade others to do what it wants without force or coercion. **Smart power** is a skilful combination of hard and soft power.

Soft power

Soft power is about shaping the long-term attitudes and preferences of others using identification and attraction. It is about the attractiveness of one's culture and values or the ability to set the agenda to make others' wishes seem too unrealistic to pursue. Soft power comes from three different resources:

 Culture (where it is attractive to others): For example, Silicon Valley, Hollywood and the American Dream make the USA attractive to much of the public across the globe.

 Political values: when those values are upheld at home and abroad. For example, Canada's commitment to openness and diversity at home and abroad.

 Diplomacy/foreign policy: where they are seen as legitimate and having moral authority through having the support of the international community.

The effectiveness of soft power

Coercion   Inducement   Agenda setting   Attraction

Hard power   **Soft power**

Due to globalisation, there has been a growth in complex interdependence, which has driven the shift from hard power to soft power.

👍 In a world of complex interdependence, goals are better achieved through cooperation not conflict.

👍 The freer flow of information and communication across borders means people are increasingly informed about foreign cultures and values, which they can compare against their own.

👍 The spread of democracy, education standards and literacy increases this tendency, especially as democracies operate on the soft power of consensus and persuasion.

👎 Hard power can undermine soft power. For example, the US war in Iraq without international agreement has undermined US power and increased anti-American sentiment. It has alienated moderate Muslim opinion and has been linked to the spread of terrorism.

👎 Soft power has been challenged as some goals, such as stopping North Korea from developing nuclear weapons, can arguably only be achieved by hard power while many, such as terrorists, are unlikely to be persuaded through attraction.

👎 Soft power is difficult to use as it can only promote, not control, popular culture while it can control foreign policy.

Smart power

The election of Barack Obama to the US presidency in 2008 coincided with a change in US strategy to 'smart power': a skilful combination of hard and soft power. It is about choosing the right tools – diplomatic, economic, military, political, legal and cultural – for each specific situation. In the case of Iran, for example, the Obama administration used damaging economic sanctions, diplomacy and Obama's attempts to reach out to the Iranian public to bring about the Iran Nuclear Deal, which restricted Iran's nuclear programme.

Now try this

1 What are the three main sources of soft power?
2 Why has the effectiveness of soft power been challenged?

Classification of state power

State power can be classified in global politics through the terms great powers, superpowers and emerging powers.

Why and how is state power classified?

Global politics traditionally sees power in terms of **capabilities**. Power is something a state possesses, based on certain advantages the state enjoys. Kenneth Waltz, a realist thinker, lists these criteria as size of population and territory, resource endowment, economic capability, military strength, political stability and competence. By measuring these advantages, states can be classified and placed within a hierarchical structure to explain the international system.

Great powers

A great power can be placed towards the top of the hierarchical state system. Great powers are seen to have:

- enough military power to provide for their own survival, and possibly to influence other states
- significant economic power
- the ability to engage globally, not just regionally, using military and economic strength, as well as diplomatic and soft power influence
- a foreign policy that can impact on international affairs and have a significant say within global governance organisations.

The term 'great power' is most commonly associated with the major states (the USA and the USSR) in the pre-Second World War era. Today, however, the term could be applied to the UK, France and possibly China, Russia and India.

Superpowers

A superpower is traditionally seen as exhibiting greater power than a great power. The definition was created to describe the USSR and the USA after the Second World War and focuses on their capabilities and ability to project their power across the globe. Superpowers are seen to have:

- the ability to achieve global political objectives through cultural, military and economic strength, as well as diplomatic and soft power influence
- pre-eminent military capability, including nuclear weapons and the means to deliver them across the planet
- pre-eminent economic and strategic powers within their ideological bloc or region – in this case, the USA and the West, and the USSR and the East.

The status of superpower today applies to the USA, and possibly will apply to China in the future.

Emerging powers

Emerging powers refer to states that are emerging as powerful modern economies. These states are becoming more economically important within the global market and are starting to be more assertive in the institutions of global governance, such as the WTO (see page 248 for more on how this institution operates) and the G20 (read about this group on page 249).

The states most commonly described as emerging are the BRICS (Brazil, Russia, India, China, South Africa). Together, the BRICS represent 26 per cent of the planet's land mass, are home to 46 per cent of the world's population and account for 19.8 per cent of global GDP and 16.9 per cent of global trade.

The rise of China

China has set itself the task of becoming a 'global leader' by 2049, the centenary of the founding of the People's Republic. Based on its vast territory and population, its incredible economic growth and growing military power, China aims to develop into a force leading the world on political, economic, military and environmental issues.

Can China and the USA escape the 'Thucydides Trap'? Thucydides, a Greek historian, showed that the rise of Athens had inspired fear in Sparta, making war inevitable. In 12 of the 16 times an emerging power has confronted a ruling power in the last 500 years, it has ended in bloodshed.

Now try this

1 Why is state power classified?
2 What is the difference between a superpower and a great power?

Polarity

Polarity describes the number of significant states (poles) within the international system, and how this impacts on the behaviour of other states and the chances for peace and prosperity.

Polarity

Realists see a global system of international anarchy, where states must rely on themselves for security and survival, where other states will look to take advantage of them and there is little reason to trust each other. The fact that this does not necessarily lead to war can be explained by the **balance of power**. The key factor which determines the balance of power, and therefore the chances of peace, is the number of poles within the system:

1 **Unipolarity**: a global system where there is only one superpower that is not constrained by any potential rival.
For example, the USA following the collapse of the USSR.

2 **Bipolarity**: the existence of two dominant poles (states) in the international system. For example, this is most closely associated with the Cold War: the USA and the West formed one pole, while the USSR and the East formed the second pole.

3 **Multipolarity**: an international system where there are three or more poles. For example, this was seen in the multipolar world of great powers that existed before the Second World War.

Unipolarity

The one power with considerable military and economic advantage over great powers, with a good prospect of winning wars against weaker rivals, becomes a potential regional or global **hegemon** (the domination of one element of the system over the rest). The hegemon, on top of military and economic power, will have structural power to shape the desires and actions of other states, leading to some level of willing consent. The stability of this system is a topic for debate:

 In **hegemonic stability theory**, imbalanced power can produce peace as one side has so much power, no one dare attack it. One state can act as the enforcer, protecting the political framework that supports the global market, preventing war and humanitarian crises in the interests of all states, and particularly to further the interests of the hegemon.

 Critics suggest potential hegemons are constantly striving for more power. At the same time, they increase fear among other great powers that follow risky policies to correct the imbalance of power. This leads the hegemon to increase its power, thus creating a spiral of fear that is hard to control. The whole system is unstable.

Bipolarity versus multipolarity

For **neo-realists**, peace and stability is far more likely in bipolarity than multipolarity because:

- There are more opportunities for war in a multipolar system. In a bipolar world, there is only one conflict relationship. The two main powers dominate; minor powers attach themselves to one of the great powers, making it hard for a superpower to pick a fight with a minor power allied to the other superpower.

- Bipolar systems tend towards balance and equality. During the Cold War, the USA and the USSR were militarily balanced, with nuclear weapons (a system of mutually assured destruction) making deterrence effective. In a multipolar world, power imbalances are more likely and this increases the chance of conflict.

- The potential for miscalculation is far greater under multipolarity. In a bipolar world, the rules of the game are far simpler, making it easier to read the intentions and capability of the rival superpower. In a multipolar world, there is a far greater chance a state will miscalculate the capabilities of another state and attempt to coerce or defeat them, thus increasing the chance of war.

 Now try this

1 Why do neo-realists see multipolarity as more unstable and dangerous than bipolarity?
2 What is a hegemon?

Changing nature of world order

You need to know about the changing nature of world order since 2000 and understand the debate relating to the polar structure since the end of the Cold War.

A unipolar world?

During the 1970s–1980s, the USA, one of two superpowers, reordered the institutions of global governance around the **Washington Consensus** (revise this collection of policies on page 246) to spread neo-liberalism globally to enhance the interests of the US economy. This asserted their position as a regional hegemon.

The critical event was the collapse of the USSR in 1991, which removed the key constraint on the USA. According to some theorists, this allowed it to spread its values across the whole globe to become a global hegemon while simultaneously taking up the role of the world's enforcer. The USA was both willing and able to enforce the international political framework of international organisations, treaties and laws that ensure the stability of the global market, as that stability was central to their long-term interests.

The impact of 9/11

The 2001 terror attacks by Al-Qaeda on the USA, which targeted the World Trade Center in New York and killed nearly 3,000 people, play a crucial role in understanding the modern global order, although not as critical as the USSR's collapse. Following the attacks, the USA, under George W. Bush, positioned itself as the world's police officer and a force for good. It increased its military power, treated states that harboured terrorists as terrorists themselves and spread democracy. However, its 2003 invasion of Iraq (without UN authorisation), use of torture and extraordinary rendition showed a hegemon acting without restraint and destabilising the global political order. This undermining has continued with the decision to withdraw from the ICC and Kyoto under Bush. Trump's election signifies a further step in this direction with his wish to pursue national interest, not global leadership, as seen in his position on the Paris Agreement, free trade deals and NATO.

The USA as a global hegemon and its decline

	USA: global hegemony	USA: declining global hegemony
Military power	Global military reach, technological edge; the USA accounts for about one-third of global military spending.	Hard power is weakening as terrorism and guerrilla tactics in Afghanistan and Iraq showed the limits of the USA's advanced military power.
Structural power	The USA plays the biggest role in most international organisations from the UNSC to the G7, the IMF and the World Bank (see pages 243, 249 and 246).	The rise of the BRICS (see page 268) has challenged the USA's structural power, limiting its power to take action over Crimea or Syria. The USA's role as enforcer of the international political framework is declining as it increasingly focuses on national interests.
Economic power	The USA is the world's largest economy and has established the dominant global economic model, neo-liberalism.	China is due to overtake the USA as the world's leading economy during the 2020s, and the dominance of the USA's neo-liberal economic model has been called into question by the global crash of 2007–2009. For example, in 2016 China launched the Asian Infrastructure Investment Bank as a rival to the US-dominated World Bank as it seeks to replace the dollar with the yuan as the global currency.
Soft power	The culture, ideology and institutions of the USA are attractive to and identified with by states and peoples across the globe.	The growing view is that soft power is becoming more significant; however, the USA's decision to invade Iraq without UN approval and its tactics have weakened its soft power.

Now try this

Why is the collapse of the USSR seen as a critical event in modern global politics?

A multipolar world

There is a debate about whether the global order is becoming multipolar. You need to know about the implications of this.

A multipolar world?

The evidence for a multipolar world can be found in two particular developments.

 The changing nature of great power politics, including:

- the decline of the USA since the start of the 21st century
- the rise of the BRICS.
  For example, the rapid economic growth of India, Russia's emergence as an energy power able to control Eastern Europe through gas and oil allied to its nuclear weapons arsenal, and China's rapid economic growth and emerging military power.

 Broader developments that have changed the nature of global power and challenged the traditional polarity models:

- Globalisation has created **complex interdependence**, meaning states are more fixated on making money than making war, so cooperation and soft power play a more important role than conflict and hard power (revise the nature of smart and soft power on page 265).
- Growing levels of global governance reflecting the rise of global issues, meaning cooperation, not conflict, is increasing in importance.
- The rise of non-state actors, such as NGOs, TNCs and terror networks, and global civil society as new centres of power in global politics.

The pessimistic view

Since the collapse of the Cold War bipolarity, many **neo-realists** see the emergence of an unbalanced multipolar system, which creates instability and conflict. There are two scenarios worth considering:

 The USA is a potential hegemon, with a clear advantage over other great powers and a greater chance of winning wars, so it starts conflict. The USA has engaged in six conflicts with weaker powers since 1991. At the same time, it wants to increase its power to increase its security and so it is constantly upgrading its military power. This sparks fear in other states, hence they follow risky polices to increase their security, such as Russia's invasion of Crimea or North Korea's pursuit of nuclear weapons.

 The rise of China as a potential regional hegemon. China will seek to grow its power in the Asia-Pacific region, which will create fear in adjoining great powers such as Russia, Japan and India, which in turn will seek to grow their power. The declining hegemonic power – the USA – will seek to prevent China's rise in order to protect its own security, probably by building an alliance like NATO in the region to contain China. This will lead to a spiralling security competition between the two sides, thus increasing instability.

The optimistic view

This view argues that the move to a multipolar world is positive. For **liberal theorists**, multipolar worlds have a tendency towards multilateralism, as reflected by the USA's turn from a unilateral approach under George W. Bush back to a multilateral foreign policy under Obama. For example, Obama was only willing to take multilateral action in Libya in 2011 with the full support of the UN in comparison to Bush's actions in Iraq in 2003. This is down to the fact that power is more evenly distributed in multipolar worlds, encouraging peace, stability, cooperation and integration, rather than the intense rivalry of the bipolar world, which creates tension, instability and an emphasis on hard power.

Now try this

Identify two developments that suggest there has been the drift towards a multipolar world.

Different systems of government

You need to know about the characteristics and consequences for global order of different types of government, including **democratic**, **semi-democratic**, **non-democratic** and **autocratic states**. For failed and rogue states, see page 271.

Democratic states

Countries such as the UK, the USA and Germany are good examples.

1 Civil liberties and rights

2 Constitutional government

Characteristics

3 Free, fair and regular elections

4 Healthy civil society

5 Capitalist economy

Consequences

In the **liberal** view, democratic states are seen to be peaceful and predictable in their decision-making, and as key drivers of **complex interdependence** (see page 265 for more on this theory), which creates global stability and order. This is achieved in two ways:

1 Democratic states seek to form trade links and establish institutions of global governance, which promotes complex interdependence. There is a correlation between the growth in numbers of democracies and the growth in global trade and international bodies, creating shared norms and values.

2 Democratic peace thesis – democracies tend not to go to war with other democracies, but will enter into war with states that are not democracies. As democracy has spread, it has created zones of peace, like Europe and North America.

Different systems of government

	Semi-democratic states	Non-democratic states	Autocratic states
Characteristics	A combination of democratic and authoritarian elements. Many have a dominant party model where elections take place but may involve fraud/unfair electoral campaigns to secure single-party dominance.	Lack almost all the key features that make up a liberal democracy. They tend to be authoritarian, with rule from above, and repress opposition and political liberty.	Ruled by a single person with unlimited power. There are no limits imposed by the rule of law, a constitution or other social and political institutions.
Examples	Russia under Putin; many states across Latin America, Africa and Asia; Hungary under the Fidesz Party since 2010.	China under the Communist Party; Turkey under Erdoğan since 2016.	Libya under Gaddafi; Germany under Hitler; North Korea under Kim Jong-un.
Consequences	They are less predictable than democracies but more predictable than autocratic states, which impacts on global order. Their unpredictability means they may or may not behave like democracies in regard to human rights and international law.	They are more likely to flout international law and repress human rights as Erdoğan has done since the failed coup attempt of 2016, and are less predictable in their decision-making. They decrease global stability and order.	They are unpredictable in their decision-making (one individual with no restraints) and are likely to violate international law and human rights. They weaken global order and stability.

Now try this

Define a democratic state.

Failed and rogue states

A **failed state** state is one that has lost control of its borders and legitimacy, while a **rogue state** is considered a threat by the international community.

Failed states and rogue states

	Failed states	Rogue states
Characteristics	They do not exhibit internal sovereignty, as they are unable to make decisions that are binding on individuals and groups in the territory or maintain order. There is no real system of law and order. There are often deep ethnic, religious or tribal divisions; sometimes civil war. The state lacks basic infrastructure and the ability to provide even a basic level of personal or economic security for its citizens.	A state that is judged to be a threat to other states and global order through its: • aggressive foreign policy • creation and stockpiling of weapons, especially nuclear weapons • support for terrorism. The real issue is who decides which state is a rogue state, and for what reason.
Examples	South Sudan, Somalia, Yemen and the Central African Republic.	The 'axis of evil' states – Iran, Iraq and North Korea (George W. Bush, 2002). The 'wicked few' states – North Korea, Iran and Syria (Donald Trump, 2017).
Consequences	They have terrible consequences for their populations and a number of different consequences for global order: • triggering refugee crises • generating regional instability • becoming a haven for international crime, terrorism and the illegal arms trade • triggering humanitarian intervention.	They are perceived as a real threat to regional or global order. Some argue that the definition of rogue state is used to justify intervention in that state by another state, often for self-interested reasons rather than global stability. For example, the USA identifying Iraq as a rogue state. Critics felt this was a cover for the USA's self-interest in gaining access to Iraqi oil and a key power base in the Middle East.

Evaluation of different systems of government

👍 The **liberal** view holds that the nature of the state is very important to global order, and hence their faith that the spread of democracy will spread peace, order and stability (see how this connects with globalisation on page 235).

👎 **Realists** believe that all states have the same interests and objectives, irrespective of their characteristics. Their key interest is survival or security as well as the attempt to possess and apply power for their own self-interest and not the mutual benefit of all. In the view of realists, the nature of government has no significant impact on global order.

There are other considerations, which limit the importance of the different characteristics of states:

1 The nature of government is not as important in shaping the global order as culture and religion, as expressed in Samuel Huntington's 'clash of civilizations' idea (read more about this on page 291).

2 Globalisation and complex interdependence has meant that global governance, international law and the global market restricts the behaviour of states, lessening the importance of the nature of government.

3 The nature of polarity, and a state's position in the international hierarchy, has more impact on state behaviour than the nature of government.

Now try this

How do liberals and realists disagree about the importance of the nature of government in different states?

Global developments

You need to know about the development and spread of liberal economies, **the rule of law** and democracy.

Liberal economies

The roots of the liberal economy can be found in the ideas of David Ricardo and the Manchester Liberals, like Richard Cobden. Free trade:

- has real economic benefits as it encourages different states to produce and sell those products and services where it has a comparative advantage, bringing benefits to all
- locks states into a relationship of interdependence so that the economic cost of war becomes too great and spreads shared values and culture.

These ideas spread along with industrialisation across Western Europe and America.

1800	1900	2000

Liberal economies developed along neo-liberal lines.

- States became ever more closely linked together in the global market, with decisions or events in one location having impacts across the globe.
- This led states to be more interested in trade than war, and increasingly favour closer cooperation, like the G20 (revise this group on page 249), or even integration, like the EU (see page 279 for an overview of this union).

Liberal economies have spread due to decolonisation, the collapse of the USSR and the Washington Consensus (see page 246) in global governance.

Rule of law

The rule of law is the principle that law should govern (see page 92). Law becomes the framework within which all actions by states should take place. Liberals see this as an essential guarantee of peace, stability and order, drawing on John Locke's idea that 'where there is no law, there is no freedom' (see page 53 for more on Locke's ideas). The rule of law has spread and impacted on global politics in two ways:

1 The development of global governance, especially the UN, since 1945 has established a rule-based international system that has collective security and the respect for international law at its core.

2 The rule of law is a central feature of liberal democracies as it ensures that all people and institutions are subject to and accountable to the law. The rule of law therefore acts as a key protection of the rights of the individual. As democracy has spread, so has the rule of law.

Has the rule of law been upheld?

👍 The Gulf War of 1991 as a punishment for Iraq's invasion of Kuwait under UNSC Resolution 678.

👍 The intervention in Libya under UNSC Resolution 1973 to protect civilians and civilian populations.

👎 The infringements within states such as Myanmar, where the military has acted outside the rule of law in its treatment of Rohingya Muslims (read about the issues related to humanitarian intervention on page 258).

Democracy

Development: Liberals believe autocratic and non-democratic states are unpredictable, militaristic and aggressive as they are unconstrained by public opinion. Democratic states are predictable and peaceful as public opinion favours making money, not war.

Spread: democracy has spread across the globe as economic globalisation creates the desire for political freedom and also due to the collapse of the communist model. The USA has controversially looked to spread democracy via military intervention, as in Iraq and Afghanistan. The failure to build effective democracies within these states reflects the difficulty of imposing democracy from above through the use of force.

Now try this

1 Define what is meant by the rule of law.
2 What is the democratic peace thesis?

Contemporary political issues

The Middle East can usefully show how the changing balance of power (revise polarity on page 267) in global politics impacts on the progress made in resolving contemporary issues. For interactions between global participants to address and resolve environmental issues, see pages 259–263.

 Case study **Iraq**

Background

Iraq under Saddam Hussein was an autocratic state; post-9/11, the USA labelled Iraq a rogue state. Iraq was accused of building up weapons of mass destruction, breaking UN Resolution 1441. The USA and UK sought a second resolution to authorise intervention in Iraq, but this was opposed by France and Russia, who both felt that a political solution based around weapon inspections was possible.

The invasion of Iraq by a US-led coalition in 2003.

War

The USA, a global hegemon, launched a unilateral pre-emptive war of self-defence, claiming the weapons could be used against America or be passed to Al-Qaeda. The legality of the war remains in question; in 2004, the UN General Secretary, Kofi Annan, said that it was illegal under the UN Charter. The USA has also tried to justify the action as regime change to spread democracy, although many critics (such as political thinker Noam Chomsky) see it as neo-colonialism to gain economic and military advantage as well as control over oil.

Consequences

The war was quickly won, showing the USA's hard power. However, it's soft power was undermined by the allegation it had undermined the UN and the rule of law. Since victory, the USA's hard power has also been called into question due to its difficulty in maintaining the peace in the face of guerrilla tactics and terrorism. The spread of democracy by force has proved difficult. Iraq is likely becoming a failed state and growing internal conflict has deepened divisions between the Sunni and Shi'a branches of Islam.

 Case study **Syria**

War

The 2011 Arab Spring uprisings quickly developed into a highly complex and brutal civil war. This civil war has seen the regional powers of Iran, Turkey and Jordan, and the great powers of the USA and Russia getting involved to extend their own strategic agendas by backing different factions. The Syrian government has been backed by Russia, Iran and Lebanon's Shia Hezbollah movement, while the mainly Sunni Muslim opposition has been backed by the USA, Turkey and Jordan.

Consequences

Syria is the worst humanitarian crisis of our time, according to Amnesty International. Yet the UNSC has remained powerless to intervene as it is hamstrung by great power rivalry – the Russians had used eight vetoes by 2017 on Syria. The failure to act is seen by some to show the weaknesses of the UN, that the world is now multipolar and that Syria is a failed state. Only the chemical attack on the Ghouta region in 2013 brought a UNSC deal. That deal called on Syria to divest itself of chemical weapons, yet in 2017 over 70 people were killed in a chemical attack in northern Syria, showing the failure of the international community to uphold international law.

Now try this

1 How did the USA justify its view that Iraq was a rogue state?
2 Evaluate how the theories of polarity (see page 267) can be used to explain the Middle East situation.

Different forms of regionalism

Regionalism is the development of **institutionalised cooperation** among states from a geographical region, which expresses a particular identity and shapes collective action. It exists in a variety of different forms.

Regionalism

Institutionalised cooperation means that regions become significant political or economic entities operating in global politics. Regionalism can take three different forms: **economic**, **security** or **political** regionalism. However, while organisations may have been set up with specific aims to achieve one form of regionalism, they change and develop over time to become involved with a far wider range of issues that can include all three forms.

The European Union (EU) is the prime example of regionalism.

Economic regionalism

Economic regionalism is the coming together of states from a geographical region for the purpose of cooperation in order to increase economic opportunities (for example, NAFTA; see page 277). This has become increasingly important since the late 1980s, with the wave of new regionalism that saw the growth and deepening of regional trade blocs. Most blocs are either a:

free trade area – reduced barriers and tariffs to trade between member states	**customs union** – a free trade area plus tariffs on the rest of the world	**common market** – a customs union plus free movement of labour and capital

Growth: the growth of economic regionalism is driven by economic globalisation. Regionalism is the method that states use to manage the effects of globalisation either as a protection against globalisation or to turbo-charge their integration into the global market.

Security regionalism

Security regionalism involves institutionalised cooperation with the aim of protecting member states against their enemies, both remote or within the region.

Growth: security regionalism grew in the first phase of regionalism from the end of the Second World War to the 1990s as a response to specific threats. For example, the European Coal and Steel Community (ECSC; read about this arrangement on page 279) was established in 1952 to create peace through cooperation between France and Germany to prevent future wars. The Association of Southeast Asian Nations (ASEAN; see page 279), was established in 1967 to create a region that was strong enough to defend itself against communism.

Political regionalism

Political regionalism is where there is institutionalised cooperation among states to protect or enhance their shared values. This in turn creates greater soft power (revise how states exercise soft power on page 265) through their heightened image and reputation.

Growth: political regionalism is driven by the desire for greater political influence. For example, this can be seen in the establishment of the Arab League in 1945 and the Organisation of African Unity in 1963 (transformed in 2002 to the African Union or AU; see page 277). The vision of the AU is for 'an integrated, prosperous and peaceful Africa, driven by its own citizens and representing a dynamic force in the global arena'.

Now try this

1 Give two regional organisations that are examples of political regionalism.
2 What has driven the growth of economic regionalism?

Regionalism and globalisation

Regionalism is the method that states use to manage the effects of globalisation.

Reasons for 'new' regionalism

Since the late 1980s, there has been a second wave of regionalism, known as 'new' regionalism. This has seen the creation of the North American Free Trade Association (NAFTA; see page 277) and the introduction of the ASEAN free trade area (read more about this agreement on page 278). 'New' regionalism has been mostly economic and has been created by a range of different factors:

- The acceleration of globalisation appeared to be reducing the sovereignty of the state over economic issues due to the growth of TNCs, international trade and the globalised financial system. This is regarded as the most significant driver.

- The collapse of the USSR meant many states had new opportunities within their regions to cooperate in economic and security matters, as seen in the eastward expansion of the EU.

- The establishment of the WTO (see page 248 for more on this institution) in 1995 and the growing role of economic governance meant economic regionalism was viewed as a key way to gain greater structural power within these bodies.

- The dynamic relationship between different parts of the world. For example, the establishment of the EU single market in 1986 may have triggered the creation of NAFTA and the ASEAN free trade area as a response.

Regionalism vs globalisation

Regionalism can be seen as either helping to protect against globalisation or to turbo-charge it.

Protection against globalisation	Turbo-charge globalisation
• Regional bodies use tariffs and subsidies to limit the impact of the global market. For example, the EU's Common Agricultural Policy (CAP) is used to protect EU farming from foreign competition. • The region is seen as a 'fortress' against global competition leading to the creation of competing blocs. For example, the growth of regional blocs since the creation of the single market in the EU in 1986. • Regionalism is a counterweight to economic superpowers. In 2004, for example, the EU forced the USA to drop its increased steel tariffs. In 2018, the EU imposed tariffs on a range of US products including orange juice, bourbon and motorcycles in response to the USA's tariffs on steel and aluminum. • Regionalism can prevent a 'race to the bottom' between states in a region created by competition in the global market, where they keep cutting regulations to lure TNCs. For example, environmental and workers' rights laws apply across all states in the EU stop this from happening.	• Economic regionalism increases the size of markets, attracting the investment, technology, jobs and skills training of TNCs as well as increasing economic specialisation. For example, the ASEAN Economic Community has a market of over 622 million people and $2.6 trillion. • Regionalism leads to increased structural power within the WTO and other bodies of global governance. For example, the EU accounts for 23 per cent of world GDP. This gives the EU far greater say in global economic decision-making than any individual EU member state could achieve on its own. • Economic regionalism is built on economic liberalisation, in line with the Washington Consensus (see page 246 for more on this policy), which increases access to the global market. For example, the South American Mercosur bloc saw intra-regional trade and world trade rise in the 1990s.

Now try this

How do regional organisations look to limit the global market?

Regionalism and sovereignty

You need to know about the prospects for **political regionalism** and the debate about the impact of regionalism on **state sovereignty**.

Prospects for political regionalism and regional governance

Since the end of the Cold War, there has been a rise in political projects, constructed by states to reorganise political space through cooperation (for example, ASEAN) or even integration (for example, the EU). The current view is that this project is now going backwards.

Forces for greater regionalism	Forces against greater regionalism
Many pressing issues for states remain global and regional in nature so there is a real need for regional governance. *For example, climate change, security challenges and transnational crime.*	The return of the nation-state. • For example, the UK's Brexit vote to leave the EU and the revival of right-wing, nationalist political parties in France, Netherlands, Poland. • Trump and 'America first' – renegotiation of NAFTA and the threat to pull out. • ASEAN Summit 2017 – ongoing debate over disputed territorial rights in the South China Sea.
The election of French President Emmanuel Macron, who speaks of 'European sovereignty', brings fresh impetus to the Franco-German drive to greater economic and political union, while Brexit removes a powerful state that was opposed to further integration.	The current crises in the EU. *For example:* • The Eurozone banking and debt crisis (see page 281 for more on this crisis), allied to low growth and declining competitiveness. Crises in Greece, Spain and Portugal. • The expansion of membership from six countries to 28 has meant there is now more diversity than unity, lessening the drive to political and economic union. Diversity is an issue across all regional blocs. • The migrant crisis – how should the EU handle migration and, in particular, the flow of refugees fleeing wars and, conflicts who are seeking asylum? This pits the southern EU states, who have to deal with migrant arrivals, against northern EU states.

State sovereignty

One key debate that needs to be explored is whether state sovereignty has been eroded by regionalism.

State sovereignty eroded	State sovereignty is unaffected
The growth of regional bodies and the policy areas they cover, especially since the late 1980s.	States are the main building blocks of global politics in institutions like the UN.
Some regional bodies represent their region in global decision-making (for example, the EU as a member of the G20 and the WTO).	There has been a rise in scepticism about regional bodies, leading to the return of the nation-state.
In certain policy areas, states pool their sovereignty, gaining greater capability and influence than they have when they operate on their own.	Most regional bodies are economic, not political. These blocs are used to protect state sovereignty from globalisation, not erode state sovereignty.
Supranational bodies of the EU – the use of qualified majority voting on the European Council, and the principle that EU law is binding on members, which has been enforced by the European Court of Justice (ECJ).	Attempts to create supranational bodies have been resisted outside the EU, in bodies such as ASEAN, which is based on **intergovernmentalism**, and the AU, which pledges to defend the sovereignty of its members.

Now try this

Why might there be reasons to be optimistic about the prospects for greater political regionalism and regional governance?

NAFTA and the AU

You need to know about the development of different regional organisations and their differing approaches to regionalism. This page covers the North American Free Trade Agreement (NAFTA) and the African Union (AU).

NAFTA and the AU

	NAFTA	AU
Formation	NAFTA was created by the USA, Canada and Mexico and came into force in 1994.	The Organisation of African Unity (OAU) was formed in 1963, with 32 states, and was replaced by the AU in 2002, now consisting of 55 African states.
Aims	The elimination of tariffs and barriers to trade between the three countries. The organisation has an intergovernmental decision-making process.	• To promote peace, security, and stability, democratic principles and institutions, popular participation and good governance. • To defend the sovereignty, territorial integrity and independence of its member states. • To achieve greater unity and solidarity between African countries and peoples of Africa.
Development	👍 Trade among the NAFTA countries has more than tripled. 👍 Side agreements have been created, such as the North American Agreement on Environmental Cooperation (NAAEC) which aims to work cooperatively to better understand and improve the protection of their environment. 👍 The North American Agreement on Labor Cooperation (NAALC) aims to improve working conditions and living standards, and to protect, enhance, and enforce basic workers' rights. 👎 NAFTA remains controversial, with Trump threatening withdrawal in 2017 due to the perceived impact on US jobs, and the stark differences economically, politically and socially between the partners makes deeper integration unlikely.	👍 The AU has changed focus from supporting liberation movements in the colonial and apartheid territories under the OAU to an organisation spearheading Africa's development and integration. 👍 It has far-reaching plans, including tackling poverty, establishing a human rights court, a central bank and a single market with a single currency. 👍 It has deployed its forces for peacekeeping purposes in Burundi, Sudan and Somalia as it believes peace must come before prosperity. 👎 Its plans for further integration are limited by its lack of finances, the fact many member states are autocracies, disagreements about the best way to develop and by its failure to act in Libya.

Now try this

Give two reasons why further integration in NAFTA is unlikely.

The Arab League and ASEAN

Two further regional organisations are the Arab League and the Association of Southeast Asian Nations (ASEAN).

The Arab League and ASEAN

The Arab League	ASEAN
Formation	

The Arab League (Formation)

PALESTINE, MOROCCO, LIBYA, LEBANON, IRAQ, TUNISIA, EGYPT, SYRIA, JORDAN, KUWAIT, BAHRAIN, UAE, QATAR, OMAN, SAUDI ARABIA, YEMEN, ALGERIA, COMOROS, DJIBOUTI, MAURITANIA, SUDAN, SOMALIA

It was formed in 1945 by six states. Today, it is made up of 22 Arab-speaking states.

ASEAN (Formation)

LAOS, VIETNAM, PHILIPPINES, MYANMAR, THAILAND, CAMBODIA, MALAYSIA, SINGAPORE, INDONESIA, BRUNEI DARUSSALAM

It was founded in 1967 by five member states. There are now ten nations.

Aims

The Arab League
- To strengthen relations between the member states.
- To coordinate their policies in order to achieve cooperation between them.
- To safeguard their independence and sovereignty, and a general concern with the affairs and interests of the Arab countries.

ASEAN
- To accelerate economic growth, social progress and cultural development in the region and promote regional peace and stability.

Development

The Arab League
- 👍 Originally the League's agenda was about ending colonial rule but its aims are now much broader.
- 👍 Since the Arab Spring in 2011, it has been more proactive, backing UN action in Libya and suspending Syria over its repression of the protests.
- 👍 It is agreed in its support for Palestinians and has been successful at a cultural level across member states, for instance with shaping school curricula.
- 👎 However, it is badly split and decisions are only binding on members who voted for them, so has made very little progress towards its own aims.

ASEAN
- 👍 Originally formed to settle intra-region disputes and resist superpower influence, ASEAN was about security regionalism.
- 👍 Perhaps on the surface, it looks more like the EU than other regional blocs. It has developed three pillars: the ASEAN Political-Security Community, the ASEAN Economic Community and the ASEAN Socio-Cultural Community.
- 👎 However, it has remained purely an intergovernmental body as it has as its core principle the respect for state sovereignty.
- 👎 It is further hampered by differences in the political stability, economic development, values and religious beliefs of the member states.
- 👍 In 2017, it was negotiating the Regional Comprehensive Economic Partnership to establish a free trade bloc with its member states and China, Japan, South Korea, Australia, New Zealand and India. This would become the world's largest trading bloc.

Now try this

Why is further integration unlikely within ASEAN?

European integration

Since the Second World War, Europe has experienced a unique process of integration. This page looks at the factors that have fostered European integration.

European integration

Some view the eventual goal of European integration as a United States of Europe, based on the principle of federalism to tackle conflict between sovereign states in an international system. This idea of a federal Europe, seen in the ideas of French politicians Monnet (1888–1978) and Schuman (1886–1963), involves sovereignty being shared between European institutions and member states, each of them enjoying a sphere of autonomous policy jurisdiction. One of the key questions is the extent to which this has been achieved.

Jean Monnet: 'We are not forming coalitions of states, we are uniting men.'

Formation and the forces of integration

During the process of regional integration since 1945, European institutions have moved from regulation of the coal and steel industries to a much broader economic and political project. There were very specific historical pressures at the time of creation that have shaped and continue to shape the structure of those institutions:

- The key factor was the post-war need to reconcile the tensions and rivalry between France and Germany; this continues to influence the shaping of the EU.
- The structural, economic and social devastation caused by the war.
- The desire for a federal Europe and to limit the power of the nation-state.
- The need to build up Europe politically and economically to resist the USSR and communism and provide a market for US goods.

Since the 1980s, three new driving forces have emerged:

- The need to meet the challenges presented by globalisation.
- The desire to ensure peace in Europe by expanding the EU to incorporate the states transitioning from communism following the collapse of the USSR.
- Further political and economic integration to enable the EU to respond to crises, both current and future. Crises may be financial or related to health pandemics, migration, energy supplies or the environment.

European Coal and Steel Community

The **1951 Treaty of Paris** was the first step towards integration as it created the European Coal and Steel Community (ECSC).

It had two main aims:

1 To create a common market for coal and steel to ensure economic expansion, the growth of employment and a rising standard of living.

2 To strengthen Franco-German relations to prevent war and open the way to further integration.

In 1951, the ECSC comprised France, West Germany, Italy, Belgium, Luxembourg and the Netherlands.

Now try this

1 What is meant by the term 'federalism' in relation to the EU?
2 What are the historical circumstances that shaped the formation of European regionalism?

The development of the EU

You need to know about the development of the EU, its key institutions and its expansion.

Timeline

1957 Treaty of Rome
The **European Economic Community (EEC)** and **European Atomic Energy Community (Euratom)** are established. The EEC was committed to a common market for all goods and economic integration for its members

1986 The Single European Act to complete the common market by 1992; a response to globalisation

1951 Treaty of Paris
The **ECSC** is created – a coal and steel common market

1967 European Community is created by merging the ECSC, the EEC and Euratom

1993 Maastricht Treaty brings the **European Union** into existence. Moved beyond economic union to political union; a response to globalisation

Key institutions of the EU

Institution	Structure	Powers
The Council (of Ministers)	Ministers from 28 member states, each accountable to their own parliament. *Intergovernmental body/supranational body*	Important decisions such as new treaties or new members are made by unanimous decision. Most other decisions are made by Qualified Majority Voting (supranationalism; see page 281).
European Council	Presidents/prime ministers of member states meet four times per year. *Intergovernmental body*	Leadership and direction.
European Parliament	750 members, who are directly elected. *Supranational body*	Key powers include rejecting the EU budget and removing the European Commission. Law-making powers in certain policy areas.
European Commission	28 European Commissioners, one per state, working on behalf of the EU. *Supranational body*	Proposes legislation, implementation of policy, including guarding EU treaties to check they are respected.
European Court of Justice (ECJ)	One judge from each state, working on behalf of ECJ. *Supranational body*	Interpret and enforce EU law and treaties. EU law has primacy over national law, as in the Factortame case.
European Central Bank (ECB)	19 of the 28 states have adopted the euro. *Supranational body*	To safeguard the value of the euro as price stability is seen as key to economic growth and job creation.

Now try this

What is the difference between the Council of Ministers and the European Council?

Key treaties of the EU

You need to know about the key treaties of the EU and how they have deepened integration, and also the unique case of economic and monetary union.

Key treaties and the deepening of integration

The deepening of the EU has seen the powers and policy areas of European institutions gradually grow in a move from economic integration towards political integration:

> **1957 Treaty of Rome:** seen by many as the founding treaty as it commits to a common market, 'ever closer union' and establishes the Council of Ministers, the Commission, the Parliamentary Assembly (now European Parliament) and the Court of Justice.

> **1986 Single European Act:** revised the Treaty of Rome to complete the common market by changing the decision-making process. It changed voting on the Council of Ministers for certain policy areas to **Qualified Majority Voting (QMV)**. States' voting power is weighted by size and different majorities are needed for different decisions, removing the need for unanimous decisions in these areas, so reducing the power of the veto. More areas have been moved to QMV under the Treaties of **Maastricht 1992, Amsterdam 1997, Nice 2001 and Lisbon 2007**.

> **1992 Maastricht Treaty:** this is a key move towards political union as it adds to the European Community, a home affairs and social policy and a common foreign and security policy. It laid the ground work for the creation of an economic and monetary union with a single currency.

> **2007 Treaty of Lisbon:** in 2004, there was an attempt to create a European Constitution, to codify all main principles and ideas and to replace the existing treaties. Despite approval by heads of government, it was defeated in referenda in France and the Netherlands over fears of its impact on national sovereignty. Much of the Constitution was incorporated in the Lisbon Treaty, which further expanded the powers of the EU, including the creation of the post of High Representative for Foreign Affairs and Security Policy and the removal of the veto over climate change, energy security and emergency aid policy.

Economic and monetary union

The EU is unique among regional blocs in actively pursuing monetary union to create **the Eurozone**. Economic and monetary union on the surface appears to be about economic efficiency and providing price stability. On deeper inspection, it is clear it has deep political ramifications:

👍 Sovereignty over monetary policy is transferred to the ECB.

👍 Nation-states lose economic sovereignty as they must follow the stability rules over debt and deficits set by the ECB.

👍 The creation of a single currency increases the pressure for closer political union.

Eurozone crisis

Since 2009, the Eurozone has been in an ongoing crisis due to the debt crisis in five euro states and the banking crisis. These crises have gone hand in hand with low growth and falling competitiveness within the EU states.

- The inflexibility of monetary policy by the ECB has arguably worsened the crisis in countries like Greece and Spain, creating an age of debt and austerity, which is stirring up social tensions and a political backlash against further integration.

- Some in the EU have argued that the answer to the crisis is more integrated fiscal union, with powers over taxation and spending to ensure that the euro can survive and flourish.

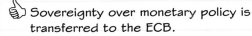

Now try this

How might the Eurozone crisis drive deeper integration?

Key debates about the EU

There are several key debates related to the EU: enlargement, Brexit and supranational vs intergovernmental approaches.

EU enlargement

Between 1951, when the ECSC was founded by six members, and 1995, a further nine states joined the EU. This included the UK, Denmark and the Republic of Ireland in 1973, who wanted to be part of the faster growing EEC, and Greece (1981), Spain and Portugal (1986), who emerged from dictatorships to become democracies. The collapse of the USSR was a key turning point, and has seen a further 13 states join the EU since 2004, most of them ex-Soviet bloc countries in Eastern Europe. This widening has increased the diversity of the states under the EU banner in terms of their economies, political structures and cultures, which makes decision-making slower, more cumbersome and so the EU lacks clear direction. This means that the process of widening has undermined the process of deepening. This **widening–deepening** raises the following questions:

1958	France, Germany, Italy, Luxembourg, Belgium, Netherlands
1973	The UK, Ireland, Denmark
1981	Greece
1986	Spain, Portugal
1995	Sweden, Austria, Finland
2004	Slovenia, Slovakia, Poland, Lithuania, Latvia, Hungary, Estonia, Cyprus, Malta, Czech Republic
2007	Romania, Bulgaria
2013	Croatia

EU membership by date.

Will the enlarged EU be able to effectively make decisions and have a coherent integration strategy?	Does diversity mean it is not possible to develop one-size-fits-all policies that suit all states?
The failure of the Constitutional Treaty of 2004 suggests not.	The monetary policy of the ECB has to work for the powerhouse economy of Germany and the debt-laden, struggling economies of Spain and Portugal.

Brexit

The UK's decision in 2016 to exit the EU will potentially have a large impact on the EU in a number of ways:

- It will increase the power of Germany within the EU.
- With Macron's election in France in 2017, it may lead to France and Germany striving for deeper integration of the EU.
- It may weaken the EU's global role as the UK is the foremost military power in the bloc and possesses considerable soft power globally.
- It may cause a possible domino effect in leading other EU states, such as Austria, Denmark and Sweden holding their own referenda on membership, weakening integration and in, the most extreme scenario, the disintegration of the EU.

Supranational vs intergovernmental approaches

The EU is unlike other regional blocs in that it has developed a closer political union. This is clear in the development of **supranational** authority, where institutions can impose certain decisions and rules on member states. This can be seen in the Commission, the Parliament, the ECJ, the ECB for Eurozone states and the extension of QMV in the Council of Ministers. These are examples of federalism and can be seen to be replacing the role of the nation-state. However, the EU still maintains an **intergovernmental** approach, where states remain in control of the process and the institutions are just there to help decision-making between states. This is the case in the European Council and in the Council of Ministers, with key decisions such as admitting new members, agreeing new treaties and in foreign policy. So, the EU can be seen to have a mixed intergovernmental and supranational approach.

Now try this

1 Why does the widening of the EU undermine its deepening?
2 What is Qualified Majority Voting and why is it important?

The EU as a global actor

There is considerable debate around whether the EU is a **global actor**, with a significant role in global politics.

The EU as a global actor

The EU is seen by some as a significant global actor; however, it faces numerous constraints and obstacles:

EU as global actor	Constraints and obstacles
Economic influence • It is the world's largest single market, with a population of 510 million people, a currency that covers 19 states and accounts for 23 per cent of the world's GDP.	**Brexit** • This will weaken the EU economically with the removal of the second largest economy – the UK. • It will reduce its structural influence as the UK is such a powerful economy, and the EU will lose one of its two member states who sit on the UNSC. • The loss of soft power (the UK is ranked second in soft power in the world). • The UK is the largest military power in the EU.
Structural influence • The Commission negotiates trade deals with other regional blocs and states. It is the top trading partner of 80 states, while the USA is the top partner of 20 states. • It is the only regional bloc represented at the G7, G20 and WTO.	**Eurozone crisis** • The crisis weakens the EU's economic influence and structural power as it is struggling to deal with the crisis. It needs to stabilise the euro and generate economic recovery to make it more attractive.
Political influence • The establishment of the Common Foreign and Security Policy (CFSP) in the 1992 Maastricht Treaty and the creation of EU High Representative for Foreign Affairs in the 2007 Lisbon Treaty. • Soft power. For example, the diplomatic role in helping broker the 2008 peace deal between Russia and Georgia, deploying EU monitors to observe. The development of the Paris Agreement (2015) on the environment and key player in bringing Iran to the table for the Iran Nuclear Deal.	**Common Foreign and Security Policy** • Decisions in this area need to be unanimous, representing the member states' desire to maintain these powers as a key element of state sovereignty. • Splits over policy direction over whether EU defence policy should operate outside or inside NATO. • Splits over policy, with only 23 states recognising Kosovo as a state, and disagreement about conflict in Iraq. • The failure to develop a significant military arm of the EU.
Military influence • Since 2003, over 30 civilian and military missions, becoming a key security provider. For example, protecting refugees in Mali and the Central African Republic and fighting piracy off Somalia and the Horn of Africa. EU Operation Sophia, a naval mission in the Mediterranean, was established in 2015 to tackle the people-smuggling industry.	**Military influence** • The EU can mobilise a rapid reaction force, but its lack of a standing army reduces its ability to be seen as a serious global player on the world stage.

Now try this

1   What is meant by the term 'global actor'?

2   Why has the Common Foreign and Security Policy been seen as ineffective?

Regionalism and global issues

Regionalism is a recognition of the shared interests of states. The resolution of contemporary issues that one country cannot achieve alone may be achieved through collective action.

Global issues

Contemporary global issues are transnational in nature as they have impacts both regionally and globally. Does regionalism help to resolve those issues or potentially make them worse?

👍 **Cooperation:** regional bodies are political spaces where states can cooperate for their mutual benefit. For example, agreeing regional environmental regulations. Collective action has a greater chance of success than individual states acting on their own.

👍 **Interdependence:** regionalism creates growing interdependence between states that will lessen the chance of conflict.

👍 **Global:** issues such as climate change, poverty and free trade are both global and regional issues. Regional cooperation becomes the basis for wider global cooperation as seen in the EU's role in the Paris Agreement (see page 260 for more on this agreement).

👍 **Free trade:** economic blocs should drive economic growth and development, reducing economic instability and poverty within regions.

👍 **Rule-based system:** regional blocs are part of an emerging rule-based international system that has collective security (to ensure peace) and international law (protects human rights) at its core.

👎 **State sovereignty:** states pursue their own national interest and will resist binding agreements that are not in their interest. For example, the tragedy of the commons in tackling environmental issues (see page 262).

👎 **Deepening integration:** as economic regionalism becomes political regionalism, individuals feel a loss of democratic power and that their national culture and identity is under threat. This may lead to the rise of political extremism, social tensions and conflict within regional blocs.

👎 **Regions not states:** if regions are replacing states as the key actors in global politics, then they exhibit the same desire for power, survival and security, which leads to conflict.

👎 **Free trade:** may create greater inequality between regions and within regions and greater economic instability. This is likely to increase the chances of conflict.

👎 **International law:** the sovereignty of states is being undermined. By increasing the chance of intervention in other states, it increases the chance of conflict.

🔍 Case study **Air pollution**

The 2016 Clean Air Programme sets national reduction commitments for five key pollutants, which have significant impacts on the environment and human health. This will improve air quality across the EU in a way that could not be achieved independently, because:

- it stops member states racing to gain competitive advantage by cutting environmental regulations as the EU ensures a level playing field for businesses through Europe-wide environmental standards
- air pollution is a transnational issue and so requires concerted action
- there is a practical advantage of a joint approach where high levels of scientific and administrative work are needed.

🔍 Case study **Climate change**

The EU has played a key role in the negotiations about tackling climate change. It was the first major economy to submit its nationally determined contributions (NDC), setting itself a target to reduce emissions by at least 40 per cent by 2030 compared to 1990. It used its power to build a coalition of developed and developing countries to set a high target, which shaped the success of the Paris Agreement.

Recently, the EU has criticised Trump's withdrawal and is looking instead to build global partnerships with US states and corporations. The EU and China have also strengthened their positions, jointly agreeing to raise $100bn by 2020 for developing states to tackle climate change.

Now try this

What is meant by a 'race to the bottom', and how does regionalism stop it?

Realism in global politics

Theories help us to explain, understand and judge the world that we live in. The two main theories that help us understand global politics are **realism** and **liberalism**.

Overview of realism

Realism has been the dominant theory of global politics, and claims to have its roots in classical political thinkers such as Thomas Hobbes or Jean-Jacques Rousseau. Realism is **state** centric, arguing that states operate in a system of international anarchy. This makes the international system a **self-help** system, where it is rational for states to compete for power and security in order to **survive**.

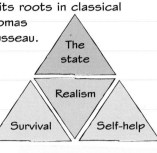

The three S elements of realism.

The state

Realists see the state as the key actor in global politics, and the distinctive feature of the state is sovereignty (see page 233 for more on sovereignty). Since the Treaty of Westphalia (revise this key agreement on page 232), the state has been the cornerstone of international relations, forming the building blocks of most international organisations like the UN, which is based on the sovereign equality of all members. At the same time, the primacy of states is central to global politics through the principle of non-intervention in the internal affairs of sovereign states, as laid out in Article 2 (7) of the UN Charter.

Classical realism and the state

Classical realists, particularly Hans Morgenthau, base their theory on a pessimistic view of human nature that draws on the political ideas of Thomas Hobbes (read about Hobbes's ideas on page 43). This view has three key elements:

 Human nature is fixed and unchanging.

 Human nature is driven by 'a perpetual and restless desire of power after power, that ceaseth only in death', rather than intellect and reason (Hobbes's *Leviathan*).

 In Hobbes's state of nature, all individuals have a right to everything and there are no rules to limit behaviour. In this state, the desire for power leads to 'a war of all against all' (Hobbes's *De Cive*).

In global politics, as there is no world government, there is a state of nature which is **anarchic**. The state, as created by humanity, shows the same flaws as humans in its ceaseless desire to dominate. This is the main cause of international conflict. As Morgenthau states in his 1948 work, *Politics Among Nations: The Struggle for Power and Peace*, 'international politics, like all politics, is a struggle for power'.

The state and national interest

In its dealings in global politics, the state is a rational actor that acts in the **national interest**. Realist diplomacy means the state has only the best interests of its citizens as a guiding principle and should ignore any supposed wider ethics of the international community as that community does not exist. Although realists recognise that war is sometimes necessary, it must meet the standard of advancing the national interest. This means a state should only engage in a conflict or intervention in another state if it ensures its own national security or other vital interests.

For example, Morgenthau opposed the Vietnam War on this basis, and 33 international relations scholars took out an advert in the *New York Times* in 2002 titled 'War with Iraq is **not** in America's national interest'. The reasons given by the scholars included the predictions that the war would spread instability in the Middle East, threatening American interests, and that there was no plausible exit plan so the USA would be embroiled in Iraq at significant cost for years to come.

Now try this

Why is international politics a struggle for power in classical realism?

Realism in international anarchy

In realist theory, **international anarchy** describes a system operating in the absence of a world government. This does not mean chaos, but it does have implications for the behaviour of states.

International anarchy

In 1979, Kenneth Waltz published *Theory of International Politics*, which took realism in a different direction from Morgenthau. Instead of focusing on human nature to explain the behaviour of states, Waltz developed Hobbes's view about **international anarchy** into the theory of **neo-realism**. Hobbes wrote that states 'for their own security, enlarge their dominions upon all pretences of danger and fear of invasion' and 'endeavour as much as they can, to subdue and weaken their neighbours by open force, and secret arts' (Hobbes's *Leviathan*).

Waltz argued that this system of international anarchy creates the structural problem that there is no higher power to prevent the use of force, so states can only ensure their survival through self-help.

- A state must provide for its own security, by increasing its power (normally military power).
- By doing so, it creates greater insecurity in other states as to what it intends to do with that power.
- States aim to increase their power relative to other states, so any form of international cooperation is unlikely. There is limited interest in treaties, laws or policies that benefit all states as the only issue for each state is whether it increases its own power versus other states ('relative gain').

(Thomas Hobbes (1588–1679) was an influential conservative thinker. For more about his ideas, see page 43.)

The implications of anarchy

- States cannot rely on international organisations, such as the UN or international law.
- The law or the decisions of international bodies cannot be enforced as there is no world government.
- States, especially powerful states, will evade the justice of international courts, as can be seen through America, China and Russia refusing to accept the jurisdiction of the ICC.
- States can and will ignore the UN. For example, the UK and USA's decision to go to war in Iraq. At the same time, powerful states will use their structural power to influence the workings of international organisations like the UN, the WTO and the World Bank.

The inevitability of war

For **classical realists**, war is inevitable due to the desire for power ingrained in human nature and the state. As states pursue their national interest, it will naturally bring them into conflict. On the other hand, **neo-realists** argue that the structure of the international system means that, where states believe they can ensure their survival by entering into conflict with another state, they will. Here, neo-realism splits into two groups:

```
Neo-realism
```

 Offensive realists: states, particularly great powers, are motivated by the desire to acquire more power to improve their rank in the global hierarchy and so states aim to be a global hegemon, as hegemony is the ultimate form of security. As great power states aim to maximise their power to ensure survival, war is inevitable.

 Defensive realists: states are motivated by the desire to maximise security not power, so only need the necessary amount of power to maintain their position in the global hierarchy. States are reluctant to go to war but will if necessary.

Now try this

1 What is the key difference between classical realism and neo-realism?
2 What is the key difference between offensive and defensive realism?

Conflict and the balance of power

From the realist view of international anarchy emerges the **security dilemma**, which increases tension and conflicts between states.

Security dilemma

One state increases its military strength to ensure its own security, which is interpreted by other states as aggressive.	→ ←	This creates fear in other states, leading them to increase their own military strength, which decreases the security of the first state in turn.

The result is a spiral of fear and tension, making insecurity an integral part of the international system of anarchy. This can cause weaker states, with the aim of survival, to enter into alliances with other weaker states to create a **balance of power** against a rising or great power. This process of balancing is crucial to neo-realists' understanding of why the anarchical international system is not one of constant, open warfare.

Balance of power

Despite the insecurity and tension, realists believe that conflict can be prevented by a **balance of power** (see page 267 for more on international polarity). For **classical realists**, balance must be carefully constructed by the diplomacy and policy of state leaders. For **neo-realists**, balance is the result of the structure of international anarchy and the distribution of power in global politics. The structural tendency for states to form a balance explains realists' interest in polarity, power as capability and their perception that hard power is the most crucial form of power. Polarity is seen in the following ways:

1. **Unipolarity:** a global hegemon can produce peace and stability as it is secure, and so does not need to start wars to gain more power; the lesser powers can't challenge it, so they can relax and accept the situation.

2. **Bipolar world:** this structure is likely to create a balance of power, where there is less chance of miscalculation and less opportunity for war than under a multipolar system.

3. **Multipolar system:** where there are three or more great powers and there is no potential hegemon with a power advantage. This is more balanced and peaceful than an unbalanced multipolar system but less peaceful than a bipolar system.

4. **Unbalanced multipolar system:** where the potential hegemon, with a considerable power advantage over other great powers, will not be satisfied that they have enough power so initiate war and the other great powers will fear the potential hegemon's rise so take greater risks to enhance their security. This system is very unstable and prone to war.

China

The rise of China poses interesting questions for realists. With its fast growth, it is a potential hegemon and threat to its immediate neighbours, especially Japan, Russia and India, and the USA in the long term.

Offensive realists would expect China to try to maximise its power gap with its neighbours and push the USA out of the Asia-Pacific region. The USA is unlikely to tolerate this and is likely to aim to contain China, much like it did the USSR, while China's neighbours (Singapore, Vietnam and South Korea) are likely to form a coalition with the USA to balance China. This could see the emergence of an intense security dilemma with real potential for conflict.

For **defensive realists**, the growth of China is likely to create less instability as China is unlikely to pursue hegemony as it knows this may provoke the USA and its neighbours to balance them or even try to crush them. China's aims are likely to be more limited and based around security, not power. This cautious approach is made more likely because Russia, India and the USA have nuclear weapons and it has been argued that Japan could quickly go nuclear if it wished.

Now try this

Why is the unbalanced multipolar system considered so dangerous?

Liberalism in global politics

Liberalism (see pages 46–55) has been the main challenger to realism and its historical roots can be traced back to thinkers like John Locke (see page 53 for an overview on Locke's views). Liberalism challenges the power politics of realism in favour of compromise, cooperation and peace.

Liberal theory and human nature

Liberals, such as Locke, generally hold an optimistic view of human nature, because they argue that humans are guided by reason. Humans are still self-seeking and self-interested, but their reason means that 'no one ought to harm another in his life, health, liberty, or possessions' (John Locke, *Two Treatises of Civil Government*). Reason also leads to disputes and disagreements being settled by discussion and negotiation. This view of humanity means that humans in the state of nature can live in peace, harmony and mutual respect, and so the same is true for states in global politics. The consequences of this are that:

- war and conflict is the last resort, justifiable in self-defence or to end oppression; war is seen as a failure of discussion and negotiation
- the moral aspect of reason means that all humans should treat each other with respect; this principle underpins the idea of **universal human rights** (read about this principle on page 253).

Possibility of harmony and balance

Liberals, like realists, accept that states are important actors within the international system. However, they believe the following:

- Non-state actors are also important and that realists underestimate the chances of cooperation.
- The international framework is one of harmony as it provides lots of opportunities for states and non-state actors to work in cooperation to pursue goals that are beneficial to all.
- This underpins the creation of **global governance**, like the UN and ICC, as well as the emergence of international law.
- Unlike realists, liberals view the nature of government within the state to be crucial in how the state behaves. This has given rise to the **democratic peace thesis** (see page 270), which sees the possibility of harmony and balance.

The democratic peace thesis

Central to this thesis is that democratic states do not go to war with other democratic states. This idea underpinned the Western policy since the Cold War of spreading democracy, and especially in the eastward expansion of the EU. The belief is that democratic government has benefits:

👍 Democratic representation means that government is constrained by public opinion, which is generally anti-war as it is normally the people who suffer.

👍 Democracies are built on the principles of negotiation, compromise and discussion, and so use this approach rather than the use of force to resolve conflict between them.

👍 Democracies are based on a healthy civil society, with civil rights and liberties, and view other democratic states with the same principles as natural friends, not threats.

The End of History

In his 1992 book *The End of History and the Last Man*, Francis Fukuyama argued that the universalisation of liberal democracy and capitalism was inevitable following the fall of the USSR and would become the final form of human government. This predicts a peaceful era of liberal democracy, where war is very unlikely. In the 21st century, it appears that Fukuyama could not have been more wrong. Capitalism is under threat after the global economic crash of 2007–2009 and the rise of China. Liberalism and democracy is under threat by the rise of autocratic states and hard-right governments who wish to roll back basic rights. Finally, peace has not broken out, with international terrorism and civil wars becoming more commonplace.

Now try this

Why are relations between democratic states seen as peaceful?

Complex interdependence and global governance

Complex interdependence is a theory that sees a growing interconnectedness between states, which means decisions taken by one state will have impacts on others (see page 265 for an overview on smart and soft power). This growth of interconnectedness is linked to the move towards cooperation, integration and a reduction in conflict.

Complex interdependence

Complex interdependence, a theory developed by Joseph Nye and Robert Keohane, offers an alternative model of global politics to realism. It has three main characteristics:

 Multiple channels connect societies: this challenges the realist idea that states are the predominant actors in global politics. Multiple channels mean that there are not only state-to-state relations, but also relations between states and non-state actors, as well as between non-state actors. These relations are all transnational.

 The absence of hierarchy among issues: military power and state security does not dominate the international agenda. Multiple issues can dominate at different times (human rights, poverty or the environment) and inadequate policy coordination on these issues has significant costs. This drives greater cooperation and integration.

 Military force plays a minor role: the importance of hard power, the immediate fear of attack and the security dilemma are in decline within global politics, where there is complex interdependence, as in Western Europe. States tend to prioritise making money, not making war.

Likelihood of global governance

The likelihood of global governance is explained by liberals in two different ways:

Social contract theory

Thinkers such as Locke use this theory to explain that humans in the state of nature come together to form a limited government in order to escape injustices. Applying this theory to global politics explains why states should contract together to form a rules-based international system. This would be based on the rule of law, collective security through international organisations and the development of international law, which will safeguard states from the problems associated with an anarchical international system.

Neo-liberal theory

Modern liberals argue that international organisations grow out of complex interdependence. In a world with multiple channels, an absence of hierarchy of issues and the decline of military force, international organisations play a key role in political bargaining. They help set the international agenda by defining which issues are the most important and grouping issues together, build coalitions to tackle those issues and provide a forum where political initiatives and links between states can develop. Each state is willing to cooperate as it is in its interest to do so. The states, by working together, will make absolute gains and this is more important than their fears about relative gains.

Impact and growth of international organisations

International organisations have grown considerably since the Second World War as there are now more areas where it is rational for states to work together. However, cooperation is not always easy, especially where there is the fear that states may act in their own best interests rather than upholding international agreements. International organisations build stronger bonds and trust between states to reduce this fear, they provide mechanisms by which disputes can be settled without the use of force and provide collective security, which ensures that conflict is avoided as the cost will be too high and the gains too small for aggressor states.

Now try this

What are the three main characteristics of complex interdependence?

Realism vs liberalism

You need to know about the key divisions between realism and liberalism.

Divisions between realism and liberalism

	Realism	Liberalism
Human nature	Pessimistic about human nature, seeing it as fixed, driven by a restless lust for power rather than reason or intellect. States reflect human nature, so cooperation is unlikely while rivalry and conflict is inevitable.	Optimistic about human nature, which is self-interested, but guided by reason. States use reason not force, cooperation not conflict. There is a moral dimension to both human and state behaviour.
Power	Survival is the main aim of the state, so it must seek power to protect itself. The realist approach focuses on hard power, especially military power, as the most important type of power in a self-help system.	Liberals argue that military power has become less reliable and therefore focus on the rise of soft power. The emergence of international organisations, economic globalisation and the spread of democracy reduce the likelihood of conflict so military power is in decline.
Order/security/ conflict	International anarchy is the constant of the international system, but war is not. The balance of power is key. A global hegemon is seen by some as a guarantee of peace, while some see a bipolar world as the most peaceful. An unbalanced multipolar system is the most dangerous.	The international system is one of complex interdependence. This brings order and security as it lessens the chance of conflict between states. There are channels to resolve disputes and the cost of conflict in an interdependent world outweighs its benefits. States are now focused on trade not conflict.
International organisations	Realists are sceptical about international organisations as global politics is the struggle for power. States are only interested in relative gains to increase their power versus others, so there is no compulsion to cooperate. In **hegemonic stability theory** (read more about this theory on page 267), a global hegemon can enforce the rules of international organisations, making them effective.	International organisations are products of complex interdependence and reflect the idea that states can gain more by working together than competing. States are focused on absolute, not relative, gains. International organisations are a forum to build trust and links between states and do not require a hegemonic state to be effective.
Significance of states	States are the predominant actors in global politics, with sovereignty as their defining trait. The main aim of states is survival. States differ in terms of power but the nature of their government is irrelevant to global politics. Globalisation is created by the states in their own interests and international organisations only have influence as far as states allow them to.	The nature of government of the state is crucial in defining its behaviour. It sees the state as an important actor in global politics but not the only actor. The rise of non-state actors, international organisation and globalisation means the power of the state is in decline.

Now try this

What is the difference between relative and absolute gains?

The anarchical society

Hedley Bull's *The Anarchical Society* (1977) became the key text of the 'English School' of international relations. His theory is an integration of neo-realist and liberal thinking.

Anarchy in the global system

In line with neo-realism, Bull argues that the starting point of global politics is the existence of states, where states are equal, independent and sovereign. They are not under any higher political authority so there is anarchy in the global system. However, Bull takes issue with the idea that global politics should be understood in 'Hobbesian' terms, where global politics is a cold, hard and brutal struggle for power between self-interested states.

Anarchical society and society of states

States become conscious of their common interests, such as limiting the chances of war and maintaining the stability of the international system, and values.

⬇

This leads states to form a society, where they see themselves as bound together by a common set of rules in their dealing with each other, and share the working of international institutions.

⬇

The common rules and international institutions, such as international law and diplomacy, regulate the anarchical society. They bring an element of order to global politics which is necessary for security and prosperity, whilst preserving state sovereignty.

'The Clash of Civilisations'

Samuel Huntington's article, 'The Clash of Civilisations?', published in 1993, also challenges liberalism and realism. Huntington argued that post-Cold War, the state remains the principal actor in global politics but there would be cooperation within civilisations and conflict between civilisations. Civilisations are defined based on religion and culture, and Huntington predicts growing conflict between the declining West and the Islamic world, as well as the declining West and the rising Sinic (East Asia) world, built around Chinese cultural values. Huntington appears to offer a theory that predicted the rising tensions in the 21st century between the West and elements of the Islamic world. The challenges to this idea include the failure to recognise or take into account:

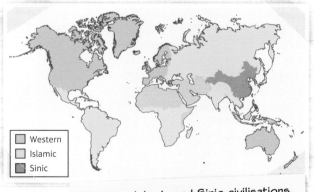

Western, Islamic and Sinic civilisations.

- the vast divisions within civilisations

- that most conflicts take place between states within a civilisation

- the impacts of globalisation, especially cultural globalisation which flattens cultural differences.

Now try this

How can the anarchical society be seen to draw on both neo-realism and liberalism?

Globalisation and global governance

 Synoptic link You need to be able to recognise and apply the tension between realism and liberalism to sovereignty and globalisation (pages 233–241) and global governance (pages 242–252).

The state and globalisation

Realism		Liberalism
• The state remains the predominant actor in global politics. • The power of the state has increased in response to 9/11 and the global financial crisis, 2007–2009. • Sceptical about globalisation. Globalisation is made by states for states, and works to the benefit of powerful states.	**VS**	• The importance of the state is declining as interdependence grows. • Positive about globalisation. Economic globalisation increases wealth, benefits everyone, and promotes political and cultural globalisation. • Growing interdependence will bring peace and cooperation.

Case study: Free trade

Globalisation has been seen as an unstoppable force for the last 25 years, particularly in terms of economic globalisation, which can be explained by liberal theory. The signing of CETA in 2016, a free-trade deal between the EU and Canada to remove 98 per cent of tariffs, is just the latest example. Despite this, there appears to have been a return of the state, as realism predicts, with the collapse of the Doha round of WTO talks, the USA withdrawing from the Trans-Pacific Partnership, the Transatlantic Trade and Investment Partnership free trade deals and aiming to dismantle and renegotiate NAFTA, while the UK has voted to leave the EU.

Global governance: political and economic

Realism		Liberalism
• Sceptical about global governance. • In an anarchical system, there is little prospect for harmony and cooperation as states are focused on relative gains. • Global governance is a potential threat to state sovereignty. • Global governance is used by powerful states for their own gains.	**VS**	• Positive about global governance. • It promotes peace and cooperation. • Economic governance promotes the free market, which creates wealth that benefits all. • States cooperate as it is in their interest to do so as the focus is on absolute gains. • Cooperation brings mutual benefits.

Case study: The 2007–2009 global financial crisis

The 2007–2009 global financial crisis and recession was the deepest crisis in global capitalism since the 1930s, with a fall in global GDP and the volume of world trade. The crisis can be seen as a failure of global economic governance as it had overseen the development of deregulated financial markets that was at the heart of the crisis. The G20 took immediate action to develop a unified strategy in line with liberal theory, where states cut interest rates, boosted demand through fiscal stimulus and committed not to return to protectionism. This allowed for a more effective global recovery than after the Wall Street Crash of 1929. Yet this unified approach quickly disintegrated as realism predicts, with many states promoting austerity, not stimulus. The development of the Eurozone crisis in 2011 then further challenged global governance. The IMF, the World Bank and the WTO look weakened organisations, unable to move beyond the Washington Consensus or reform themselves to more effectively represent the economic power shift to the BRICS.

Now try this

How does realism approach recent developments in free trade?

Global governance and regionalism

> **Synoptic link** You need to be able to recognise and apply the tension between realism and liberalism to human rights and environmental governance (pages 253–263) and regionalism and the EU (pages 274–284).

Global governance: human rights and environmental

Realism
• Sceptical about international law.
• International law has to recognise the principle of state sovereignty to be legitimate.
• Human rights law, which promotes individual rights over states' rights, undermines sovereignty.
• Supranational law undermines state sovereignty.

Liberalism
• Positive about international law.
• International law deepens interdependence and trust between states.
• International law is an expression of the mutual interests of states and brings mutual benefits.

The Paris Agreement, 2015 (Case study)

'As of today, the United States will cease all implementation of the non-binding Paris accord and the draconian financial and economic burdens the agreement imposes on our country.' (Donald Trump, June 2017)

By November 2017, 168 countries had ratified the Paris Agreement (see page 260) on climate change, which highlights the debate about global governance and international law. The Agreement allows for mutual action by states for their mutual benefit in line with liberal thinking. But it is non-binding as states set their own targets and there is no enforcement mechanism; so it respects state sovereignty. Trump, however, takes a realist approach in following his policy of 'America first'; in effect, the deal is not in the USA's national interest. The US withdrawal will weaken interdependence and trust between states, and may have significant impacts on the USA's soft power as the rest of the world moves forward on the deal without them.

Regionalism and the EU

Realism
• Cooperation at an international level is limited and this applies to regionalism.
• Such cooperation is rejected as states are concerned with relative gains.
• The emergence of supranational institutions is particularly difficult for realists to explain as they undermine sovereignty.

Liberalism
• Cooperation is much more likely as states are focused on absolute gains.
• The mutual benefits of political, economic and/or security regionalism explain why states engage in integration and cooperation.

The EU (Case study)

There has been a deepening of the EU since the 1986 Single European Act, with increasing integration such as the rise of QMV, monetary union and the emergence of a Common Foreign and Security Policy. At the same time, the EU has widened with its eastward expansion. This fits with liberal thinking and raises questions as to how realism can explain this **widening–deepening**. However, the Eurozone crisis and the Brexit vote seem to have halted further integration, with some predicting this could see further disintegration of the EU project in line with the realist approach.

> **Now try this**

Does liberalism or realism explain the widening and the deepening of the EU more effectively?

Had a look ☐   Nearly there ☐   Nailed it! ☐

Power and developments

There are tensions between realism and liberalism around power and developments in global politics.

Synoptic link You need to be able to recognise and apply the tension between realism and liberalism to human rights and environmental governance power and developments (pages 264–273).

Power and developments

Realism	Liberalism
• The balance of power and hard power are important.	• Bipolarity breeds tension, rivalry and an emphasis on military power.
• They believe in hegemonic stability theory, which argues a hegemon can and will enforce the rules of international organisations.	• Multipolar systems tend towards greater cooperation and interdependence.
• A bipolar world is safer than a multipolar world.	• Liberals place an emphasis on the rise of soft power.
• An unbalanced multipolar world is the most unstable world.	• Complex interdependence brings stability, peace and cooperation.

VS

📖 Case study The rise of China

The rise of China has led offensive realists like John Mearsheimer to see the future as an unbalanced multipolar world, marked by deep instability. The growing economic power of China will naturally lead to a growing desire for military power and the ability to control the Asia Pacific region. This could lead to increased conflict with Japan, Russia and India, as well as numerous weaker nations with whom China has territorial disputes. This rising power will challenge the USA, which has been strengthening military ties across Asia since 2010 to contain China, creating the possibility of war between the two powers.

However, the rise of China is taking place in a world of complex interdependence according to liberal theory, where China is locked into the global market, limiting its appetite for conflict. China's growing interdependence with the world economy means any conflict would have enormous economic losses and repercussions. China's military power is also a long way behind the USA

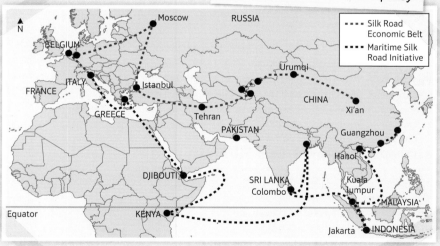

China's One Belt, One Road policy

···· Silk Road Economic Belt
▬▬ Maritime Silk Road Initiative

so it seems likely that China will continue to focus on economic power and soft power, leading to a peaceful rise. This can be seen in the One Belt, One Road policy of China which will invest $900bn in infrastructure in Asia and beyond to promote deeper economic cooperation. In essence, this is an attempt by China to increase its global economic and political leadership role. This is further reflected by the growing role China plays in international organisations and frameworks such as the UN, the G20 and the Paris Agreement, which fits with the liberal understanding of global politics.

Now try this

Define the One Belt, One Road policy.

Exam skills 1: Section A

This question will help you to revise for **Section A** of your A Level **Paper 3** exam. The first question you will encounter is the **comparative** question. This will ask you to compare two political elements, such as institutions, organisations, practices or issues, from sections 1–5 of Global politics.

Section A

- Section A of your Paper 3 exam consists of two 12-mark questions and you will have to choose **one** of them to answer.
- You will be assessed on AO1 and AO2 skills, with each skill being worth six marks.
- You must make reference to both elements in your answer.
- You should aim to spend around 15 minutes on your answer.

Assessment objectives

- **AO1 knowledge and understanding.** You need to express what you know and show you understand how it relates to the question you are answering.
- **AO2 analysis.** You need to show how the political aspect you are examining can be broken down and how it relates to the question. You should show comparisons, similarities, differences and/or parallels between the two political elements.

Command word: Examine

You need to look at the aspect of politics named in the question. You need to make a comparison between the two political elements, showing similarities and differences in how they deal with this aspect.

Planning

It is not really necessary to plan a 12-mark question. However, picking the right question is crucial. You could make a very brief list of three or four bullet points to identify the factor you will discuss in each paragraph to ensure you have enough factors to discuss before you begin.

Worked example

This question does not need an introduction.

1 Examine the main issues relating to UN Special Tribunals and the International Criminal Court's ability to deal with human rights abuses. **(12 marks)**

The key word here is 'issues' – and looking to explore any similarities or differences between the issues that affect both institutions.

A key issue that surrounds both Special Tribunals and the International Criminal Court (ICC) is that they are seen by some states to exhibit a form of Western imperialism. The International Criminal Tribunal for the former Yugoslavia is based on events in a transitioning country, while the International Criminal Tribunal for Rwanda is based on events in a developing country. It has been alleged by the African Union that the ICC shows a similar bias as it has concentrated on prosecuting black African leaders from developing states, such as Thomas Lubanga and Laurent Gbabgo, rather than tackling alleged human rights abuses by Western states or their allies. In both cases, the courts and human rights are seen as based on Western values and ideals and are used to enforce these values on countries that are seen as backward in Western eyes. This has undermined the legitimacy of the Courts in tackling human rights abuses...

At the beginning of each paragraph, clearly identify the factor that you are going to discuss – in this case, 'Western imperialism'.

The student has identified an issue that is seen as a major criticism of these courts in how they deal with human rights.

Using examples is important, but they must have a little explanation to make them relevant. Here, the focus is on how the examples illustrate the bias of the ICC in the eyes of the African Union.

Try to avoid summing up a paragraph by repeating the question. Here, the student has drawn together how the same controversy affects both institutions.

This worked example continues on the next page.

Exam skills 2: Section A
continued...

Here, we continue looking at **Section A** of your A Level **Paper 3** exam and the question you were asked on page 295. Your answer to this question is likely to be about two sides in length in your exam booklet.

Comparison

A 12-mark question should identify three or four points of **comparison**. It is important that in each paragraph you explicitly **show** the comparison. Make sure you include reference to both elements in the question.

Answering the question

A key part of analysis is making sure you are actually answering the question set. You must show you can relate your issues to both the stated institutions. In this case, while 'issues' was the factor, the ability of both institutions to tackle human rights abuses is the analytical focus. Describing what issues they have is AO1; showing how this affects the Tribunals' and Court's ability to tackle human rights abuses is AO2.

Worked example

... The speed and cost of prosecutions is a major issue that limits the ability of the Court's to successfully protect human rights. The International Criminal Tribunal for the former Yugoslavia took over 24 years to bring about 90 prosecutions and the total cost looks like it will run to over $2bn. The ICC took over ten years to bring its first successful prosecution. The absence of major powers such as the USA, China and Russia means that the high cost of the Court is an increased burden on the other member states. The speed of the Court undermines its legitimacy and effectiveness in dealing with human rights abuses. The ongoing cost of the Tribunals into Rwanda and Yugoslavia were time limited and so cost limited. However, the ICC is permanent and the ongoing cost and lack of value for money has led to member states looking to cut the budget, which will only serve to further reduce the ability of the Court to tackle human rights issues in the future...

 Read the question and the partial student answer on page 295 again before continuing below.

 Most of your paragraphs will follow the same basic structure once you get into the flow of an essay. In this case, identify a controversy and compare and contrast its impact on the two institutions.

You must ensure your paragraphs are on different points. In this paragraph, speed and cost are seen to undermine the ability of the Court to tackle human rights issues.

 This paragraph also shows how the differing nature of the Court (permanent/temporary) means the issue has different impacts.

 For each paragraph, ask yourself
- ✓ Does this paragraph deal with a clear and unique factor?
- ✓ Have I shown an explicit comparison?
- ✓ Have I used a relevant example?
- ✓ Does my paragraph relate to the question?

To complete this answer, the third paragraph could cover the issue of the impact on the Courts of state sovereignty. A key focus might be the difficulty that the ICC has had in getting all states to sign up to it due to the conflict between the Court and sovereignty. Remember, this question does not need a conclusion.

Exam skills 3: Section B

This question will help you to revise for **Section B** of your A Level **Paper 3** exam. This section consists of **one compulsory question**. It is worth 12 marks and should be structured in roughly the same way as Section A (see pages 295–296). The key difference here is that you must deploy your **comparative theories** to help explain your answer.

Comparative theories

These are political theories that help to explain why similarities or differences exist in global politics. The key theories are:

✓ realism (see page 285)

✓ liberalism (see page 288).

Synopticity

In this question, you are expected to make links between comparative theories and the content in Component 1: Core political ideas (see pages 36–67). To do well, you should draw any comparison back to your study of conservatism, liberalism and socialism where appropriate. You can link back to the idea as a whole or to the key ideas of individual thinkers, such as Locke or Hobbes.

Worked example

2 Analyse the disagreements between liberals and realists over the likelihood of war and conflict in global politics. **(12 marks)**

In your answer you must discuss any relevant core political ideas.

In analysing the likelihood of war and conflict in global politics, both realists and liberals turn to human nature to enable them to understand the behaviour of states. Classical realists, like Morgenthau, are pessimistic about human nature and draw heavily on the thinking of Thomas Hobbes. In line with Hobbes, they see human nature as driven by a restless desire for power, not intellect and reason. As states are created by humanity, they exhibit the same traits as human nature in their constant desire to dominate and this can only lead to war and conflict between states. In contrast, liberal theory has an optimistic rather than pessimistic view of human nature. Drawing on liberalism, liberals view states, like humans, as self-interested but also guided by intellect and reason. This means that there is a moral dimension to human behaviour and relationships between states are built on reason, not force, leading to cooperation rather than war and conflict...

It is vital that you cover **both** named theories within your answer. This reminder will appear below the question to remind you to link back to core ideas.

There is no need for an introduction here, get straight into your answer.

This answer links back to Hobbes's view of the state of nature (see page 43) and so meets the requirement of discussing any relevant core political ideas.

Human nature is linked here to the behaviour of states to explain how realism explains the likelihood of conflict.

This paragraph looks at the differences between the two theories over human nature and the likelihood of conflict between states in order to develop its AO2 analysis marks.

Liberal theory is linked back to liberalism as a whole, rather than a specific thinker. This approach is fine.

Turn the page to see more on this 12-mark comparative theories question.

Exam skills 4: Section B
continued...

Read the question and accompanying information on page 297 before continuing below. Here, we continue looking at **Section B** of your A Level **Paper 3** exam. While the essay structure, length and timing is the same as Section A, the inclusion of comparative theories makes your paragraphs look a little different.

Command word: Analyse

You need to look at the idea or issue and break it down. In this kind of question, that means looking for similarities and differences and showing why or how they exist. Remember, you must refer to **both** key theories.

Timing

Make sure you know how much you can write in 15 minutes before you get into the exam. Practise at home in timed conditions as often as you can. There is not much point trying to write three or four long paragraphs if you know you are going to run out of time.

Worked example

... Liberals see the international order as one of complex interdependence. The creation of multiple channels between states and non-state actors that connect society brings order and security to global politics as conflict is resolved through discussion, cooperation and negotiation, not force. This emergence of intergovernmental organisations such as the UN, WTO and ICJ reflects this growing interdependence and reveals that it is rational for states to work together as together they achieve more. Realists oppose this view, as they believe that states are only actors in global politics and are interested in relative gains not absolute gains, so are unlikely to cooperate meaningfully or over a longer period of time. States are constantly striving for power, creating a system of international anarchy. However, for realists, this does not make war inevitable. The likelihood of war and conflict is driven by the balance of power in the system, with bipolarity, as in the Cold War era, reducing the chances while unbalanced multipolarity increases the chances. For realists, like Mearsheimer, the emergence of China is a threat to its immediate neighbours like Russia and Japan as well as the USA. Its rise will create an unbalanced multipolar world, with an intense security dilemma that would increase the chance of conflict and war.

Read the question and the partial student answer on page 297 again before continuing below.

Using effective political vocabulary and key terms such as 'complex interdependence' within the right context illustrates your knowledge.

The second sentence shows that the student can explain complex interdependence and its relationship to the likelihood of conflict.

The student has explained how intergovernmental institutions are an illustration of complex interdependence.

This paragraph, in line with the first paragraph, aims to draw differences and parallels between the two key theories in explaining the issue of conflict.

There is no link back to core political ideas in this section, as that was established in the first paragraph.

To finish this answer, you would need to include a third paragraph covering another difference or parallel between the two key theories.

There is no need to write a conclusion in this type of question, as it is only assessing AO1 and AO2.

If a question focuses on the main ideas of the anarchical society and society of states theory, associated with Hedley Bull, you can still draw similarities or differences between liberalism and realism because he draws on both traditions in his theory of global politics. See page 291 for more on Bull.

Exam skills 5: Section C

This question will help you to revise for **Section C** of your A Level **Paper 3** exam. This section consists of three 30-mark questions – you will need to choose **two** of them to complete.

Section C

- You should aim to spend around 45 minutes on each essay.
- Each essay needs to be fully structured, including an introduction and a conclusion.
- You will be assessed on AO1, AO2 and AO3 skills.
- Questions may cut across specification sections, so you should be ready to establish links between different areas of the specification – not just sections 1–5 of Global politics.

Assessment objectives

- **AO1 knowledge and understanding.** You need to express what you know and show you understand how it relates to the question you are answering.
- **AO2 analysis.** You need to show how the aspects of politics you are examining can be broken down and how they relate to the question. You should also be able to make clear connections between ideas and concepts.
- **AO3 evaluation.** This is your ability weigh up the quality of differing arguments. This weighing up based on the evidence should lead to clear, supported conclusions throughout the essay, not just at the end.

Planning

Planning is vital. It will ensure your essay makes sense, is focused and gains marks more quickly. You should only spend a couple of minutes planning your essay. If it becomes clear that you do not have enough information to answer the question, quickly pick a different question to answer – this is not wasted time.

Steps to planning

1. **Introduction:** define key terms and introduce the argument.
2. **Body:** what points are you going to discuss and what examples are you going to use to support them? What connections are there between points?
3. **Conclusion:** which side of the debate wins and why does it win?

---

3 Evaluate the extent to which the European Union (EU) is now a significant global actor on the world stage. **(30 marks)**

You must consider this view and the alternative to this view in a balanced way.

Plan

Introduction: define 'global actor' and outline both sides of the argument.

Body:

For	Against
• Economic power (1)	• Brexit (1)
• Market size	• UK's role and power
• Aid budget	• Eurozone crisis (3)
• Structural power (2)	• Euro and economic recovery
• Trade deals	• Common Foreign and Security Policy (CFSP) (2)
• G7/20 and WTO	• State sovereignty
• Political power (3)	• No military
• CFSP	• Splits (NATO) and failures (Iraq)
• Soft power	
• Military power (4)	
• Missions (Mali and Somalia)	

Conclusion: the EU has emerged as a global actor but its future as a global actor is in doubt due to Brexit and the Eurozone crisis.

Start by listing your key points on both sides of the debate, with examples.

Rank the points 'for' in order of importance, then do the same for the points 'against'. Rank the arguments in order of their importance to the question.

Think about how you can draw links between the points.

Decide which side of the debate wins and why.

Exam skills 6: Section C
continued...

This is a continuation of the question and sample answer given on page 299. Read the question and sample student answer on that page before continuing below.

Introduction

Your introduction should show that you understand what you have been asked to do. It should therefore define the key terms of the question, outline what you are going to discuss and perhaps even hint at what you may argue.

Command words: Evaluate the extent

This command term will be followed by a statement that suggests one side of an argument. You need to show that you **know and understand** (AO1), can **analyse** (AO2) and **evaluate** (AO3) this **and the other side** of this argument. You need to review the points that affect your argument and judge their importance or effectiveness.

Timing

You should plan to spend 45 minutes on each 30-mark question. Do not think that you must spend the whole of this time writing, however. You should keep a few minutes to plan your work and proofread it at the end. You have plenty of time to do this and it will ultimately help you produce better work.

Worked example

The European Union (EU) is a difficult organisation to categorise as it has been continuously redesigned and reshaped since the establishment of the European Coal and Steel Community in 1952. It has become a unique political and economic union between 28 states that is seen by many now as a significant global actor. The concept of global actor really focuses on the idea it has the capacity to act as a single body in global politics, particularly in terms of foreign and defence policy. Its capacity to act has been strengthened as the Union has become ever closer with growing economic, political, structural and military power. Recent EU crises and the constant conflict between the EU and state sovereignty have called into question its role as a global actor and suggest that the future of the EU is less certain...

 The EU and the concept of global actor are defined here.

 The references to how the EU has changed over time and to recent events reflect the importance of the word 'now' in the question.

 Reference to economic, political, structural and military power establishes the points for discussion.

 The final sentence hints at how the student will argue. An introduction like this identifies that a student understands all three of the assessment objectives and sets the essay up excellently.

This worked example continues on the next page.

300

Exam skills 6: Section C
continued...

Read the question and sample student answer on page 300 before continuing below.

Body
Structuring the main part of your essay requires some individual style. The more you practise, the better at this you will become.

Worked example

... The EU is the world's largest single market, with a population of over 510 million and accounts for 23 per cent of the world's GDP, making it far more economically influential than any other trading bloc, such as Mercosur or NAFTA. It has its own currency (the euro), which is now used by 19 countries that have adopted it since 1999, and acts as a rival to the dollar as the world currency. This economic power is wielded by the Commission, rather than individual states as the EU is a customs union, allowing the EU to act as one on economic issues. The Commission carries out trade negotiations with the WTO, other trading blocs and individual nations. It is now the top trading partner for 80 states while the US is only the top trading partner of 20 states, suggesting it is challenging US hegemony. The EU's capacity as a global actor is further enhanced by having the world's largest development aid budget, which is channelled to the global South to develop its influence in the region as this remains a market that is growing in importance for EU exports.

The massive growth in the economic power of the EU has enhanced its ability to act as a global actor in other respects. The EU is the only trading bloc currently represented at the G7, the G8 and the WTO. Its economic powers and ability to act with one voice on economic issues gives it structural power to shape the institutions that shape global economic policy. The pooled sovereignty of the individual states gives them a far more powerful voice in organising the global economy than they could ever achieve on their own. This structural power can be seen in the global role played by the EU in tackling climate change. The EU was the first major economy to submit its nationally determined contribution target, which was used as a basis to build a coalition of states to support the Paris Agreement and ambitious targets. Since the US's withdrawal, the EU has been a key global actor in building partnerships directly with US states and corporations to ensure that the Paris deal can still be delivered, and has agreed with China to raise $100bn by 2020 to assist developing states tackle climate change. This shows that there is little doubt that the EU is rivalling the power of China and the US in global politics...

 This paragraph uses examples to illustrate the argument and draws connections to other trading blocs and countries to enhance the point.

 This focuses on the 'now' element of the question, using current evidence and referring to how the EU has changed over time.

This shows a clear understanding of how the EU works and allows it to act as global actor.

 This answer shows how questions cut across specification sections, as it is drawing on both the regionalism and the EU section and the section on power and developments.

This paragraph has a clear opening that links economic power with structural power and addresses the question.

 Correct use of political vocabulary in the right context here, which reveals clear understanding.

 A good example here, which enhances the point by clearly illustrating the argument.

 Having established the EU as a significant global actor in terms of economic and structural power, the answer would then challenge this by looking at how Brexit and the Eurozone crisis undermine the structural and economic power of the EU and possibly threatens its status as a global actor going forwards.

This worked example continues on the next page.

Exam skills 8: Section C
continued...

This is a continuation of the sample answer given on pages 299–301. Read the question and sample student answer on those pages before continuing below.

Conclusion

Your conclusion should give a definitive answer to the question and show how you reached that conclusion. With the command word 'evaluate the extent', the conclusion must be more than simply 'yes' or 'no'.

> **Worked example**

The widening and deepening of the EU, in particular since the Maastricht Treaty, has significantly enhanced the capacity of the EU as a significant global actor. The growing economic and structural power of the EU has seen it rival the power of China and the USA. However, its ability to develop a Common Foreign and Security Policy has been far more problematic due to tensions over state sovereignty and splits over its foreign policy role in relation to NATO. The absence of coherent EU policy in relation to many of the critical issues facing global politics reflects its current weakness as a global actor. Perhaps more significantly, Brexit and the Eurozone crisis have undermined the power of the EU on the global stage and created greater tensions within the EU, limiting its ability to act as a single entity moving forward.

The opening line of the conclusion shows the student understands the broad context of the question – they are not repeating what they have already written.

Both sides of the argument are referenced but a clear case is made for supporting one of those sides. This shows the student is making a justified argument.

The final sentence directly addresses the question and places the whole question in its most current context.

Just like the introduction, you will not be awarded marks for your conclusion alone. The conclusion should, however, be predictable. It should be clear what you are going to conclude from how you have written your essay.

Conclusion checklist

Have I...

✓ answered the question directly?

✓ explained how and why I reached this conclusion?

✓ written a conclusion that matches the tone of my essay?

Have I avoided...

✗ simply repeating paragraphs or examples?

✗ writing only one sentence?

✗ introducing new information?

Exam-style practice

Practise for **Paper 3** of your A Level exam with these exam-style questions. There are answers on page 319. Paper 3 is made up of three sections, and in total you will have to answer four questions: **one** from Section A, **one** from Section B and **two** from Section C.

Section A

1 Examine the factors that make international cooperation on the environment between developed and developing states hard to achieve. **(12 marks)**

Aim to spend around 15 minutes on the Section A question. It is worth 12 marks – six marks each for AO1 and AO2.

Look at the different views on causes, measurement and responsibility to tackle environmental problems and how these limit cooperation. Make sure you include examples to support your points.

Again, spend around 15 minutes on the Section B question. It is worth 12 marks – 6 marks each for AO1 and AO2.

Section B

2 Analyse the divisions between realists and liberals over the nature of the international system.

In your answer you must discuss any relevant core political ideas. **(12 marks)**

Make sure you refer back to both liberalism and realism in your answer, and also link back to core political ideas (see pages 36–67) where relevant to the question.

You could link the realist view about international anarchy back to Thomas Hobbes (see page 43).

Remember that you need to answer **two** questions in Section C; each should take about 45 minutes. Each question is worth 30 marks – 10 marks each for AO1, AO2 and AO3.

Section C

3 **(a)** Evaluate the extent to which state sovereignty is now an outdated concept due to the impact of globalisation.

You must consider this view and the alternative to this view in a balanced way. **(30 marks)**

(b) Evaluate the extent to which economic globalisation is the solution to poverty and inequality.

You must consider this view and the alternative to this view in a balanced way. **(30 marks)**

Make sure your answers are properly structured, each with an introduction and a conclusion that reaches a well-argued judgement.

For each question, you need to draw on relevant ideas from across the specification and include examples to illustrate your points.

Try to place each question in a modern context to stay as contemporary as possible.

Answers

1. Representative democracy

Your reasons could include two from:
- Elections are regular, competitive and secretive. They must be held every five years using the first past the post system.
- There are established civil rights and freedoms enshrined in law by the Human Rights Act 1998.
- There are numerous political parties to contest elections.
- Constitutional checks exist to prevent a concentration of power. The UK constitution sets the boundaries of the democratic system.
- An assembly exists which reflects the make-up of society. Political decisions are made by MPs, who are expected to represent the views of the electorate.
- Pressure groups have the opportunity to put forward their views and are seen as an integral part of the UK democratic, representative system.
- An independent judiciary is separated from the executive and legislature.

2. Direct democracy

Direct democracy does not have a government, while representative democracy does have a government.

Direct democracy requires constant participation, while representative democracy requires only occasional participation.

3. How healthy is UK democracy?

(i) Limited government is where the power of the government is limited by law, usually (but not always) though a codified constitution.

(ii) Judicial independence is where the judiciary is free from interference from the government, allowing them to make all decisions based purely on the rule of law and not taking into account any political considerations.

4. Participation crisis

Anti-politics has shown itself in the election of Donald Trump in the USA, the success of Jeremy Corbyn in the UK and Bernie Sanders in the USA, and the Brexit referendum vote in the UK.

5. Reforming UK democracy

Your answer could include any three from
- MPs' blogs, which usually take the form of an online diary. For example, www.power-to-the-people.co.uk/mps-blogs/ has a comprehensive list of blog sites for UK MPs from the three major political parties.
- Commentators blogs, such as https://order-order.com or leftfootforward.org.
- Social networking sites like Snapchat, Facebook, Twitter and YouTube allow citizens to interact and share images or audio/video clips.
- Many MPs have Facebook pages. Parliament and 10 Downing Street started its own YouTube channels in 2007.
- The government e-petition website https://petition.parliament.uk.
- Other informal online petitions, such as 38degrees.org or change.org.

6. Group politics

Despite being a corporation, Uber is campaigning against Transport for London's (TFL) decision to withdraw its licence in London. Hence it is acting as a pressure group, seeking to influence the public to try to get TFL to change its mind. It launched an e-petition and a Twitter campaign (#saveuber), as well as a legal challenge to its decision. These are classic pressure-group methods.

7. Methods used by pressure groups

Possible answers include:
- Insiders need to ensure that they are seen as responsible in order to maintain their legitimacy. Their methods do not need to influence the public; they have the government's ear already.
- Small outsider groups often use 'stunts' or celebrities to gain greater visibility.
- Large outsider groups are able to mount major campaigns of direct action to mobilise public support.
- Some outsiders use civil disobedience as a way of getting the attention of government.
- Wealthy groups may use their economic power to persuade government.

8. Factors influencing the success of groups

For example:
1 Insider – having the ear of the government is the most likely chance of successfully achieving their aims.
2 Wealth – being wealthy may mean that you are a powerful economic group which governments usually listen to in order to ensure economic prosperity. Equally, wealthy groups can pay lobbying firms to help them get better access to governments.
3 Public support – a group with wide public support is likely to concern the government as ultimately, in a democracy, the government needs to listen to the people.

9. Groups and democracy

Strengths – one from:
- They enable individuals to participate in the political process before elections
- Pressure groups reflect the system of pluralist democracy, which gives citizens another voice in the decision-making process beyond parties.
- Pressure groups counter-balance the tyranny of the majority by lobbying on behalf of minorities. They ensure that minorities, such as gay people, the elderly and students, can have their voice heard.
- They can bring expert knowledge to the government's attention on an important issue. Ministers and MPs are rarely experts on every issue.
- Pressure groups keep government on its toes, and encourage government to be responsible, democratic and answerable. They act as a limit to government power.
- Pressure groups promote debate and educate and inform the electorate. They ensure healthy debate occurs.

Weakness – one from:
- Pressure groups can be divisive and selfish and can dominate an issue.
- Pressure groups are very good at stopping things that others feel are needed.
- Pressure groups are not accountable to the public as a whole despite the fact that their influence on policy can be large. They often work with governments behind closed doors.
- Pressure groups have reduced the power of Parliament and undermined its sovereignty by working closely with ministers and civil servants. By the time Parliament sees legislation, it is all but decided.
- They make the country difficult to manage and govern. 'Hyper-pluralism' depicts the difficulty a government may encounter when it is perplexed by a multitude of pressure groups blocking their actions.

10. Rights in the UK

Until the Human Rights Act (HRA) was passed in 1998, UK citizens had only negative rights, i.e. as murder was illegal that 'told' us we had a right to life. The HRA gave us positive rights enshrined in UK law for the first time, i.e. the right to life.

11. Are our rights protected?

Abu Qatada – the right to be free from torture

Belmarsh – *habeus corpus* – people cannot be unlawfully detained

Poundland – freedom from forced labour

Segregation in schools – equal treatment of the sexes

12. Political parties

Left wing, any one from:
- a desire to introduce change
- making society more equal
- favouring the group solution above the individual
- supporting state intervention and collectivism
- associated with welfare, economic intervention and wealth redistribution

Right wing, any one from:
- acceptance of the status quo
- a need for stability in society
- giving individuals more freedom
- favouring the individual over the group
- favouring the market and individualism
- supporting low taxes, limited welfare and free-market economics.

13. Enhancing democracy and funding

Any two from:
- Political parties encourage people to participate in politics via party activity, election campaigning, voting and standing for office.
- They provide voters with choices and help to make electoral choice clearer and more coherent.
- They help to educate and inform the electorate about key political issues through political debate and by presenting a range of arguments.
- They administer elections, encouraging people to vote and presenting election issues clearly to the electorate.
- They uphold the authority of Parliament and reinforce respect for political institutions.
- They facilitate representation by serving as a channel of communication between government and people.
- They identify political talent and recruit appropriate candidates for office.
- Legitimate political parties ensure that there is a peaceful transition of power after elections.

14. The history of the Labour Party

One key difference between Old and New Labour is Old Labour's commitment to equality and New Labour's greater interest in individuals achieving their potential.
Other differences include:
- nationalisation vs free market economics
- cradle-to-grave welfare vs targeted welfare
- recognition of class divisions vs rejection of this view.

15. The Labour Party today

In 2017, it supported left-wing policies, including:
- the re-nationalisation of water, railways and Royal Mail and regulation of the energy market
- the reintroduction of the 50p tax rate
- an increase in corporation tax
- the establishment of a National Investment Bank with £250bn for infrastructure
- the re-introduction of maintenance grants for university students and abolition of tuition fees.

16. The history of the Conservative Party

David Cameron can be seen to be both a One Nation Conservative and a Thatcherite.
One Nation Conservative:
- on record as saying 'I am a One Nation conservative'
- 'Big Society' programme
- big supporter of NHS
- raising of tax threshold.
Thatcherite:
- cuts in welfare
- austerity
- reducing of 50p tax rate.

17. The Conservative Party today

'Big beasts' are very important members of the party who cannot be ignored by a PM. They are significant because they have power to motivate restless backbenchers, which can make the position of a relatively weak PM difficult.

18. The Liberal Democrats

As part of the Coalition Agreement, the Lib Dems accepted that their pledge to abolish tuition fees could not happen, choosing perhaps instead to insist on a pupil premium and a raise in income tax thresholds and a referendum on electoral reform. They subsequently supported the Conservative's introduction of legislation to increase university tuition fees to a maximum of £9,000.

19. Emerging and minor parties

In 2015, UKIP faced a problem that affects many minor parties, namely that their support is spread relatively evenly across the country. FPTP requires a party's support to be concentrated in constituencies so they can win them. Despite UKIP's 3.8m votes, they only came first in 1 seat. Interestingly, they came second in 120 seats.

20. Other emerging and minor parties

Any one from:
- UKIP – influenced Cameron to hold a referendum on EU membership; helped turn public opinion in favour of Brexit.
- SNP – influenced Cameron to hold a referendum on Scottish independence, making it an issue for the first time in generations; pushed the government to give more power to the Scottish Parliament (devo-max).
- DUP – propped up May's government, allowing them to govern.

21. Parties and party systems

Traditionally in Westminster, the UK has been seen as a two-party system, although since the 1970s the description of a two-and-a-half party system has been more accurate, with the Lib Dems increasing its size in the Commons. The 2015 elections saw three additional parties get between 1 and 5 million votes – the Greens (1.2m), SNP (1.5m) and UKIP (3.8m) votes – leading many to suggest that the UK was entering a period of multi-party politics, despite the reality that the Greens and UKIP each received only one seat. However, 2017 saw a return to two-party dominance, with Labour and the Conservatives dominating the results with 82 per cent of the vote between them and 89 per cent of the seats.

22. Factors affecting party success

Factors:

- Campaigns – a terrible campaign by May and an excellent one by Corbyn was the main story of 2017.
- Leader – linked to above, the focus on May in the campaign showed all her weaknesses as party leader, whereas Corbyn's personal strengths were on show throughout.
- Policies – thinking they had a strong 20-point lead, the Conservative manifesto had very few giveaways and the social care policy (changed midway through the campaign) was a disaster. The Labour manifesto was full of popular policies, such as abolishing tuition fees.
- Media – the Labour Party's use of social media was fundamental to their success in motivating young people to vote while the 'old' media's support of the Conservatives appeared to make little headway.

23. The role of elections in democracy

An electoral mandate is the permission to govern and is received when a party wins an election. It is important because it shows the electorate giving consent to the government to carry out their political programme (as shown in their manifesto). This gives the government of the day and their programme legitimacy to govern. In a democracy, it is essential that the people consent to those who rule over them.

24. First-past-the-post

1. Safe seats are constituencies where the winner wins by a very large amount of votes and there is very little chance of a seat changing hands. The Electoral Reform Society suggests that approximately 370 out of 650 seats in a UK general election are safe. This means that politicians tend not to bother campaigning in these seats as the result is a forgone conclusion. Voters in these seats may feel their vote is not as important as voters in other areas.

2. FPTP wastes votes in safe constituencies. If you live in a safe seat, where the same party wins the seat at every election, your vote is worth very little. The results of elections under FPTP are decided by a few thousand voters in a small number of marginal constituencies. Politicians concentrate their efforts on these voters as they know they are the key to winning elections. The Electoral Reform Society calculated that 74 per cent of votes cast in 2015 were wasted: cast either for losing candidates or for winning candidates above and beyond the amount needed to win in a particular constituency and they had no impact on the final result of the general election.

25. Supplementary Vote

SV is a majoritarian system as the winner in a constituency is required to have a majority of votes in order to win. This does not need to be a majority of first-preference votes.

26. Additional Member System

In 2016, after the constituency results 73/129:

- The SNP had 81% of MSPs on only 47% of the vote; once top-up MSPs were added, they had 49% of the seats on 45% of the vote.
- The Conservatives had 10% of MSPs on 22% of the vote; once top-up MSPs were added, they had 24% of the seats on 23% of the vote.
- Labour had 4% of MSPs on only 23% of the vote, once top-up MSPs were added, they had 19% of the seats on 21% of the vote.
- Greens had 0% of MSPs on only 1% of the vote; once top up MSPs were added, they had 4% of the seats on 4% of the vote.
- Lib Dems had 5% of MSPs on only 8% of the vote; once top-up MSPs were added, they had 5% of the seats on 7% of the vote.

This shows that having top-up MPs makes the system highly proportionate.

27. Single Transferable Vote

MMCs provide greater choice for the voter as they can choose between parties or between candidates in the same party or both.

MMCs offer voters a wider choice of representatives to approach with their concerns after the election, rather than just one who they may not have voted for or whose policies they don't agree with.

MMCs mean lines of accountability for representatives are less clear.

28. Use of referenda

Cameron said that the UK's membership of the EU was 'poisoning' the Conservative Party. The party had been split on the EU since the late 1980s, and the rise of UKIP had begun to unnerve Cameron, with many voters appearing to desert the Conservatives for them due to their stand on the EU. He also believed that people were frustrated with the EU but the UK hadn't had a referendum on this issue for 40 years, despite the fact that the EU was changing. Cameron felt the issue needed to be resolved once and for all with a referendum.

29. Impact of different electoral systems

UKIP won 12 per cent of the vote (3.8m) under FPTP, but won only one seat in the House of Commons. They won 24 seats under PR in the European Parliament in 2014.

The Green Party has one seat in Westminster under FPP, but has six seats in the Scottish Parliament, two seats in the Greater London Assembly and three seats in the European Parliament, all under PR.

30. Trends in voting behaviour

There is a link between class and regional voting because working-class voters (C2, D, E) tend to live in urban areas whereas middle-class voters (A, B, C1) tend to live in rural and suburban areas. Moreover, the further north you go, the more likely you are to see greater support for the Labour Party (in England) and the same is true of Conservative support in the south. However, the Brexit debate compromised this idea with many Leave voters in the north of England switching support to the Conservatives in 2017.

31. Short-term factors affecting voting behaviour

Prior to the election, the Conservative government led by John Major had lost the voter's trust on economic competency over the European Exchange Rate Mechanism (ERM). In addition, by 1996–1997 the government had appeared to run out of steam and was plagued by scandals in the press. In contrast, Blair's Labour Party seemed to have new solutions to the country's problems and had won the support of the city, big business and the media. These issues helped to forge a sense of competency, which gave voters the confidence to vote for them in 1997.

32. Case study: the 1997 general election

The Conservatives had a historically terrible result, winning only 30.7 per cent of the vote. While the economy was recovering from the recession of the early 1990s, voters failed to see the economic improvement as it had failed to visibly benefit them via tax cuts or increased investment in public services. Financial and sexual scandals further weakened the appeal of the Conservatives along with internal divisions over the European Union. Major was seen as a weak leader and out of touch with the times.

From very early on, monthly opinion polls were showing that Labour was ahead of the Conservatives. New Labour under Blair successfully appealed to all age groups, ethnicities, class and gender with a well-managed campaign that modernised Labour. Policies moved away from traditional Labour policies such as nationalisation and tax increases, and towards a more centre-ground position, which appealed to middle-class voters. The media also heavily backed Labour over the Conservative party.

33. Case study: the 2017 general election

The 2017 general election produced surprising results in many areas. One of the biggest factors was age. In ten constituencies with the highest proportion of 18–24-year-olds, there were increases of 14% in the Labour vote. Class did not appear to be a significant factor, with 2–4% difference in support for the Labour and Conservative parties. Employment status appears to have been significant in 2017, with the Conservatives 39 points ahead among retirees and Labour 45 points ahead among full-time students. The Brexit factor was also significant and helped to shore up support for the two main parties with the smaller parties, which had been so successful in 2015, losing out.

34. The influence of the media

The 2017 general election shows that print media is losing influence over voters. This can be seen as most newspapers did not support the Labour Party and were particularly disparaging about Jeremy Corbyn. *The Sun*'s front page on election day, for example, had a picture of Corbyn's head in a bin, suggesting that electing him would not be good for the country. It drew parallels with their infamous front page in 1992 with Neil Kinnock's head in a lightbulb, asking, 'Would the last person to leave Britain if Kinnock become PM please turn out the lights.' Whereas in 1992, this front page was seen as a key contributor in Kinnock's loss (even Kinnock said so), the 'CorBIN' front page had a very limited effect. In fact, the Labour Party polled 40% of the vote – an increase of 10% from the 2015 election.

35. Media and electoral outcomes

Labour focused on social media because they wanted to reach out to younger voters who were more likely to support the Labour Party but who are also not known for high levels of turnout at elections. By effective use of social media, the Labour Party was able to motivate them to support their party.

36. Pragmatism and tradition

Conservatives argue that:

- Humans cannot fully understand reality due to their limited capabilities. Therefore, it makes sense to reject abstract or ideological blueprints in favour of previous practical experience when deciding on a future course of action.
- The introduction of ideological or abstract principles into society can lead to radical and destabilising change that worsens rather than improves conditions.
- A cautious approach to reform which emphasises gradualism and continuity will introduce necessary change or reform to key institutions without jeopardising social cohesion or stability.
- A pragmatic 'middle way', or mixed economy creates wealth, promotes growth and provides funded state welfare for the most vulnerable.

37. Human imperfection and the organic state

- Since the organic society functions like a living organism, with its various parts working together harmoniously, it fulfils the human need for stability and social cohesion.
- The emphasis placed on traditional institutions in the organic society provides humans with a strong sense of security and predictability
- The emphasis placed on hierarchy and authority in the organic society reflects the unequal distribution of ability and talent, and provides humans with direction, security and a sense of where they 'fit in'.

38. Paternalism and libertarianism

A paternalistic conservative would make the following criticisms of libertarianism:

- Libertarianism underestimates how important the concept of social responsibility is to human nature.
- A minimal state would offer little welfare provision, leaving the poor and vulnerable to fend for themselves.
- Unregulated free-market competition would sharpen social and economic inequalities and potentially destabilise society.

39. Traditional conservatism

- Aristocratic rule was 'natural' because the upper class (unlike other classes) had been brought up and educated to govern at local and national level.
- As the largest property owners, the aristocracy had a significant stake in society, which entitled them to rule.
- Aristocratic rule was based on paternalism and noblesse oblige so that privilege and power was counter-balanced by duty, obligation and social responsibility.

40. One Nation conservatism

Modern One Nation conservatives endorsed the mixed economy because in their view:

- the mixed economy represented a moderate 'halfway house' between unrestricted capitalism and state socialism
- the mixed economy would permit state-funded welfare to guarantee a minimum standard of living
- the mixed economy would deliver managed and 'orderly capitalism' to preserve the social cohesion of the nation and prevent discontent.

41. New Right

Some have maintained that the New Right is not a coherent doctrine because it contains three apparently incompatible ideological elements:

- A radical element that rejects government intervention in economic and social affairs and endorses an anti-permissive approach to social attitudes and moral choices.
- A traditional element that champions the benefits of hard work, respect for all forms of authority and the importance of family values.
- A reactionary element that harks back to a supposed 'golden age' (which has since slipped away) dominated by economic freedom and individual moral responsibility.

42. Neo-liberalism and neo-conservatism

Neo-liberals oppose state intervention because in their view:

- State welfare provision grows, irrespective of demand, driven by the vested interests of the professionals involved (e.g. doctors) and political parties (who promise to raise welfare funding to attract votes). This produces increasingly inefficient state welfare services, rising taxation and higher inflation.
- Economic inefficiency and lack of incentive are the inevitable consequences of state planning, nationalisation and high taxation.
- Humans are self-interested, self-sufficient and rational. Consequently, individual freedom can only be protected by 'rolling back' the state in order to release and fulfil human potential and create natural harmony through free relations between people. State intervention (e.g. in the form of welfare provision) weakens atomistic individualism by promoting a dependency culture.

43. Key thinkers: 1
Hobbes and Burke both argue that:
- humans are vulnerable, limited and security-seeking – in short, imperfect
- society has to be based on order and hierarchy to ensure social cohesion and harmony
- peace and stability are preserved by the authority of the state and its institutions.

44. Key thinkers: 2
- Oakeshott rejects rationalism as dangerous whereas Rand and Nozick view it positively and see it as central to human nature.
- Oakeshott places significant emphasis on pragmatism whereas Rand and Nozick adopt a more rigid ideological position (e.g. on the economy).
- Oakeshott's views suggest both society and the state have important roles to play whereas Rand and Nozick emphasise individualism and the minimal state.

46. Individualism and freedom
Liberals stress the importance of the individual because in their view:
- each person is unique and all individuals have equal worth and their own intrinsic value
- each person exhibits egoistical individualism – the idea that humans are essentially self-seeking and self-reliant
- tolerance is a natural right to which every person is entitled.

Modern liberals also argue in favour of developmental individualism whereby society is created in such a way that permits every individual to experience personal growth and achieve their potential.

47. The state and rationalism
Rationalism is central to the liberal outlook because liberals believe that:
- humans are guided by reason and so they have the capacity to make their decisions about their own interests
- rationalism benefits individuals because it enables people to take responsibility for themselves rather than depend on the state or other external body
- rationalism is essential for the development of a progressive society because personal growth and fulfilment (achieved by individual rational decision-making) leads to wider social advancement
- rationalism, in the form of reasoned negotiation and discussion, should be employed to resolve conflicts and disagreements.

48. Equality/social justice and liberal democracy
Some liberals are uneasy about liberal democracy because in their view:
- sections of the electorate who are poorly educated will not be able to vote in an informed way
- mass democracies inevitably promote collectivism, increasing state intervention and curbing individual liberty
- liberal democracy may result in the 'tyranny of the majority', adversely affecting minority rights, tolerance and individual freedoms.

49. Liberalism and freedom
Classical liberals support negative freedom because in their view:
- it is linked to egoistical individualism – the idea that humans are basically self-seeking and self-reliant
- individual liberty can be maximised by minimising state power, thereby encouraging people to assume greater responsibility for their own lives rather than being reliant on the state
- dependence on the state undermines individual responsibility and autonomy; it also weakens the human entrepreneurial initiative required for economic growth.

50. Liberalism and the state
Liberals oppose the state on the grounds that:
- growing state power threatens individual liberty
- state intervention (e.g. in the form of welfare provision) encourages dependency and undermines individual responsibility and self-reliance.

Liberals embrace the state on the grounds that:
- state intervention can promote positive freedom by helping individuals to achieve liberty and fulfil their potential
- the enabling state is consistent with government by consent because humans desire a society where the lot of the poor is improved.

51. Liberalism and the economy
Liberals agree on the economy in the following ways:
- Both classical and modern liberals believe in a market-based capitalist economy because this form of economic organisation supports the liberal belief that private property is a natural right.
- Both classical and modern liberals believe in a market-based capitalist economy because this form of economic organisation promotes liberal individualism through the personal pursuit of economic betterment.

Liberals disagree agree on the economy in the following ways:
- Classical liberals argue that under laissez-faire capitalism, the 'invisible hand' of market forces delivers prosperity to individuals and society as a whole; modern liberals maintain that the free market is not self-regulating and susceptible to cyclical slumps, leading to mass unemployment and loss of individual liberty.
- Modern liberals contend that state or government-directed capitalism is necessary to steer the economy and regulate demand to achieve sustainable economic growth and maintain full employment; classical liberals reject economic interventionism, arguing that the state has to adopt a 'hands off' approach to the economy so that the free market can generate wealth that trickles down to the wider population.

52. Contradiction or continuation?
Classical liberalism has little in common with modern liberalism in the following areas.
- Classical liberals emphasise negative freedom whereas modern liberals see positive freedom as more important.
- Classical liberals have sometimes regarded taxation as 'state theft' but modern liberals view taxation as a means to achieve positive freedom through state intervention.
- Classical liberals endorse laissez-faire capitalism and call for minimal state involvement in economic affairs; modern liberals argue for a Keynesian-style approach to manage market forces and level of demand in the economy.
- Classical liberals are uneasy about democracy, particularly fearing 'the tyranny of the majority', but modern liberals accept liberal and representative democracy.
- Classical liberals call for a minimal state but modern liberals champion the enabling state with its wider economic and social functions.

Classical liberalism still has much in common with modern liberalism in the following areas.
- Both forms of liberalism are based on an optimistic view of human nature and regard individualism as the core element of society and politics.
- Both forms of liberalism regard tolerance as a natural right to which all humans are entitled.
- Both forms of liberalism regard capitalism as the best economic system because it promotes private property, individualism and the progress of society.
- Both forms of liberalism desire a constitutional state and government by consent.

53. Key thinkers: 1
The key features of Locke's social contract are:
- The state is established by humans to serve their interests; this state is based on the voluntary consent of those governed by it. The state is not God-given or based on the divine right of monarchs to govern.
- People accept the authority of the state as long as it fulfils its side of the 'contract' by upholding natural rights (e.g. the right to property and liberty).
- If the state breaks its contract with the people (by disregarding their natural rights), they are entitled to oppose or even remove it.
- The social contract is based on reason: rational people will not willingly submit to arbitrary rule (power without legal restraints) because it is not in their interests to do so. The state serves the individual, not the other way round.

54. Key thinkers: 2
Wollstonecraft's feminist ideas are linked to liberalism in the following ways:
- Women, like men, are rational and independent human beings and so should be entitled to the same rights as men.
- The state and social attitudes restricted individual freedom for women (e.g. the idea that women were not rational) and offered few opportunities for female personal growth and development via education or a career.
- Denying women the vote conflicted with the liberal concept of government by consent.
- Marriage undermined a woman's individual liberty because, as a wife, she was not legally independent.

55. Key thinkers: 3
Friedan's feminism is liberal in the following ways:
- It rests on the core liberal belief that all individuals (including women) are of equal worth and therefore entitled to equal rights.
- The state should intervene to curb (through legislation) discrimination that harms the liberty of women and prevents equality of opportunity.
- Progress can only come about through legal change which in turn is based on rational discussion and debate.
- Legal equality for women is an example of the liberal belief in tolerance.

57. Collectivism and common humanity
Socialists support collectivism on the following grounds:
- Human nature: humans are social creatures with a natural tendency towards cooperation and collective effort for the common good.
- Society: the interests of society (or community) should take priority over individual self-interest; collectivism also contributes to the betterment of society.
- Economy: collective endeavour harnesses the economic potential of society more efficiently than wasteful competitive individual effort.
- State: collective action via the state ensures a fairer distribution of goods and services (through state intervention and state planning) than free-market forces.

58. Equality
Fundamentalist socialists and Marxists endorse equality of outcome and absolute equality respectively to remove the capitalist system with its inherent inequalities; social democrats and advocates of the Third Way reject these approaches on the grounds that they do not accord with human nature (incentives provide motivation), are unworkable in practice and may undermine social stability.

Social democrats and the Third Way call for equality of opportunity because they believe that everyone should progress as far as their talents and work ethic will take them, creating a meritocratic society. They also support equality of welfare so that the state can guarantee an equal minimum standard of living for everyone. Marxists reject both these concepts of equality because neither removes the unequal capitalist system.

59. Social class and workers' control
Marxists argue that a person's relationship to the means of production determines their class position – crucially whether a person owns the means of production (a member of the ruling class) or has to sell their labour to survive (a member of the exploited class). Conflict between these two groups is inevitable. Under capitalism, for example, the capitalists or bourgeoisie (the owners of productive wealth) are locked in a class struggle with the working class or proletariat (the wage labourers). The ruling bourgeoisie use the state apparatus to maintain their dominance but, ultimately, intensifying class conflict results in a proletarian revolution, which overthrows capitalism and leads to a classless, equal society and the withering away of the state.

Social democrats are less rigid in their definition of social class, which tends to link occupational differences more fluidly to income and status. Unlike Marxists, social democrats look to state intervention to reduce, not remove, class differences and inequalities through welfare and redistribution schemes. Furthermore, instead of advocating class conflict, social democrats emphasise the need for class consensus and the peaceful reform of society.

60. Revolutionary socialism

Revolutionary socialism has tended to produce fundamentalist socialist regimes for the following reasons:

- Such regimes often emerge from violent struggle since revolutionary socialists argue that the ruling class has to be forcibly removed to bring about a complete transformation of society.
- Once in power, revolutionary socialists seek to impose centralised state control over the economy to determine the production and distribution of goods and services.
- To maintain political power, revolutionary socialists tend to establish regimes based on hierarchical parties led by dominant leaders and repressive political methods to crush all opponents and introduce totalitarian forms of control.

61. Social democracy

Social democracy found it difficult to sustain both dynamic economic growth and fairness in society for the following reasons:

- Social democracy's twin aims of economic growth and fairness in society became increasingly difficult to sustain as economic problems mounted in the 1970s and early 1980s. As unemployment increased, the demand for welfare provision (e.g. unemployment benefit) increased but tax-based funding for such welfare assistance declined (as the jobless total increased and business profits fell). This left social democracy with a stark choice: either cut taxes and curb inflation to rejuvenate the economy or make funding of the welfare state the key objective.
- Social democracy's difficulties in this area were compounded by (a) the loss of its electoral base due to the contraction of the working class as a result of deindustrialisation (b) the collapse of the Soviet bloc, which discredited socialist solutions that regarded the state as an important agency of economic and social reform.

62. The Third Way

Critics argue that the Third Way is not socialist because it:

- supports a capitalist market economy and an enterprise culture – key features of neo-liberalism
- distances itself from the socialist policy of wealth redistribution through progressive taxation
- supports social consensus and harmony, an approach that departs from the traditional socialist focus on class differences and inequality.

Supporters argue that the Third Way is socialist because it:

- emphasises equality of opportunity and a meritocratic social system in a similar way to social democracy
- endorses 'traditional' socialist values such as mutual dependence and fairness
- has introduced measures to foster social justice and improve conditions for the socially and economically disadvantaged.

63. Key thinkers: 1

Social class is central to Marxism because Marxists argue that:

- Class and economic factors shape historical and social development; class relations are conditioned by the economic system (e.g. capitalism) which influences all other aspects of society.
- Change within each stage of human history is driven by the struggle between the exploiting class and the exploited class (e.g. the bourgeoisie and proletariat under capitalism). This process culminates in the creation of a classless communist society.
- In order to overthrow the exploiting class, the exploited class must develop a revolutionary class consciousness in order to overthrow their oppressors. Thus, under capitalism, to remove the bourgeoisie, the proletariat has to become a 'class for itself', meaning it recognises its own interests and is resolved to pursue them.

64. Key thinkers: 2

- Webb believed in a gradual parliamentary route to socialism whereas Luxemburg advocated Marxist class struggle and revolution to create a socialist society.
- Webb contended that, because of its limitations, the working class would have a restricted role in the transition to socialism; Luxemburg argued that spontaneous proletarian revolutionary consciousness was the essential element in a socialist takeover of power.
- Webb maintained that the existing state, with its collectivist ethos, would play a key role in establishing socialism; Luxemburg argued that the capitalist state would have to be overthrown by the workers before a socialist system could be introduced.

65. Key thinkers: 3

According to Giddens, the role of the modern state is as follows:

- The modern state can no longer follow the social democratic interventionist role because circumstances have changed due to the impact of globalisation, the new knowledge economy and more individualistic aspirations.
- A new 'social investment' state has to be introduced which:
  (i) rejects the social and economic aims of the welfare/redistribution programmes of earlier social democratic governments, partly because these encouraged a dependency culture
  (ii) is based on a contract between the state and the citizen, whereby the state invests in education and infrastructure and, in return, people have an obligation to take advantage of this to better their situation
  (iii) promotes equality of opportunity but also acts to ensure that inequalities of outcome do not become pronounced.

67. Exam-style practice

1 Conservatism

Think about pessimistic and optimistic conservative assessments of human nature.

- Introduction – set up debate; define key terms.
- General conservative pessimistic outlook on human nature – humans are flawed, incapable of reaching a state of perfection and immutable (link to work of Hobbes). Humans are morally, psychologically and intellectually imperfect.
- Traditional, One Nation and neo-conservatives share this pessimistic view of human nature. Hence, their emphasis on authority, hierarchy and order (link to the work of Burke and Oakeshott).
- Neo-liberal conservatives disagree with this pessimistic assessment of human nature and instead stress atomistic individualism – the idea that individuals are rational, self-interested and self-sufficient (link to the work of Robert Nozick).
- Conclusion – most conservatives have a pessimistic view of human nature but the neo-liberal wing of the New Right provides an important exception.

2 Liberalism

Think about where classical and modern liberals agree and disagree on the economy.

- Introduction – set up debate; define key terms.
- The general liberal outlook on the economy is shaped by its support for private property, individualism and a positive view of human nature – so both liberal strands endorse a capitalist economic system (link to the work of Locke).
- Classical liberalism, with its emphasis on the rights of the individual, advocates a free market capitalist economy with limited or minimal state intervention (link to the work of Mill).
- Modern liberals take a more cautious view of the workings of the market economy and call for state intervention to ensure long-term economic growth and tackle the social and economic problems associated with unregulated capitalism (link to the work of Rawls).
- Conclusion – both liberal strands agree that a capitalist economy is necessary because it fits with core liberal values but classical and modern liberals disagree over the appropriate level of state intervention in the economy.

3 Socialism

Think about how different strands of socialism view society:

- Introduction – set up debate; define key terms.
- Traditionally, socialists have viewed society mainly in terms of class inequalities, economic divisions and significant disparities in property ownership.
- Marxists see capitalist society as dominated by class conflict and only communism, with its commitment to classlessness and absolute equality, can deliver a stable and unified society (link to work of Marx and Engels).
- Social democrats view society in more fluid terms, arguing that class inequalities and social differences can be reduced through welfare and redistribution schemes (link to work of Crosland). Social democrats also recognise that the rise of the service economy has made society increasingly 'middle class'.
- The neo-revisionist view of society rejects the traditional socialist emphasis on class distinctions and inequality, stressing instead harmony, consensus and social inclusion (link to work of Giddens).
- Conclusion – in recent decades, socialist views on society have become more diverse with social democrat and

Third Way thinking moving away from the traditional socialist focus on social and economic inequalities.

68. Types of constitutions

A codified constitution is judiciable. This means it gives powers to judges to decide if ordinary laws are in line with the constitution. Parliamentary sovereignty means that Parliament has the final say on laws. A codified constitution means that judges, not Parliament, would have the final say.

69. Sources of the UK constitution

Some sources are seen to be more rigid than others. In many ways EU laws and treaties may be seen as the most rigid of all sources as they require all member states to agree to any changes. Statute law is also quite rigid as it can only be changed by Parliament. Common/case law is more flexible as it requires judges to make a ruling (although the ruling is likely to go all the way to the Supreme Court, which may take a while). Conventions are traditions which theoretically do not have to be kept. However, it is very difficult to go against behaviour or procedures that are expected by many. Equally, works of authority act merely as guidance, but in the UK's evolutionary system, 'guidance' is expected to be adhered to.

70. Constitutional reforms since 1997

Electing chairs and members of select committees instead of them being appointed by whips made an enormous difference to the conduct of these committees. When selected by whips, members of key committees tended to be ones who would be loyal to and supportive of their party. Once they were elected by backbenchers, many independently minded MP's were elected to key roles on committees. As a result, select committees became much more effective in doing their job of scrutinising government departments.

71. UK devolved bodies

The Scottish Parliament was initially given more powers than the Welsh Assembly as the desire for self-rule was far greater in Scotland than in Wales, as shown in the result and turnout in the referendum of 1997. Subsequently, both in Scotland and (surprisingly) in Wales, there has been greater demand for more powers for their Assembly and Parliament. Despite all the changes to their powers (as outlined on page 71), the Scottish Parliament still has greater powers than the Welsh Assembly.

72. Devolution and its impact

Metro mayors can help the economic regeneration of a city by representing the city abroad to encourage investment in the city. They can pitch for business contracts or encourage businesses to relocate to their area. This would bring investment and job prospects to an area. Metro mayors also have control over long-term budgets from central government. They have more control over roads and transport, housing, and strategic planning, they can set the focus for their whole region and have a long-term plan for a city, rather than a short-term plan. It is expected that metro mayors will go to central government and demand more powers over transport, housing or economic development.

73. Are further reforms desirable?

An English Parliament would resolve the West Lothian question as issues discussed in the Westminster Parliament would then mainly be about issues affecting the whole of the UK, which all MPs would discuss. Other matters relating to the four regions would be discussed in their own Parliaments and Assemblies.

It would also improve the symmetry of devolution in the UK as areas of the UK would have a second level of representative below a Westminster MP.

Despite both these points, however, an English Parliament is an unlikely prospect.

74. Other possible reforms

Legitimacy means having the right to rule. In a democracy, the right to rule is usually conferred on our legislators via an election. Currently, even though they have a substantial say in the UK's legislative process, the Lords are unelected and hence lack legitimacy. Reforming the Lords, by electing them, would radically enhance the legitimacy of Parliament.

75. Parliament

The executive's role is to run the country and to propose legislation for the legislature to pass. The role of the legislature is to consider and (probably) pass the executive's proposal, possibly amending it first. It has an additional function of holding the executive to account in Parliament.

76. The structure of the Houses

The whips are crucial in maintaining party unity. Their role is to act as a channel of communication between the PM and their backbenchers, letting backbenchers know what the PM thinks and, just as crucially, making the PM aware of concerns of backbenchers. Whips are powerful people in Parliament as they decide if backbenchers are permitted to miss votes, go on trips abroad and of course, recommend them for promotion to the government. Whips are likely to help backbenchers who support the government's agenda by voting for their legislation, whereas rebellious backbenchers are unlikely to win many favours from the whips.

77. Functions: legislating and debating

There is significant overlap between these two functions as a large part of the legislative process involves debating legislation in Parliament. So, part of the legislative function is to debate the proposed legislation. However, there are aspects of the legislative function that are not related to debating legislative proposals, e.g. public bill committees.

Additionally, while a large part of the debating function is interconnected with the legislative function, since the Wright Reforms were introduced, the Commons has had a boost to its non-legislative debating function. Since then, many debates take place in the Commons which are unrelated to legislation.

78. Representative function

Parliament carries out its representative function in a number of ways:

- All MPs in the Commons are elected to represent a geographical area.
- The vast majority of MPs are members of a political party, so they represent the party and its manifesto commitments.
- MPs are socially representative, in that there is growing representation of women and minorities in society.

79. Composition and powers of the Houses

The term 'crossbenchers' refers to those members of the House of Lords who do not sit on either of the party benches, choosing instead to act as independents. They sit in a specific section of the chamber reserved for those members without party affiliation. They are significant because they tend to number approximately a third of the Lords, meaning that neither of the two main parties has a majority.

80. Relative power of the Houses

One reason for the growing significance of the Lords is that since the removal of hereditary peers in 1999, the Lords has felt rejuvenated and has flexed its muscles more towards the Commons.

Another reason is that combined with above, the Blair government between 1997 and 2005 had very large majorities in the Commons which made it difficult for them (the Commons) to hold the government to account; as such, the Lords felt in a better position to hold the government to account than the Commons.

A final reason is that since when in coalition with the Conservatives, the Lib Dems had 100 people appointed to the Lords. They have been prepared to stand up to the government on regular occasions since 2015, especially over Brexit.

81. The legislative process

Arguably the most important stage of a bill is the second reading in the Commons. This is widely accepted as being the biggest hurdle as this is where the main debate occurs and a crucial vote is taken. It is extremely rare for a government to lose a vote at second reading in the Commons.

Although the Lords can 'ask the Commons to reconsider' up to three times before the government invokes the Parliament Act, this is a **very** rare occurrence as the Lords usually accepts the will of the elected commons.

82. Parliamentary scrutiny

One key criticism is that questions on the floor of the Commons are too short to get a real answer. Often, the emphasis is on embarrassing or catching out the minister/PM rather than seeking information. This is illustrated most weeks particularly at Prime Minister's Questions where MPs are not shown in their best light. Another problem is that the governing party uses its own backbenchers to ask friendly, planted questions enabling the minister/PM to give the pre-planned answer.

83. Backbenchers

A government with a large majority (e.g. those of Blair, Thatcher) tends to weaken backbenchers' power. This is because it takes a lot of government backbenchers to rebel for the government to lose a vote. A government with a large majority is usually a very popular government with a PM who may well be around for many years. Backbenchers are less likely to upset the PM if they are likely to be in their position for a while as it reduces their chance of being promoted off the backbenches.

Equally, a government with a small or no majority (e.g, those of Cameron, May) tends to result in backbenchers feeling emboldened, as only a handful of government backbenchers are needed to stop the government's legislative agenda. Governments with small or no majority tend not to be very popular and there is usually a great deal of debate as to how much longer the PM will be in their position. Backbenchers are less likely to feel the need to be loyal to a PM who may only be in power for a very short time.

84. Structure and role of the executive

It is very easy to get the terms 'Parliament' and 'government' confused in the UK due to the fusion of powers that exists between the legislature and executive (see page 75). As the UK's government (executive) sits in Parliament (legislature), it is difficult to see them as two distinct 'institutions' as they both sit in the Commons (primarily). Members of the UK government 'wear two hats'. In 2017, for example, Amber Rudd was the Home Secretary as well as being the MP for Hastings and Rye. As a member of the government, she voted on legislation, while in theory, as an MP, she had a different representative role.

85. The Cabinet

Cabinet committees reduce the importance of the Cabinet as they are a way a PM can bypass Cabinet by making decisions with small groups of Cabinet ministers rather than allowing them to be debated in full Cabinet. It was suggested that many Brexit issues were discussed in a Cabinet committee, not in full Cabinet.

86. Collective ministerial responsibility

Collective responsibility was weakened in June 2017 as many members of May's Cabinet felt able to speak out and air their disagreements in public. Traditionally, Cabinet ministers do not behave in this way for fear of being sacked by the PM. However, May did not feel she could face the consequences of sacking these ministers and them fighting against her on the backbenches, so she ignored their breaking of this important convention.

87. Individual ministerial responsibility

It can be argued that IMR has lost its significance as there are many examples of it being broken and ministers not resigning. It is perhaps correct to say that legal responsibility has shifted in interpretation, with responsibility now meaning 'staying on as minister and dealing with the problem' rather than resigning. Political responsibility is perhaps kept more often when there is a clear case of a minister bringing the office into disrepute.

88. The power of the prime minister

Perhaps the first priority for a PM is to have their close, trusted allies in the Cabinet. Secondly, perhaps (depending how strong their position is within their party), they may seek to balance the wings of their party. This may well include giving important positions to 'big beasts' in their party as well as potential rivals. Nowadays, a PM must also consider the gender and ethnic balance of their Cabinet as PMs who have not done this recently have found themselves in trouble.

89. The Cabinet and the prime minister

When looking at Tony Blair as PM, early in his premiership you can see that he had a charismatic personality, a Cabinet who were prepared to yield to him and large majorities of over 150. He was also extremely popular in the country and faced a weak opposition for most of his time in office. He worked hard to keep the media on side and in the first few years had no major events to deal with. This made him an extremely strong PM.

However, much changed in the last few years of his premiership. His decision to take the country to war in Iraq led to a huge decrease in his popularity both in the public and the media, and his Cabinet became fed up by his authoritarian approach to decision-making. In 2005, his majority went down to 65 and David Cameron took over as leader of the opposition. All these factors led to a great weakening of his position, culminating in him being forced from office by his own party in 2007.

90. The executive and coalition government

The Quad were significant because the success of the coalition depended on being able to keep both parties satisfied. By working through policies in the Quad, they could ensure that are policies would be acceptable to both Conservatives and Lib Dems. However, some people argue that the Quad was significant because it was a way of avoiding full Cabinet and that key decisions were made there and not at Cabinet.

91. The Supreme Court

The CRA enhanced the independence of the judiciary as it separated the judiciary from the other two branches of government, legislature and executive. It did this by separating the position of Lord Chancellor into three distinct positions held by three different people: the Chief Justice, who is now a judge and head of the judiciary; the Speaker of the Lords, who is now a member of the Lords; and the Lord Chancellor, aka Justice Secretary, who is a member of the Cabinet.

92. Judicial neutrality and independence

Judicial independence, the idea that judges are not influenced by any other branch of government, is a central tenet of the constitutional set-up of the UK. In order for the rule of law to exists, judges must make ruling purely on the basis of the law.

93. The influence of the Supreme Court

Miller v Secretary of State for Exiting the European Union is an example of the Supreme Court being involved in interpreting the complex notion which is the UK's constitution. The outcome of the Supreme Court's ruling was that the government had to get Parliament's approval to trigger Article 50, which caused considerable trouble for Theresa May.

94. Important Supreme Court cases

If judges were to monitor parliamentary debates, this would undermine the separation of powers between the judiciary and the legislature as the only role the courts have is to rule on cases brought before them. Judges in the UK have no role in overseeing parliamentary procedures and this would therefore undermine that important separation.

95. Aims and influence of the EU

International trade has been dramatically affected by EU membership. As members of the Customs Union, the UK was unable to make trade deals with countries outside the UK (this does not mean the UK does not trade with other countries).

Also, immigration policy has been affected because, as members of the single market, the UK must allow free movement of people within the EU.

96. Impact of the EU on UK government

Factortame was considered significant because it showed, in no uncertain terms, that the UK's Parliament had been restricted by EU membership. Parliamentary sovereignty now had to be considered in association with our obligations under membership of the EU.

97. Sovereignty in the UK

Parliament's sovereignty is undermined by EU membership. Despite the fact that Parliament passed a law acceding to EU membership, while the UK is a member of the EU, decisions from the EU and its institutions take priority over UK laws.

In addition, devolution of powers, especially in the case of Scotland, has undermined the sovereignty of Parliament. Despite the legal position that Parliament is capable of passing a law to abolish the devolved assemblies, the political reality is that is its unable to do so without causing enormous disruption to the UK – to do so would be considered folly.

110. Exam-style practice 1, AS Level Paper 1

Section A: question 1

- They contest elections at various levels – so the party's candidates get elected or to win power and form the government.
- They have shared political views and values – parties are united around similar preferences and by ideology.
- Organisation – formal membership, structure to develop policy, identify and select both candidates and leaders.
- Broad issues focus – develop goals and policies across all major political issues, manifesto.

Section B: question 2

- Confusion – simple answer to a complex question and issue. Hard to understand the issues and the question is more complicated than yes or no, leaving the EU.
- Interpreting the result – how does the government interpret the result e.g. the 2011 vote in the AV referendum, a vote for FPTP or against AV?
- Decided by the minority, who get to impose their will on the public, especially true with low turnout, e.g. Welsh devolution, but even in EU where turnout was higher – only 37 per cent of total electorate voted to leave.
- Hot button issues – debate gets too simplified, moves away from key issues and question marks over the information e.g. EU referendum – immigration, the NHS pledge or poor quality of the debate in the 2011 electoral reform referendum.

111. Exam-style practice 2, AS Level Paper 1
Section B: question 3

- Sources 2 and 3 both agree that there is a participation crisis in politics and a collapse in the 18–24 vote is seen in both sources and that letting them vote is one potential solution.
- Sources 2 and 3 disagree about whether there is evidence to support the lowering of the voting age.
- Sources 2 and 3 both agree that there is and has been limited support for this change, but Source 2 shows that support for lowering the age can increase after the change is made.
- Source 2 suggests that 16- and 17-year-olds have the political maturity to vote – they had access to wider sources of information before voting in referendum,
- Source 3 suggests that the state has enhanced the number of laws to protect under 18s reflects that under 18s don't have the political maturity to vote.

Section C: question 4

- Introduction: define terms – two-party system, multiparty system. direction – the UK operates a two-party system but this does not apply across the different parts of the UK, e.g. – the SNP and Scotland.
- Votes and seats: two-party system – prior to 1980s, Labour and Tories win over 90 per cent of vote, nearly all the seats. Yet from 1980 to 2015 this vote share, and seat share, declined – multi-party. 2017 return to two parties.
- Forming governments: two parties – only Tories and Labour have a realistic chance of forming the government. Yet the 2010 coalition and the 2017 DUP confidence and supply agreement suggests a multi-party system but both deals saw one of the main parties as the dominant partner and came about not because of the rise of the Lib Dems or the DUP.
- Regional variations: multi-party – Northern Ireland, Scotland and regional variations in England. Two-party – Northern Ireland is a separate party system, Scotland does appear multi-party but most regions have a two-party system and some are dominated by one party – Labour in the North East or the Tories in South East.
- Conclusion: 2017 was a return to the two-party system in the UK but this cannot be applied to all parts of the UK as different regions seem to have different systems.

112. Exam-style practice 3, AS Level Paper 2
Section A: question 1

- Legislation – private members' bills and scrutiny of bills on public bill committees.
- Representation – of their constituents.
- Debate – main issues of the day and debates set by Backbench Business Committee.
- Hold the government to account – PMQs, Ministerial Question Time and Select Committees.

Section B: question 2

- Call witnesses – the ability to question in depth ministers and civil servants and really drill down into their answers, unlike PMQs or Ministers' Questions in the House.
- Reports – generally unanimous so gives them extra weight and often picked up by the media putting further pressure on the government to respond and make changes.
- Chairs elected and paid – makes this an attractive career option so attracts good candidates, voted for by MPs based on their abilities not loyalty to party leaders, e.g. Dr Sarah Wollaston, Chair of Health Select Committee.
- Independence – parties act free of party control and now members are elected and their appointment is not controlled by the Whips. Free to scrutinise the government.

113. Exam-style practice 4, AS Level Paper 2
Section B: question 3

- Sources 2 and 3 both agree that the Lords does an effective job at amending legislation, especially since the removal of the bulk of the hereditary peers in 1999.
- Source 2 and 3 both argue that an elected chamber would reduce the experience of the upper chamber, limiting its effectiveness in scrutinising law.
- Source 3 argues that its lack of legitimacy due to being unelected means the House of Lords is still not that assertive – it backs down when government backbench rebellions melt away. Elections would change this.
- Source 2 suggests that elections would lead to a chamber that either meekly accepted the will of the Commons or directly challenged it, both in effect leading to ineffective law making.

Section C: question 4

Think about how far reforms have modernised the constitution, satisfied public opinion and extended democracy and citizens' rights.

Introduction – set out the debate, key terms, what the reforms are. How you will argue.

How these have modernised the constitution:

- Devolution – has modified the centralised nature of the UK constitution; devolved bodies are able to shape policies to suit local needs, e.g. Right to Buy in Scotland and defeat of the independence referendum in 2014. Little evidence of desire for further reform in Wales, while devolution in Northern Ireland has helped end violence and created a power-sharing system.
- Electoral reform – more proportional results in elections to the Scottish Parliament, Welsh Assembly and Northern Ireland Assembly. Rejection of AV in the 2011 referendum indicates there is no public appetite for the extension of reform to Westminster.
- House of Lords reform – removal of most hereditary peers and the creation of an independent commission to appoint non-party peers have created an upper house based on merit and experience. The Lords have been more assertive in holding the government to account in recent years (e.g. opposition to George Osborne's attempt to cut tax credits in 2015). A fully elected chamber would produce a house of professional politicians and reduce the range of expertise.
- Human Rights Act 1998 – brought the UK into line with other European states. Provides protection of citizens' rights, without threatening parliamentary sovereignty. Judges can highlight laws that are incompatible with the Act but they cannot strike them down. It is not entrenched, so the government can modify the way it operates.

How these have not modernised the constitution:

- Devolution – there is a case for moving towards a federal solution that creates greater uniformity across the UK (increased strength of SNP).
- Electoral reform – declining levels of support for the two largest parties make FPTP seem out of step with political change. The underrepresentation of small parties and the way FPTP produces governments with a majority of seats but a minority of votes are powerful arguments for further reform.
- House of Lords reform – the Lords continues to lack an elected element. The main parties are all agreed on the case for change.
- Human Rights Act 1998 – there is a case for strengthening the HRA; governments can take away important liberties via a majority vote. The Conservative Party wants to replace the Act with a British Bill of Rights, making the UK Supreme Court the final arbiter of citizens' rights instead.
- Conclusion – a fully supported conclusion, reaching an overall judgement on the adequacy of constitutional reforms since 1997.

114. Exam-style practice 5, A Level Paper 1
Section A, question 1

- Introduction – set up the debate, define key terms.
- Age as a factor in determining the outcome of the 2015 general election: what information does the source offer to support this?

The Conservatives gained the support of 47 per cent of the 65+ age-group. Labour won only 23 per cent of this group. Conversely, the only section of the electorate by age, among whom Labour had a lead, was 18- to 34-year-olds. Use your own knowledge and understanding to expand on this and to explain why older people were more likely than the young both to vote Conservative and to turn out at all (e.g. wealth protection, inclusion in society, less idealism, 2015

policies for older people, such as pensions, issues for young people).

- The importance of other factors in determining the outcome of the 2015 general election. For example: class and ethnicity. Start with the evidence in the source and back this up with your own knowledge. You could link both class and ethnicity to wealth and property ownership; turnout; particular policies that might appeal to different ethnicities and class backgrounds, such as Labour's emphasis on anti-discrimination policies; the exception of those from an Asian background having more of a tendency to vote Conservative and why.
- Conclusion: reach an overall judgement on the relative importance of the various factors. The age profile of the electorate was a very important factor in producing the Conservative victory in 2015. There was a clear divide between the voting habits of the oldest and youngest sectors of the electorate. However, this links to two other features: likelihood to vote, correlation between class and property ownership.

Section A, question 2

Consider the ways in which resources (size of membership, finance) give pressure groups influence, before going on to balance this against other relevant factors.

- Introduction – set up debate, define key terms. Outline your argument.
- Resources – focus on up to three major factors: these could be the quality of leadership, the attitude of public opinion and whether the pressure group is in step with the government's agenda. Make sure that you give proper coverage to the issue of resources before moving on to the other factors. Explain why resources are important: because they enable the group to run a permanent organisation, attract media coverage and so on. Balance this with examples of well-funded, large groups that have not achieved their objectives to make the point that resources are not always the key to success.
- Assess the significance of the other factors that you listed in your introduction. In each case you must refer to specific examples . It is important to support your answer with examples of pressure groups that you have studied; your knowledge and understanding of the subject must underpin the analysis and evaluation throughout the essay.
- Conclusion – finally, you need to provide a short conclusion in which you decide which of the factors, on balance, is the most important one. Your conclusion must be fully focused on the question and justified, with your reasons clearly explained.

115. Exam-style practice 6, A Level Paper 2
Section A, question 1

- Introduction – set up the debate, define key terms.
- The Lords should remain unelected. What information does the source offer to support this?

It will help maintain the current broad range of membership of the Lords; it doesn't threaten the supremacy of the Commons; appointment is more cost effective than election.

Use your own knowledge and understanding to expand on these points and explain why these points would make the Lords more effective than it currently is.

- The Lords should be reformed but remain partly unelected. What information does the source offer to support this?

It combines the best of both systems; the Commons would retain its supremacy; it would be a more straightforward system to introduce.

Use your own knowledge and understanding to expand on these points and explain why these points would make the Lords more effective than it currently is.

Are these points more convincing than the arguments in the paragraph above? Compare and contrast the different advantages expressed in these two options and come to a judgement about which one provides a stronger case.

- The Lords should be reformed and be fully elected. What information does the source offer to support this?

It addresses the democratic deficit; more people will be given the opportunity to stand for Parliament; more young people will sit in the Lords.

Use your own knowledge and understanding to expand on these points and explain why these points would make the Lords more effective than it currently is.

Are these points more convincing than the arguments in the paragraphs above? Compare and contrast the different advantages expressed in these three options and come to a judgement about which one provides a stronger case.

- Conclusion – reach an overall judgement on the relative importance of the various options. In a case like this, there is no clear correct answer, so you must choose a side and argue that throughout your answer, using as much evidence from the source as you can. Your conclusion should simply confirm what you have made clear throughout your essay.

Section A, question 2

You should cover both individual and collective responsibility, although you do not necessarily have to divide your time equally between the two. Make sure, however, that you look at both sides of the argument: at ways in which ministerial responsibility remains important, and at how its importance has been eroded in recent decades. The list below sets out the main points. Remember to give specific examples to support your points.

Individual responsibility

Reasons for continued importance:
- In a parliamentary system, it is vital for ministers to be held to account by the elected representatives of the people. This is why misleading Parliament carries the ultimate sanction of loss of office (e.g. Immigration Minister Beverley Hughes, 2004). The people have a right to expect high standards of their representatives.
- It is a means of maintaining the traditional demarcation of roles between ministers and civil servants.

Ways in which importance has decreased:
- Individual responsibility is an elastic concept whose application depends on particular circumstances. When things go wrong, much depends on the level of criticism faced by the minister (e.g. Charles Clarke, 2006), and on the willingness of the prime minister to maintain or withhold support.
- Accountability is hard to define precisely in a complex political environment, with executive agencies existing alongside traditional government departments, and a 24-hour news culture placing both ministers and officials under unrelenting scrutiny.

Collective responsibility

Reasons for continued importance:
- It sustains the unity of the government against external attacks, by insisting that ministers jointly support an agreed line (e.g. May's Cabinet and the third Heathrow runway).
- The doctrine also emphasises the importance of confidentiality in Cabinet and Cabinet committees, even if this is not always observed.
- It strengthens the authority of the prime minister over their colleagues by requiring a minister who cannot accept the agreed position to resign (e.g. Blair's Cabinet following Robin Cook's 2003 resignation).

Ways in which importance has decreased:
- It is ignored by ministers who maintain their opposition to their colleagues from within the government, and who may leak information to the media in order to promote their own viewpoint (e.g. Major's Cabinet in the mid-1990s undermined by rival MPs leaking rumours).
- In practice there have been important exceptions to the rule of collective responsibility (e.g. in the formation of the Cameron coalition and the two European referendums of 1975 and 2016).

116. Rejection of the state

Anarchists reject the state on the following grounds:
- The state has a negative impact on human nature since it can:
  - (a) coerce an individual to act against their will, undermining their autonomy
  - (b) suppress human initiative, creativity and self-realisation
  - (c) corrupt people in authority since their wealth, power and status makes them lose touch with the collaborative and altruistic essence of human nature
  - (d) uphold inequality and use force to impose its will, thereby abusing the people under its authority.
- The state is unjust and exploitative in its defence of economic inequality since it:
  - (a) imposes taxation, which amounts to a form of state 'theft'
  - (b) protects the elites of the developed nations through international institutions such as the World Bank
  - (c) defends the privileges of the wealthy and private property.

117. Liberty and order

Anarchism's view of human nature underpins the anarchist perspective on liberty in the following ways:

- For individualist anarchists, humans are rational, autonomous, competitive and self-interested. However, since all types of authority are commanding and controlling, people are deprived of their autonomy, rationalism and individuality. Therefore, in order to express their true human nature, people have to be liberated from all forms of authority.
- For collectivist anarchists, the oppressive state prevents humans from realising their true unselfish and collaborative nature. In their view, individual liberty is achieved only when everybody is free to fulfil their potential, thus making liberty dependent on the existence of social and economic equality. Hence, the liberty to express true human nature is achieved by removing the class-based, hierarchical state and society which supports socio-economic inequality.

118. Economic freedom and utopianism

Anarchists oppose capitalism because in their view:
- capitalism promotes private property, inequality and exploitation; it also uses the state apparatus to deny real freedom by safeguarding the position of the privileged and oppressing the rest of the population
- under capitalism, state intervention in the economy skews the market and creates public and private monopolies, resulting in restricted competition, limited choice and a loss of economic freedom.

119. Collectivist anarchism: anarcho-communism

Collectivist anarchism is similar to socialism in the following ways:
- Both have a positive view of human nature, in particular stressing that people are sociable, cooperative and altruistic.
- Both maintain that collective action in the pursuit of their aims is superior to competitive individual effort.
- Collectivist anarchism and most forms of socialism endorse the idea of common ownership.
- Most collectivist anarchists and some socialists call for the revolutionary overthrow of capitalism.

Collectivist anarchism is different from socialism in the following ways:
- Collectivist anarchism calls for the abolition of the state; most socialists advocate the permanent or temporary retention of the state.
- Collectivist anarchists call for the complete removal of capitalism; moderate socialists aim to reform or 'humanise' capitalism.
- Collectivist anarchism rejects the positive emphasis placed on the individual and the free market by the Third Way.

120. Mutualism and anarcho-syndicalism

The main differences between mutualism and anarcho-syndicalism are:
- Mutualism provides a link between collectivist and individualist anarchism, whereas anarcho-syndicalism falls squarely into the collectivist anarchist category.
- Although both view the state as oppressive, mutualism argues for the peaceful removal of the state based on some form of democratic consent, whereas anarcho-syndicalism calls for the destruction of the state through a general strike, mass demonstrations and violence.
- Anarcho-syndicalists view the trade unions as the basis of a stateless, free, stable and classless anarchist society; mutualism calls for small communities and associations that do not use the trade unions as an organisational template.

121. Individualist anarchism

Individualist and collectivist anarchists differ over human nature in the following ways:
- Individualist anarchists, such as egoists, maintain that humans lack morality, want total personal autonomy and are self-interested. People are driven by egoism and should act as they see fit without any constraints. The most extreme egoists (nihilists) regard humans as fundamentally individualistic, not sociable. In contrast, collectivist anarchists argue that human nature is sociable, cooperative and altruistic. Consequently, human relationships are naturally based on mutual assistance, social unity and harmony.
- Individualist anarchists, such as anarcho-capitalists, regard humans as competitive, rational, economic and autonomous. Motivated by an innate sense of entitlement, people work to possess private property. Thus, it is natural for people to act in a self-serving manner and enter into free, self-interested economic relationships. Collectivist anarchists, such as anarcho-communists and anarcho-syndicalists, reject the argument that humans are self-seeking and competitive. Instead, they maintain that people are essentially sociable, cooperative and empathetic, with a natural capacity for social solidarity.

122. Anarchist key thinkers

Goldman's and Proudhon's views on the state overlap in the following ways:
- Both see the state as immoral – a negative presence.
- Both call for the state to be removed.

Goldman's and Proudhon's views on the state do not overlap in the following ways:
- Proudhon explicitly calls for the peaceful removal of the state but Goldman does not.
- Proudhon's 'peaceful removal' strategy implies a longer time frame is required to dismantle the state.

124. Ecology and holism

Enlightened anthropocentrism is different as it extends rights to both the current generation and future generations, seeing humans as the stewards of nature rather than its master.

125. Environmental ethics and consciousness

It has moved beyond traditional ethical thinking in several ways – by extending rights to future generations, animals and the wider biotic community or by saying that the traditional ethical framework is part of the problem and there is the need to radically change our world view to one of environmental consciousness.

126. Materialism, consumerism and sustainability

Materialism links happiness with the consumption of goods, while consumerism is constantly creating new demand for the consumption. This increase in consumption drives production, which uses up finite resources while increasing pollution.

127. Deep green ecologism

1 This is a nature-centred approach rather than a human-centred approach that emphasises the maintenance of ecological balance over any human-centred goals.
2 Intrinsic value refers to the idea of nature having value in its own right, rather than nature only having value due to the benefits it brings to humanity.

128. Shallow green ecologism

Some shallow greens believe the state should withdraw from the market, leaving the market as the best solution to environmental profit. The desire for profit will mean companies take a sustainable approach to win the business of ethical consumers and to drive down the cost of increasingly scarce resources. Other shallow greens see the state taking a leading role, using increased regulation or green taxes to drive companies to innovate and adopt more sustainable technologies.

129. Social ecology

1 All three are united by the view that ecological disaster is caused by existing structures in society based on the domination of human by human. For ecosocialists, this is capitalism with the domination of one class by another. For ecofeminism, this is patriarchy, the domination of women by men. For eco-anarchists, it is the state and hierarchical structures which divide people into the few who give orders and the many who have to take them. All agree that these structures must be overthrown and radical social change brought about.
2 Both deep greens and ecoanarchists envision a future society without the state, based around decentralised, self-organising communes that use direct democracy with economies that work in harmony with local ecosystems to reach strong sustainability.

130. Agreement and tensions within ecologism

1 Industrialism is a view that underpins core political ideas like socialism, conservatism and liberalism and is based on a belief in large-scale production, faith in science and technology and limitless growth.
2 The idea of environmental consciousness is one of a spiritual, inner revolution, or 'eco-la-la' as Bookchin described it. The spiritual element takes it away from rational argument and it is hard to see how this revolution will take place. Holistic ethics struggles as it appears to place all life on an equal footing, meaning that the human species and viruses have an equal right to life.

131. Ecologist key thinkers

Aldo Leopold – deep green, Rachel Carson – shallow green, E.F. Schumacher – deep green, Murray Bookchin

– social ecology (eco-anarchist) and Carolyn Merchant – social ecology (ecofeminist).

133. Sex and gender
Words may include the following:
Men – strong, brave, assertive, ambitious, firm
Women – sensitive, anxious, bossy, hard.

134. Patriarchy and 'the personal is political'
Historically, the media perpetuated patriarchy through adverts which emphasised a woman's primary role in a domestic setting. Nowadays, media focuses on unreasonable expectations of the way women should look.

135. Equality and difference feminism; intersectionality
• Black women have had a different experience of oppression as they have had to tackle racism and sexism within society. They have argued that they are at the very bottom of a hierarchy that has white men at the top, then white women, then black men and lastly black women.
• Working-class women have also had a very different experience of oppression. They argued that while second-wave feminism had been partly focused on the right of women to enter the workplace, they had always had to work. Their experience of oppression was the unequal and usually extremely unfair way they were treated in the workplace, often with few if any rights compared to working-class men.

136. Liberal and socialist feminism
Freidan was referring to the feelings women had when they had achieved everything they were supposed to achieve in order for them to feel fulfilled, i.e. marriage and family, but yet they did not feel fulfilled. Instead they felt unhappy but could not understand why.

137. Radical feminism
For radical equality feminists, difference feminists threaten the very premise that radical feminism is based on. For a radical equality feminist, patriarchy bases its oppression on the myth that men and women are biologically different and that the difference is a hierarchal one, i.e. women's differences make them inferior to men. Thus, when difference feminists argue that men and women **are** different, they feel this is the same argument used to justify patriarchy.

138. Post-modern feminism
The different attitudes of feminists identified on this page highlight how many different views and experiences exist for women. This is what post-modern feminists seek to identify and highlight. In many ways, post-modern feminism is saying that it's impossible to give a view about what 'women' think, or how 'women' feel, as there are as many differences between women as there are between men and women (and probably between men, too).

139. Differences within feminism
All feminists agree that one's gender plays a significant role in the way you are treated by society; i.e. that men and women are treated differently. Moreover, all feminists believe that this can be changed. Nonetheless, it is accurate to say that there are many differences between feminist beliefs.

140. Feminist key thinkers
Charlotte Perkins Gilman – socialist feminist based on her analysis of the economy.
Simone de Beauvoir – a radical feminist based on her work on sex and gender and patriarchy.
Kate Millett – a radical feminist based on her work of the role of family and literature on patriarchy.
Sheila Rowbotham – a socialist feminist based on her analysis of capitalism.
bell hooks – a post-modern feminist based on her analysis of the role of women of colour.

142. Politics of recognition
Misrecognition is where racism, stereotyping and stigmatisation of a community by other cultures can damage the sense of self-worth and well-being of the members of that community. It can make those individuals feel like an outsider or a second-class citizen even though they have formal equality, and weakens their commitment to wider society.

143. Culture and identity
Communitarianism is the idea that individuals are 'culturally embedded'; they are shaped by the communities which they belong to and grew up in.

144. Minority rights
1 Even where the state is seen as or professes to be neutral between different cultures, the official language of the state, public holidays and the curriculum are all examples of how the state is aligned with the dominant culture and this places minorities at a disadvantage within society.
2 Minority rights can be viewed as reverse discrimination, making minority cultures inward-looking not outward-looking, therefore likely to segregate themselves from wider society, and can lead to minority cultures restricting the freedoms of their members.

145. Diversity
Shallow diversity only values diversity within a liberal framework. Diversity does not extend to cultures which are illiberal – a threat to personal autonomy. Deep diversity criticises this approach, arguing that it absolutises liberalism (makes it an absolute value that all cultures must subscribe to), when it is only one conception of the good life and cannot be seen as superior to other cultures and their values. Deep diversity is the idea that all cultures have some value and so deserve recognition.

146. Liberal multiculturalism
1 Autonomy is the liberal idea that an individual must be able to choose their version of the good life in line with their own beliefs, values and ideas and that these ideas are subject to evaluation and change.
2 Tolerance only extends to cultures, their practices and ideas which are compatible with the liberal framework, in particular autonomy, freedom and liberal democracy.

147. Pluralist multiculturalism
Universalism is the idea that there are some values which apply to all individuals and societies, regardless of culture or any other difference. For example, the liberal multiculturalist approach can be seen to universalise or absolutise autonomy.

148. Cosmopolitan multiculturalism
Cosmopolitan multiculturalism wishes to promote and support diversity, as different cultures provide the freedom for individuals to pick and mix their identity. The issue is that the creation of these new identities weakens the commitment to cultures and could ultimately lead to the dissolving of cultural groups and diversity.

149. The conservative criticism
Assimilation is the process of encouraging minority cultures to conform to the majority culture. Minorities are expected to adopt the values, beliefs and customs of the majority culture to create a homogenised national identity that is seen as the basis for a stable society.

150. Multiculturalist key thinkers
• Assimilation is the state-led policy of dissolving minority cultures into the majority culture by getting them to accept the values, customs and beliefs of the majority.
• Individualist integration involves granting rights and equality to members of minority groups and immigrants as individuals.
• Multiculturalist integration is a two-way process that shapes minority and majority cultures. Individuals from minority groups are granted equal rights and the state must implement laws both to protect and promote those cultures.
• Cosmopolitan integration means the state must protect cultures so that minority, as well as majority, individuals, can mix with, borrow and learn from all cultures.

152. Nations
A group may consider themselves a nation if they have a shared history, e.g. the UK. Here the experiences gone through as a nation forge a sense of unity among people.

Another way a group may consider themselves a nation is by sharing values, e.g. the USA in the 1940s and 1950s. Here the concept of the 'American dream' was that anyone, no matter what their background, could have the opportunity to be successful if they really wanted to work hard, respect American values and become a part of society.

153. Self-determination and nation-states
Germany is considered a nation-state as Germany is ruled in a clearly defined territory by Germans. This was not always the case as Germany was split until 1990 into West Germany and East Germany.

Italy is a nation-state as Italy is ruled in a clearly defined

territory by Italians. It was unified in 1871. Between 1815 and 1871, the different states of the Italian peninsula Italy united to become one country. Mazzini was involved in this movement towards unification.

154. Culturalism and racialism
Culturalism is considered to be exclusive as one cannot understand or even feel the culture of a nation immediately. It takes time to understand the cultural aspects that different nations exhibit. However, eventually one may hope to feel part of the cultural identity of a nation, so although it is somewhat exclusive, it is not totally so.
Racialism, which is based on alleged biological differences between nations, is considered to be completely exclusive as theoretically, one cannot change one's race. Thus if one is born into a race, one cannot change it.

155. Internationalism
Liberal internationalism is consistent with liberal nationalism as they argue the best way to guarantee a peaceful world is for independent nation-states (liberal nationalism) to cooperate with other nations, making them interdependent and working within supranational institutions (liberal internationalism). They believe this is the best way to secure peaceful coexistence in the world.

156. Different types of nationalism
The terms 'inclusive' and 'exclusive', when referred to a form of nationalism, are linked to how easy it is to become part of a nation. This is directly linked to whether they express nationalism as civic, cultural, ethnic or racial.
• Civic nationalism merely requires people to support the values of their society; hence they are highly inclusive.
• Cultural nationalism requires people to have shared values, such as language, culture, tradition. These take time to develop so are less inclusive and more exclusive.
• Ethnic nationalism requires more than cultural assimilation, it requires a shared heritage and ancestry. This can take a generation or more to develop so is quite exclusive.
• Racial nationalism requires the biological clarity of the race/nation, as it rejects the view that there is only one human race. If you are not born into the race, you can never become part of it, irrespective of where you were born, what values you share with those who are part of the 'race'. This is highly exclusive as it is impossible to join if you are not born into it.

157. Liberal and conservative nationalism
Liberal nationalism supports the idea that many cultures should be encouraged within society as it promotes the important values of tolerance, pluralism and diversity. Liberal nationalism believes in civic nationalism, that one simply needs to share the values of a nation in order to become a part of it. They don't support the idea that one must share the same culture to identify with a nation.
Conservative nationalism supports monoculturalism – the idea that society is united within one cultural identity. This is linked to their idea of an organic society. Conservatism believes that humans seek the security of the known and familiar, while change makes humans feel insecure and afraid. Hence immigrants should be encouraged to reject their cultural heritage and adopt the culture of their new home nation.

158. Expansionist and anti/post-colonial nationalism
Anti-colonial nationalism is the rejection of expansionist nationalism as they are the 'victims' of expansionist oppressors. The scramble for Africa in the 19th century saw European powers carve Africa up and 'take' parts of it as their own; they expanded their rule over these nations, oppressing them and not allowing the indigenous population any rights in their own country. Eventually, these nations rose up against their colonial masters; this is what we understand as anti-colonial nationalism.

159. Differences within nationalism
There is no doubt that the many differences between the different strands of nationalism make it hard to see this as a single coherent ideology. However, all the strands of nationalism are focus their attention on the role of the nation and the importance (or not) of the nation-state and self-determination. While there is no doubting the enormous variations in the ideology, it is still reasonable for it to be studied under the single heading of 'nationalism'.

160. Nationalist key thinkers

Rousseau – liberal nationalist based on his idea of civic nationalism.

Herder – a conservative nationalist based on his ideas of culturalism.

Mazzini – liberal nationalism based on his ideas of self determination.

Maurras – expansionist nationalism based on his idea of ultra-nationalism.

Garvey – anti/post-colonial nationalism based on his ideas of black nationalism.

162. Exam-style practice

Anarchism

Think here about the debate around the nature of the state and how to remove it.

- Introduction: define key terms; set the debate.
- Agreement: the state is immoral because it restricts liberty, unjust because it defends economic inequality, and has a negative impact on human nature (Kropotkin, Stirner, Goldman).
- Disagreements: most collectivist anarchists call for revolutionary action to overthrow the state (Kropotkin, Bakunin). Others call for the peaceful and gradual abolition of the state through a democratic political process as anarchist ideas become more popular (Proudhon). Some egoists call for insurrection, a process where self-interested individuals elevate themselves above the state so the latter is ignored and fades away (Stirner).
- Conclusion: collectivist and individualist anarchists largely agree about the oppressive nature of the state, but there are disagreements about how to remove the state.

Ecologism

Think here about the debate around human nature and anthropocentrism.

- Introduction: define key terms; set the debate.
- Agreement: anthropocentrism and the separation of humans from nature, mechanistic world-view, and lessons of holism and ecology.
- Disagreements: enlightened anthropocentrism, the lessons of holism and ecology – Carson, intergenerational equity and animal rights. Ecocentrism – lessons of holism and ecology, holistic ethics, Leopold and environmental consciousness. Social ecology – the debate about anthropocentrism is irrelevant. Bookchin: tackle hierarchical structures and domination to change human behaviour.
- Conclusion: largely agree that anthropocentrism is a key issue, but disagreement about the type of change needed is fundamental and unresolvable.

Feminism

Think here about the debate around patriarchy among feminists.

- Introduction: define the key terms; set the debate.
- Agreement: all feminists recognise that society benefits men more than women. Radical, socialist and post-modern feminists believe that patriarchy is a dominant form of oppression against women in society, which must be reformed by social revolution (Perkins Gilman).
- Disagreement: radical feminists are the only feminists who believe that patriarchy is the main oppressive force in society (Millett). Socialist feminists believe that capitalism oppresses women at least as much as patriarchy in society (Rowbothom). Post-modern feminists believe that there are other forces alongside patriarchy that oppress women, e.g. race, hooks. Many liberal feminists reject the idea of patriarchy as a form of oppression that can only be removed by social revolution, preferring instead to believe that there is discrimination in society, which can gradually be reformed.
- Conclusion: largely agree that patriarchy is a key issue but disagreement over the type of change as well as the existence of other forces at work alongside patriarchy.

Multiculturalism

Think here about the role of the state in promoting diversity.

- Introduction: define the key terms; set the debate.
- Conservative criticism – any state support to promote diversity undermines unity. State should promote assimilation to create unity.
- Criticisms of assimilation as creating disunity, the idea of individualist integration to balance diversity and unity.
- Does individualist integration go far enough? Multicultural integration – Taylor and politics of recognition; Kymlicka – group differentiated rights balances diversity and unity.
- The state – needs to go further to promote not just tolerate diversity. Parekh – multicultural integration and tackle social and economic inequality to create unity.
- Conclusion: the state has a key role to play, but deep disagreements over the approach that should be adopted by the state.

Nationalism

Think here about differences between types of nationalism.

- Introduction: define the key terms; set the debate.
- Agreement: all types of nationalism agree that the nation is the key unit of identity in society – Rousseau.
- Disagreements: how a nation is defined is a key area of disagreement between liberal and anti-colonial nationalists, and expansionist nationalists and conservative nationalists – Garvey. Self-determination is a key area of disagreement between liberal and anti-colonial nationalists and expansionist nationalists – Mazzini. How welcoming society should be to other cultures is a key area of difference between liberal and anti-colonial nationalists and expansionists nationalists and conservative nationalists – Maurras.
- Conclusion: a few common areas, but overwhelmingly more differences between the different types than similarities.

163. Comparative theories

1 Rational theory is best understood as 'selfish' because it looks at individuals acting in a way that gets the best outcome for them personally. Cultural theory is best understood as 'shared' as it looks at similarities and differences that exist in terms of ideologies. Structural theory is best understood as 'institutions' as it aims to explain differences and similarities through the political processes which exist with the institutions of government.

2 You would use these theories **only** to explain differences and similarities **between** two systems. The theories cannot be used to explain the action within one country, only between two or more countries.

164. The US Constitution

1 The US Constitution is short, and therefore easy to understand, and lends clarity to the US political system. It is kept up to date, despite being codified, due to its vagueness and the amendment process, but it is also protected from continual change which prevents any government manipulating it to control too much individual power.

2 The 'right to bear arms' in the second amendment is no longer necessary. The Electoral College prevents direct elections for the US president.

165. The constitutional framework

1 Congress has power of the purse as representatives of the taxpayers (e.g. the annual budget), approves treaties between the USA and other nations (e.g. the START Treaty 2010) and approves judicial and ambassadorial appointments (e.g. Neil Gorsuch to the Supreme Court 2017). They can also declare war on other nations but this was last used officially in the Second World War. The president is the Commander-in-Chief and can move troops (e.g. Iraq 2003). He also negotiates treaties (e.g. START 2010), nominates judicial and ambassadorial appointments (e.g. Neil Gorsuch, 2017) and can veto legislation (e.g. Obama's Keystone Pipeline veto, 2015).

2 The president puts forward nominees for appointments and treaties; Congress can merely accept or reject these, rather than suggesting their own. The president suggests both the budget and legislation (at the State of the Union address) for Congress to act upon. As Commander-in-Chief, numerous US presidents have involved the USA in military conflict, yet the last time that Congress used its power to declare war was in the Second World War.

166. The amendment process

1 The process requires super-majorities on both Houses of Congress, which is difficult to achieve in a country as diverse and divided as the USA; the same is true of the difficulty of gaining agreement from three-quarters of states. This makes the process very lengthy, meaning any public desire for an amendment often wanes. Given the vagueness of the US Constitution, there is little necessity or public pressure for amendments as the Supreme Court can update the Constitution through judicial interpretative amendments.

2 Some of the arguments for changing the process are:
- It is too long and prevents change from happening, meaning the Constitution is out of date.
- It allows for a tyranny of the minority, meaning that representative democracy is undermined.
- The difficulty of the process has led to so few amendments that, conversely, the Supreme Court has gained too much power as an unelected branch.
- The requirements for bipartisanship do not work in a USA that is so deeply divided, but do help to continue the existence of just a two-party system.

167. Principles of the US Constitution

1 'Separation of powers' refers to the independent powers and actions of one branch to act alone. 'Checks and balances' refers to the powers that directly allow one branch to impede the action of another branch.

2 Arguably, each of the principles is under threat. However, most under threat seems to be either federalism or limited government. The other three are all threatened due to current political circumstances. Comparatively, federal government has continually grown in size over centuries and in doing so has increasingly eroded the powers of the individual states.

168. Federalism

1 The 10th amendment protects the generic rights of the states and other Articles in the Constitution protect their rights to run, for example, their own elections. The role of the Supreme Court ensures both states and federal government have an independent body they can appeal to in the case of conflict. For federal government, as well as the enumerated powers, the 'necessary and proper' clause and the 'commerce clause' allow the federal government enough power to react to threats to the whole of the USA.

2 While state governments retain constitutional power under the 10th amendment and demonstrate their individuality in areas such as elections and death penalty legislation, the ultimate power seems to rest with federal government. States look to federal government for money when major events happen that are very costly, federal law is superior to state law and even when there is conflict it is the Supreme Court – one of the branches of federal government – which is the final referee.

169. Evaluation of the US Constitution

1 The US Constitution could be considered out of date with amendments such as the 'right to bear arms' still upheld, and with the notable power of an unelected and unaccountable judiciary. It could also be considered out of date having been written over 200 years ago when the USA was much smaller and less diverse, meaning some processes (such as the Electoral College and Amendment Process) are no longer effective or necessary today.

2 Your answer may depend on the current political circumstances. For example, during the time of Obama's presidency, the growth of federal government through legislation such as Obamacare might have been the biggest weakness. However, President Trump may argue that power of unelected judges is the biggest weakness, having had many of his executive orders challenged in the courts.

170. The US Constitution and democracy

1 The USA clearly has aspects of a number of differing types of democracy. However, it seems most closely aligned to liberal democracy having a limited government and rights protected. It does not fulfil all aspects of a liberal democracy, as there is a question over the extent to which US elections are 'fair', for example given the Electoral College.

2 The amendment process and the requirement for super-majorities allows for 'tyranny of the minority', which undermines the will of the majority. The Supreme Court is unelected and unaccountable and therefore in being able to overrule the will of the elected representatives it undermines representative democracy, as does the Electoral College which prevents direct elections for the president. The codification of the Bill of Rights also prevents the changing views of the electorate being effectively reflected by their representatives.

171. Federalism today

1 The death penalty shows the USA remains federal in a number of ways. Each state in the USA is free to decide whether it wishes to use the death penalty at all, and if so, by which method. Where methods have proven difficult, for example, with the acquisition of drugs being increasingly difficult, states have made their own decisions on which combination of three drugs can be used and in what quantities. Even when this has been challenged at federal level, the court has upheld the states' rights to make decisions over the death penalty for themselves.

2 The Supreme Court poses a threat to federalism as they are able to overturn state laws as unconstitutional, or uphold federal law over state law. The Electoral College threatens federalism as it encourages presidential candidates to focus only on

the bigger states and appeal to their voters, therefore creating policies which ignore US diversity.

172. Constitutions compared

1 One reason they are different is because the US Constitution is codified and the UK constitution is not. This means the US Constitution has a formal amendment process within the text of the document. They are also different due to the location of sovereignty. As the US Constitution is sovereign, it should be difficult to change. Comparatively, sovereignty in the UK resides in Parliament giving them power to change the constitution frequently. Finally, they are different due to the roles of the Supreme Courts. The US Supreme Court is able to rule on the Constitution and make 'interpretive amendments' that are effectively sovereign whereas the UK Supreme Court could be ignored by the government.

2 Differences could be explained using cultural theory as federalism in the USA reflects vast differences in ideology between the states in the USA. California, for example, is often considered more 'liberal' whereas Texas is considered more 'conservative'. Comparatively, the ideological differences between the countries in the UK are far more marginal meaning differences are less pronounced. However, structural theory is also useful as federalism is a key part of the US Constitution, protecting the rights of states in the 10th amendment. Comparatively, in the UK, devolved bodies only exist having been allowed to by central government, and have their power only because central government has given it to them, while maintaining its own supremacy.

173. The structure of Congress

1 It is clear that the US Congress is becoming more representative of minority groups, with women, African-Americans and Hispanics all gaining more representation. However, the number of women is still not reflective of the population generally, and is only increasing slowly. Hispanic representation is increasing more quickly than the African-American population, and the Hispanic community has better representation in the Senate than African-Americans, despite having less representation in Congress as a whole.

2 Congress has become more effective at representation over the past ten years, with more women, African Americans and minorities being elected. It best represents African Americans, with 9.4 per cent of Congress representing a group which makes up 14 per cent of the US population. Hispanic representation has increased most quickly over the past five Congresses and if it continues to increase the Hispanic population will be appropriately represented in Congress. However, whilst the representation of women has improved, it has done so only marginally, and women remain hugely under-represented in Congress when compared to the national population.

174. Powers within Congress

1 The Senate alone limits the power of the president by being able to reject his nominees for positions, such as judicial and cabinet appointments, and being able to reject his treaty proposals. As the House which tries impeachment, their vote can remove a president from office. However, the Senate also limits the power of president as part of Congress, being necessary to pass his suggested legislation and budgets. They are also required to vote as part of the declaration of war; however, this has not been used since 1942.

2 The House of Representatives could be considered superior as they always have the most recent mandate from the people, having a full election every two years. As representatives of the taxpayers, they get to initiate money bills, and they decided on the charges against a president in impeachment proceedings. Equally, when the Electoral College is deadlocked, they get to decide the president alone, whereas the Senate gets only to decide on the vice-president.

175. Representative function

1 Incumbents are highly likely to retain their seats in an election, although this seems more likely in the House of Representatives than in the Senate. The main reasons for this is the benefits that being an incumbent gives to a candidate, notably their name recognition and political support such as franking and website support.

2 A Congressional politician is likely to be influenced by each of the factors when considering his vote. However, with frequent elections they must be certain to pay attention to their constituents, especially in the House of Representatives where everyone is elected every two years.

176. Legislative function

In the House, the role of a party is crucial whereas in the Senate, just one Senator can hold up the legislation. The party in the House determines the timetabling and just a simple majority is needed. In the Senate, a filibuster can be held by one member and much of the business is conducted by unanimous consent, reducing the importance of the party.

177. Oversight function

1 Congressional oversight over the Supreme Court is limited as all the methods are rather extreme. Before a justice gets on to the Supreme Court, they could reject them as a nominee; however, this does not affect the power of the Court. They can remove justices or initiate constitutional amendments but both of these are incredibly difficult and each has only been used once.

2 There are a number of challenges to effective congressional oversight. Probably the most important, as the most frequent and predictable, is congressional elections and this turns their attention away from the business of government and towards their constituents. However, national emergencies, such as 9/11, can mean that Congress defers some of their power to the president and this is a significant limit on oversight but usually for a shorter time.

178. Effectiveness of representation

1 The Constitution ensures adequate representation of the population through the use of a frequent election cycle which requires representatives to be accountable for their actions, and by the representation of districts (in the House of Representatives) and states (in the Senate) to ensure that both are well represented regardless of population size

2 The House of Representatives is elected more frequently and therefore more responsive to constituents' demands, and they represent smaller numbers of people giving each person arguably greater representation. However, Senators are individually more powerful and are therefore better able to advance the views of the state they represent.

179. Changing role and powers of Congress

1 While Congressional power is set in the Constitution, their ability to exercise this power depends on current political circumstances as the evolution of the USA, and technology over the past 200 years have made some of the powers less important. For example, the power to declare war is unlikely to be used; however, Congress does give authorisation for military force. Equally, if a president is popular, Congress is more likely to do what he wants if they are from the same party; if not, the partisanship of Congress makes it less likely that much will be achieved at all.

2 The two-party system seems to make parties very important, with an increasing number of votes being taken along party lines and an increasing level of partisanship being evident in Congress. However, with both parties covering a wide ideological spectrum – a 'broad church' – and frequent elections, it could be argued that the parties are merely vehicles by which to win elections.

180. The effectiveness of Congress

Congress is somewhat effective at all the functions. It has demonstrated its ability to carry out all the functions, including passing law, representing the electorate and scrutinising both the president and the Supreme Court. When both Houses and the Presidency are held by one party, Congress is often most effective at legislation, being able to work together to get laws passed relatively quickly, such as Obamacare. When the branches are controlled by different parties, Congress becomes more effective at oversight, being more willing to challenge the president on his actions.

181. Legislatures compared

1 The House of Commons has more power over legislation as the government usually has a majority in this House and the House of Lords has only a limited ability to prevent their work. The House of Representatives is more powerful at oversight, with separation of powers allowing for better scrutiny of the executive branch and more direct powers, such as the veto override, to prevent action by the executive.

2 Congressional ability to oversee the actions of the president depend crucially on whether government is united or divided. In times of divided government, Congress can act more forcefully to control the executive branch, refusing to pass legislation, passing budgets, ratifying appointments and treaties and even using the veto override or impeaching the president. However, in times of united government in the USA, Congress is often less willing to challenge the president and use the powers they are given. In the UK, effectiveness is determined by the size of the government majority. Parliament is dominated by the government in the UK, usually with a government majority in the lower chamber and a limited power of the upper chamber to prevent the government doing as it pleases. However, the last three elections have produced governments of either no, or small, majorities, and therefore Parliament has been more able to control the executive.

182. The US president

1 The president needs Congress in order to gain money for any of his initiatives, pass any legislation that he wants, approving treaties and appointments, all as outlined in the US Constitution (separation of powers, and checks and balances).

2 Both roles are important for the president. As a world leader, the president speaks on behalf of the USA to the rest of the world and is the figure by whom the USA is often judged. This role has fewer constitutional checks and so can be important when a president is unpopular. The Head of Government role is important as it is on domestic policies that most presidents run an electoral campaign, and therefore they have to achieve in this area to get re-elected. However, there are more constitutional checks in this area.

183. Informal sources of power

1 Informal sources of power could improve the president's popularity as he could use them in order to make substantial changes very quickly, therefore pleasing the electorate. However, overuse of these powers could seem autocratic and might end up costing him popularity.

2 Given that both Trump and Obama controlled both Houses of Congress, the key factor that enabled one to be successful while the other was not was their individual popularity. Powers of persuasion depend on popularity and at the beginning of Obama's term in office, his electoral mandate, a reflection of his popularity, was stronger than Trump's.

184. Executive Office of the President

1 The EXOP is clearly important as they speak on behalf of the president and are his closest and most trusted advisors. This gives them a lot of power to decide who gets access to the president and their appointment reflects the view of the president. By appointing Steve Bannon to the NSC, Trump indicated a more right-wing and political approach to this body but made the body look weak by appointing someone with no experience. Comparatively, however, the EXOP has no constitutional power. In the case study, the swift removal of Bannon suggests that the EXOP does have some power.

2 During times of military action, the NSC is likely to be a more important part of the EXOP, advising the president military policy. However, in times of economic crisis, it is more likely that the OMB would be more important, and in times of scandal, the WHO is likely to be who he relies on.

185. Relationship with other institutions

1 During a formal lame-duck session, both Congress and the president become lame ducks. While both still formally hold the Constitutional powers allocated to them, they lack a mandate to exercise them. Arguably, therefore, the Supreme Court would be the most powerful branch during this time, not relying on an electoral mandate for its power.

2 The factors that affect presidential power all link. The timing of the electoral cycle is clearly crucial, however, as it is for this reason that there are parties in the USA, and this determines the control of the Houses of Congress, as well as determining how strong the presidential mandate is, which directly affects his ability to persuade.

186. Limits on the president's power

The two presidents did not achieve very much for quite different reasons. In the case of Obama, the Constitution coupled with powerful interest groups and the opposition party controlling Congress preventing him from achieving gun control. Comparatively, Trump has struggled to make substantive achievements due to poor popularity ratings which have fractured the Republican Party despite controlling both Houses of Congress and the Presidency.

187. Achieving their aims

1 George W. Bush was probably the most successful in carrying out what he promised in the electoral campaign and his reforms were substantial. However, much of his agenda got shaped early on in his presidency when 9/11 occurred. While all of the presidents have had some successes many of these were earlier in their presidencies, and Bush had a huge poll rating boost after 9/11.

2 Their popularity, control of Congress and national events are key factors in a president having enough power to carry out his promises.

188. The imperial presidency

1 The imperial presidency is one in which checks and balances that are placed upon the president are deemed to be ineffective.

2 The imperial presidency is difficult to maintain as a frequent election cycle means that maintaining control of both Houses of Congress is unlikely, and a president can only serve for eight years. Equally, the Supreme Court has the power to overturn presidential actions.

189. The president and foreign policy

1 Ford meant that reactions to foreign affairs needed to be done swiftly, and having 535 Congressmen discussing it would be inappropriate, and very slow. The Constitution reflects this by making the president commander-in-chief while Congress can agree or not on declaring war.

2 In the short term, the president is more powerful in foreign policy, being able to speak, and in some cases act, on behalf of the USA. This is somewhat dependent on their popularity but usually in the short term the president can control foreign policy. Over the longer term, however, Congress is able to scrutinise the president's actions, including withholding money and launching investigations, which gives them greater power in the long run.

190. Executives compared

1 The US president is more dependent on 'persuasion' due to the separation of powers meaning his influence over Congress is limited. The fused powers of the UK legislature and executive mean that the prime minister is more able to force things through Parliament with strong party discipline and little need for persuasion.

2 The effectiveness of each legislature does depend on circumstances such as popularity, but largely Congress has more formal power to limit the president. Parliament has been increasingly effective given the lack of, or limited, majority in the 2010, 2015 and 2017 elections. Both legislatures are less effective in time of a large majority by one party, and this is less likely to occur in the USA.

191. Nature of the Supreme Court

1 Judicial review is the power of the Supreme Court to rule laws or actions unconstitutional and therefore 'null and void'.

2 The Supreme Court does remain largely independent due to limited ways in which other branches can influence justices once they are on the Supreme Court. As part of the appointment process, Congress can allow or reject a justice, but they can do little once they are on the Court given their life tenure and protected salary. Congress do control the numbers of justices on the Supreme Court but this has not changed since 1869.

192. The appointment process

1 If a president can appoint a Supreme Court nominee, he can help to shape the ideological balance of the Supreme Court, which may end up ruling on his laws or actions.

2 The president may consider a candidate's ideology, their chances of successfully passing through the appointment process, their experience and even their gender or ethnicity.

193. Public policy

1 The Supreme Court is considered to be quasi-sovereign as it interprets the meaning of the sovereign document and therefore its rulings are effectively sovereign.

2 While the Supreme Court simply upheld a congressional law in this case, therefore seemingly not a sign of its power, in doing so they effectively gave constitutionality to aspects of Obamacare. As a law of Congress, signed by the President, the Supreme Court were really the last branch that could have removed it; by upholding it, the immediate future of Obamacare seemed safe, demonstrating the significant impact of the Supreme Court even when agreeing with the elected branches.

194. Political role of the Court

1 Traditionally, conservative justices would be assumed to be more restrained, placing value on the role of elected branches and believing in smaller government. This is not always the case, however, and the issue they are ruling on does affect this interpretation.

2 In certain issues, the Roberts Court has seen a degree of conservative activism – this is ruling on cases to with a view to achieving conservative values in society. They have been more willing to hear cases regarding gun control (DC *v* Heller, 2008 and McDonald *v* Chicago, 2010) and have ruled to uphold gun owners' rights. Equally, in the case of Carhart *v* Gonzales, 2007, they ruled to place restrictions on abortion. In these cases, the justices are acting in an 'activist' manner, but the values that they are achieving in their rulings are conservative.

195. Rights today

1 Probably the most controversial is the 2nd amendment, which guarantees the 'right to bear arms'. Right to gun ownership continues to be problematic when there are so many mass shootings in the USA. Equally, the 8th amendment prohibits cruel and unusual punishment and yet the death penalty still exists. Many of the amendments are controversial in some way.

2 The Supreme Court is an effective protector of rights given its power of judicial review. However, in hearing only 60–80 cases a year. It limits the amount of rights it can uphold. Equally, what is a 'right' is not commonly accepted and justices disagree on this depending on their political philosophy. In this way, the Supreme Court has worked to uphold some rights successfully, while others remain limited in their protection.

196. Race and rights

1 While racial equality has advanced, most notably with the appointment of Obama, it clearly remains an issue, with under-representation in Congress and the Supreme Court agreeing that race is still a factor worthy of considering in college applications. The need for a movement such as Black Lives Matter suggests that the African-American community still believes this is a problem.

2 For racial equality to be achieved, one or more of the branches of government needs to support it. However, both elected branches of government are likely to be more interested in the majority given the use of the FPTP electoral system in the USA. Therefore, the Supreme Court should be relied upon to take and rule upon cases of racial equality in order to protect the minority of US citizens.

197. Affirmative action

1 The cartoon suggests that African-Americans have helped the USA become a success and instead of helping African-Americans now achieve equality, the USA is being hypocritical and suggesting they should earn their equality alone. Under the policy of affirmative action, it could be said that this cartoon is less accurate. However, with the demise of this policy and increasing challenges to it, while inequality remains, it could be argued that in fact this cartoon is increasingly relevant.

2 As a liberal democracy, affirmative action does have a place in the USA today as it aims to solve the clear inequality that exists. However, the 'American Dream' also places a huge emphasis on meritocracy, and it could be argued that affirmative action gives preference to those who have not earned it.

198. Judicial vs political

1 'Legislating from the bench' means that the Supreme Court is effectively creating new law through its judicial decisions.

2 The Supreme Court could arguably be political as there is nothing explicitly in the Constitution regarding same-sex marriage and therefore the ruling from this case is based on broad interpretation of the Constitution in order to achieve a socially progressive outcome. This 5–4 ruling allowed for same-sex marriage in every state, despite 13 states having outlawed it in the state legislatures. However, it could be argued that they were being judicial by interpreting the 'equal protection' clause of the 14th amendment to allow the same protection with regards to marriage for homosexual couples that heterosexual couples have.

199. Effectiveness of rights protection

The main reason is that whether a right is protected or not is often down to the ideological interpretation of those involved, and rarely does a 'right' have one side. For example, gun ownership could be argued to be a right, while those opposed would argue their right to life and safety is being impinged. Abortion could be argued to be a women's right, while others would argue the foetus has a right to life. Free speech seems relatively uncontentious, until the free speech of someone controversial is upheld. The disagreement over what rights in the Constitution are supposed to mean, and how they should be interpreted today, means it is difficult to see whether they have been upheld.

200. Immigration reform

1 Immigration reform has been attempted through legislation, at state and federal level, through executive orders and through the Supreme Court.

2 The continuing growth of the Hispanic population is a crucial reason for the importance of immigration reform today. However, the failure of Congress to reach an agreement, and that Obama resorted to executive orders which were ultimately struck down by the Supreme Court, suggests that some resolution to this problem is needed.

201. Judiciaries compared

1 Life tenure and security of pay, as well as separation of powers (both physical and theoretical), ensure the independence of the Supreme Court in the USA and the UK.

2 The Supreme Courts in the USA and UK have an increasing number of similarities following the Constitutional Reform Act of 2005 in the UK, which physically separated the UK Supreme Court from the legislature. However, in one crucial regard the courts differ – the sovereignty they hold. The US Supreme Court is quasi-sovereign, responsible for interpreting the sovereign document of the Constitution, while in the UK Parliament remains sovereign, meaning the Supreme Court could be ignored. However, given that the likelihood of this is minimal, the courts do actually share a degree of similarity in both power and appearance.

202. Rights compared

1 In both countries, pressure groups can appeal to the Supreme Court and lower courts. In the USA, however, groups can submit *amicus curiae* briefs without bringing a case, but in the UK groups can appeal higher to the ECHR if their case fails in the UK Supreme Court. Devolution and federalism give a different access point at a more local level.

2 Having quasi-sovereignty has meant rulings of the Supreme Court in the USA are seldom ignored and therefore rights are well protected when they are ruled upon. However, in practice, when it comes to terrorism and Guantanamo Bay, their rulings have been somewhat ignored. Comparatively in the UK, while the Supreme Court lack quasi-sovereignty, the authority it has gained as a separated institution means its rulings are also unlikely to be ignored. Therefore, sovereignty does not seem to have allowed the US Supreme Court to have protected rights much better than in the UK.

203. The electoral process

1 Front-loading is where states move their primaries earlier in the electoral calendar in order to have a greater role in the selection of the presidential candidates.

2 The electoral process is so long due to the number of stages that must take place. Importantly, it is long because voters do not just elect the president, they also elect presidential candidates in the primaries which elongates the process. It is also lengthy because it is not a direct election, meaning the Electoral College stage at the end adds to the time an election takes.

204. The Electoral College

1 It is not a direct election because voters are actually voting for the party that the state's ECVs will be pledged to, rather than directly voting for the president.

2 Trump won because he took more states than Clinton, 30 in total, which added up to more than the 270 ECVs which are required to win the presidency. It does not matter what percentage of the popular vote a candidate wins; the winner is decided by the Electoral College.

205. Significance of the electoral process

1 The Electoral College helps to provide a clear winner in the US presidential election, even when the popular vote is close. In both 2000 and 2016, while the winner of the popular vote did not win the election, the ultimate winner did take the most number of states, which helps to protect federalism. However, with two of the last five elections producing a result which does not reflect the popular vote, the USA claims of being a liberal and representative democracy could be challenged, and can lead to increasing voter apathy.

2 Each part of the electoral process has aspects which could be reformed. It is important to consider what is trying to be achieved with each reform. If the aim is to ensure the winner of the popular vote ultimately wins, then the Electoral College is probably the area most in need of reform. However, if the aim is to allow more parties to compete, the length of the process and the electoral system used is more in need of reform. If the aim is to increase voter interest and the resulting mandate, then the value of primaries and caucuses, with the low turnout they have currently, can be questioned.

206. Incumbency

1 Government control is the ability of the incumbent president to control the workings of government, such as suggesting legislation, controlling departments and exercising the powers of the president, which can help him to pass popular policies just before an election. However, having to run a government as head of state and head of government, and run for an election could mean that the president is distracted from the campaign trail, which can make their campaign more difficult.

2 If it is presumed an incumbent president will win, they have little to gain in, for example TV debates, and lots to lose. This is because the expectations on them are high and therefore it is easier to underperform against expectations of the electorate.

207. Campaign finance and reform

1 The main differences are the amount of money that each group is allowed to raise and whether they are allowed to use it directly for a campaign. Only Super PACs and 527s can raise unlimited amounts but neither can give it directly to a campaign. PACs and Super PACs can support or oppose a specific candidate.

2 The main reason that campaign finance proves so difficult is that by the time politicians are in a powerful enough position to do something about it, many are so dependent on campaign finance for their position that it is not in their interest to enact changes. The Constitution and Supreme Court have also posed a significant barrier creating constitution protection for campaign spending as 'free speech'.

208. Electoral reform

1 The NPVIC circumvents the Electoral College by placing greater emphasis on the result of the popular vote nationally rather than the result within each individual state.

2 The Electoral College was designed to protect the voice of small states and guard against populism. In this way, the Electoral College is therefore operating as intended by the Founding Fathers. This may not be in keeping with modern views on democracy, but it does prevent big states like California swaying the election.

209. Elections compared

1 Providing state funding would help because the cost of elections is so high and increasing. This means that third parties find it harder to compete with the main parties who often have more money and are better at raising it. If the state funded parties, third parties would stand a better chance of being able to compete against the major parties.

2 The increasing cost of elections, evident in both the USA and UK, is controversial due to how such money is raised. In both the USA and UK, campaign finance has caused controversy, with scandals in the UK in 2015 and Supreme Court cases like Citizens United *v* FEC 2010 in the USA. With money playing such a big role in elections, it could be argued that elections can be 'bought', which does not seem to be in line with representative or liberal democracy.

210. Party principles

The main parties in the USA are described as broad churches as the policies, views and ideologies within each party are wide-ranging. Warren and Manchin are both Democrats and yet score vastly different results from the NIAC, reflecting a difference in their view of this issue. Equally, Americans for Prosperity seems like a group which would be naturally aligned with the Republicans given its aims, yet Susan Collins only scores 49 per cent from them, reflecting a lukewarm attitude from her towards them. Comparatively, Ted Cruz, also Republican, gained 98 per cent, showing the difference in attitude towards this group within the Republican Party.

211. Party factions

In some respects, there is an overlap between the two parties, with the 'moderates' and 'conservatives' within the Democrat Party being willing to accept some fiscal conservativism similar to that of the Republican Party. Equally the 'moderates' in the Republican Party can be willing to accept more socially progressive policy in more line with that of the 'liberals' in the Democrat Party. However, such overlaps are quite minimal.

212. Party power

1 Party decline is the idea, perhaps outdated, that parties in the USA are becoming less relevant and important. This is supported by the decline in their role in nominating presidential candidates. Party renewal suggests the opposite, that despite the decline in this area, parties remain, or indeed are increasingly, relevant in other areas, for example with the growing partisanship in USA politics.

2 Parties are crucial to the organisation of Congress. With almost every member of Congress belonging to either the Republicans or the Democrats, the structure of Congress largely revolves around a two-party system. The leadership positions are set up to reflect a two-party system and the parties both operate their own structure within Congress to ensure they can achieve their own policy aims.

213. Voters

1 Voting patterns in the 21st century have remained remarkably consistent. The most notable change is the growth in the Hispanic vote for the Democratic Party over the last four elections. Women seem to have become less likely to vote Republican and men less likely to vote Democrat but this has not increased the vote of the opposite side, suggesting perhaps that their votes have gone elsewhere to third parties. Those with higher levels of education seem to have become marginally more likely to vote Democrat and those with lower level of education marginally more likely to vote Republican.

2 The reason that each group tends to associate with one party or the other is the support that party lends to policies which is important to that group. For example, younger and more educated people tend to be more liberal and socially progressive, whereas older and less educated people tend to be more conservative in outlook, corresponding with a marginal trend to vote Democrat and Republican respectively.

214. Two-party system

1 Third parties may have gained votes in 2016 for a number of reasons. Trump winning the nomination for the Republicans and Clinton for the Democrats could have been important. Both were unpopular in some ways (Trump for his inexperience and Clinton for various scandals such as Benghazi) and so voters may have looked elsewhere. Equally, the two parties, even with Trump as the Republican nominee, did not offer anything radically different from one another. With some media attention being placed on Bernie Sanders in the early primaries, however, and the increasing presence of parties such as the Green Party, it was clearer that there were other options, even if the Electoral College would mean they had little real chance.

2 The most important reason that the USA remains a two-party system is a combination of the use of first-past-the-post and the Electoral College, both of which encourage the development of a two-party system.

215. Democracy compared

1 First-past-the-post encourages a two-party system. By only rewarding the candidate who gains a plurality of votes, third parties gain nothing for coming anywhere other than first, meaning they achieve little or nothing for the votes they actually achieve. Comparatively, the main parties tend to be over-rewarded, achieving seats with less than a majority of the vote.

2 Labour is currently divided over the direction of the party under the leadership of Jeremy Corbyn while Brexit remains a divisive issue within the Conservative Party. The Republicans are divided over their loyalty to Trump and the factions like the Freedom Caucus. This suggests the Democrats are the 'most unified', although given their lack of success in 2016 and the controversies that Clinton's campaign created, perhaps 'least disunified' is more accurate!

216. Significance of interest groups

1 The USA is hospitable for interest groups due to the wide number of access points – three branches of federal government and many levels of state and local government, all of which can be targeted. Equally, the frequent election cycle means groups can try and gain through donations to candidates or use of PACs and Super PACs. With the two-party system being so dominant, for many, the only way to achieve other change may be though pressure groups.

2 Money is crucial to pressure group success as they can use money for campaign donations, adverts, protests and lobbying. If this gains media attention, then it may be hugely influential. However, more important is probably any access they can gain through connections – the table on page 210 shows how groups rate Representatives and Senators. Having a member of Congress who is sympathetic to your cause could be far more influential than money.

217. Resources and tactics of interest groups

1 Lobbying is the act of seeking the ear of government, where a group will try to achieve influence over a lawmaker or piece of legislation so that it is in-keeping with their aims and beliefs.

2 Lobbying firms could be controversial as they could be seen as elitist. Those with the most money or the most important contacts often have the most success. SPB acquiring John Boehner for their firm brought with it a lot of insider knowledge of Congress and contacts that he has. This places smaller, citizen-led groups at a disadvantage.

218. Interest group typology

The main difference between pressure groups comes from what they are aiming to achieve. Those aiming to achieve influence over wide policy areas are 'policy groups' and their success may affect a vast array of people. Comparative single-issue group success, while also affecting many people, will only affect a small issue in their lives. Professional groups are almost a mix of these two – they can affect wide policy areas but for only a smaller group of people, defined by certain characteristics.

219. Interest groups and democracy

Pressure groups are good for liberal democracy as they advocate for the protection of rights, but could be bad as the money they pour into elections is perhaps not 'free and fair'. They are good for representative democracy as citizens who do not feel represented by their member of Congress can instead join a pressure group; however, small groups can gain undue influence which undermines representative democracy. They are good for pluralist democracy as the huge number of pressure groups represents tolerance; however, those with the most money are often most influential, which is not therefore a 'wide dispersal of power'. Finally, pressure groups are good for US constitutional democracy, helping to ensure rights are protected; however, they potentially undermine the elections outlined in the Constitution through the vast use of money.

220. Interest groups and influence

Pressure groups can be influential in the USA in a range of ways beyond lobbying and campaign finance. As experts in their policy area, they are able to provide information to government through congressional committee hearings and *amicus curiae* briefs to the Supreme Court. More directly, they can even write legislation and hope to gain a congressional sponsor, or bring a case to the Supreme Court.

221. Interest groups compared

1 The main reason that US groups use electioneering methods more than UK groups is due to the sheer volume of money involved in US elections. While the cost of UK elections is increasing, it is nowhere near the cost of US elections, so for a candidate to be competitive in the USA they may be more willing to listen to pressure groups in return for campaign finance. The courts are more widely used in the USA due to their constitutional standing and having quasi-sovereignty. In the UK, with sovereignty resting in Parliament, groups may have a better chance of success using MPs, rather than the courts.

2 Pressure groups in both countries have some influence and have had notable successes. They act quite differently in both countries. The successes are probably more prominent in the UK as pressure group activity is less linked with money and the

potential political scandals that that can create. In the USA, because money and electioneering are so closely aligned, it can often be more difficult to see exactly where a pressure group has had success.

231. Exam-style practice

Section A

One way of answering this question might be:

- Legislative differences – the House of Lords only has the power of delay and can be usurped by the House of Commons, whereas the Senate and House of Representatives have equal legislative power.
- Scrutiny power – the House of Lords has a substantial power of delay supported by a lesser degree of party unity in the Lords, however has little noted power to scrutinise the government more broadly. The Senate has constitutionally protected powers such as approval of treaties and cabinet ministers.
- Representative differences – the House of Lords, being unelected, does not directly represent any constituencies in the UK, whereas the Senators are directly elected within each state and represent not just the electorate, but state interests and the party for whom they were elected.

Section B

One way of answering this question might be:

- The principle of checks and balances are limited in the UK due to fused powers of executive and legislature, but are strong in the USA as outlined through Articles I, II and III. This is best explained using cultural theory, as the UK constitution has evolved over time with no distinct need for codified separation of powers, whereas the US Constitution was written as a reaction to previous British rule and perceived 'tyranny'.
- Bipartisanship is enforced through supermajorities in the US Constitution, but is usually unnecessary in the UK due to large electoral majorities of the winning party. This is best understood structurally as the US Constitution requires super-majorities in processes such as the veto override and has separately elected Houses, raising the prospect of a divided Congress. Comparatively, the simple majority required for passing legislation in the UK and ability of the government to dominate both Houses removes much need for bipartisanship.
- US government is limited through checks and balances which allows one branch to oversee and have an impact upon the actions of another; this can lead to government shutdowns. Conversely, the power of the UK executive in the legislature can lead to an 'elective dictatorship' (Hailsham, 1976). This is best understood both rationally and structurally as in both cases those who hold power are using it to serve themselves, yet the outcome is vastly different due to the political context in each country.

Section C

(a) One way of answering this question might be:

Intro – following the 2016 election, both the Republicans and Democrats have shown considerable division within their parties. However, the growing partisanship in US politics and culture suggests parties are more important than ever. With Trump as a leading figure within the Republican Party and his limited successes in his first year, the divisions among Republicans do seem more pronounced than among Democrats.

The Democratic Party is more unified than the Republican Party:

- The 'no bill no break' sit-in and response to Parkland shooting suggest a far more unified approach to gun control than the Republican Party. Trump initially supported a bump-stock ban and Congressmen Curbelo called for gun control, but the party remains divided, with wide support for training and arming of teachers.
- The failure of the Republicans to pass a 'repeal and replace' to Obamacare was due largely to their indecision over what should replace it, while the Democrats remained broadly in favour.
- Immigration remains a unifying factor for most Democrats but a divisive factor for Republicans, with a Democrat filibuster leading to the 2018 government shutdown over immigration.

The Democratic Party is not more unified than the Republican Party:

- Republican cohesion to conservative ideals remains strong, as seen in their refusal to hold hearings for Merrick Garland and their vote for Neil Gorsuch to the US Supreme Court.

- Both parties seem equally united in the face of Trump's tax reform bill, with the vote in both houses being almost entirely a party-line vote.
- Despite seeming unified, Democrats have proven divided on arming school teachers following gun control debates, compared to a broadly pro-2nd amendment stance from Republicans.

Conclusion – the key division within the Republicans currently seems to be over their view of Trump and the issues he advances. While this makes the Democrats on the face of it seem less divided, they also have less holding them together, which is of concern when they occupy the opposition in all branches of federal government. Despite some deep divides in the Republicans, these seem to stem from strongly held beliefs and have not proven insurmountable.

(b) One way of answering this question might be:

- Separation of powers should ensure that each branch of US federal government has its own powers, personnel and buildings. Constitutionally, this separation remains unhindered today and the powers of each branch has not changed. In reality, however, some of these powers seem to have been usurped, such as a lack of congressional control over foreign policy in the 21st century.
- Federalism, while not mentioned in the Constitution explicitly, is threaded throughout the document. While Supreme Court cases and federal laws such as Obamacare may have chipped away at this, the huge variation in state laws on public policy issues such as death penalty, abortion and marijuana suggest the USA remains broadly federal.
- The federal government was envisaged as a 'limited government' by many of the Founding Fathers, who tried to ensure it would not become unwieldy and tyrannous. It has grown considerably in size, with the annual budget now around $4 trillion, and is probably larger than original intended. However, the same is true of the USA – in terms of geographical size, population and number of states, it has grown tremendously since.

232. The state: nation-state

1 The nation-state is an autonomous political community held together by citizenship and nationality. It comprises the elements of a state as a territorially based unit and a nation, which is a community of people held together by shared values and traditions.

2 The term is highly problematic as most states are diverse in terms of traditions, values and ethnicity. Some, like Iraq, are so diverse that they are states without nations. On the other hand, some nations don't have their own states but have to live in other states, like the Kurds.

233. The state: national sovereignty

1 National sovereignty refers to the state's absolute and unlimited power both within its own territorial borders and in global politics. This can be divided into internal sovereignty and external sovereignty, and sovereign states are the building blocks of global politics.

2 The Treaty of Westphalia (1648) establishes the three key principles of international law, which are all built on the principle of the sovereignty of states. The three principles are the sovereignty of states, the legal equality of states and the principle of non-interference in states.

234. The state and globalisation

Globalisation can be seen as the emergence of a complex web of interconnectedness that means that people's lives are now shaped by decisions made a great distance away. This shrinking of the world has had a significant impact on the territorial borders of states.

235. Economic and cultural globalisation

1 There has always been international trade. Under globalisation, however, that trade has grown. With the emergence of global production chains, there has been a huge increase in trade within TNCs across borders, while the globalised financial system suggests the shrinking of the world and the weakness of the idea of territorial borders.

2 Economic globalisation has created TNCs, which have promoted global goods and brands and spread global news, which have shaped cultural globalisation. In particular, economic globalisation has been seen to Westernise global culture around Western ideals of individualism, materialism, consumerism and support for universal human rights.

236. Political globalisation

1 Political globalisation lags behind economic and cultural globalisation as there is opposition to the idea of placing limits on the sovereignty of individual states. This means most institutions are based on intergovernmentalism, not supranationalism, and there is no desire for world government.

2 The spread of wealth, ideas and information across the globe changes societies. With these ideas and increased wealth comes the desire of ordinary people to achieve political freedom as well as economic freedom.

237. Globalisation and international law

1 The rise of international human rights law can be linked to some of the mass atrocity crimes of the 20th century under the Nazi and Stalinist states. The crises in Yugoslavia and Rwanda sped up this demand, as images of the crimes were broadcast across the globe. International law will promote the rules and norms of international behaviour that lessen the chance of mass atrocity crimes and conflict.

2 International law challenges the Westphalian order, as it looks to regulate the actions of states within their own territorial borders in contravention of the principle of sovereignty and may trigger humanitarian intervention within states, contravening the rule of non-intervention.

238. Humanitarian and forcible intervention

In the new post-Westphalian order, sovereignty is conditional on the state living up to international law and protecting its own population. Failure to do so is seen as invalidating state sovereignty, legalising external intervention within states.

239. Globalisation and the nation-state

1 Transformationalists disagree with both hyperglobalisers, who see the state as massively weakened by globalisation, and sceptics, who see the state as remaining powerful or even increasing in power. They argue that this approach is too simplistic as it shows change only in one direction and in a uniform way for all states. Globalisation has had different impacts on different states, changing their nature, and has had an uneven impact on communities and individuals, integrating some while leaving others behind.

2 There are disagreements about whether globalisation is significant, the nature of its impact on the state, the importance of global governance and whether globalisation brings peace and cooperation.

240. The impact of globalisation

1 The realist view of globalisation is generally sceptical. Sceptics argue that the impact of globalisation is exaggerated. Most economic activity takes place within state borders, and national economic policies are still the key to growth as China has shown. International institutions remain weak and states are still the main actors on the world stage. It may even be that international institutions become the instruments through which major powers aim to achieve their goals.

2 This would be the case for liberals, and especially hyperglobalisers. The weakening of states and the emergence of global institutions, the move towards a global culture and the spread of wealth will create a world where peace and cooperation become the norm.

241. Globalisation and contemporary issues

Economic globalisation is uneven as it benefits certain regions, countries and people within states more than others. This creates winners and losers from the process. Winners would be TNCs, Western states like the USA and some emerging states like China and India, while the states of sub-Saharan Africa have suffered, as have the poor, especially marginalised groups, within states.

242. The United Nations (UN)

The UN Charter protects state sovereignty by ensuring that its organisation is based around the principle of equality of all member states. Article 2 (7) protects state sovereignty by ensuring that the United Nations cannot intervene in the domestic jurisdiction of any state.

243. The UN Security Council (UNSC)

1 It does not represent the modern balance of power in the world today, it is not regionally balanced and the P-5 use the veto for their own ends rather than building collective security.

2 The veto is so problematic as it makes it very hard to the UNSC to take action. Instead, the veto allows the P-5 to further their own objectives, rather than collective security, as can be seen by the failure to reach agreement over action in Syria.

244. UN General Assembly, ECOSOC and ICJ

The key difference is in the membership and voting structure. First, the Assembly includes all nations, while the Council only has 15 members. Secondly, in the Assembly, each nation has one vote and a two-thirds majority is needed to make decisions. In the UNSC, however, the P-5 each have a veto and can block any decision. Lastly, decisions by the UNSC are binding while decisions by the Assembly are only recommendations.

245. North Atlantic Treaty Organization (NATO)

NATO has needed to find a new role for itself since the collapse of the Cold War. It has expanded its membership eastwards and become a specialist in peacekeeping and humanitarian intervention, and this role has developed beyond Europe.

246. The IMF and the World Bank

There are three main policy conditions – austerity, trade liberalisation and export-led growth. Austerity involves shrinking the role of the state, trade liberalisation involves opening up domestic markets and exports are seen as the key source of economic growth.

247. IMF and World Bank: significance and reform

Both are based in the USA, have Western leadership at the head of the organisations and a voting structure that favours the largest economies. This gives the USA, and the West, the power to shape the agenda of both organisations.

248. The World Trade Organization (WTO)

1 Comparative advantage works by states using their advantages to focus on the goods they can produce best. If different countries can produce different goods/services at a lower cost, then all countries will benefit by trading with each other. If Portugal was relatively better than England at producing wine, for example, and England relatively better at producing clothes, it benefits both parties to trade goods.
2 The strengths are the consensus process can be seen as democratic and ensures the protection of developing states, who make up about two-thirds of the membership. Consensus decision-making is incredibly slow and difficult, with the process often grinding to a halt, as seen in the case of the Doha round.

249. The G7(8) and G20

The G20 can be seen as more legitimate as it more accurately reflects the balance of the global economic order and has greater regional balance than the G7(8). It is more effective due to its legitimacy and its resources, which can be seen in its response to the global economic crash.

250. Global governance and poverty

1 It has been challenged as there is so much variation within the regions of the North and South. At the same time, it has been challenged as there is increasingly inequality within states in both the North and the South. This means that as a term, it is unable to effectively describe the current situation regarding poverty and inequality.
2 Import substitution industrialisation (ISI) is a form of economic policy, adopted by Southern states as a response to the perception that structural relationships were stopping the South from developing and were entrenching poverty. It argues that the state should protect infant industries with tariffs and subsidies to decrease dependency on developed countries. This allows these industries to develop so that they can then compete with imported goods.

251. Poverty and development

Orthodox theories see poverty purely as the inability to buy food and satisfy basic material needs: absolute poverty. Alternative theories see poverty as both the ability to fulfil basic material needs and non-material needs, and measurements of poverty should be based on more than absolute poverty. They should take into account relative poverty and/or human development.

252. Global governance and contemporary issues

Global civil society acts as the democratic voice of ordinary people, especially the marginalised, to counterbalance the power of international organisations

and TNCs. It forces global governance to listen to ideas, which challenge the orthodoxy of free trade and free markets and adapt to take those voices into consideration in decision making. This has been seen to force international organisations to reform to focus more on poverty, environmental concerns and human rights issues. NGOs have also become a key channel for aid to tackle humanitarian crises, poverty and to encourage development.

253. International law and human rights

1 The two key sources are International Conventions and Treaties such as the Nuclear Non-Proliferation Treaty or the UN Charter and customary law, which is where the common behaviour of states over time becomes an accepted norm. The UDHR is an example of this.
2 Human rights have been controversial as they have resulted in intervention, which undermines national sovereignty, as it is contested whether liberal human rights are universal or can be seen as a form of neo-colonialism.

254. International Court of Justice

The key weaknesses of the ICJ are that its jurisdiction only extends to states, not individuals or non-state actors, it has no enforcement powers and it appears to favour the interest of Western states, the P-5 in particular, thereby undermining its legitimacy.

255. UN tribunals and the ICC

The ICC is a permanent rather than a temporary body, with global jurisdiction rather than focusing on crimes in one particular state, and it is not reliant on the UNSC for its authority. It was created by states ratifying the Rome Statute while the ICTY and ICTR were set up by the UNSC. The UNSC can only delay a prosecution for one year, not block it, if it interferes with their primary aim of maintaining peace and security.

256. Human rights and international justice

1 The ECHR can be seen as the most effective due to very high level of compliance with its rulings by signatory states, even where they disagree with the ruling.
2 The absence of the USA means the burden of the cost of the ICC is greater for its current members, that its jurisdiction is limited and its legitimacy and effectiveness are reduced as the USA remains the most powerful state in global politics.

257 Humanitarian intervention

1 Yes. Realists would still argue that the principle of non-intervention established in the Treaty of Westphalia and confirmed in Articles 2 (4) and 2 (7) of the UN Charter is undermined by humanitarian intervention and do not accept the concept of sovereignty presented in the R2P. Realists fear that the R2P will undermine sovereignty and, with it, international order.
2 The R2P establishes the principle that sovereignty is contingent on the state providing security for all its peoples. When the state fails to stop harm coming to its peoples, then the principle of intervention overrides the principle of national sovereignty.

258. Humanitarian intervention: controversy

1 It is selective as intervention can only legally take place based on a Resolution by the UN Security Council. This means intervention can only take place where all the P-5 agree – this would mean as a minimum that none of the interests of the P-5 were in conflict in the case of any intervention, as was seen in Libya. Where interests clash, like Syria, intervention will be vetoed.
2 Human Rights Watch (www.hrw.org/) and Amnesty International (www.amnesty.org/en/) are examples of NGOs.

259. The UNFCCC and Kyoto Protocol

1 Climate change is transnational; the effects of climate are global and can only be solved by global cooperation, while climate change is the exploitation of the global commons, shared by all countries and consequently beyond national jurisdiction.
2 The Kyoto Protocol is considered an advance as it introduced for the first time binding targets for carbon dioxide emissions and established a global emissions trading system.

260. Other international agreements

1 The Conference was considered a failure as no binding targets were set. This was down to great

power politics, particularly the positions of the USA and the China, and due to the fact that the global financial crisis imposed significant economic pressures on states, who were therefore unwilling to commit to targets which may have associated financial costs.
2 The strengths are that NDCs are determined by states, so it committed states to sign up to the Paris Agreement due to its limited impact on state sovereignty. The NDCs were also supposed to reflect the highest possible ambition of individual states to cut or limit emissions, and each five-year plan was to progress further than the last. The key weaknesses are that the NDCs are voluntary targets and there are no enforcement measures, so the approach can be seen as very weak.

261. The IPCC

Economic globalisation has spread global capitalism across the world. The ideology of global capitalism is driven by a relentless desire for profit, seeing nature in purely economic terms and believing in limitless growth. Any attempts to tackle climate change involve challenging these ideas by moving to much greater state and international regulation. Culturally, the Americanisation of the world has spread the idea that happiness is linked to the consumption of material goods. Any attempts to tackle climate change need to challenge this world view in order to reduce consumption, which is a key source of resource depletion and pollution.

262. International cooperation

It is a tragedy of the commons problem as the Earth's atmosphere is a global commons. States can rationally keep producing the cheapest possible goods, even if this increases greenhouse emissions as the cost of the emissions is shared globally by all countries, species and even future generations. As a result of all states behaving rationally, the global commons will be over exploited and be irreparably damaged.

263. Competing views

1 The anthropocentric view sees nature as only having value through its use to humanity. The ecocentric view sees nature as having value in its own right, independent of any value placed on it by humanity. This extends our ethical community and rights from humans to the whole of nature.
2 Deep green thinking emphasises strong sustainability, which preserves and sustains the Earth through zero-growth economies. Shallow greens support weak sustainability, which argues for slower, smarter growth that limits the environmental impact.

264. Power and hard power

There has been this shift because of the failure of hard power due to guerrilla and terrorist tactics allied to the fact it has been argued that economic globalisation has made war too costly. States need access to the global market to provide economic security to their citizens and to grow, so economic sanctions and inducements are cheaper to use and more likely to work.

265. Soft and smart power

1 The three main sources of soft power are seen as culture, political values and diplomacy/foreign policy. Attraction and identification almost certainly relies on a blend of all three.
2 Soft power has been challenged as it can only work in certain circumstances – American culture, values and diplomacy will work effectively in some cultures and states, but also act as a repulsion to others, meaning that hard power is required in certain cases. While diplomacy is controlled by the state, culture is not, so soft power is far harder for the state to control and use effectively.

266. Classification of state power

1 Realists classify state power in terms of capabilities – they do this in order to measure the advantages possessed by a state so as to classify them and place them within the hierarchical structure of international relations as they see it.
2 A superpower moves beyond having significant power of a great power to pre-eminent power politically and economically, and specifically has the ability to project that power across the globe to successfully pursue its own political objectives.

267. Polarity

1 There are more opportunities for war in multipolarity – in bipolarity, there is one potential conflict, while a system with five potential great powers has ten potential great-power-to-great-power conflicts. In multipolar systems, power imbalances

are more frequent. The potential for miscalculation is therefore far greater.

2 A hegemon is a state which can dominate the whole global system through economic, military and structural power.

268. Changing nature of world order

It is considered a critical event as it ended the Cold War bipolarity that had existed since the Second World War, which is seen as an era of relative peace by the realist tradition. It arguably led to the unipolar moment, where the USA emerged as a global hegemon – the USA saw itself as a benevolent hegemon while others viewed it as a malign hegemon.

269. A multipolar world

The first is the way that great power politics has changed with the slow decline of the USA allied to the rise of the BRICS. Secondly, the idea of a polarity has been challenged by the way in which power has diffused through the global system through the rise of complex interdependence, global governance and the rise of non-state actors, all of which have created new potential poles of power.

270. Different systems of government

A democratic state is defined by having government of the people, by the people and for the people, which means that in theory all the people are involved in making decisions about its affairs. Most democratic states are seen to have the following key features: civil liberties and rights; constitutional government; free, fair and regular elections; a healthy civil society and a form of capitalist economy.

271. Failed and rogue states

Liberals see the nature of the government as very important to the global order as it shapes the way states behave, arguing that the spread of democracy across the globe will bring peace, order and stability – eventually leading to Fukuyama's 'end of history' concept. However, realists argue that the nature of the government in a state is not important as all states are fundamentally alike; their key interest is security and survival and they will strive to gain the power to achieve that goal.

272. Global developments

1 The rule of law is the principle that law should govern and is seen by liberals as crucial to the protection of liberty. In global politics, law should be the framework within which all actions by states should take place.

2 The democratic peace thesis is the idea that democracies do not go to war with other democracies, although conflict with non-democratic states still occurs. The logical result of this thesis is that the spread of democracy across the globe will massively reduce the likelihood of conflict.

273. Contemporary political issues

1 The USA's disputed claim was that Iraq was building up an arsenal of weapons of mass destruction, which it could deploy against other countries or could be sold or passed onto the terrorist organisation Al-Qaeda, hence Iraq was a rogue state and a clear threat.

2 In hegemonic stability theory, the global hegemon (the USA) can act as the world's police officer, thereby ensuring peace and the protection of human rights in the Middle East. However, this assumes that the hegemon's interests are aligned with global interests in the Middle East rather than the USA using its power just to further its own power and goals. An aggressive hegemon pursuing its own interest may undermine the peace, stability and cooperation in the region. If there is multipolar system, with an even division of power between states, the states will work together to ensure peace and stability. However, an unbalanced multipolar system may see rivalries and conflicts between the rival states pursuing their own national interest dominate the politics of the region, decreasing the chances of international cooperation to resolve the ongoing issues.

274. Different forms of regionalism

1 The Arab League and the African Union.

2 It has been driven by economic globalisation – either as a method to protect against or limit the impacts of globalisation or as a method to speed up further integration into the global market to gain its benefits.

275. Regionalism and globalisation

They introduce subsidies to support their businesses against global competition, or tariffs to protect businesses against imports. The best example of this is the use of the CAP by the EU to support and protect the farming industry.

276. Regionalism and sovereignty

First, many of the key issues facing states today are both regional and global – terrorism, immigration, the environment. It makes sense for states within a region to come together to tackle issues that cross borders. Secondly, the chance for further integration within the EU may be enhanced by the election of the heavily pro-EU Macron and the departure of the UK from the EU as the UK has been sceptical about the desirability of further integration.

277. NAFTA and the AU

First, the election of Donald Trump, who is sceptical of NAFTA and has threatened to withdraw the USA if he cannot renegotiate the deal to America's advantage. Secondly, there are such stark differences between the states politically, economically and culturally that deeper integration would be very difficult to achieve.

278. The Arab League and ASEAN

ASEAN is unlikely to pursue further integration as it has as its core principle the respect for state sovereignty. At the same time, the ten nations of ASEAN are very diverse, with differences in political, stability, economic development, values and religious beliefs.

279. European integration

1 Federalism in this sense means the development of a federal system in Europe, where European institutions and states form two distinct levels of government, each with a sphere of autonomous policy jurisdiction.

2 The formation of the EU is shaped by the immediate circumstances of the post-Second World War period – the devastation of mainland Europe, the desires for federalism to limit the power of the nation-state, the need for a prosperous Europe to resist the USSR and trade with the USA, and the need to bring France and Germany together as their rivalry had been at the heart of recent conflicts.

280. The development of the EU

The European Council is made up of heads of government from the member states, while the Council is made up of ministers from each of the member states, who are accountable to their own legislatures. The European Council takes a leadership role and sets the direction of the EU. The Council, however, is where all the key decisions are made, either by unanimous decision or Qualified Majority Voting.

281. Key treaties of the EU

It has been argued that the debt crisis is down to a lack of integration rather than too much integration. The Eurozone needs to integrate further to create an EU fiscal union, where powers over taxation and spending will be transferred from states to the EU.

282. Key debates about the EU

1 The widening of the EU to include the countries from Eastern Europe has increased the diversity of the states within the regional bloc. This diversity makes decision-making slower and more cumbersome and creates a lack of a clear direction and desire for deeper integration. Deeper integration would only be possible where there was a greater political, cultural and economic similarity between member states.

2 States' voting power is weighted by size and different majorities are needed for different decisions. This is important as it removes the need for unanimous voting, which streamlines the decision-making process by removing the veto. It is seen by many as a move from an intergovernmental approach to a more supranational approach.

283. The EU as a global actor

1 A global actor is a body that can participate or act in global politics.

2 The CFSC has been so ineffective as it requires unanimous decision-making, which is very difficult when member states are so split over the general direction – should defence policy operate within or outside of NATO – and over specific issues such as whether Kosovo should be recognised as a sovereign state or intervention in Iraq. There is also no permanent military arms and the EU relies on ad hoc forces contributed by member states.

284. Regionalism and global issues

The race to the bottom refers to a process whereby states compete with each other by cutting environmental regulations or workers' rights to attract or retain businesses and investment in their territory. The spiral of cutting regulations between states to attract businesses will mean the destruction of the natural environment.

285. Realism in global politics

This idea, associated with Morgenthau, is drawn from the Hobbesian view of human nature. As human nature is fixed and driven by the desire for power, life in the state of nature will be a war of all against all. As states are made in the image of humanity and as global politics is equivalent to the state of nature since there is no world government, politics will always be a ceaseless struggle for power between states.

286. Realism in international anarchy

1 For classical realists, human nature explains the behaviour of states in global politics, while for neo-realists it is the structural system of international anarchy, not human nature, which dictates the behaviour of states.

2 The key difference is that offensive realists argue that the national interest of states is to maximise their power to ensure their survival while defensive realists argue that states should maximise security, not power.

287. Conflict and the balance of power

The unbalanced multipolar system has three or more great powers, where one, a potential hegemon, has a considerable power advantage over the others. This can lead to the potential hegemon initiating conflict to grow its powers to create a unipolar world, where its security is guaranteed. The rising power of the potential hegemon creates a security dilemma for the other great powers, triggering a spiral of fear and tension that could lead to conflict.

288. Liberalism in global politics

As it is governments who make war, it is important to have democratic checks and controls on the government by the people to limit the chances of conflict. At the same time democracies have a lot in common with each other which is a basis for friendship. Democracies work internally to resolve conflict through discussion, compromise and negotiation and so take this approach when dealing with conflicts with other democratic states as they know they will do the same.

289. Complex interdependence and global governance

The three main characteristics are the development of multiple channels that connect societies, the absence of a hierarchy of issues and the declining importance of military power.

290. Realism vs liberalism

Absolute gains are total gains made by the state, irrespective of the gains made by other states. Relative gains are gains made by a state that increase their power comparative to other states.

291. The anarchical society

The anarchical society agrees with neo-realism that the state is predominant in global politics, which is anarchical as there is no higher political authority than the state. However, the theory disagrees that the anarchical system leads to a constant struggle for power. Instead, drawing on liberalism and John Locke, states form a society based around common rules as it preserves order, which is crucial for states to both survive and thrive.

292. Globalisation and global governance

Realism doesn't believe that economic globalisation and free trade have altered the role of the state as the predominant actor. States can and will cooperate if they judge it in their best interest. However, the collapse of the Doha round of talks, Brexit and the weakening of free trade agreements show that globalisation has not undermined the state. In fact, it may have led to the state making a comeback.

293. Global governance and regionalism

Liberalism can easily explain the widening and deepening of the EU as an example of harmony and balance being developed. States have integrated and cooperated with each other in order to make absolute gains in political, economic and/or security terms. Realist theory does not adequately explain the widening and deepening and struggles in particular with the emergence of supranationalism in the EU such as the ECJ and the ECB.

294. Power and developments

One Belt, One Road is a Chinese policy developed under Xi Jinping. It involves the investment of $900bn in infrastructure to build a belt road across mainland Asia into Europe as well as a maritime sea road connecting Asia, Africa and Europe. The main aim is to promote deeper economic integration and increase China's role as a leading economic and political power in global politics.

303. Exam-style practice

Section A

In your answer, you should consider:
- Who is responsible for causing environmental problems?
- Who is responsible for taking actions to solve environmental problems?
- How should environmental impact be measured? Current or cumulative emissions? Should population size be taken into account?
- How should the right to development and environmental regulations be balanced?

Section B

In your answer, think about the following contrasting views:
- Liberalism: humans are led by reason and are willing and able to cooperate (Locke) and this is reflected in the society of states. Realism: humans are egotistical and self-interested and states replicate this (Hobbes).
- Liberalism: using either social contract theory or complex independence, liberals argue that a peaceful world with mutual benefits and general prosperity for all is inevitable. Realism sees international anarchy as inevitable, either using human nature as the cause

(Morgenthau) or the structural problem created by the existence of states with no higher authority (Waltz).
- Liberalism: a balance of interests will develop between states and a world of peaceful coexistence, underpinned by global governance. Realism: states emphasise survival and security and so emphasise hard power, meaning they are sceptical of global governance and see a tendency towards conflict and war.

Section C

Question 1

Aim to cover the following:
- Introduction: define terms – sovereignty, globalisation; signpost to your argument – state sovereignty is still central to global politics despite globalisation.
- Interdependence and interconnectedness: state borders are porous – capital, culture and people; criticism – the borderless world does not exist. Re-emergence of the state and state sovereignty post-9/11 and global crash 2007–2009.
- Rise of non-state actors (TNCs, NGOs): they operate outside the state system and cross borders; criticism – international law and system is based around states and state sovereignty.
- Rise of regional (EU) and global governance (UN) undermines sovereignty: criticism – these are generally intergovernmental, not supranational, so protect sovereignty and may increase state power and reaction against collective action, e.g. Trump and America First.
- Humanitarian intervention: ICC and R2P mean international law is moving away from state sovereignty as its core principle. Criticism – the status of humanitarian intervention is a very debatable,

Western ideal – rise of China and their view.
- Conclusion: state sovereignty is not outdated – it may even be growing in importance based on the modern global context.

Question 2

Aim to cover the following:
- Introduction: define key ideas – globalisation and economic global governance, poverty and inequality; signpost to your argument – has reduced global poverty but inequality has risen during the same period.
- Globalisation benefits all economies, including the global South (World Bank poverty figures) – liberal view of development; criticism – globalisation is built on structural inequalities and so has widened the gap between North and South.
- Success stories: Asian Tigers, India and China – engaged with globalisation and global free market has grown, those such as North Korea have fallen behind. Criticism – growth in between-country and within-country inequality.
- Global governance (IMF, World Bank, WTO, G7/G8 and G20): has adapted and changed to focus on new realities to deliver a solution; criticism – global governance is based on the Washington Consensus, favouring developed states over developing states. Think SAPs.
- TNCs: bring with them jobs, workforce training and upskilling and access to modern technologies and so are welcomed by states; criticism – TNCs are about opening up markets and profit, not development.

Conclusion: globalisation has delivered a partial solution to poverty but still has work to do, but at the same time it has promoted inequality both within and between states and regions.

Glossary

Additional Member System (AMS): a hybrid electoral system that has two components or elements. The voter makes two choices. Firstly, the voter selects a representative on a simple plurality (FPTP) system then a second vote is apportioned to a party list for a second or 'additional' representative.

Affirmative action: a policy of favouring historically disadvantaged members of a community.

Altruism: concern for the interest and welfare of others based on rational self-interest or a belief that humans are social beings with a capacity for social solidarity.

Anarchical society and society of states: the theory that the states of the world can be members of a society despite the anarchical nature of the international system.

Anthropocentric: the non-human world is there purely as a means to human ends and non-human nature has only human instrumental value.

Anti-permissiveness: a rejection of permissiveness, which is the belief that people should make their own moral choices, suggesting there is no objective right and wrong.

Assimilation: the processes affecting change and the relationship between social groups are one way, with minorities adopting the values, customs and beliefs of the majority.

Atomism: that society is made up of self-interested and self-sufficient individuals (also known as egoistical individualism).

Authoritative works: works written by experts describing how a political system is run; they are not legally binding but are taken as significant guides.

Authority: for conservatives, this is the idea that people in higher positions in society are best able to make decisions in the interests of the whole society; authority thus comes from above; from the anarchist perspective, authority is the right of one person or institution to influence the behaviour of others and is seen as commanding, controlling and corrupting.

Autocratic state: a state that is ruled by a single person with unlimited power.

Autonomy: a form of self-government or legislation, a combination of freedom and responsibility, in which the individual is not subject to the will of the state or any other person.

Backbenchers: MPs or Lords who do not hold any government office.

Biocentric equality: the radical idea that all beings within the biotic community have equal intrinsic value.

Biodiversity: the diversity of species within a biotic community, which brings the benefits of health and stability to the community.

Bipartisanship: attempts within the structure of the US Congress to try and ensure that the two main parties must work together in order to fulfil Congressional functions.

Bipolarity: an international system revolving around two poles.

Black nationalism: a reaction to white oppression originating in the mid-20th century.

Buddhist economics: the idea that economics should be built on the principles of 'right livelihood', which is an economics as if people mattered.

Cabinet: the prime minister and senior ministers, most of whom lead a particular government department.

Campaign finance: funds raised to promote candidates, political parties or policy initiatives and their agendas during an election.

Capitalism: an economic system, organised by the market, where goods are produced for profit and wealth is privately owned.

Change to conserve: that society should adapt to changing circumstances rather than reject change outright and risk rebellion and/or revolution.

Chauvinistic nationalism: a form of nationalism that believes its nation is superior to others, seeing them as a threat to their survival.

Checks and balances: the division of power between the three branches of government where each branch has a direct ability to prevent action from another branch.

Civic nationalism: a form of nationalism based on the active participation of its citizens and a shared vision of equal citizens.

Class consciousness: the self-understanding of social class that is a historical phenomenon, created out of collective struggle.

Class dealignment: the process where individuals no longer identify themselves as belonging to a certain class and for political purposes fail to make a class connection with their voting pattern.

Classical liberals: classical liberalism is a philosophy developed by early liberals who believed that individual freedom would best be achieved with the state playing a minimal role.

Coalition government: a government that is formed of more than one political party. It is normally accompanied by an agreement over policy options and office of state, as was the Conservative-Liberal-Democrat coalition from 2010–2015.

Codification: the process whereby a constitution is written down in one document.

Codified: a constitution contained in a single written document.

Collective responsibility: the principle by which ministers must support Cabinet decisions or leave the executive.

Collectivisation: the abolition of private property and its replacement by a system of common ownership.

Common law: laws made by judges where the law does not cover the issue or is unclear.

Common ownership: is the common ownership of the means of production so that all are able to benefit from the wealth of society and to participate in its running.

Communism: the communal organisation of social existence based on the common ownership of wealth.

Complex interdependence: the theory that states and their fortunes are inextricably tied together.

Confidence and supply: the rights to remove the government and to grant or withhold funding. Also used to describe a type of informal coalition agreement where the minority partner agrees to provide these things in exchange for policy concessions.

Congressional caucuses: these are groups of legislators who share special interests and meet to pursue common legislative objectives, e.g. black caucus, women's caucus, Hispanic caucus.

Conservative justice: a justice with a strong belief in *stare decisis*, with a more narrow view of the Constitution, more likely to believe in a literal interpretation of the wording and believing in a generally smaller government.

Constitution: a set of rules determining where sovereignty lies in a political system, and establishing the relationship between the government and the governed.

Constitutional rights: the rights specifically outlined for citizens within the US Constitution, Bill of Rights and subsequent amendments.

Consumerism: a psychological and cultural view that focuses on consuming goods and services as a means to feel good about ourselves and drive economic growth.

Conventions: traditions not contained in law but influential in the operation of a political system.

Cooperation: working collectively to achieve mutual benefits.

Cosmopolitan integration: the maximum freedom for minority, as well as majority, individuals, to mix with, borrow and learn from all cultures.

Cultural feminism: a form of difference feminism that seeks to challenge the dominance of male culture in society, instead seeking to promote 'women's values'.

Cultural globalisation: growing transmission of ideas, meanings and values around the world.

Culture: involves values, customs and beliefs that are passed on through the generations via learning.

Decentralisation: decentralised societies based around communes, villages or bioregions that can achieve sustainability through a high level of self-sufficiency, making them dependent on their natural environment.

Democratic deficit: a flaw in the democratic process where decisions are taken by people who lack legitimacy, not having been appointed with sufficient democratic input or subject to accountability.

Democratic state: a state with a system of government in which all the people are involved in making decisions about its affairs.

Dependency theory: emphasises structural imbalances within capitalism that impose dependency on poorer states.

Developmental individualism: the idea that individual freedom is linked to human flourishing.

Devolution: the dispersal of power, but not sovereignty, within a political system.

Dialectic: a process of development that occurs through the conflict between two opposing forces. In Marxism, class conflict creates internal contradictions within society, which drives historical change.

Direct action: a whole range of political actions from non-violent to violent actions taken outside of the legal and constitutional framework.

Direct democracy: all individuals express their opinions themselves and not through representatives acting on their behalf. This type of democracy emerged in Athens in classical times and can be seen today in referenda; from an anarchist perspective, citizens making law and policy decisions in person rather than through elected representatives in a form of popular, self-government.

Discrimination: less-favourable treatment of one group of people compared to other groups.

Disillusion and apathy: a process of disengagement with politics and political activity. Having no confidence in politics and politicians as being able to solve issues and make a difference. Manifested in low turnout at elections and poor awareness of contemporary events.

Diversity: different races and cultures within a state are possible, is positive and should be celebrated, although the extent to which diversity should extend is contentious.

Divided government: when the House of Representatives, Senate and presidency are not all controlled by one party.

Domestic politics: issues within the USA that directly concern citizens, e.g. healthcare, gun control, racial issues.

Ecocentric: a nature-centred rather than a human-centred system of values that gives priority to ecological balance.

Economic globalisation: the growing economic integration and interdependence of economies through intensified cross-border movement of goods, services, technologies and capital.

Egoistical individualism: the idea that individual freedom is associated with self-interest and self-reliance (see also atomism).

Elective dictatorship: a government that dominates Parliament, usually due to a large majority, and therefore has few limits on its power.

Electoral mandate: an electoral mandate is the permission granted to a political leader or winning party to govern and act on their behalf, e.g. to President Obama in 2008 and 2012. The mandate is more or less in effect for as long as the government is in power.

Emerging power: a state that is considered to be rising, primarily in economic power and influence.

Empiricism: the idea that knowledge comes from real experience and not from abstract theories.

Enabling state: a larger state that helps individuals to achieve their potential and be free.

Entrenched: a constitution with a special procedure for amendment.

Entrenchment: a system by which the US Constitution is protected from change by law; in this case, by the amendment process of Article V.

Enumerated powers: such powers are stated explicitly in the US Constitution – for example Article 1, Section 8 provides a list of Congressional powers.

Environmental consciousness: a state of being where your sense of self is fully realised by a deep identification with the non-human world; this is the basis for a new form of ethics and social organisation.

Equality and difference feminism: feminists who argue that men and women are equal and fundamentally different from one another.

Equality of opportunity: the idea that all individuals should have equal chances in life to rise and fall.

Essentialism: the belief that biological factors are significant in the different character and behaviour of men and women.

Ethnicity: the sense of belonging to a social group that shares a common and distinctive culture, religion, language, or the like.

European integration: the process of industrial, political, legal, economic, social and cultural integration of states in Europe.

European Union (EU): a political and economic union of a group of European countries.

Evolutionary socialism: a parliamentary route, which would deliver a long-term, radical transformation in a gradual, piecemeal way through legal and peaceful means, via the state.

Exclusive nationalism: a form of nationalism that believes that it takes time to be a part of the nation, as membership is based on shared history and language.

Executive: the collective group of prime minister, Cabinet and junior ministers, sometimes known as 'the government'.

Executive branch: the executive branch, headed by the president, is one of the three branches of government; the other two are the legislative branch (headed by Congress) and the judiciary (headed by the Supreme Court).

Executive orders: a direction to the federal bureaucracy on how the president would like a piece of legislation to be implemented.

Factions: the groups (factions) that make up political parties – ideological wings, particular age and occupation groups, citizens concerned about particular issues – are now a feature of modern politics.

Failed state: a state that is unable to operate as a viable political unit.

Federal: a political system where all legal sovereignty is not contained in a single place.

Federalism: the legal and political structures where power is distributed between two distinct levels of government on the basis that neither is subordinate to the other.

Filibuster: when a Senator gives a prolonged speech on the floor of the Senate in order to obstruct legislative progress of a bill or confirmation of appointments to the executive or judiciary.

First-past-the-post (FPTP): an electoral system where the person with the most number of votes is elected. Victory is achieved by having one more vote than other contenders – it is also called a plurality system.

Formal equality: the idea that all individuals have the same legal and political rights in society.

Foundational equality: the rights that all humans have by virtue of being born which cannot be taken away (also known as natural rights and inalienable rights).

Four freedoms (EU): the principle of free movement of goods, services, capital and people within the EU's single market.

Franchise/suffrage: franchise and suffrage both refer to the ability/right to vote in public elections. Suffragettes were women campaigning for the right to vote on the same terms as men.

Fraternity: the bonds of comradeship between human beings.

G7(8): an organisation – Group of Seven states/Eight states.

G20: an organisation – Group of Twenty states.

Gender equality: the idea that society should treat everyone the same, irrespective of their gender.

Gender stereotypes: the different way society expects men and women to behave according to gender roles.

Global actor: an entity that participates or acts in international relations.

Global commons: areas and resources that are un-owned and consequently beyond national jurisdiction.

Global governance: the movement towards political integration of transnational actors aimed at negotiating responses to problems that affect more than one state or region.

Globalisation: the emergence of a complex web of interconnectedness in many forms.

Governing competency: the perceived ability of the governing party in office to manage the affairs of the state well and effectively. It can also be a potential view of opposition parties and their perceived governing competency if they were to secure office.

Government: from an anarchist perspective, government is a particular system of rule, from monarchism to dictatorship to liberal democracy, based on deceit and violence.

Government department: a part of the executive, usually with specific responsibility over an area such as education, health or defence.

Great power: a state that is recognised as having the ability and expertise to exert its influence on a global scale.

Green capitalism: the market will deliver environmental solutions based on a strong faith in technology solutions and capitalism's response to ecologically aware consumers.

Gridlock: a situation in US politics where the president and Congress are equally powerful, constantly preventing each other from acting, resulting in difficulty passing legislation.

Group differentiated rights: rights that belong to a group, in contrast to a right held by individuals, includes self-government rights, polyethnic rights and representation rights.

Hard power: the use of military and economic means to influence the behaviour or interests of other political bodies.

Harm principle: the idea that individuals should be free to do anything except harm other individuals.

Hierarchy: the conservative belief that society is naturally organised in fixed tiers, where one's position is not based on individual ability.

Historical materialism: a Marxist theory that the economic base (the economic system) forms the superstructure (culture, politics, law, ideology, religion, art and social consciousness).

Homogenisation and monoculture: the coming together of global cultures and development of a single, homogeneous culture without diversity or dissension.

House of Commons: the primary chamber of the UK legislature, directly elected by voters.

House of Lords: the second chamber of the UK legislature, not directly elected by voters.

Human imperfection: the traditional conservative belief that humans are flawed in a number of ways which makes them incapable of making good decisions for themselves.

Human rights: rights that people are entitled to by virtue of being human.

Humanitarian intervention: military intervention carried out in pursuit of humanitarian rather than other objectives.

Identity politics: advances a critique of liberal universalism as cultural oppression, where minorities are marginalised and the claiming of an authentic sense of identity by groups is an act of political liberation.

Imperial judiciary: a judiciary that is all powerful and on which checks and balances are weak and ineffective.

Imperial presidency: a dominant presidency with ineffective checks and balances from the other branches.

Imperialism/colonialism: the extension of control by one country over another by settlement or economic domination.

Imperilled presidency: this is the contrasting theory to that of an imperial presidency – it is claimed that the president does not have enough power to be effective.

Inclusive nationalism: a form of nationalism that believes that joining a nation is straightforward and quick, as it is not based on shared previous experiences.

Incumbency: the current holder of a political office re. House or Senate seat or presidency.

Individual responsibility: the principle by which ministers are responsible for their personal conduct and for their departments.

Individualist integration: institutional adjustments for migrants or minorities as those of individual claimants and bearers of rights as equal citizens.

Industrialism: based on large-scale production, a faith in science and technology, and the accumulation of capital and continuous growth to satisfy material needs, which is the super ideology of the complete left-right political spectrum.

Informal powers: the powers of the president not listed in the Constitution but taken anyway.

Insurrection: not synonymous with revolution but rather egoistic, not a political or social act, that allows individuals to elevate themselves above the established institutions, leaving the establishment to decay and die.

Integral nationalism: an intense, hysterical form of patriotism in which the individual is absorbed into the nation.

Interconnectedness: the mutual reliance of two or more groups.

Intergovernmental Panel on Climate Change (IPCC): the UN body set up as an internationally accepted authority on climate change.

Intergovernmentalism: the interaction among states based on sovereign independence.

International anarchy: the concept that the world system is leaderless: there is no universal sovereign or worldwide government.

International Court of Justice (ICJ): the principal judicial organ of the United Nations.

International Criminal Court (ICC): the organisation that prosecutes individuals for the international crimes of genocide, crimes against humanity and war crimes.

International law: the law that governs states and other international actors.

International Monetary Fund (IMF): the international organisation working to foster global monetary cooperation, secure financial stability, facilitate international trade, promote high employment and sustainable economic growth, and reduce poverty around the world.

International tribunals: organisations set up to prosecute individuals in specific states for the crimes of genocide, crimes against humanity, and war crimes.

Intersectionality: an idea that challenged the notion that 'gender' was the singular factor in determining a woman's fate, arguing that black and working class women's experiences of patriarchy are different from that of white, middle-class women.

Invisible primary: the period between when a candidate announces their bid for public office and when the actual primaries take place. It is also sometimes called the 'money primary' since candidates spend most of their time during this period raising money in an effort to show political strength.

Judicial activism: an approach to judicial decision making that holds that a justice should use their position to promote desirable social ends.

Judicial independence: the principle that judges should not be influenced by other branches of government, particularly the executive.

Judicial neutrality: the principle that judges should not be influenced by their personal political opinions and should remain outside of party politics.

Judicial restraint: an approach to judicial decision making that holds that a justice should defer to the executive and legislative branches, which are politically accountable to the people, and should put great stress on the principle established in previous court decisions.

Judicial review: the power of the judiciary to review, and sometimes reverse, actions by other branches of government that breach the law or that are incompatible with the Human Rights Act; the ability of the Supreme Court to declare acts of Congress, and acts or actions of the presidency, unconstitutional and therefore null and void.

Keynesian economics: government intervention – can stabilise the economy and aims to deliver full employment and price stability.

Keynesianism: an economic system that requires government involvement to stimulate the economy to achieve full employment and price stability.

Laissez-faire: a preference towards minimal government intervention in business and the state.

Laissez-faire capitalism: an economic system, organised by the market, where goods are produced for exchange and profit, and wealth is privately owned.

Left wing: a widely used term for those who desire change, reform and alteration to the way in which society operates. Often this involves radical criticisms of the capitalism made by liberal and socialist parties.

Legal equality: that the law applies equally to all and that no one is above the law.

Legal sovereignty: the legal right to exercise sovereignty, i.e. sovereignty in theory.

Legislative bills: proposed laws passing through Parliament.

Legitimacy: the rightful use of power in accordance with pre-set criteria or widely held agreements, such as a government's right to rule following an election or a monarch's succession based on the agreed rules.

Liberal internationalism: the idea that sovereign nations should cooperate and create a level of interdependency to avoid international conflict.

Liberal justice: a justice who interprets the Constitution more broadly in order to give the people more freedom and bring about social change.

Liberalism: a wide school of thought in international relations theory that rejects power politics as the sole outcome of international relations and emphasises mutual benefits and cooperation.

Limited government: the role of government is limited by checks and balances, and a separation of powers because of the corrupting nature of power; the power of the US federal government over its states and citizens is subject to limitations as laid out in the Constitution.

Limits to growth: the finite Earth, with the scarcity it implies, places limits on industrial growth.

Living constitution: the idea that the Constitution is an evolutionary document that can change over time through re-interpretation by the Supreme Court (linked to loose constructionism).

Lobbyists: a lobbyist is paid by clients to try to influence the government and/or MPs and members of the House of Lords to act in their clients' interests, particularly when legislation is under consideration.

Loose constructionist: a legal philosophy that favours a broad interpretation of a document's language. This term is often used to contrast with strict construction.

Mandate: the successful party following an election claims it has the authority (mandate) to implement its manifesto promises and also a general permission to govern as new issues arise.

Manifesto: in its manifesto, a political party will spell out in detail what actions and programmes it would like to put in place if it is successful in the next election – a set of promises for future action.

Marginal seat: a seat held by the incumbent with a small majority. There is no precise percentage or winning margin to which this aligns but a 10 per cent margin would need only a swing of 5 per cent to the rival party to take it. Marginal seats are important as they are where the outcomes of elections are decided. Only a minority of seats in UK Westminster constituencies are marginal.

Marxism: an ideological system, within socialism, that drew on the writings of Marx and Engels and has at its core a philosophy of history that explains why it is inevitable that capitalism will be replaced by communism.

Mechanistic theory: the idea that the state was created by 'man' to serve the people and act in their interests.

Mechanistic world view: post-Enlightenment science sees nature exist for the convenience of humankind and nature as a machine where the parts can be understood, fixed or replaced in isolation from the whole.

Meritocracy: a society organised on the basis that success is based on ability and hard work.

Mid-term elections: Congressional elections held mid-way through a president's four-year term.

Minimal state: the idea that the role of the state must be restricted in order to preserve individual liberty.

Minister: an MP or member of the House of Lords appointed to a position in the government, usually exercising specific responsibilities in a department.

Minority government: a government that enters office but which does not have a majority of seats in the legislature (Parliament). This makes passing legislation very difficult.

Modern liberals: modern liberalism emerged as a reaction against free-market capitalism, believing this had led to many individuals not being free. Freedom could no longer simply be defined as 'being left alone'.

Multicultural integration: the processes of integration are seen as two way, different for different groups and individuals, to create a new national identity, where all citizens have not just rights but a sense of belonging to the whole, as well as to their own group identity/identities.

Multipolarity: an international system revolving around three or more poles.

Mutual aid: the most successful species are those that employ solidarity and cooperation rather than individualistic competition.

Mutualism: a system of equitable exchange between self-governing producers, organised individually or in association and small-scale private property based on use or possession.

Nation-state: an autonomous political community held together by citizenship and nationality.

NATO: North Atlantic Treaty Organisation – a military alliance based on the North Atlantic Treaty, signed in 1949.

Negative freedom: the absence of external constraints in society as well as no interference in the private sphere.

New Labour (Third Way): a revision of the traditional Labour values and ideals represented by Old Labour. Influenced by Anthony Giddens, the 'Third Way' saw Labour shift in emphasis from a heavy focus on the working class to a wider class base, and a less robust alliance with the trade unions.

New Right: there are two elements – (i) the neo- (or new) conservatives who want the state to take a more authoritarian approach to morality and law and order and (ii) the neo-liberals who endorsed the free-market approach and the rolling back of the state in people's lives and businesses.

Noblesse oblige: the duty of the wealthy and privileged to look after those less fortunate.

Non-democratic state: a state that lacks the central characteristics of a democratic state.

Non-governmental organisations (NGOs): this is any non-profit, voluntary citizens' group organised on a local, national or international level, e.g. Christian Aid. NGOs perform a variety of service and humanitarian functions, bring citizens' concerns to governments, advocate and monitor policies and encourage political participation through provision of information.

Non-state actors: participants in international relations with significant power and influence, which are not states.

North–South divide: global socio-economic and political divide.

Old Labour (social democracy): key Labour principles embodying nationalisation, redistribution of wealth from rich to poor and the provision of continually improving welfare and state services, which largely rejected Thatcherite/free-market reforms or a Blairite approach.

One Nation: a paternalistic approach adopted by Conservatives under the leadership of Benjamin Disraeli in the 19th century and continued by David Cameron and Theresa May in the 21st century, that the rich have an obligation to help the poor.

Opposition: the MPs and Lords who are not members of the governing party or parties.

Originalism: the idea that the meaning of the US Constitution is fixed and should not be subject to interpretation.

Otherness: the idea that women were considered to be fundamentally different from men, who were seen as the 'norm' and women, deviants from this norm.

Oversight: the ability of one branch of government to supervise the work of another.

Parliament: the British legislature made up of the House of Commons, the House of Lords and the monarch.

Parliamentary privilege: the right of MPs or Lords to make certain statements within Parliament without being subject to outside influence, including law.

Parliamentary sovereignty: the principle that Parliament can make, amend or unmake any law, and cannot bind its successors or be bound by its predecessors.

Participation crisis: a lack of engagement by a significant number of citizens to relate to the political process either by choosing not to vote or to join or become members of political parties or to offer themselves for public office.

Partisan dealignment: the process where individuals no longer identify themselves on a long-term basis by being associated with a certain political party.

Partisanship: a situation in which Congressmen/women are incredibly loyal to their party, even when it means that the result is gridlock.

Party system (UK): the way or manner in which the political parties in a political system are grouped and structured. There are several variants that could apply to the UK; these include one-party dominant, two-party, two-and-a-half party and multi-party systems.

Party system (USA): the number of parties that have a realistic chance of forming government within a political system.

Pluralist democracy: a type of democracy in which a government makes decisions as a result of the interplay of various ideas and contrasting arguments from competing groups and organisations.

Polarity: describes the nature of the international system at any given time in terms of how power is distributed.

Policy group: a group that attempts to influence a whole policy area, e.g. American Israeli PAC (AIPAC).

Political Action Committee (PAC): this raises and spends money in order to elect/defeat electoral candidates, with a donation limit of $5,000 per candidate per election.

Political equality: equal right to vote, one person one vote, equal right to protest.

Political globalisation: the growing importance of international organisations.

Political sovereignty: the political ability to exercise sovereignty, i.e. sovereignty in practice.

Positive discrimination: preferential treatment for groups in society to correct structural inequality or compensate for historical wrongs.

Positive freedom: the idea that freedom is about personal fulfilment and realisation of potential.

Power: from the anarchist viewpoint, power is the means or instruments such as the law, the police and the use of ideology, by which the state and other social institutions secure their authority.

Powers of persuasion: this is an informal power of the president in which they can use the prestige of their job, and other bargaining methods in order to get people to do as they wish.

Presidential government: an executive dominated by one individual; this may be a president but is also used to describe a strong, dominant prime minister.

'Principle': a fundamental and 'organising' idea that runs throughout the US Constitution, e.g. democracy or accountability.

Private sphere: the area in society where relationships are seen as private, specifically home and domestic life.

Professional group: a group that represents the economic interests of its members, e.g. American Medical Association (AMA), American Bar Association (ABA).

Progressive: ideas that move towards improving society.

Public bill committees: committees responsible for looking at bills in detail.

Public policy: legislation and judicial decisions made on any policy that affect the whole of the population.

Public sphere: the area in society where relationships are public, specifically life outside the home, particularly society and work.

Racial equality: racial equality is an equal regard to all races. It can refer to a belief in biological equality of all human races and to social equality for people of different races. In the USA, there remain calls for desegregation and voter registration in the south, and better jobs, housing and school integration in the north.

Radical: a belief whose ideas favour drastic political, economic and social change.

Rational: the idea that humans are capable of reasoned thought and are able to make logical decisions for themselves.

Realism: a wide school of thought in international relations theory that has a belief that world politics will remain a field of conflict among actors pursuing power.

Reformist: seeking to change society gradually and peacefully.

Regionalism: the creation and implementation of institutions that express a particular identity and shape collective action within a geographical region.

Regressive: ideas that seek to revert society to a former or less advanced state.

Religious right: a movement which generally gives support to the Republican Party; it is an ultra-conservative religious response to the sexual revolution and an attempt to translate this into public policy, promoting family values, opposing abortion and the 1973 Roe v Wade judgement, opposing same-sex marriage, civil partnerships and non-discrimination laws.

Representative democracy: a more modern form of democracy through which an individual selects a person (and/or political party) to act on their behalf to exercise political choice.

Reserve army of labour: the idea that women constitute a spare workforce that can be called on as and when needed.

Revisionism: a move to re-define socialism that involves a less radical view of capitalism and a reformed view of socialism.

Right wing: this term reflects support for the status quo, little or no change, stressing the need for order, stability and hierarchy – generally relates to conservative parties.

Rogue state: a state that has a foreign policy that poses a threat to other states.

Royal prerogative: a set of powers and privileges belonging to the monarch but normally exercised by the prime minister or Cabinet, such as the granting of honours or of legal pardons.

The rule of law: the principle that all people and bodies, including government, must follow the law and can be held to account if they do not.

Safe seat: a seat in which the incumbent has a considerable majority over the closest rival and which is largely immune from swings in voting choice. The same political party retains the seat from election to election. A majority of seats in UK Westminster constituencies are safe seats.

Salisbury Convention: the convention whereby the House of Lords does not delay or block legislation that was included in a government's manifesto.

Secondary legislation: powers given to the executive by Parliament to make changes to the law within certain specific rules.

Security Council: the United Nations' most powerful body, with primary responsibility for the maintenance of international peace and security.

Security dilemma: the theory that actions by a state intended to increase its security, such as increasing its military strength, can lead to other states responding with similar measures, producing increased tensions that create conflict.

Segregation: the belief that humans can be divided along racial and ethnic lines.

Select committees: committees responsible for scrutinising the work of government, particularly of individual government departments.

Semi-democratic state: a stable state that combines democratic and authoritarian elements.

Separation of powers: the three key bodies of government, legislature, executive and judiciary each have their own powers, personnel and buildings.

Single-interest group: a group that advocates policy surrounding a small specific issue, e.g. National Rifle Association (NRA).

Single Transferable Vote (STV): this system allows voters to rank their voting preferences in numerical order rather than simply having one voting choice. In order to obtain a seat, a candidate must obtain a quota. After the votes are cast, those with the least votes are eliminated and their votes transferred and those candidates with excess votes above the quota also have their votes transferred.

Social contract: the idea that the state/society is set up with agreement from the people to respect its laws which serve to protect them.

Social justice: a distribution of wealth that is morally justifiable and implies a desire to limit inequality.

Socialist internationalism: the idea that class solidarity is more powerful and politically significant than national identity. As Marx said: 'Working men of all countries, unite!'.

Soft power: the ability to attract and co-opt and to shape the preferences of others through appeal and attraction.

Soft money: when cash is contributed to a political party with no limits attached to the amount that can be received, this is a 'soft money' contribution.

Solidarity: from an anarchist perspective, a relationship of sympathy, cooperation and harmony between people, which means that they have no need to be regulated by the state and any regulation makes solidarity impossible.

Sovereignty: absolute and unlimited power and authority.

Stare decisis: this doctrine is built on the idea of standing by decided cases, upholding precedents and maintaining former adjudications – thus tends to favour the status quo – this is the opposite of the 'living Constitution' approach.

State: from an anarchist perspective, the state is seen as a sovereign body that exerts total authority over all individuals and groups living within its defined geographical limits.

Statute law: laws passed by Parliament.

Strict constructionist: a legal philosophy that favours looking solely at the written text of the law. This term is often used to contrast with strict construction.

Structural Adjustment Programme (SAP): conditional loans provided by the International Monetary Fund (IMF) and the World Bank to countries that experience economic crisis.

Super PACs: a Super-Political Action Committee (Super PAC) raises and spends unlimited amounts of money to support or oppose political candidates but without directly donating to or coordinating with these candidates (a result of Citizens United v FEC [2010]).

Superpower: a state with a dominant position in international relations, pre-eminent among great powers, and characterised by its unparalleled ability to exert influence or project power on a global scale.

Supplementary Vote (SV): this is a majoritarian system. The voter makes two choices (hence the term 'supplementary'). If one candidate obtains over 50 per cent on the first vote then the contest is complete, if no candidate attains this level, all but the top two candidates remain. Then the supplementary choices are re-distributed and whoever gets most votes from the remaining two wins the seat.

Supranationalism: refers to a large amount of power given to an authority, which, in theory, is placed higher than the state.

Supreme Court: the highest courts in the UK and US political systems.

Sustainability: the capacity of the ecological system to maintain its health over time, one of the most contested ideas in ecologism.

Sustainable development: development that meets the needs of the present, without compromising the ability of future generations to meet their own needs.

Swing justice: an informal name for the justice on the Supreme Court who falls ideologically in the centre of the nine current justices.

Syndicalism: revolutionary trade unionism that uses direct action and the mass strike as an expression of working-class power to inspire popular revolt.

Think tanks: a body of experts brought together to collectively focus on a certain topic(s) – to investigate and offer solutions to often complicated and seemingly intractable economic, social or political issues.

Tolerance: a willingness to respect values, customs and beliefs with which one disagrees.

Tragedy of the commons: the situation within a shared-resource system where individual users acting independently and rationally according to their own self-interest behave contrary to the common good of all users by depleting that resource.

Treaties: formal agreements with other countries, usually ratified by Parliament.

Ultra vires: literally 'beyond the powers'. An action that is taken without legal authority when it requires it.

Unanimous consent: a Senator or Congressman/woman may request unanimous consent on the floor to set aside a specified rule of procedure so as to expedite proceedings.

Uncodified: a constitution not contained in a single written document.

Unentrenched: a constitution with no special procedure for amendment.

Unified government: where both Houses of Congress and the presidency are controlled by people from the same political party.

Unipolarity: an international system in which there is one dominant pole.

Unitary: a political system where all legal sovereignty is contained in a single place.

United Nations (UN): an organisation created in 1945, following the Second World War, to promote international cooperation and to prevent another such conflict.

United Nations Framework Convention on Climate Change (UNFCCC): an international environmental treaty negotiated at the Earth Summit in Rio de Janeiro in 1992.

Universal human rights: rights that apply to people of all societies regardless of cultural or other differences.

Universalism: from a multiculturalist view, universalism is where certain values are applicable to all individuals and all societies, regardless of culture, history, geography or any other differences.

Value pluralism: there is no one absolute conception of the 'good life' but rather multiple, competing and equally legitimate conceptions.

Volksgeist: the 'spirit' of a nation, the unique identity of a people based on their culture.

Widening–deepening: the process by which the EU has attempted to expand membership while furthering integration.

World Bank: the international organisation that offers concessional loans and grants to the world's poorest developing countries in order to reduce poverty.

World government: the idea of a common political authority with legislative and executive power over states.

World Trade Organization (WTO): the organisation that regulates international trade.

THOMAS TALLIS SCHOOL LIBRARY